Value Sharing for Sustainable and Inclusive Development

Mario Risso
Niccolò Cusano University, Italy

Silvia Testarmata
Niccolò Cusano University, Italy

A volume in the Advances in Business Information Systems and Analytics (ABISA) Book Series

IGI Global
DISSEMINATOR OF KNOWLEDGE

Published in the United States of America by
IGI Global
Business Science Reference (an imprint of IGI Global)
701 E. Chocolate Avenue
Hershey PA, USA 17033
Tel: 717-533-8845
Fax: 717-533-8661
E-mail: cust@igi-global.com
Web site: http://www.igi-global.com

Library of Congress Cataloging-in-Publication Data

Names: Risso, Mario, 1972- editor. | Testarmata, Silvia, 1977- editor.
Title: Value sharing for sustainable and inclusive development / Mario Risso and Silvia Testarmata, editors.
Description: Hershey, PA : Business Science Reference, [2018] | Includes index.
Identifiers: LCCN 2017015899| ISBN 9781522531470 (hardcover) | ISBN 9781522531487 (ebook)
Subjects: LCSH: Sustainable development. | Economic development--Social aspects. | Social responsibility of business. | Value.
Classification: LCC HC79.E5 V254 2018 | DDC 306.3--dc23 LC record available at https://lccn.loc.gov/2017015899

This book is published in the IGI Global book series Advances in Business Information Systems and Analytics (ABISA) (ISSN: 2327-3275; eISSN: 2327-3283)

British Cataloguing in Publication Data
A Cataloguing in Publication record for this book is available from the British Library.

Advances in Business Information Systems and Analytics (ABISA) Book Series

Madjid Tavana
La Salle University, USA

ISSN:2327-3275
EISSN:2327-3283

Mission

The successful development and management of information systems and business analytics is crucial to the success of an organization. New technological developments and methods for data analysis have allowed organizations to not only improve their processes and allow for greater productivity, but have also provided businesses with a venue through which to cut costs, plan for the future, and maintain competitive advantage in the information age.

The **Advances in Business Information Systems and Analytics (ABISA) Book Series** aims to present diverse and timely research in the development, deployment, and management of business information systems and business analytics for continued organizational development and improved business value.

Coverage

- Data Management
- Information Logistics
- Business Information Security
- Business Intelligence
- Forecasting
- Decision Support Systems
- Legal information systems
- Data Analytics
- Management Information Systems
- Data Governance

IGI Global is currently accepting manuscripts for publication within this series. To submit a proposal for a volume in this series, please contact our Acquisition Editors at Acquisitions@igi-global.com or visit: http://www.igi-global.com/publish/.

The Advances in Business Information Systems and Analytics (ABISA) Book Series (ISSN 2327-3275) is published by IGI Global, 701 E. Chocolate Avenue, Hershey, PA 17033-1240, USA, www.igi-global.com. This series is composed of titles available for purchase individually; each title is edited to be contextually exclusive from any other title within the series. For pricing and ordering information please visit http://www.igi-global.com/book-series/advances-business-information-systems-analytics/37155. Postmaster: Send all address changes to above address.

Titles in this Series

For a list of additional titles in this series, please visit: www.igi-global.com/book-series

Smart Technology Applications in Business Environments
Tomayess Issa (Curtin University, Australia) Piet Kommers (University of Twente, The Netherlands) Theodora Issa (Curtin University, Australia) Pedro Isaías (Portuguese Open University, Portugal) and Touma B. Issa (Murdoch University, Australia)
Business Science Reference • copyright 2017 • 429pp • H/C (ISBN: 9781522524922) • US $210.00 (our price)

Advanced Fashion Technology and Operations Management
Alessandra Vecchi (London College of Fashion, University of London Arts, UK)
Business Science Reference • copyright 2017 • 443pp • H/C (ISBN: 9781522518655) • US $200.00 (our price)

Maximizing Business Performance and Efficiency Through Intelligent Systems
Om Prakash Rishi (University of Kota, India) and Anukrati Sharma (University of Kota, India)
Business Science Reference • copyright 2017 • 269pp • H/C (ISBN: 9781522522348) • US $175.00 (our price)

Maximizing Information System Availability Through Bayesian Belief Network Approaches Emerging Research and Opportunities
Semir Ibrahimović (Bosna Bank International, Bosnia and Herzegovina) Lejla Turulja (University of Sarajevo, Bosnia and Herzegovina) and Nijaz Bajgorić (University of Sarajevo, Bosnia and Herzegovina)
Information Science Reference • copyright 2017 • 180pp • H/C (ISBN: 9781522522683) • US $140.00 (our price)

Handbook of Research on Advanced Data Mining Techniques and Applications for Business Intelligence
Shrawan Kumar Trivedi (BML Munjal University, India) Shubhamoy Dey (Indian Institute of Management Indore, India) Anil Kumar (BML Munjal University, India) and Tapan Kumar Panda (Jindal Global Business School, India)
Business Science Reference • copyright 2017 • 438pp • H/C (ISBN: 9781522520313) • US $260.00 (our price)

Exploring Enterprise Service Bus in the Service-Oriented Architecture Paradigm
Robin Singh Bhadoria (Indian Institute of Technology Indore, India) Narendra Chaudhari (Visvesvaraya National Institute of Technology, Nagpur, India) Geetam Singh Tomar (Machine Intelligence Research (MIR) Labs, India) and Shailendra Singh (National Institute of Technical Teachers' Training and Research, India)
Business Science Reference • copyright 2017 • 378pp • H/C (ISBN: 9781522521570) • US $200.00 (our price)

Applying Predictive Analytics Within the Service Sector
Rajendra Sahu (ABV-Indian Institute of Information Technology and Management, India) Manoj Dash (ABV-Indian Institute of Information Technology and Management, India) and Anil Kumar (BML Munjal University, India)
Business Science Reference • copyright 2017 • 294pp • H/C (ISBN: 9781522521488) • US $195.00 (our price)

IGI Global
DISSEMINATOR OF KNOWLEDGE

701 East Chocolate Avenue, Hershey, PA 17033, USA
Tel: 717-533-8845 x100 • Fax: 717-533-8661
E-Mail: cust@igi-global.com • www.igi-global.com

Table of Contents

Detailed Table of Contents

The aim of this chapter is to enter into the debate on the objective of the firm and more in general of the organizations, in order to discuss the contribution that the Italian doctrine Economia Aziendale (EA) can give to this debate and to the sustainable economic development. To this end, it is pro-posed the concept of primary interest of the organizations, the aziende according to the EA (i.e., business entities, public administrations and non-profit organizations), which is to satisfy human needs through the production of useful goods and services (the objective of the azienda) ensuring a sustainable value creation in the short and long term (the condition for the survival and growth of the azienda). For business entities, the primary interest supports the so called 'integration thesis' according to which business and ethics can be achieved together, since the profit is considered as a condition that allows the survival and growth of the firm favouring all stakeholders and the community.

A sense of responsibility keeps human on the edge which continuously reminds one of where their pursuit lies. Of course, Responsibility keeps piling up as one grow. In a society where the globe is technologically upgrading every second, the businesses are assigned the challenge to keep the surroundings at balance; this is where the term corporate social responsibility gains momentum. In constantly growing economies, Corporate Social Responsibility (CSR) is the force which keeps organizations stay afloat and is the make or break point. Realising this, the economies of world are jointly or individually pursuing the corporate goals towards society in different areas. CSR is the vantage point which is titled to aid an organization's mission as well as a guide to what the company stands for its consumers. The aim of the chapter is to articulate how corporate social responsibility has become the most valuable touch point of the society to survive among different companies and highlight the various issues and challenges in CSR implementation and regulation.

While more and more businesses incorporate sustainability in their core business strategy, there has recently been a shift from corporate social responsibility (CSR) to the notion of creating shared value (CSV). This thesis investigates the emergence of new hybrid enterprises and innovative business models. Starting from a literature review about CSR and its evolution into the "Big Idea" proposed by Porter and Kramer, the chapter will analyse the link between business and society, especially in the developing countries where this link is stronger. The main aim is to identify the most effective business models that enhance the competitiveness of a company, while simultaneously advancing the economic and social conditions in the communities in which it operates. The general idea is that enterprises should have longer-term perspective on how they operate in relation to the external society and environment, addressing societal needs and challenges through the business itself, within a business model.

The created shared value represents a paradigm shift in business corporate social responsibility (CSR) and sustainability strategy. Apart from addressing the limitations inherent in the traditional CSR which is mainly philanthropic, short-lived and separated from the core business strategy and activities, it enhances the company's competitiveness while simultaneously advancing the economic and social conditions in the community of operation. Companies can create shared values through re-conceiving products and markets, redefining productivity in the value chain and building supportive industry clusters at the company's locations and solving society problems. Despite the criticisms and challenges of the shared value concept, there are convincing evidences that the created shared value is a veritable instrument for addressing the bottom of the pyramid resulting in inclusive, sustainable development of developing countries and it has the potentials to unleash the next wave of global economic growth, prosperity and sustainable development when governments, companies and non-government organizations in developing countries demonstrate commitment to their roles in shared value creation and companies start to think and take long-term views of social investments and economic prosperity, and look at corporate decisions and opportunities through the lens of shared value by incorporating social and societal values into their economic agenda.

Companies benefit society by supplying products and services to customers, creating jobs for people, providing incomes for their employees, investing in knowledge or developing communities. The last decades have witnessed significant developments in re-conceptualizing the role of companies in society. By creating shared value, companies consider society as an integral part of their businesses and link economic performance with societal progress. In order to meet this challenge one of their most valuable options is the implementation of the lean management approach. The chapter aims to explore the theoretical foundation of the shared value concept and to exemplify the case of Toyota Motor Company. The research method is the case study. The study shows that there is a Toyota Way in creating shared value.

This chapter argues about some of the main effects generated by cultural events on the host territory with the aim at verifying under which conditions an event creates value for all stakeholders and is sustainable. Sustainability is not a static condition but an ever-changing process, which should lead to enhanced life conditions from an economic, social and environmental point of view. This requires that all stakeholders not only participate but also deeply share values as well as local resources, take part in common projects and act to achieve mutual goals. In this regard, Expo Milano 2015 is analyzed as a significant example, because not only it promotes a virtuous theme but also it represents the product of intents and values shared by different organizations. However, despite the undisputed value generated by the event, the aim is to call into question its degree of sustainability, in relation to the policies implemented for promoting the event, the firms' strategy, as well as the social and economic effects in Milan and in Italy.

The global waste market is estimated at US$410 billion a year and growing, while only 25 per cent of total waste is known as recovered and recycled. Besides, this figure does not include the informal segment in which around 20 million people work as waste pickers in developing countries. Solid waste management policy and recycling practices differ among certain parts of the world to a large extent. Industrialized countries generally have formal and automated waste management systems, whereas developing countries rely on the informal sector. In Istanbul, which is one of the few megacities in the world appear to be at the crossroad of a policy choice. Authorities will either privatize the recycling business for large firms or try to follow more inclusive approach for more than 100,000 waste pickers in the city. Based on the literature, this study will review the formal waste management systems and describe the integration of informal recycling sector in particular world regions that may have policy implications for Istanbul.

The concept of smart cities has recently emerged to highlight the significance of innovation and information technologies in urban planning. In this chapter, after a discussion of different conceptions and important dimensions of smart cities, a wealth of information technologies that have been used in cities for a variety of services is presented. The authors advocate that smart urban solutions should be designed within a smart cities vision and strategic plan, defined by people's needs. They propose an integrated strategic policy making model for smart, sustainable and inclusive cities and they make recommendations for policies and education for smart cities. The special character of public and private spaces, the significance of everyday life, the pivotal role of open governance and meaningful citizen participation, as well as the balance between the desired surveillance for efficient resource management and freedom and creativity have been highlighted as challenges that should inform the design of smart urban solutions and future research on smart cities.

Foreword

Value sharing is a new emerging phenomenon to build new relationships between business, government and civil society. Recently, companies are increasingly promoting innovation through collaborative initiatives among business, non-profit organizations and public institutions for facilitating economic development. Often, innovation systems are based on the cross-fertilization between economic and social actors. It is relevant to better understand how the actors involved could develop new models of governance and innovation strategies. Corporate strategies, management practices, government policies, cultural norms and values, as well as individual decision and actions all influence the nature and speed of innovations in a sustainable environment.

The aim of the setting management activities according to the sharing values among the stakeholders (owners, managers, employees, public and private institutions, consumers, and other related enterprises) becomes even more challenging when the company takes part in a global environment. Against this background, it is crucial to define the responsibilities of the different actors involved, as per their actual role, and identify a culture of the sharing values both within companies, both in the inter-organizational relationships. In addition, it is relevant to better understand how the actors involved in value sharing processes could develop new models of governance and innovation strategies. Finally, it is essential to analyse new entrepreneurial approaches where economic and social aspects become mutually supportive to enhance their impact on communities' development.

The readers of this volume will gain new insights into the dynamics of the management and organizational culture as a key factor in determining the performance through the behaviour of all actors and the decision-making system. In particular, the aim of this book is to investigate how a culture of sharing values inside the business organizations could generate a sustainable, inclusive and human development.

The value sharing is an emerging issue in business. There are some experiences and applications on this topic but there is a lack of a systematic analysis of the value sharing approaches from both a theoretical and practical point of view. The book aims at providing a systematic review on this emerging issue to point out relevant theoretical frameworks and the best practices about value sharing to assess the opportunities and constraints of the value sharing approaches oriented to value creation for smart, sustainable and inclusive development. In particular, the goal is to enhance knowledge and application about value sharing in different industries, geographic regions, and personal/professional contexts.

The challenges in innovation by value sharing are both difficult and interesting. People are working on them with enthusiasm, tenacity, and dedication to develop new methods of analysis and provide new solutions to keep up with the ever-changing threats. In this new age of global interconnectivity and interdependence, it is necessary to provide academics and practitioners, both professionals and students, with state-of-the art knowledge on the frontiers in value sharing approaches and models. This book is a good step in that direction.

Fabio Fortuna
Niccolò Cusano University, Italy

Fabio Fortuna *is the Chancellor of the Niccolò Cusano University of Rome, Former Dean of the Faculty of Economics, Full Professor of Accounting and PhD Coordinator of the PhD in Governance and Management for Business Innovation of the Niccolò Cusano University. Currently, he is member of various scientific committees and editorial boards in the field of business and management issues. He is the author of many publications on business administration, accounting and finance. His fields of expertise are in business administration, accounting and finance. His current research interests are corporate governance, corporate social responsibility and corporate disclosure in organizations. He has published several articles and books. In particular, he is co-author of the widely recognized article on business models published in the Journal of Management and Governance in 2016.*

Preface

INTRODUCTION

Heightened attention to sustainable and inclusive development has fostered a rethinking of business activities, calling for bold and transformative steps to shift the economic and social world onto a resilient path (Elkington, 1994). The 2030 Agenda for Sustainable Development of the United Nations (United Nations, 2015) identifies 17 goals with 169 targets. In order to achieve these objectives a new approach to sharing values is needed among all actors involved.

Businesses, governments and civil society should work together to identify opportunities through which business activities can make a significant positive contribution to sustainable and inclusive development (Porter & Kramer, 2006, 2011; Pepe, 2013). This requires a collective assessment of existing capacity and an inclusive participatory process to inform strategic planning, required skills upgrading and technical training activities (Tagliaventi & Mattarelli, 2006; Risso, 2012; Bocken, Short, Rana, & Evans, 2013).

Opportunities for sustainable value creation can be found by prioritising approaches that enable progress towards achieving common objectives, goals and targets tailored to specific contexts and sectors (Risso, 2012; Boons, Montalvo, Quist, & Wagner, 2013). Establishing trustful relationships among all actors involved is also a key factor for an open and constructive dialogue leading to innovative solutions for sustainable and inclusive development (Gillespie & Mann, 2004; Cheng, Yey, & Tu, 2008; Wu, Chen, & Chung, 2010; Lee, Olson, & Trimi, 2012).

The usefulness of shared value approach has also been criticized. Further work is needed to refine the approach and investigate practical experiences (Beschorner, 2013; Crane, Palazzo, Spence, & Matten, 2014).

ORGANIZATION OF BOOK

This volume aims to analyse the role of sharing values as a driver for sustainable and inclusive development. It collects the contributions of young academics from different countries all over the world and is divided into two sections and 15 chapters.

The first section addresses the relationship between sharing values and entrepreneurship.

Chapter 1 examines the fundamentals of the search for the value sharing model. Creating shared value refers to innovation by businesses, governments and non-profit organizations working collaboratively and strategically to find areas where core businesses operations on commercial terms can create shared benefits with scalable development impact. The Authors provide a structured literature review on shared value creation. Starting with the famous contribution of Porter and Kramer "Creating Shared Value: Redefining Capitalism and the Role of the Corporation in Society", the review offers insights into emerging business practices.

Chapter 2 focuses on education as a critical determinant of human development and economic growth. An educated man is central to a sustainable economy, one that promotes values and rationality. The holistic analysis elaborates on what an entrepreneurial system should look like, how creative thinking could help and to what extent it will contribute to an "educated development".

Chapter 3 identifies the sustainable development challenges in business management. The aim of this chapter is to enter into the debate on the core purpose of firms and more generally of organizations, in order to discuss the contribution that the Italian doctrine Economia Aziendale can make to sustainable development.

Chapter 4 reviews how corporate social responsibility (CSR) has become a critical element in the interactions between society and companies in the global economy. It highlights the various issues and challenges in CSR implementation and regulation.

Chapter 5 describes the recent shift from the concept of CSR to the notion of creating shared value. In particular, the Authors investigate the emergence of new hybrid enterprises identifying how innovative business models can enhance the competitiveness of companies and simultaneously advance the economic and social conditions in the communities in which they operate.

Chapter 6 shows how companies can create shared value through re-conceiving products and markets, redefining productivity in the value chain and building supportive industry clusters. The study provides perspectives from developing countries. Despite the criticism and challenges related to the shared value concept, the Author demonstrates how shared value can be a useful tool for addressing the bottom of the pyramid resulting in sustainable and inclusive development of developing countries.

The second section describes local experiences in different national contexts and industries. Tailoring shared value approaches to specific conditions can support implementation efforts and yield successful results that can be replicated or adapted to scale.

Chapter 7 sets out the theoretical foundations of the shared value concept and presents the case of Toyota Motor Company.

Chapter 8 analyses the main effects generated by cultural events on the host territory with the objective of verifying under which conditions an event creates value for all stakeholders. In this regard, Expo Milano 2015 provides an interesting case in point.

Chapter 9 illustrates formal waste management systems and describes the integration of the informal recycling sector in Istanbul, including through more inclusive approaches to involve informal waste pickers in the city.

Chapter 10 focuses on modern knowledge societies and smart cities. Cities are the hubs of a global network of interactions that require urban planning to balance new technologies and people's needs. The Authors propose an integrated strategic policy making model for smart, sustainable and inclusive cities, highlighting the pivotal role of open governance and meaningful citizen participation for efficient resource management of public and private spaces.

Chapter 11 discusses how to improve sustainability by sharing resources and services in a new sharing economy paradigm. The Authors build a conceptual model for taxi ridesharing to describe the value potential of increasing the efficiency of taxi businesses. The model shows that it is possible to have a system that creates value for both the taxi driver and the passenger, while simultaneously leading to significant reduction in CO_2 emissions.

Chapter 12 considers the financial dimension of sustainability. In particular, the Authors investigate the reaction of investors to the inclusion of firms on the BIST Sustainability Index of the Borsa Istanbul.

Chapter 13 proposes a holistic approach to strategic regional development in Romania. The Authors offer a critical qualitative description of the Romanian ecosystems focusing on public policies and entrepreneurial attitudes towards sustainable development.

Chapter 14 reviews issues surrounding renewable energy sources and their large potential contribution to sustainable development. The Authors synthesise the literature on renewable energy technologies and sustainable development in Turkey, contributing to develop a conceptual framework for measuring the impact of renewable energy on sustainability.

Chapter 15 outlines the potential benefits that the recent oil and gas discoveries in Kenya herald to the country's population. The Author describes and analyses the global oil and gas industry with a focus on its strategic, financial, and business aspects. He also identifies investment opportunities for promoting the participation of the local industry in the value chain of oil and gas projects.

Mario Risso
Niccolò Cusano University, Italy

Silvia Testarmata
Niccolò Cusano University, Italy

REFERENCES

Beschorner, T. (2013). Creating shared value: The one-trick Pony approach – A comment on Michael Porter and Mark Kramer. *Business Ethics Journal Review*, *17*(1), 106–112. doi:10.12747/bejr2013.01.17

Bocken, N., Short, S., Rana, P., & Evans, S. (2013). A value mapping tool for sustainable business modelling. *Corporate Governance*, *13*(5), 482–497. doi:10.1108/CG-06-2013-0078

Boons, F., Montalvo, C., Quist, J., & Wagner, M. (2013). Sustainable innovation, business models and economic performance: An overview. *Journal of Cleaner Production*, *45*, 1–8. doi:10.1016/j.jclepro.2012.08.013

Cheng, J. H., Yeh, C. H., & Tu, C. W. (2008). Trust and knowledge sharing in green supply chains. *Supply Chain Management*, *13*(4), 283–295. doi:10.1108/13598540810882170

Crane, A., Palazzo, G., Spence, L. J., & Matten, D. (2014). Contesting the Value of Creating Shared Value. *California Management Review*, *56*(2), 130–153. doi:10.1525/cmr.2014.56.2.130

Elkington, J. (1994). Towards the Sustainable Corporation: Win-Win-Win Business Strategies for Sustainable Development. *California Management Review*, *36*(2), 90–100. doi:10.2307/41165746

Gillespie, N. A., & Mann, L. (2004). Transformational leadership and shared values: The building blocks of trust. *Journal of Managerial Psychology*, *19*(6), 588–607. doi:10.1108/02683940410551507

Lee, S. M., Olson, D. L., & Trimi, S. (2012). Co-innovation: Convergenomics, collaboration, and co-creation for organizational values. *Management Decision*, *50*(5), 817–831. doi:10.1108/00251741211227528

Pepe, C. (2013). *Values and corporate responsibility in globalization processes*. Milan, Italy: McGraw-Hill Education.

Porter, M. E., & Kramer, M. R. (2006). Strategy & Society: The Link between Competitive Advantage and Corporate Social Responsibility. *Harvard Business Review*, *84*(12), 78–92. PMID:17183795

Porter, M. E., & Kramer, M. R. (2011). Creating Shared Value: Redefining Capitalism and the Role of the Corporation in Society. *Harvard Business Review*, *89*(1-2), 62–77.

Risso, M. (2012). A horizontal approach to implementing corporate social responsibility in international supply chains. *International Journal of Technology Management*, *58*(1-2), 64–82. doi:10.1504/IJTM.2012.045789

Tagliaventi, M. R., & Mattarelli, E. (2006). The role of networks of practice, value sharing, and operational proximity in knowledge flows between professional groups. *Human Relations*, *59*(3), 291–319. doi:10.1177/0018726706064175

United Nations. (2015). *Transforming Our World: The 2030 Agenda For Sustainable Development, A/RES/70/1*. New York: United Nations.

Wu, J. J., Chen, Y. H., & Chung, Y. S. (2010). Trust factors influencing virtual community members: A study of transaction communities. *Journal of Business Research*, *63*(9-10), 1025–1032. doi:10.1016/j.jbusres.2009.03.022

Acknowledgment

The editors would like to acknowledge the help of all the people involved in this project and, more specifically, to the authors and reviewers that took part in the review process. Without their support, this book would not have become a reality.

First, the editors would like to thank each one of the authors for their contributions. Our sincere gratitude goes to the chapter's authors who contributed their time and expertise to this book.

The editors also wish to acknowledge the valuable contributions of the reviewers regarding the improvement of quality, coherence, and content presentation of chapters. Most of the authors also served as referees; we highly appreciate their double task. The editors extend a special note of thank to members of the Scientific Board of the PhD programme on "Governance and Management for Business Innovation" of the Niccolò Cusano University for their contribution as reviewers of the chapters. Finally, the editors gratefully acknowledge the assistance of the PhD students in Governance and Management for Business Innovation who have helped to review the editing of the manuscript.

Mario Risso
Niccolò Cusano University, Italy

Silvia Testarmata
Niccolò Cusano University, Italy

Section 1

Sharing Values and Entrepreneurship

Chapter 1
The Advent of the Value Sharing Model

Silvia Testarmata
Niccolò Cusano University, Italy

Mario Risso
Niccolò Cusano University, Italy

Fabio Fortuna
Niccolò Cusano University, Italy

ABSTRACT

This chapter reviews the field of Shared Value (<SV>) to develop insights into how <SV> research is developing, offer a critique of the research to date, and outline future research opportunities. The authors find that most published <SV> research presents normative arguments for <SV> and there is little research examining <SV> in practice. Thus, the authors call for more research that critiques <SV>'s rhetoric and practice. Thus, this chapter offers an insightful critique into an emerging management issue and widespread business practice. The research findings provide insights into future research needs on Shared Value.

INTRODUCTION

Value creation and value appropriation are core concepts in management because the two processes critically shape the financial performance of firms and the economic returns to key stakeholders, including employees, suppliers, customers, financiers (including shareholders, bondholders, debtholders), and communities. Yet, the recent evolution of the concept of corporate social responsibility, which is increasingly entering into corporate strategies and activities, fosters a sustainable and shared value creation by firms in collaboration with all the actors involved in the economic, social and environmental processes (Golinelli 2005; Cafferata, 2009; Pepe, 2013). Practitioners and scholars struggle to understand the motives and strategic orientations of governments, non-profits, and private firms that seek to interact to create and allocate value among partners and stakeholders.

DOI: 10.4018/978-1-5225-3147-0.ch001

The advent of value sharing model refers to the business innovation that comes from the collaboration among firms, public and private institutions and third sector organizations to identify areas of activity in which the value creation is sustainable and inclusive, meaning that it goes strategically with the pursuit of social and environmental objectives.

The process of value sharing, is based on the simultaneous realization of mutual benefits and new value for all stakeholders that requires an overall vision, able to include different perspectives to find a balance among:

- Economic growth, social development and environmental protection;
- Technological progress and involvement of human resources;
- Short term objectives and medium and long-term objectives;
- Development of creativity and recovery of social and cultural identities.

Ever since Michael Porter and Mark Kramer proposed Creating Shared Value (CSV) as a cure for the ailing legitimacy of business - originally in 2006 and more prominently in 2011- the idea of shared value replaced the concept of value sharing and has earned a central place in the conversation about the impacts - positive and negative - of business in society. McKinsey & Co. gave its award for the best article in Harvard Business Review in 2011 to Porter and Kramer's contribution, which to date has already been cited nearly 5,000 times according to Google Scholar. The core idea in Creating Shared Value is that companies should not ignore society, as under the narrow conception of capitalism that has done so much harm to the legitimacy of business, but rather should search for business opportunity in society's needs. Strategies that respond to the challenges presented by society and the environment and also reinforce the competitive advantage of a company create shared value.

Academics who study business ethics and corporate responsibility remain skeptical about Creating Shared Value, but even they confirm the significance of the idea by publishing critical articles in leading journals (e.g., Beschorner, 2013; Crane, Palazzo, Spence, & Matten, 2014; Dembek, Singh, & Bhakoo, 2016). Outside the academy, in the realm of corporate practice, Creating Shared Value has become a buzzword and a call to business action to address matters of sustainability. Creating Shared Value as a strategy tool has taken off, already adopted by leading international companies ranging from Allianz to Mattel and Nestlé to Unilever, to name only a few noteworthy examples. Despite the far-reaching influence of Porter and Kramer's work on Creating Shared Value, the idea remains largely underdeveloped in its applications and in response to its criticisms, with few exceptions (e.g., Pfitzer, Bockstette, & Stamp, 2013).

In the meanwhile, since the book published by Botsman and Rogers (2010) on the rise of collaborative consumption, Sharing Economy (SE) has become a popular buzz word in public media (Hern, 2015). SE indicates the peer to peer sharing of access to underutilized goods and services, which prioritizes utilization and accessibility over ownership (Schor & Fitzmaurice, 2015). The sharing economy may take a variety of forms, including using information technology to provide individuals with information that enables the optimization of resources through the mutualization of excess capacity in goods and services. A common premise is that when information about goods is shared (typically via an online marketplace), the value of those goods may increase for the business, for individuals, for the community and for society in general. Other most popular terms to describe this emerging business practice are 'collaborative consumption' and 'peer to peer economy' (Belk, 2014).

In this context scholars have devoted greater attention to the issues of shared value (or sharing value) and sharing economy, which are different aspects of an emerging business practices, that is the value sharing model. So our purpose is to provide an overview of the current state of the literature by developing a structured literature review on this stream of research, namely shared value.

We structure the remainder of this chapter as follows. Section 2 describes and justifies the use of a structured literature review methodology to investigate <SV> research. Section 3 describes an SLR method for selecting and analyzing the articles and provides insights and critique of the <SV> literature. Section 4 proposes a critique of the current literature through descriptive statistics and an analysis of the research results. Section 5 offers our arguments on the future of <SV> research practice and policy and presents several relevant unanswered research questions. The final section provides some closing remarks and the limitations of our analysis.

METHODS

Our research examines the <SV>'s research foundations, so that we can establish the focus of <SV> literature and offer some insights into how it may develop in the future. For this study we use the structured literature review (<SRL>) methodology as developed by Massaro, Dumay and Guthrie (2016), that is a method for studying a corpus of scholarly literature, to develop insights, critical reflections, future research paths and research questions.

Massaro et al., (2016, p. 769) argue that:

[...] for experienced academic researchers an SLR offers an alternative approach that can either confirm one's knowledge or open up new avenues for research to which the traditional approach may not provide access. The latter is the likely outcome, therefore, an SLR can help experienced scholars develop new and interesting research paths by accessing and analysing a considerable volume of scholarly work.

Additionally, the SLR method complements traditional literature reviews because the approach helps to yield different outcomes that are defensible. The SLR can be useful for higher degree students and emerging scholars, allowing them to demonstrate that their literature reviews are defensible (Massaro et al., 2016, p. 769).

THE STRUCTURED LITERATURE REVIEW

In our study we adopt an SLR method to provide insights and critique that will help identify future research agenda for <SV>. Essentially a structured literature review is a form of content analysis whereby the unit of analysis is the article, as opposed to words, sentences or paragraphs, as is commonly found in content analysis research (Massaro et al., 2015, p. 533). Accordingly, the review process is conducted in ten different stages shown in Figure 1.

Figure 1. The process to develop the structure literature review
Source: Massaro et al., 2016

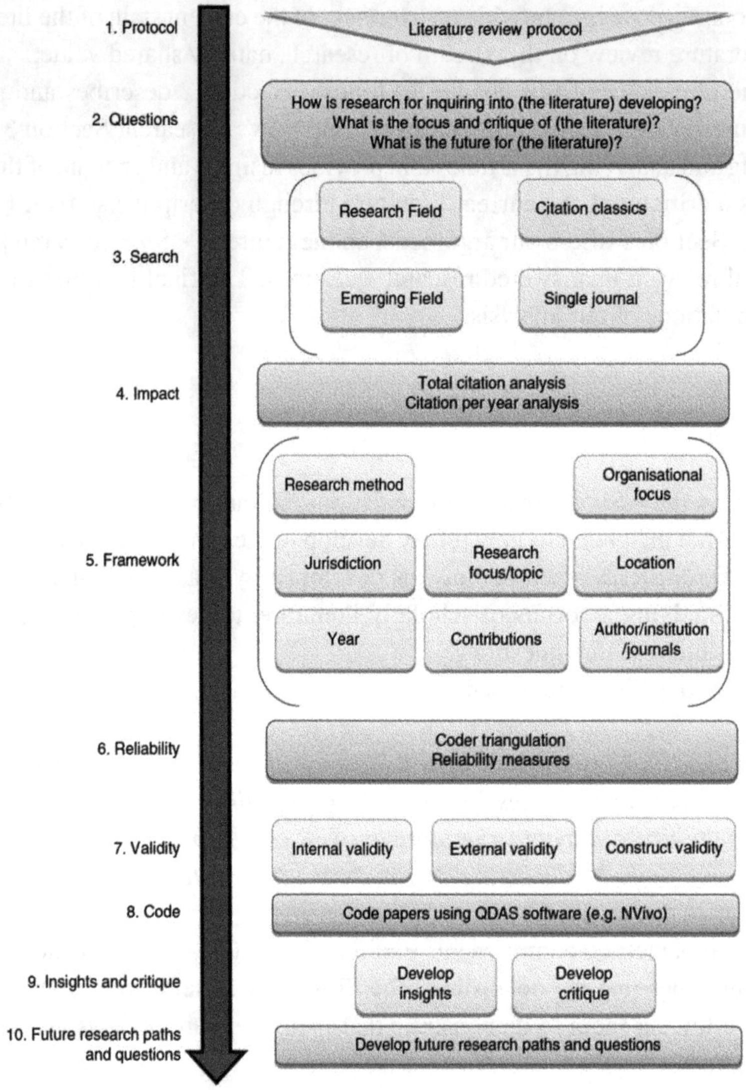

The Literature Review Protocol

In the first stage, we outline how to set up the research project. First, we identified that to date there has been only one literature review on shared value recently published in Journal of Business Ethics by Dembek et al. in 2016. The authors provided a systematic and thorough analysis of shared value, focusing on its ontological and epistemological properties. However, that research focuses exclusively on the shared value concept, without considering other aspects of the value sharing model such as sharing economy and sharing value. While this is not a research gap, there is a need for such a review, especially in the first phase of a contemporary research field such as <SV>. According to Petty and Guthrie (2000), there are two main goals for investigating an emerging field such as <SV>. First, it is necessary to categorise it in a way that provides a useful understanding of how and why the <SV> movement has developed in the way it has and, second, a platform to identify those avenues for future research that we consider likely to deliver results for understanding the nature, impact and value of <SV>. Thus, the aim of the chapter is to follow these goals and provide empirical justification for the research gaps we discover and the subsequent research questions we outline.

To develop our research we adopt the structured literature review protocol, proposed by Massaro et al., (2016), consisting of the following steps: statement of research questions, literature search, articles impact analysis, definition of analytical framework, reliability, validity, articles coding, insights and critique, further research on <SV>.

Research Questions

Researchers use SLRs to map and assess the existing intellectual territory to identify future research needs (Dixon-Woods, 2011, p. 331). Before proposing a path of future research development with the literature review, we need to analyse from a critical point of view the existing field of knowledge by developing research issues. Subsequently, in the second stage we adapt the three generic research questions of a SLR to focus specifically on the <SV> literature.

1. How is research for inquiring into <SV> developing?
2. What is the focus and critique of the <SV> literature?
3. What is the future for <SV> research?

The Literature Search

The third stage involves the selection of data sources for the review. We select articles from internationally recognised academic journals covering different disciplines, including, but not limited to, the management literature based on the terms 'shared value', 'sharing economy', 'sharing value' and 'value sharing' appearing in the title, abstract or keywords of the article.

We focus on three types of academic articles (based on Scopus, the largest abstract and citation database of peer-reviewed literature): articles by citations, articles in press and conference papers, using specific keywords. In fact, "*a keyword search can help researchers to find relevant articles that extend existing topics in a particular field. Although a keyword search is a powerful tool, researchers have to be careful in the keyword selection criteria*" (Massaro et al., 2016, p. 777). Furthermore, according to Cronin, Ryan and Coughlan (2008, p. 40) "*keywords need careful consideration to select terms that will generate the data being sought*".

We retrieve data from Scopus database on 18 March 2017, for a period of 20 years. We used 1 January 1997 as a starting date and adopted a cut-off date of 31 December 2016. As a result, we identify 517 academic contributions, consisting of 458 articles by citations, 24 articles in press and 35 conference papers. From the analysis it emerges that scholars pay increasing attention and growing emphasis to the concept of shared value as showed in Table 1.

According to Table 2, the main focus of academic research is the concept of shared value. Starting from that the well known contribution of Porter and Kramer "Creating Shared Value: Redefining Capitalism and the Role of the Corporation in Society", published on Harvard Business Review in 2011, and cited more than 1,050 times according to Scopus Database, this stream of research has received growing attention in recent management studies.

Table 1. Literature review by year

Year	1997	1998	1999	2000	2001	2002	2003	2004	2005	2006
Articles	4	6	6	7	5	7	9	13	3	19
Year	**2007**	**2008**	**2009**	**2010**	**2011**	**2012**	**2013**	**2014**	**2015**	**2016**
Articles	14	15	20	31	22	35	51	69	81	100

Source: Our elaboration, 2016

Table 2. Literature review by key term

Key Term	Shared Value	Sharing economy	Value Sharing	Sharing Value
Articles	405	81	18	13

Source: Our elaboration, 2016

Then, we examine the titles, abstracts and keywords of all the retrieved academic journals and conference papers and select articles examining shared value to ensure the articles are relevant. For example, an article may claim to discuss a model of sharing value, but in reality do not explore any concept or aspect related to shared value. As a result, we identify 78 articles focusing on shared value (see Appendix).

We then download the PDF versions of these articles and stored them in a shared Dropbox folder with full referencing details.

Article Impact

In the forth stage we determine the articles' impact according to the number of Scopus citations. To do so we download from Scopus the articles' citation data as of 15 June 2017.

We used the citation metrics to measure the article's impact because interesting insights can come from an analysis of the number of articles in terms of citation metrics (Dumay, 2014). Citation metrics allow researchers to understand how the literature develops and if the research topic is important, by examining the impact different articles have over time (Massaro et al., 2016, p. 774). In fact, as Serenko and Bontis (2013, p. 309) outline, "*a key assumption is that there exist a strong positive relationship between the number of citations attracted by a journal and its overall quality*".

But this method can have some problems. Dumay and Cai (2014, p. 270) outline that "*One problem with determining the impact from citations alone is that older articles can accumulate more citations*". For this reason to determine the articles' impact we have set the period analysed from 1991 to 2015 excluding the articles published in 2016 because they may have less citations.

In Table 3 we report the top ten articles by Scopus citations, highlighting the authors name, the publication year, the article's title and the total number of citations. For example, the article by Porter and Kramer (2011) has been cited 1,051 times indicating that it has a strong impact on the academic <SV> debate. Similar considerations could be done for the article by Dhanaraj, Lyles, Steensma, and Tihanyi (2004), that has been cited 363 times; the article by Hartline, Maxham III, and McKee (2000), that has been cited 336 times; and the article by Young-Ybarra and Wiersema, that has been cited 317 times.

Table 3. Top ten articles by Scopus citations - As of June 15, 2017

Number	Reference	Publication Year	Article	Scopus Citations
1	Porter & Kramer	2011	Creating shared value	1,051
2	Dhanaraj, Lyles, Steensma, & Tihanyi	2004	Managing tacit and explicit knowledge transfer in IJVs: The role of relational embeddedness and the impact on performance	363
3	Hartline, Maxham III, & McKee	2000	Corridors of influence in the dissemination of customer-oriented strategy to customer contact service employees	336
4	Young-Ybarra & Wiersema	1999	Strategic flexibility in information technology alliances: The influence of transaction cost economics and social exchange theory	317
5	Maxham III & Netemeyer	2003	Firms reap what they sow: The effects of shared values and perceived organizational justice on customers' evaluations of complaint handling	240
6	Burke, Sims, Lazzara, & Salas	2007	Trust in leadership: A multi-level review and integration	180
7	Goodman & Svyantek	1999	Person-organization fit and contextual performance: Do shared values matter	176
8	Mukherjee & Nath	2007	Role of electronic trust in online retailing: A re-examination of the commitment-trust theory	153
9	Cheng, Yeh, & Tu	2008	Trust and knowledge sharing in green supply chains	142
10	Lee, Olson, & Trimi	2012	Co-innovation: Convergenomics, collaboration, and co-creation for organizational values	138

Source: Our elaboration, 2016

Subsequently, in Table 4 we report the top ten articles by Scopus citations per year (Massaro et al., 2016). From a comparative analysis with the results of the previous tables, we observe that two articles published more that ten years ago (Gillespie & Mann, 2004; Tagliaventi & Mattarelli, 2006) appear in the list of Table 4, and each has been cited more that one hundred times, indicating that they have already had an impact on the <SV> debate. In addition, we observe that some more recent articles (Crane et al., 2014; Markham, Yammarino, Murry, & Palanski, 2010; Cohen & Kietzmann, 2014; Michelini & Fiorentino, 2012; Pfitzer et al., 2013) appear in the list of Table 4, and each has been cited more that twenty times, indicating that they have already had an impact on the <SV> debate. In particular, we would like to draw readers' attention to the fact that the article by Crane et al., (2014) has been already cited 57 times, that denotes the strong impact of the main critique to the 'Creating Shared Value' model proposed by Porter and Kramer (2011). Therefore, there is an academic interest in <SV> as an emerging field of management research.

Define the Analytical Framework

To pursue an SLR, we must identify units of analysis within selected papers and treat them as independent elements to be analysed. Thus, in the fifth stage, we define an analytical framework, as shown in Table 5, in order to help us to organize the existing literature on <SV>.

Table 4. Top ten articles by citations per year (CPY) - As of June 15, 2017

Number	Reference	Publication Year	Article	Scopus Citations per Year
1	Porter & Kramer	2011	Creating shared value	1051
2	Maxham III & Netemeyer	2003	Firms reap what they sow: The effects of shared values and perceived organizational justice on customers' evaluations of complaint handling	240
3	Goodman & Svyantek	1999	Person-organization fit and contextual performance: Do shared values matter	176
4	Gillespie & Mann	2004	Transformational leadership and shared values: The building blocks of trust	111
5	Tagliaventi & Mattarelli	2006	The role of networks of practice, value sharing, and operational proximity in knowledge flows between professional groups	105
6	Crane, Palazzo, Spence, & Matten	2014	Contesting the value of 'creating shared value'	57
7	Markham, Yammarino, Murry, & Palanski,	2010	Leader-member exchange, shared values, and performance: Agreement and levels of analysis do matter	34
8	Cohen & Kietzmann	2014	Ride On! Mobility business models for the sharing economy	32
9	Michelini & Fiorentino	2012	New business models for creating shared value	23
10	Pfitzer, Bockstette, & Stamp	2013	Innovating for shared value	22

Source: Our elaboration, 2016

To develop this framework, we adopted the criteria proposed by (Massaro et al., 2016). As part of developing the framework the authors initially coded ten articles to determine the suitability of the adopted frameworks and to determine if any other criteria or attributes needed changing, adding or deleting according to the analytical procedure adopted by Dumay, Bernardi, Guthrie, and Demartini (2016). Also, during and after our initial coding we reviewed the criteria and attributes again. As a result, we add two additional criteria: E: Academic, practitioners and consultants (as authors) and F: Academic, practitioners and consultants (as readers). In addition, we delete Year and Authors/institutions/journals as criteria, because it seems that they are not significant for our analysis. This means there are seven different criteria, with three to seven attributes each.

The Literature Review Reliability

In the sixth stage we illustrate the literature review reliability. As structured literature review is a form of content analysis, we use subjective coding to analyse the selected articles because the "*research is based on data generated by human beings asked to make some kind of judgment*" (Hayes & Krippendorff, 2007, p. 77). So, it is important to develop particular forms of control and triangulation that reduce the "*bias by integrating theories, methods, data sources and researchers with complementary strengths and non-overlapping weaknesses*" (Modell, 2009, p. 209). In fact, if researchers could reduce bias they would be able to argue that their coding and analytical framework are reliable (Yin, 2014).

Table 5. Results of analysis of <SV> articles

Article Code	Criterion	Number of Articles	Article Code	Criterion	Number of Articles
A	JURISDICTION		B	ORGANISATIONAL FOCUS	
A1	Supra-national/ International/ Comparative - General	28	B1	Publicly listed	4
A1.1	Supra-national/ International/ Comparative - Industry	16	B2	Private-SMEs	3
A1.2	Supra-national/ International/ Comparative - Organizational	1	B3	Private-Others	17
A2	National - General	5	B4	Public sector	2
A2.1	National - Industry	25	B5	Not-for-profit	0
A2.2	National - Organizational	3	B6	General/Other	52
A3	One Organization	0		Total	78
	Total	78			
C	COUNTRY OF RESEARCH		D	FOCUS OF <SV> LITERATURE	
C1	USA/Canada	22	D1	Business Ethics	5
C2	Australasia	4	D2	Strategy and Business Models	37
C3	European Union	18	D3	Human Relations	7
C4	Asia	13	D4	Management	6
C5	Other (including General)	21	D5	Marketing	6
C6	Total	78	D6	Tourism	17
				Total	78
E	ACADEMIC, PRACTITIONERS AND CONSULTANTS (as authors)		F	ACADEMIC, PRACTITIONERS AND CONSULTANTS (as readers)	
E1	Academic(s)	75	F1	Academic(s)	16
E2	Practitioner(s) and consultant(s)	1	F2	Practitioner(s) and consultant(s)	7
E3	Academics, practitioners and consultants	2	F3	Academics, practitioners and consultants	55
	Total	78,00		Total	78
	RESEARCH METHODS				
G	Case/Field study/Interviews	23			
G1	Content analysis/Historical analysis	0			
G2	Survey/Questionnaire/Other empirical	19			
G3	Commentary/ Normative/Policy	34			
	Literature review	2			
	Total	78			

Source: Our elaboration, 2016

Thus, reliability measures can help researchers to demonstrate that their data: *"(a) have been generated with all conceivable precautions in place against known pollutants, distortions and biases, intentional or accidental, and (b) mean the same thing for everyone who uses them*" (Krippendorff, 2013, p. 267).

We use Krippendorff's alpha (K-alpha) as the reliability measure (Krippendorff, 2013). Accordingly, when coding the first ten articles, the lead author independently read the articles and recorded the codes on a separate spread sheet and the other authors independently repeated this process. Based on our first attempt at coding we had a K-alpha score of 0,81 which is just over the recommended score of 0,80. Then, we discuss the coding system together and, after having clarified the questionable issues, we develop the remain part of the analysis.

Testing Literature Review Validity

In the seventh stage we explain the validity of our literature review in terms of internal and external validity (Massaro et al., 2016).

Internal validity seeks to establish causal relationships (White & McBurney, 2012, p. 142). We use a pattern-matching logic that compares an empirically based pattern with a predicted one made before colleting data (Yin, 2014). Starting with a small group of articles we analysed data to develop first conclusions and identify elements for deeper analysis and, then, we use the expanded framework to analyse all articles.

External validity in concerned with whether the results of a study can be generalised (White & McBurney, 2012, p. 145). In our study, we select the most representative articles of the available literature. Firstly, we do a content analysis of the selected articles reading the abstracts and, in some cases, the full content of the articles to select the articles that are more representative of the current literature on <SV>.

As a result, we identify several articles as being not relevant to the literature review. Rejected articles were either not scholarly articles or articles in which the author of the article referred to <SV> ambiguously or they use the term in a general or unrelated way.

Article Coding

In the eighth stage, after defining the analytical framework and checking the framework's reliability, we coded the articles recording the results in an Excel spread sheet. Furthermore, we retained an open coding approach alongside coding for the pre-established categories in the analytical framework, in case we discovered any relevant new article attributes or categories.

As such, we added two extra criteria to the analytical framework, after the first pass at coding, because we found new insights as we read and coded the articles. This highlights how the SLR process is not just a rigid approach, but is flexible and develops iteratively (Dumay et al., 2016, p. 172).

In the 'Insights and critique' section that follows we discuss the research results and develop the critique from the analysis of each criterion, that is the ninth stage of the structured literature review protocol.

INSIGHT AND CRITIQUE

In this section we present the main research results of our analysis of <SV>'s articles and attempt to answer to the research question one 'How is research for inquiring into <SV> developing?' and two

'What is the focus and critique of the <SV> literature?'. Thus, we provide some reflections and insights on the current state of <SV> literature and offer a critique of the field resulting from an in-depth analysis of a defined body of literature.

First, we examine the research results of the preliminary literature search that identifies 517 articles in terms of timeline, source, author, author affiliation and country.

Figure 2 shows a noticeably growing trend of <SV> articles since 2011, when Porter and Kramer published their seminal article on 'Creating Shared Value', that reaches a peak in 2016. This is explained by the fact that this issue is an emerging stream of research.

Looking at the type of academic journals, we note a predominant interest for the <SV> literature from both business ethics and strategic management journals, such as Harvard Business Review, Journal of Business Ethics, Journal of Cleaner Production, and Journal of Business Research as we expected (see Figure 3).

Figure 4 shows the main authors that publish articles on <SV>. They are Appelbaum, S. H. and Maxham III, J. G. However, most authors published two or three articles on these issues thus this result is not significant.

More interesting is Figure 5, that explains the most recurring affiliations. At the top lies the National University of Singapore, Copenhagen Business School ranks second and the Université Concordia of Montreal is the third. There are also a remarkable component in the US (Louisiana State University, Harvard Business School and University of Virginia). The other recurring universities are situated in Finland (Aalto University), China (Hong Kong University) and the UK (University of Leeds and University of Virginia). These results show that the <SV> research is widespread all over the world.

Figure 6 shows the documents by country/territory. The first three countries where <SV> is investigated are United States, Unites Kingdom and Australia; so, these results highlights a strong interest on

Figure 2. Articles by year
Source: Our elaboration on Scopus Database, 2017

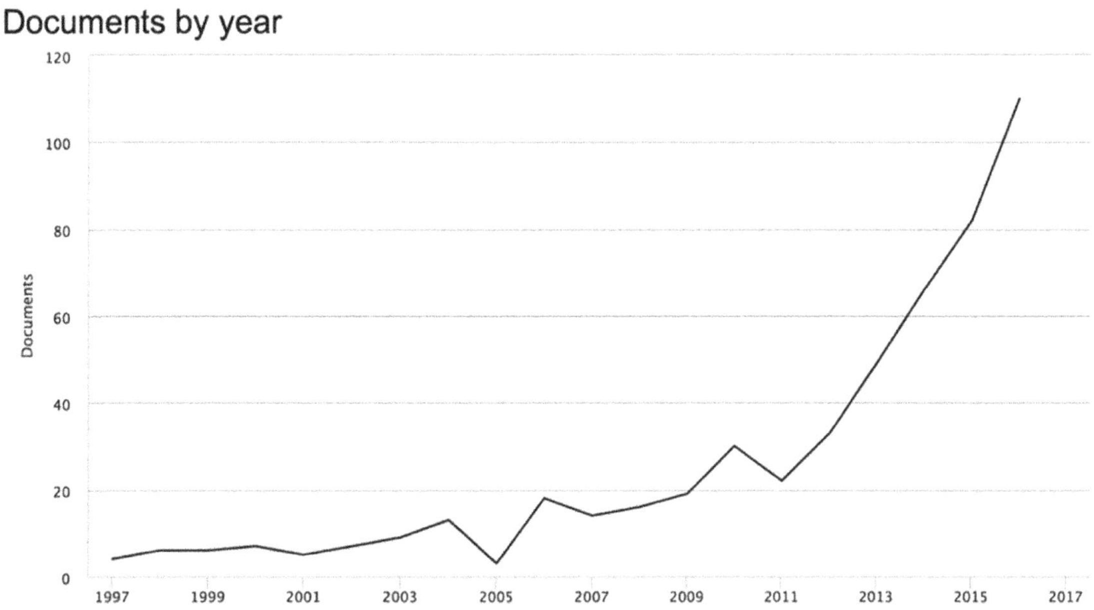

Figure 3. Articles per year by source
Source: Our elaboration on Scopus Database, 2017

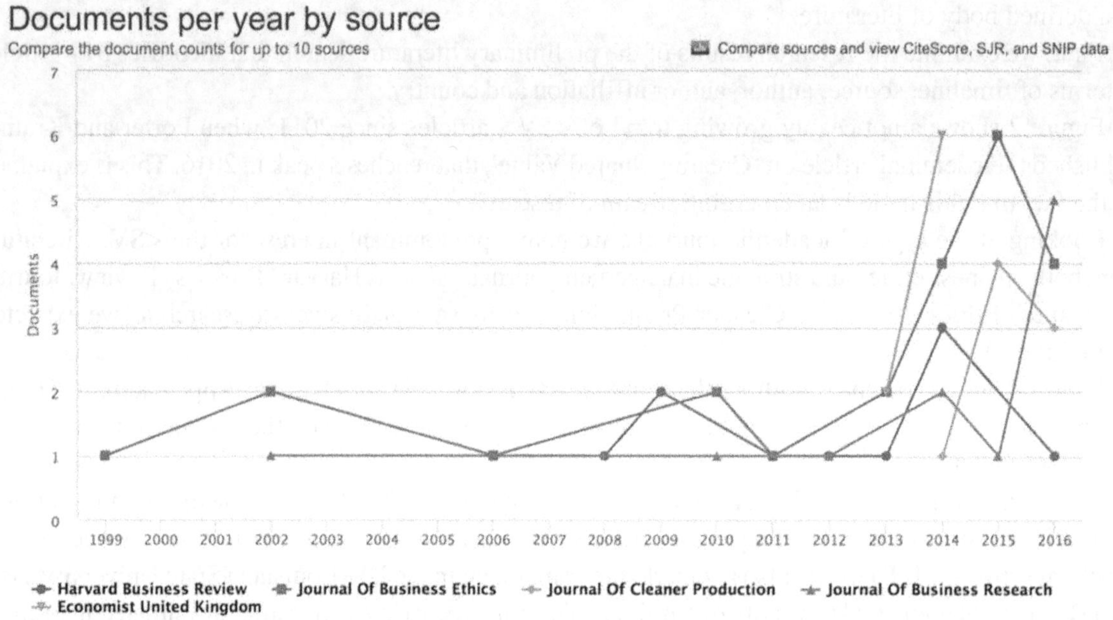

Figure 4. Articles by author
Source: Our elaboration on Scopus Database, 2017

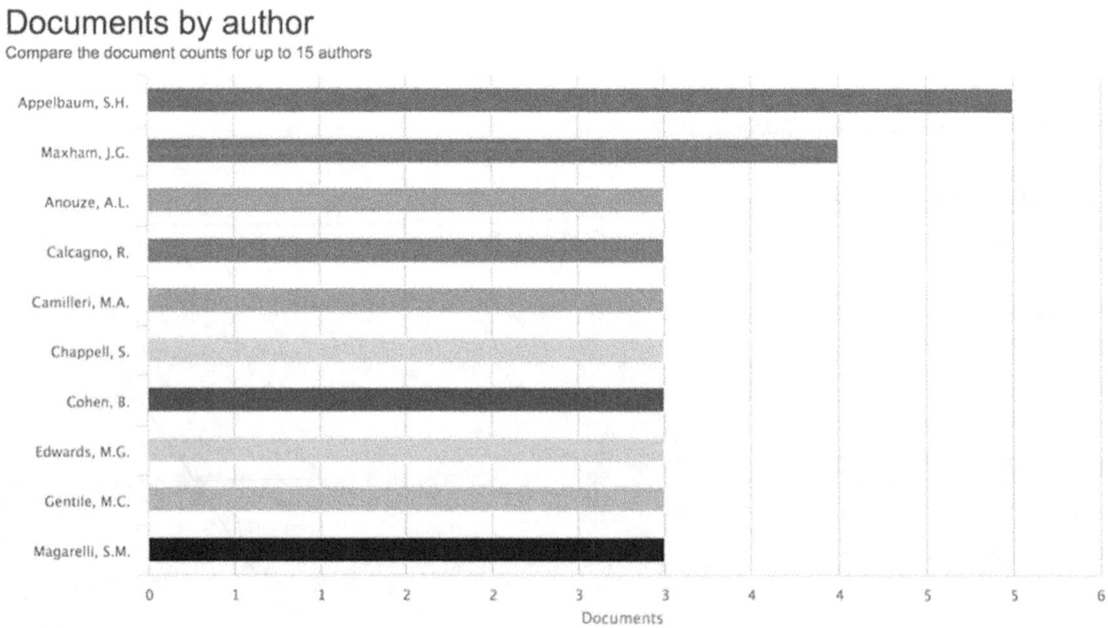

Figure 5. Articles by affiliation
Source: Our elaboration on Scopus Database, 2017

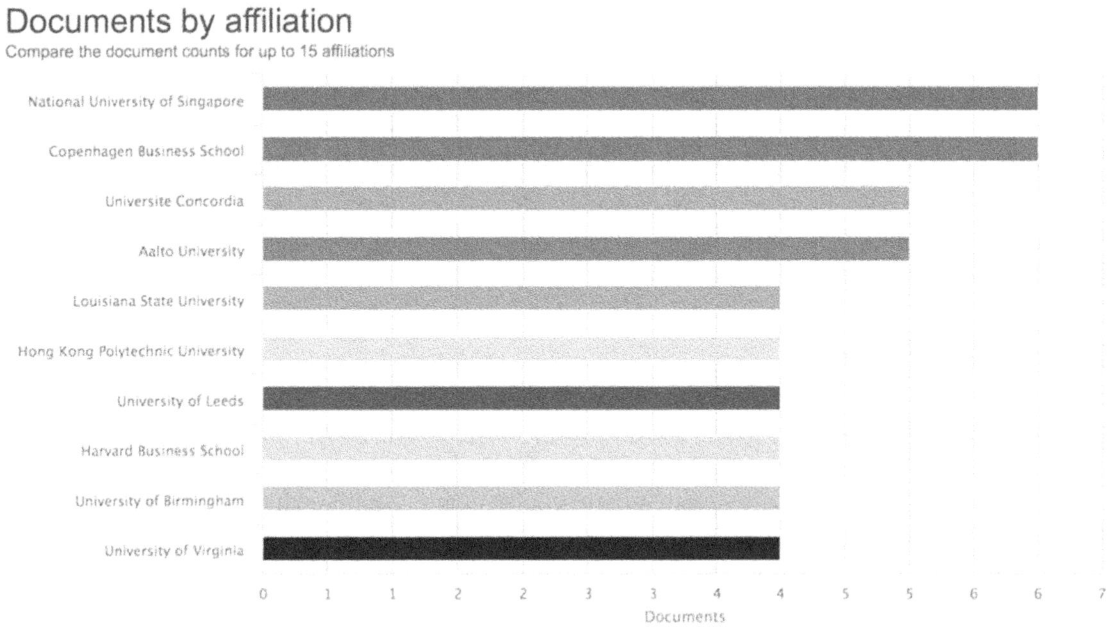

Figure 6. Articles by country
Source: Our elaboration on Scopus Database, 2017

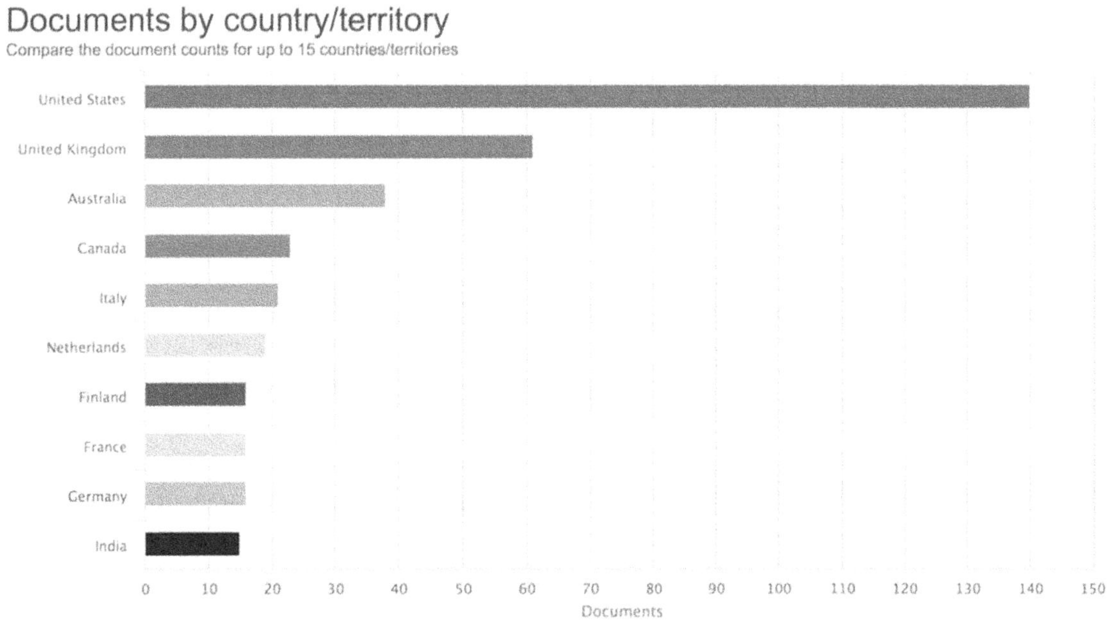

<SV> research in Anglo-Saxon culture. This evidence is partly explained by the leadership of American business schools in corporate strategy studies.

After the preliminary analysis, we selected 78 articles examining the titles, abstracts and keywords of all the retrieved academic journals and conference papers and, in some cases, the full content of the articles to ensure the articles are relevant.

The research follows the SLR method, classifying the articles according to the SLR schema and the changes we include for analysing <SV> criteria (see Table 5), and provide insights and critique into the evolution of the <SV> literature. However, rather than describe the entire SLR framework, we first address each criterion by describing the reason we chose the criteria for our analysis and the insights and the critique we develop from the results.

Jurisdiction

We adopt the Jurisdiction (A) criterion from Guthrie, Ricceri, and Dumay (2012, p. 71). It shows where the papers are emanated from (Massaro et al., 2016, p. 783) and examines the context of <SV> research. In the 'Supra-national' perspective, we categorize articles in which authors have compared two or more countries. For example, we classify articles that do not have an empirical based as 'Supra-national/International/Comparative-General'. Whereas articles focusing on specific nations or regions, fall into 'National-General' perspective.

We further sub-classify these attributes into 'Industry' or 'Organizational' subcategories either from 'Supra-national' or 'National' perspective. For example, the sub-category 'National-Industry' includes papers based on a specific industry belonging to a single country. On the contrary, the 'National-Organizational' subcategory includes articles whose analysis concerns a single organization belonging to a single country.

As shown in Table 5, in the 'Supra-national' perspective the articles analyzed are concentrated in the 'General' and 'Industry' subcategories, that include respectively 28 and 16 articles; instead, in the 'National' perspective the majority of articles adopt an industry approach because there is a greater concentration in the subcategory 'National-Industry', with 25 articles.

Organizational Focus

The Organizational Focus (B) criterion helps to identify the type of organizations that a research paradigm investigates (Massaro et al., 2016). According to Guthrie et al. (2012, p. 71) in our research this criterion consists of six attributes: 'Publicly listed', 'Private-SMEs', 'Private-Others', 'Public sector', 'Not-for-profit', 'General/Other'.

As showed by Table 5 we find that the majority of <SV> studies focusing on 'General/Other' (with 52 articles), this evidence confirms that <SV> research regards mainly the entrepreneurial and managerial approach to business activity. 'Private-Others' companies has 17 contributes, so these are the most commonly researched type of organizations (e.g., Airbnb, Uber). Surprisingly, only 2 articles focus on 'Public Sector' whereas no articles focus on 'Not-for-profit' organizations. This result denotes that <SV> studies concerns almost exclusively private firms on the basis of Creating Shared Value approach (Porter & Kramer, 2011), leaving room for more sustainable and inclusive approaches, in which there is a collaboration among firms, government and third sector.

Country of Research

The Country of research (C) criterion shows what are the geographic areas that are more investigated and if there are other countries/ regions that require attention (Massaro et al., 2016, p. 783). We develop this criterion from Guthrie et al.'s (2012) original classification scheme. However, we change the original attributes because we would expect a significant number of contributions from Asia. Additionally, we merge United Kingdom with Continental Europe, then we change the label to European Union, so we are more specific and because companies in this area are subject to EU directives. Therefore, we build a classification scheme dividing the Country of research in seven regions: 'USA/Canada', 'Australasia', 'European Union', 'Asia', and 'Other (including General)'. If the regional focus or the geographical location of the research cannot be determined, we classify the article in the 'Other (including General)' category.

The results suggest that the most studied locations are the USA/Canada and the European Union, respectively with 22 and 18 articles, so these are the contexts dominating the <SV> research agenda (see Table 5). Unsurprisingly, 21 articles adopt a general approach to <SV>, which we expect because <SV> claims to be the next step in the evolution of corporate strategy (Porter & Kramer, 2011).

Focus of <SV> Literature

The research focus refers to the specific topic developed by previous studies (Massaro et al., 2016, p. 783). We develop the Focus of <SV> literature (D) criterion from Guthrie et al. (2012) original classification scheme. In particular, we change the original format to highlight the specific research topics of our analysis, so we classify the categories as follows: 'Business Ethics', 'Strategy and Business Models', 'Human Relations', 'Management', 'Marketing' and 'Tourism'.

Unsurprisingly, we find that the most popular category is 'Strategy and Business Models' with 37 articles, which we expect that because since the seminal article of Michael Porter and Mark Kramer in 2006 the idea of shared value has earned a central place in the conversation about the impacts - positive and negative - of business in society as showed by Table 5. Another specific focus of <SV> literature is 'Tourism', which we expect because value sharing models are widespread in this industry (e.g., Ert, Fleischer, & Magen, 2016; Cheng, 2016; Heo, 2016; Font, Guix, & Bonilla-Priego, 2016; Fang, Ye, & Law, 2016; Forno, & Garibaldi, 2015; Hsiao & Chuang, 2016).

Academics, Practitioners and Consultants

In our study we add Academics, Practitioners and Consultants as double criteria to determine the authors of the articles and the subjects to which the articles are addressed (see Table 5). We develop the Academics, Practitioners and Consultants (as authors) (E) criterion and Academics, Practitioners and Consultants (as readers) (F) criterion from Dumay et al. (2016, p. 172) classification scheme. In particular, we change the original format to highlight the different perspective of Academics, Practitioners and Consultants as authors and readers. For this reason, we identify three categories: 'Academic(s)', 'Practitioner(s) and Consultant(s)' and 'Academics, practitioners and consultant(s)' for both criteria.

We find most articles are written by academics (75 articles) and only 2 are co-written by academics and practitioners. Additionally, practitioners and consultants contribute little to the <SV> research debate with only one article (Ukolov, Solomatin, Solomatin, Chernikov, & Ukolov, 2016).

Concerning the audience of the <SV> literature, we find that the majority of articles is directed to the broad category of Academics, practitioners and consultant(s) with 55 contributions, whereas only 16 articles address theoretical issues directed solely to academics.

Research Methods

The research method criterion (G) adapted from Guthrie et al. (2012) includes five attributes. In particular, the first three attributes relate to studies that are empirical in nature (Dumay et al., 2016): 'Case/Field study/Interviews', 'Content analysis/Historical analysis', 'Survey/Questionnaire/Other empirical'. The next two attributes are normative in nature and include 'Commentary/Normative/Policy' and 'Literature review'.

The results of our analysis show that the research method most commonly employed is 'Commentary/Normative/Policy' with 34 articles. Next, 'Case/Field study/Interviews' has 23 contributions followed by 'Surveys/Questionnaire/Other empirical' with 19 contributions, so both of them are research methods popular for investigating <SV> as showed by Table 5. Additionally, only two articles adopt a 'literature review' method, the first is a literature review on shared value made by Dembek et al. (2016), whereas the second regards a literature review on sharing economy written by Cheng in 2016.

The last stages of the structured literature review protocol, developing further research paths and question on <SV>, is presented in the next section.

FUTURE RESEARCH DIRECTIONS

In this section, we answer research question three 'What is the future for <SV> research?' and outline the new directions in research on <SV>. In doing so we want to point out that while we are skeptical about Creating Shared Value as concept based only on Porter and Kramer approach (Porter & Kramer, 2006; 2011), we see great potential for the wider concept of <SV>, that refers to broader value sharing models.

Thus, there are still significant opportunities for researchers to investigate it, especially if <SV> proliferates and builds a corpus of reports and organizational <SV> practice. Thus, <SV> is a significant movement and, for this reason, its existence and impact merit investigation (Dembek et al, 2016; Cheng, 2016). However, we see some significant challenges researchers and practitioners need to overcome.

As confirmed by our analysis, under the umbrella of <SV> there are different concepts and models of value sharing. Particularly, the focus of <SV> literature results highlights that 'Strategy and Business Models' and 'Tourism' are the main topics of <SV> literature. However, within these to categories there are different concepts relating to <SV> literature, including Shared Value and Sharing Economy.

From a strategic point of view, the concept of Creating Shared Value - that replaced the concept of value sharing - proposed by Porter and Kramer (2006, 2011) is an emerging stream of research. For example, Dembek et al. (2016) identify four major avenues for future research on Creating Shared Value. First, it is necessary for research to address the question of exactly what Creating Shared Value means to convert Shared Value from a buzzword and another marketing tool to shape organizational image to a reputable strategic concept. The authors propose as way to establish what Creating Shared Value means to clarify the means, outcomes, and beneficiaries of the outcomes of Shared Value, and focus on satisfying human needs. Second, future research should investigate how Shared Value should be measured, in fact the current efforts to measure Shared Value do not appear to offer a solution. Third, future research should carefully consider the levels of analysis of Creating Shared Value and their implications. Forth, future research should further investigate the tensions between business and society. To do this, it is necessary to consider broader impact (in terms of both costs and benefits) of Creating Shared Value and to use data from multiple stakeholders (Dembek et al., 2016, p. 244).

From a business modeling point of view, Sharing Economy is an emerging stream of research. According to Cheng (2016), in business practice are emerging various types of Sharing Economy business models, comprising different collaborative and peer-to-peer business models e.g., Airbnb and Uber), and their potentials, particularly service models' impacts on the personal aspects of consumers and goods that requires further research. Additionally, there is a growing interest recognizing the relationship between innovation and sustainability development in Sharing Economy, that should be further investigated. This theme is particularly connected to the 'Sustainability' theme by the concept of housing reflecting the strong relationship between the accommodation sector in Sharing Economy (e.g., Airbnb) and sustainable sharing practices (e.g., shared mobility and collaborative consumption).

Finally, looking at tourism and hospitality the literature review reveals a specific interest on two aspects: Sharing Economy's impacts on destinations and tourism services and Sharing Economy's impacts on tourists. It is well known that the traditional accommodation industry is threaded by Airbnb business model, that is at the frontier of Sharing Economy, other industries in tourism and hospitality are also facing increasing pressures, such as peer-to-peer financing, transport and restaurants, but no attention has been devoted to these areas to date (Cheng, 2016). Therefore, there is a need of further research.

CONCLUSION

In conclusion, this chapter examines the <SV>'s research foundations, establishes the focus of <SV> literature and offers guidelines for future research and suggests to move beyond the first stage towards second stage research on <SV>.

Based on the results and analysis, we argue that the way forward for <SV> research is an emerging research field. Researchers need to be innovative in searching for <SV>, for example investigating new business models and organizational structures. Additional evidence that current <SV> research is the persistence with which the majority of studies are theoretical and examine the issue from a general point of view suggests to focus on organization types especially Private-SMEs, Public Sector and Not-for-profit organizations, that seem under investigated topics. One last comment relates to the different concepts related to <SV> that we identified in this literature review (e.g., corporate social responsibility, sustainability, shared value, sharing economy). Another way that could contribute to clarifying the meaning of <SV> would be to conduct a meta-level study to clarify the meaning and use of different concepts related to <SV>.

Finally, as with all interpretive research, the findings are limited to the breadth and depth of the data analysed and our interpretation of the results. While the SLR method employed offers more reliability than a traditional authorship literature review, researchers using the same method may interpret the results differently. Thus, we take all responsibility for our interpretation of the findings including any errors or omissions.

REFERENCES

Belk, R. (2014). You are what you can access: Sharing and collaborative consumption online. *Journal of Business Research*, *67*(8), 1595–1600. doi:10.1016/j.jbusres.2013.10.001

Beschorner, T. (2013). Creating shared value: The one-trick Pony approach – A comment on Michael Porter and Mark Kramer. *Business Ethics Journal Review*, *17*(1), 106–112. doi:10.12747/bejr2013.01.17

Botsman, R., & Rogers, R. (2010). *What's Mine Is Yours: The Rise of Collaborative Consumption*. New York: Harper Business.

Burke, C. S., Sims, D. E., Lazzara, E. H., & Salas, E. (2007). Trust in leadership: A multi-level review and integration. *The Leadership Quarterly*, *18*(6), 606–632. doi:10.1016/j.leaqua.2007.09.006

Cafferata, R. (2014). Management in adattamento. Bologna, Italy: Il Mulino.

Cheng, J.-H., Yeh, C.-H., & Tu, C.-W. (2008). Trust and knowledge sharing in green supply chains. *Supply Chain Management*, *13*(4), 283–295. doi:10.1108/13598540810882170

Cheng, M. (2016). Sharing economy: A review and agenda for future research. *International Journal of Hospitality Management*, *57*, 60–70. doi:10.1016/j.ijhm.2016.06.003

Cohen, B., & Kietzmann, J. (2014). Ride on! mobility business models for the sharing economy. *Organization & Environment*, *27*(3), 279–296. doi:10.1177/1086026614546199

Crane, A., Palazzo, G., Spence, L. J., & Matten, D. (2014). Contesting the value of creating shared value. *California Management Review*, *56*(2), 130–153. doi:10.1525/cmr.2014.56.2.130

Cronin, P., Ryan, F., & Coughlan, M. (2008). Undertaking a literature review: A step-by-step approach. *British Journal of Nursing (Mark Allen Publishing)*, *17*(1), 38–43. doi:10.12968/bjon.2008.17.1.28059 PMID:18399395

Dembek, K., Singh, P., & Bhakoo, V. (2016). Literature review of shared value: A theoretical concept or a management buzzword? *Journal of Business Ethics*, *137*(2), 231–267. doi:10.1007/s10551-015-2554-z

Dhanaraj, C., Lyles, M. A., Steensma, H. K., & Tihanyi, L. (2004). Managing tacit and explicit knowledge transfer in IJVs: The role of relational embeddedness and the impact on performance. *Journal of International Business Studies*, *35*(5), 428–442. doi:10.1057/palgrave.jibs.8400098

Dixon-Woods, M. (2011). Systematic reviews and qualitative methods. In D. Silverman (Ed.), *Qualitative Research. Issues of Theory, Method and Practice* (3rd ed.; pp. 331–346). London, UK: Sage Publications.

Dumay, J. (2014). 15 years of the journal of intellectual capital and counting: A manifesto for transformational IC research. *Journal of Intellectual Capital*, *15*(1), 2–37. doi:10.1108/JIC-09-2013-0098

Dumay, J., Bernardi, C., Guthrie, J., & Demartini, P. (2016). Integrated reporting: A structured literature review. *Accounting Forum*, *40*(3), 166–185. doi:10.1016/j.accfor.2016.06.001

Dumay, J., & Cai, L. (2014). A review and critique of content analysis as a methodology for inquiring into IC disclosure. *Journal of Intellectual Capital*, *15*(2), 264–290. doi:10.1108/JIC-01-2014-0010

Ert, E., Fleischer, A., & Magen, N. (2016). Trust and reputation in the sharing economy: The role of personal photos in Airbnb. *Tourism Management*, *55*, 62–73. doi:10.1016/j.tourman.2016.01.013

Fang, B., Ye, Q., & Law, R. (2016). Effect of sharing economy on tourism industry employment. *Annals of Tourism Research*, *57*, 264–267. doi:10.1016/j.annals.2015.11.018

Font, X., Guix, M., & Bonilla-Priego, M. J. (2016). Corporate social responsibility in cruising: Using materiality analysis to create shared value. *Tourism Management*, *53*, 175–186. doi:10.1016/j.tourman.2015.10.007

Forno, F., & Garibaldi, R. (2015). Sharing economy in travel and tourism: The case of home-swapping in Italy. *Journal of Quality Assurance in Hospitality & Tourism*, *16*(2), 202–220. doi:10.1080/1528008X.2015.1013409

Gillespie, N. A., & Mann, L. (2004). Transformational leadership and shared values: The building blocks of trust. *Journal of Managerial Psychology*, *19*(6), 588–607. doi:10.1108/02683940410551507

Golinelli, G. M. (2005). L'approccio sistemico al governo dell'impresa. L'impresa sistema vitale (vol. 1). Padua, Italy: Cedam.

Goodman, S. A., & Svyantek, D. J. (1999). Person-Organization fit and contextual performance: Do shared values matter. *Journal of Vocational Behavior*, *55*(2), 254–275. doi:10.1006/jvbe.1998.1682

Guthrie, J., Ricceri, F., & Dumay, J. (2012). Reflections and projections: A decade of intellectual capital accounting research. *The British Accounting Review*, *44*(2), 68–82. doi:10.1016/j.bar.2012.03.004

Hartline, M. D., Maxham, J. G. III, & Mckee, D. O. (2000). Corridors of influence in the dissemination of customer-oriented strategy to customer contact service employees. *Journal of Marketing*, *64*(2), 35–50. doi:10.1509/jmkg.64.2.35.18001

Hayes, A. F., & Krippendorff, K. (2007). Answering the call for a standard reliability measure for coding data. *Communication Methods and Measures*, *1*(1), 77–89. doi:10.1080/19312450709336664

Heo, C. Y. (2016). Sharing economy and prospects in tourism research. *Annals of Tourism Research*, *58*, 166–170. doi:10.1016/j.annals.2016.02.002

Hern, A. (2015). *Why the Term 'Sharing Economy' Needs to Die*. Retrieved on March 30, 2017 from http://www.theguardian.com/technology/2015/oct/05/why-the-term-sharing-economy-needs-to-die

Hsiao, T.-Y., & Chuang, C.-M. (2016). Creating shared value through implementing green practices for star hotels. *Asia Pacific Journal of Tourism Research*, *21*(6), 678–696. doi:10.1080/10941665.2015.1068194

Krippendorff, K. (2013). *Content Analysis. An Introduction to Its Methodology*. Thousand Oaks, CA: Sage Publications.

Lee, S. M., Olson, D. L., & Trimi, S. (2012). Co-innovation: Convergenomics, collaboration, and co-creation for organizational values. *Management Decision*, *50*(5), 817–831. doi:10.1108/00251741211227528

Markham, S. E., Yammarino, F. J., Murry, W. D., & Palanski, M. E. (2010). Leader-member exchange, shared values, and performance: Agreement and levels of analysis do matter. *The Leadership Quarterly*, *21*(3), 469–480. doi:10.1016/j.leaqua.2010.03.010

Massaro, M., Dumay, J., & Guthrie, J. (2016). On the shoulders of giants: Undertaking a structured literature review in accounting. *Accounting, Auditing & Accountability Journal*, *29*(5), 767–801. doi:10.1108/AAAJ-01-2015-1939

Maxham, J. G. III, & Netemeyer, R. G. (2003). Firms reap what they sow: The effects of shared values and perceived organizational justice on customers evaluations of complaint handling. *Journal of Marketing*, *67*(1), 46–62. doi:10.1509/jmkg.67.1.46.18591

Michelini, L., & Fiorentino, D. (2012). New business models for creating shared value. *Social Responsibility Journal*, *8*(4), 561–577. doi:10.1108/17471111211272129

Modell, S. (2009). In defence of triangulation: A critical realist approach to mixed methods research in management accounting. *Management Accounting Research*, *20*(3), 208–221. doi:10.1016/j.mar.2009.04.001

Mukherjee, A., & Nath, P. (2007). Role of electronic trust in online retailing: A re-examination of the commitment-trust theory. *European Journal of Marketing*, *41*(9-10), 1173–1202. doi:10.1108/03090560710773390

Pepe, C. (2013). Values and corporate responsibility in globalization processes (EMEE vol. 32). Milan, Italy: McGraw-Hill Education.

Petty, R., & Guthrie, J. (2000). Intellectual capital literature review: Measurement, reporting and management. *Journal of Intellectual Capital*, *1*(2), 155–176. doi:10.1108/14691930010348731

Pfitzer, M., Bockstette, V., & Stamp, M. (2013). Innovating for shared value. *Harvard Business Review*, *91*(9), 1–9.

Porter, M. E., & Kramer, M. R. (2006). Strategy & Society: The Link between Competitive Advantage and Corporate Social Responsibility. *Harvard Business Review*, *84*(12), 78–92. PMID:17183795

Porter, M. E., & Kramer, M. R. (2011). Creating Shared Value: Redefining Capitalism and the Role of the Corporation in Society. *Harvard Business Review*, *89*(1-2), 62–77.

Schor, J. B., & Fitzmaurice, C. J. (2015). Collaborating and connecting: the emergence of the sharing economy. In L. Reisch & J. Thogersen (Eds.), *Handbook of Research on Sustainable Consumption*. Cheltenham, UK: Edward Elgar. doi:10.4337/9781783471270.00039

Serenko, A., & Bontis, N. (2013). Global ranking of knowledge management and intellectual capital academic journals: 2013 update. *Journal of Knowledge Management*, *17*(2), 307–326. doi:10.1108/13673271311315231

Tagliaventi, M. R., & Mattarelli, E. (2006). The role of networks of practice, value sharing, and operational proximity in knowledge flows between professional groups. *Human Relations*, *59*(3), 291–319. doi:10.1177/0018726706064175

Ukolov, V. F., Solomatin, A. V., Solomatin, Y. V., Chernikov, S. U., & Ukolov, A. V. (2016). Food-sharing economy pattern comparison in UK and Russian markets. *International Business Management*, *10*(18), 4268–4282.

White, T., & McBurney, D. (2012). *Research Method* (9th ed.). Belmont, CA: Wadsworth.

Yin, R. K. (2014). *Case Study Research: Design and Methods* (5th ed.). Los Angeles, CA: Sage Publications.

Young-Ybarra, C., & Wiersema, M. (1999). Strategic Flexibility in Information Technology Alliances: The Influence of Transaction Cost Economics and Social Exchange Theory. *Organization Science*, *10*(4), 439–459. doi:10.1287/orsc.10.4.439

KEY TERMS AND DEFINITIONS

Creating Shared Value: According to a Creating Shared Value approach companies should not ignore society, as under the narrow conception of capitalism that has done so much harm to the legitimacy of business, but rather should search for business opportunity in society's needs. Creating shared value means to adopt business strategies that respond to the challenges presented by society and the environment and also reinforce the competitive advantage of a company.

Shared Value (or Sharing Value): While the origins of all the definitions of Shared Value - that replaced the concept of value sharing - can be seen in Porter and Kramer's (2006, 2011) work that define the shared value as policies and operating practices that enhance the competitiveness of a company while simultaneously advancing the economic and social conditions in the communities in which it operates. However, according to an overall definition of Shared Value it allows simultaneous creation of economic value for the firm and social and environmental value for the places in which they do business in a inclusive and sustainable manner.

Sharing: Can be anything to which access is enabled through pooling of resources, products or services.

Sharing Economy: It indicates the phenomenon as peer to peer sharing of access to underutilized goods and services, which prioritizes utilization and accessibility over ownership. The sharing economy may take a variety of forms, including using information technology to provide individuals with information that enables the optimization of resources through the mutualization of excess capacity in goods and services. A common premise is that when information about goods is shared (typically via an online marketplace), the value of those goods may increase for the business, for individuals, for the community and for society in general. Other most popular terms to describe this emerging business practice are 'collaborative consumption' and 'peer to peer economy'.

Structured Literature Review: The SLR is a method for studying a corpus of scholarly literature, to develop insights, critical reflections, future research paths and research questions. The SLR method complements traditional literature reviews because the approach helps to yield different outcomes that are defensible. The SLR can be useful for higher degree students and emerging scholars, allowing them to demonstrate that their literature reviews are defensible. Unlike a seasoned academic, who has immersed him or herself in a chosen field, these emerging scholars do not yet have the familiarity with the literature to develop a comprehensive review that sufficiently identifies worthwhile gaps for research. Additionally, for experienced academic researchers an SLR offers an alternative approach that can either confirm one' s knowledge or open up new avenues for research to which the traditional approach may not provide access. The latter is the likely outcome, therefore, an SLR can help experienced scholars develop new and interesting research paths by accessing and analyzing a considerable volume of scholarly work.

APPENDIX

Shared Value Publications Reviewed (1997-2016)

Acquier, A., Valiorgue, B., & Daudigeos, T. (2015). Sharing the shared value: A transaction cost perspective on strategic CSR policies in global value chains. *Journal of Business Ethics*. doi:10.1007/s10551-015-2820-0

Amah, E., & Ahiauzu, A. (2014). Shared values and organizational effectiveness: A study of the Nigerian banking industry. *Journal of Management Development*, *33*(7), 694–708. doi:10.1108/JMD-09-2010-0065

Bergquist, A. K., & Lindmark, M. (2016). Sustainability and shared value in the interwar Swedish copper industry. *Business History Review*, *90*(2), 197–225. doi:10.1017/S0007680516000374

Bertini, M., & Gourville, J. T. (2012). Pricing to create shared value. *Harvard Business Review*, *90*(6), 96–104.

Boria-Reverter, S., Crespi-Vallbona, M., García-González, A., & Vizuete-Luciano, E. (2013). Shared values in the Spanish company [Los valores compartidos en la empresa española]. *Universia Business Review*, *37*, 68–85.

Bouncken, R. B., & Reuschl, A. J. (2016). Coworking-spaces: How a phenomenon of the sharing economy builds a novel trend for the workplace and for entrepreneurship. *Review of Managerial Science*, 1–18. doi:10.1007/s11846-016-0215-y

Camilleri, M. A. (2016). Responsible tourism that creates shared value among stakeholders. *Tourism Planning and Development*, *13*(2), 219–235. doi:10.1080/21568316.2015.1074100

Cheng, M. (2016). Current sharing economy media discourse in tourism. *Annals of Tourism Research*, *60*, 111–114. doi:10.1016/j.annals.2016.07.001

Cheng, M. (2016). Sharing economy: A review and agenda for future research. *International Journal of Hospitality Management*, *57*, 60–70. doi:10.1016/j.ijhm.2016.06.003

Choi, H. R., Cho, M. J., Lee, K., Hong, S. G., & Woo, C. R. (2014). The business model for the sharing economy between SMEs. *WSEAS Transactions on Business and Economics*, *11*(1), 625–634.

Chu, W. (2001). Contingency organizations and shared values: Multiple logics in managing diversification. *Asia Pacific Journal of Management*, *18*(1), 83–99. doi:10.1023/A:1010617323691

Cohen, B., & Kietzmann, J. (2014). Ride on! mobility business models for the sharing economy. *Organization & Environment*, *27*(3), 279–296. doi:10.1177/1086026614546199

Comelli, M., Fenies, P., & Lemoine, D. (2009). Tactical planning for optimal cash flow and value sharing in supply chain. *International Journal of Logistics Systems and Management*, *5*(3-4), 323–343. doi:10.1504/IJLSM.2009.022500

Corner, P. D., & Pavlovich, K. (2016). Shared value through inner knowledge creation. *Journal of Business Ethics*, *135*(3), 543–555. doi:10.1007/s10551-014-2488-x

Crane, A., Palazzo, G., Spence, L. J., & Matten, D. (2014). Contesting the value of creating shared value. *California Management Review*, *56*(2), 130–153. doi:10.1525/cmr.2014.56.2.130

Dembek, K., Singh, P., & Bhakoo, V. (2016). Literature review of shared value: A theoretical concept or a management buzzword? *Journal of Business Ethics*, *137*(2), 231–267. doi:10.1007/s10551-015-2554-z

Dempsey, J. (2015). Moral responsibility, shared values, and corporate culture. *Business Ethics Quarterly*, *25*(3), 319–340. doi:10.1017/beq.2015.31

Dreyer, B., Lüdeke-Freund, F., Hamann, R., & Faccer, K. (2016). Upsides and downsides of the sharing economy: Collaborative consumption business models' stakeholder value impacts and their relationship to context. *Technological Forecasting and Social Change*. doi:10.1016/j.techfore.2017.03.036

Eisen, D. (2015). The sharing economy may reek of desperation, but it's a threat to your bottom line. *Hotel Management*, *230*(12), 4.

Ert, E., Fleischer, A., & Magen, N. (2016). Trust and reputation in the sharing economy: The role of personal photos in Airbnb. *Tourism Management*, *55*, 62–73. doi:10.1016/j.tourman.2016.01.013

Esposito, M., Kapoor, A., & Goyal, S. (2012). Enabling healthcare services for the rural and semi-urban segments in India: When shared value meets the bottom of the pyramid. *Corporate Governance (Bingley)*, *12*(4), 514–533. doi:10.1108/14720701211267847

Fang, B., Ye, Q., & Law, R. (2016). Effect of sharing economy on tourism industry employment. *Annals of Tourism Research*, *57*, 264–267. doi:10.1016/j.annals.2015.11.018

Florin, J., & Schmidt, E. (2011). Creating shared value in the hybrid venture arena: A business model innovation perspective. *Journal of Social Entrepreneurship*, *2*(2), 165–197. doi:10.1080/19420676.2011.614631

Font, X., Guix, M., & Bonilla-Priego, M. J. (2016). Corporate social responsibility in cruising: Using materiality analysis to create shared value. *Tourism Management*, *53*, 175–186. doi:10.1016/j.tourman.2015.10.007

Forgacs, G., & Dimanche, F. (2016). Revenue challenges for hotels in the sharing economy: Facing the Airbnb menace. *Journal of Revenue and Pricing Management*, *15*(6), 509–515. doi:10.1057/s41272-016-0071-z

Forno, F., & Garibaldi, R. (2015). Sharing economy in travel and tourism: The case of home-swapping in Italy. *Journal of Quality Assurance in Hospitality & Tourism*, *16*(2), 202–220. doi:10.1080/1528008X.2015.1013409

Fox, J. (2016). Airbnb: How the sharing economy is affecting new york city hotels. *Hotel Management*, *231*(1), 90–92.

Gillespie, N. A., & Mann, L. (2004). Transformational leadership and shared values: The building blocks of trust. *Journal of Managerial Psychology, 19*(6), 588–607. doi:10.1108/02683940410551507

Goodman, S. A., & Svyantek, D. J. (1999). Person-organization fit and contextual performance: Do shared values matter. *Journal of Vocational Behavior, 55*(2), 254–275. doi:10.1006/jvbe.1998.1682

Heo, C. Y. (2016). Sharing economy and prospects in tourism research. *Annals of Tourism Research, 58*, 166–170. doi:10.1016/j.annals.2016.02.002

Houjeir, R., & Brennan, R. (2016). Trust in cross-cultural b2b financial service relationships: The role of shared values. *Journal of Financial Services Marketing, 21*(2), 90–102. doi:10.1057/fsm.2016.4

Hsiao, T.-Y., & Chuang, C.-M. (2016). Creating shared value through implementing green practices for star hotels. *Asia Pacific Journal of Tourism Research, 21*(6), 678–696. doi:10.1080/10941665.2015.1068194

Huefner, R. J. (2015). The sharing economy: Implications for revenue management. *Journal of Revenue and Pricing Management, 14*(4), 296–298. doi:10.1057/rpm.2015.18

Iriyadi. (2016). Performance measurements: From accounting to shared values. *International Journal of Applied Business and Economic Research, 14*(3), 1571-1585.

Jones, D. T., Huchzermeier, A., & Mitchell, A. (2011). Creating shared value with consumers. *International Commerce Review, 10*(1), 2–3. doi:10.1007/s12146-011-0075-y

Jones, S., & Wright, C. (2016). Fashion or future: Does creating shared value pay?. *Accounting and Finance*. doi:10.1111/acfi.12243

Jose, P. D. (2016). Business and society: Creating shared value: In conversation with N. R. Narayan Murthy, founder, Infosys. *IIMB Management Review, 28*(1), 43–51. doi:10.1016/j.iimb.2016.02.003

Kashyap, V., & Sivadas, E. (2012). An exploratory examination of shared values in channel relationships. *Journal of Business Research, 65*(5), 586–593. doi:10.1016/j.jbusres.2011.02.008

Kathan, W., Matzler, K., & Veider, V. (2016). The sharing economy: Your business models friend or foe? *Business Horizons, 59*(6), 663–672. doi:10.1016/j.bushor.2016.06.006

Kramer, M. R., & Pfitzer, M. W. (2016). The ecosystem of shared value. *Harvard Business Review, 94*(10), 80–89.

Lee, D., Moon, J., Cho, J., Kang, H.-J., & Jeong, J. (2014). From corporate social responsibility to creating shared value with suppliers through mutual firm foundation in the Korean bakery industry: A case study of the SPC group. *Asia Pacific Business Review, 20*(3), 461–483. doi:10.1080/13602381.2014.929301

Leighton, P. (2016). Professional self-employment, new power and the sharing economy: Some cautionary tales from Uber. *Journal of Management & Organization, 22*(6), 859–874. doi:10.1017/jmo.2016.30

Marchi, A., & Parekh, E.-J. (2016). How the sharing economy can make its case. *The McKinsey Quarterly*, (1): 112–116.

Markham, S. E., Yammarino, F. J., Murry, W. D., & Palanski, M. E. (2010). Leader-member exchange, shared values, and performance: Agreement and levels of analysis do matter. *The Leadership Quarterly*, *21*(3), 469–480. doi:10.1016/j.leaqua.2010.03.010

Matinheikki, J., Rajala, R., & Peltokorpi, A. (2015). From the profit of one toward benefitting many - crafting a vision of shared value creation. *Journal of Cleaner Production*. doi:10.1016/j.jclepro.2016.09.081

Matzler, K., Veider, V., & Kathan, W. (2015). Adapting to the sharing economy. *MIT Sloan Management Review*, *56*(2), 71–77.

Maxham, J. G., III, & Netemeyer, R. G. (2003). Firms reap what they sow: The effects of shared values and perceived organizational justice on customers evaluations of complaint handling. *Journal of Marketing*, *67*(1), 46–62. doi:10.1509/jmkg.67.1.46.18591

Mcmullin, W. (2007). Comments on lasting change: The shared values process that makes companies great. *Leadership and Management in Engineering*, *7*(2), 47–48.

Meulensteen, T. M., Vermeulen, W. J. V., & Meerman, S. (2016). Creating shared value in the buyer-supplier relationship through the implementation of sustainability requirements. *Global Business and Economics Review*, *18*(6), 656–678. doi:10.1504/GBER.2016.079410

Michelini, L., & Fiorentino, D. (2012). New business models for creating shared value. *Social Responsibility Journal*, *8*(4), 561–577. doi:10.1108/17471111211272129

Morgan, A., Adair, D., Taylor, T., & Hermens, A. (2014). Sport sponsorship alliances: Relationship management for shared value. *Sports. Business and Management*, *4*(4), 270–283.

Muñoz, P., & Cohen, B. (2016). Mapping out the sharing economy: A configurational approach to sharing business modelling. *Technological Forecasting and Social Change*. doi:10.1016/j.techfore.2017.03.035

Orr, S., & Sarni, W. (2015). Does the concept of creating shared value hold water? *The Journal of Business Strategy*, *36*(3), 18–29. doi:10.1108/JBS-10-2013-0098

Parguel, B., Lunardo, R., & Benoit-Moreau, F. (2016). Sustainability of the sharing economy in question: When second-hand peer-to-peer platforms stimulate indulgent consumption. *Technological Forecasting and Social Change*. doi:10.1016/j.techfore.2017.03.029

Pavlovich, K., & Corner, P. D. (2014). Conscious enterprise emergence: Shared value creation through expanded conscious awareness. *Journal of Business Ethics*, *121*(3), 341–351. doi:10.1007/s10551-013-1726-y

Pfitzer, M., Bockstette, V., & Stamp, M. (2013). Innovating for shared value. *Harvard Business Review*, *91*(9), 1–9.

Pongwiritthon, R. (2015). Creating shared value of Thai SMEs for competitive advantage. *International Journal of Applied Business and Economic Research*, *13*(5), 3109–3120.

Popovič, A., Hackney, R., Coelho, P. S., & Jaklič, J. (2014). How information-sharing values influence the use of information systems: An investigation in the business intelligence systems context. *The Journal of Strategic Information Systems*, *23*(4), 1–26. doi:10.1016/j.jsis.2014.08.003

Porter, M. E., & Kramer, M. R. (2011). Creating Shared Value: Redefining Capitalism and the Role of the Corporation in Society. *Harvard Business Review*, *89*(1-2), 62–77.

Raghavan, S., & Shreen, K. (2015). Shared value, conscious business, and spirituality in a fashion enterprise in south India. *Organizational Cultures*, *15*(1), 15–29.

Riad, S. (2007). Of mergers and cultures: What happened to shared values and joint assumptions? *Journal of Organizational Change Management*, *20*(1), 26–43. doi:10.1108/09534810710715261

Richard, B., & Cleveland, S. (2016). The future of hotel chains: Branded marketplaces driven by the sharing economy. *Journal of Vacation Marketing*, *22*(3), 239–248. doi:10.1177/1356766715623827

Sarmah, B., & Rahman, Z. (2016). NEDFi: Transforming lives through shared value creation. *Asian Journal of Management Cases*, *13*(1), 40–55. doi:10.1177/0972820116631413

Serra, J., Font, X., & Ivanova, M. (2015). Creating shared value in destination management organisations: The case of Turisme de Barcelona. *Journal of Destination Marketing and Management*. doi:10.1016/j.jdmm.2016.06.005

Spitzeck, H., & Chapman, S. (2012). Creating shared value as a differentiation strategy - the example of BASF in brazil. *Corporate Governance (Bingley)*, *12*(4), 499–513. doi:10.1108/14720701211267838

Szmigin, I., & Rutherford, R. (2013). Shared value and the impartial spectator test. *Journal of Business Ethics*, *114*(1), 171–182. doi:10.1007/s10551-012-1335-1

Tagliaventi, M. R., & Mattarelli, E. (2006). The role of networks of practice, value sharing, and operational proximity in knowledge flows between professional groups. *Human Relations*, *59*(3), 291–319. doi:10.1177/0018726706064175

Tatham, P. (2013). An exploration of trust and shared values in UK defence supply networks. *International Journal of Physical Distribution & Logistics Management*, *43*(2), 148–166. doi:10.1108/IJPDLM-03-2011-0044

Toggenburg, G. N., & Grimheden, J. (2016). Upholding shared values in the EU: What role for the EU agency for fundamental rights? *Journal of Common Market Studies*, *54*(5), 1093–1104. doi:10.1111/jcms.12404

Topal, J., & Toledano, P. (2013). Why the extractive industry should support mandatory transparency: A shared value approach. *Business and Society Review*, *118*(3), 271–298. doi:10.1111/basr.12011

Turnbull, C. (2016, Sept.). Strength in numbers: Opportunities in china's sharing economy. *China Business Review*.

Ukolov, V. F., Solomatin, A. V., Solomatin, Y. V., Chernikov, S. U., & Ukolov, A. V. (2016). Food-sharing economy pattern comparison in UK and Russian markets. *International Business Management*, *10*(18), 4268–4282.

Van Swol, L. M. (2011). Forecasting another's enjoyment versus giving the right answer: Trust, shared values, task effects, and confidence in improving the acceptance of advice. *International Journal of Forecasting*, *27*(1), 103–120. doi:10.1016/j.ijforecast.2010.03.002

Wagner, S. M., & Lindemann, E. (2008). Determinants of value sharing in channel relationships. *Journal of Business and Industrial Marketing*, *23*(8), 544–553. doi:10.1108/08858620810913353

Watrous, K. M., Huffman, A. H., & Pritchard, R. D. (2006). When co-workers and managers quit: The effects of turnover and shared values on performance. *Journal of Business and Psychology*, *21*(1), 103–126. doi:10.1007/s10869-005-9021-2

Weber, T. A. (2014). Intermediation in a sharing economy: Insurance, moral hazard, and rent extraction. *Journal of Management Information Systems*, *31*(3), 35–71. doi:10.1080/07421222.2014.995520

Zhang, Z., Wan, D., Jia, M., & Gu, L. (2009). Prior ties, shared values and cooperation in public-private partnerships. *Management and Organization Review*, *5*(3), 353–374. doi:10.1111/j.1740-8784.2009.00154.x

Chapter 2
Entrepreneurial Thinking in the Educational System

Cătălin Grădinaru
University of Bucharest, Romania

Sorin-George I. Toma
University of Bucharest, Romania

Paul I. Marinescu
University of Bucharest, Romania

ABSTRACT

Education is the critical vein for human development, for society and economic growth. Because the context nowadays is vacillating, sometimes turbulent even, mankind needs empowerment through a belief system. We believe that an educated man is key to a sustainable economy, one that promotes values, lucidity and rationality. Education is modelled by and models society, through the way we think, act and react. The individual is the main actor on life's scene and he is responsible of the various shapes and forms of the socio-economic systems, of different contexts and behaviours in general. In this chapter, we aim to highlight the importance of entrepreneurship, management, creativity in managing an educational institution (system). We will analyse how an entrepreneurial system should look like, how creative thinking helps and how it will contribute to an "educated development".

INTRODUCTION

We live in an environment where it is critical to adapt as quickly as possible to all sorts of stimuli and it is this ability that may give us the competitive advantage we need to succeed. Nowadays situations are hard to handle in an isolated manner. We live in networks, in networks of networks and in networks that generate networks. As the wheels keep turning at a faster pace than ever, soft skills required to handle situations are becoming indispensable. This is the globalized society, a concept that interlinks all interested parties around the world, pushes the educational system forward, forces institutions to overcome more and more complex problems, leads towards general reconfigurations and is inherently linked to

DOI: 10.4018/978-1-5225-3147-0.ch002

a constant adaptation to the variable geometry of the fast-paced shifting of the economical context. In order to function adequately, to create and be part of projects (internal, local, regional, national and international), the managerial system of the educational system should act in an entrepreneurial way. In "global knowledge societies and economies" (Aleandri & Refrigeri, 2013) the responsibility of all interested parties such as the manager (leader), other employees, students, companies, etc. is to think differently, effectively and creatively in any undertaken project.

Education and its management should be regarded as one would look at a company: it should thrive using its resources, optimizing its processes, satisfying clients and taking into consideration stakeholders' thoughts, involving them into its activities, thus making them part of the organization. It is essential to get continuous feedback using all sorts of methods, because we consider this to be one of the top priorities when anything is subject to perfection. Education is not a business but it definitely should use entrepreneurial thinking so that it will boost its components, providing synergic effects. Universities cannot exist on their own, even though they can be self-sufficient from an economic standpoint; they are part of the worldwide educational network. They are responsible over the way they act, react and serve society and economy though its main result (outcomes): students.

Using creative thinking, educational institutions should promote student initiative in all its forms: spin-offs, personal projects, or any other form of materializing any type of fruitful opportunities. The university is now responsible not only for knowledge creation and transfer, but also for developing an entrepreneurial spirit and solid civic sense. Thus, it should be "concerned with the creation and exploitation of creative or intellectual capital" (Bujor & Avasilicai, 2016), pursuing greatness at its best. It is essential to state that in an entrepreneurial society, innovation can be found everywhere: things, procedures, thoughts. Humans constantly need to educate themselves, sometimes using sophisticated algorithms. While economy provides the means, the educational system stands for the framework support.

A knowledge-based society regards education as the base of sustainable development. Thus, investments in this area are considered to be a sine qua non condition for evolution. One should also take into consideration that "durability" in education usually resides in the echoes it has over one's life throughout the years.

Entrepreneurship, in general, is more about facing and handling challenges, dealing with contexts whilst thinking in a creative manner. In a fluid economy, entrepreneurs must act quickly and use resources at their maximum potential. An entrepreneurial educational system should be the answer to providing the human resources economy critically needs.

A respectable university should make sure high-quality standards are met and never stop raising the bar. Education may also be synonymous to social responsibility if the students that graduate have embraced and absorbed in their DNA this kind of ethics. The manager of the system (depending on the institution, for instance the dean of an university) should regard the components of the system in an entrepreneurial manner so that everything would not only function, but work in such a way that efficacy becomes the engine of thoughts. This is how one creates an ecosystem that can represent the core of a society's development in the future.

In such an entrepreneurial educational system, one main topic is how to evaluate organizational performance. The methods of evaluation are various and sometimes hard to grasp, especially when human capital is involved. Another important part is the motivational system and the rewards used in order to promote performance. Intellectual capital should be used within the entrepreneurial educational system so that it creates added value. The organization is responsible for providing the necessary means to achieve a high standard of individual, team and organizational performance.

An entrepreneurial educational system is not only about enhancing the entrepreneurial potential in graduates or seeking to provide the necessary knowledge in order to succeed in an economic activity. It is also about creating a system that is effective, creative and resourceful, about motivating stakeholders to be part of that particular system; it may even be about creating a global entrepreneurial-educational-social system that would integrate all existing and future networks in such a way that every element becomes a part of the whole. Among the pillars supporting the system one must refer to the prevalence of educational enterprises. This particular entrepreneurial mind-set should be practised at all educational levels, both from the organizational chart and students' side. This system may also be about not only return on investment, but return to society (social entrepreneurship from institutions form the educational field of activity). The university may become a business incubator of knowledge and business, constantly seeking to thrive in an ethical manner. This is one difficult opportunity that the system has and should profit from.

THE ENTREPRENEURIAL SPIRIT AND THINKING

The entrepreneurial spirit may be regarded in a sense "that one is working for oneself rather than for someone else. Those with entrepreneurial spirit feel they have a stake in the business and can directly affect the success of that business" (Denton, 1993). The entrepreneurial spirit is not innate. Such a spirit is achieved primarily through education, experience, effort and, obviously, will. But, in this complicated process of achieving the abilities of an entrepreneur, motivation is definitely very important (perhaps the most important of all). The configuration of this motivation is neither simple, nor linear. It is built over time, through endogenous factors which depend therefore on personality, ability, attitude and even on everyone's character, as well as through exogenous factors, which are defined generally on the requirements, demands and constraints and, of course, freedoms of society and, especially, of the business environment.

But the most important question, both for society, as well as for the individual is the one that refers to the universe of the entrepreneurial spirit, the entrepreneurial thinking. In other words, are the entrepreneurial spirit (or having enterprising spirit in a sense that you have to constantly notice and pursue opportunities in everything and not necessarily be a business owner) and the entrepreneurial thinking (or possessing enterprising thinking) part of the strategic component, or are they just a helpful instrument of such component? What is the "essence of being entrepreneurial" (Krueger, 2007)?. It is said that entrepreneurs have "extraordinary ways of thinking" that "could be called entrepreneurial thinking or entrepreneurial mindset" (Hnatek, 2015). Generally, literature does not deal with the taxonomy of such spirit and, therefore, of such a way of thinking, but it covers only the management of this spirit, namely the way in which a man, especially an intelligent and enterprising young man, can initiate and implement a business. Such an activity is not at all easy under some current conditions, especially referring to barriers certain countries have (e.g. an inadequate legislation), it is very complicated and therefore requires a lot of courage and many qualities from the person who desires to become an entrepreneur.

Certain questions related to this topic arise:

- Does entrepreneurship bring a touch of cognition or does it just use in a more or less intelligent manner what already exists within the field, aiming to obtain profit or simply to carry out a useful and profitable activity?

- Does entrepreneurship manifest itself only in its pragmatic side, meaning in the process of generating various projects and profitable activities or does it also concern the fields of scientific research as well?
- Does it represent a consequence of liberalism, neo-liberalism, market and the social market economy, a product of the new type of society in which everyone is seeking a place and a role, or the modus vivendi of a man (especially the modus vivendi of a young man) who is seeking his place and role in a society that has no idea that he exists and in which he must live?

One probably cannot answer clearly to this kind of questions which are closer to a strategic economic and social concept rather than the pragmatism and efficiency of such a concept. But precisely such pragmatism and such development of a spirit located somewhere between initiative (the effective search of a field of achievement) and the establishment of a business constitutes nowadays one of the most accessible and, after all, most successful sides that one can find in a profitable modus vivendi.

Generally, society, through the level of cognition achieved and through openings it operates towards the future, but especially through its educational system (formal, informal and non-formal) meets this field, shapes it and ensures a very rich cognitive support which consists in the existence of adequate courses, various databases, certain eLearning educational packages and even a substantial culture in the field. Education should be a "real locomotive of integration" (Dobrescu, 2014) on all levels that concern welfare and well-being. In fact, ever since the beginning of the world, there has been, in one way or another, almost for each intelligent individual on this planet, a spirit of entrepreneurship, which, over time, has generated an entrepreneurial thinking (enterprising), resulting in notable achievements. In ancient times, peasant households – which were generally very well organized – were the product of such an entrepreneurship spirit. Peasants' children were taught in school how to establish a household, how to use their minds and knowledge to get the most from working the land, the livestock, the forestry and natural conditions. It is really astonishing to observe that, throughout history, man has never been without initiative, courage, creative intelligence, entrepreneurial spirit and entrepreneurial and creative thinking.

After all, the entrepreneurial spirit (enterprising) is part of the defining qualities of man, even of human nature. This is the reason why man learns, in and through all forms and formulas of training (formal, non-formal and informal), how to become an entrepreneur, how to educate, to develop and to put into practice its innate qualities (qualities present in each man in the form of predispositions, certain abilities). The number of schools, courses, identities participating in education and training of future entrepreneurs is extremely large.

It is usually suitable that an entrepreneur should possess certain characteristics and abilities before endeavoring in business creation (Gedik, Miman & Kesici, 2015):

1. Planning skills.
2. Good communicator.
3. Interpersonal skills (great at establishing and maintaining positive relationships).
4. Positivist (learning from mistakes).
5. Persistent.
6. Problem solver.
7. Passionate.
8. Advice seeker.

All these qualities have nothing to do with being cunning, resourceful, with cruising through difficulties, with misleading the enemy, nor with diddling, tricking the other, with selfishness, greed, arrogance and the desire to have more and more and, often, at any cost, in the shortest time, or with stinginess, nor with other such "qualities" which populate or, to be more precise, pollute and vitiate our today's society. Nevertheless, these are realities which cannot and must not be eluded within an analysis of the procedural feature of the entrepreneurial thinking.

In the process of educating entrepreneurs in general and especially the youth who must form a solid and consistent entrepreneurial thinking, respect for the moral values of a business, of any type of activity – profitable or not – must be included. If not from a very solid morality, no human action can exist on a long term run; otherwise, consequences will always be a step back from evolution and may even be harmful or disastrous. Although, in derogatory terms, it is said that the concept of honest business represents an oxymoron, or that it does not matter how one (once) made his fortune, we believe that such a concept (to the extent in which we can consider dishonesty a concept), even if it is part of human reality, has no reason to be within an entrepreneurial thinking and even less in an entrepreneurial spirit. An entrepreneurial project and all the solutions designed and applied must not only be legal and legit, but under no circumstances are they to accept malicious practices such as immoral stratagems, being resourceful by any means necessary, misleading competition, tricking the customer, etc. Unfortunately, such attitudes are still present within the business world – there are not meant to serve the entrepreneurial spirit and thinking, and their effects in time will be disastrous including for the entrepreneur regardless of how great his success will be at a certain point or how much money or assets he owns.

The entrepreneurial spirit and, generally, the entrepreneurial thinking, are related to a series of essential components of the human personality, of which, the most important to this topic are the following:

1. Intelligence.
2. Will.
3. Initiative.
4. Cognition.
5. Culture.
6. Vocation.
7. Character.

Some of these (such as intelligence) are innate and present themselves as predispositions. Others are acquired within the process of training and continuous education. Intelligence is trained as well; it does not remain in its primitive, natural form. It is hard all those components separately because they form a whole. For instance, it is difficult to assume that intelligence alone would suffice for a young man to become a good entrepreneur thus lacking other qualities listed above, but such a thing is almost impossible without intelligence. A man without intelligence or a man having a poor intelligence coefficient simply may prove that he cannot become a good entrepreneur. There are very few things he may become in the system of an efficient economy, maybe a simple worker who, generally, cannot do anything else but some routine operations. But one must not conclude from this, that individuals who do not have a high enough intelligence coefficient cannot find an honourable place within society, but only the fact that they cannot become, only with very few and rare exceptions, great entrepreneurs.

Intelligence

Probably the most valuable quality of a future entrepreneur is intelligence. Without intelligence, it is highly unlikely to become a good entrepreneur. But this does not mean that intelligence is suffice. Intelligence, when uneducated and lacking the moral qualities an individual living within a society must have, may easily slip into various shapes, some of them even dangerous. Often, in popular terms, it is said that "where there is mind, there is also stupidity" (Anonymous), which means that uneducated intelligence and without the control of reason, may easily slide into other areas having a highly diversified and some very harmful effects for man and society. Or, as it is well known, the most important role in educating the intelligence of a man is played by school.

Intelligence can be: creative, intuitive but also speculative, imitating, strategic, emotional (meaning a type of social intelligence that involves the ability to monitor one's own and others' emotions) (Mayer & Salovey, 1993), spiritual and even perverse. All these are "nurturing creativity and innovation" (Chin, Raman, Yeow & Eze, 2012). To a very large extent it depends on what type of intelligence characterizes the one who wants to become an entrepreneur but no one can know for sure if a future entrepreneur is characterized by a positive, creative or highly speculative or even perverse intelligence. Some want to use their minds just to reach certain targets thus outreaching by any means any type of constraints, including the legal ones and even more so the moral ones.

One may have a very sharp mind that makes anything possible. But, of course, it depends what one wants to do with it. Entrepreneurial thinking cannot be deprived of a quick mind, but this quick mind must be forever associated with those principles from which an entrepreneur cannot ever deviate from without the risk of disqualification.

Will

"Sun would have not been up in the sky if I had not been there to see it" – this phrase is believed to have been said by young Schopenhauer, the author of the later and famous work "The World as Will and Representation". P. P. Negulescu writes that Goethe would have replied on that day, that actually he, young Schopenhauer, would not have been there if it were not for the sun up in the sky to see him. This, of course, is very true. But Schopenhauer was revealing precisely the role of the subject in knowledge, as well as the willingness to learn, to know, to discover. For a future entrepreneur, such will is part of the set of vital abilities. Will is the one which can stimulate that energy to help the entrepreneur move mountains (of course, provided he has the right instruments for that). It is obviously very important to want to, but willingness is scarcely combined with possessing the proper abilities.

Initiative

The initiative, materialized in a spirit of initiative, lies in the capacity and ability to do something new, to find a solution to a problem that is bothering you, without waiting for it to solve by itself or be solved by others. Initiative does not only mean to be one step ahead or to surpass others (although in a society based on a market economy, it is very normal to do so, and, for the entrepreneurial spirit, such a quality is even essential), but it implies taking responsibility and assuming risk. But the initiative is neither isolated, nor lacking the effects of some competitive factors. Furthermore, like any other human activity on Earth, the initiative is conditioned and interdependent. This is the reason why, a man of initiative, even if he tricks his way out through regulations, he cannot elude the key references, he cannot avoid the mandatory "gates" as the process of avoiding such a gate automatically leads to disqualification, exactly as it happens with the slalom on the ski track. Nowadays society pushes us towards "strategic initiative" (Ahmad, Nasurdin, Halim & Tahizadeh, 2013) in order enhance productivity.

Cognition

In this context, we understand cognition both as an ability to know, as well as a procedural feature of knowledge, as a heritage of knowledge and as a very complex effect of the whole cognitive procedural feature. Cognition equals the meaning of "to know" (in French: "savoir"). Cognition represents not only the foundation of any activity, of any human action (as any human action - even the one held by virtue of reflexes, as an instant reaction, is preceded by a representation, a thought, even though, in certain circumstances, it is just an inspiration of the thought or just a spark). Entrepreneurial spirit and even less so entrepreneurial thinking cannot exist without a sufficient level of knowledge of the field or frame, circumstances, conditions, causes and effects that can generate entrepreneurial attitudes and behaviours. It is best that before starting an activity, one should know very well what he wants to do, in what way, with whom, with what, when, where and, especially, with what results and effects.

The necessary cognition to generate ability, an attitude and an entrepreneurial behaviour produces, in turn, an entrepreneurial cognition, namely an entrepreneurial concept: all these can be found in an entrepreneurial spirit and, as we mentioned above, in an entrepreneurial thinking. But such thinking is not done from one day to another, as it takes time. Here too, as in any other field, rush can ruin things. Therefore, an appropriate and adequate method must be associated with the entrepreneurial intelligence, entrepreneurial will, entrepreneurial cognition and, especially, entrepreneurial thinking.

Ability, Skill, and Experience

This set of qualities and, at the same time, this set of conditions refers to knowing what to do, having the skills that usually "are socially conditioned by the family and the school as fundamental agencies of socialization" (Manzanera-Roman & Brandle, 2016) and the necessary experience or even the belief that you need such qualities to thrive in an entrepreneurial endeavor. Subsequently, one will strive to develop them, both through own efforts, as well as by collaborating with others, with the personnel of the enterprise (organization), with other entrepreneurs, following different courses, trying hard to make a decision only when they have used all stages and all means of analysis and evaluation of the situation, including thorough consultation with those who have a particular expertise in the field.

Culture

Culture could be defined as "the common features of people in group and it is transmitted from generation to generation" (Duman, Beduk, Koyluoglu & Kezban, 2015). Even though society may promote an entrepreneurial culture and could act in a synergistic manner as a business (businessman) potentiator, a strong business culture within the organization is required. Knowing the system values underpinning the field in which the future entrepreneur wishes to carry out an activity and not in an isolated way, but in line with areas of intersection, with areas of the market and obviously, with those of the cognitive space is considered to be a key success factor. If, for instance, a future entrepreneur wishes to start a business aimed at teaching students how to use certain graphic design software and wants to offer authorized certificates that would help them find a suitable job in any economic entity that requires such skills, then he would have to know the value systems in this particular type of education, the legislation in force, experience gained in the field, achieved performance, brands etc.

Vocation

The future entrepreneur must choose not only a field where he thinks he could be successful, but that particular field he thinks he knows, for which he has a certain calling, a certain interest, a certain predisposition and a certain level of knowledge. Such a level of knowledge makes him aware of the opportunities he has, as well as his abilities which may lead him (or not) to success. Knowledge helps him identify the vocation and the elements which are in perfect agreement or harmony with this field. Usually, the entrepreneurs who are bound to succeed have a vocation for their job, for the chosen field of activity, and for the business they aim to develop. The best examples are provided precisely by the fields that require vocation, such as literature and art, creation, design, etc. Obviously, the entrepreneur's vocation must firstly be a managerial vocation. For instance, in order to establish a successful publishing house, you do not necessarily have to be a writer, but a very good manager in the field. This means that you should like working with books, you should be passionate about printing books and making electronic books, you should have a serious culture and knowledge in the field even though you are not a writer. But if you are a writer who also possesses such managerial abilities in the field, then your chances of achieving an exceptional result dramatically increase at least in terms of the quality of the published works.

Ethics

Ethics "commonly means rules or principles that define the rights and wrongs of conduct" (Sroka & Lorinczy, 2015). It is a great in the environment nowadays for ethical attitude in people everywhere. Napoleon, for instance, said that if he were to choose between an intelligent officer and a moral officer, he would choose the latter. Ethics is very important for any man on Earth and even more so for an entrepreneur (usually society appreciates and rewards through goods/services acquisition such an individual / economic entity). The individual who wants to become an entrepreneur bears a very consistent set of responsibilities, including the important decisions that are to be taken and that can affect the fate and destinies of some people, the relationships with other companies which can generate success or failures, losses or gains, performance or, on the contrary, extreme situations. Sometimes an entrepreneur is forced to stand very high risks, and the aftermath can be abrupt: either success or failure. The entrepreneur's verticality, his behaviour in such situations, his attitude towards his employees and collaborators, partners and competitors is extremely important because he is facing a "contradiction with the request of ethics and deontology in business" (Vadastreanu, A.M. Maier & D. Maier, 2015) and strictly pursuing profits in an "efficient" manner. Often, this verticality is synonymous with his character, education and quality as human and manager. Therefore, a good entrepreneur must always be ethical and the one that must be a constant reminder of this is nobody but his very person.

THE ROLE OF EDUCATION IN THE DEVELOPMENT AND TRAINING PROCESS OF THE ENTREPRENEURIAL THINKING

Entrepreneurial learning often stresses out "the role of experience and previous knowledge" (Fust & Tobias, 2014), thus a highlight should be placed on forming and developing the entrepreneurial thinking within the process of education. In all the stages of this process, starting with family and preschool and continuing with elementary school, gymnasium, secondary education, postgraduate, doctoral and even postdoctoral there is and there must always be a constant interest towards training managers, cultivating the entrepreneurial spirit, training the entrepreneurial thinking (enterprising initiatives) of the graduates. The same spirit should be applied also with other forms and formulas of education such as non-formal education that "relies on the objectives and the contents of activities structured and organized in an institutionalized framework, with an optional character, complementary to school" (Moldovan & Bocoş-Binţinşan, 2015) and informal education that is considered a "lifelong process whereby every individual acquires attitudes, values, skills and knowledge from daily experience and the educative influences and resources in his or her environment" (Farahani, Mirzamohamadi & Noroozi, 2014).

There are two important ways of training the entrepreneurial thinking within the educational processes:

1. One way belongs to the explicit type and consists of the existence in the curricula of several programs with explicit components, as well as several special programs for training of abilities in this regard and, based on this, for training this type of thinking.
2. The other way belongs to the implicit type and it is given by the purpose of any course and any manual, namely the one to form knowledge and abilities particular to that field and applied within an efficient human activity.

The methodological and practically applicable field by which they materialize within the educational processes is very extensive and, from this perspective, it seems that nothing is missing in the educational processes with entrepreneurial and managerial purpose. In reality, things are more complicated. The purpose and the objectives of the process of training entrepreneurs weaken themselves in the vastness of requirements and real possibilities, restrictions and bureaucratic networks. Often, to complete a business idea, one must climb many Everest mountains of restrictions and bureaucracies - some absolutely necessary because one must navigate through ice packs and sharks formations, others unnecessary, stressful and time consuming, as man has invented various types of policies, strategies, tactics and procedures to make a rod for his own back.

By simplifying the explanations and reducing the tasks and abilities of the processes of the educational training and development of skills, attitudes and qualities of a productive entrepreneurial thinking to their essence, there are 12 stages of its formation, as follows: family, elementary school, gymnasium, high school (college), vocational schools, professional schools, undergraduate education, graduate education – Masters, graduate education – PhD, graduate education – postdoctoral schools, the units and identities of continuous professional training and other elements of non-formal education and elements of informal education.

Family

Family is the first and most interested in identifying, educating and encouraging the children's abilities and attitudes, qualities which are useful in their choice of a proper career and, clearly, useful for the development of his enterprising spirit (the entrepreneurial spirit) and, based on this, even for the development of an entrepreneurial thinking. Obviously, not all families are able to provide their children support in terms of high quality entrepreneurship, but many of them are trying hard to, in most cases reaching out to counselling or specialised help. Many parents are hiring tutors for their children, and, by talking to them, they strive together to identify their children's abilities and qualities, to guide them as much as possible towards careers for which they have vocations for or fields where they can put into practice and value their qualities, abilities, attitudes, ethics and, generally, their personality, culture and knowledge.

We are witnessing more and more incredible performances (in various fields such as art, painting, music, mathematics, physics, sports, etc.), obtained by preschool children (4-5-6 years old), teenagers, students etc., and this is due in a large extent to a very good collaboration between the family and education specialists. Family is the first to prove their child's entrepreneurial spirit and the quality of the entrepreneurial thinking. Family is the one who always encourages the initiative of the family's new members, and teaches them to be bold, thorough, attentive, and critical, to think tenfold prior to action.

A family stands by their child, be they teenagers or adults. A family helps their child unconditionally in all circumstances, and pays special attention to the proper use of skills and knowledge gained by the child throughout his life. A family is part of the system of ongoing education and it provides all its members with entrepreneurial assistance which is very special. Family represents the shoulder on which an entrepreneur will find support all his life, thus always finding warmth, understanding, good advice and unconditional support.

Elementary School

Together with family, elementary school is the first specialist for the general and special education of a student. School is the one that identifies ahead of time the student's abilities and the one which does continuously and from the beginning an assessment of the student's intelligence and knowledge level, the quality of his abilities and attitudes, vocation and even character. School is very concerned and attentive in terms of cooperation with the family in order to train the student in the spirit of a realistic and enterprising thinking. The elementary school has practical activities programs and projects where the students' creative intelligence, abilities and knowledge are stimulated. Since the early years, a primary-school teacher already has a very clear idea about the qualities and capabilities of his students and encourages them to continuously develop them, while the elementary school teacher is already working with his students in this regard. They will know who has abilities towards abstract thinking, pragmatism, initiative and who is talented (gifted). It is true that the excessive mobility of the workforce, emigration and other phenomena, together with pressures on educational processes, have greatly diminished the spirit of the elementary school and, therefore, it should be regained taking into account the new conditions and the immanence of the network effect, including the one generated by the network and the educational networks.

Gymnasium

Gymnasium is the one that adjusts the procedural feature of entrepreneurship in terms of culture and cognition. From here, each student chooses an already oriented educational space, a place where they will probably accomplish themselves according to their intelligence, aptitudes and qualities. Many will definitely manage to identify their future path, their entrepreneurial and managerial qualities and capabilities. For one's career, this stage is very important, even decisive. For instance, students with no vocation for theoretical thinking and abstraction will face difficulties should they decide to follow humanities, mathematics or sciences because the pattern in terms of human and occupation incline them towards this field of interest. And other students, who want to earn money at all costs – in their opinion money being forever the most important thing in life - but have almost no ability in terms of business organization and management, may cause a real disaster given his great love for money, but not for a correct, thorough and intelligent business management, to be more precise, the entrepreneurial spirit.

High School (College)

High school can be seen as the last bastion, namely, as one of the highest schools of general encyclopedic knowledge, identity culture and culture essential for a cognitive type of society, for a knowledge society and for a civilization of knowledge. With great belief, the precursors endowed with remarkable cognitive capabilities, may be selected only from high school and, after graduating the university, masters and PhD, they will be able to access the areas of excellence of the superior management which is specific to the knowledge-based society, professions and enterprises which embody in their physiognomy and philosophy epistemological components.

High school is not a filter, but a laboratory of cognition, a place where the future entrepreneur will be equipped with that "savoir" (to know, knowledge, cognition) that will enable him access to a "savoir faire" (the ability to do, superior abilities, special skills, high qualification), all which are absolutely necessary for an entrepreneurship from the high fields of society.

Vocational Schools

Vocational schools are actually the institutions which guide thinking from the start towards vocational cardinal directions. For instance, a student who has musical inclinations will probably become a musician. If he possesses an entrepreneurial thinking as well and the qualities of a good manager, he might start up a successful music band. Generally, vocational schools do not create managers, but individuals with a very high qualification - musicians, painters, writers, dancers, artisans, genius IT specialists, mathematicians, physicists, athletes etc. - due to their special abilities, talents and focus on the content of that vocation. Among such individuals, those that are highly intelligent and with managerial vocation have a great chance of not only becoming entrepreneurs in that particular field but can also be successful in creating businesses in many fields of activity. Of course, entrepreneurship requires particular competencies that they have to particularly develop.

Professional Schools

Generally, professional schools train workers. They select people who are inclined to different trades and train them so that they will have the required (particular) knowledge and skills. Professional schools train and provide society and the labour market the following: lathe operators, milling-machine operators, cooks, confectioners, waiters, tractor drivers, locomotive engineers, sailors, drivers etc., to make a long trade list short, individuals who are extremely useful for society and who have their precise place within the system. Of these individuals, the most intelligent and oriented managers can become entrepreneurs in the sense of designing and running a business, usually in the areas where they are specialized in and not only. Obviously, the entrepreneurial activity implies the achievement or training various competences which are required by the entrepreneurial position.

Undergraduate Education

The university represents the most powerful and useful formative stage generating entrepreneurial thinking. Not only is that knowledge creation a prerequisite, but universities also play the role of transferring useful knowledge (diffusing it) into the economic system. Their mission is „to develop the creative and innovative spirit among students" (Contiu, Gabor & Stefanescu, 2012). Here, the student becomes familiar with the systems of economic, social, cognitive values, with specific scientific research and with the process of carrying out activities that require a deep knowledge of the field, spirit of initiative, ability to monitor, assess and experience, epistemological competences and the ability to assume important responsibilities. It is a well-known fact that entrepreneurial thinking has been present since childhood or even the first years of school. Nevertheless, the university represents the actual school where entrepreneurial thinking and enterprising thinking are formed and trained – fact which does not only imply the desire and will to start a business, but much more than that. At the university, students learn to analyse and evaluate their abilities, attitudes and competences, to have a sense of measure, to understand their limits and also the ways in which such limits may be overcome, how they can be really down to earth, understand and apply that principle which, in logics, is called the principle of sufficient reason. At the university, students learn the values and features of the entrepreneurial spirit, of assuming the responsibilities of a job well and thoroughly done. But most of all, they learn to question those absolute truths that often have nothing in common with the highly dynamic and complex reality of a business, and even much less with the entrepreneurial thinking. Here, students are involved in drafting scientific research projects, in designing and setting up a business, in the process of correlating all the factors that can contribute to a healthy and rational thinking which is beneficial to the concept of entrepreneurship.

Graduate Education: Masters

Masters actually represent not only a specialisation in a particular field, but also a continuation of development, a demonstration and application of entrepreneurial thinking, both in the form of the Self which appears and asserts itself in a being materialized not only in a better knowledge of the self, in an otherness of the cognitive Self, but also in the effect on the team's or group's creative and entrepreneurial thinking. Master studies help the future entrepreneur project himself into a dynamic of designed, elaborated and rigorous planned processuality, having clear objectives that are well divided into stages and materialized into actions which are very accurate, perfectly connected and interconnected to the financing procedures, to market research, identification, monitoring procedures and to the process of trends forecasting. Master studies help the future entrepreneur escape to a secure and elegant way from negation, from that fateful "It is not possible!" and calculate boldly and knowingly the conditioning elements of probability and the ones that allow him taking a conscious, calculated but not hazardous risk. Only now can we state that we are dealing with a mature, responsible and very efficient entrepreneurial thinking.

Graduate Education: PhD

PhD represents the most elevated form of higher education and it is actually a warranty for a knowingly inclusion into the scientific research field. A PhD possesses more than an entrepreneurial thinking. As of now, he is gifted, thus having scientific abilities and competences, as well as a remarkable epistemological capability. A PhD has a rigorous, experimental thinking that is focused on clear research directions and objectives that should lead to performance. The main quality of this specialist, to the extent that he assumes an entrepreneurship or taking a business into enterprise, is represented by the scientific rigour and long drawn method by which all objectives and all planned parameters are accomplished. Thus, a PhD graduate is not an entrepreneur but an expert in a field, an authority that can manage an entrepreneur and, at the same time, it can help him so that he would not make (at least major) mistakes.

Graduate Education: Postdoctoral Schools

Postdoctoral schools also have their importance in generating scientific cognition, the epistemological dimension of highly qualified human action. They generate and maintain the level of scientific and epistemological cognition (here with the meaning of experiment, testing the certainty of cognition) necessary to the scientific and academic management of any enterprise and much more to the enterprising spirit and thinking. For it is one thing to want to conduct a business, to think you have all the chances of success and quite another to have the opportunity to relate to an academic level of cognition in any field, to know that up there, in the world of scholars, the scientific approval may or may not exist, meaning the credible and profitable endorser for your business.

THE UNITS AND IDENTITIES OF CONTINUOUS PROFESSIONAL TRAINING AND OTHER ELEMENTS OF NON-FORMAL EDUCATION

Non-formal education is increasingly spread across the globe. The network allows everyone access to databases, to large libraries, to eLearning educational packages and, especially, to the precise information an entrepreneur needs in order to understand ab initio whether he has a chance or not, whether with his knowledge and abilities he is capable or not to start a business. Nevertheless, the opportunity to consult and access such sources does not replace formal education, the thorough education and school an entrepreneur has attended over the years, but it does help him to better understand the phenomenon, to gather new knowledge in real-time and even to form some abilities that are necessary for the action to be initiated later on.

Elements of Informal Education

Informal education, meaning the education that you need immediately, is quite beneficial to the training and developing of an entrepreneurial thinking. There are people who have created complicated mechanisms, drones and all kinds of technical systems simply by doing research on the Internet. Therefore, informal education, meaning the education one needs at any time and can be found in almost any situation, without specific steps, the education that helps you to be informed, to understand a phenomenon, to comprehend the dimension of a business and even of an entrepreneurial thinking, is quite modern and beneficial. Of course, it requires a thorough culture and a superior comprehension of the network philosophy and physiognomy within the space of cognition.

A possible graphical representation of the 12 stages of training and development of an efficient entrepreneurial thinking is suggested in Figure 1.

All these stages are closely linked. Their contribution in the formation and development of the entrepreneurial spirit and, on this basis, of the entrepreneurial thinking (enterprising) is conditional and interactive. The next stage includes in its structure the contribution of the previous stage and influences this stage through a strong feedback relationship. All these must be translated into rational algorithms to implement such thinking, in the sense of assuming an entrepreneurial approach. How can one really do this?

First, it must be stated that an entrepreneurial thinking is not formed overnight, but through a long process and in an appropriate environment where an entrepreneurial (enterprising) spirit should exist effectively in the whole community. As demonstrated above, each of the stages of forming such thinking requires a set of educational, formative, stimulating and persuasive activities.

After going through all these stages - or was even involved in their process - a future entrepreneur must reflect very seriously on his condition. Regarding his own person, he must answer at least four necessary questions:

1. Which is the accessible and affordable field a future entrepreneur should propose in an enterprising endeavor and which are its demands or requirements?
2. Which are the necessary knowledge, abilities and competences?

Figure 1. Stages (steps) of training and development of the entrepreneurial thinking

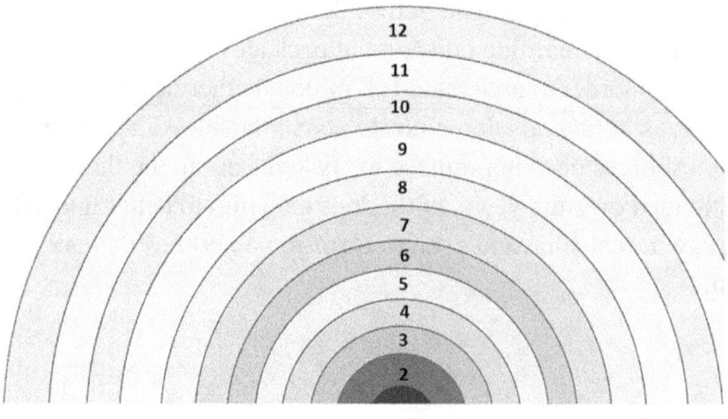

3. To what extent the future entrepreneur's knowledge, abilities, competences and experience in this field are compatible with the requirements?
4. What project should be proposed?

The method of answering the first three questions has been practised throughout the entire educational process, starting with the family experience. All the time, throughout the whole educational system, the future entrepreneur has been taught to ask such questions and to seek and find the most suitable answers. Specific topics have been created, scenarios have been compiled, all sorts of answers have been formulated and analysed, and the future entrepreneur, the one that would move to the next educational stage or would solve a real problem of this type, was forced to formulate answers.

In our case, the entrepreneurial project to be proposed (D) is defined by the intersection of sets A, B and C. Thus, $D = A \cap B \cap C$

Figure 2 shows such a stage of generating an entrepreneurial project.

By such operations, the compatibility of the personality of the future entrepreneur is identified and assessed in relation with the project that he wants to initiate. There may be compatibilities and incompatibilities, problems that can be solved easily and issues requiring further efforts and acquiring new abilities. The future entrepreneur should focus on the process of finding solutions in a timely manner, as he did dozens of times within the process of education, family and the primary school to the last level of higher education. Here, the entrepreneur must compose a CV encompassing all data and qualities he possesses and he must identify who he is and how he is in relation to the actual requirements of a project within his chosen field.

Regarding the actual situation of the future entrepreneur, he must consider and analyse his own state of affairs in relation to the legislation in force, to identify his strengths and weaknesses (vulnerabilities), as well as the opportunities of the process of preparing and launching an entrepreneurial project, as well as the inherent difficulties, to be more precise, the threats. In this case using a SWOT (Strengths, Weaknesses, Opportunities, Threats) methodology is more than advisable, since such analysis helps to correctly "assess alternatives and complex decision situations" (Helms & Nixon, 2010) and to choose the right strategy. All the other elements matter a lot: the level of education, the professional experience, gender,

Figure 2. The method of identifying the field where an entrepreneurial project can be generated

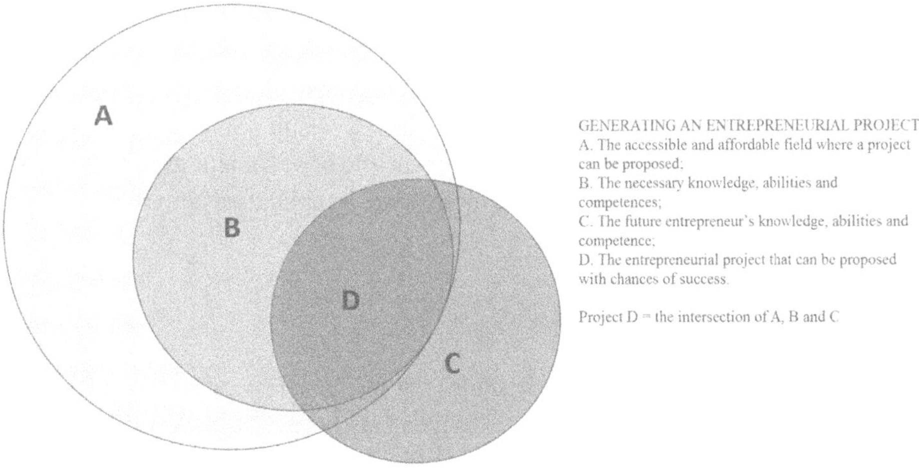

marital status, hired or unemployed, having a disability or not, whether he intends to work alone, within his family or in a team, whether he wants to be the sole owner or associate, what kind of planning he chooses for his project (the targets, tasks, stages, etc.), which are his envisaged financing resources, etc.

Of great avail is the use of a GANTT chart so as not to omit anything from a rigorous planning of all the necessary activities. This chart is widely used as a great management tool, Henry L. Gantt being "known as their developer" even though it's "origins and provenance are less well understood" (Wilson, 2003).

One possible rational algorithm for the initiation and the proposal of an entrepreneurial project should include, among other things, very well thought answers to a series of questions (ordered alphabetically) such as:

1. Are there any possible interactions with other similar projects?
2. Are you a risk taker?
3. Are you a traditionalist?
4. Have you assessed your chances of success?
5. Have you made a market research?
6. Have you made a social, economic and environmental impact study?
7. Have you thought about a way of protecting your entrepreneurial idea?
8. Do you have a clear idea regarding your entrepreneurial project?
9. Do you know the legislation in the eligible fields for your project?
10. Do you know the projects' strengths, weaknesses, opportunities and difficulties (obstacles, threats)?
11. Do you know your strengths, weaknesses, opportunities and difficulties (obstacles, threats)?
12. Do you think that you have the necessary abilities?
13. Do you want to be the sole owner or do you wish to associate?
14. For how long are you planning to pursue this economic endeavor if you encounter difficulties?
15. How long will it take for this project to integrate in the market and become profitable?
16. Is this a long term project or a short term project?
17. What are the constraints?
18. What are the freedoms?
19. What is the vision of the project?
20. What would be the needed (critical) financing resources?
21. Where do you see yourself in the next 5-10 years?
22. Would you like to become an entrepreneur?

Such questions are numerous. They must be analysed and answered with appropriate responses, in a process of profound entrepreneurial reflection from which to result a series of important conclusions for the ongoing process of carrying out, based on the principle of sufficient reason, the monitoring, assessment and early forecasting stages, as well as, the practical-applicative activities.

CONCLUSION

Man (used as a general term) cannot live only under the more or less protective wing of the society. Regardless of how important the social dimension of man may be, man is nevertheless the vital element of the society, its core, and its cognitive and creative monad. A society of men is always composed of men, and not of something else. Man is always the one who lays at the foundation of the development of the society. He is and, will probably always be, the most important element of whom and through whom a society is built, even if the inter-determination is mutual and by default. Man represents the vital element of society and this is the reason why he and only he represents the extent and even the mirror of that society.

Society by itself cannot give, create or solve. This is not its purpose. Thus, society represents only a framework, meaning a complex identity and yet, of holistic characteristic, which sometimes presents itself rather as a set of constraints than a set of freedoms. Society does not provide solutions, but it formulates requirements. The individual must find solutions. The individual, the cognitive man, the creator man, has a specific function within society. Through his cognitive ability, through his power of creation, man and man alone, is the one who generates that unbreakable capital, that intangible potential which pushes the society ahead, which raises to the rank of ontological, gnosiological, logical and security frame, where he lives and survives. Because, from this perspective, society, as a holistic system, represents more than the set of brilliant individuals who are part of it.

Undoubtedly, even if it exists in nearly every human under the shape of some predispositions, certain abilities, the entrepreneurial (enterprising) spirit is formed through education. Therefore, the role of family, school and community in the generation of an entrepreneurial cognitive support, an entrepreneurial culture, and, finally, an entrepreneurial thinking, is essential. In all the stages, school must meet an essential requirement of a society based on a market economy, namely the requirement to form and train in every individual an entrepreneurial thinking on the core axes of this society: competition, initiative, compliance with the law, efficiency.

Nevertheless, this objective - essential for the functioning of a society based on market economy – is not done at once, but over time through sustained efforts and through the process of effective generating of such needs, both at the level of society and the communities, as well as at an individual level. The entrepreneurial spirit, and, as effect and support of it, the entrepreneurial thinking, although they are strictly individual and concern the individual human, are related, however, to a much broader vision and consider the relationships existing within society, the effects generated by such a spirit and the process of correcting those side effects that stimulate individualism, selfishness, unfair competition, greed or corruption.

Through the education system, the entrepreneurial spirit must be integrated in an appropriate moral concept, so as to prevent ab initio behavioural deviations that can cause serious injuries to such projects. Therefore, the formation of this spirit and the formation of an adequate entrepreneurial thinking must be part of a coherent system of regulations and customs based on honesty, fairness, honour, dignity, respect for others, cooperation, solidarity, legality.

The shifting of the society to a cognitive dimension brings to the entrepreneurial thinking new coordinates of inherent responsibility. It is very important that, beyond the systems of regulation, constraints and endogenous limits of any initiative, there should be a synergistic effort of the whole society and all its components to be found in the consciousness, the idea and horizons of every entrepreneur as an important and absolutely necessary support for the generation and success of a project.

REFERENCES

Ahmad, N. H., Nasurdin, A. M., Halim, H. A., & Taghizadeh, S. K. (2013). The Pursuit of Entrepreneurial Initiatives at the Silver Age: From the Lens of Malaysian Silver Entrepreneurs. *Procedia: Social and Behavioral Sciences*, *129*, 305–313. doi:10.1016/j.sbspro.2014.03.681

Aleandri, G., & Refrigeri, L. (2013). Lifelong Learning, Training and Education in Globaized Economic Systems: Analysis and Perspectives. *Procedia: Social and Behavioral Sciences*, *93*(21), 1242–1248. doi:10.1016/j.sbspro.2013.10.022

Bujor, A., & Avasilicai, S. (2016). The creative entrepreneur: A framework of analysis. *Procedia: Social and Behavioral Sciences*, *221*, 21–28. doi:10.1016/j.sbspro.2016.05.086

Chin, S. T. S., Raman, K., Yeow, J. A., & Eze, U. C. (2012). Relationship Between Emotional Intelligence And Spiritual Intelligence In Nurturing Creativity And Innovation Among Successful Entrepreneurs: A Conceptual Framework. *Procedia: Social and Behavioral Sciences*, *57*, 261–267. doi:10.1016/j.sbspro.2012.09.1184

Contiu, L. C., Gabor, M. R., & Stefanescu, D. (2012). Hofstedes cultural dimensions and students ability to develop an entrepreneurial spirit. *Procedia: Social and Behavioral Sciences*, *46*, 5553–5557. doi:10.1016/j.sbspro.2012.06.474

Cordos, R. C., Bodea, A., Avasilicai, S., Bacali, L., Pop, C., & Anguelov, K. (2008). *Entrepreneurship*. Cluj-Napoca: Todesco Publishing House.

Dobrescu, E. M., & Dobrescu, E. M. (2014). Theories Regarding the Role of the Growth Poles in the Economic Integration. *Procedia: Social and Behavioral Sciences*, *8*, 262–267.

Duman, L., Beduk, A., Koyluoglu, A. S., & Kezban, A. (2015). Entrepreneurship Culture at SMEs: A Case Study in Konya. *Procedia: Social and Behavioral Sciences*, *207*, 492–501. doi:10.1016/j.sbspro.2015.10.119

Farahani, M. F., Mirzamohamadi, M. H., & Noroozi, N. (2014). The Study On Features Of Informal Education In Postmodernism. *Procedia: Social and Behavioral Sciences*, *136*, 559–563. doi:10.1016/j.sbspro.2014.05.376

Fust, A., & Tobias, J. (2014). *Self-Regulation and Entrepreneurial Learning*. Paper presented at the 59th Annual ICSB World Conference, Dublin, Ireland.

Gedik, Ş., Miman, M., & Kesici, M. S. (2015). Characteristics and Attitudes of Entrepreneurs Towards Entrepreneurship. *Procedia – Social and Behavioral Sciences*, *195*, 1087-1096.

Grădinaru, C. (2015). *University education and its contribution to increasing the management system performance of the Romanian companies* (PhD Thesis). Bucharest.

Helms, M. M., & Nixon, J. (2010). Exploring SWOT analysis – where are we now? A review of academic research from the last decade. *Journal of Strategy and Management*, *3*(2), 215–251. doi:10.1108/17554251011064837

Hnatek, M. (2015). Entrepreneurial thinking as a key factor of family business success. *Procedia: Social and Behavioral Sciences*, *181*, 342–348. doi:10.1016/j.sbspro.2015.04.896

Krueger, N. F. Jr. (2007). What lies beneath? The experimental essence of entrepreneurial thinking. *Entrepreneurship Theory and Practice*, *31*(1), 123–138. doi:10.1111/j.1540-6520.2007.00166.x

Manzanera-Roman, S., & Brandle, G. (2016). Abilities and skills as factors explaining the differences in women entrepreneurship. *Suma de Negocios*, *7*(15), 38–46. doi:10.1016/j.sumneg.2016.02.001

Mayer, J. D., & Salovey, P. (1993). The intelligence of emotional intelligence. *Intelligence*, *17*(4), 433–442. doi:10.1016/0160-2896(93)90010-3

Moldovan, O., & Bocoş-Binţinţan, V. (2015). The necessity of reconsidering the concept of non-formal education. *Procedia: Social and Behavioral Sciences*, *209*, 337–343. doi:10.1016/j.sbspro.2015.11.245

Réfléchir à la création de mon entreprise. (n.d.). Retrieved from https://www.jesuisentrepreneur.fr/creer-une-entreprise/comment-proteger-idee.html

Sroka, W. & Lorinczy, M. (2015). The perception of ethics in business: analysis of research results. *Procedia – Economics and Finance*, *34*, 156-163.

Vadastreanu, A.M., Maier, D. & Maier, A. (2015). Is the Success Possible in Compliance with Ethics and Deontology in Business?. *Procedia – Economics and Finance*, *26*, 1068-1073.

Vaduva, S. (2004). *Entrepreneurship*. Bucharest: Economica Publishing House.

Wilson, J. M. (2003). Gantt charts: A centenary appreciation. *European Journal of Operational Research*, *149*(2), 430–437. doi:10.1016/S0377-2217(02)00769-5

KEY TERMS AND DEFINITIONS

Education: Education should be regarded as a prerequisite for human evolution, a continuous and everlasting learning process regarding the knowledge, skills and understandings an individual receives or gives.

Entrepreneurial Spirit: Entrepreneurial spirit is a mindset, an attitude and a special approach to life and endeavors. It is specific to those that approach life through such a way of thinking that they constantly and actively seek out change, see opportunities everywhere, embracing change and continuous improvement. It develops in individuals who have a true passion for building greatness from nothing, willing to manifest themselves in any creation endeavor. Such people usually show a collection of characteristics such as creativity, adaptability and grit; they are risk takers, business savvy and have strong developing potential.

Entrepreneurial Thinking: Entrepreneurial thinking refers to having the ability to capitalize in the most adequate manner (when and how) opportunities identified (discovered) on the marketplace.

Entrepreneurship: Entrepreneurship refers to the process of developing, organizing, managing and leading a business, taking on risks and pursing profit.

Intellectual Capital: Intellectual capital describes intangible assets and incorporates human capital (egg. competence, know-how, skills, etc.), structural/organizational capital (egg. patents, trademarks, processes, etc.) and relational capital (egg. strategic alliances, relationships with customers, suppliers, etc.).

Knowledge-Based Society: In an ever-changing environment, the model needed in order to compete and thrive is that of a well-educated society, using knowledge as a growth engine (driver) so that its people would prosper and thrive.

Liberalism: Liberalism relates to the concept of freedom and the autonomy of the individual.

Modus Vivendi: Modus vivendi aims at a peaceful coexistence between conflicting parties, trying to bypass difficulties.

Neo-Liberalism: Neo-liberalism is a modified form of liberalism aiming at transferring the control of economic factors from the public to the private sector, tending to favor a free-market capitalism.

Savoir-Faire: Defines the ability of taking an appropriate action; knowing how to do.

Chapter 3
The Italian Doctrine *Economia Aziendale* and the Primary Interest of the Organizations

Emiliano Di Carlo
University of Rome "Tor Vergata", Italy

ABSTRACT

The aim of this chapter is to enter into the debate on the objective of the firm and more in general of the organizations, in order to discuss the contribution that the Italian doctrine Economia Aziendale (EA) can give to this debate and to the sustainable economic development. To this end, it is pro-posed the concept of primary interest of the organizations, the aziende according to the EA (i.e., business entities, public administrations and non-profit organizations), which is to satisfy human needs through the production of useful goods and services (the objective of the azienda) ensuring a sustainable value creation in the short and long term (the condition for the survival and growth of the azienda). For business entities, the primary interest supports the so called 'integration thesis' according to which business and ethics can be achieved together, since the profit is considered as a condition that allows the survival and growth of the firm favouring all stakeholders and the community.

INTRODUCTION

In the aftermath of the global financial crisis, several scholars of the Italian discipline *Economia Aziendale* (*EA*) have been committed in recognizing its possible causes in the alienation of individuals involved in business from what are the right rules to well conduct the business itself, suggested by the *EA* (Cavalieri, 2009; Coda, 2010). In this line, the lecture by Prof. Massimo Saita, held at the University of Milan Bicocca in December 2014, entitled 'The foundations of *Economia Aziendale* forgotten before the crisis.'

The aim of this chapter is to enter into the debate on the objective of the firm and more in general of the organizations, the *aziende* according to the *EA* (i.e. business entities, public administrations and non-profit organizations), in order to discuss the contribution that the *EA* can provide to this debate and to the sustainable economic development.

DOI: 10.4018/978-1-5225-3147-0.ch003

The need to explore the suggestions of that doctrine comes from at least the following considerations:

1. The limits of some of the most popular theories on the objective of the firms, in particular shareholder theory and agency theory, that diffused the gloomy vision of human nature (Hirschman, 1970) in universities and business schools around the world (Agle, Donaldson, Freeman, Jensen, Mitchell, & Wood, 2008; Ghoshal, 2005; Giacalone & Wargo, 2009);
2. The alternatives to the shareholder theory (e.g. stakeholder theory) often do not clarify how and in what time companies should create value, with the risk to be vague and ambiguous, favouring the opportunistic behaviour of the insiders (i.e. managers and controlling shareholder) (Phillips, Freeman, & Wicks, 2003, p. 495);
3. The possibility to focus the attention on the concept of *azienda* (almost unknown outside the Italian context) using the heritage of teachings of some Masters of the *Economia Aziendale* (Amaduzzi, 1978; Ferrero, 1968; Giannessi, 1960; Masini, 1982; Onida, 1971; Zappa, 1957) about the finalism and the conditions that all *aziende* must achieve in order to survive and growth;
4. The ability to broaden the observation from the business entities (firms) to all types of economic entities (public administrations and non-profit entities), all considered as cells of the society (Amaduzzi, 1978, p. 19; Cassandro, 1969). Indeed all the economic entities can ensure the development of the economy and society (Cavalieri, 2009), participating to the common good (Caldarelli, Fiondella, Maffei, Spanò, & Zagaria, 2011);
5. With specific regards to for profit entities, the scope of analysis covers not only large, publicly held corporation, but also small and medium-sized companies, contrasting 'the tendency of management scholars more generally to concentrate on large, multinational corporations as the objects of their research' (Phillips et al., 2003, p. 495).
6. The *Economia Aziendale* connects the ethics with business decisions (Costa & Ramus, 2012; Signori & Rusconi, 2009), giving elements to support the integration thesis, in the sense that moving from the interest of the shareholders to that of the firm it can be said that not only 'good ethics is good business' (Davis, 1994), but also 'good business (for the firm) is good ethics (for all stakeholder)', in the sense that if you really care about stakeholders you should conduct the business in a profitable way.

It is then proposed the concept of 'primary interest of the *azienda*', as a principle of good governance for all organizations. This interest includes two elements: 1) the objective of the *azienda* (i.e. satisfy human needs through the production of useful goods and services); 2) a condition for the survival and growth of the *azienda* (i.e. ensuring a sustainable value creation in the short and long term). The primary interest of the *azienda* wants to support the so-called 'integration thesis' (Agle et al., 2008), according to which business and ethics can be achieved together. The term "primary" is used in order to distinguish that interest from the particular (and sometimes temporary) interest of the stakeholders, which become secondary when in contrast with the primary interest of the *azienda*.

Such a proposal tries to answer the following questions which find only partial answers in the Anglo-American theories: "for whom", "how" and "in what times" companies should create value?

From a methodological point of view, the choice of the elements included in the primary interest is based on the following criteria:

1. Consider the effect of the objective of the *azienda* on its continuity as well as on the economic problem resolution and the ability to steer the governance toward the common good;
2. Mitigate the opportunistic behaviour against the *azienda* by the various stakeholders;
3. Avoid that the goal of the *azienda* coincides with the particular (and sometimes temporary) interest of a specific stakeholder or group of stakeholders, and at the same time avoid assigning more objectives, or an objective that is vague and ambiguous;
4. Promote the dissemination of a culture of sustainable value creation even in public administration and in non-profit organizations.

The methodological approach used in the analysis of the literature is descriptive/narrative and the points listed above represent the criteria that led to select certain authors instead of others. Thus the limit of that approach derives from the goodness of these criteria.

The chapter consists of five sections. In section two the main Anglo-American theories on corporate objective are analysed. Section three is dedicated to the description of the *Economia Aziendale* and to the concept of *azienda*. Section four proposes the concept of primary interest of the *azienda*. Section five concludes.

THE ANGLO-AMERICAN THEORIES ON CORPORATE OBJECTIVE

The Anglo-American theories on the objective (or purpose) of the corporation are shown in Table 1. The debate on what should be the most appropriate purpose of the firm aims to achieve the best solution, according to an utilitarian perspective (Singer, 2010), for what concern the effect that it may have on both the survival and growth of the firm and the social well being.

For example, according to the shareholder theory the welfare is maximized when firms create value for their shareholders, while for the stakeholder theory this purpose could be unsustainable, being necessary take into account and satisfy the expectations of all stakeholders.

Normally, the objective is referred to the individual, i.e. "for whom" the corporation should create value (e.g. shareholder, stakeholder, corporation itself). In addition Table 1 also contains "*how*" and "*in what time*" these theories suggest to create value. In this regards, Cavalieri (2010) argues that 'talk about creating value without any clarification on the content of that term is meaningless. Indeed, one must understand for whom, by what time references and how (i.e., under what equilibrium conditions) the *azienda* must create value' (p. 25, our translation). The specification of these elements is central for the continuity of the *azienda*, as well as for giving a guide to managers, mitigating their eventual opportunistic behaviour.

According to Meynhardt (2009) the term "Values" 'is one of those ambiguous container terms with enormous promise of insight but no widespread consensus' (p. 196). Rescher (1969) states that 'Philosophers and social scientists concerned with value questions have long recognized the need for a more precise value terminology to facilitate the exact formulations needed in scholarly and scientific contexts' (p. 2).

Table 1. Anglo-American theories on the objective of the corporation: 'for whom', 'how' and 'in what time' create value

	Idea of Corporation as a Separate Institution	*"For Whom"* Create Value	*"How"* Create Value	*"In What Time"* Create Value	Authors
Shareholder theory	Absent	Shareholders	Resolving conflicts with stakeholders, in order to maximize profit for shareholders. The corporation is an instrument of the shareholders	Not specified, but the market pushes toward the short term	Friedman, 1970
Stakeholder theory	Absent	Stakeholders	Managing relationships with stakeholders who have conflicting interests, through the balance between contributions and rewards. The corporation is an instrument of the stakeholders	Not specified	Freeman, 1984
Enlightened value maximization theory	Absent	Shareholders	Managing relations with stakeholders, in order to maximize profit for shareholders. The corporation is an instrument of the shareholders	Long term	Jensen, 2001
Organic theory	Strong	Corporation	Not specified	Not specified	Arthur, 1987
Social entity theory	Strong	Community	Not specified	Not specified	Allen, 1992

Source: Our elaboration

Only the enlightened value maximization theory explicits all the value creation conditions. As part of the theories mentioned, it is possible to distinguish those with a strong idea of the firm as a separate institution from its stakeholders and, therefore, with its own purpose, from those for which the company is an instrument to satisfy the interests of a group of individuals (e.g. shareholder or stakeholders).

The *shareholder theory* has influenced the attention of scholars of management and governance for several years clarifying strategies and behaviour of firms (Friedman, 1970; Rappaport, 1990). For that theory, the agents (managers) have a moral obligation to maximize the principals (shareholders) wealth, i.e. 'conduct the business in accordance with their desires, which generally will be to make as much money as possible' (Friedman, 1970). Being the firm a legal fiction, an instrument owned by the shareholders to maximize their profit (Jensen & Meckling, 1976), the interests of the firm and shareholders coincide (Allen, 1992). This is confirmed by the fact that in some cases the concept of creating value for the shareholders is used as a synonym for creating value of the corporation (e.g. Alexander & Cohen, 1999, p. 3). The short-term orientation of that theory comes from the fact that markets are not likely to capture the ability of the company to create value in the medium and long term (myopic market model), or they are simply interested in the short term (Dallas, 2011; Hayes & Abernathy, 1980).

Unlike the shareholder theory, the *stakeholder theory* (Freeman, 1984) draws attention to the need to balance the value creation for shareholder with the value creation of all the other stakeholders. The firm is an instrument to create value for all its stakeholders. The reason behind that theory derives from two approaches: normative and instrumental (Donaldson & Preston, 1995). The normative approach recognizes the existence of an ethical dimension (Phillips et al. 2003, p. 481) in addition to the economic and legal ones, a moral duty for those who governs the company to consider the rights of all those involved.

According to the instrumental approach, managers have to pay attention to the other stakeholders because is the best way to create value for the shareholders (Jones, 1995; Plender, 1997).

However, one of the limits of the stakeholder theory is viewed as leaving too much discretion to managers (Keay, 2008, p. 20). In this regards (Tirole, 2010) states that 'management can almost always rationalize any action by invoking its impact on the welfare of some stakeholder' (p. 62). Moreover, Jensen (2001) points out that stakeholder theory 'allows managers and directors to devote the firm's resources to their own favourite causes—the environment, art, cities, medical research (...) By expanding the power of managers in this unproductive way, stakeholder theory increases the agency costs in the economic system.' (p. 14). Phillips et al. (2003, p. 495), analysing the challenges of stakeholder theory, state that managerial opportunism still represents a threat to the organizational effectiveness.

The shareholders *vs* stakeholders debate has interested many scholars in the last decade (Asher et al., 2005; Freeman, et al. 2004; Jensen, 2001; Keay, 2008; Sundaram & Inkpen, 2004; Tirole, 2010). Comparing shareholder theory and stakehodler theory, Jensen (2001) argues that shareholder theory and stakeholder theory can be considered jointly in what he calls '*enlightened value maximization*' (also called 'enlightened stakeholder theory'). This approach draws many concepts of the stakeholder theory, but at the same time puts the maximization total long-term firm market value as a necessary criterion to define a compromise between the various stakeholders. In other words, the long-term orientation is the element that allows, in maximizing the shareholder value, to take into account the expectations of the other stakeholders.

This orientation provides the solution to the problems that arise in the identification of multiple objectives of stakeholder theory, providing managers with the criteria for the right balance between stakeholders. In this regards, Jensen (2001) points out that 'telling a manager to maximize current profits, market share, future growth in profits, and anything else one pleases will leave that manager with no way to make a reasoned decision. Indeed, it leaves the manager with no objective. The result will be confusion and a lack of purpose that will handicap the firm in its competition for survival' (p. 11), increasing the agency costs and damaging the social wealth.

Unlike the settings that move between shareholder and stakeholder theory, organic theory and social entity theory consider the firm as a separate institution from all its stakeholders and with its own interest (Lan & Heracleous, 2010).

The *organic theory* does not accept that only the individual can be considered as a legal person worthy of protection. In fact, with specific reference to the corporation, they are separate legal entities with respect to the owners (Arthur, 1987). For this reason, corporations, having legal personality, should be compared to a citizen with its responsibilities (Dodd, 1932). The assumption that the enterprise is comparable to an individual is clearly opposed to the agency theory (Jensen & Meckling, 1976) and contractual theory (Coase, 1937, p. 311), which sees the company as a set of contracts, an artificial person created by the law.

The *social entity theory* considers the corporation as a social entity formed through political and legal processes, in order to meet social welfare (Allen, 1992). In this sense, the corporation can be considered as a political tool for social purposes. The company would be formed through political and legal processes, in order to meet social welfare (Allen, 1992; Arthur, 1987; Lan & Heracleous, 2010). The company, therefore, would not only have financial obligations towards the shareholders, but also to the community. As good citizens, businesses should contribute to the social well-being.

The problem with organic theory and social entity theory is that the concept of value creation is vague and ambiguous, since they do not clarify: 1) how the corporation should create value, in particular how to solve the trade-off between the interest of the company and the interest of its stakeholders; 2) what is the role of stakeholders in the value creation for the corporation; 3) in what time the corporation should create value; 4) how to minimize the managerial opportunism against the interest of the company and its stakeholders.

THE *ECONOMIA AZIENDALE* AND THE CONCEPT OF *AZIENDA*

Economia Aziendale (*EA*) is an Italian doctrine founded in 1927 by Gino Zappa (1927) who focuses on the '*azienda*' as a coherent unity (i.e. inseparability) of 'economic operations' (Cinquini & Marelli, 2007; Viganò & Mattessich, 2007, p. 25), which characterises institutions (i.e. for-profit organization, public administrations, and non-profit organizations). Zappa (1956) defines the *azienda* as an 'economic institution intended to last for an indefinite length of time and that, with the aim of meeting human needs, manages the production, procurement or consumption of resources in continuous coordination' (p. 37, our translation), and *EA* as a unitary science that studies the 'existence conditions and life manifestations of the *azienda*' (Zappa, 1927).

The Italian School of Accounting and *Economia Aziendale* (Sidrea, 2009) proposes the following three attributes that allow distinguishing the *azienda* from the world of economic organizations (see also Cavalieri, 1999):

- Systemic coordination;
- Decision-making autonomy;
- Economicità;

The *azienda* is a system in the sense that its parts (e.g. assets such as machinery, equipment) and participants (i.e. persons involved in the production process) are not separated; instead they are coordinated and integrated, they are bounded together in order to achieve the *azienda*'s interest (Bertini, 2014; Coda, 2010). The *azienda* 'is not identified with the owners, the capital, the assets, the people taking part in it or with the contracts or the relationships among its components, but rather it is an autonomous and real entity composed of all these elements and the relationships among them. It is very important to point out the concept of system which is used by Zappa but not fully explored (…) In the *azienda*, the components will change, the elements will modify, but the whole will persist' (Signori & Rusconi, 2009, p. 308). Onida (1971) emphasizes this concept, defining the *azienda* as a dynamic system in which the 'unity in the variety and permanence in mobility, comes true in a vital synthesis' (p. 4, our translation).

Amaduzzi (1936) points out that the *azienda* is 'a system with economic dynamics for the achievement of one given purpose' (p. 18, our translation). Such a system 'can be understood and studied only as a coordination of forces which act and change without interruption' (p. 18, our translation).

The systemic vision basically involves the integration of all operations in order to achieve the objective of the organization and allows understanding the importance and the relativity of each behaviour and operation.

The *azienda* should have a decision-making autonomy (the second attribute) in the sense that in achieving its purpose it should be not subjected to the direction of other individuals or organizations (Airoldi, Brunetti & Coda, 2005; Cavalieri, 1999, p. 119). In other words, the *azienda* must be independent from external dominant pressures. For instance, if Entity A controls and manages Entity B (i.e. Entity A and Entity B form a business group), thus entity B does not have a decision-making autonomy, being a sub-system of entity A, consequently A and B are parts of the same *azienda*. More precisely, the *azienda* has a decision-making autonomy when it can autonomously achieve its objective. The objective can be also assigned by other entities (e.g. entity A gives the objective to Entity B), what it is relevant is that the *azienda* is autonomous in achieving that objective and that its activity is not related to the activity of other entities (e.g. entity A has a business model related to that of entity B, since the former produces cars while the latter trucks). Thus, if: 1) entity A controls entity B without manage it; 2) its objective is different from the entity B's objective and; 3) the activity of Entity A is not related to the activity of entity B (e.g. because of entity A produces cars, while entity B produces computers), thus entity A and entity B are two autonomous *aziende*, even if they belong to the same business group (Di Carlo, Fortuna & Testarmata, 2015).

The *economcità* (the third attribute) implies that the entire activity of the *azienda* is permanently inspired by the logic of strategic effectiveness and operational efficiency (Cavalieri, 1999; Onida, 1971, pp. 55-112). The strategic effectiveness is the ability of the *azienda* to allocate the available resources to the achievement of winning objectives, or, rather, to select suitable products to meet and satisfy the overall expectations of the customers/users. Operational efficiency is the *azienda*'s ability to achieve these productions reducing the use of resources.

The *aziende* can then be classified as: business entities, public administrations and non-profit organizations (Cavalieri, 2010). Business entities, unlike the other categories, operate in the market, both for the acquisition of factors production, and for the placement of products. From the legal point of view, there are three different types of business entities: sole proprietorships, partnerships and corporations. The corporation is therefore a type of *azienda* that has the legal status of corporation, that is, a juridical person with juridical personality. It means that the corporation is an incorporated business (i.e. the business is recognized as a separate legal entity).

However, unlike shareholder and stakeholder theories, according to the *EA* the *azienda*-corporation is an institution intended to last for an indefinite length of time. It allows distinguishing the particular (and sometimes temporary) interests of the stakeholders from the interest of the *azienda*.

Thus, all the *aziende* are organizations while there are some organizations that cannot be qualified as *aziende*, because they do not possess all the three attributes listed above. For instance a subsidiary within a group of companies is a productive organization but is not an *azienda* if, for example, its business model is integrated with that of the other affiliated group companies and/or is directed by the parent company of the group (Di Carlo, Fortuna & Testarmata, 2015).

The attributes of *aziendalità* are not always present and do not emerge, therefore, as a predetermined condition following the mere establishment of a legal institution (Cafferata, 2016). Conversely, they are rather difficult to possess, but at the same time necessary for a long-term continuity of the *azienda*.

THE PRIMARY INTEREST OF THE *AZIENDA*

The Need of the Organizations' Objective

Any type of productive organization must be oriented to the achievement of an objective (Parsons, 1960; Simon, 1964). For corporations, Keay (2008) points out that 'establishing the objective is critical. First, it provides some guidance for directors in the carrying out of their functions. Secondly, it enables us to assess whether directors have done what they should have done. Thirdly, it helps us to formulate corporate governance mechanisms' (p. 665).

Following the *EA* thought, the objective is important to give a sense to the three attributes (systemic coordination, decision-making autonomy and *economicità*) that allow recognizing the *azienda* among the world of organizations. Indeed, the *azienda* is a finalized system, in that it must be aimed at achieving a specific *objective*, its governing bodies must have decision-making autonomy in the attainment of the assigned *objective*, and the *economicità*, as method of action, should have an objective as a guide for the behaviour. Indeed, two managers, both acting with *economicità*, may behave in different way considering the same situation, because of the different objective to achieve (e.g. Do an investment in research and development? The one oriented to the profit maximization in the short term will refuse it, while the other with a long term orientation will accept the investment).

The research of a single objective for the universe of all *aziende*, that is valid regardless of the context and time, cultural and regulatory system in which the *aziende* operate, should take into consideration at least the following elements:

1. The effect that the objective has on the *azienda* continuity and on the resolution of the so-called economic problem, i.e. the ability to meet – in a sustainable way, – unlimited needs in the presence of scarce resources, and thus the ability to orient the governance and management toward the common good of the stakeholders and community;
2. The answer that business entities can give to the pressure generated by contemporary business regulations towards 'internal mechanisms to bring management standards and business practices in line with prevailing legal requirements including corporate compliance and ethics programs and employee grievance procedures' (Peterson, 2003, p. 1029);
3. Avoiding that the objective of the *azienda* coincides with the particular interest of a specific stakeholder or a group of stakeholders (Koslowski, 2000, p. 138), since the *azienda* needs the contribute of all its stakeholders, and at the same time avoid assigning more purposes that could lead trade-off difficult to manage (Argenti, 1997; Jensen, 2001), increasing the agency costs due to the managerial opportunistic behaviour.

The first two elements are particularly relevant considering the global financial crisis, which saw its genesis in the lack of ethics in financial market as well as in the purpose of the corporation mainly focused on the profit maximization in the short-term (Kemper & Martin, 2010; Lazonick, 2011; Zamagni, 2009).

The *azienda* should be seen as a cell of the economic system that contributes to the social well-being. Indeed, there cannot be the growth of the country economy without the growth of the singular cells, the *aziende*, where national wealth is concretely produced (Amaduzzi, 1978, p. 19; Cassandro, 1969).

The sustainable growth of the economy asks for the 'sustainable growth of the *aziende* that can promote, slowed down or prevent the economic growth' (Cavalieri, 2010, pp. 10-11, our translation). This approach broadens the range of responsibilities, in the sense that the irresponsible (or unsustainable) behaviour of the *azienda* is determined not only by those who govern and manage it, but also by the irresponsible behaviour of the funders, customers/users, citizens (with their vote), politicians and so on.

The Primary Interest of the *Azienda* in Its Mission Statement

The mission statement is a key elements to orient the governance and management of the *azienda*, for both private and public sectors (Bolon, 2005).

According to Arthur (1987) a mission is 'the charter that defines the basic business or businesses in which the enterprise will engage, the type of products it will make or the services it will provide, the markets it will serve, and how the company will conduct its affairs' (pp. 65-66). In this definition, there are two elements commonly identified in the company's mission, which are the 'what' the company produces and 'how' it produces.

Bart (2001) defines the mission statement as 'a formal written document intended to capture an organization's unique *raison d'etre*. It should answer such vital questions as: why do we exist, what is our real purpose and what are we trying to accomplish' (p. 360). That definition underlines the purpose of the organization, the 'why' it produces. The term '*unique*' indicates the necessity to differentiate the organization from other organizations that produce similar goods or services.

Even if there is not consensus as to what mission statements should include or should not include, the purpose appears to be the most common dimension (Baetz & Kenneth, 1998). The purpose (or objective) is central also because it allows to understand the responsibilities of the organization in conducting the activity (Gallino, 2005, p. 7). Omran, Atrill and Pointon (2002) point out that 'one way of discovering whether a company adopts a shareholder or stakeholder orientation is through an examination of its mission statement' (p. 319).

Since the aim of this chapter is to propose an objective that is able to orient the *azienda* towards the common good of the community, integrating business and ethics, we embrace the definition proposed by Melé (2009) who states that 'a corporate mission consistent with the principle of the common good becomes a practical way of introducing business ethics at the top of a company, and an effective implementation of such a mission a way of implementing business ethics' (p. 238). Moreover, 'the common good principle provides a compass for social life, including business. Business as a part of society should contribute to the common good through its specific mission. Within the business firm, all must contribute to the common good of the firm, which should be consistent with the common good of the society at large' (p. 238).

According to Argandoña (1998) the common good consists 'in producing useful goods and services, and producing them efficiently (so as to create wealth) and sustainably, so as to guarantee the conditions in which each participant receives from the company what he or she can reasonably expect' (p. 1097).

Figure 1 contains a purpose of framework for the *azienda*'s mission. The framework includes two elements: 1) the primary interest of the *azienda*; 2) as well the 'what' the *azienda* produces (i.e. the object), and the 'how' it produces (i.e. its business model).

The primary interest of the *azienda* includes two elements: the objective of the *azienda* (the 'why' produce i.e. satisfaction of client/user needs through the production of useful goods and services) and the condition of survival and growth, summarised with the term sustainable value creation. Thus organizations that meet human needs can be distinguished in two categories: those that create value and those that destroy value (and lives). The social function of the company lies in its primary interest, in the sense that

Figure 1. Primary interest as a part of the Azienda's mission
Source: Our elaboration

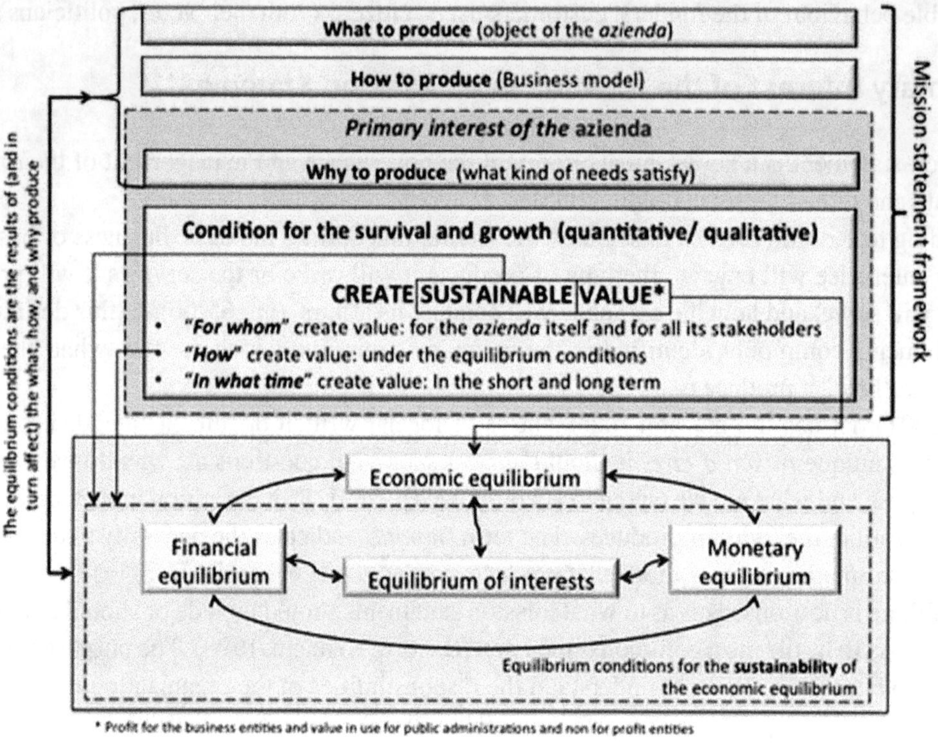

achieving that interest contributes to the common good of the *azienda*'s stakeholders and community. In this regards, several articles compared the *EA* to the theory of the common good (Caldarelli et al., 2011; Costa & Ramus, 2012).

The proposed framework reduces the ambiguity and vagueness of the organization's objective leaving low margins of discretion in the interpretation of the company mission. This allows the mission to serve as a compass to guide both top and middle level managers and to limit their opportunistic behaviour also clarifying under which balance's conditions the firm must create value. Moreover the primary interest model gives a framework that allows an integrated thinking, connecting the management choices with the effect of those choices on the equilibrium conditions.

Distance Between the Interest of the Controlling Party and the Interest of the *Azienda*

The framework proposed in Figure 1 allows measuring the eventual distance between the peculiar interest of the controlling party (e.g. the dominant shareholder in a company with concentrated ownership, managers in a widely held corporation, politicians in a public administration) and that of the *azienda*. Figure 2 shows two extreme situations: 1) perfect alignment between the two interests, as can happen in a company governed and managed by an entrepreneur who looks for the satisfaction of its customers' needs, posing as a condition for the survival and growth of his/her business the sustainable value creation (i.e. sustainable profit) over time, 2) maximum misalignment between the two interests as happens in widely held corporations where the controlling party is represented by managers who, in making the interests of shareholders motivated only by profit in the short term, run the company irresponsibly, leading the company toward the crisis.

The maximum misalignment can also occur in a municipality governed and managed, for political will, in uneconomic and predatory way.

Sometimes, the controlling party while wanting to achieve the primary interest of the *azienda*, participating to the common good of the society, he/she is forced to move away from that interest as certain environmental variables could undermine the viability of the company. For example, consider the contexts in which the irresponsible companies have a better durability conditions than those responsible because of the poor legislation regulating deviant behaviours.

So, the primary interest of the *azienda* expresses an interest to which it is appropriate to tend, but the striving for such interest depends on internal and external variables to the company, not always under the control of the dominant party. In other words, not always the ethics expressed in the concept of primary interest is sustainable from an economic point of view.

From the Objective of the Corporation to the Objective of all *Aziende*: The Why to Produce Goods and Services

According to distinguished scholars of Italian *EA*, the general purpose of all *aziende* is to satisfy human needs, through the production of useful goods and services (Amaduzzi, 1978, p. 19; Amodeo, 1964, p. 12; Cavalieri, 1999, p. 118; Coda, 2006, p. 11; De Dominicis, 1966, p. 43; Ferrero, 1968, pp. 3-4; Onida, 1971, p. 3; Sidrea, 2009; Zappa, 1957, p. 37).

Often *EA* scholars do not specify to what needs they refer (Signori & Rusconi, 2009). However, the needs to be met can be divided into two categories: those of the recipients of goods and services produced

Figure 2. Distance between the interest of the controlling party and the interest of the Azienda
Source: Our elaboration

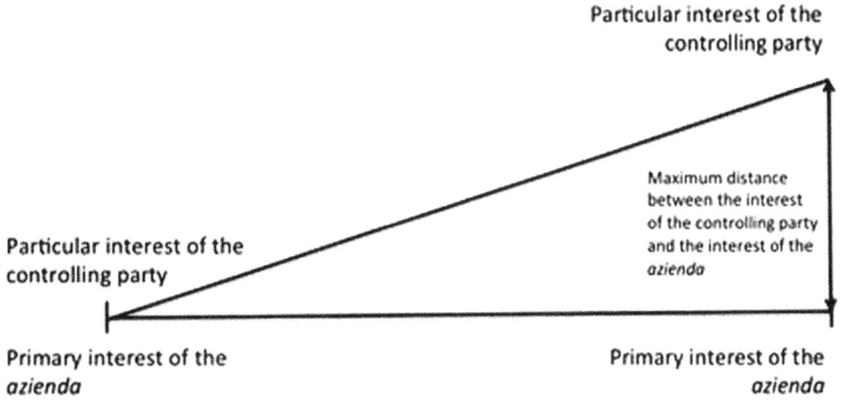

by the economic activity and those of the other stakeholders. The aim of the *azienda* is here referred to the first category. Thus, according to the proposed framework, needs satisfaction is the first element of the primary interest of the *azienda* that is its objective, its *raison d'etre*.

Since the 'what' to produce is not included within the primary interest, the framework of the mission is more user-oriented than product-oriented. Indeed, the 'what' and 'how' are excluded from the primary interest (even if included in the mission statement) because the *azienda* must be ready, in its interest and thus in the interest of its stakeholders and community, to react (i.e. to change its own 'what' and / or 'how to' produce) when the productions are no longer able to meet the needs of the client/user. An excessive focus on the 'what' and 'how' is likely to orient toward the short term, not to look at the real needs of the market (or users), and thus making difficult to get out of moments of economic crisis.

Needs satisfaction, through the production of useful goods and services, should be the objective of all *aziende*, not only of business entities. Coda (2010) points out that 'Each kind of productive institution – be it a for profit or not-for-profit organization as well as a local public entity – exists to implement and achieve its mission, consisting in the production of goods or services intended to meet specific needs, in compliance with certain rules involved in business. It follows that, if this mission comes to be vague and confused and the firm is not completely focused and devoted to its fulfilment, a crisis due to a lack of sense will have its way opened' (p. 25, our translation).

This approach is based on a broad concept of production that is separate from the fact that the production is destined to the market exchange. Therefore, even economic entities that do not sell on the market but give the produced goods and services to the users (i.e. public administrations and non-profit organizations), sometimes for free, are considered as productive economic entities.

Moreover, this approach allows interpreting the economic activity of all *aziende* as a phenomenon of production. Considering the production process also in the non-business entities gives relevance to the attribute the *economicità* and to the value creation condition also in those organizations. Indeed, also the non-business entities must be managed with strategic effectiveness and operational efficiency, guaranteeing a value creation in the short and long term.

This is the reason why, instead of distinguish the producing economic entities (in Italian, *aziende di produzione* or *imprese*) from the consuming economic entities, (in Italian, *aziende di erogazione*, such as public administrations and non-profit organizations), following Cavalieri (1999) *aziende* are distinguished in organizations that produce for the market (business entities) from those that do not produce for the market (public administrations and non-profit organizations). In this regard, according to Coda (2006) 'all *aziende* – whether business or government or non-profit organizations – perform a function of production (goods or services) to the satisfaction of certain needs' (p. 11, our translation).

Being an institution, the objective (the purpose) of the *azienda* is distinguished from the scope of the individual or group of people that establish the *azienda* (e.g. the entrepreneur, the owner, the founder of the *azienda*), as well as from the scope of all of those that participate in various ways to the economic activity (e.g. employees, lenders, suppliers).

The purpose of those who decide to establish the *azienda* becomes important to understand why he/she wants to meet certain needs: while in some cases individuals have the profit (particular interest of the owner) as an extrinsic motivation, in other cases is, for example, a philanthropic interest (e.g., in certain foundations or associations). As Adam Smith said with specific reference to the business entities, 'it is not from the benevolence of the butcher, the brewer, or the baker that we expect our dinner, but from their regard to their own interest' (i.e. the interest to the profit). Thus the butcher, the brewer and the baker want to satisfy their clients needs because they can earn profit from those activities. However, their economic activities are oriented to satisfy people needs. In other terms, the profit could be considered as the financial result of the needs satisfaction.

Value Creation as a Condition for the Survival and Growth (Quantitative and/or Qualitative) of the *Azienda*

In meeting human needs the *azienda* must achieve a condition of survival and growth (quantitative and/or qualitative), summarized by the term 'value creation' (Figure 1). This implies that 'the value of the resources consumed to make and distribute the product is systematically lower than the value of production, to be placed on the market or to assign to the users' (Cavalieri, 2012, p. 12, our translation). Thus, the value creation is referred to the typical input-transformation-output process (Argandoña, 2011), and according to our framework it is the second element of the primary interest of the *azienda* (Figure 1).

The condition of value creation that all *aziende* in satisfying human needs should meet can be summarized as indicated in Table 2 (Cavalieri & Ferraris Franceschi, 2008, p. 218):

Therefore, the value creation condition (the economic equilibrium in Table 2) requires that the utility generated (i.e. the economic value of the production to be placed on the market or assign to the users in case of a public administration or a non-for profit organization - vp^t) is systematically (in the short and long term) higher than the utility consumed (i.e. the value of input that are consumed in the production process - vf^t); the difference is the value created by the economic activity (v).

Thus, the economic entity could satisfy human needs creating and destroying value.

With specific reference to the business entities (i.e. the firms), since they operate on the market, the value of productive inputs (vf^t) derived from the purchase price multiplied by the quantity of inputs acquired (costs), while that of the output from the sale price multiplied by the quantity of products sold (revenues) (vp^t). For business entities meeting human needs is necessary but not sufficient for their survival and growth (Amaduzzi, 1978, p. 192; Cavalieri & Ferraris Franceschi, 2008, p. 221). For business entities 'v' is represented by the profit that is a difference between revenues and costs. Since the costs include the satisfactory remuneration of the owners in terms of distributed dividends, the profit (also called economic residual) is what remains after the remuneration of the various factors of production (such as labour, capital, and the State). According to the *EA* the 'pure' profit is what it should be left in

Table 2. Condition of Economic Value Creation (or economic equilibrium) applicable to all economic entities

$$\sum_{t=t_0}^{t_z} vp^t = v + \sum_{t=t_0}^{t_z} vf^t$$

where:
vp^t = value of production over time;
vf^t = value of factors of production consumed to enable the production (realized in the time frame of reference);
v = new value created by the economic activity;
t_0-t_z = entire lifetime of the *azienda*, tending to infinity

Source: Cavalieri & Ferraris Franceschi (2008, p. 218)

the company in the form of non-distributed income, and then used by the firms to finance its quantitative and/or qualitative growth (Amaduzzi, 1948, p. 305; Cassandro, 1969; Onida, 1971 p. 84). Thus, the economic value is created when the net income (revenues minus costs) is positive (net profit) and includes two elements: a) the profit for the owners (distributed dividends); b) the profit for the firm and all its stakeholders (undistributed income that remains in the business entity allowing its growth).

Consequently the profit is not a positive net income, since it arises when revenues suitably remunerate all the factors of production, including the ownership and the entrepreneur for the work done in the firm. The undistributed profit increase also the value of the owners share – indeed, owners have a double remuneration: dividend and capital gain – as well as it satisfy all the stakeholders since it favourites the continuity of the firm. Thus, all stakeholders should be interested to the profit, not only the shareholders.

'Consider the profit, according to its true nature, as an indispensable means of the existence and growth of the firm it allows also to remove every weapon at those critics (…) who would attack it in moral terms, seeing it as something reprehensible' (Cassandro 1969, p. 828, our translation).

As a result, the firm is in economic equilibrium when it is able to congruously remunerate all the factors of production (Ferrero, 1968, p. 200; Onida, 1971, p. 18). The value creation condition must be met in the long-term. This obviously does not mean that the short-term equilibrium is not important, but rather that imbalances in the short term do not affect the going concern assumption, when it derives from accidental factors that will be absorbed by an effective and efficient management.

Following this logic, the profit is not the objective of the firm (which is, in the primary interest view, the needs satisfaction), but a condition for its survival and growth. The profit is what remains after suitably remunerated subjects who participated in the value creation, such as labour, capital, loan and property, and the State (Cassandro, 1969). According to Cassandro, with regard to the business entities, 'limiting the objective of the company to the profit maximization will diminish the fundamental economic and social functions of the company. The most important ones are to create new wealth for the community and distribute it among those that to it have contributed' (Cassandro, 1969, p. 826, our translation).

Therefore, profit and corporate objective should not be confused; it would be like saying, because I need to work for live the end of my life is work. In this regard, it was noted that 'profits and purpose are two different ideas, and collapsing them is like concluding from the fact that I need red blood cells to live, that the purpose of my life is to make red blood cells' (Agle et al., 2008, p. 166). 'The profit, even if it were, at best, the only stimulus for private initiative (...) could never constitute the objective of the business entity' (Ferrero, 1968, pp. 30-31, our translation).

It follows a central aspect that leads to distinguish the business entities from the non-business entities, i.e. the possibility to verify if the *azienda* is run with *economicità* (i.e. efficiently and effectively) using its financial results (for example, the result for the period, the revenue growth, return on investment). Moreover, for business entities meeting human needs is a necessary condition for the survival and growth, not being able to see their durability guaranteed by the support of third economies.

Explained the concept of 'value creation', it remains to be clarified 'for whom', 'how' and 'in what time' the *azienda* must create value.

The answer to this question wants to find inspiration in the proposal of Sidrea (*Società Italiana dei Docenti di Ragioneria ed Economia Aziendale*) that suggests that the *azienda* must create value for 'itself and for the different categories of stakeholders involved and socially recognized, in a long and short-term' (Sidrea, 2009, p. 31, our translation; see also Cavalieri, 2012, p. 12).

'For Whom' Create Value: The *Azienda* and Its Stakeholders

Stakeholders to take care during the value creation process are widely intended here, including the azienda itself, its primary stakeholders (owners, employees, customers, suppliers, lenders) and secondary stakeholders (media, activist, government authorities) (Clarkson, 1995). This approach is closed to the setting of those scholars who consider the corporation as a distinct stakeholder (Clarke, 1998; Kay, 1997; Magill, Quinzii, & Rochet, 2015; Metcalfe, 1998).

Stakeholders participate to the economic activity in the expectation of an adequate remuneration for their contribution. In this sense, they have a particular, and sometimes temporary, interest that motivates (intrinsically and extrinsically) their behaviour (Argandoña, 2011).

The primary interest logic has some important differences compared to the following theories on the company objective (see Table 1):

1. Shareholder theory and enlightened value maximization theory;
2. Stakeholder theory;
3. Organic theory and social entity theory.

With regard to the business entities, unlike the shareholder theory, according to the primary interest idea the agents are responsible not only towards shareholders, but also towards a plurality of stakeholders, and the profit is not considered as an end but as a condition of survival and growth of the firm. This last aspect also distinguishes the primary interest idea from the enlightened value maximization theory.

Thus, the proposed approach may seem to be aligned with the stakeholder theory of the firm. However, it also requires responsibility towards the survival and growth (qualitative and/or quantitative) of the azienda that is seen as an economic institution (Zappa, 1957) separated from its stakeholders.

In particular, following the EA, the azienda is not here conceived as a juridical fiction, as just a set of contracts with its stakeholders, instead it is viewed as an institution (Costa & Ramus, 2012) that is distinct from its stakeholders, with its own interest to survive and develop, in order to satisfy human needs and create sustainable value. According to this approach it can be also said, for example as regards to the business entities, that the shareholder interest toward the profit maximization is particular and should be compatible with the interests of the azienda and other stakeholders. In other words, when the profit is achieved in an irresponsible or fictitious way, it becomes secondary if compared to the primary one that considers the firm as part of the community, that contribute to the common good. Considering the azienda as an organization that contributes to the common good it allows adding the interest of the azienda among the peculiar interests of the stakeholders (Masini, 1970, p. 11), that is, the interest of the azienda becomes part of the interest of its stakeholders. 'The common good has to do with creating the conditions that will enable those involved in the business to achieve their personal goals, we can say that there is no conflict between the common good and the individual or personal good' (Argandoña, 1998, p. 1097).

The proposed approach is also different from the one followed by those who ask to create value for the company (e.g. organic theory and social entity theory), taken for granted that by doing so, they strive to create value for all stakeholders. Brief, Buttram & Dukerich (2001) state that belief in the sanctity of the firm is so a strong message that managers tend to believe that by serving the corporation's interests they are also serving the interests of the community: what's good for Microsoft is good for the country.

However, the corporate scandals show that this automatism does not always occur. For example, a company could improve its value destroying the environment, by failing to ensure appropriate working conditions for its employees especially if they have very limited possibility to change their job.

For this reason, in order to achieve its primary interest the azienda has to maintain good relations with the stakeholders, while stakeholders, including community, should understand the problems of the azienda. Thus, reciprocal duties exist among corporate stakeholders, as well as between stakeholder and the azienda. According Fassin (2012) 'Whereas stakeholders are widely seen as having rights, they may also have duties and obligations' (p. 85).

In other words, the proposed approach differs from the theory of value creation for the organization as it offers practical solutions to reconcile the interests of the azienda with those of its stakeholders.

Cavalieri (2010) argues that 'it is just in this subtle game of balance between the value recognized to different stakeholders and the value recognized to the organization itself useful to ensure it's survival and growth, that the professionalism of those who do business is expressed' (pp. 26-27).

As pointed out by Adams, Licht and Savig (2011), 'we contrast shareholderism with stakeholderism as ideal-type, polar strategies. Between them resides a continuum of intermediate stances that find merit in both views. There may be purists who subscribe to strong versions of either view regardless of the circumstances. Most decision makers, however, will follow their principles to find a middle ground depending on the context' (p. 1332). It is almost evident that this middle ground derives from the consideration of a further interest, which can only be that of the firm.

'How' Create Value: The Sustainability of the Economic Equilibrium

The 'how' question wants to specify under what conditions the economic equilibrium expressed in Table 2 should be achieved and it is related to the sustainability of that equilibrium over time. Two organizations can be distinguished by the different ways on how they create value, even if they make the same product and satisfy the same needs. The answer to the 'how' question is necessary in order to mitigate the opportunistic behaviour of the management.

Indeed, the economic equilibrium condition does not say anything yet about the sustainability of that value. In other words, a car company, while operating with efficiency and effectiveness, may not be ethical, social and environmental responsible, as well as a public administration that create an economic value, it may not behave in a sustainable way in respect to certain stakeholders (think of the delay in payments to suppliers).

- *Financial, Monetary and Interests Equilibriums*

The conditions to achieve in order to create sustainable value, or sustainable economic equilibrium, are: financial, monetary and interests equilibriums. The first three conditions (economic, financial and monetary equilibriums) derived from the theory of the business entity equilibrium proposed by Aldo Amaduzzi (1948), one of the Zappa's pupils. The theory of equilibrium, which initially covered only the business entities, was later revisited by Cavalieri (2010), an Amaduzzi's pupil, who expands the scope of the theory of equilibrium to all types of organizations, adding a fourth condition, the so-called *overall strategic equilibrium* intended as 'equilibrium position simultaneously against the different social partners and the markets' (Cavalieri, 2010, p. 28, our translation). However, in the primary interest model the *overall strategic equilibrium* was substitute with the equilibrium of interests. For non-business entities the concept of revenue is substitute by that of value of production over time, while the concept of cost by the value of factors consumed in the production process.

In particular, the sustainability over time of the economic value creation includes three conditions: 1) have a balanced capital structure (financial equilibrium) in order to guarantee the solidity of the *azienda* and overcome unfavourable economic periods that have a negative impact on the economic equilibrium, because of losses that decrease the level of the equity; 2) meet regularly its payments (monetary equilibrium); 3) be socially and environmentally sustainable (equilibrium of interests).

- *Financial equilibrium* is the necessity (of the *azienda*) to develop appropriate correlations (in quantitative and qualitative terms) between investments (assets) and financial sources (liability and equity), in order to maintain a systematic capability to satisfy its obligations timely and in a correct manner, without prejudice in the future.
- *Monetary equilibrium* is achieved when the company is able to meet at any time, the payment commitments, for example, with employees, suppliers, financiers. This equilibrium then binds to the concept of liquidity, through which measures the company's solvency in the short term.
- *Equilibrium of interests* is intended as a balancing of interests of stakeholders who participate in various ways to the value creation. This equilibrium is connected to the shared value creation and it is reached when the rewards (not only monetary) received by stakeholders are aligned to the contributions they provide to the *azienda*.

Under the *azienda*'s equilibrium model the stakeholder management does not see any contrast between normative and instrumental approach (Donaldson e Preston, 1995), due to the fact that the instrumental approach is not referred to the shareholder's interest, but rather to the company's interest. Indeed, managers have to deal with the stakeholders – in order to achieve the equilibrium of interest – in accordance to the company's interest and, by trying to find (according to internal and external contingencies) the right balance between a fair behaviour (regardless of the economic results) and a behaviour that has to be instrumental to the survival and growth of the company itself. However, going deeply in the investigation, the primary interest theory sees the instrumental approach as a way to exalt the fairness approach toward all other stakeholders. The need to preserve the business continuity has to be considered in fact the right behaviours even if a possible consequence could be the short-term sacrifice of some stakeholders' expectations.

- *The Overall Equilibrium*

The *azienda* achieves the *overall equilibrium* when it cannot improve a single equilibrium (economic, financial, monetary and interests) without damaging, in the long term, its condition of survival and growth. It can be also stated, in the mathematical sense, that the overall balance is a system of four interrelated equilibriums that the solution of the system (survival and growth in the long term) should meet simultaneously. The equation is solved when it has chosen the best composition of the balance for the survival and/or growth of the *azienda*. The manager can evaluate the impact of his/her choices on the overall equilibrium. Improve that equilibrium is a fair behaviour towards all the stakeholders.

Thus, an increase of welfare of a single stakeholder is acceptable when it has a positive effect on the overall balance. Indeed, the unitary vision of the *azienda* suggests connecting the effect of the stakeholder management to the economic, financial and monetary equilibrium. If increasing the well being of a stakeholder improves, in the long term, the overall equilibrium the *azienda* the manager should do that, also because increasing the possibility of the *azienda* to survive and growth is the right thing to do for all the actual and future stakeholders.

'In What Time' Create Value

The last element of the value creation condition is referred to the period in which that value should be created. The short-termism has been considered as one of the causes of the global financial crisis (Dallas, 2011; Treviño & Nelson, 2011).

The value creation condition must be achieved in the short and long term. Cavalieri (2010) observes that 'the simultaneous long and short-term management of a business has to belong to the set of task of a conscious management team' (p. 27, our translation). The short, as well as the long run, can be referred to the economic, financial, monetary and interest equilibriums. The value creation condition should be read in the short and long term, in order to understand how today's behaviors may impact on the overall balance of tomorrow. An orientation to the income in the short-term reduces the importance assumed by the other equilibriums, necessary to ensure that the former is durable and sustainable in the long term.

The azienda is not an organization with a short life-time, instead is an organization set to continue. In this regard, the term azienda is normally translated with the term 'going concern'.

Bertini (2013) argues that 'on one hand, whether management uncertainties are experienced focusing on a long-term perspective, all issues are reconsidered in the light of the company continuity dominant theme. (...) profit in turn becomes an instrument useful to ensure to the company an higher level of stability. (...) On the other hand, if a short term approach prevails, everything tends to be exasperated: the daily search for profit would sacrifice future profit opportunities; conflicts of interest among different stakeholders would be dominated by the need for an immediate and self-interested achievement of each related expectations; therefore, the entire system equilibrium would be close to reach the point of crisis' (p. 99, our translation).

'The organization durability goes beyond the permanence of that people constituting in a specific moment the organization itself. A group or a single individual who is committed to tie the life of the organization to its own interests or specific objectives, would surely produce economic damages with moral effects both for other organization's members as well as for the whole economy' (Airoldi et al., 2005, p. 163, our translation). Thus, 'human beings could not defeat the course of time while aziende could reach the immortality' (Anselmi, 2014, p. 39, our translation).

In other words, it is the consideration of the azienda as an economic institute interested in its time continuity and in the creation of a sustainable value that lead to a long-term focus rather that a short-term one.

The 'how' and 'for whom' create value assumes a significant relevance in the choice between short and/or long-term orientation. Creating value in a sustainable way means having a better perception of how an irresponsible behavior (i.e. disequilibrium of interests) of today may affect the survival and growth of the azienda. In other words, sustainability can bring out future costs and benefits associated with the current choices.

The temporal problem of the value creation becomes particularly relevant looking to the peculiar interests of the party (or parties) that govern the azienda. Indeed, a dominant party that is oriented to the short term will lead the company following this logic, jeopardizing the azienda's continuity, while long-term oriented dominant party might not realize the effects that poor management of the short term may have in the long term and indeed hope that in the long run the short imbalances can be reabsorbed. In other terms, it cannot be underestimated the effect of the short term on the long-term. However, sometimes the problem is not thinking to the long term, but have adequate decision-making tools to link the effect of short-term choices with long-term consequences, and to contrast psychological factors that lead the agent to the short term even if he/she is oriented to the long term (Ariely & Zakay, 2001).

In this regard, an important factor that may caused the corporate fraud – at least in the initial stage – was that related to the good profitability condition of the defrauded corporations (think of Parmalat, called after the default "the European Enron"), and the prospects for future growth that they would have to absorb, in the long term, the costs of expropriation generated by the controlling party (the so called wishful thinking effect). In other words, the predators "entrepreneurs" seem not to have perceived the risk that the destruction of the economic equilibrium in the short-term could cause catastrophic consequences in the medium-long term. Moreover, the manipulation of the financial statements gave to the market just the appearance of equilibrium conditions, not allowing the external observers, even to the actors involved in the expropriation, to understand the severity of the situation and, therefore, to take action to avoid disaster.

To conclude, what it has to be underlined is that, the long-term orientation, thus, the endless life of the firm, concerns the survival and growth conditions of the azienda (that is the creation of sustainable value) and not the achievement of those goals useful to reach these conditions.

All economic and extra-economic goals could concern even very short periods. The sustainability of value creation in a long-term perspective allows to set goals that are coherent with such condition, solving possible trade-off between economic and extra-economic purposes.

CONCLUSION

The analysis of the main Anglo-American theories on corporate objective shows several weak points for what concern 'for whom', 'how' and 'in what time' corporations must create value.

The most critical aspect is connected to the fact that some theories ask for the value creation of specific actors (e.g. the owners in the shareholder theory), or for several stakeholders, without considering the distance between those interests and the primary interest of the corporation to survive and growth. On this aspect the Italian doctrine Economia Aziendale gives an important contribution.

From the critical review of the thoughts of the Masters of the EA, at least three significant aspects emerge: 1) having considered the interest of the all the economic organizations as a central governance issue, instead of the peculiar (and sometimes temporary) interests of certain individuals (e.g. shareholders, managers, politicians), emphasizing the importance of protecting the azienda equilibrium over time and, therefore, its survival and growth (quantitative and / or qualitative); 2) having had as object of study not only the entity that produce for the market (i.e. the business entities, or for-profit organization), but also the non-business entities (i.e. public administrations and non-profit entities) 3) having assigned to all the aziende the common goal of meeting the needs, while the distinction between profit, non-profit organizations and public institutions is based on the scope of the individual or group of people that establish the azienda; 4) providing different insights on 'for whom', 'how' and 'what time' such organisations should create value, specifying that the azienda must create value not only for its stakeholders but also for itself.

The main contribution of this chapter is to propose a principle of governance (an objective) common to all types of organizations. The nature of this need comes from the proliferation of the last twenty years' corporate scandals and economic crisis, whose origin lies in the violation of those rules of good conduct recommended and transmitted by Economia Aziendale. Indeed, the searching for common rules and principles is one of the main objectives of this discipline.

The main point of the analysis is the distinction between the primary interest of the azienda and the interests of the controlling party as well as of the other stakeholders. The corporate governance literature is often focused on conflict of interest between owners and managers in companies with disperse ownership (i.e. the agency problem type I, Berle & Means, 1932; Fama & Jensen, 1983; Jensen & Meckling, 1976) and between controlling shareholder and minority shareholders in companies with concentrated ownership (i.e. the agency problem type II, Claessens, Djankov, & Lang, 2000; Shleifer & Vishny, 1997). This study suggests a third type of agency problem, that is, the conflict of interest between the primary interest of the firm and its managers and/or shareholders. That third type of conflict may coexist with the type I and II. Thus, further studies should explore this type of conflict in different types of ownership (e.g. widely held corporation, family firms, State owned firms).

Another key aspect of the Masters of Economia Aziendale is reflected in their consideration of the azienda as a mean for the improvement of the collective welfare, thus its consideration as a common good, rather than as an instrument for some groups to achieve their personal (and sometimes temporary) interests. Therefore, the discipline of corporate behaviours cannot be only left in the hands of the market and regulators, finding some interesting guidance in the Economia Aziendale rules of good conduct.

REFERENCES

Adams, R. B., Licht, A. N., & Sagiv, L. (2011). Shareholders and stakeholders: How do directors decide? *Strategic Management Journal*, *32*(12), 1331–1355. doi:10.1002/smj.940

Agle, B. R., Donaldson, T., Freeman, R. E., Jensen, M. C., Mitchell, R. K., & Wood, D. J. (2008). Dialogue: Toward superior stakeholder theory. *Business Ethics Quarterly*, *18*(2), 153–190. doi:10.5840/beq200818214

Airoldi, G., Brunetti, G., & Coda, V. (2005). *Economia Aziendale*. Bologna, Italy: Il Mulino.

Alexander, C. R., & Cohen, M. A. (1999). Why do corporations become criminals? Ownership, hidden actions, and crime as an agency cost. *Journal of Corporate Finance*, *5*(1), 1–34. doi:10.1016/S0929-1199(98)00015-7

Alexander, D., & Servalli, S. (2011). Economia Aziendale and financial valuations in Italy: Some contradictions and insights. *Accounting History*, *16*(3), 291–312. doi:10.1177/1032373211407052

Allen, W. T. (1992). Our schizophrenic conception of the business corporation. *Cardozo Law Review*, *14*, 261–281.

Amaduzzi, A. (1936). Aziende di erogazione. Primi problemi di organizzazione gestione e rilevazione. Casa editrice Giuseppe Principato.

Amaduzzi, A. (1948). *Il sistema produttivo dell'impresa nelle condizioni del suo equilibrio e nel suo andamento*. Rome, Italy: Kappa Edition.

Amaduzzi, A. (1977). Situazione e prospettive degli studi aziendali. *Rivista Italiana di Ragioneria e di Economia Aziendale*, 1.

Amaduzzi, A. (1978). *L'azienda nel suo sistema e nell'ordine delle sue rilevazioni*. Turin, Italy: Utet.

Amodeo, D. (1964). *Ragioneria generale delle imprese*. Naples, Italy: Giannini.

Anselmi, L. (2014). *Percorsi aziendali per le pubbliche amministrazioni*. Turin, Italy: Giappichelli.

Argandoña, A. (1998). The stakeholder theory and the common good. *Journal of Business Ethics*, *17*(9-10), 1093–1102. doi:10.1023/A:1006075517423

Argandoña, A. (2011). *Stakeholder theory and value creation*. Working paper, IESE Business School, 922, 1–13.

Argenti, J. (1997). Stakeholders: The case against. *Long Range Planning*, *30*(3), 442–445. doi:10.1016/S0024-6301(97)00004-6

Ariely, D., & Zakay, D. (2001). A timely account of the role of duration in decision making. *Acta Psychologica*, *108*(2), 187–207. doi:10.1016/S0001-6918(01)00034-8 PMID:11569762

Arthur, E. E. (1987). The ethics of corporate governance. *Journal of Business Ethics*, *6*(1), 59–70. doi:10.1007/BF00382949

Baetz, B., & Kenneth, C. (1998). The relationship between mission statements and firm performance: An exploratory study. *Journal of Management Studies*, *35*(6), 823–853. doi:10.1111/1467-6486.00121

Bart, C. K. (2001). Exploring the application of mission statements on the world wide web. *Internet Research: Electronic Networking Applications and Policy*, *11*(4), 360–368. doi:10.1108/10662240110402812

Berle, A. A., & Means, G. C. (1932). *The modern corporation and private property*. New York: MacMillan.

Bertini, U. (2013). *Scritti di politica aziendale. Quarta edizione riveduta e ampliata* (Vol. 33). Turin, Italy: Giappichelli.

Bertini, U. (2014). *La corporate governance, fattore di superamento della crisi e di sviluppo dell'economia*. Opening speech at the inauguration of the academic year of Unicusano University.

Bolon, D. S. (2005). Comparing mission statement content in for-profit and not-for-profit hospitals: Does mission really matter? *Hospital Topics*, *83*(4), 2–9. doi:10.3200/HTPS.83.4.2-10 PMID:16425696

Borgonovi, E. (2014). La rilevanza del concetto di istituto per l'economia aziendale. *Economia Aziendale Online*, *5*(1), 3–10.

Brief, A. P., Buttram, R. T., & Dukerich, J. M. (2001). Collective corruption in the corporate world: Toward a process model. In M. E. Turner (Ed.), *Groups at Work: Theory and Research* (pp. 471–499). Mahwah, NJ: Erlbaum.

Cafferata, R. (2016). Darwinist connections between the systemness of social organizations and their evolution. *Journal of Management a Governance*, *20*(1), 19–44. doi:10.1007/s10997-014-9303-z

Caldarelli, A., Fiondella, C., Maffei, M., Spanò, R., & Zagaria, C. (2011). The common good and Economia Aziendale theory: Insights for corporate social responsibility from the Italian perspective. *Journal of the Asia-Pacific Centre for Environmental Accountability*, *7*(4), 197–216.

Cassandro, P. E. (1969). Il profitto dell'impresa, mezzo e non fine. *Dirigenti Industria*, 7-8.

Cassandro, P. E. (1978). Sul concetto di impresa come "comunità". *Rassegna Economica*, 1.

Cavalieri, E. (1999). Organizzazioni produttive, aziende e imprese: considerazioni di carattere istituzionale. *Rivista Italiana di Ragioneria e di Economia Aziendale*, 3/4.

Cavalieri, E. (2009). Una riflessione sulle cause e sulle responsabilità della crisi globale. *Rivista Italiana di Ragioneria e di Economia Aziendale*, 5/6.

Cavalieri, E. (2010). *Le nuove dimensioni dell'equilibrio aziendale: Contributo alla rivisitazione della teoria*. Turin, Italy: Giappichelli.

Cavalieri, E. (2012). Dottrina e organizzazioni produttive verso nuovi modelli di sviluppo. *Rivista Italiana di Ragioneria e di Economia Aziendale*, 1/2.

Cavalieri, E., & Ferraris Franceschi, R. (2008). Economia aziendale: Vol. I. *Attività aziendale e processi produttivi*. Turin, Italy: Giappichelli.

Cinquini, L., & Marelli, A. (2007). Accounting history research in Italy, 1990–2004: An introduction. *Accounting Business & Financial History*, *17*(1), 1–9. doi:10.1080/09585200601127509

Claessens, S., Djankov, S., & Lang, L. H. P. (2000). The separation of ownership and control in East Asian corporations. *Journal of Financial Economics*, *58*(1), 81–112. doi:10.1016/S0304-405X(00)00067-2

Clarke, T. (1998). The stakeholder corporation: A business philosophy for the information age. *Long Range Planning*, *31*(2), 182–194. doi:10.1016/S0024-6301(98)00002-8

Coase, R. H. (1937). The nature of the firm. *Economica*, *4*(16), 386–405. doi:10.1111/j.1468-0335.1937.tb00002.x

Coda, V. (2006). Economia Aziendale: alla ricerca di punti di convergenza. In Società Italiana dei Docenti di Ragioneria e di Economia Aziendale (Eds.), Manifesto dei soci fondatori, in "Appunti per un dibattito sulla cultura aziendale". Academic Press.

Coda, V. (2010). Insegnamenti dalle "crisi di senso". *Sinergie*, *81*, 25–30.

Costa, E., & Ramus, T. (2012). The Italian Economia Aziendale and catholic social teaching: How to apply the common good principle at the managerial level. *Journal of Business Ethics*, *106*(1), 103–116. doi:10.1007/s10551-011-1056-x

Dallas, L. (2011). Short-termism, the financial crisis, and corporate governance. *The Journal of Corporation Law*, *37*, 264–363.

Davis, J. J. (1994). Good ethics is good for business: Ethical attributions and response to environmental advertising. *Journal of Business Ethics*, *13*(11), 873–885. doi:10.1007/BF00871701

De Dominicis, U. (1966). *Lezioni di ragioneria generale*. Bologna, Italy: Azzoguidi.

Di Carlo, E., Fortuna, F., & Testarmata, S. (2015). Boundaries of the business model within business groups. *Journal of Management and Governance*, *20*(2), 321–362. doi:10.1007/s10997-015-9338-9

Dodd, M. E. (1932). For whom are corporate managers trustees. *Harvard Law Review*, *45*(7), 1145–1163. doi:10.2307/1331697

Donaldson, T., & Preston, L. (1995). The stakeholder theory of the corporation: Concepts, evidence and implications. *Academy of Management Review*, *20*(1), 65–91.

Fama, E., & Jensen, M. C. (1983). Separation of ownership and control. *The Journal of Law & Economics*, *26*(2), 301–325. doi:10.1086/467037

Fassin, Y. (2012). Stakeholder management, reciprocity and stakeholder responsibility. *Journal of Business Ethics*, *109*(1), 83–96. doi:10.1007/s10551-012-1381-8

Ferrero, G. (1968). *Istituzioni di economia d'azienda*. Milano, Italy: Giuffrè.

Freeman, R. E. (1984). *Strategic management: A stakeholder approach*. Prentice-Hall.

Friedman, M. (1970). The social responsibility of business is to increase its profits. *New York Times Magazine, 33*, 122–126.

Ghoshal, S. (2005). Bad management theories are destroying good management practices. *Academy of Management Learning & Education*, *4*(1), 75–91. doi:10.5465/AMLE.2005.16132558

Giacalone, R. A., & Wargo, D. T. (2009). The roots of the global financial crisis are in our business schools. *Journal of Business Ethics Education*, *6*, 147–168.

Giannessi, E. (1960). *Le aziende di produzione originaria: Vol. 1. Le aziende agricole*. Pisa, Italy: Cursi.

Hayes, R. H., & Abernathy, W. J. (1980). Managing our way to economic decline. *Harvard Business Review*, *58*, 67–77.

Hirschman, A. O. (1970). The search for paradigms as a hindrance to understanding. *World Politics*, *22*(3), 329–343. doi:10.2307/2009600

Jensen, M. C. (2001). Value maximization, stakeholder theory, and the corporate objective function. *Journal of Applied Corporate Finance*, *14*(3), 8–21. doi:10.1111/j.1745-6622.2001.tb00434.x

Jensen, M. C., & Meckling, W. (1976). Theory of the firm: Managerial behavior, agency costs, and capital structure. *Journal of Financial Economics*, *3*(4), 305–360. doi:10.1016/0304-405X(76)90026-X

Jones, T. M. (1995). Instrumental stakeholder theory: A synthesis of ethics and economics. *Academy of Management Review*, *20*(2), 404–437.

Kay, J. (1997). The stakeholder corporation. In G. Kelly, D. Kelly, & A. Gamble (Eds.), *Stakeholder capitalism* (pp. 125–141). London: Macmillam Press.

Keay, A. (2008). Ascertaining the corporate objective: An entity maximization and sustainability model. *The Modern Law Review*, *71*(5), 663–698. doi:10.1111/j.1468-2230.2008.00711.x

Kemper, A., & Martin, R. L. (2010). After the fall: The global financial crisis as a test of corporate social responsibility theories. *European Management Review*, *7*(4), 229–239. doi:10.1057/emr.2010.18

Koslowski, P. (2000). The limits of shareholder value. *Journal of Business Ethics*, *27*(1-2), 137–148. doi:10.1023/A:1006438000855

Lan, L. L., & Heracleous, L. (2010). Rethinking agency theory: The view from law. *Academy of Management Review*, *35*(2), 294–314. doi:10.5465/AMR.2010.48463335

Lazonick, W. (2011). From innovation to financialization: how shareholder value ideology is destroying the US Economy. The Handbook of the Political Economy of Financial Crises.

Magill, M., Quinzii, M., & Rochet, J. C. (2015). A Theory of the stakeholder corporation. *Econometrica*, *83*(5), 1685–1725. doi:10.3982/ECTA11455

Masini, C. (1982). *Lavoro e risparmio*. Turin, Italy: Utet.

Melé, D. (2009). Integrating personalism into virtue-based business ethics: The personalist and the common good principles. *Journal of Business Ethics*, *88*(1), 227–244. doi:10.1007/s10551-009-0108-y

Metcalfe, C. E. (1998). The stakeholder corporation. *Business Ethics (Oxford, England)*, *7*(1), 30–36. doi:10.1111/1467-8608.00083

Meynhardt, T. (2009). Public value inside: What is public value creation? *International Journal of Public Administration*, *32*(3-4), 192–219. doi:10.1080/01900690902732632

Moore, M. H. (1995). *Creating public value: Strategic management in government*. Harvard University Press.

Omran, M., Atrill, P., & Pointon, J. (2002). Shareholders versus stakeholders: Corporate mission statements and investor returns. *Business Ethics (Oxford, England)*, *11*(4), 318–326. doi:10.1111/1467-8608.00291

Onida, P. (1971). *Economia d'azienda*. Turin, Italy: Utet.

Parsons, T. (1960). *Structure and process in modern societies*. New York: The Free Press.

Peterson, E. A. (2013). Compliance and ethics programs: Competitive advantage through the law. *Journal of Management and Governance*, *17*(4), 1027–1045. doi:10.1007/s10997-012-9212-y

Phillips, R., Freeman, R. E., & Wicks, A. C. (2003). What stakeholder theory is not. *Business Ethics Quarterly*, *13*(4), 479–502. doi:10.5840/beq200313434

Plender, J. (1997). *A Stake in the Future: The Stakeholding Solution*. London: Nicholas Brealey.

Rappaport, A. (1990). *La strategia del valore*. Milano, Italy: Franco Angeli.

Rescher, N. (1969). *Introduction to Value Theory*. Washington, DC: University Press of America.

Shleifer, A., & Vishny, R. (1997). A survey of corporate governance. *The Journal of Finance*, *52*(2), 737–783. doi:10.1111/j.1540-6261.1997.tb04820.x

Signori, S., & Rusconi, G. (2009). Ethical thinking in traditional Italian Economia Aziendale and the stakeholder management theory: The search for possible interactions. *Journal of Business Ethics*, *89*(3), 303–318. doi:10.1007/s10551-010-0391-7

Simon, H. A. (1964). On the concept of organizational goal. *Administrative Science Quarterly*, *9*(1), 1–22. doi:10.2307/2391519

Singer, A. E. (2010). Integrating ethics and strategy: A pragmatic approach. *Journal of Business Ethics*, *92*(4), 479–491. doi:10.1007/s10551-009-0176-z

Società Italiana dei Docenti di Ragioneria e di Economia Aziendale (SIDREA). (2009). L'oggetto degli studi di Economia Aziendale. In Atti del I convegno Nazionale su 'La Ragioneria e L'Economia aziendale: dinamiche evolutive e prospettive di cambiamento'. Milan, Italy: Franco Angeli.

Sundaram, A., & Inkpen, A. (2004). The corporate objective revisited. *Organization Science*, *15*(3), 350–363. doi:10.1287/orsc.1040.0068

Tirole, J. (2010). *The theory of corporate finance*. Princeton University Press.

Treviño, L. K., & Nelson, K. A. (2011). *Managing business ethics. Straight talk about how to do it right* (5th ed.). New York, NY: Wiley.

Vigano, E., & Mattessich, R. (2007). Accounting research in Italy: Second half of the 20th century. *Review of Accounting and Finance*, *6*(1), 24–41. doi:10.1108/14757700710725449

Vilanova, L. (2007). Neither shareholder nor stakeholder management: What happens when firms are run for their short-term salient stakeholder? *European Management Journal*, *25*(2), 146–162. doi:10.1016/j.emj.2007.01.002

Zamagni, S. (2010). La lezione e il messaggio di una crisi annunciata. In *Crisi economica, crisi antropologica. L'uomo al centro del lavoro e dell'impresa*. Rimini, Italy: Il Cerchio.

Zappa, G. (1927). *Tendenze Nuove negli studi di Ragioneria, Opening Speech of the Academic Year 1926–1927*. University of Venice.

Zappa, G. (1950). Il reddito di impresa. Giuffré Editore.

Zappa, G. (1954). La nozione d'azienda nell'economia moderna. *Il Risparmio*, *8*, 1255–1278.

Zappa, G. (1956). *Le produzioni nell'economia dell'impresa. Tomo primo*. Milan, Italy: Giuffré Editore.

KEY TERMS AND DEFINITIONS

***Azienda*:** Economic organization with three attributes: systemic vision, decision-making autonomy, and *economicità*.

Business Model: An organization's business model is its system of transforming inputs, through its business activities, into outputs and outcomes that aims to fulfil the organization's strategic purposes and create value over the short, medium and long term.

***Economia Aziendale*:** Is an Italian doctrine founded in 1927 by Gino Zappa as a unitary science that studies the 'existence conditions and life manifestations of the *azienda*'.

***Economicità*:** Is one of the attributes used to define the concept of *azienda*. It is a method of action, in the sense that the *azienda* operates with *economicità* when it is effective and efficient.

Primary Interest of the *Azienda*: Is a principle of good governance for all organizations. This interest includes two elements: 1) the objective of the *azienda* (i.e. satisfy human needs through the production of useful goods and services); 2) a condition for the survival and growth of the *azienda* (i.e. ensuring a sustainable value creation in the short and long term).

Chapter 4
Corporate Social Responsibility:
A Conscientious Take

Chandra Sekhar Patro
Gayatri Vidya Parishad College of Engineering (Autonomous), India

K. Madhu Kishore Raghunath
National Institute of Technology – Warangal, India

ABSTRACT

A sense of responsibility keeps human on the edge which continuously reminds one of where their pursuit lies. Of course, Responsibility keeps piling up as one grow. In a society where the globe is technologically upgrading every second, the businesses are assigned the challenge to keep the surroundings at balance; this is where the term corporate social responsibility gains momentum. In constantly growing economies, Corporate Social Responsibility (CSR) is the force which keeps organizations stay afloat and is the make or break point. Realising this, the economies of world are jointly or individually pursuing the corporate goals towards society in different areas. CSR is the vantage point which is titled to aid an organization's mission as well as a guide to what the company stands for its consumers. The aim of the chapter is to articulate how corporate social responsibility has become the most valuable touch point of the society to survive among different companies and highlight the various issues and challenges in CSR implementation and regulation.

INTRODUCTION

Today organizations are living in a world like never before, times have changed and of course the priorities that every organization have. Yes, corporate social responsibility (CSR) is the theme for all organizations of this generation. Most of the organizations are thinking beyond the primary interests of the firm that is benefiting the society. CSR is not only drawing the corporate magnates into its circumference, but is also luring educationists, social activists, reformists, from all over the world to delve deeper into this subject. Corporate social responsibility is a strategy, be it for enhancing corporate image or to be in competition. One cannot pick up a newspaper, magazine or journal without encountering some discussion of the issue, some recent or innovative example of what business is thinking or doing about CSR,

DOI: 10.4018/978-1-5225-3147-0.ch004

or some new conference that is being held in Specific journals, news magazines, books, dictionaries, encyclopedias, and websites.

The acronym "CSR" (Corporate Social Responsibility) became popular in the 1960s and has remained a term used indiscriminately by many to cover legal and moral responsibility more narrowly construed. Earlier a few organizations focused on economic, responsibility, philanthropic, and legal responsibilities. But nowadays with the changing market situation this focus is shifting and including three other factors: environmental, educational and health responsibilities (Patro & Raghunath, 2016). Companies or organizations have started spending their social responsibility money for environmental benefits, public health care initiatives and for providing free education to the wads of employees and underprivileged (Carroll, 1991). Observers increasingly note that corporate social responsibility has become a mainstream business activity. Firms are investing ever more resources in public goods provision and many companies reduce negative externalities below levels required by law (Turban & Greening, 1997).

As the world is shrinking due to globalization the concept of Corporate Social Responsibility (CSR) has acquired an undeniably high degree of relevance and scope in a large number of sectors. The social responsibility of business encompasses the economic, legal, ethical, and discretionary expectations that society has of organizations at a given point in time (Carroll, 1979). More than one third of large firms have voluntary external certifications for social and environmental standards, and nearly 11 per cent of professionally managed US investment was certified as socially responsible. It is estimated that US and European markets have over 2 trillion USD and 300 billion EURO in certifies socially responsible assets (Espenson, 2014). Firms such as IBM, General Motors or Microsoft even inform potential employees about their CSR efforts. The aim of the chapter is to articulate how corporate social responsibility has become the most valuable touch point of the society to survive among different companies and highlight the various theories and dimensions for emerging markets. This chapter also emphasizes on the contribution of CSR towards the economy and recent trends in CSR implementation and regulation.

BACKGROUND

During the last two decades, there has been a major change in the nature of the triangular relationship between the companies, the state and the society. The evolution of the relationship between companies and society has been one of slow transformation from a philanthropic coexistence to one where the mutual interest of all the stakeholders is gaining paramount importance. Companies are beginning to realize the fact that in order to gain strategic initiative and to ensure continued existence, business practices may have to be moulded from the normal practice of solely focusing on profits to factor in public goodwill and responsible business etiquettes (Raynard & Forstater, 2002). The current trend of globalization has brought a realization among the firms that in order to compete effectively in a competitive environment; they need clearly defined business practices with a sound focus on the public interest in the markets (Gray, 2001). It has been observed that consumers consider switching to another company's products and services, speak out against the company to family/friends, refuse to invest in that company's stock, refuse to work at the company and boycott the company's products and services in case of negative corporate citizenship behaviors (Edenkamp, 2002). Warhust (2001) points out, the three major elements of CSR are product use which focuses on contribution of industrial products which help in well-being and quality of life of the society, business practice which focuses on good corporate governance and gives high impetus for the environmental well-being and equity which tries for distribution of profits equitably across different societies especially the host community.

Emergence of different marketing innovations seeks direct linkage of corporate social responsibility practices with the business corporate strategies (Sharma & Kiran, 2013). CSR refers to one process by which an organization expresses and develops its 'corporate culture' and social consciousness (Rupp, Ganapathi, Aguilera, & Williams, 2006). Dating back several decades ago (Carroll, 1999), CSR has been conceptualized as activities, decisions, or policies that 'organizations' engage in to effect positive social change and environment sustainability. CSR is typically identified as a macro-level activity that has macro level consequences (Orlitzky, Schmidt, & Rynes, 2003), and as a result it has received scant attention within the micro organizational behavior.

Corporate Social Responsibility in India

Asian firms often lag behind their Western counterparts on CSR practices (KPMG, 2005). However, advent of liberalization and globalization, entry of MNCs in Asian markets, rising consumer expectations towards business, and emergence of pressure groups have made the case of CSR stronger in Asian countries including India. But Indian companies mostly focus their CSR activities on community development (Partners in Change [PiC], 2004). Philanthropic orientation of Indian businessmen has its roots in history. In the early nineteenth century India, CSR was mainly found in the form of philanthropic contributions by Gujrati and Parsi merchant communities, who provided funds for building schools, pilgrim rest houses, places of worship like temples, distributing relief items during disasters, and helping the poor.

A 20-country public opinion survey finds that India is the last in the level of CSR demanded from companies in any country. Lack of provable link between CSR and firm performance often discourages companies from engaging in CSR (British Council, UNDP, CII, & Pricewaterhouse Coopers, 2002). Obstacles to CSR are found to be adhoc approach by the top management towards CSR, lack of consensus on priorities within the firm, and problems related to measurement and evaluation of CSR activities (Krishna, 1992). Unclear policies, bureaucracy, poor monitoring, complicated tax systems, and poor infrastructure are a few more hindering factors (Centre for Social Markets, 2001). However, there is a growing feeling among the Indians that business organizations must play a wider role in the society besides providing quality products at reasonable rates, making their operations environmentally sound, adhering to high labor standards, and reducing human rights abuses at the work place (Kumar, Murphy, & Balsari, 2001). Consequently, Indian companies have started changing their outlook towards CSR by looking beyond passive philanthropy. Companies are considering CSR for improved brand image and stronger ties with the local community (PiC, 2004).

In its historical form, CSR in India has been dominated by a philanthropic approach consistent with the long-standing tradition of close business involvement in social development needs. More recently, CSR has received an impetus from the emergence of nonfamily businesses, 'corporate will,' and government and public expectations (Mohan, 2001). Indian CSR is now an important part of the movement away from rapid-growth, export-oriented, cost advantaged-focused strategies to longer-term, business development initiatives (Balasubramanian, Kimber, & Siemensma, 2005). On the role of MNCs operating in multiple geographies, Chen, Newburry and Park (2009) found that with the progression in the development framework, the importance of stakeholders and sustainability has gone up. Hence, the challenge for MNCs seems to be to redesign business models, along with their attitudes and cognitions towards emerging markets, that can help provide suitable products with good quality, sustainability and profitability combined (Joshi & Shah, 2016).

Since the liberalization of the Indian economy, western-style ethical stances are being promoted hence even though the ethical, statist, and stakeholder models may be idealized, the liberal (Friedman) model may be more influential in India (Balasubramanian, Kimber, & Siemensma, 2005). Considering institutional changes, particularly to economic sectors, firms in Asian countries can report overlaps between two or more approaches, and in some cases, multiple orientations to these four models. There is a definite trend in India towards looking at CSR in a positive manner (Narwal & Sharma, 2008). Earlier it was perceived that the firms' CSR activities were not motivated by the desire for social service, but was instead motivated by the desire to avail themselves of tax exemptions and other government incentives and therefore society did not really trust business. Post-liberalization, the Indian government, along with NGOs and the media are becoming agents of change with regard to the CSR activities of firms (Baskin, 2006).

Even though CSR in India may be in a more advanced state than previously thought, but much improvement is needed in how CSR strategies are implemented and integrated within Indian firms. Though several companies in India have climbed on to the CSR bandwagon and are engaged in causes like health care, education, empowerment of women, micro-credit and rural development, CSR seems to be in a confused state in the country (Arora & Puranik, 2004). Graafland and van de Ven (2006) identified two dimensions which motivates the firms to pursue CSR as strategic motives and moral motives. The strategic motive suggests that firms pursue CSR in the hopes of achieving profitability. The moral motive suggests that firms have a moral duty towards society. Therefore, CSR is driven by the personal values and beliefs of individual managers.

CORPORATE SOCIAL RESPONSIBILITY THEORIES

According to Parsons (1961), in any social system; adaptation to the environment (related to resources and economics), goal attainment (related to politics), social integration and pattern maintenance or latency (related to culture and values) are necessary. According to Garriga and Melè (2004), CSR theories are categorized into four groups: Instrumental theories, Political theories, Integrative theories, and Ethical theories.

Instrumental Theories

In this theory, CSR is seen only as a strategic tool to achieve economic objectives and, ultimately, wealth creation. Friedman (1970) viewed that the only responsibility of business towards society is maximization of profits to the shareholders within the legal framework and the ethical custom of the country. As Windsor (2001) has pointed out recently that a leitmotiv of wealth creation progressively dominates the managerial conception of responsibility. It has been argued that in certain conditions the satisfaction of these interests can contribute to maximizing the shareholder value (Ogden & Watson, 1999). An adequate level of investment in philanthropy and social activities is also acceptable for the sake of profits (McWilliams & Siegel, 2001). Three main groups of instrumental theories are identified depending on the economic objective.

Figure 1. Corporate Social Responsibility Theories

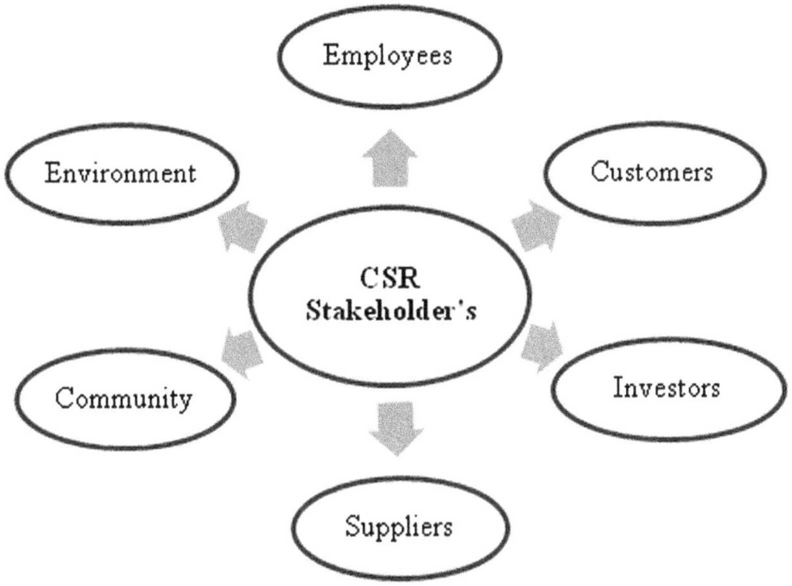

1. **Maximizing Shareholder Value:** A well-known approach is that which takes the straightforward contribution to maximizing the shareholder value as the supreme criterion to evaluate specific corporate social activity. Currently, this approach usually takes the shareholder value maximization as the supreme reference for corporate decision-making. Jensen (2002) proposed the 'enlightened value maximization' concept which specifies long-term value maximization or value-seeking as the firm's objective.
2. **Achieving Competitive Advantages:** A second group of theories are focused on how to allocate resources in order to achieve long-term social objectives and create a competitive advantage (Husted & Allen, 2000). In this group three approaches can be included: social investments in competitive context; natural resource-based view of the firm and its dynamic capabilities; and strategies for the bottom of the economic pyramid (Prahalad & Hammond, 2002). Disruptive innovations can improve the social and economic conditions at the 'base of the pyramid' and at the same time they create a competitive advantage for the firms in telecommunications, consumer electronics and energy production and many other industries, especially in developing countries (Hart & Christensen, 2002).
3. **Cause-Related Marketing:** Cause-related marketing is the process of formulating and implementing marketing activities that are characterized by an offer from the firm to contribute a specified amount to a designated cause when customers engage in a revenue providing exchanges that satisfy organizational and individual objectives (Varadarajan & Menon, 1988). Its goal then is to enhance company revenues and sales or customer relationship by building the brand through the acquisition of, and association with the ethical dimension or social responsibility dimension (Murray & Montanari, 1986).

Political Theories

This theory focuses on interactions and connections between business and society and on the power and position of business and its inherent responsibility. They include both political considerations and political analysis in the CSR debate (Davis, 1960; Carroll, 1999). Although there are a variety of approaches, two major theories can be distinguished: Corporate Constitutionalism and Corporate Citizenship.

1. **Corporate Constitutionalism:** Davis (1960) was one of the first to explore the role of power that business has in society and the social impact of this power4. In doing so, he introduces business power as a new element in the debate of CSR. He held that business is a social institution and it must use power responsibly. Davis (1967) formulated two principles that express how social power has to be managed: "the social power equation" and "the iron law of responsibility". The social power equation principle states that "social responsibilities of businessmen arise from the amount of social power that they have". The iron law of responsibility refers to the negative consequences of the absence of use of power.
2. **Corporate Citizenship:** Although the idea of the firm as citizen is not new (Davis, 1973) a renewed interest in this concept among practitioners has appeared recently due to certain factors that have had an impact on the business and society relationship. The term corporate citizenship was introduced into the business and society relationship mainly through practitioners (Altman & Vidaver-Cohen, 2000). Matten, Crane and Chapple (2003) have distinguished three views of corporate citizenship: a limited view, a view equivalent to CSR, and an extended view of corporate citizenship, which is held by them.

Integrative Theories

Integrative theory looks at how business integrates social demands, arguing that business depends on society for its existence, continuity and growth. Social demands are generally considered to be the way in which society interacts with business and gives it a certain legitimacy and prestige (Preston & Post, 1975). Basically, the theories of this group are focused on the detection and scanning of, and response to, the social demands that achieve social legitimacy, greater social acceptance and prestige.

1. **Issues Management:** Social responsiveness, or responsiveness in the face of social issues, and processes to manage them within the organization (Sethi, 1975) was an approach which arose in the 70s. Ackerman (1973) analyzed the relevant factors regarding the internal structures of organizations and integration mechanisms to manage social issues within the organization. According to Jones (1980), corporate behavior should not in most cases be judged by the decisions actually reached but by the process by which they are reached. The concept of social responsiveness was soon widened with the concept "Issues Management". The latter includes the former but emphasizes the process for making a corporate response to social issues (Wartick & Rude, 1986).
2. **Principle of Public Responsibility:** The responsiveness approach and the purely process approach was criticized and instead proposed the "principle of public responsibility" (Jones, 1980). They choose the term "public" rather than "social", to stress the importance of the public process, rather than personal-morality views or narrow interest group defining the scope of responsibilities (Preston & Post, 1981). The development of this approach was parallel to the study of the scope regarding

business–government relationship (Vogel, 1986). This focused on government regulations, their formulation and implementation, corporate strategies to influence these regulations, including campaign contributions, lobbying, coalition building, grassroots organization, corporate public affairs and the role of public interest and other advocacy groups.

3. **Stakeholder Management:** Instead of focusing on generic responsiveness, specific issues or on the public responsibility principle, the approach called 'stakeholder management' is oriented towards 'stakeholders' or people who affect or are affected by corporate policies and practices. Stakeholder management includes topics such as how to determine the best practice in corporate stakeholder relations (Bendheim, Waddock, & Graves, 1998), stakeholder salience to managers (Agle & Mitchell, 1999), the impact of stakeholder management on financial performance (Berman, Wicks, Kotha, & Jones, 1999), the influence of stakeholder network structural relations and how managers can successfully balance the competing demands of various stakeholder groups (Ogden & Watson, 1999). Now some corporations are seeking corporate responses to social demands by establishing dialogue with a wide spectrum of stakeholders.
4. **Corporate Social Performance:** The corporate social performance (CSP) includes a search for social legitimacy, with processes for giving appropriate responses. Carroll (1979), generally considered to have introduced this model, suggested a model of 'corporate performance' with three elements: a basic definition of social responsibility, a listing of issues in which social responsibility exists and a specification of the philosophy of response to social issues. A new development came with Wood (1991) who presented a model of corporate social performance composed of principles of CSR, processes of corporate social responsiveness and outcomes of corporate behavior.

Ethical Theories

The fourth group of theories focuses on the ethical requirements that cement the relationship between business and society. They are based on principles that express the right thing to do or the necessity to achieve a good society. As main approaches we can distinguish the following.

1. **Normative Stakeholder:** Stakeholder management has been included within the integrative theories group because some authors consider that this form of management is a way to integrate social demands. Donaldson and Preston (1995) held that the stakeholder theory has a normative core based on two major ideas i.e. stakeholders are persons or groups with legitimate interests in procedural and/or substantive aspects of corporate activity; and interests of all stakeholders are of intrinsic value.
2. **Universal Rights:** Human rights have been taken as a basis for CSR, especially in the global market place (Cassel, 2001). In recent years, some human-rights-based approaches for corporate responsibility have been proposed. It was first presented by the United Nations Secretary- General Kofi Annan in an address to 'The World Economic Forum' in 1999. Although for many people universal rights are a question of mere consensus, they have a theoretical grounding, and some moral philosophy theories give them support (Donnelly, 1985). It is worth mentioning the Natural Law tradition, which defends the existence of natural human rights.
3. **Sustainable Development:** Another values-based concept, which has become popular, is "sustainable development". Although this approach was developed at macro level rather than corporate level, it demands a relevant corporate contribution. Wheeler, Colbertm, and Freeman, (2003)

stated, sustainability as an ideal toward which society and business can continually strive, the way we strive is by creating value, creating outcomes that are consistent with the ideal of sustainability along social environmental and economic dimensions. Van Marrewijk and Werre (2003) argued that maintaining corporate sustainability is a custom-made process and each organization should choose its own specific ambition and approach regarding corporate sustainability.

4. **Common Good Approach:** This third group of approaches, less consolidated than the stakeholder approach but with potential, holds the common good of society as the referential value for CSR (Velasquez, 1992). This approach maintains that business, as with any other social group or individual in society, has to contribute to the common good, because it is a part of society. Although there are several ways of understanding the notion of common good (Sulmasy, 2001), the interpretation based on the knowledge of human nature and its fulfillment seems to us particularly convincing. It permits the circumnavigation of cultural relativism, which is frequently embedded in some definitions o sustainable development.

CSR: AN OMNIPRESENT PHENOMENA

The approach of business organizations to CSR has transcended from merely displaying social concerns to being sensitive and alert to the constituents in the internal and external business environment. These constituents, known as stakeholders, are potent forces to accelerate or decelerate a firm's performance. With globalization of national boundaries and information technology revolution, companies are under tight scrutiny from multiple stakeholders including regulators, investors, customers, pressure groups, and the public at large. Corporate scandals are making big news leading to crumbling of well settled business empires. When stakeholders lose confidence in a firm's performance, the firm loses its critical support structure and customer base (Lee, 2008). Customers stop buying products or go for legal suits, shareholders sell their stocks, employees do not perform, and environmental advocates sue (Wood, 1991), all of which directly affect firm performance.

A firm's survival and success depends on the ability of its managers to create sufficient wealth and satisfaction for its primary stakeholders (employees, shareholders, customers, suppliers, communities, and natural environment). If any of the primary stakeholder groups withdraws its support to the firm, the firm's operation is adversely affected (Clarkson, 1995). Firms that establish relationship with primary stakeholders beyond market transactions gain competitive advantage (Barney & Hansen, 1994). Effective management of key stakeholders acts as a value driver by leveraging performance and reducing stakeholder-inflicted costs. Lower employee turnover reduces hiring and training costs, loyal suppliers reduce quality certification costs, supportive communities reduce legal and public relations overhead, and stable shareholders reduce stock market volatility (McVea & Freeman, 2005). In order to achieve sustainability in business, firms must identify key stakeholders affecting the firm, identify their needs, and design organizational policies and practices to cater to them.

CSR Towards Employees

Proactive policies and practices towards employees reflect organizations' intention to address the interests of its employees and satisfy their needs. Policies and practices towards union relations, employees' participation in decision making, remuneration policy, working conditions, and elimination of forced/

Figure 2. Corporate Social Responsibility Stakeholder's

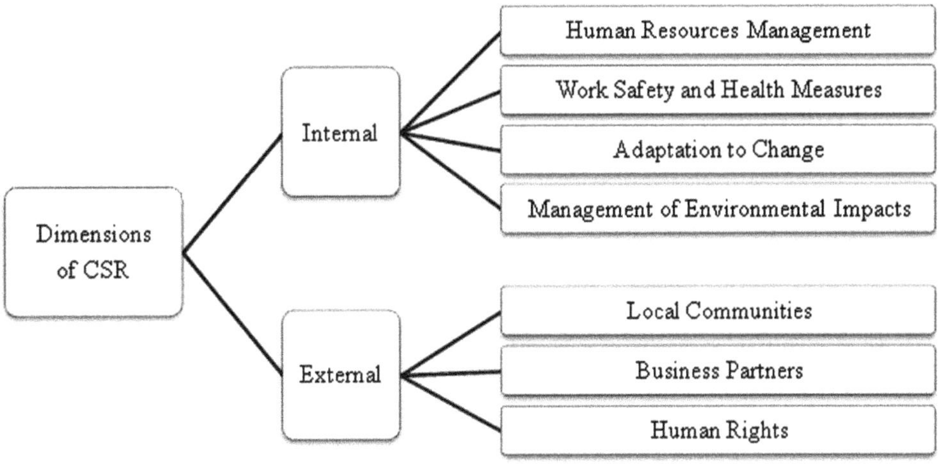

child labor, portray a firm's CSR towards employees enhancing overall efficiency and effectiveness. Working conditions that respect human dignity, equality, and social protection result in a productive workplace (Somavia, 2000). Social responsibility of a company is a reputation factor and is an attractive force for potential and current employees (Turban & Greening, 1997). Ethical reputation contributes to job satisfaction and lower employee turnover by evoking positive reactions from employees' families and friends (Riordan, Gatewood, & Bill, 1997).

CSR Towards Customers

Positive customer perception about product quality and safety leads to increased sales or decreased costs associated with stakeholder relationships (Waddock & Graves, 1997). Higher product safety and quality improves the bottom line. In product retailing, market reactions are found to be negative for socially irresponsible companies (Bromiley & Marcus, 1989). Event studies establish that market value of a company decreases when corporate irresponsibility and illegal behavior is observed (Frooman, 1997). Continuous deterioration in quality directly affects firm performance. Hence, companies need to be careful about factors such as ethical advertising standards, customer health and safety during product use, company-wide quality programs for providing better products at right prices and the like (Landon & Smith, 1997). Company policies and practices to address such issues give a positive signal about a company's responsible attitude towards its customers and can improve firm performance.

CSR Towards Investors

Firms can strengthen their investor relations by adopting proper governance standards. After the corporate governance debacles in 1990s such as that of Enron in the US, the stock market crisis in India, and falling corporate governance standards across the globe, a lot of importance is being given to governance codes and laws for protecting the interests of shareholders and investors. CSR towards investors examine firm policies and practices towards such issues including shareholders' participation in decision making, auditors' independence, and policies towards insider trading. Investors show willingness to pay a premium for the stocks of well-governed companies compared to poor-governed companies (Landon & Smith, 1997). Positive relations are found between corporate governance and stock price performance and financial ratios in emerging markets.

CSR Towards Suppliers

Influence of suppliers has become crucial in recent years as companies have started focusing more on their core competencies, outsourcing other functions to suppliers (Prahalad & Hammond, 2002). Recent years have seen growing importance of suppliers' issues such as health and safety, environmental impact, community involvement, and the payment of living wages to employees at both outsourced plant locations and home locations of suppliers. Standards on CSR towards suppliers incorporate issues such as ethical procurement of raw materials by suppliers, and elimination of child labor and human rights' violation at suppliers' locations. By ensuring adherence of CSR standards by suppliers, a firm sends strong signals about its commitment towards CSR, which improves its image and performance. Violation of CSR standards by suppliers adversely affects a firm's performance (Mishra & Suar, 2010).

CSR Towards Community and Society

Typical involvement of business with the community is seen in areas of education, health, and income generation. CSR towards community is seen in terms of philanthropic giving, public–private partnerships, community relationships, and participation in social and economic development issues (Singh & Bhagat, 2004; Dunn & Yamashita, 2003). When firms focus their social actions on communities in and around their area of operation, they reap the benefits of a socially responsible image among their employees and the local community (Husted, 2003). Berry (2007) has suggested that in effectively generous firms, the relationship between social and financial performance is mutually reinforcing, creating a virtuous circle benefiting the firm and its employees, customers and the community. Poole (2009) has arrived at the conclusion that Companies recognised as role models over time by their peers, seem to exhibit not only Vision, but also stand for something beyond mere profits. Burns and Schapper (2008) have built a case for the reinforcement of affirmative action, which provides a group of people with an opportunity to cut away from an inheritance that has placed them in an inequitable economic and social position.

CSR Towards Environment

In recent times, the term Corporate Social and Environment Responsibility (CSER) seems to have gained popularity. Lynes and Andrachuk (2008) have developed a model by which various external, sector-specific and internal influences for CSER are interpreted, and then shaped into action at the level of the firm. Environmental performance is enhanced by improvements in three aspects such as product technologies, process technologies, and management systems. The impact of firms' proactive environmental practices on market share, profitability, and return on investment is better in environmentally conscious companies compared to not so conscious companies (Ahmed, Montagno, & Firenze, 1998). Pirson and Lawrence (2010) have built the case for a new paradigm of sustainable development of business in the future, where the economic system can be reconnected to its humanistic roots. Porter and Kramer (2002) focused upon the new paradigm of being green and competitive, and the need to use resources productively. It is important to use resources productively, whether those resources are natural and physical, or human and capital. Lyon and Maxwell (2008) believe that business often takes proactive steps to avert political conflict. This is also the dominant line of thinking in linking up CSR and the Environment, with a view that pollution reduction and cost reduction go together to create win-win opportunities.

CSR AND FIRM'S PERFORMANCE

The relations between CSR and FP are mostly inconclusive, but positive relations between the two have been reported in most of the studies (Margolis & Walsh, 2003) suggesting an instrumental orientation of CSR initiatives. An instrumental orientation towards CSR suggests the alignment of the social goal with the business goal where CSR is considered as a strategic tool to promote the economic objective of the firm. Managers foresee significant value additions in firm performance due to strengthened stakeholder relations. Management theorists argue that by improving CSR towards stakeholders, firm performance is augmented (Waddock & Graves, 1997). The influence of stakeholder oriented CSR on firm performance can be understood with the help of three theories:

1. Consumer Inference making theory suggests that if a consumer knows that the manufacturer of the product is a responsible firm, people can infer positively about the product (Brown & Dacin, 1997). Such inferences induce consumer goodwill (Handelman & Arnold, 1999) that influences purchase intention (Gildea, 1994).
2. Signaling theory suggests that in situations where there is information asymmetry between buyers and sellers, consumers look for information/signals that distinguish companies performing well on attributes of interest compared to companies performing poorly (Kirmani, 1997).
3. Social Identity theory emphasizes that one's self-concept is influenced by membership in different social organizations, including the company for which an individual works (Dutton, Dukerich, & Harquail, 1994). Employees' self-image is influenced by the image and reputation of their employers, consumers identify themselves with organizations or brands involved in discretionary citizenship (Aaker, 1994), and institutional investors like to be associated with socially responsible firms (Hoeffler & Keller, 2002). Such bonds of identification encourage positive evaluations of a firm's products, and reap value addition through customer loyalty, advocacy, positive words-of-mouth, and resilience to negative brand information (Sen, Bhattacharya, & Korschun, 2006).

Alternatively, irresponsible behavior by firms agitates stakeholders. They often react by boycotting the company (Hayes & Pereira, 1990), reducing consumption of the company's products (Sen & Bhattacharya, 2001), initiating legal action against the company (Greeno & Robinson, 1992), and/or spreading bad words-of-mouth about irresponsible business practices. Boycotting of Nike products due to human rights' abuse and unsafe working conditions at suppliers' locations in Asia or sharp reaction from environmentalists and consumers to the pesticide content in Pepsi and Coca-Cola beverages in India are few such instances (Herbert, 1996). While improved stakeholder relations have the potential to improve a firm's reputation and performance, strained relations have the risk of adversely affecting a firm's performance.

CSR CONTRIBUTION TOWARDS ECONOMY

According to the India CSR Outlook Report (2015 & 2016), there is substantial improvement in the actual CSR spend to the prescribed CSR in FY 2015-16. The prescribed CSR was INR 7,143 crores, while the actual CSR spent was INR 6,578 crores. It was 79 per cent in FY 2014-15 and has increased to 92 per cent in last financial year. Almost one third of the companies spent more than the prescribed CSR while one fifth of the companies spent exactly as the prescribed CSR. 58% of the companies have spent either exactly as the prescribed CSR or more than the prescribed CSR, while in 2014-15 it was only 48 per cent.

The Table 1 gives us the overall picture of the top 10 companies listed in the BSE sensex with the prescribed and actual CSR spent during 2014-15 and 2015-16, and percentage change in CSR contribution towards the development of economy. At the outset the table shows the overall percentage contributions by all the top 10 companies in year 2014-15 was INR 2,884 crores, and the actual spent CSR was INR 2,702 crores. The same prescribed CSR contribution in 2015-16 was INR 3,062 crores and the actual spent CSR was INR 3,100 crores, where it is visible that not just the role of CSR in statements but also there was a significant increase in the overall CSR contribution in the year 2015-16 when compared to 2014-15 by 14.73 per cent. So, it can be ideated that the role of CSR has taken a big leap when compared to previous years since the Companies Act - 2013 has come into force (India CSR Report, 2015; 2016).

The Table 2 shows the Companies with highest CSR contribution on par with the prescribed CSR during the year 2015-16. Economy can benefitted largely by the way companies are contributing to the CSR, as it is evident that out of the top 10 companies with highest CSR contribution top three companies have spent more than 39 per cent above their prescribed CSR contribution and remaining other companies have spent at an average of 11 per cent above their prescribed CSR. It can be observed that

Table 1. Top 10 companies (prescribed and actual CSR spent)

Sl. No.	Companies	2014-15 (INR Cr.)			2015-16 (INR Cr.)		
		Prescribed CSR	Actual CSR	% Increase/ Decrease	Prescribed CSR	Actual CSR	% Increase/ Decrease
1	Reliance Industries Ltd.	533	761	43	558	652	17
2	NTPC Ltd.	283	205	(28)	350	492	41
3	Oil & Natural Gas Corp Ltd	660	495	(25)	594	421	(29)
4	TCS	285	219	(23)	360	294	(18)
5	ITC Ltd.	213	214	0	247	248	0
6	Tata Steel	168	171	2	150	213	42
7	NMDC	210	189	(10)	193	210	9
8	Infosys Ltd.	243	240	(1)	253	202	(20)
9	Power Finance Corp Ltd.	117	52	(56)	145	196	35
10	ICICI Bank Ltd.	172	156	(9)	212	172	(19)
Total		**2884**	**2702**	(6)	**3062**	**3100**	1

Source: Authors computation based on India CSR Outlook Report (2015 & 2016)

Table 2. Highest CSR contribution by companies in % (In INR Cr.) 2015-16

Sl. No.	Company Name	Prescribed CSR	Actual CSR	% Increase
1	Tata Steels Ltd.	150	213.24	42
2	NTPC Ltd.	349.65	491.8	41
3	Power Finance Corp Ltd.	145.09	196.2	35
4	Maruti Suzuki India Ltd.	65.4	78.46	20
5	Larsen &Toubro Ltd.	101.46	119.9	18
6	Reliance Industries Ltd.	557.78	651.57	17
7	Indian Oil Corp Ltd.	141.5	156.68	11
8	NMDC	193.28	210.09	9
9	Wipro Ltd.	156	159	2
10	ITC Ltd.	246.76	247.5	0

Source: Authors computation based on India CSR Outlook Report (2015 & 2016)

the companies in year 2015-16, have been all big players showing path to other upcoming medium and small companies.

The Table 3 shows the companies with highest CSR contribution on par with the prescribed CSR during the year 2014-15. In this year apart from big players we have other companies coming into the list with highest CSR contribution, where top three companies have spent more than 168.67 per cent above their prescribed CSR contribution and remaining other companies have spent at an average of 54 per cent above their prescribed CSR.

To have birds eye of the CSR flowing on a whole in our economy, the Table 4 shows the sector wise actual contribution of CSR for the year 2014-15 and 2015-16. Where it is evident that all the sectors on the list have a positive sign of CSR growth except Oil, Drilling and Refineries sector which is going

Table 3. Highest CSR contribution by companies in % (In INR Cr.) 2014-15

Sl. No.	Company Name	Prescribed CSR	Actual CSR	% Increase
1	Kirloskar Brothers Ltd.	1.39	4.5	224
2	Sobha Developers Ltd.	5.97	14.4	141
3	Indian Metals & Ferro Alloys	1.68	4.05	141
4	Indiabulls Housing Finance Ltd.	23.2	43.5	88
5	Tech Mahindra Ltd.	30.88	53.21	72
6	Bharat Forge Ltd.	7.12	11.23	58
7	UPL Ltd.	6.93	10.62	53
8	Reliance Industries Ltd.	532.96	760.58	43
9	Kirloskar Ferrous Industries Ltd.	1.22	1.63	34
10	NIIT Technologies Ltd.	3.63	4.72	30

Source: Authors computation based on India CSR Outlook Report (2015 & 2016)

Table 4. Sectors wise performance (Actual CSR Spent)

Sl. No.	Sector	2014-15 (INR Cr.)	2015-16 (INR Cr.)	% Increase
1	Auto and Auto Ancillaries	183	249	36
2	Banking and Finance	702	1178	68
3	Computers (Software and Hardware)	690	774	12
4	Pharmaceuticals	143	189	32
5	Oil, Drilling and Refineries	1568	1368	(13)
6	Steel (all)	-	378	
Total		3286	4136	26

Source: Authors computation based on India CSR Outlook Report (2015 & 2016)

through a rough phase right now, moreover even Steel industry have started contributing in year 2015-16 onwards. The overall increase of CSR contribution in the year 2015-16 is up by 26 per cent.

As it is said that unity is strength everywhere, same applies to CSR also, with the given rise in social awareness towards our country, all the states are coming ahead to do their bit in CSR. Table 5 shows the top 10 states with their CSR contributions. It can be observed that the states West Bengal, Andhra Pradesh, Gujarat, Odisha, and Telangana had a rise in the CSR fund flow, whereas the funds flow has been decreased for the states of Maharashtra, Rajasthan, Karnataka, and Tamil Nadu compared to the year 2014-15 and 2015-16.

DIMENSIONS OF CSR FOR EMERGING MARKETS

The Commission of the European Communities identifies two main dimensions of CSR, an internal dimension relating to practices internal to the company and an external dimension involving the exter-

Table 5. CSR funds flow- state wise (INR Cr.)

Sl. No.	State	2014-15		2015-16	
		Amount	% Ratio	Amount	% Ratio
1	Maharashtra	1012	18	986	15
2	West Bengal	205	4	571	8.7
3	Andhra Pradesh	176	3	417	6.3
4	Rajasthan	552	10	342	5.2
5	Gujarat	234	4	343	5.2
6	Karnataka	421	8	337	5.1
7	Tamil Nadu	273	5	319	4.8
8	Odisha	253	4	291	4.4
9	Telangana	172	3	292	4.4

Source: Authors computation based on India CSR Outlook Report (2015 & 2016)

nal stakeholders (Green Paper, 2001). The dimensions and its components are shown in Figure 2 and discussed below.

Internal Dimension

This relates to practices internal to the company which need to be modified to incorporate CSR practices. The various components of the internal dimension of CSR as shown in Figure 2 are discussed.

1. **Human Resources Management:** Corporate Social Responsibility can be successfully implemented in an organization through precise management of its own work force. The internal dimension of CSR includes elements like providing an environment for life-long learning for employees, employee empowerment, better information flow, improving the balance between work, family, and leisure, diversified work force, profit sharing and share ownership schemes, concern for employability as well as job security among others. Dawar and Chattopadhyay (2000) infer that many times, emerging markets are able to provide cheap skilled and unskilled labour at wages which would be substantially cheaper than the normal cost of automation of the job positions.
2. **Work Safety and Health Measures:** Worker safety and labour health have been documented to be having a direct impact on productivity of the labour force. Although legal measures exist in most nations on maintaining standards for ensuring worker safety and providing health benefits, recent trends have made it imperative for companies to adopt a proactive approach to this issue (Green Paper, 2001). In emerging markets having significant cost advantages in labour, outsourcing of

Figure 3. Dimensions of Corporate Social Responsibility

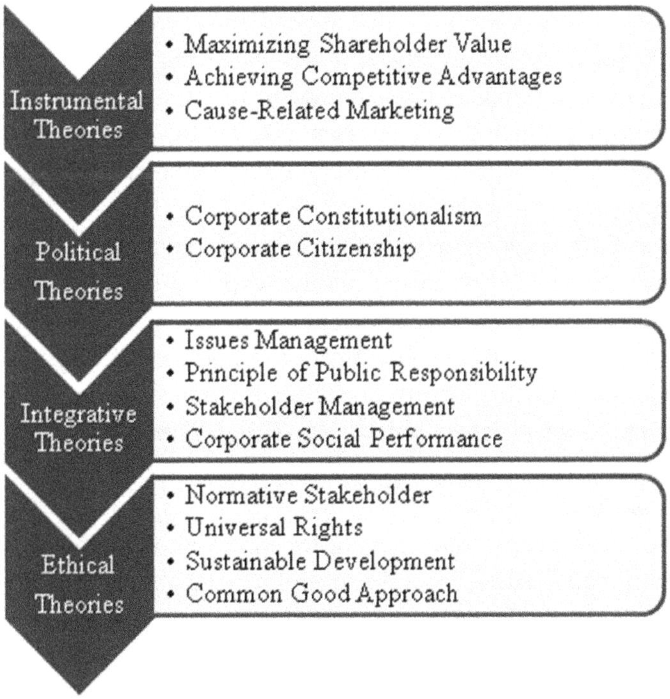

labour and processes have led to the situation where companies not only need to maintain high safety levels in their own premises but also ensure that their suppliers and other connected parties comply with these principles (Dawar & Chattopadhyay, 2000).

3. **Adaptation to Change:** A recent trend in the global business scenario has been the wide spread use of mergers and acquisitions for business expansion. Also downsizing has been used, often ineffectively, as a cost cutting measure by firms in their relentless push for profits. According to Green Paper (2001), restructuring in a socially responsible manner means to balance and take into consideration the interests and concerns of all those who are affected by the changes and decisions. Bhattacharyya and Rahman (2003) point out that although most emerging economies have labour laws preventing labour retrenchment even in the event of declining sales, in practice lobbying with the bureaucracy and government is an aspect which firms cannot chose to ignore.
4. **Management of Environmental Impacts:** The importance of the aspect of corporate social responsibility cannot be over emphasized. Optimization of resource utilization and reducing environmentally damaging effluents can reduce the environmental impact. Many firms in emerging markets have had to face serious repercussions from the state and society for over exploitation of natural resources and disregard for environmental safety measures (Green Paper, 2001). Many multinational companies are realizing to their cost that early compliance with accepted standards will provide strategic advantages in the long run even though cost inefficient in the near future.

External Dimension

This dimension relates to practices concerning external stakeholders. The significance of this dimension of corporate social responsibility has come to the forefront with the advent of globalization leading to the development of international standards for business practices.

1. **Local Communities:** The development of positive relations with the local community and thereby the accumulation of social capital is particularly relevant for non-local companies. These relations are being increasingly used by multinational companies to support the integration of their subsidiaries into various markets in which they are present (Dawar and Chattopadhyay, 2000). In emerging markets this is more relevant than ever because of the availability of cheaper labour from the local communities and reaps the cost benefits.
2. **Business Partners:** Building long term relationships of sound ethical foundation with suppliers, customers will enable companies to meet customer expectations better while reducing complexity and costs. The effect of corporate social responsibility activities will not remain limited to the company itself, but will also touch upon their economic partners. Companies in emerging markets actually take on additional CSR responsibilities because of the existence of outsourcing opportunities in the form of suppliers and outsourcing agents (Green Paper, 2001). Thus in emerging markets, consumer based business strategies would enable companies to build long lasting relationships with consumers based on trust.
3. **Human Rights:** Companies operating in countries where human rights are regularly violated may experience a climate of civil instability and corruption that makes for uneasy relations with government officials, employees, local communities and shareholders. In the context of emerging markets,

firms also need to build confidence in the local community that people (including union members) participating in peaceful protests against company operations are not intimidated, arrested or in any other way threatened (Robbins, 2000). Companies need to ensure that human rights principles are withheld in all their operations and related activities in emerging markets.

RECENT TRENDS IN CSR

Today, CSR is on the agenda of CEO's of many companies. Now it is also being considered seriously by on the agenda of governments (national and local), both national and local as well as NGOs', consumer groups, investors and other actors in civil society (Das Gupta & Das Gupta, 2005). Business organizations across the world are realizing the benefits of adopting socially responsible behavior. If a company engages with its stakeholders effectively, it can enjoy a strong and enduring reputation in the market and community. This idea still needs to be understood and implemented in a better manner by the business sector in India. CSR experts blame the lack of trained personnel, non-availability of accurate information and lack of understanding of the necessity, objectives and the benefits for the slow acceptance of CSR in the country. But the present condition seems to be changing as many companies are making the efforts take their CSR beyond 'planting trees or giving away to charity for the needy'. The trend is to move away from just doing a 'social good' to viewing CSR as a business necessity. The corporate social responsibility trend in India is also undergoing change.

Corporate Social Responsibility is not a new concept in India. Corporates like the Tata Group, the Aditya Birla Group, and Indian Oil Corporation, to name a few, have been involved in serving the community ever since their inception. Several other organizations have been doing their part for society through donations and charity events. Today, CSR in India has gone beyond merely 'charity and donations'; and is approached in a more organized fashion. It has become an integral part of the corporate strategy (Das Gupta, 2010). Companies have CSR teams that devise specific policies, strategies and goals for their CSR programs and make budgetary provisions to support them. These programs, in many cases, are based on a clearly defined social philosophy or are closely aligned with the companies' core business expertise. Employees become the backbone of these initiatives and volunteer their time and contribute their skills, to implement them. CSR programs could range from overall development of a community to supporting specific causes like education, environment, healthcare, etc.

CSR has come a long way in India. From responsive activities to sustainable initiatives, corporations have clearly demonstrated their ability to make a significant difference in society and improve the overall quality of life. In India, it is difficult for one single entity to bring about change, as the scale is enormous. Corporations have the expertise, strategic thinking capabilities, manpower and money financial resources to facilitate extensive social change. CSR encompasses the entire gamut of activities that are involved in the management of a business. Starting from stakeholder engagement and management, it covers relationships with the supply chain, consumer and customer relations, labour relations, corporate governance, Human Resources (HR), environment, etc (Pramar, 2012). All activities under CSR should rightly be handled by the business and its employees, with or without a partnership with civil society organizations. Handing over its responsibilities, even partially, to the government or bureaucracy would weaken the CSR agenda and deny the company its rightful standing among the stakeholders.

CONCLUSION

Every organization irrespective of its core objective have to compliment the society in which they sustain, it can't be better than inculcating Corporate Social Responsibility programmes. CSR has always been a double edged tool which either makes or breaks. In such a situation organizations have an important role to decide the extent of economic development at sight, and of course it is at full length. Developing countries has a job to complete by contributing towards aggregate world cause in improving the environment considering the depth of the situation and the present scenario which is prevailing all over. After analyzing the various dimensions of CSR for emerging markets and also multiple theories, it has become and will be a perquisite for all organizations to contribute their share towards what they can do to make the world a better place. And now is best time to react and incorporate CSR.

Now it is timely to propose an agenda for further multi-disciplinary research. Concepts of CSR are often addressed by multiple agencies with different goals, cultures and values, working together in networks. Further research into how to lead and manage such networks more effectively could be helpful. More efforts could also be made to integrate management tools into the practice of CSR. Future research could explore the mechanisms linking CSR, ethics, and poverty alleviation. Further attention could be paid to the importance of intercultural factors, leadership and values in institutions, and MNEs when crafting strategies for emerging markets. Corporate Social Responsibility has been an open challenge to nations, societies, politicians, scholars, managers, organizations, and communities where all can contribute and collaborate under one umbrella to exploit this opportunity for welfare of nation as *"Unity is the pillar of Strength"*.

REFERENCES

Aaker, D. (1994). Building a Brand: The Saturn Story. *California Management Review*, *36*(2), 114–121. doi:10.2307/41165748

Ackerman, R. W. (1973). How Companies Respond to Social Demands. *Harvard University Review*, *51*(4), 88–98.

Agle, B. R., Mitchell, R. K., & Sonnenfeld, J. A. (1999). Who Matters to CEOs? An Investigation of Stakeholder Attributes and Salience, Corporate Performance and CEO Values. *Academy of Management Journal*, *42*(5), 507–526. doi:10.2307/256973

Ahmed, N. Z., Montagno, R. V., & Firenze, R. J. (1998). Organizational Performance and Environmental Consciousness: An Empirical Study. *Management Decision*, *36*(2), 57–62. doi:10.1108/00251749810204124

Altman, B. W., & Vidaver-Cohen, D. (2000). Corporate Citizenship in the New Millennium: Foundation for an Architecture of Excellence. *Business and Society Review*, *105*(1), 145–169. doi:10.1111/0045-3609.00069

Arora, B., & Puranik, R. (2004). A review of corporate social responsibility in India. *Society for International Development*, *47*(3), 93–100.

Balasubramanian, N. K., Kimber, D., & Siemensma, F. (2005). Emerging opportunities or traditions reinforced? An analysis of the attitudes towards CSR, and trends of thinking about CSR in India. *Journal of Corporate Citizenship*, *17*(2), 79–92. doi:10.9774/GLEAF.4700.2005.sp.00010

Barney, J. B., & Hansen, M. H. (1994). Trustworthiness as a Source of Competitive Advantage. *Strategic Management Journal*, *15*(S1), 175–190. doi:10.1002/smj.4250150912

Baskin, J. (2006). Corporate responsibility in emerging markets. *Journal of Corporate Citizenship*, *24*(4), 29–47. doi:10.9774/GLEAF.4700.2006.wi.00006

Bendheim, C. L., Waddock, S. A., & Graves, S. B. (1998). Determining Best Practice in Corporate-Stakeholder Relations Using Data Envelopment Analysis. *Business & Society*, *37*(3), 306–339. doi:10.1177/000765039803700304

Berman, S. L., Wicks, A. C., Kotha, S., & Jones, T. M. (1999). Does Stakeholder Orientation Matter? The Relationship between Stakeholder Management Models and the Firm Financial Performance. *Academy of Management Journal*, *42*(5), 488–509. doi:10.2307/256972

Berry, L. (2007). The Best Companies are generous Companies. *Business Horizons*, *50*(4), 263–269. doi:10.1016/j.bushor.2007.02.003

Bhattacharyya, S. K., & Rahman, Z. (2003). Why large local conglomerates may not work in emerging markets. *European Business Review*, *15*(2), 105–115. doi:10.1108/09555340310464731

British Council, UNDP, CII, & Pricewaterhouse Coopers. (2002). Corporate Social Responsibility Survey. A Survey by British Council, UNDP, CII and Pricewaterhouse Coopers.

Bromiley, P., & Marcus, A. (1989). The Deterrent to Dubious Corporate Behavior: Profitability, Probability, and Safety Recalls. *Strategic Management Journal*, *10*(3), 233–250. doi:10.1002/smj.4250100304

Brown, T. J., & Dacin, P. A. (1997). The Company and the Product: Corporate Associations and Consumer Product Responses. *Journal of Marketing*, *61*(1), 68–85. doi:10.2307/1252190

Brugmann, J., & Prahalad, C. K. (2007). Co-Creating Business's New Social Compact. *Harvard Business Review*, *85*(2), 80–90. PMID:17345682

Burns, P., & Schapper, J. (2008). The Ethical Case for Affirmative Action. *Journal of Business Ethics*, *83*(3), 369–379. doi:10.1007/s10551-007-9625-8

Carroll, A. B. (1979). Three-dimensional conceptual model of corporate performance. *Academy of Management Review*, *4*(4), 497–505.

Carroll, A. B. (1991). The pyramid of corporate social responsibility: Toward the moral management of organizational stakeholders. *Business Horizons*, *34*(4), 39–48. doi:10.1016/0007-6813(91)90005-G

Carroll, A. B. (1999). Corporate social responsibility: Evolution of a Definitional Construct. *Business & Society*, *38*(3), 268–295. doi:10.1177/000765039903800303

Cassel, D. (2001). Human Rights Business Responsibilities in the Global Marketplace. *Business Ethics Quarterly*, *11*(2), 261–274. doi:10.2307/3857749

Clarkson, M. B. E. (1995). A Shareholder Framework for Analyzing and Evaluating Corporate Social Performance. *Academy of Management Review*, *20*(1), 571–610.

CSM (Centre for Social Markets). (2001). *Corporate Social Responsibility: Perceptions of Indian Business.* A Report by CSM, Calcutta, India. Retrieved May 10, 2016, from www.csmworld.org/public/pdf/social_respons.pdf

Das Gupta, A. (2010). *Ethics, business and society*. Singapore: Sage Publications.

Das Gupta, A., & Das Gupta, A. (2005). Corporate social responsibility: the Indian context. In D. Crowther & R. Jatana (Eds.), *Representations of social responsibility* (Vol. 2, pp. 31–73). Hyderabad, India: ICFAI University Press.

Davis, K. (1960). Can Business Afford to Ignore Corporate Social Responsibilities? *California Management Review*, *2*(3), 70–76. doi:10.2307/41166246

Davis, K. (1967). Understanding the Social Responsibility Puzzle. *Business Horizons*, *10*(4), 45–51. doi:10.1016/0007-6813(67)90007-9

Davis, K. (1973). The Case For and Against Business Assumption of Social Responsibilities. *Academy of Management Journal*, *16*(2), 312–322. doi:10.2307/255331

Dawar, N., & Chattopadhyay, A. (2000). *Rethinking Marketing Programs for Emerging Markets*. Davidson Institute Working Paper Series. Retrieved on May 28, 2016, from http://eres.bus.umich.edu/docs/workpap-dav/wp320.pdf

Donaldson, T., & Preston, L. E. (1995). The Stakeholder Theory of the Corporation: Concepts, Evidence, and Implications. *Academy of Management Review*, *20*(1), 65–91.

Donnelly, J. (1985). *The Concept of Human Rights*. London, UK: Croom Helm.

Dunn, D., & Yamashita, K. (2003). A Changed World, Micro capitalism and the Mega-Corporation. *Harvard Business Review*, *81*(8), 46–54. PMID:12884667

Dutton, J. E., Dukerich, J. M., & Harquail, C. V. (1994). Organizational Images and Member Identification. *Administrative Science Quarterly*, *39*(2), 239–263. doi:10.2307/2393235

Edenkamp, P. (2002). Insights into how consumers are thinking, how they are acting and why. *Brandweek*, *43*(36), 16–20.

Espenson, A. (2014). *5 Companies Doing Corporate Social Responsibility Right*. Retrieved May 20, 2016, from http://www.business2community.com/social-business/5-companies-corporate-social-responsibility-right-0951534#rYj9voqGiqDJ3B3A.97

Frooman, J. (1997). Socially Irresponsible and Illegal Behavior and Shareholder Wealth: A Meta- Analysis of Event Studies. *Business & Society*, *36*(3), 221–249. doi:10.1177/000765039703600302

Garriga, E., & Melè, E. (2004). Corporate Social Responsibility Theories: Mapping the Territory. *Journal of Business Ethics*, *53*(1-2), 51–71. doi:10.1023/B:BUSI.0000039399.90587.34

Gildea, R. L. (1994). Consumer Survey Confirms Corporate Social Action Affects Buying Decisions. *Public Relations Quarterly*, *39*(4), 20–22.

Graafland, J., & van de Ven, B. (2006). Strategic and moral motivation for corporate social responsibility. *Journal of Corporate Citizenship*, *22*(3), 111–123. doi:10.9774/GLEAF.4700.2006.su.00012

Gray, R. (2001). *Social and Environmental Responsibility, Sustainability and Accountability, Can the Corporate Sector Deliver?*. Centre for Social and Environmental Accounting Research, University of Glasgow. Retrieved on May 28, 2016, from www.agenda-scotland.org/documents/ Can%20business%20 deliver%20Gray.pdf

Greening, D. W., & Turban, D. B. (2000). Corporate Social Performance as a Competitive Advantage in Attracting a Quality Workforce. *Business & Society*, *39*(3), 254–280. doi:10.1177/000765030003900302

Greeno, J. L., & Robinson, S. N. (1992). Rethinking Corporate Environmental Management. *The Columbia Journal of World Business*, *27*(3-4), 222–232.

GreenPaper EU. (2001). *Promoting a European Framework for Corporate Social Responsibility*. Brussels: Commission of the European Communities. Retrieved on May 28, 2016, from www.btplc.com/ Societyandenvironment/ Reports/GreenpaperonCSR.pdf

Handelman, J. M., & Arnold, S. J. (1999). The Role of Marketing Actions with a Social Dimension: Appeals to the Institutional Environment. *Journal of Marketing*, *63*(3), 33–48. doi:10.2307/1251774

Hart, S. L., & Christensen, C. M. (2002). The Great Leap. Driving Innovation from the Base of the Pyramid. *MIT Sloan Management Review*, *44*(1), 51–57.

Hayes, A. S., & Pereira, J. (1990). Facing a Boycott, Many Companies Bend. *Wall Street Journal, 24*, 1.

Herbert, B. (1996). Nike's Pyramid Scheme. *New York Times*, pp. 17-23.

Hoeffler, S., & Keller, K. L. (2002). Building Brand Equity through Corporate Societal Marketing. *Journal of Public Policy & Marketing*, *21*(1), 78–89. doi:10.1509/jppm.21.1.78.17600

Husted, B. W. (2003). Governance Choices for Corporate Social Responsibility: To Contribute, Collaborate or Internalize? *Long Range Planning*, *36*(5), 481–498. doi:10.1016/S0024-6301(03)00115-8

Husted, B. W., & Allen, D. B. (2000). Is It Ethical to Use Ethics as Strategy? *Journal of Business Ethics*, *27*(1-2), 21–32. doi:10.1023/A:1006422704548

India C. S. R. Outlook. (2015). *A Snapshot of CSR Spend In FY 2014-15' 250 BSE-Listed Companies*. Retrieved September 20, 2016, from http://www.ngobox.org

Jensen, M. C. (2002). Value Maximization, Stakeholder Theory, and the Corporate Objective Function. *Business Ethics Quarterly*, *12*(2), 235–256. doi:10.2307/3857812

Jones, T. M. (1980). Corporate Social Responsibility Revisited, Redefined. *California Management Review*, *22*(2), 59–67. doi:10.2307/41164877

Joshi, Y. C., & Shah, D. (2016). Transforming Corporate Social Responsibility towards Socially Responsible Corporation. *Synergy*, *18*(1), 1–9.

Kirmani, A. (1997). Advertising Repetition as a Signal of Quality: If Its Advertised So Much, Something Must Be Wrong. *Journal of Advertising*, *26*(3), 77–90. doi:10.1080/00913367.1997.10673530

KPMG. (2005). *KPMG International Survey of Corporate Responsibility Reporting 2005*. KPMG Global Sustainability Services. Retrieved May 05, 2016, from http://www.kpmg.org

Krishna, C. G. (1992). *Corporate Social Responsibility in India*. New Delhi, India: Mittal Publications.

Kumar, R., Murphy, D. F., & Balsari, V. (2001). *Altered Images: The 2001 State of Corporate Responsibility in India Poll. In Understanding and Encouraging Corporate Responsibility in South Asia – Update 1*. New Delhi, India: Tata Energy Research Institute.

Landon, S., & Smith, C. E. (1997). The Use of Quality and Reputation Indicators by Consumers: The Case of Bordeaux Wine. *Journal of Consumer Policy*, *20*(3), 285–297. doi:10.1023/A:1006830218392

Lee, M. P. (2008). A Review of the Theories of Corporate Social Responsibility: Its Evolutionary Path and the Road Ahead. *International Journal of Management Reviews*, *10*(1), 53–73. doi:10.1111/j.1468-2370.2007.00226.x

Lynes, J., & Andrachuk, M. (2008). Motivations for corporate social and environmental responsibility: A case study of Scandinavian Airlines. *Journal of International Management*, *14*(4), 377–390. doi:10.1016/j.intman.2007.09.004

Lyon, T., & Maxwell, J. (2008). Corporate Social Responsibility and the Environment: A Theoretical Perspective. *Review of Environmental Economics and Policy*, *2*(2), 240–260. doi:10.1093/reep/ren004

Margolis, J. D., & Walsh, J. P. (2003). Misery Loves Companies: Rethinking Social Initiatives by Business. *Administrative Science Quarterly*, *48*(2), 268–305. doi:10.2307/3556659

Matten, D., Crane, A., & Chapple, W. (2003). Behind de Mask: Revealing the True Face of Corporate Citizenship. *Journal of Business Ethics*, *45*(1-2), 109–120. doi:10.1023/A:1024128730308

McVea, J. F., & Freeman, R. E. (2005). A Names-and-Faces Approach to Stakeholder Management. *Journal of Management Enquiry*, *14*(1), 57–69.

McWilliams, A., & Siegel, D. (2001). Corporate Social Responsibility: A Theory of the Firm Perspective. *Academy of Management Review*, *26*(1), 117–127.

Mishra, S., & Suar, D. (2010). Does Corporate Social Responsibility Influence Firm Performance of Indian Companies? *Journal of Business Ethics*, *95*(4), 571–601. doi:10.1007/s10551-010-0441-1

Mohan, A. (2001). Corporate citizenship: Perspectives from India. *Journal of Corporate Citizenship*, *2*(3), 107–117. doi:10.9774/GLEAF.4700.2001.su.00012

Moreno, C. (2015). *Doing Their Part: 3 Excellent Examples of Corporate Social Responsibility*. Retrieved May 20, 2016, from http://lineshapespace.com/doing-their-part-3-excellent-examples-of-corporate-social-responsibility

Murray, K. B., & Montanari, J. R. (1986). Strategic Management of the Socially Responsible Firm: Integrating Management and Marketing Theory. *Academy of Management Review*, *11*(4), 815–828.

Narwal, M., & Sharma, T. (2008). Perceptions of corporate social responsibility in India: An empirical study. *Journal of Knowledge Globalization, 1*(1), 61–79.

Ogden, S., & Watson, R. (1999). Corporate Performance and Stakeholder Management: Balancing Shareholder and Customer Interests in the U.K. Privatized Water Industry. *Academy of Management Journal, 42*(5), 526–538. doi:10.2307/256974

Orlitzky, M., Schmidt, F. L., & Rynes, S. L. (2003). Corporate social and financial performance: A meta-analysis. *Organization Studies, 24*(3), 403–441. doi:10.1177/0170840603024003910

Parsons, T. (1961). An Outline of the Social System. In T. Parsons, E. A. Shils, K. D. Naegle, & J. R. Pitts (Eds.), *Theories of Society*. New York: Free Press.

Patro, C. S., & Raghunath, K. M. K. (2016). Corporate Social Responsibility: A Manifestation in FDI. In M. Ojo (Ed.), *Analyzing the Relationship between Corporate Social Responsibility and Foreign Direct Investment* (pp. 215–240). Hershey, PA: Business Science Reference. doi:10.4018/978-1-5225-0305-7.ch014

PiC (Partners in Change). (2004). *Third Report on Corporate Involvement in Social Development in India*. New Delhi: PiC.

Pirson, M., & Lawrence, P. (2010). Humanism in Business - Towards a Paradigm Shift? *Journal of Business Ethics, 93*(4), 553–565. doi:10.1007/s10551-009-0239-1

Poole, E. (2009). Organizational Spirituality - A Literature Review. *Journal of Business Ethics, 84*(4), 577–588. doi:10.1007/s10551-008-9726-z

Porter, M., & Kramer, M. (2002). The Competitive Advantage of Corporate Philanthropy. *Harvard Business Review, 80*(12), 56–69. PMID:12510538

Prahalad, C. K., & Hammond, A. (2002). Serving the World's Poor, Profitably. *Harvard Business Review, 80*(9), 48–58. PMID:12227146

Pramar, S. K. (2012). *Companies Should Implement Their CSR Projects Themselves*. Retrieved June 05, 2016, from http://www.indiacsr.in/en/?p=7797

Preston, L. E., & Post, J. E. (1981). Private Management and Public Policy. *California Management Review, 23*(3), 56–63. doi:10.2307/41172602

Raynard, P., & Forstater, M. (2002). *Corporate Social Responsibility: Implications for Small and Medium Enterprises in Developing Countries*. United Nations Industrial Development Organization. Retrieved May 16, 2016, from http://unido.org/userfiles/BethkeK/csr.pdf

Riordan, C. M., Gatewood, R. D., & Bill, J. B. (1997). Corporate Image: Employee Reactions and Implications for Managing Corporate Social Performance. *Journal of Business Ethics, 16*(4), 401–412. doi:10.1023/A:1017989205184

Robbins, N. (2000). *Position Paper on Emerging Markets and Human Rights*. Retrieved May 28, 2016, from http://ampcapital.com.au/_PDF/adviser/sri/papers/Emerging_Markets.pdf

Rupp, D. E., Ganapathi, J., Aguilera, R. V., & Williams, C. A. (2006). Employee reactions to corporate social responsibility: An organizational justice framework. *Journal of Organizational Behavior*, *27*(4), 537–543. doi:10.1002/job.380

Sen, S., & Bhattacharya, C. B. (2001). Does Doing Good Always Lead to Doing Better? Consumer Reactions to Corporate Social Responsibility. *JMR, Journal of Marketing Research*, *38*(2), 225–243. doi:10.1509/jmkr.38.2.225.18838

Sen, S., Bhattacharya, C. B., & Korschun, D. (2006). The Role of Corporate Social Responsibility in Strengthening Multiple Stakeholder Relationships: A Field Experiment. *Journal of the Academy of Marketing Science*, *34*(2), 158–166. doi:10.1177/0092070305284978

Sethi, S. P. (1975). Dimensions of Corporate Social Performance: An Analytical Framework. *California Management Review*, *17*(3), 58–65. doi:10.2307/41162149

Sharma, A., & Kiran, R. (2013). Corporate Social Responsibility: Driving Forces and Challenges. *International Journal of Business Research and Development*, *2*(1), 18–27. doi:10.24102/ijbrd.v2i1.182

Singh, R., & Bhagat, K. (2004). Corporate Initiatives in Indian Agriculture. *Indian Management*, *43*(2), 72–79.

Somavia, J. (2000). Business: Its Direct Stake in Putting Human Needs First. *UN Chronicle*, *37*(2), 42.

Sulmasy, D. P. (2001). Four Basic Notions of the Common Good. *St. John's Law Review*, *75*(2), 303–311.

Turban, D. B., & Greening, D. W. (1997). Corporate Social Performance and Organizational Attractiveness to Prospective Employees. *Academy of Management Journal*, *40*(3), 658–763. doi:10.2307/257057

Van Marrewijk, M., & Were, M. (2003). Multiple Levels of Corporate Sustainability. *Journal of Business Ethics*, *44*(2/3), 107–120. doi:10.1023/A:1023383229086

Varadarajan, P. R., & Menon, A. (1988). Cause-Related Marketing: A Coalignment of Marketing Strategy and Corporate Philanthropy. *Journal of Marketing*, *52*(3), 58–58. doi:10.2307/1251450

Velasquez, M. (1992). International Business, Morality and the Common Good. *Business Ethics Quarterly*, *2*(1), 27–40. doi:10.2307/3857220

Vogel, D. (1986). The Study of Social Issues in Management: A Critical Appraisal. *California Management Review*, *28*(2), 142–152. doi:10.2307/41165191

Waddock, S. A., & Graves, S. B. (1997). The Corporate Social Performance - Financial Performance Link. *Strategic Management Journal*, *18*(4), 303–320. doi:10.1002/(SICI)1097-0266(199704)18:4<303::AID-SMJ869>3.0.CO;2-G

Warhust, A. (2001). Corporate Citizenship and Corporate Social Investment: Drivers of Tri-Sector Partnerships. *Journal of Corporate Citizenship*, *1*(1), 57–73. doi:10.9774/GLEAF.4700.2001.sp.00008

Wartick, S. L., & Rude, R. E. (1986). Issues Management: Corporate Fad or Corporate Function? *California Management Review*, *29*(1), 124–132. doi:10.2307/41165231

Wheeler, D., Colbertm, B., & Freeman, R. E. (2003). Focusing on Value: Reconciling Corporate Social Responsibility, Sustainability and a Stakeholder Approach in a Network World. *Journal of General Management*, *28*(3), 1–29. doi:10.1177/030630700302800301

Wood, D. J. (1991). Corporate Social Performance Revisited. *Academy of Management Review*, *16*(4), 691–718.

KEY TERMS AND DEFINITIONS

Corporate Social Responsibility: It is the activity and status related to a company's perceived societal or stakeholder obligations.

Customer Satisfaction: It is the overall evaluation based on the customer's total purchase and consumption experience with a good or service over time.

Economic Responsibility: The economic responsibility of business is to produce goods and services that society desires and to sell them at a profit.

Explicit CSR: It refers to corporate policies to assume responsibility for the interests of the society. It normally consist of voluntary, self-interest driven policies, programmes and strategies by corporations addressing issues perceived as being part of their social responsibility by the company and/or its stakeholders.

Implicit CSR: It is the entirety of a country's formal and informal institutions assigning corporations an agreed share of responsibility for society's interests and concerns. It consists of values, norms and rules which result in requirements for corporations to address issues stakeholders consider a proper obligation upon corporate actors.

Instrumental Theory: The corporations are seen as only an instrument for wealth creation, and its social activities are only a means to achieve economic results.

Political Theory: It distresses themselves with the power of corporations in society and a responsible use of this power in the political arena.

Chapter 5
Social Responsibility, Shared Value, and Business Modelling:
An Integrated Approach

Alessandro Giosi
Lumsa University, Italy

Eleonora Zaccaro
Luxottica Group Spa, Italy

Silvia Testarmata
Niccolò Cusano University, Italy

ABSTRACT

While more and more businesses incorporate sustainability in their core business strategy, there has recently been a shift from corporate social responsibility (CSR) to the notion of creating shared value (CSV). This thesis investigates the emergence of new hybrid enterprises and innovative business models. Starting from a literature review about CSR and its evolution into the "Big Idea" proposed by Porter and Kramer, the chapter will analyse the link between business and society, especially in the developing countries where this link is stronger. The main aim is to identify the most effective business models that enhance the competitiveness of a company, while simultaneously advancing the economic and social conditions in the communities in which it operates. The general idea is that enterprises should have longer-term perspective on how they operate in relation to the external society and environment, addressing societal needs and challenges through the business itself, within a business model.

INTRODUCTION

Businesses' responsibility in terms of economic, social and environmental impact has always been a very thorny subjected in the business community's debate, evidencing alignments and conflicts between external and internal stakeholders (Sheehy, 2015).

DOI: 10.4018/978-1-5225-3147-0.ch005

Nevertheless, the recent global agreement on the importance of the role of business in society for the international development, economic growth and poverty reduction (Nwagbara & Kamara, 2015) has reached the audience and the attention of academics and industry experts.

Despite in recent years business has been increasingly viewed as one of the major cause of society's problems, the big idea claimed by Porter and Kramer (2011) presents a new business perspective that aims to reconnect company success to with social progress.

Adopting the concept of creating shared value is a journey companies need to embark on to overcome the "blindness" that made them ignore all the big opportunities that rise once this fundamental link is restored.

The solution lies in the shift from Corporate Social Responsibility, a concept still powerful but not efficient in the contemporary competitive environment, to a new paradigm of business focused on Shared Value principle that enhance company's competitiveness while simultaneously creates value for society. In any different conceptual framework the problem still remain how to help companies to response to stakeholder expectations through their management systems and value chain linkages (Visser & Kymal, 2015). This means, in the lens of Italian doctrine of Economia Aziendale, re-discover the company systemic relationships.

The logic of shared value becomes more influential when companies decide to operate into developing countries (Cavaco & Crifo, 2014) where the interconnection between business and society is definitely stronger, since these countries offer great opportunities to develop new business but they are also characterized by deep social disadvantages (Michelini & Fiorentino, 2011).

Thus, businesses' response to low-income markets problems has contributed to blur the lines between for profit and not for profit organizations and the rise of hybrid enterprises is one of the strong signs of this transformation (Beugré, 2017).

According to this new perspective, this research intends to identify the business models that allow companies to invest in new markets (mature or developing countries) adopting a shared value approach based on addressing social needs by creating economic value.

This study is exploratory in nature, since it aims to provide both theoretical and empirical backgrounds analysing the transformation process from Corporate Social Responsibility to Creating Shared Value and highlighting the distinctive features and the level of criticality of both the managerial approaches to sustainability.

Finally, not all societal problems can be solved through shared value solutions. However, shared value offers corporations the opportunity to utilize their skills, resources, and management capabilities to lead social progress in ways that provide economic and societal benefit both for businesses and the communities in which they operate.

BACKGROUND

From Corporate Social Responsibility to Creating Shared Value

Corporate social responsibility thinking has evolved over the past few decades from a traditional positioning, mainly focused on philanthropic initiatives, to a more strategic approach that incorporates social issues into businesses core strategies to benefit both society and their own long-term competitiveness (Blodgett, Hoitash, & Markelevich, 2014). Although corporations without good performance of CSR can make profits occasionally in a short term game, they have greater difficulty winning in a repeated game. The reason is that any stakeholders are not willing to deal with corporations that lack of CSR (Wang, 2014).

In addition, the expansion of corporate responsibility in the social environment is increasingly connected to the development strategies of the company, which to successfully pursue its business purpose, cannot ignore the characteristics of the context in which it operates.

In 2006 Porter evaluating the CSR theory, traditionally driven by reputational reasons (Plewa, Conduit, Quester, & Johnson, 2015), has pointed up the importance of going beyond the "doing good, being good avoiding risks" attitude, embracing a new management thinking that reinforces corporate engagement in society.

For this reason, the transformation process from CSR to CSV is necessary to reshape the capitalistic system (now under siege) and find new links that are profitable for both the company and the society (Kramer, 2011).

Figure 1, introduced by Porter at the Annual Summit for Shared Value Leadership, shows that not many years ago businesses were mainly focused on philanthropic activities, like donations to worthy social causes or volunteering. Philanthropy is about personal value or corporate reputation and usually understates the problems.

Progressively, businesses become more aware of societal issues and start to use their core resources and capabilities to find solutions.

At the very basic level, businesses are getting more sensible engaging in "good activities" that show off how they spend money for projects of corporate social responsibility. However, this approach presents some limits on the implementation of these perspectives inside and outside the organizations. This is the fundamental reason why recently companies have lost their legitimacy and have been widely perceived to be prospering at the expense of the broader community.

Hence, Porter's idea of a socially integrated company refers to the policies and practices that enhance competitiveness while advancing economic and social conditions.

Figure 1. Corporate Thinking Has Evolved Over the Past Decade
Source: FSG, 2011.

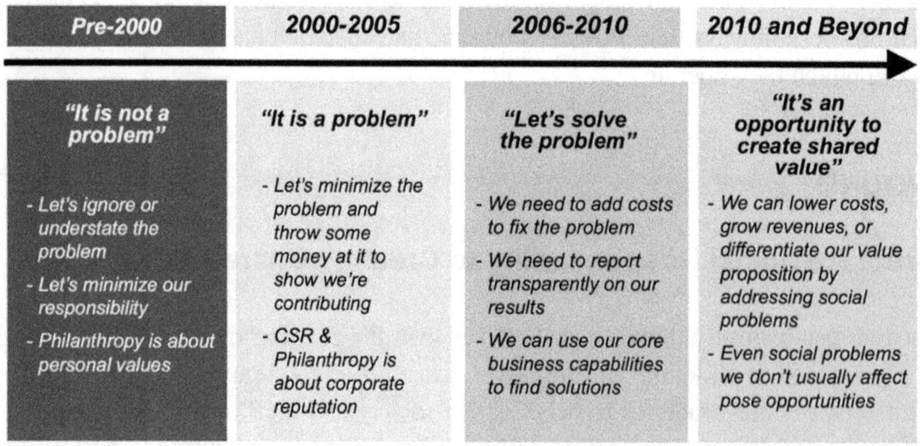

In 2010 the transformation process seemed to be definitive: businesses began to embrace the shared value concept, meant as an opportunity to abandon the short term perspective and supersede the CSR logic by generating benefits for both companies and society. However, moving a corporation toward a shared value approach require a major mindset change that will differ for each company, depending on its goals, context and culture.

The concept of shared value can be defined as policies and operating practices that enhance the competitiveness of a company while simultaneously advancing the economic and social conditions in the communities in which it operates. Thus, CSV focuses on identifying the connection between societal and economic progress that should always be addressed using value principles. Value is defined as benefits relative to costs, not just benefits alone (Porter & Kramer, 2011).

Although a growing number of companies have integrated the shared value concept into their business strategies, until now societal issues have been rarely approached from a value perspective but have been treated as peripheral matters. In accordance to Porter and Kramer point of view, CSV should supersede CSR in guiding the investments of the companies in the society and as a consequence assimilating economic and social objectives together in order to look at shared value through entirely different lenses.

In the past, all the corporate social responsibility programs have emerged as an attempt of the firm to improve their own reputation and their role of corporate citizenship, thus they have been seen as "necessary" costs. Basically, CSR initiatives are short term oriented and have a limited link to the business or sometimes a non-existing one. Shared value perspective, instead, is functional to the profitability and the competitive advantage of the company since profit maximization and investments in social issues are not separated (Kramer, 2011). Sure the boundaries, the overlapping or the contrasts between CSR and CSV is still discussed in the literature, in particular the CSV is questioned from scholars advocates for a strategic CSR, defining CSR in a different way of a corporate image management (Jean & Yazdanifard, 2015). Moreover, Dembek, Singh and Bhakoo (2015), after a greater literature review concludes that share value has spread into the language of multiple disciplines, but that its current conceptualization is vague, and it presents important discrepancies in the way it is defined and operationalized from scholars. The authors recommended for defining and measuring the concept even through case studies. Despite these critics and following the latter suggestion carry out by the authors about case studies, we are still moving in the context of the Porter's framework.

According to Porter and Kramer, one of the strengths of the shared value approach is its connection with the long-term business strategy of the company and for this reason Porter's idea could be defined as a real business model. In order to adopt a shared value approach a change of business strategy is needed: corporate engagement in society will lead to the next major transformation of business thinking.

The Three Level of Shared Value: How It Is Created

In general, companies can create shared value in three basic ways: reconceiving products and markets, redefining productivity in the value chains and enabling local clusters development.

For what concern the first level of creating shared value, it refers to the huge numbers of unmet social needs. For a company, the starting point for creating this kind of shared value is to identify all the societal needs, benefits, and harms that could be embodied in companies' products. Thus, meeting needs in underserved markets is a great opportunity for businesses to redesign their products or to enter in new markets that could offer strategy differentiation and company repositioning. In addition, the societal needs in developing countries or disadvantaged communities are even more pressing and the attention of big leading companies, focused on the needs of emerging markets, offers the possibility to access billions of new customers at the so called Bottom of the Pyramid (Panapanaa, Bruce, Virkki-Hatakka, & Linnanen, 2016; Ansari, Muni, & Gregg, 2012).

Every company had a well-developed value chain, made of primary activities like sourcing and procurement, inbound logistic, operation assembly and sales and customer services, and support activities, like research and development, human resources management and marketing and advertisement activities. In this case, opportunities to create shared value arise because societal problems can create economic costs in the firm's value chain. This leads consequently to a redefinition of the productivity of the value chain, definitely more effective, in order to avoid externalities or societal costs generated by companies that could compromise the health of the overall society.

Finally, the third way of creating shared value is linked to the external environment with which companies dialogue. Indeed, companies do not operate in isolation from their surrounding but their success is defined by the context in which they operate. To support clusters development, companies need to identify gaps and deficiencies in different areas, like logistics, suppliers, distribution channels, etc.. Focusing on these weaknesses that constrain company's productivity and growth will be the greatest opportunity to create shared value.

Hence, shared value creation is strictly related to the relationship between companies and local clusters that could improve businesses performances in terms of productivity, innovation and competitiveness, simultaneously generating benefits for the communities.

This three methods for creating shared value are mutually reinforcing, as they create a *virtuous circle* in which businesses tend to incorporate social issues into their core business strategies to gain social benefits and a long-term competitive advantage.

To sum up, the shared value concept arise new social needs to meet, new products to offer, new ways to refine the value chain, allowing companies to leverage their expertise and competences to drive economic and social development.

Shared Value Concept Into the Strategic Planning Process

A growing numbers of companies are adopting this new pragmatic approach and increasingly recognize that their contributions can be more effective if they align them with core competencies.

General Electric, IBM, Unilver and obviously Nestlè are pioneers in this corporate (re)evolution since they have already started to contribute to social problems redefying their own strategies and business models in order to create a connection between social and business performances.

Such companies seek to create "shared value" incorporating social issues into their core business strategies to benefit both society and their own long-term competitiveness as shown in Figure 2.

Shared value framework defines a new role for business in society that goes beyond the traditional CSR perspective, usually seen as a response to external stimulus, to government regulation or pending regulation. Shared value reconnects company success with social progress and could also drive the next wave of innovation and productivity growth in the global economy as it opens managers' eyes to immense human needs that must be met, large new markets to be served, and the internal costs of social deficits as well as the competitive advantages available from addressing them (Porter & Kramer, 2011).

Thus, Porter's concept is not just to redistributing value previously created through philanthropic or CSR activities, but consist mainly in having a robust strategy to solve social issues and make profit.

Figure 2. Shared Value
Source: Bockstette & Stamp, 2011.

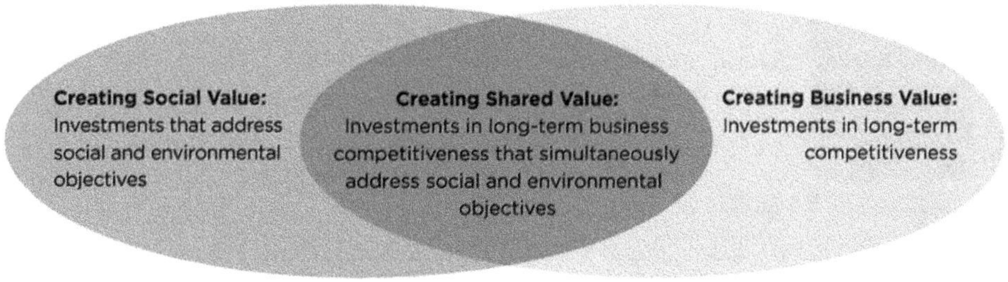

According to Porter and Kramer (2011), the logic of creating shared value could be defined as a reshaped capitalism that, connecting companies' success with societal improvement, inevitably opens up new ways addressing societal needs while simultaneously create economic value in a long-term perspective.

Building Blocks

Creating shared value can be broken out into ten key building blocks that help any kind of businesses or organizations to build a strong and effective strategy (Bockstette & Stamp, 2011). Basically we can compare these building blocks to a sort of blueprint that translate the shared value idea into concrete actions (see Figure 3).

The shared value approach is unique for every single company and its strictly linked to the company strategy, context and competitive advantage. Nevertheless, FSG a non-profit consulting firm for leaders in search of large-scale, lasting social change, working with different leading corporations, has identified some common points to generate shared value.

Creating shared value starts with an explicit strategic decision by top management that need to delineate company's vision and ensure that all the business areas are actively engagement.

Vision is fundamental to the strategic long-term direction of the company; indeed the second step focuses on the strategy.

In order to create shared value, the vision needs to be translated into a robust strategy that identifies a clear focus and articulates ambitious goals. A good strategy should be tailored to reflect a company's unique positioning, capabilities, and competitive environment and should also identify social challenges that represent cost-reduction or growth opportunities.

The third block refers to the management of the delivery process that leverage and add value to the internal and external assets of the company.

Once ambitious goal are set, companies need to regroup all the business units and mobilize a wide range of internal and external resources. This process could be broken down into three essential practices.

- **Deploy a Range of Assets to Address the Issue:** These assets can include goods and services, skills, political influences, etc.. The most effective companies are the ones able to combine in a strategic way the different assets in the areas where they have an edge over other actors.

Figure 3. The Building Blocks of Creating Shared Value
Source: Bockstette & Stamp, 2011.

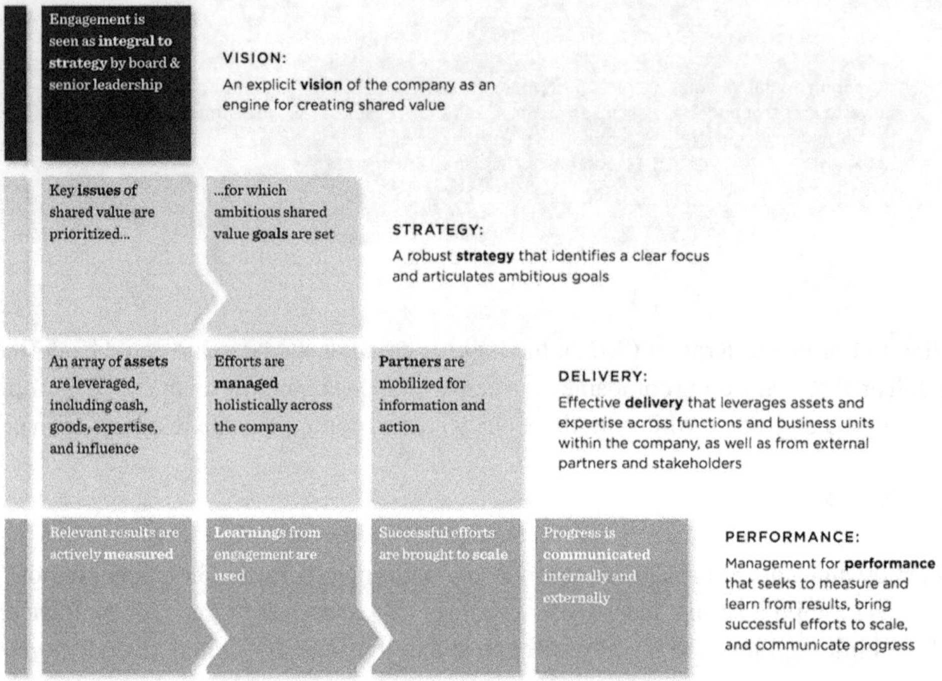

- **Manage Efforts Holistically Across the Organization:** In many companies' social engagement is not confined to an isolated silo, but instead is integrated into a wide variety of roles and functions, and often overseen at the board level.
- **Collaborate With Partners:** Creating shared value requires new and strong forms of collaborations. Indeed, most companies consult with stakeholders and work with NGOs to embrace competences and resources useful to the company's success.

Finally, the last building block of shared value is linked to the company's modus operandi that, if well manage, could deliver high performance.

Usually companies measure their progress and learn lessons from their activities, structured for continuous improvement.

New Business Models for Creating Shared Value

One central goal for companies nowadays is to create shared valued, for this reason new type of innovative business model are arising and represent a hybrid managerial choices between profit and non-profit oriented models. As suggested by Porter during an interview for the Western State Colorado University (Driver, 2012), new hybrid enterprises are rapidly appearing due to the blurring of the boundary between successful for-profit and non-profit organizations.

Hybrid enterprises are those enterprises straddling the boundary between the for- profit business world and the social mission-driven public and not for profit organizations (Daw, 2013; Wilson & Post, 2013). Thus, they belong to the Social Entrepreneurship category that could be defined as an important transitional vehicle toward the creation of shared value and a capitalist system in which meeting social needs is not just a peripheral activity but a core aspect of every business (Driver, 2012).

In other words, Social Entrepreneurship is a step of the creating shared value process through which a social oriented company gain the right competences in order to incorporate social issues into their core business strategies. Social Entrepreneurship may be defined along a continuum from the creation of positive social change to earned income in the pursuit of social change (Driver, 2012).

Despite Social Entrepreneurship concept is relatively new and still need to be properly defined it could open up new ways of doing business and bring a whole new sensibility and a whole new set of tools and attitudes to addressing social issues.

As previously mentioned, hybrid organizations strive to combine their own economic benefits to the societal benefits of the developing countries through managerial strategies and models, based on social entrepreneurship and shared value concepts. Indeed, social entrepreneurship includes the use of market principles and economic value to meet social needs of the underserved communities that should be considered not just as "exploratory territories" but as real markets with specific needs to address through ad hoc business models.

At this point in the study it is useful to underline the connections between hybrid enterprises and the rise of innovative business model, based on social innovation whose main aim is to improve community well-being while simultaneously guarantee economic and financial sustainability. Based on companies' decision to expand their businesses into low-income markets, Michelini and Fiorentino (2011) identified two innovative business models (social and inclusive business models) that generate shared value.

Social Business Model

Social Business Model represents a new way for the companies to address unmet social needs through combining business know-how with the desire to improve quality of life of the developing countries.

The Nobel Prize Muhammad Yunus introduce this new dimension for capitalism: a business model that does not strive to maximize profits but rather to serve humanity's most pressing needs (Yunus, 2010). Nevertheless, many authors agree that meeting societal needs is a governments' responsibility since they should represent all the society interests. Instead, the right kind of government regulation can encourage companies to pursue shared value investing in the economic and social development of the society.

Contrary to the traditional business models, in the Social Business Model there are no losses nor dividends for shareholders and the company is led exclusively by predetermined social objectives. Obviously there is still profit though it is only used to keep the company alive and further develop it. Investors should not focus only on profit from their own activities; they should also be incentivised by the success that could be obtained if their social needs were fulfilled.

The European Commission uses the term "social business" to cover

...businesses providing social services and/or goods and services to vulnerable persons (access to housing, health care, assistance for elderly or disabled persons, inclusion of vulnerable groups, child care, access to employment and training, dependency management, etc.); and/or businesses with a method of production of goods or services with a social objective (social and professional integration via access

to employment for people disadvantaged in particular by insufficient qualifications or social or professional problems leading to exclusion and marginalization) but whose activity may be outside the realm of the provision of social goods or services. (European Commission, 2011, p. 3)

Social Business Model is characterized by two mains typologies: social business that includes all the companies that do not distribute dividends and social business adopted by all the companies whose mission is social oriented independently from the financial management (Clark & Brennan, 2012).

According to Yunus's idea, type one focuses on businesses dealing with social objectives only, as has just been mentioned. Type two, instead, can take up any profitable business so long as the poor and the disadvantaged, who can gain through receiving direct dividends or by some indirect benefits, own it.

The key element of the first type of Social Business Model is to not allow any dividends (share of profits) for shareholders due to the fact that profit seeking companies with a strong CSR commitment try to make their pursuit of profit consistent with social considerations (Yunus, 2007). Hence, even if this model could generate profits shareholders would not benefit of any dividend because all the revenues will guarantee company sustainability. Any surplus coming from company's activities will be return to the investor or reinvested into the company itself.

A concrete example of this type of social business model could be a limited company (Ltd) resulted from a strategic alliance between profit organization and no profit local organization. Sharing their know-how, both organizations realize together a sort of new activity, linked to the traditional business of the company while simultaneously creating social value in the community in which it operates. Indeed, social benefits derives from the company's goods and services (Kroeger & Weber, 2015).

Although the second type of Social Business Model is more profit oriented, its social purpose consists on making underserved communities autonomous in order to improve their economic and social condition through dividends and profit generated by the company.

In general, companies that adopt a Social Business Model are tied to the creation of a joint venture with local non-profit organizations: sharing resources and competences both companies and organizations create shared value.

Inclusive Business Model

As previously said, in attempting to apply the principle of creating shared value many companies have started to implement alternative models of governance and management, which can be referred to the social entrepreneurship concept. One of these models is the Inclusive Business Model that aims to build bridges between businesses and the disadvantaged communities for mutual benefit: making profit and improving social conditions of local population. Thus, the term "inclusive" refers to active engagement of low-income sector into the core business of the company and vice versa (Halme, Linderman, & Lima, 2012).

Inclusive Business Model has its roots into the Bottom of Pyramid Theory proposed by Prahalad, which is based on the concept of "serving the poor profitability" (Prahalad, 2004).

According to this socio-economic concept, that refers to more than 4 billion people all over the world living with less than 1 dollar per day, developing countries should no longer be considered as a territory to exploit but a market composed of producers and consumers with specific need, which could be met through innovative business models.

The main pillar on which the Inclusive Business Model is founded is the strategic relationship between a local dimension (the low income communities) and a global dimension (companies) that offers new opportunities to conduct business responsibly creating – at the same time – economic and social value (Hann, 2012).

According to the World Business Council for Sustainable Development definition, the Inclusive Business Model is:

one which seeks to contribute toward the alleviation of poverty by including lower-income communities within its value chain while not losing sight of the ultimate goal of business, which is to generate profits. (WBCSD-SNV, 2010, p. 2)

The integration of low- income communities into company's value chain could be represented by two broad categories (WBCSD-SNV, 2010, p. 3):

- **Low Income People as Consumers:** Companies male available quality goods and services which underserved populations need and want at prices they can afford;
- **Low Income People as Suppliers or Distributors:** Low income populations are business partners, suppliers and/or distributors. By including small local entrepreneurs in their value chain, companies create jobs and speed up the transfer of skills.

For this reason, the inclusive business model could be seen also as a co-working model, where goods and services come from the merger between the bottom and the top of the pyramid.

Inclusive and Social Business Models

Based on the definitions of these two models, it is necessary to outline the main characteristics of both Inclusive and Social Business Models highlighting common points and differences (Speiss-Knafl, Mast, & Janse, 2015).

Despite both models can create shared value their strategies and governance systems are completely aligned.

First of all, the main objective of the two models are different: Inclusive Business Model aims to economic and societal benefits; while Social Business Model focuses principally on societal benefit without excluding the economic ones. As outlined by Michelini and Fiorentino (2011), Inclusive Business Model could represent an evolution of the traditional business to a model based on a mutual co-dependence between the company and its social environment. Social Business Model, instead, can be considered as an advanced philanthropic approach that improves social conditions of the underserved communities while simultaneously pursuing companies' economic sustainability.

In accordance to the framework proposed by Michelini and Fiorentino (2011), it is possible to categorize these two models by using two variables: economic return on investments and social/economic benefits (see Figure 4). In the quadrant at the top left section of the matrix below are located philanthropic initiatives that do not represent a conventional form of business model since they aim to generate social benefit, without providing any economic returns for the company. Inclusive and Social Business Models are positioned into the second quadrant at the top right of the matrix. Both models, indeed, are focused on addressing social needs generating positive effects for the communities and for the companies in terms of social and economic value. Finally, the traditional business model is located in the bottom right quadrant of the matrix and is solely profit- oriented without consideration of any social effects

Hence, due to the limits of the traditional business to embrace type of hybrid enterprises, where the social dimension is crucial, it is necessary to explore and consider alternative business models definitely more appropriate to the transformation outlined.

CASE STUDY ANALYSIS

Despite the growing importance of the issues previously analysed, the concrete examples of new forms of business models aimed at creating shared value is still limited. For this reason, this study intends to provide an analytical and exhaustive representation of the shared value concept and its role into the economic and social environment. Therefore, the aim of this study is to identify the key elements of OneSight's business model in order to define a new paradigm of business, focused on expanding the connection between economic and societal progress.

To accomplish this goal, a case study of a not for profit organization was conducted based on a qualitative analysis. This approach consists of two consecutive phases. The first phase aims to collect and explore different documents coming from internal and external sources. In the second phase, semi-structured interviews were conducted to a remarkable number of employees belonging to different business areas in order to have an homogenous and holistic point of view of the case study. Specifically the people involved in the interview were:

- **Lukas Ruecker:** *President Lux Vision Care EyeMed*
- **Paul Case:** *OneSight Sr Manager Clinics Operations Shared Services*
- **Emily Ryan:** *OneSight Sr. Manager Communications*
- **Mony Iyer:** *OneSight Sr Director Strategy Shared Services*
- **Gloria Bondi:** *OneSight Fundraising Manager*

Figure 4. Social and Inclusive Business Models
Source: Adapted from Michelini & Fiorentino, 2011.

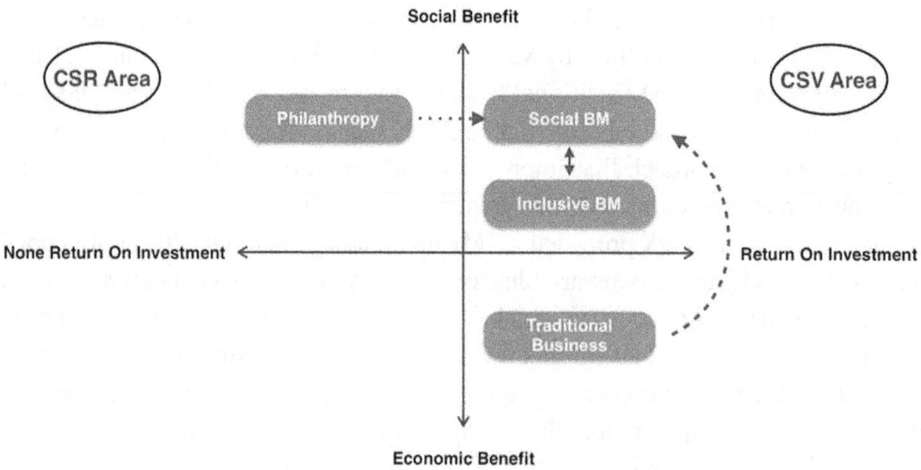

- **Mustapha Njie:** *OneSight Project Manager Gambia*

The method used is exploratory and is also characterized by a strong focus on resultus measurement, meant as fundamental tool of this research. Most interviews were conducted in English, face to face, some by telephone due to the inability of some employees to be physically present during the conversations.

The purpose of these interviews was to gain richer and deeper information about Onesight and its business model, for this reason questions were asked following a specific funnel: starting from the generic information about the overall organization to the most accurate ones. In each interview some open-ended questions were asked, so respondents were encouraged to speak freely, creating a dynamic relationship (Qu & Dumay, 2011).

In the following pages we meticulously explain the insights and outcomes linked to the adoption of the shared value approach by OneSight.

OneSight Profile

OneSight is an independent non-profit organization providing access to quality vision care and glasses in underserved communities worldwide, mobilizing eye care professionals, industry experts, volunteers and partners. The real strength of the company lies in its partnerships with global organizations, businesses and mainly with Luxottica, funding partner and global sponsor.

Luxottica's commitment to OneSight consists on funding administrative costs and providing annual operating support, glasses and engagement of its employees. Every year more than a thousand of Luxottica employees travel the globe to be part of OneSight programs, using their skills and expertise in day-to-day activities.

Since 1988, year of foundation, OneSight programs had impacted more than 9 millions lives across 41 countries. Thanks to partnerships with local health organizations, 8 sustainable vision centres, that provide permanent vision care access to two million people around the globe, have been opened.

Unfortunately, the number of people that require access to eye treatment continues to grow, for this reason OneSight is highly committed to pursuing its mission: eradicating the global vision care crisis and building permanent solutions to help the world see better.

Indeed, since every community is different, OneSight develops customized solutions to meet the local needs at best: patients can count on comprehensive eye exams and top high quality glasses coming from the OneSight's collection made by Luxottica. (OneSight, 2016).

Global Need for Glasses

Together with Deloitte (2015), OneSight conducted an extensive study to determine the number of people in the world who need glasses but are living without access to vision care. The study defined visual impairment in relation to a child's ability to perform well in school and an adult's ability to be productive at work; access is determined by the availability of glasses at an affordable price.

About 1.1 billion people around the globe need glasses but lack access; specifically the crisis is most acute in Sub-Saharan Africa and Southeast Asia. In addition, the research has outlined that 1 in 7 people across the globe can't get eye exams and thus do not have access to glasses due to the economic and social condition in which they live.

This situation brings necessarily not just physical consequences – an eye exam and a pair of glasses could definitely improve people's sight – but mainly psychological and social consequences since these problems are not linked only to a single person but in general address the whole community. For this reason, vision care is not just a healthcare issue; it is also an education and an economic development issue: 80% of learning is visual and in wider terms studies show that people are 35% more productive at work when they can see clearly.

In order to establish exactly the problems of each single country in which OneSight operates, Deloitte has suggested to refine the "vision-crisis sizing approach" to enhance and improve in a more strategic way OneSight's sustainable business model.

By employing a strategy of both immediate and long-term solutions, OneSight provides on-going, top quality vision care to adults and children throughout temporary and permanent initiatives, sponsored by capable local partners to serve each community's distinct needs.

In general, lack of access can mean not living near an eye doctor or not being able to afford an eye exam and a pair of glasses. As previously discussed, those who lack access are hindered by poor eyesight in school, in jobs and in relationships. Thus, to avoid all these problems OneSight offers two different solutions: charitable solutions (or the so-called Vision Care Clinics) and Sustainable Vision Centers.

At OneSight Vision Care Clinics, adults and children receive comprehensive eye exams and free eyeglasses over the period of a few days or weeks. Through more than 50 Vision Care Clinics each year, OneSight brings the right tools and expertise to both remote villages and bustling cities–wherever the need takes them. Naturally, in order to make these charitable solutions efficient - as Paul Case (OneSight Sr. manger Clinics Operation) said - it is necessary to partner with local governments, health departments and volunteers that actively contribute to the temporary equipment of the clinics and to the distribution of the glasses coming from the special collection made by Luxottica.

Because OneSight mission is to eradicate the global vision care crisis around the globe, short-term clinics are just one piece of the solution; indeed, OneSight has developed a new long term approach by building permanent clinics. The Sustainable solution brings together public sector, private industry leaders and no-profit partners to create a new optical micro-economy in underserved communities. In other words, by empowering and training local communities OneSight creates permanent and affordable Vision Centers that are independently run by local teams through existing hospitals and healthcare systems. Within this sustainable model permanent vision care access is guaranteed.

Despite OneSight's different initiatives could be included in the large category of not for profit organizations, it is possible to put into practice all the theoretical principles outlined before and try to define what is the most efficient business model for OneSight, always keeping in mind the "social nature" of the organization in a shared value point of view.

The Gambia Project

As previously stated, the main focus of this study is to analyse the strategical transformation process of OneSight from traditional and charitable solution to the new sustainable model.

Launched in 2013, Sustainable Vision Centers are revolutionising the way OneSight is operating in the underserved countries, creating permanent and autonomous system for local communities. During the interview, Paul Case outilined how in order to accomplish its mission and meet the objectives, OneSight strategy was transformed in a long-term plan, which basically consists in building permanent infrastructures with support from governments and local partners within their own healthcare system.

Through the Vision Care Clinics, OneSight makes a purely philanthropic investment whereas thanks to the adoption of a new sustainable business model, that is the Sustainable Vision Centers, it is clear that the organization is changing its mind-set into a shared value approach (Porter & Kramer, 2011). The idea at the behind these projects is to build specialized infrastructures that help communities to develop an economic independence and to acquire the right expertise.

To sum up, OneSight establishes sustainable clinics staffed by local, capable partners to serve each community's distinct needs and patients pay an affordable price defined by the local market. Central manufacturing and supply chains are centralized and support local demand for clinic supplies and glasses.

OneSight's first global sustainable project was developed in Gambia: the smallest country in Africa with 1.9 million inhabitants with 1/3 of the population living under the international poverty line of $1.25/ day. The situation is so critical that Gambia is ranked 151 of 160 on the "Human Development Index" (Deloitte, 2015).

Although the small dimensions, the need of eye exams and glasses is impressive: as stated by Mustapha Nije, OneSight Project Manager in Gambia, almost one in three Gambians need refraction error corrections (especially cataract and trachoma) but only half of them are aware they have a problem or do not have sufficient resources to afford an eye exam.

Unfortunately, people have to travel for kilometres just to have access to refractive correction services. On top of this fact one has to consider that the cost of a pair of glasses is prohibitive: before OneSight's project a pair of glasses where worth almost an entire month's pay. After OneSight's arrival, the situation has definitely improved and from 2013 up to now the project is continuously growing.

In total OneSight opened 6 vision Centers in all the strategic locations of the country (administrative regions) and one in-country optical manufacturing lab in Kanifing, providing access to all the Gambians. Also, OneSight volunteers cooperated to make this shift in execution feasible and thanks to all their support about 236 Gambians were trained, with the positive results of 186 new jobs created.

All these Vision Centers are equipped with the most modern and advanced equipment, in order to allow local doctors and optometrists to practice all the knowledge and skills acquired during the training period.

Throughout local marketing strategies, the level of awareness about how a pair of glasses can correct refractive errors and change someone's life, has generated an increase of sales (about 6 thousand pair of glasses were sold by OneSight) with also an increase of revenues re-invested in OneSight's activities.

The success of a sustainable project like the one carried out by OneSight in Gambia is not measured only by the number of people who receive access to vision care with an immediate effect, but also considering the long-term impact that such project could have on an entire country.

The case study of Gambia is explicative of the fundamental shift in execution from philanthropic initiatives, like the charitable solutions developed in the traditional clinics, to the most advanced permanent centers based on a model strategically sustainable with long-term objectives (Porter & Kramer, 2011).

Hence, this new type of business model is completely different form the previous one and as Mustapha Njie said, what OneSight is doing in Gambia has a deep significance: OneSight not only helps people to see better but also allows local underserved communities to gain new skills, develop their economic and makes each single country a better place to live in.

OneSight Sustainable Model

OneSight business model is based on three important pillars: Access, Awareness, Affordability (OneSight, 2016).

The terms Access refers to the spaces provided by the government, hospital and existing health care systems managed independently by local teams (Optical Lead). Basically, once trained local teams introduce the new Vision Center into their own community and serve neighbours together.

In many communities, vision care is a foreign concept. People are unaware that vision care exists, that their poor eyesight can be corrected, or that there is significant value in investing in a pair of eyeglasses. For this reason, one of the main objectives of this project is to increase awareness on the Vision Centers and drive traffic to them across localized marketing strategies.

Finally, once the clinics are built in permanent and well-equipped infrastructures it is necessary to make them visible to the population with appropriate marketing and communication campaigns aimed at launch the activities. In general, patients pay an affordable price defined by local market. Indeed, despite the economic condition of the countries in which OneSight operates are extremely poor, all the services offered (eye exam, glasses etc..) are not free but have a "convenient" and value for money price for the target.

Therefore, if the eye exam and the glasses were free, patients and local doctors will depend on OneSight's philanthropic donations and in this case the model will not be sustainable anymore. At this point of our study we can confirm that a sustainable solution like the one promoted by OneSight requires a steady economic situation and a change of mindset of all the stakeholder involved, definitely more oriented to a social dimension of the problem and willing to build long-lasting relationship with local partners (Porter & Kramer, 2011).

In the analysis of the business case has been widely utilized the research developed by Deloitte to examine the first implementation of the sustainable model in Gambia (Deloitte, 2015)

Specifically, the aim of the study was to analyse Gambian current state operations to understand the viability and sustainability of the OneSight model and its applicability to other contexts, in order to learn from operations and inform future expansion.

The Deloitte team conducted over 128 customer interviews/focus groups and 28 employee interviews in Farafenni, Basse, and Kanifing as part of the in-country data collection process.

Results can be summarized in three different categories:

- **Sustainability of the Program:** The steady state model in the Gambia is sustainable since the revenues coming from Vision Care Centers are able to cover operating costs and the cost of goods sold with profits. Also, some profits are allocated for building a fund to cover long-term equipment maintenance to ensure program longevity.
- **Increased Impact:** When profits comfortably cover operating costs with a surplus, funds are freed for strategic investments to advance OneSight's mission (e.g., free glasses for extreme poor or children) Surplus funds also become available to support outreach and education or program expansions.
- **Replicable Model:** The business model is efficient and sustainable so should be replicable in other markets.

In order to better evaluate the sustainability of the model in terms of market potential and cost structure, Deloitte has developed in detail what was the relationship between the need for eye care in Gambia (market penetration) and the ability of the National Health Program to cover costs through the revenue generated from the sale of glasses or from the services offered. Only through the correlation of these two indicators it can be assessed how the model adopted is efficient and effective.

In brief, we can affirm that OneSight can definitely provide access to vision care and top quality eyewear through the new sustainable approach based on strategic partnerships and the development of local clusters.

Should OneSight Adopt CSV Approach?

According to the theoretical background previously outlined, it is now necessary to delineate a business model framework to understand the interactions between OneSight sustainable model and Porter and Kramer's shared value approach.

Shared value creation focuses on identifying the connections between societal and economic progress and should be applied by all type of organizations across the well-known three operating methods. Hence, a new and stronger linkage between business and society is needed to create economic value in a way that also creates value for society by addressing its needs and challenges.

Moreover, this win-win relationship becomes more relevant when companies decide to expand their businesses into developing countries or low-income markets, that are characterized by deep social disadvantages but could also offer great opportunity in terms of developing innovative business model, like social and inclusive business model.

OneSight's sustainable model lies exactly between this two new business models and cover all the three ways identified by Porter and Kramer to create shared value (Porter & Kramer, 2011). Throughout the Sustainable Vision Centers Gambian population could benefit (at the very beginning of the project) of the access to the health care system and therefore of an improvement of economic and social conditions of the local communities: reinforcing local economies, re-launching productivity and also creating new jobs.

In order to evaluate the possible alternatives for a company to create shared value, this study postulates a new framework, based on the one already defined by Michelini and Fiorentino (2011), to graphically highlight the evolution of the shared value approach.

Figure 5 shows how the traditional business is definitely more oriented to create economic value than social value, focusing on maximizing profit per se and generating – as a consequence – "negative externalities".

Externalities arise when firms create social costs that they do not have to bear, such as pollution. Thus, society must impose taxes, regulations, and penalties so that firms "internalize" these externalities and influence many government decisions (Porter & Kramer, 2011). Meanwhile, philanthropic initiatives – by their nature – are mainly focused on societal needs not just conventional economic needs. The transition between these two distinct but correlated businesses, inevitably leads to the creation of shared value where the economic value accurately approximates the social value and vice versa.

Despite these models could be used by the same type of hybrid enterprises, they have different roots: Social Business Model, addressing predominantly social benefits, could be considered as a progressive philanthropic approach; while Inclusive Business Model has its roots in the traditional business given the emphasis on both social and economic benefits (Michelini & Fiorentino, 2011).

Figure 5. The evolution of social and Inclusive Business Models
Source: Our elaboration.

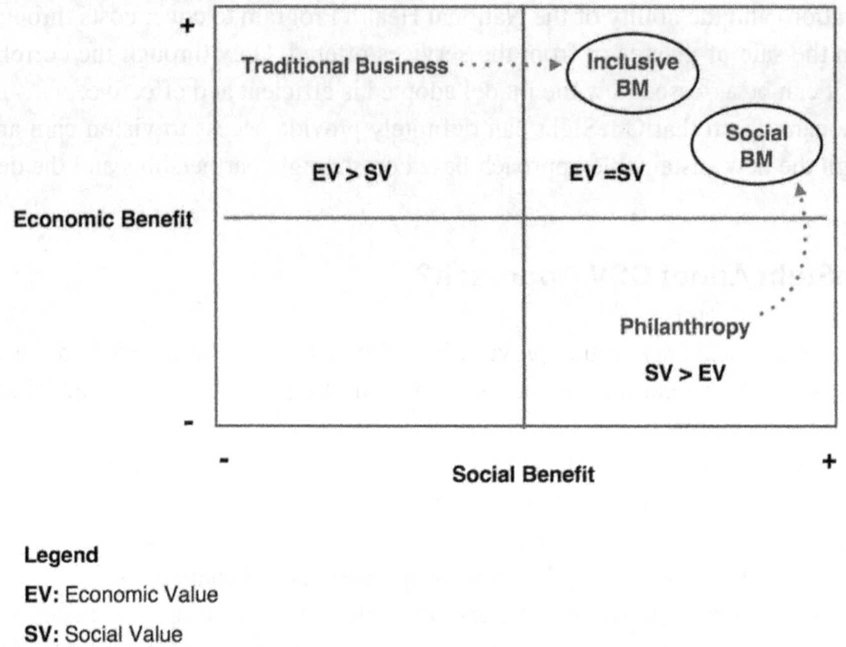

In addition to this theoretical framework, it could be useful to adopt the "building blocks method" to OneSight in order to clearly define which is the most efficient and effective strategy that the organization should pursue (Bockstette & Stamp, 2011).

Based on the blueprint developed by FSG, we can identify how the managerial approach of OneSight is intrinsically linked to the creation of shared value, although the not for profit disposition could lead to a philanthropic or CSR approach.

Figure 6 shows the steps of the creating shared value process, based on OneSight's sustainable model.

Each single block includes Onesight information on vision, strategy, delivery and performance so it is easy to extrapolate the business strategy developed in order to meet the goals and realize OneSight's mission.

Specifically, OneSight strategy aims to guarantee vision care access across the globe through sustainable solutions with support from industry experts, volunteer and partners.

Therefore, all the donations and support coming from partners and mainly form Luxottica, OneSight is able to manage in an holistic and cross-functional way the overall organization and the delivery of the planned initiatives.

To evaluate the sustainability of the business model, it needs to be constantly monitored highlighting its strengths and weakness. OneSight has a true P&L that brings together all the main KPI's to measure the results and the effectiveness of the plan.

Hence, the building blocks translate the shared value idea into concrete actions tailored to the context, the strategy and the measurement process.

Figure 6. The Building Blocks of Creating Shared Value in OneSight
Source: Our elaboration.

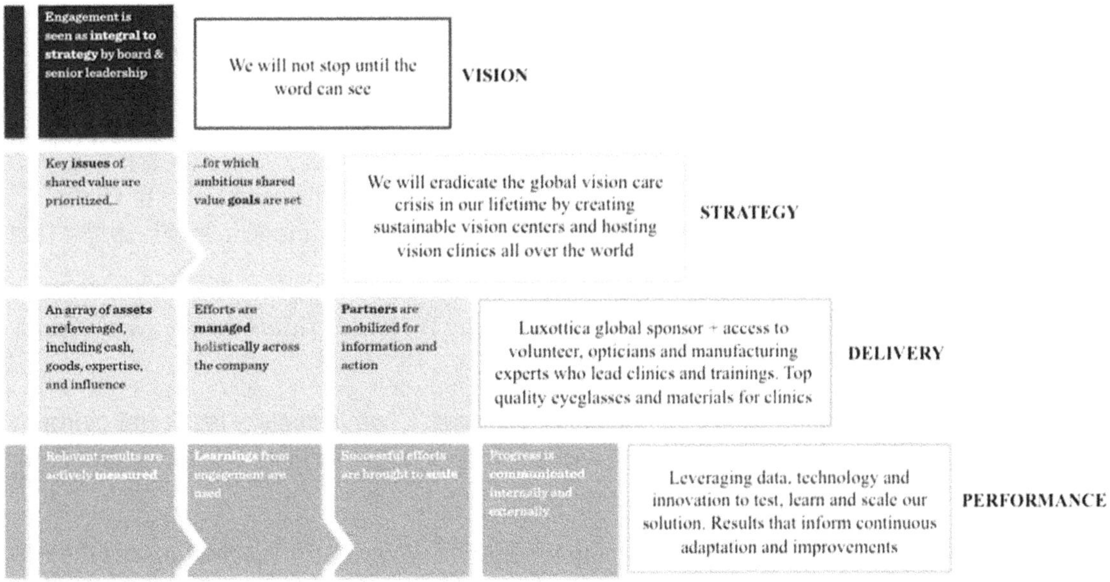

CONCLUSION

First of all, despite the corporate social responsibility is still fundamental for the business management, the principle of shared value is becoming a growing trend into the contemporary economic environment.

According to the evolution postulated in this study, shared value holds the key to unlocking the next wave of business innovation and growth. It will also reconnect company success and community success in ways that have been lost in an age of narrow management approaches, short-term thinking, and deepening divides among society's institutions.

Due to its versatile nature, the concept of shared value blurs the line between for-profit and not for profit organizations and new kinds of hybrid enterprises are rapidly appearing into the broad category of Social Entrepreneurship.

Hence, this study contributes on identifying a theoretical framework useful to analyse the rise of new business models for creating shared value: OneSight's sustainable model belongs to this new category and is a prime example of Social Entrepreneurship.

In a high level interpretation of the case study, it is also possible to analyse how OneSight's sustainable model and Luxottica business model could be integrated. Indeed, thanks to OneSight's initiatives Luxottica realize its CSR approach primarily through creating and strengthening local cluster in underserved communities.

The finding of the research outlines some open points especially regarding the concrete implementation of these business model. For this reason, further research should strive to extend the analysis of the relationship between hybrid enterprises and society to deep dive the development of shared value approach to definitely more "challenging" areas.

REFERENCES

Ansari, S., Muni, K., & Gregg, T. (2012). Impact at the Bottom of the Pyramid: The Role of Social Capital in Capability Development and Community Empowerment. *Journal of Management Studies*, *49*(4), 813–842. doi:10.1111/j.1467-6486.2012.01042.x

Beugré, C. (2017). *Social Entrepreneurship. Managing the Creation of Social Value*. New York: Routledge.

Blodgett, M. S., Hoitash, R., & Markelevich, A. (2014). Sustaining the Financial Value of Global CSR: Reconciling Corporate and Stakeholder Interests in a Less Regulated Environment. *Business and Society Review*, *119*(1), 95–124. doi:10.1111/basr.12026

Bockstette, V., & Stamp, M. (2011). *Creating Shared Value: A How-to Guide for the New Corporate (R)evolution*. Boston: FSG.

Cavaco, S., & Crifo, P. (2014). CSR and Financial Performance: Complementary between Environmental, Social and Business Behaviours. *Applied Economics*, *46*(27), 3323–3338. doi:10.1080/00036846.2014.927572

Clark, C., & Brennan, L. (2012). Entrepreneurship with Social Value: A Conceptual Model for Performance Measurement. *Academy of Entrepreneurship Journal*, *18*(2), 17–32.

Committee for Economic Development. (1971). *Social Responsibilities of Business Corporations. A Statement on National Policy by the Research and Policy Committee of the Committee for Economic Development*. New York: Committee for Economic Development.

Daw, J. (2013). *What Does Creating Shared Value Mean for the Non-profit Sector?*. Retrieved May 30, 2016 from https://sharedvalue.org/groups/shared-value-initiative-community/what-does-creating-shared-value-mean-nonprofit-sector

Deloitte. (2015). *Gambia Steady State Model Analysis*. Deloitte Consulting LLP.

Dembek, K., Singh, P., & Bhakoo, V. (2016). Literature Review of Shared Value: A Theoretical Concept or a Management Buzzword? *Journal of Business Ethics*, *137*(2), 231–267. doi:10.1007/s10551-015-2554-z

Driver, M. (2012). An Interview with Michael Porter: Social Entrepreneurship and the transformation of Capitalism. *Academy of Management Learning & Education*, *11*(3), 421–431. doi:10.5465/amle.2011.0002A

European Commission. (2011). *A renewed EU strategy 2011-14 for Corporate Social Responsibility*. Brussels: European Commission.

Hahn, R. (2012). Inclusive Business, Human Rights and the Dignity of the Poor: A Glance beyond Economic Impacts of Adapted Business Models. *Business Ethics (Oxford, England)*, *21*(1), 47–61. doi:10.1111/j.1467-8608.2011.01640.x

Halme, M., Linderman, S., & Lima, P. (2012). Innovation for Inclusive Business: Intrapreneurial Bricolage in Multinational Corporations. *Journal of Management Studies*, *49*(4), 743–758. doi:10.1111/j.1467-6486.2012.01045.x

Jean, W. A., & Yazdanifard, R. (2015). The Review of Shared Value in Contemporary CSR Run by Two Successful Companies to Sustain the Business in Recent Years. *International Journal of Management. Accounting and Economics*, *2*(9), 1122–1129.

Kramer, M. (2011). *CSR vs. CSV - What's the difference?*. Retrieved May 30, 2016 from http://www.fsg.org/blog/csr-vs-csv-what's-difference

Kramer, M. R. (2009). Catalytic Philanthropy. *Stanford Social Innovation Review*, *7*(3), 29–35.

Kroeger, A., & Weber, C. (2015). Developing a Conceptual Framework for Comparing Social Value Creation. *Academy of Management Review*, *30*(4), 513–540.

Michelini, L. (2012). *Social Innovation and New Business models. Creating shared value in low income markets*. Heidelberg, Germany: Springer. doi:10.1007/978-3-642-32150-4

Michelini, L., & Fiorentino, D. (2011). Nuovi modelli di business per la creazione di valore condiviso: Il social e l'inclusive business. *Impresa Progetto - Electronic Journal of Management*, *1*(1), 1–20.

Nwagbara, U., & Kamara, H. Y. (2015). Corporate Social Responsibility (CSR) Leadership and Poverty Reduction: The Case of Nigeria and Sierra Leone. *Economic Insights – Trend and Challenge*, *67*(2), 21-30.

OneSight. (2016). *OneSight Overview Presentation*. Retrieved May 30, 2016 from https://onesight.org

Panapanaa, V., Bruce, T., Virkki-Hatakka, T., & Linnanen, L. (2016). Analysis of Shared and Sustainable Value Creation of Companies Providing Energy Solutions at the Base of the Pyramid (BoP). *Business Strategy and the Environment*, *25*(5), 293–309. doi:10.1002/bse.1866

Pfitzer, M., Bockstette, V., & Stamp, M. (2009). Innovating for Shared Value. *Harvard Business Review*, *91*(9), 100–107.

Plewa, C., Conduit, J., Quester, P. G., & Johnson, C. (2015). The Impact of Corporate Volunteering on CSR Image: A Consumer Perspective. *Journal of Business Ethics*, *127*(3), 643–659. doi:10.1007/s10551-014-2066-2

Porter, M. E., Hills, G., Pfitzer, M., Patscheke, S., & Hawkins, E. (2012). *Measuring Shared Value How to Unlock Value by Linking Social and Business Results*. Boston: FSG.

Porter, M. E., & Kramer, M. R. (2002). The competitive advantage of corporate philanthropy. *Harvard Business Review*, *80*(12), 56–68. PMID:12510538

Porter, M. E., & Kramer, M. R. (2006). Strategy and Society. The Link Between Competitive Advantage and Corporate Social Responsibility. *Harvard Business Review*, *84*(12), 78–92. PMID:17183795

Porter, M. E., & Kramer, M. R. (2011). Creating Shared Value. *Harvard Business Review*, *89*(1-2), 62–77.

Prahalad, C. K. (2005). *The Fortune at the Bottom of the Pyramid*. Pearson Education Inc.

Qu, S. Q., & Dumay, J. (2011). The Qualitative Research Interview. *Qualitative Research in Accounting & Management*, *8*(3), 238–264. doi:10.1108/11766091111162070

Sheehy, B. (2015). Defining CSR: Problems and Solutions. *Journal of Business Ethics*, *131*(3), 625–648. doi:10.1007/s10551-014-2281-x

Speiss-Knafl, W., Mast, C., & Janse, S. A. (2015). On the Nature of Social Business Model Innovation. *Social Business. An Interdisciplinary Journal*, *5*(2), 113–130.

United Nations Development Programme. (2008). *Creating Value for All: Strategies for Doing Business with the Poor*. New York: United Nations Development Programme. Retrieved May 30, 2016 from http://growinginclusivemarkets.org/media/gimlaunch/Report_2008/GIM%20Report%20Final%20August%202008.pdf

Visser, W., & Kymal, C. (2015). Integrated Value Creation (IVC): Beyon Corporate Social Responsibility (CSR) and Creatong Shared Value (CSV). *Journal of International Business Ethics*, *8*(1), 29–43.

Wang, S. (2014). On the Relationship between CSR and Profit. *Journal of International Business Ethics*, *7*(1), 51–57.

Wilson, F., & Post, J. E. (2012). Business Models for people, Planet (&Profits): Exploring the Phenomena of Social Business, a Market Based Approach to Social Value Creation. *Small Business Economics*, *40*(3), 715–737. doi:10.1007/s11187-011-9401-0

World Business Council for Sustainable Development (WBCSD) & SNV Netherlands Development Organization. (2008). *Inclusive Business: Profitable Business for Successful Development*. Geneva: WBCSD & SNV. Retrieved May 30, 2016 from http://wbcsdservers.org/wbcsdpublications/cd_files/datas/business-solutions/social-impact/pdf/InclusiveBusiness-ProfitableBusinessForSuccessfulDevelopment.pdf

Yunus, M. (2007). *Creating a World Without Poverty: Social Business and the Future of Capitalism*. New York: Public Affairs.

Yunus, M. (2010). *Building Social Business: The New Kind of Capitalism that Serves Humanity's Most Pressing Needs*. New York: Public Affairs.

KEY TERMS AND DEFINITIONS

Building Blocks: A blueprint developed by FSG that help companies to translate the shared value idea into concrete actions tailored to the context, the strategy and the measurement process.

CSV: The concept of shared value can be defined as policies and operating practices that enhance the competitiveness of a company while simultaneously advancing the economic and social conditions in the communities in which it operates.

Hybrid Enterprises: Hybrid enterprises are those enterprises straddling the boundary between the for- profit business world and the social mission-driven public and not for profit organizations. Hybrid Enterprises belong to the broad category of Social Enterprises.

Inclusive Business Model: Inclusive business models are commercially viable and replicable business models that include low-income customers, retailers, suppliers, or distributors in core operations, recognizing the untapped opportunities this market segment represents. Companies with an inclusive business model are directly contributing to reducing poverty and promoting shared prosperity through better income opportunities and access to goods and services for 4.5 billion individuals who are often called the "Base of the Pyramid".

Social Business Model: Social business is a new category of business. Specifically is a cause drive business model. In a social business, the investors/owners can gradually recoup the money invested, but cannot take any dividend beyond that point. Purpose of the investment is purely to achieve one or more social objectives through the operation of the company.

Social Entrepreneurship: Social Entrepreneurship is a step of the creating shared value process through which a social oriented company gain the right competences in order to incorporate social issues into their core business strategies. Social Entrepreneurship may be defined along a continuum from the creation of positive social change to earned income in the pursuit of social change.

Sustainable Model: OneSight's sustainable model results from the transformation process from traditional and charitable solution to the new permanent vision care clinics. OneSight business model is based on three important pillars (Access, Awareness, Affordability) and it was developed for the first time in Gambia.

Chapter 6 Created Shared Value and Sustainable, Inclusive Development of Developing Countries

James Odia
University of Benin, Nigeria

ABSTRACT

The created shared value represents a paradigm shift in business corporate social responsibility (CSR) and sustainability strategy. Apart from addressing the limitations inherent in the traditional CSR which is mainly philanthropic, short-lived and separated from the core business strategy and activities, it enhances the company's competitiveness while simultaneously advancing the economic and social conditions in the community of operation. Companies can create shared values through re-conceiving products and markets, redefining productivity in the value chain and building supportive industry clusters at the company's locations and solving society problems. Despite the criticisms and challenges of the shared value concept, there are convincing evidences that the created shared value is a veritable instrument for addressing the bottom of the pyramid resulting in inclusive, sustainable development of developing countries and it has the potentials to unleash the next wave of global economic growth, prosperity and sustainable development when governments, companies and non-government organizations in developing countries demonstrate commitment to their roles in shared value creation and companies start to think and take long-term views of social investments and economic prosperity, and look at corporate decisions and opportunities through the lens of shared value by incorporating social and societal values into their economic agenda.

DOI: 10.4018/978-1-5225-3147-0.ch006

INTRODUCTION

The concept of Created Shared Value (CSV) has been pioneered by Professor Michael Porter and Mark Kramer of the Harvard University since 2011. Although the idea of shared value was first expressed in their publication in the Harvard Business Review on "Strategy and society: The link between competitive advantage and corporate social responsibility" in 2006 where they advocated a mutual dependence between corporations and society or a win-win business-society relationship. There would be a symbiotic relationship and reciprocity between business and society as firms redefine and readjust their concept of value in a broader, more "shared" perspective (Davenport, 2011). It is business paving ground for its own success by curing the defects of a dysfunctional society through provision of infrastructure (such as roads, water supplies, schools) required for its production and produce shared value for the whole area (Kleemann & Krieger-Boden, 2011).

The CSV is a new revolutionary way of business thinking in the business-society relationship, which integrates social goals within business practice without distracting a firm from its primary purpose of achieving profit (Porter & Kramer, 2011; Rocchi & Fererro, 2014). This could trigger once again the greatest economic wealth, growth and innovation for humanity and business (Porter & Kramer, 2011). According to Porter and Kramer (2011), shared value can be defined as policies and operating practices that enhance the competitiveness of a company while simultaneously advancing the economic and social conditions in the community in which it operates and companies can create shared values through re-conceiving products and markets, redefining productivity in the value chain and building supportive industry clusters at the company's locations.

Porter and Kramer's propositions for the CSV have been laudable and applauded by many supporters (Bockstette & Stamp, 2011; Hills, Russell, Borgonovi, Doty, & Lyer, 2012; Pfitzer, Bockstette & Stamp, 2013; Visser, 2013) in re-connecting the disconnected corporations' successes to society's development, particularly in the advancement of social causes to strategic level, specifying the roles of government in enhancing shared value and introducing a broader conception of capitalism- the "caring or conscious capitalism". Without doubts, the world has experienced unparalleled prosperity following the industrial revolution and the free-market economy. Nevertheless Ringmar (2005) argued that although capitalism has produced comparable levels of economic prosperity, it has brought to human beings and societies the consequences of income inequality, erosion of non-market values, commodification and alienation of people and hence it should be controlled.

The arguments on CSR have revolved around the CSR continuum of Professor Friedman's neo-classical economic theory and Professor Freeman's stakeholder theory. Although Porter and Kramer (2011) argued that CSV is not social responsibility, philanthropy or even sustainability, it does appear that CSV is beyond CSR of business! In fact, In every country, particularly the developing ones, CSR has become inescapable priority for businesses (Porter & Kramer, 2006; Jean & Yazdanifard, 2015) and they are being blamed for every society's failures (Porter & Kramer, 2011), as corporate prosperity at the expense of the society's deep poverty and problems. Moreover, most of companies' efforts have not pay off greatly in their productivity due to the disconnect from or the ditch against society and the failure to link CSR to their strategy (Porter & Kramer, 2006). Porter and Kramer (2011) argued that there is a growing perception of companies' successes at the expense of society's social, environmental and economic problems. The companies' CSR have not been strategic to be a source of business opportunity, innovation, revenue growth, competitive advantage and benefits to society (Moore, 2014).

The CSV represents a win-win situation where an organization creates value for the society by tackling its needs and challenges in a way, which also creates economic value to them. Epstein (2012) remarks that CSV will grow future markets as well as strengthen economies and communities The CSV challenges the academic literature on corporate social responsibility as well as business practice in the few years of its existence. No wonder, CSV has been studied from different point of views, contexts such as industrial sectors and multinationals, social entrepreneurship (Pirson, 2012) and countries e.g. Brazil (Spitzek & Chapman, 2012), India (Vaidyanathan & Scott, 2012), and Australia (Leth & Hems, 2014). Some have tried to reconstruct/redesign or extend the original CSV framework by Porter and Kramer (Michelini & Fiorentino, 2012; Moon, Pare, Yim & Park, 2011) and/or widely applied the CSV to regional development, poverty reduction and to other disciplines like finance and banking (Bockstette, Pfitzer, Smith, Bhavaraju, Priestley & Bhatt 2014), education (Kramer &Tallant, 2014), global health (Peterson, Rehrig, Stamp & Kim, 2012), oil, gas and mining companies (Hidalgo, Peterson, Sith & Foley, 2014), agriculture, business corporate strategy, low-income markets and emerging markets (Hills, Russell, Borgonovi, Doty & Iyer, 2012).

A global assessment of CSV projects by Kreckova (2015) shows that CSV by regions is very uneven with South America, Central America and Caribbean region (22%), Africa (18%), North America (14%) and Asia (14%). The top social incidents are health and nutrition projects (21%), education, including workforce development (19%), financial inclusion, human rights and poverty with 9% each. Again AT Kearney (2015) study of over 200 social impact initiatives of United Nations Global Compact led companies reveals that 40% was shared value, 35% fall into philanthropy and 25% in community investments. This study was different from 2011 study where 75% of corporate social investment was philanthropy. The reason for the shift was attributed to the increased focus on minimizing environmental impacts and expanding employment and educational opportunities.

There are lots of literature and empirical evidences that the CSR approach in the developing countries of Africa including Nigeria has been mainly philanthropic and normative CSR (Visser, 2006, 2008; Visser, Matten, Pohl & Tolhurst, 2007; Amaeshi, Adi, Ogbechie & Amao, 2006; Odia, 2016). There are also increasing expectations by various stakeholders that corporate organizations, especially the multinational companies (MNCs) and transnational companies (TNCs) should go beyond profit maximization and regulatory compliance to take up responsibilities that make significant impact on society by helping to remedy the social problems including the ones caused by them (Odia, 2016). Some of the multinational oil companies in Nigeria like Shell Petroleum and Chevron have tried to move towards value sharing in their social responsiveness to oil producing communities in the Niger Delta region through partnership and social investments in host communities. Chevron's Partnership Initiatives in the Niger Delta (PIND) through the collaborative venture with the United States Agency for International Development (USAID), the Department for International Development (DFID), and others was aimed at enabling economic growth in the nine (9) oil-producing States of the Niger Delta area of Nigeria through investment of over $100 million in five years to create opportunities in other areas other than its value chain.

The CSV may just be the desired solution that the stakeholders have been waiting for to make corporations break away from the restricted CSR involvement to embrace the broader view of "caring, conscious capitalism" and respond to social issues and problems (Visser, 2013; Kreckova, 2015). While there are social and economic benefits, and prospects associated with CSV to the society and businesses at least from evidences of companies that have keyed into the CSV, a research gap exists on how CVS is linked to the sustainable, inclusive development of developing countries. There are also numerous limitations and criticisms regarding CSV such as: measurement issues, changing corporate mindsets to view environmental and social problems not as constraints but as business opportunities, gaining support of top management of MNCs, TNCs and other companies to key in and their voluntary CSV compliance and getting support of governments and agencies at the local, national and international levels to encourage more businesses to adopt shared value strategies.

Therefore, based on the review of extant literature and case studies on CSV, the objective of the chapter is to examine the relationship between CVS and sustainable, inclusive development from the perspective of developing countries like Nigeria. The rest of the chapter is divided into four sections: The immediate section clarifies the concept of CSV and differentiates it from CSR. Section three considers the issues, controversies and problems relating to CSV such as the problems with the presents CSR, the creation of shared value, shared valued opportunities in the extractive industries including the roles of government, extractive industries and civil society in creating in-country shared value, CSV opportunities and benefits in developing countries, criticisms and limitations of CSV measurement and the inclusive, sustainable development through CSV. Section four proffers solutions and recommendations to the constraints of the effective implementation of CSV in developing countries. Section five is the conclusion and suggestions for further study.

BACKGROUND

The Concept of Created Share Value

According to Porter and Kramer (2011), shared value can be defined as policies and operating practices that enhance the competitiveness of a company while simultaneously advancing the economic and social conditions in the community in which it operates. Shared value was born due to the need to address societal needs, mostly in the bottom-of-the-pyramid segments of the customers (Kreckova, 2015). Shared value creation focuses on identifying and expanding the connections between societal and economic progress. It describes how firms can incorporate CSR activities to their overall business strategy so that they not solely represent a cost but also create value for the firm in terms of a unique market position. Creating shared value implies ethical standards and complying with the law, and it also considers any mitigation after harms that may affect results of business practices. Shared value involves creating economic value in a way that also creates value for society by addressing its needs and challenges. It aligns CSR activities with core business activities to generate business returns and thereby create a business case for sustained commitment and investment (Porter & Kramer 2011). Shared value positions social engagement as a "long-term investment that is intrinsic to business success." (Bockstette & Stamp 2011, p. 21). A shared value perspective recognizes the interdependency between business and society. It is creating economic value in a way that also creates value for society by addressing its needs and challenges. The idea is combining "traditional objectives with additional benefits for society" (Altman & Berman, 2011).

Again shared value is being referred to as a new way to address the underlying root causes of community concerns and unlock economic opportunities for companies in the extractives sector which have made little progress using current approaches (philanthropy, reputation building, local content requirements), with rising disputes, unending conflicts, violence and militancy like in the Niger Delta Region of Nigeria. CSV is a differentiation strategy (Spitzeck & Chapman 2012) that creates business value by tackling social issues or converting social issues into tangible business opportunities based on three pillars of (i) re-conceiving products and markets, (ii) re-defining productivity in the value chain and (iii) enabling local clusters development (Porter & Kramer, 2011; Porter, Hills, Pfitzer, Patscheke & Hawkins, 2012).

Although there are numerous social issues as generic, value chain social impacts and social dimensions of competitive context impacts, the CSV concept focuses particularly on those issues within the business context that have significant impact on firm competitiveness. The CSV is about creating social and business values simultaneously. The social values refer to positive improvements in the social issues targeted by the firm, and social outcomes or social changes that are needed to be achieved. The business values are the actual economic benefits to the firms (Porter et al., 2012). According to Porter and Kramer (2011), the most pressing social issues that could be targeted by shared value strategy include supplier access and viability, employee skills, worker safety, employee health, water use, energy use, and environmental impact. It is argued that businesses acting as businesses, not as charitable, philanthropic givers, are arguably the most powerful force to address pressing society's issues. It is believed that businesses' quest to create economic value while simultaneously creating shared value for society will give rise to far broader opportunities for strategy and profitability that would drive the next wave of innovation, productivity and economic growth while also motivating and attracting consumers, business partners, employees, shareholders, and the public to them (Porter, 2014). This is because only the companies who address social issues strategically and understand the interdependence between business and society (Porter & Kramer, 2006, 2011) would be able to compete in this new world (Bockstette, 2011; Porter & Kramer, 2011). It must be emphasized that solving social problems requires innovation (Pfitzer et al., 2013), collective impact (Kania & Kramer, 2011) and changes to the traditional CSR mindset.

While many researchers have presented corporate responsibility with regard to social and environmental problems as an ethical duty (Donaldson & Dunfee, 1999), a political responsibility (Scherer & Palazzo, 2007, 2011; Whelan, 2012; Néron, 2013; Whelan, 2013; Scherer, Palazzo & Matten, 2014) or a response to business risks (Fombrun, Gardberg & Barnett, 2000), the CSV makes corporations to see social and environmental problems not as disconnected and externally imposed but as real opportunities and serious strategic targets for genuine business decisions. According to Brown and Knudsen (2013), the shared value replaces and expands the notion of CSR, which as a practice has too often become affiliated with misguided initiatives, costly sideshows and shallow public relation activities.

Camilleri (2012) has argued that there seems to be Adam Smith's "invisible hand" in force with regard to the CSV conceptualization since businesses contribute to society's value creation when they pursue their own interests. Thus the CSV argument tends to support Adam Smith's (1776) remark that it is not from the benevolence of the butcher, the brewer or the baker, that we can expect our dinner, but from their regard to their own interest. Again, Moczadlo (2015) argues that taking into account the examples cited by Porter and Kramer in their 2011 article, their understanding of CSV seems to correspond in some respects with strategic CSR. Strategic CSR can be located between strict compliance of given rules and regulations and good corporate citizenship (Windsor, 2013). Nonetheless, CSV is going beyond the pure business case approach of CSR because it requires integrating shared value into the core business and the long-term strategic alignment of companies. Porter and Kramer (2011) posit that strategic CSR, value co-creation, social innovation and inclusive business model follow the principle of the CSV. Young (2012) argues that CSV represents one particular model for implementing strategic CSR in larger organizations. Like CSV, strategic CSR reframes sustainability and social benefits as a driver of business innovation, value creation and competitive advantage.

The Differences Between CSR and CSV

CSV goes beyond CSR because shared value creates long-term potential for a company's profitability and competitive position in the market, while corporate social responsibility is a short-term remedy that is hard to justify in the long run. While CSR is based on being responsible, philanthropy and doing good for society, its impacts are too reactionary and cursory to make a significant impact in improving either society or the company's earnings potential. On the other hand, CSV is a readjustment of the company's overall operations in order to create new value. Again, whereas CSR is a short-term solution, CSV is a long-term realignment of the company's entire budget, market position and overall mission. CSV is distinct from CSR where companies are challenged to sponsor the (costly) production of social goods, or like social businesses and social entrepreneurs that refrain from profit maximization in favour of a social goal and accept forgoing a higher income. Nevertheless, compliance with laws and ethical standards and reducing harm from corporate activities are assumed in both CSR and CSV (see Table 1).

The European Commission changed the definition of CSR in 2011 to include CSV as a core element for companies with their owners and shareholders respectively, as well as for other stakeholders and the society. Moreover, the Commission sees strategic CSR as an important tool for the competitiveness of companies and a measure for business to contribute to inclusive growth, employment and well-being of the society. Therefore, companies should take into account economic, social and environmental targets

Table 1. Differences between CSR and CSV

	Bases	CSR	CSV
1	**Motivation/focus**	Corporate reputation	Competitive advantage
2	**Main driver**	External stakeholders	Corporate strategy
3	**Approach**	Reactive and defensive	Proactive
4	**Measurement**	Spending, standard ESG metrics	Social and economics values
5	**Management**	CSR/ public affairs	Across the firm
6	**Business Benefits**	Risk reduction and goodwill	New business opportunities
7	**Social benefits**	Successful projects	Large scale, sustainable chain
8	**Value**	Doing good	Economic and societal benefits relative to cost
9	**Type**	Citizenship, philanthropy, sustainability	Joint company and community value creation
10	**Profit definition**	Separate from profit maximization	Integral to profit maximization
11	**Motives**	Discretionary in response to external pressures	Integral to competing strategy
12	**Budget**	Impact limited by company's footprint and CSR budget	Realign the entire company's budget.
13	**Agenda**	Defined by external reporting and personal preference	Company's specific and internally guidelines
14	**Person(s) in charge**	Typically led by CSR, marketing, corporate communications, external/public/government affairs, community relations, sustainability and foundation departments	Typically led by CEO, senior executive team and individual champions across the company in close collaboration with corporate affairs and sustainability departments
15	**Example**	Fair trade purchasing	Transforming procurement to increase quality and yield

Source: Adapted from Porter and Kramer (2011)

including ethical human rights and consumer concerns when developing their long-term business strategy. Maczaldo (2015) differentiates between the CSV of the European Commission and Porter and Kramer (see Table 2). First, the CSV of Porter and Kramer goes beyond the pure business case of CSR because CSV is a long-term measure integrated systematically into the strategic core business of companies. The Commission sees the shareholders as just one common group of a company's stakeholders and gives no preference to them. For Porter and Kramer the simultaneous creation of profit and societal value are decisive. While the European Commission sees CSR as a driving concept, Porter and Kramer differentiate CSV from CSR-development of a new strategic business concept which can simultaneously create economic and societal value as well as increase the competitiveness of companies.

ISSUES, CONTROVERSIES, AND PROBLEMS

What Is Wrong With the Present (Traditional) CSR?

Basically, traditional CSR activities in most developing countries of Africa encompass employment benefits, community development and philanthropy which is not linked to the core business strategy. Porter and Kramer (2006) argued that the prevailing approach of CSR is so fragmented and so disconnected from business and its strategy that many of the greatest opportunities of companies to benefit society are obscure and lost. Again all four schools of CSR (moral obligation, license to operate sustainability, reputation) focus on the tensions between society and business rather than the interdependence; and they are not sufficient enough to enable a company to identify, prioritize and address social issues it can make the biggest impact.

According to Browne and Nuttall (2013), this CSR has failed to fulfill its core purpose in building stronger relationships with the external world because of the following. First, the head-office initiatives rarely gain the full support of the business and tend to break down in discussions over who pays and who gets the credit. Second, centralized CSR teams can easily lose touch with reality- they tend to take too narrow view of the relevant external stakeholders. Firms' investments in CSR are moderate and mini-

Table 2. Distinction between European Commission (2011) CSR and Porter and Kramer (2011) CSV

Category	European Commission (2011)	Porter and Kramer CSV
Role of business in society	CSR as core element for legitimation of business	
Pre requisite	Companies fulfill their legal obligations; collective between social partners	Companies fulfill their legal obligations
Aims	Contribution to inclusive growth and well-being of the society; triple-bottom	To reach simultaneously economic and social progress through value creation quantified by the relation of benefits to costs
Stakeholder	Shareholders, other stakeholders, the whole society	Varied with the concrete projects
Strategic orientation	CSR/CSV is a long-term strategy and included in the core activities of business	
Role of government	No strict regulation but flexible for businesses; Government procurement directives can be used to enhance CSR	Government should set clear and measurable social goals; public authorities should support business rather than over-regulate them

Source: Maczaldo (2015)

mum because they consider such investments as a cost or expense factor only which takes its share of the firm's profit (Christmann & Taylor, 2006). Corporate social responsibility is considered as a means to an end, and the bare-minimum mentality de-motivates companies from further pursuing any other sort of contributory value to society (Davenport, 2011). Third, CSR focuses too closely on limiting the downside. Companies often see it only as an exercise in protecting or enhancing their reputations- to get away with irresponsible behavior elsewhere. Fourth, CSR programs tend to be short-lived and because they are separated from the company's commercial activity, they survive on the whims and caprices of senior executives rather than the value they deliver. Therefore the programs are vulnerable when there are changes in management or costs are cut. Besides, they fail to see the future business opportunities and competitive advantages that may accrue to them over their competitors in the longer term. Fifth, there is wrong perception of CSR and lack of top management support. Also, it is hard to determine the social impact and business benefits of CSR.

Many MNCs do only what they must in order to please stakeholders and obtain legitimacy, seeking to keep their actions to a minimum (Chen & Bouvain, 2009; Christmann & Taylor, 2006). According to Salzmann (2004), firms are only interested in making profits while supporting employment, investments, purchases, wages and taxes without any consideration of the welfare of the community around them. The responsible actions were due to external pressure and reputation enhancing, public relation and gaining a positive score on CSR scorecards which ultimately failed to connect CSR activities to their core business strategy; and not the desire to do good (Aspelund, Fjell & Rødland, 2015; Milliman, Ferguson & Sylvester, 2008). Porter and Kramer (2006) summed up the traditional CSR as a hodgepodge of uncoordinated CSR and philanthropic activities disconnected from the company's strategy that neither make any meaningful social impact nor strengthen the firm's long-term competitiveness.

Furthermore, scholars have argued that CSR has not proved itself in businesses of the current century because it lacks criteria of differentiation for businesses to follow this theory (Szmigin & Rutherford, 2013). The benefits of traditional CSR are often nebulous, difficult to define and measure, externally influenced, and only indirectly connected to the action being taken (Bockstette & Stamp, 2011). The traditional CSR is differentiated in motivation, implementation, and impact from strategic CSR (Werner, 2009). The CSR is carried as a reactionary and reputation-enhancing agenda with no clear strategic framework link to core business. Hence the result has suboptimal economic or social impacts on stakeholders and society. The present CSR does not fully comply with the society needs; CSR means a reduction of profits for the sake of an environmental or social environmental end (Bosch-Badia, Montllor-Serrats & Tarrazon, 2013), and stakeholders' interests are being ignored (Székely & Knirch, 2005). Although CSR has some potentials to deal with environmental issues such as carbon emission, pollution, waste disposal and oil spills (Frynas, 2009), and also emphasizes various activities including corporate governance, sustainability, stakeholders management, relationship with employees, unions, suppliers and community representatives, commitment to transparent reporting and harm reduction (Petrovic-Lazarevic, 2008), it is reactive, defensive, lack active strategic choices within companies, and fail to deal with key challenges in the business-society relationships (Frynas, 2009). Jonikas (2013) contends that CSR can often create use-value for stakeholders and society but little value for companies in terms of profit increases. He suggests that CSR should become more oriented towards CSV to help companies gain sustainable competitive advantage and make significant social impact on society.

Salzmann (2005) argues that corporations currently used both social benefits theory and practice to fulfill the requirements of environmental and social issues by rising up, at the same time, the financial aspects of the firms themselves. There has been a shift from philanthropic or ancillary CSR to a more strategic perspective because the current models of CSR have been largely ineffective at addressing society's pressing and urgent challenges (Visser, 2010; McWilliams & Siegel, 2011; Young, 2012). This requires that firms should move away from the emphasis on image to emphasis on substance; from fragmented, defensive CSR posture to an integrated, affirmative approach; go beyond good corporate citizenship, philanthropy and pre-occupation with measuring shareholders' satisfaction to creating shared value by becoming more selective in mounting initiatives whose social and business benefits are larger and distinctive (Porter & Kramer, 2006). Strategic CSR helps firms to build trust and reputation, increase financial performance, minimize risk, gain competitive advantage, enhance strategic positioning and synergistic value creation (Porter & Kramer, 2006; Juscius & Jonikas, 2013; Fleming & Jones, 2013). Strategic CSR unlocks shared value by investing in social impacts that strengthen company's competitiveness. The CSV theory recognizes the social needs rather than focusing only on the economic needs to define markets. It also goes beyond the strategy theory by motivating companies to look at opportunities that strive to satisfy fundamental social needs of the community (Porter & Kramer, 2011).

Creation of Shared Value

Bockstette and Stamp (2011) identify ten common building blocks to create shared value to include: articulate a vision, prioritize key issues, set specific ambitious goals, deploy a wide range of assets to address the issue, manage efforts holistically across the organization, collaborate with partners, measure progress on key indicators, learn from measurement to improve efforts, address issues at scale, and communicate progress to internal and external audiences. Pfitzer et al. (2013) provide a five-step framework

Table 3. Philanthropic and created shared value approach

Philanthropic Approach	Areas of Investments	CSV Approach	Business Benefit	Social Benefit
Drinking water/wells for local communities	Infrastructure e.g. water	Develop sustainable water utility leveraging business process	Reduce water treatment costs by charging commercial water rates	Provide water to communities that lack access to it
Provide broad- based skills training with no link to employment opportunities	Training	Create training program based on business and supplier needs and link it to jobs	Reduce employee costs by reducing on expatriate employees	Improve employability and wage-earning capabilities of local workforce
Invest in Environmental restoration unrelated to the business	Environment	Restore degraded coastlines or wetlands to reduce risk of a natural disaster to the business	Protect assets (e.g. pipelines) near coastlines from disasters	Improve the resilience of host communities to natural disasters
Funds construction of local clinic	Health Care	Develop program to reduce disease burden among population living in mine catchment area	Improve employee productivity and reduce company's health care costs	Reduce the disease burden in local communities
Provide scholarship for local students	Education	Catalyze coalition to improve secondary school educational outcomes in host community	Improve the quality of the future talent pool in host communities	Improve educational achievement and job prospects for students

Source: Hidalgo et al. (2014)

in the development of shared value strategy as (a) embedding a social purpose; (b) rigorously defining the social need;(c) measuring the social and business value; (d) creating the optimal innovation structure; and (e) co-creating with external stakeholders like government, universities, NGOs, and other companies. There are usually many values created but Jonikas (2013) argues that only shared value creation through CSR seems to be sustainable.

According to Porter and Kramer (2011), companies can create shared values in three levels as: re-conceiving products and markets, redefining productivity in the value chain and building supportive industry clusters at the company's locations. In order to re-conceive products and markets, companies should re-evaluate the relationships they have with their consumers, and then incorporate shared value into the process of goods exchange. They can use strong advertisement, rebrand their mission to be more socially conscious and address many unmet needs in order to attract consumers to their company and products/services. This level focuses on revenue growth, market share and profitability that arise from the environmental, social, or economic development benefits delivered by a company's products and services (Porter et al, 2012). For example, Shell has established a sustainable utility company on Bonny Island, Nigeria, that serves and supply energy to over 93,000 customers (Hidalgo et al 2014).

Redefining productivity can be done in the value chain through: (a) energy use and logistics, (b) resource use, (c) procurement, (d) distribution, (e) employee productivity, and (f) location. It could also be by sub-contracting. The level focuses on improvements in internal operations that improve cost, input access, quality and productivity achieved through environmental improvements, better resource utilization, investment in employees, supplier capability and other areas. For instance, Intercontinental Hotels Group (IHG), the largest hotel company in the world, launched its Green Engage programmes in 2009 with the objective of testing dozens of options for reducing energy use, water consumption, and waste disposal in pilot hotels, and providing a detailed ranking of all possible shared value opportunities in terms of returns to IHG through substantial reductions in hotel operating costs, including energy savings of up to 25%.

Clusters include not only businesses, institutions such as academic programmes, associations and standards organizations but also broader public assets in the surrounding community such as schools and universities, clean water, fair-competition laws, quality standards and market transparency. Creating shared value from enabling local cluster development derives from improving the external environment for the company through community investments and strengthening local suppliers, local institutions, and local infrastructure in ways that also enhance business productivity. As the world's largest food and beverage company, Nestlé created clusters by implementing a rural development strategy that trains, assists and supports small diary Indian farmers with better technology in order to increase the productivity of their cattle thereby ensuring the reliable supply of high quality raw materials. In fact without a supporting cluster, productivity suffers. According to Porter and Kramer (2011), a focus on clusters and location has been all but absent in management thinking. Cluster thinking has also been missing in many economic development initiatives which have failed because they involved isolated interventions and overlooked critical complementary investments. While a key aspect of cluster building in developing and developed countries alike is the formation of open and transparent markets, companies can support cluster development in the communities in which they operate by identifying gaps and deficiencies in areas such as logistics, suppliers, distribution channels, training, market organization and educational institutions. Delgado, Porter and Stern (2010) argue that clusters help to reduce the costs and risks associated with new venture formation, and they can also increase the likelihood of survival during early years of a business' development.

They drive local competition by not only increasing operational effectiveness and strategic positioning (Porter, 2000) but also resulting in more resilient competitive advantage.

Porter and Kramer (2006) argued that firms can create shared value by using CSR strategically to achieve a competitive advantage. Companies can create and sustain a competitive advantage by cooperating with other companies in a supply chain by nurturing and building competencies through collaborative partnerships. In fact, the success of every company is affected by the supporting companies and infrastructure around it. Gradl and Jenkins (2011) noted that inclusive business model acts as a catalyst for the CSV concept. Bisgaard (2009) consideres cross-sector partnership, collaboration and alliances with non-governmental organizations (NGOs), governmental bodies and other business companies, co-creation with stakeholders and development of new business models as the strategic dimensions to create shared value. Saul (2011) focuses on social innovation to enhance shared value creation.

Fjell and Rødland (2015) found that MNCs can create shared value by pursuing the two different methods of responsible differentiations to obtain competitive advantage over competitors, and by sustainable value innovation to have a blue ocean based on responsible actions (green planet strategy). Also a company can instigate shared value by solving problems through the products and services it creates, addressing problems through company operations, including better use of natural resources and a business investing outside its operations in order to solve problems connected with company growth and productivity, such as improving growing techniques. According to Porter and Kramer (2011), to create social value companies must invest in areas that address social and environmental objective; to create share value they must invest in long-term business competitiveness that simultaneously address social and environmental objectives and to create business value, they should invest in long-term competitiveness. Effective internal communication of CSR implementation is one essential ingredient to embed value creation in a company. Companies with economies of scale can also use pricing to create shared value (Bertini & Gourville, 2012).

Table 4. Social and business benefits associated with the levels of shared value

Levels of Shared Value	Business Results	Social Results
Re-conceiving products and markets: How targeting unmet needs drives incremental revenue and profits	-Increased revenue - Increased market share - Increased market growth - Improved profitability	- Improved patient care - Reduced carbon footprint - Improved nutrition - Improved education
Redefining productivity in the value chain: How better management of internal operations increases productivity and reduces risks	-Improved productivity -Reduced logistical and operating costs -Secured supply -Improved quality -Improved profitability	- Reduced energy use - Reduced water use - Reduced raw materials - Improved job skills - Improved employee incomes
Enabling cluster development: How changing societal conditions outside the company unleashes new growth and productivity gains	-Reduced costs - Secured supply - Improved distribution infrastructure - Improved workforce access - Improved profitability	-Improved education - Increased job creation - Improved health - Improved incomes

Source: Porter et al (2012)

Shared Value Creation and Appropriation

There is distinction between value creation and value appropriation; organizations that create new value may lose except they share this value with other stakeholders such as employees, competitors or society (Nohria & Ghoshal, 1994; Makadok & Coff, 2002; Chatain & Zemsky, 2011; Porter & Kramer, 2011). According to Di Gregorio (2013), value appropriation is a two-step process through which a firm first competes against other firms to create and protect appropriation streams (inter-organizational value appropriation), and then managers, employees, shareholders and other stakeholders compete to capture the value that has been retained within the firm (intra-organizational value appropriation). Companies will not only benefit by creating and capturing value, but also by sharing or appropriating it. Both value creation and value appropriation capabilities are required for achieving sustainable competitive advantage and superior financial performance (Ghemawat, 1991; Mizik & Jacobson, 2003). But a firm must strive for balance (March, 1991; Mizik & Jacobson, 2003) or integrate the two (Di Gregorio, 2013) depending on its choice. It is argued that value appropriation is the more relevant process since it only impacts firm profitability (Barney, 2001); it is also of more immediate concern to managers and researchers than value creation (Di Gregorio, 2013).

Basically, societal value created is captured by the innovating firms, consumers, communities and other firms-competitors and non-competitors (Mansfield et al., 1977). Value creation often entails the development of strategic resources while value appropriation entails the extraction of value that is embedded in resources. Whereas value creation influences the potential magnitude of the advantage, value appropriation influences the amount of the advantage the firm is able to capture and the length of time the advantage persists. Nevertheless there is a trade-offs in the strategic emphasis by firms between developing customer-value creation and value appropriation capabilities. Various organizational resources and capabilities such as technological (R&D), financial, physical, legal, human, organizational, informational, and relational capabilities influence value creation and value appropriation (Mizik et al., 2003). Di Gregorio (2013) argued that value is not created by resources, but by the actions of individuals and organizations in factor markets, internalized transactions, and product markets (dynamic capabilities). However, resources plays key role because they are the result of value creation processes and they are exploited in value appropriation processes. Di Gregorio (2013) identifies four elements of value appropriation that apply to both inter- and intra-organizational contexts to include: market-based bargaining power, relation-based power, isolating mechanisms, and opportunity-based action.

CREATED SHARED VALUE IN THE EXTRACTIVE INDUSTRIES: FROM LOCAL CONTENT TO CREATED SHARED VALUE

According to Porter (2014), the extractives sector represents a significant opportunity for impact on society given its unique characteristics which include: $3.5 trillion in annual revenues (about 5% of global GDP as at 2012); long time horizon for operations; multiple points of interaction with local communities; and often located in remote areas with major societal needs and poor infrastructure, generate employment, revenues for the government and with significant impact on procurement and the gross domestic product (GDP). The economic value created by extractive companies can transform the lives of millions living in resource-rich, cash-poor countries. The extractives sectors are a critical source for economic and social development in many of these countries. But most developing countries have failed to fully capitalize on the societal opportunities created by oil and gas or mining companies. Instead there are increasing conflicts, agitations and militancy in this sector and countries like the Niger Delta region of Nigeria and the platinum mines in South Africa. Consequently, 23 out of the 25 nations that depend most heavily on minerals and fuels are poor with low Human Development Index (HDI) and GDP.

The local content, "non-technical" risk management and current CSR approach used by the extractive industries have largely limited the actualization of this objective. Therefore, shared value is advocated as a new way to address the underlying root causes of community concerns and unlock economic opportunities for companies in the extractive sector including the oil and gas industry (Hidalgo, Peterson, Sith & Foley, 2014; Organization for Economic Co-operation and Development-OECD, 2016; Swartout, 2016). The concept of shared value is becoming a linchpin of the modern mining and extractive sectors (Crosbey et al., 2016). Given advances and changes in technology, it is predicted that the mining of the future will involve decreased local equipment-related procurement resulting in drop in benefits derived from local procurement and employment. The consequence is of critical concerns to firms, host communities and countries like Nigeria which depend and earn a greater part of their revenues from the sector. Therefore, firms and countries are expected to focus on other ways in which mining can contribute to the host economy and communities. Table 5 indicates the shared valued opportunities in the extractive industries.

Outside the realms of procurement and employment, there are four other avenues through which shared value can be created (Cosbey et al., 2016). These include:

- **Downstream (Forward) Linkages:** Relate to the beneficiation of extracted commodities through refining, smelting and further downstream processing of the commodity before reaching the final consumer(s).
- **Horizontal (Lateral) Linkages:** Relate to the development of new non-mining-related industries adapting the capabilities developed to serve the mining-related value chain.
- **Knowledge (Technological) Linkages:** Relate to the transfer of knowledge and technological know- how to state-owned companies, the employees of the mine and to the labour force involved in the mine's value chain.
- **Spatial (Infrastructure) Linkages:** Relate to the benefits associated with the infrastructure developed for an extractive-industry project (such as railways) profiting other actors in the economy.

Table 5. Shared values opportunities in extractives and mining industries

Re-Conceiving Products and Market	Re-Defining Productivity in the Value Chains	Creating Enabling Local Environment
Build local markets for intermediate products created by extractive activity (e.g., water, electricity, transport, housing)	Improve local workforce capabilities Develop local suppliers Improve the health of employees Improve utilization of water, energy and other resources in operations Increase local emergency response capabilities	Develop the local cluster supporting the extractives sector Invest in shared local infrastructure and logistics networks Partner with other local clusters and government in building community infrastructure Play an active role in broad-based regional economic and community development

Source: Porter (2014)

There might be revision to the fiscal element of shared value, adoption of more progressive fiscal regimes, changes to the fundamental relationship between investor and host governments and evolution of a more collaboration and commitment to defined roles for government, extractive industries and civil societies. National or host governments can help companies create shared value by creating enabling policies and regulations as well as show collaboration by acting as knowledge broker, serving as convener of interested stakeholders, acting as operating partner for shared value strategies and incentivizing shared value investments. On the other hand companies can take a long-term view toward solving societal issues to benefit the business; they should invest in improving business unit operations' knowledge of societal issues and vice-versa, measure societal outcomes and their impact on the business, and work with other multinational companies in the extractive sectors, NGOs, and governments. The five actionable steps specified in the OECD (2016) framework on collaborative strategies for in-country shared value creation of extractive projects and the roles of government, extractive industries and civil societies are shown in Table 6.

CSV Opportunities and Benefits in Developing Countries

Despite the criticisms, CSV has been applauded for the strengths in appealing to practitioners and scholars, elevating social goals to a strategic level, defining a role for government in responsible behaviour and propagating the idea of "conscious and caring capitalism" (Crane, Palazzo, Spence & Matten, 2014). Moreover, there is growing consensus that through CSV firms can better respond to the societal, environmental and market needs, support business activities, and develop innovative capacity. Moczadlo

Table 6. Actionable steps and roles of government, extractive industries and civil societies for in-country shared value creation

Actionable Steps	Roles of Government, Extractive Industries and Civil Societies			
	Government	Extractive Industries	Government & Extractive Industries	Government, Extractive Industries & Civil Societies
1.Adopt a comprehensive long-term vision and implementation strategy to build competitive and diversified economies and create in-country shared value out of resources	Articulate vision, coordination; limit rent seeking opportunities; enhance economic competiveness; transparent reporting; counter macro-economic policies	Take long-term approach, engage with relevant stakeholders; understand local dynamics and power structures in resource-bearing communities; share best practices developed		Build inclusive fora for continuous dialogue; forecast the necessary infrastructure and capacity to achieve extractive stage; identify opportunities to which business activities can make a significant positive contribution
2.Build an empirical basis to inform decision making through an inclusive participatory process	Serve as conveners and identify the stakeholders; Identify trade-offs and associated costs/benefits; create the conditions for proactive interventions and reduce conflicts recognize areas of value creation	Provide information on an individual basis (to avoid any anti-competitive issues) to governments on future demand		Assess the extractives sector's collective current and future needs; map out potential economic opportunities and potential negative impacts and constraints of project; Identify barriers to entry for production of goods/
3.Unlock opportunities for in-country shared value creation: local workforce and supplier development; shared infrastructure (power, water and transport)				

continued on following page

Table 6. Continued

Actionable Steps	Roles of Government, Extractive Industries and Civil Societies			
	Government	Extractive Industries	Government & Extractive Industries	Government, Extractive Industries & Civil Societies
3A. Shared Power	Take a long-term perspective of potential synergies, affordability and willingness to pay design appropriate power pricing mechanisms consider other partners in development of power generation capacity; engage in regional and sub-regional policy co-ordination for infrastructure development and power sharing	Provide forecasts regarding anticipated demand for power and sourcing of power; implement energy efficient operations; develop electricity self-supply plans that align with government's plans	Undertake early discussions regarding power infrastructure needs, synergies, efficiencies and other opportunities for shared value creation with respect to power generation and distribution; articulate government and company responsibilities and liabilities for any project undertaken; consider power usage and distribution	
3B.Shared value for water	Adopt an integrated approach to water resource management; have a well-designed, adjustable and transparent plans for allocating water resources among competing uses; ensure policy coherence and adequate institutional framework for used water	Engage with local communities and water users to understand water-related issues and risks and offer solution; collaborate with other extractives; collaborate with other extractives companies for water management and allocation	Devise mutually beneficial arrangements; share knowledge, information and expertise	
3C.Shared use for transport infrastructure	Provide a clear and effective regulatory framework for multi-purpose and multi-user infrastructure; avoid exclusive access or monopoly pricing; effective coordination and policy encouraging investment in transport infrastructure	Collaborate with other extractive companies from the same basin to determine the potential for shared value by developing shared transport infrastructure	Devise mutually beneficial arrangements concerning transport infrastructure	
4.Support and contribute to innovation leading to new products and services	Identify changing trends in global consumption and production patterns; consider trade-offs associated with technological innovation; support R&D efforts to identify, adapt, and transfer technology	Invest in specialized technologies that reduce environmental impact; increase use of renewable energy; Contribute to improving the innovative capacity of subsidiaries and subcontractors and finding solutions to challenges shared by extractive industries	Engage in co-operation based on project life cycle analysis, covering the entire value chain and offering the opportunity to build on best practices of several sectors	
5.Establish effective and transparent monitoring and evaluation systems and regularly review the collaborative strategy		Integrate the standardized methodology and reporting procedures into internal local monitoring and evaluation system; Provide detailed reporting to better measure and manage company activities		Build on existing structures e.g. EITI, MSG develop governance mechanisms to ensure effective and transparent monitoring and evaluation; evaluate impact, local industry participation, efficient use of limited resources and creation of value for all stakeholders; re-evaluate measurements from time-to-time communicate results to stakeholders

Source: Adapted from OECD (2016)

(2015) argued that Porter and Kramer's CSV bring the business world closer to society's issues as it focuses on unmet needs and under-served markets or Blue Ocean Strategy (Kim &Mauborgne, 2005) and the business model innovation which is a key factor in competitiveness (Scott-Kemmis, 2012). In fact, the shared value has already made some companies like WEG Corporation in Brazil and HP to be industry leaders, improved companies' value chains as well as strengthened local economies in companies such as Intel, Nestle, Unilever and Nepresso, and led to long-term company's profitability, competitive advantage and sustainability like the case of Coca Cola Company.

There are numerous examples of multinational organizations that are either already implementing and investing in CSV or making efforts to implement CSV as part of their business strategies such as: Coca-Cola, Nestlé, Nepresso, Unilever, Intel, Nutreco, McDonald's, IBM, Cisco, Dow, Intel, Becton Dickinson (BD), Novartis, Wal-Mart, Inter-American Development bank, General Motor (GM), General Electric (GE), Google, Johnson and Johnson, InterContinental Hotels Group (IHG) and social entrepreneurs like Gramen Bank in Bangladesh among others (Porter & Kramer, 2011; Porter et al. 2012; World Bank, 2013).

A typical example of CSV is the corporate Water Stewardship Programme particularly the Replenish Africa Initiative (RAIN) water for schools created by Coca-Cola Company in 2009 but presently in 37 African countries. The programme has the intention to provide sustainable and safe water access to 6 million people across Africa by the end of 2020.Similarly, the WASH programme, particularly the RAIN Water for Schools, not only creates social value and but also indirectly promotes business value and contributes to virtuous cycles of creating value for local communities (Mitler, Rostorfer & Ledbetter, 2015). The Coca Cola Company also launched a two-month Coletivo Retail training programme for Brazilian low-income (including youth and students) in 2009 to enable retailers gain hands-on experience, placement and enhance their performance. By 2015, about 25,000 youths have graduated with over 10% of Coletivo graduates setting up their own retail stores with micro-credit support as well as the Coletivo Retail community sales growing on an annual average of 9.5% (Coca-Cola Supports, 2015). Moreover, the Coca Cola Company's 5by20 Initiatives aim to improve the economic empowerment of five million women entrepreneurs within the company's global value chain by 2020 through a combination of core business operations, cross-sector partnership and strategic social investment mostly in developing countries. The Coca-Cola Company began working toward its 5by20 commitment in Brazil, India, the Philippines, and South Africa in 2010. Over, 300,000 women have participated in 5by20 initiatives in 12 countries (Brazil, China, Costa Rica, Egypt, Haiti, India, Kenya, Mexico, Nigeria, Philippines, South Africa, and Thailand) as at 2013. The company expects 5by20 initiatives to reach 1.5 million women in 20 to 30 countries by 2015 and 5 million women in 100 countries by 2020. The Coca Cola's 5by 20 initiatives include: Coletivo Recycling and Artesians in Brazil, Project Nurture in Kenya and Uganda, the STAR Programme in the Philippines, and Kwanza's Micro Distribution Center Model in Tanzania (Jenkins, Valikai & Baptista, 2013).

The CSV of Nestle for joint value optimization with society encompasses three areas of water, rural development and nutrition. Nestlé aligned corporate vision with a social purpose and set enterprise-wide shared value goals to guide business planning. For instance, Nestlé trains and assists smallholder farmers to foster rural development while ensuring a reliable supply of high quality raw materials. Nepresso's collaboration focuses on three commitments: Coffee, Capsules and Carbon Footprint as well as creating shared value for society. The areas where value was created and shared in McDonald were: employee welfare, waste, climate/energy, animal welfare, water, raw materials and community impact. Unilever's poverty eradication, women empowerment, education of rural dwellers and hand-washing campaigns have recorded a huge success in bringing profitable micro-enterprise opportunities for rural women, reducing diseases and saving many lives of children in Asia and Africa (Kreckova, 2015). Intel tied a portion of incentive compensation to performance on social and environmental priorities.

BHP Billiton invested $50M in northern Chile to create a cluster of world-class mining suppliers. BHP created the "World Class Supplier Program" in Chile which engaged local suppliers to develop innovative solutions to manage various areas of BHP Billiton's operations such as water, energy, human capital, maintenance, air quality, acid mist control, and leaching. The goal of the initiative was for Chile to have at least 250 world-class suppliers that can export their services to mining projects around the world by 2020.The 36 suppliers involved employ 5,000 people, and BHP Billiton has achieved $121m in net present value of cost savings as at 2012 (Porter, 2014) and generated combined sales of $400 million. The social and economic benefits for BHP Billiton include: creation of world-class suppliers for the mining sector and high-quality employment, and reduced cost of inputs, goods, and services. Rio Tinto's Diavik Diamond Mine in Northern Canada worked with communities, contractors, local governments and education institutions to develop a local workforce and supplier base which enables it to hire 62% of its employees, and sources 71% of goods and services locally, saving transportation costs (Porter, 2014). For SNC-Lavalin with interest in mining and metallurgy, oil and gas, infrastructure and environment and power, the Local Resource Development Initiative ™ (LRDI) helps to maximize local benefits and create shared value with communities as the LRDI aligns project objectives with community objectives whenever possible, promotes sustainability opportunities, reduces project costs and generates values for farmers, communities and operating company in many countries of Africa, Latin America and Asia.

Criticisms of Porter and Kramer's CSV

Despite the many benefits and opportunities acclaim to CSV, there are also many critics of Porter and Kramer's CSV (such as Crane, Palazzo, Spence & Matten, 2014; Mohammed, 2013; Denning, 2011 & 2012; Hartman & Werhane, 2013; Wilburn & Wilburn, 2014; Rocchi & Fererro, 2014; Escudero, 2013 and others) who argued that CSV is not new or original; CSV ignores the tensions inherent to responsible business activity, naïve about business compliance and it is based on a shallow conception of the corporation's role in society (Crane et al., 2014). CSV is "undercooked", ignores tensions and differences between societal and economic goals, lacks specific framework upon which shared value creation can be measured (Crane et al., 2014; Mohammed, 2013), can't fix capitalism (Denning, 2011, 2012), incomplete mental model (Hartman & Werhane, 2013), misunderstood concept (Wilburn & Wilburn, 2014), incomplete and process-orientation ignoring the people in the work process (Rocchi & Fererro, 2014), akin to strategic CSR and not a new approach (Escudero, 2013). It has also been argued that the CSV is not different from Elkington's (1998) that focused on the triple-bottom line of economic, environmental and social goals. Again, the main idea is not so different from strategic CSR concept earlier defined by Porter and Kramer in 2006 (Neves, 2013). Nevertheless, Drucker (1984) has argued that the proper "social responsibility" of business is to tame the dragon, that is, to turn a social problem into economic opportunity and economic benefit". Wheeler, Colbert & Freeman2003 (2003) have also defended that "in certain circumstances the creation of communities and social networks or value-based networks is a pre-requisite to economic pay-off'. The idea that businesses should address new markets based on social issues, being profitable had been presented by Prahalad and Hart (2002) arguing that "low-income markets present a prodigious opportunity for the world`s wealthiest companies to seek their fortunes and bring prosperity to the aspiring poor".

Table 7. Examples of created shared value social and economic benefits in developing countries

S/no	Company/Organization	Country	Initiatives	Social Benefits	Economic/Business Benefits
1	Coca Cola	37African countries including South Africa	Corporate water stewardship and Replenish Africa Initiative (RAIN) water for schools	-Improvements across a wide range of capabilities, both directly and indirectly -Increase in the value of natural capital	Every US$1 invested would yield at least US$2 in benefits, and in some locations it could be over US$11 in benefits for every US$1 invested
		Brazil	A two-month Coletivo Retail training programme for Brazilian low-income (including youth and students employment) in 2009	- 30% of the young people trained immediately land their first job with Coca-Cola or one of its partners - 10% set up their own business with micro-credit support from the company	- Increased sales of Coca-Cola products - Higher penetration of consumers among the emerging lower middle class segment - Better retailer performance and a stronger Coca-Cola brand connection
2	Chevron	Nigeria	Niger Delta Partnership Initiative (NDPI) and Partnership Initiative in the Niger Delta in 9 oil producing in the Niger Delta region and creation of addition value chains	Development of economic opportunities outside of Chevron's direct oil and gas supply chains	Reduction in business disruptions due to greater economic opportunities outside of oil and gas; potential reductions in supply chain costs
			Chevron's General Memorandum of Understanding (GMOU) approach in the Niger Delta for building local governance and decision-making capabilities through delivering value for the business via reduced risk and a stronger operating environment	- Community-led disruptions to Chevron operations dropped from 81 in 1998 to 11 in 2011 to zero in 2012 - Create a platform for communities to debate, discuss, and agree on their priorities	- Create enabling environment for the company to do its business -Significant cost saving in company's operations - Saving of tens of millions of dollars in lost revenues in vandalism and theft
3	BHP Billiton	Chile	Creation of at least 250 world-class suppliers that can export their services to mining projects around the world by 2020	Creation of world-class suppliers for the mining sector and high-quality employment	Reduced cost of inputs, goods, and services
4	AngloGold Ashanti	Ghana	Addresses health problems (endemic malaria) by implementing an integrated control programme involving multiple community-level interventions	Decrease in disease incidence by over 72% in the first two years of the programme	Improved employee productivity, lowered treatment costs, with the number of person-shifts lost per month falling from 7,500 to around 90 in 2012 and declining treatment costs resulting in cost savings to the company of around $600,000 per year by 2013
5	Anglo American	South Africa	Water Reclamation Plant for treatment of water for drinking and irrigation water by the local municipality in the Malahleni and Mpumalanga provinces	Access to potable water in local community, generating 25-30 million liters per day or 12% of the water requirement	Over 60% offset of treatment costs from revenues in water sold to BHP Billiton and local community, reduction in the cost of responsible environmental management and compliance with regulation
6	Banka BioLoo	India	Bio-toilet system to dispose human waste in eco-friendly manner	Improved hygienic sanitation, treated, recycle human wastes and bio-toilet for millions of people	Increased employment opportunity, growing revenues in multi-fields
7	Capital Diamond Star Group with Action Aid	Myanmar	Provide farmers with necessary training, technical and financial skills for optimal productivity, quality livelihood and increased bottom line.	Improved livelihoods through empowerment of farmers, sustainable agriculture and better access to finance and to markets for rural communities	More productive, better quality and more reliable supplier base; stronger, more loyal and better educated customer base

Hartman and Werbane (2013) see Porter and Kramer's CSV as an incomplete mental model with imprecise conception of "profit," overemphasis on the novelty of their theory, and broadly negative description of prior attempts to achieve social progress through private enterprise. They argue that there was no explanation on the calibration of shared value from profits. Besides, some have argued that Porter and Kramer were not the first and novel to propose alternative to the single-minded pursuits of shareholders' gain, and that "shared value" is just one of the many viable means to reconstruct a corporate worldview to tackle new-world social, environmental and economic problems. Moreover, many profitable companies have been successful in addressing social problems through profitable business ventures without the need of the shared value approach. Again, the CSV omits the revision of companies' core mission to reflect the pursuit, not of "profit per se," but "profits involving social purpose". Beschorner (2013) argued that Porter and Kramer's CSV is "neither so radical nor such a departure from standard management thinking" and their ultimate reliance on economic arguments is too normatively thin to reconnect businesses with society. He suggested that prospects for a genuine reinvention of capitalism lie elsewhere. There is also criticism that ethics and integrity is left out of the CSV as well as its measurement. Companies that are most advanced in pursuing shared value lack the data they need to optimize its results. Besides, some of the companies that claim to implement CSV are not doing the right thing (Brown & Knudsen, 2013).

Challenges and Limitations of CSV

Cane et al. (2014) concluded that the short comings of CVS take us further from the solution to a challenge that we are already struggling to address. Although shared value has gained momentum, it is still largely experimental and short-term. Only a few companies particularly multinational companies like Coca-Cola, Novo Nordisk, Nestlé, Intel, and InterContinental Hotels Group among others have enshrined the shared value into their corporate objective and core business strategy due to CSR fatigue. Most companies around the world remain unaware of shared value improvement opportunities and are ill-prepared to capitalize on them when they materialize thereby limiting the company's bottom line and short- changing society of the much needed innovation to solve social problems (Porter et al., 2012). Brown and Knudsen (2013) have argued that failure to appropriately manage shared value could result in wasted resources, unsustainable projects, and in the worst cases, marred corporate reputations thereby resulting in negative social and environmental consequences. This could be as a result of companies' failure to (1) carry through responsible practice in its implementation, (2) change their overall business model to address a social or environmental problem, and (3) discuss how they should manage the complexities and trade-offs required to address social issues.

Again, studies from various sectors (food, beverages, agriculture, pharmaceutical, health care, financial services, extractives, and natural resources) advocated that firms can enhance their competitiveness by embracing the CSV concept in their business strategy (Hills et al., 2012). However, the results are mainly based on successful individual cases from large Multinational corporations and the nature of the relationships between CSV and firm competitiveness in those studies is still unclear and has not been verified empirically. Also, examples and number of local listed companies as well as small and medium scale enterprises embedding CSV in their core business or moving beyond traditional CSR to the shared value in their CSR are limited. Haxby, Compela and Weperen (2014) argued that CSV can be complicated because of the diverse interests of each stakeholder and attempts to optimize value for one stakeholder can have a negative effect for others.

It is not easy to measure social activities and their impacts on a company and the economy. There are also several problems in finding reasonable and significant key performance indicators (KPIs) or metrics to measure shared value of the social and business outputs, outcomes and impacts (Giddens, 2011). In fact, the lack of understanding of the interdependency between social and business results by companies limit the opportunities for innovation, growth and social impact (Porter et al., 2012). Despite lot of suggested frameworks and approaches to measure shared value including employee engagement, stakeholder feedback, scalability, growth opportunities, risk mitigation, public policy impact, and brand and reputation impact, there is no holistic framework or universal tool on how to measure value created through CSR. Besides decision making on CSR implementation still remains subjective and one-sided in most cases (Jonikas, 2014). Again, Porter et al. (2012) argued that the framework to link social progress directly to business success and vice versa is still missing Moreover, the relationship between social welfare and company profitability is complex (Lin et al., 2009). The analysis of sustainability results is complicated "due to the wide range of reporting practices for environmental, social and corporate governance risks/opportunities and also due to the difficulty of verifying the accuracy of the information provided by companies" (Székely & Knirsch, 2005). Hidalgo et al. (2014) summarized four interrelated and entrenched challenges that inhibit creation of shared value to include: inadequate organizational structure and behavior or culture, incomplete measurement costs and benefits, low motivation for collaboration and lack of alignment with government.

CSV AND SUSTAINABLE, INCLUSIVE DEVELOPMENT OF DEVELOPING COUNTRIES

The Brundtland Report of the World Commission for Environment and Development (1987) defines sustainable development as development that meets the needs of the present generation without compromising the ability of the future generations to meet their needs. In 2015, the world leaders agreed that the realization of the sustainable development goals (SDGs) by 2030 needs governments' partnership with businesses and other stakeholders. A recent survey by Fleishman Hillard and the U.S. Chamber of Commerce Foundation in May, 2015 identified top 5 SDGs as important to business in the post 2015 to include: build resilient infrastructure (67%), sustain economic growth (65%), achieve gender equality (60%), ensure quality education (52%) and strengthen global partnership (44%). The 'My world 2015' survey by the United Nations put the three top concerns the world over to include: good education, better health care and better job opportunities. The CSV tends to be moving corporations towards the direction of achieving these goals through shared value approach which is premised on the simultaneous realization of economic, social and societal progress. Through the inclusive business strategy, the CSV helps to integrate poor and low income communities into the leading companies' value chains in order to create new opportunities for poor people at the bottom of the pyramid, increase their incomes, improve the living standards and create a competitive value chain and long term economic value for the companies.

At its heart, the notion of shared value pertains to the sustainable development of the host community and countries. For instance, the OECD (2016) framework for collaborative Strategies for in-country shared value creation in the extractive sector is a tool for forging a public-private alliance which can be used to advance the sustainable development agenda of 2030 adopted by the United Nations in 2015. Specifically, the OECD framework supports the achievement of SDGs 8 (promote inclusive and sustainable economic growth, employment and decent work for all), 9 (build resilient infrastructure, promote sustainable industrialization and foster innovation), 6 (ensure access to water and sanitation for all) and 7 (ensure access to affordable, reliable, sustainable and modern energy for all). According to Cosbey et al. (2016), the shared-value paradigm, by promising to deliver benefits to host communities, regions and countries, has become increasingly critical for mining companies in securing their social license to operate. The delicate balance inherent in the shared-value paradigm is especially relevant for developing countries and other states (most of which are resource-driven countries) where poverty eradication, social development and environmental protection are urgent development challenges.

Due to the expectations that the application of the shared-value paradigm in the mining and extractive sector would bring substantial developmental benefits to large populations and the link to sustainable development, it has been endorsed to become the mainstay of most major mining policy frameworks such as: the Africa Mining Vision (African Union, 2009), the Mining Policy Framework (Intergovernmental Forum (IGF) on Mining, Minerals, Metals and Sustainable Development (2012), and the OECD Framework on Public-Private Collaboration for in-Country Shared Value Creation from Extractive Projects (OECD, 2016).The International Council for Mining and Metals (ICMM) also reference the shared-value concept in their good practice guidance (ICMM, 2015).Leading civil society organizations working in the area of mining and sustainable development like Columbia Center on Sustainable Investment (CCSI), 2015; International Institute for Environment and Development (IIED); International Institute for Sustainable Development (IISD), 2014; and Natural Resource Governance Institute (NRGI), 2015 have fully subscribed to shared value. Both the developed and developing countries are benefiting and enjoying from the shared value concept as more and more corporations are keying into the social change. While the focus in developed markets is less on poverty but more on education, income inequalities, health and wellness, environment and sustainability, the CSV focus by corporations in developing markets is building capacity and financing, empowerment and entrepreneurship, expansion of the value chain and raising the standard of living in the communities of operations.

Shared value approach has the potentials to foster sustainable development of developing countries as CSV concept is embraced and promoted not only by the few multinationals but all companies. For instance, the activities of Novartis to provide the locals in remote villages with health services and train some of them to be health educators in India, Vietnam, Kenya and Indonesia resulted in over 10 million receiving health education and 750,000 direct health services. The '+' projects by Phillips a multi-sector partnership with governments, NGOs and consumers in Southeast Asia reached over 50 million people in Indonesia, Thailand and Singapore, generating 28,000 social media conversations. The goal was to increase Philips' bottom line and simultaneously have positive social impact. Phillips sourced ideas from local consumers to provide insights that enabled the company to accelerate innovation and ultimately improve the health and well-being of consumers. Vodafone partnered with a Kenyan telecoms firm, Sarifoam and created a new market by launching M-Pesa in Kenya in 2007.Vodafone's goal was to support financial inclusion in Kenya through a money transfer solution with a simple key message, "Send Money Home", which enabled customers to send money directly between each other using mobile technology. By 2015, M-Pesa is now available in many countries including India, Egypt, Tanzania, South Africa, Democratic Republic of Congo, Lesotho, Mozambique, Romania and Albania with over 19.9 million active customers who used M-Pesa with over 3.4 billion transactions processed yearly.

Following the challenges of a quadruple burden of disease, an undersupply of doctors and an egalitarian healthcare system presented a significant challenge to the healthcare industry in South Africa, Discovery Insurance Company developed Vitality, a behaviour based wellness solution that incentivized healthier behavior by giving customers access to wellness partners such as gyms, empowering them with healthcare knowledge and tools, and offering financial incentives that increased as members engaged with the Vitality programme. The increased health and fitness levels, lowered the frequency and cost of hospitalization and reduced the disease burden of customers improve the financial incentives and rewards that by 2015, the company currently serves over 5.1 million clients across South Africa, the United Kingdom, the United States, China, Singapore, Australia and Hong Kong. Discovery is globally acknowledged as the pioneer of shared value insurance. The shared value presents an open window of opportunities and benefits not only for economic prosperity of business but also the sustainable development of developing economies. Therefore a high level corporate commitment to the shared value concept, and ingenuity of the private sector and business leaders in forming alliances would lead to the actualization of the United Nation's sustainable development goals (UN SDGs) by eradicating poverty in all its forms by 2030.

SOLUTIONS AND RECOMMENDATIONS

In an era of increasingly stakeholders' knowledgeable demands and expectations amidst the increasing global challenges, integrating economic and social goals will demonstrate corporation's real concerns and ability to achieve the "win-wins" of the shared value model, long-term sustainability, competitive advantage and economic prosperity. In order to give concrete meaning to the concept of CSV in developing economies, the companies must change the philanthropic way that CSR is presently conceptualized and organized because of its limitations in helping them to achieve competitive advantages and adequately address societal problems. Based on the shared value approach, companies in developing countries should restructure and prioritize CSR to be part of their organizational culture, value and core business strategy that emphasizes sustainability by redefining corporate leadership and integrating economic and social goals in their business pursuits in addressing societal problems. The integration makes CSR a core element of strategy, structure and process, eliminates distinct CSR functions in the organization and makes CSR a mutual responsibility across the firm - from top down and thereby increasing its credibility and implementation.

However, achieving shared value will require a radical and collective rethinking of management practice by all parties. There must be strong commitment at the executive, top management level and employees; Leading managers of global players as well as of small and medium companies in developing countries must discuss and take CSR very seriously by going beyond "green washing" or "window dressing". They must begin to embrace and transmit the CSV vision and ideology among all employees of their organizations through re-conceiving new products and services in new markets, improving productivity and developing clusters. Therefore, companies would need to incorporate shared value thinking into the operations of employees at all levels of their businesses to really transform capitalism and bring about inclusive and sustainable development. The realization of the SDGs in 2030 requires that companies in developing countries have a major mindset change towards the adoption of the CSV agenda. This will involve the companies working inside out and embracing top down leadership, commitment and strategy as well as a bottom up overhauling of the operating models to reflect total commitment; CSV takes time, energy, tenacity and patience to embed and thus the process requires change managers and skilled leaders rather than programme managers (Bockstette & Stamp, 2011; AT Kearney, 2015). In fact, achieving a successful, sustainable and scalable shared value requires significant changes in the way that corporations do business. Therefore, businesses in developing countries must change their business models and current CSR philosophy to include shared value creation and business value sustainability.

Government and regulators in developing countries should recognize their roles in helping businesses to create shared value by focusing on measuring environmental performance and introducing standards, phase-in periods and support for technology that would promote innovation, improve the environment and increase competitiveness of business simultaneously. They would need to limit the pursuit of exploitative, unfair or deceptive practices in which companies benefit at the expense of society. Governments can help companies create shared value by: creating enabling policies and regulations, showing collaboration by acting as knowledge broker, serving as convener of interested stakeholders, acting as operating partner for shared value strategies and incentivizing shared value investments. Regulatory authorities like the National Hydrocarbon Agency (NHA) in Columbia must promote shared value creation through its regulatory framework. Although local content presents one of the clearest opportunities to create shared value, governments in developing countries particularly those with rich minerals and extractive industries must collaborate with companies to access opportunities to deliver real value for business and society across different areas of investments based on shared value approach.

On the other hand, companies must take a long-term view toward solving societal issues that would benefit the business by investing in improved business unit operations' knowledge of societal issues. They should measure societal outcomes and their impact on the business, and work with other multinational companies, NGOs and governments to create shared value. They must also take concrete actions to shift the current dynamic relationships between the corporations and government from one that views for instance extractive companies as contractors who pay for the privilege of carrying out extraction to one that sees these companies as development partners who could help solve societal issues of concern to government and create shared values through direct engagement with various levels of governments and communities, capacity building and indirect support for independent, third-party efforts. Faculties and business schools would also need to broaden their curricula and teaching to include: efficient use and stewardship of all forms of resources, human and societal needs and how to serve non-traditional customer groups; because these would define the next-generation thinking on value chains.

CONCLUSION

The chapter examines CSV and the inclusive, sustainable development of developing countries The CSV is a (r)evolutionary strategic management thinking meant to enhance the companies' competitiveness while simultaneously advancing their economic and social conditions in the society they operate. It challenges the constrained corporate mindset of lip-service philanthropic CSR activities of business over half a century to making it a major solver of society's problems in a much beneficial and profitable ways through creation of shared values. Created shared value tasks companies in developing countries to go beyond CSR to addressing social and society's issues in addition to their pursuit of profits by incorporating social and societal values into their economic agenda. The shared values created by these companies in developing countries would give rise to long-term corporate profitability, competitiveness and sustainable development of host communities and countries. Interestingly, evidence abound of companies at least of global multinational and transnational companies in developed and developing countries, which have already keyed into the CSV enjoying immense profits, sales growth and sustainable competitive advantages through integration of social and economic goal while also addressing societal needs. Therefore, companies including extractive and mining industries in developing countries must begin to take a long-term approach to social investments and prosperity of company, host communities or countries by embracing the pillars of shared value of re-conceiving new products and services, identifying new market opportunities and enabling clusters development. It has been demonstrated that the created shared value has the potentials to foster unparalleled economic growth, prosperity and sustainable development in countries when companies start to think a new and look at decisions and opportunities through the lens of shared value.

Although, the created shared value approach is being embraced and applied by most global multinational corporations, there is no known study in Nigeria. Therefore a study of the current CSR practices is recommended on whether the shared value concept is already being practiced by indigenous companies in Nigeria, the influencing factors and challenges of creating shared value in turbulent environments.

REFERENCES

Afrin, S. (2013). Traditional vs strategic corporate social responsibility: In pursuit of supporting sustainable development. *Journal of Economics and Sustainable Development*, *4*(20), 153–157.

Altman, D., & Berman, J. (2011). The single bottom line. *Dalberg Global Development Advisor*, 1-13.

Amaeshi, K., Adi, B., Ogbechie, C., & Amao, O. (2006). *Corporate social responsibility in Nigeria: Western mimicry or indigenous practices?*. Research Paper Series, International Centre for Corporate Social Responsibility, Nottingham University.

Aspelund, A., Fjell, L., & Rødland, S. E. (2015). *Doing good and doing well - On the relationship between Internationalization and Social Responsibility.* Paper presented at the 18th McGill International Entrepreneurship Conference, Al-Ain, UAE.

Barney, J. B. (2001). Resource-based theories of competitive advantage: A ten-year retrospective on the resource-based view. *Journal of Management*, *27*(6), 643–650. doi:10.1177/014920630102700602

Bertini, M., & Gourville, J. T. (2012). Pricing to create shared value: Rethinking the way prices are set can expand the pie for everyone. *Harvard Business Review*, *90*(6), 96–104.

Beschorner, T. (2013). Creating shared value: The one-trick pony approach. *Business Ethics Journal Review*, *1*(17), 106–112. doi:10.12747/bejr2013.01.17

Bhattacharya, C. B., Sen, S., & Korschun, D. (2008). Using corporate social responsibility to win the war for talent. *MIT Sloan Management Review*, *49*(2), 37–44.

Bisgaard, T. (2009). *Corporate social innovation, companies' participation in solving global challenges*. Retrieved July 2010, from http://samfundsansvar.dk/file/319040/csi_corporate_social_innovation_juli_2010.pdf

Bockstette, V. (2011, Nov. 16). Create shared value with a trampoline approach. *Harvard Business Review Blog Network.*

Bockstette, V., Pfitzer, M., Smith, D., Bhavaraju, N., Priestley, C., & Bhatt, A. (2014). *Banking on shared value: How banks profit by rethinking their business.* Retrieved from http://www.fsg.org/publications/banking-shared-value

Bockstette, V., & Stamp, M. (2011). *Creating shared value: A how-to guide for the new corporate (r)evolution.* Retrieved from http://www.fsg.org/publications/creating-shared-value-how-guide-new-corporate-revolution

Bosch-Badia, M. T., Montllor-Serrats, J., & Tarrazon, M. A. (2013). Corporate social responsibility from Friedman to Porter and Kramer. *Theoretical Economic Letters*, *3*(3), 11–15. doi:10.4236/tel.2013.33A003

Brown, D., & Knudsen, J. S. (2013). *Generating value for investors and society*. The Conference Board.

Browne, J., & Nuttall, R. (2013). Beyond corporate social responsibility: Integrated external engagement. McKinsey & Company.

Camilleri, M. A. (2012). *Creating shared value through strategic CSR in tourism* (Doctoral dissertation). University of Edinburgh, UK.

Carroll, A. B. (1999). Corporate social responsibility evolution of a definitional construct. *Business & Society*, *38*(3), 268–295. doi:10.1177/000765039903800303

Carroll, A. B., & Shabana, K. M. (2010). The business case for corporate social responsibility: A review of concepts, research and practice. *International Journal of Management Reviews*, *12*(1), 85–105. doi:10.1111/j.1468-2370.2009.00275.x

Chen, S., & Bouvain, K. (2009). Is corporate responsibility converging? A comparison of corporate social responsibility reporting in the USA, UK, Australia and Germany. *Journal of Business Ethics*, *87*(1), 299–317. doi:10.1007/s10551-008-9794-0

Christmann, P., & Taylor, G. (2006). Firm self-regulation through international certifiable standards: Determinants of symbolic versus substantive implementation. *Journal of International Business Studies*, *37*(6), 863–878. doi:10.1057/palgrave.jibs.8400231

Coca-Cola. (2015). *Coca-Cola supports retail capacity and economic development in Brazil.* Retrieved from https://sharedvalue.org/examples/coletivo-retail-program-supporting-retail-capacity-and-economic-development-brazil

Cosbey, A., Mann, H., Maennling, N., Toledano, P., Geipel, J., & Brauch, M. D. (2016). *Mining a Mirage? Reassessing the shared-value paradigm in light of the technological advances in the mining sector.* International Institute for Sustainable Development.

Crane, A., Palazzo, G., Spence, L. J., & Matten, D. (2014). Contesting the value of creating shared value. *California Management Review*, *56*(2), 130–153. doi:10.1525/cmr.2014.56.2.130

Davenport, E. (2011). *The next catalyst for change: How corporate shared value is reshaping capitalism. CMC Senior Theses. Paper 111.* Claremont College.

Delgado, M., Porter, M. E., & Stern, S. (2010). Clusters and entrepreneurship. *Journal of Economic Geography*, *10*(4), 495–518. doi:10.1093/jeg/lbq010

Denning, S. (2011). Why "shared value" can't fix capitalism. *Forbes*. Retrieved from http://www.forbes.com/sites/stevedenning/2011/12/20/why-shared-value-cant-fixcapitalism/

Denning, S. (2012). Is shared value a new mental model for innovation?. *Forbes*. Retrieved from http://www.forbes.com/sites/stevedenning/is-sharedvalue-a-new-mental-model-for-innovation/

Di Gregorio, D. (2013). Value creation and value appropriation: An integrative, multi-level framework. *Journal of Applied Business and Economics*, *15*(1), 39–53.

Dicken, P. (Ed.). (2011). *Global shift: Mapping the changing contours of world economy* (6th ed.). New York: The Guilford Press.

Donaldson, T., & Dunfee, T. W. (1999). *Ties that bind: A social contracts approach to business ethics*. Boston, MA: Harvard Business School Press.

Drucker, P. F. (1984). The new meaning of corporate social responsibility. *California Management Review*, *26*(2), 53–63. doi:10.2307/41165066

Elkington, J. (1998). *Cannibals with forks. The triple bottom line of the 21st century* (1st ed.). Oxford, UK: Capstone Publisher Limited.

Epstein, J. (2011). *So you tall this CSR? Or one of its many other names?*. Retrieved from http://www.forbes.com/sites/csr/2011/07/28/so-you-call-this-csr-or-one-of-its-many-othernames/

Ernst & Young. (2014). *Creating shared value in Africa: Local content in the oil and gas industry*. EYGM Limited.

Escudero, G. (2013). Modelos de Empresa y Etica. *Cuadernos Empresay Humanismo, 120.*

Fava Neves, M., & Dutra de Barcellos, M. (2013). *Value creation, capture and sharing model for food companies, chains and networks (VCCS Model)*. Symposium honouring Klaus Grunert, AU, Arhus.

Fjell, L., & Rødland, S. E. (2015). *CSR in international business: Creating shared value* (Unpublished Masters' Thesis). Norwegian University of Science and Technology.

Fombrun, C., Gardberg, N., & Barnett, M. (2000). Opportunity platforms and safety Nets: Corporate citizenship and reputational risk. *Business and Society Review*, *105*(1), 85–106. doi:10.1111/0045-3609.00066

Frynas, J. G. (2009). *Beyond corporate social responsibility: Oil multinationals and social challenges*. Cambridge, UK: University Press. doi:10.1017/CBO9780511581540

Gascon, J. F. (2015). *Creating shared value: Corporate case study in developing countries*. Retrieved from https://www.mcgill.ca/isid/files/isid/gascon.pdf

Ghemawat, P. (1991). *Commitment: The dynamics of strategy*. New York: The Free Press.

Gholami, S. (2011). Value creation model through corporate social responsibility (CSR). *International Journal of Business and Management*, *6*(9), 54–57. doi:10.5539/ijbm.v6n9p148

Giddens, M. (2011). *Investment & pensions Europe: Measuring social impact*. Retrieved from http://www.ipe.com/measuring-social-impact/41198.article

Gradl, C., & Jenkins, B. (2011). *Tackling barriers to scale: From inclusive business models to inclusive business*. Retrieved from https://www.hks.harvard.edu/mrcbg/CSRI/publications/report_47_inclusive_business.pdf

Hartman, L. P., & Werhane, P. H. (2013). Proposition: Shared value as an incomplete mental model. *Business Ethics Journal Review*, *1*(6), 36–43. doi:10.12747/bejr2013.01.02

Hidalgo, C., Peterson, K., Smith, D., & Foley, H. (2014). *Extracting with purpose: Creating shared value in the oil and gas and mining sectors' companies and communities*. Retrieved from http://www.fsg.org/publications/extracting-purpose

Hills, G., Russell, P., Borgonovi, V., Doty, A., & Lyer, L. (2012). *Shared value in emerging markets: How multinational corporations are redefining business strategies to reach poor or vulnerable populations*. Retrieved from http://www.fsg.org/publications/shared-value-emerging-markets

Jean, W. A., & Yazdanifard, R. (2015). The review of shared value in contemporary CSR run by two successful companies to sustain the business in recent years. *International Journal of Management, Accounting and Economics*, *2*(9), 1122–1129.

Jenkins, B., Valikai, K., & Baptista, P. (2013). *The Coca-Cola Company's 5by20 Initiative: Empowering Women Entrepreneurs across the Value Chain*. Cambridge, MA: The CSR Initiative at the Harvard Kennedy School and Business Fights Poverty.

Jonikas, D. (2013). Conceptual framework of value creation through CSR in separate member of value creation chain. *Bulletin of Geography Socio–Economic Series*, *21*, 69–78.

Jonikas, D. (2014). Value created through CSR measurement possibilities. *Procedia: Social and Behavioral Sciences*, *156*, 189–193. doi:10.1016/j.sbspro.2014.11.169

Juscius, V., & Jonikas, D. (2013). Integration of CSR into value chain: Conceptual framework. *InzinerineEkonomika-Engineering Economics*, *24*(1), 63–70.

Kania, J., & Kramer, M. (2011). Collective impact. *Stanford Social Innovation Review*, *9*(1), 36–41.

Kearney, A. T. (2015). *Creating value by doing good*. A.T. Kearney Inc.

Kim, W. C., & Mauborgne, R. (2005). *Blue Ocean Strategy*. Boston, MA: Harvard Business School Press.

Kleemann, L., & Krieger-Boden, C. (2011). *Bridging morale and business through shared value?*. Kiel policy brief / InstitutfürWeltwirtschaftan der Universität Kiel, No. 38.

Kramer, M. R., & Tallant, K. (2014). Roundtable on shared value in education. *Stanford Social Innovation Review*. Retrieved from http://ssir.org/articles/entry/roundtable_on_shared_value_in_education

Kreckova, Z. (2015). Corporate response to concept of shared value. *European Scientific Journal*, *11*(22), 36–45.

Leandro, L., & Neffa, E. (2012). Is the integration of shared value creation (SVC) with strategy management of productive organizations an innovative approach to environmental challenges faced by companies today?. *International Journal of Business, Management, Economic Research Journal*, *3*(2), 484–489.

Leth, M., & Hems, L. (2014). *The potential for creating shared value in Australia.* CSV Green Paper. Retrieved from https://static.squarespace.com/static/52045752e4b0330b6437dade/t/52dce083e4b086a63887ccb5/1390207107654/CSV-Green%20Paper_Draft%20for%20Discussion.pdf

Lin, C. H., Yang, H. L., & Liou, D. Y. (2009). The impact of corporate social responsibility on financial performance: Evidence from business in Taiwan. *Technology in Society*, *31*(1), 56–63. doi:10.1016/j.techsoc.2008.10.004

Maczadlo, R. (2015). Creating competitive advantages – The European CSR-strategy compared with Porter's and Kramer's shared value approach. *ECONVIEWS*, *28*, 243–256.

Mansfield, E., Rapoport, J., Romeo, A., Samuel Wagner, S., & Beardsley, G. (1977). Social and private rates of return from industrial innovation. *The Quarterly Journal of Economics*, *91*(2), 221–240. doi:10.2307/1885415

March, J. (1991). Exploration and exploitation in organizational learning. *Organization Science*, *2*(1), 71–87. doi:10.1287/orsc.2.1.71

March, J. G., & Simon, H. A. (1958). *Organizations.* New York: John Wiley and Sons.

McWilliams, A., & Siegel, D. S. (2011). Creating and capturing value: Strategic corporate social responsibility, resource-based theory, and sustainable competitive advantage. *Journal of Management*, *37*(5), 1480–1495. doi:10.1177/0149206310385696

Mena, K. P. B., & Zelaya, N. S. L. (2013). *Creating shared value in the educational sector: The contributions of CSV to the educational sector through social impact organizations* (Master Thesis). Umea School of Business and Economics.

Michelini, L., & Fiorentino, D. (2012). New business models for creating shared value. *Social Responsibility Journal*, *8*(4), 561–577. doi:10.1108/17471111211272129

Milliman, J., Ferguson, J., & Sylvester, K. (2008). Implementation of Michael Porter's strategic corporate social responsibility model. *Journal of Global Business Issues*, *2*, 29–33.

Mitler, D., Rostorfer, D., & Ledbetter, K. (2015). *Water stewardship in Africa: The next frontier for building shared value.* University of Michigan.

Mizik, N., & Jacobson, R. (2003). Trading off between value creation and value appropriation: The financial implications of shifts in strategic emphasis. *Journal of Marketing*, *67*(1), 63–76. doi:10.1509/jmkg.67.1.63.18595

Mohammed, M. (2013). *Conceptual framework for corporate accountability in the context of sustainability: A literature review.* Paper presented at the 5th Annual EuroMed Conference of the EuroMed Academy of Business, Montreux, Switzerland. doi:10.1108/EMJB-05-2013-0026

Moon, H. C., Pare, J., Yim, S. H., & Park, N. (2011). An extension of Porter and Kramer's creating shared value (CSV): Reorienting strategies and seeking international cooperation. *Journal of International and Area Studies*, *18*(2), 49–64.

Moore, C. (2014). *Corporate social responsibility and creating shared value: What's the difference?*. Retrieved from https://sharedvalue.org/sites/default/files/resource-files/CFR-047%20Corporate%20Social%20Responsibility%20White%20Paper_FINAL.pdf

Néron, P. Y. (2013). Toward a political theory of the business firm? A comment on political CSR. *Business Ethics Journal Review*, *1*(3), 14–21. doi:10.12747/bejr2013.01.03

Neves, J. M. d. N. G. V. (2013). *Creating shared value. The case of Nestlé* (Dissertation). Universidade Católica Portuguesa.

Nohria, N., & Ghoshal, S. (1994). Differentiated fit and shared values: Alternatives for managing headquarters subsidiary relations. *Strategic Management Journal*, *15*(6), 491–502. doi:10.1002/smj.4250150606

Odia, J. O. (2016). Foreign direct investments, corporate social responsibility and economic development: Exploring the relationship and mitigating the expectation gaps. In M. Ojo (Ed.), *Foreign Direct Investments, Corporate Social Responsibility, and Economic Development*. IGI Global. doi:10.4018/978-1-5225-0305-7.ch015

OECD. (2016). *Collaborative strategies for in-country shared value creation: Framework for extractive projects. OECD Development Policy Tools*. Paris: OECD Publishing.

Ogrean, C. (2014). Perceptions on the strategic value of corporate social responsibility-some insights from global rankings. *Journal of International Studies*, *7*(2), 128–140. doi:10.14254/2071-8330.2014/7-2/11

Orlitzky, M., Siegel, D. S., & Waldman, D. A. (2011). Strategic corporate social responsibility and environmental sustainability. *Business and Society Review*, *50*(1), 6–27. doi:10.1177/0007650310394323

Peloza, J., & Shang, J. (2011). How can corporate social responsibility activities create value for stakeholders? A systematic review. *Journal of the Academy of Marketing Science*, *39*(1), 117–135. doi:10.1007/s11747-010-0213-6

Peterson, K., Rehrig, M., Stamp, M., & Kim, S. (2012). *Competing by saving lives: How pharmaceutical and medical device companies create shared value in global health*. Retrieved from http://www.fsg.org/publications/competing-saving-lives-0

Petrovic-Lazarevic, S. (2008). The development of corporate social responsibility in the Australian construction industry. *Construction Management and Economics*, *26*(2), 93–101. doi:10.1080/01446190701819079

Pfitzer, M., Bockstette, V., & Stamp, M. (2013). Innovating for shared value. Companies that deliver both social benefit and business value rely on five mutually reinforcing elements. *Harvard Business Review*, *91*(9), 100–107.

Pirson, M. (2012). Social entrepreneurs as the paragons of shared value creation? A critical perspective null. *Social Enterprise Journal*, *8*(1), 31–48. doi:10.1108/17508611211226575

Porter, M. (2014). *Created shared value: Becoming a movement*. Shared Value Leadership Summit, New York, NY.

Porter, M., & Kramer, M. R. (2011). Creating shared value: How to reinvent capitalism - and unleash a wave of innovation and growth. *Harvard Business Review*, *89*(1/2), 62–77.

Porter, M. E. (1998). *Competitive advantage-Creating and sustaining superior performance* (2nd ed.). New York: Free Press.

Porter, M. E. (2000). Locations, clusters, and company strategy. In G. L. Clark, M. P. Feldman, & M. S. Gertler (Eds.), The Oxford Handbook of Economic Geography (pp. 253–274). Academic Press.

Porter, M. E., Hills, G., Pfitzer, M., Patscheke, S., & Hawkins, E. (2012). *Measuring share value: How to unlock value by linking social and business results.* Retrieved from www.fsg.org: http://www.mesacc.edu/other/engagement/2013Conf/Measuring_Shared_Value.pdf

Porter, M. E., & Kramer, M. R. (2006). Strategy and society: The link between competitive advantage and corporate social responsibility. *Harvard Business Review*, *84*(12), 78–92. PMID:17183795

Prahalad, C. K., & Hart, S. L. (2002). The fortune at the bottom of the pyramid. *Strategy Business Magazine,* 26.

Reich, R. (2007). *Supercapitalism: The transformation of business, democracy and everyday life..* Retrieved from http://www.economist.com/node/18330445

Ringmar, E. (2005). *Surviving capitalism.* London: Anthem Press.

Rocchi, M., & Fererro, I. (2014). *Systematic shared value in finance: Expanding Porter's approach.* Working Paper No. 07. Pontificia Università della Santa Croce/University of Navarra.

Saul, J. (2011). *Social innovation: 5 strategies for driving business growth through social change.* San Francisco: Jossey-Bass.

Scherer, A. G., & Palazzo, G. (2007). Toward a political conception of corporate social responsibility: Business and society seen from a Habermasian perspective. *Academy of Management Review*, *32*(4), 1096–1120. doi:10.5465/AMR.2007.26585837

Scherer, A. G., & Palazzo, G. (2011). The new political role of business in a globalized world: A review of a new perspective on CSR and its implications for the firm, governance, and democracy. *Journal of Management Studies*, *48*(4), 899–931. doi:10.1111/j.1467-6486.2010.00950.x

Scherer, A. G., Palazzo, G., & Matten, D. (2017). The business firm as a political actor: A new theory of the firm for a globalized world. *Business & Society*, *53*(2), 143–156. doi:10.1177/0007650313511778

Scott-Kemmis, D. (2012). *Responding to change and pursuing growth: Exploring the potential of business model innovation in Australia.* Australian Business Foundation.

Spitzeck, H., & Chapman, S. (2012). Creating shared value as a differentiation strategy – the example of BASF in Brazil. *Corporate Governance*, *12*(4), 499–513. doi:10.1108/14720701211267838

Swartout, N. L (2016). *Exxon Mobil local content program.* Being presentation at the UNCTAD, Nairobi, Kenya.

Székely, F., & Knirsch, M. (2005). Responsible leadership and corporate social responsibility: Metrics for sustainable performance. *European Management Journal*, *23*(6), 628–547. doi:10.1016/j.emj.2005.10.009

Szmigin, I., & Rutherford, R. (2013). Shared value and the impartial spectator test. *Journal of Business Ethics, 114*(1), 171–182. doi:10.1007/s10551-012-1335-1

Vaidyanathan, L., & Scott, M. (2012). Creating shared value in India: The future for inclusive growth. *Vikalpa: The Journal for Decision Making, 37*(2), 108–113.

Visser, W. (2006). Revisiting Carroll's CSR pyramid: An African perspective. In E. R. Pedersen & M. Hunicke (Eds.), *Corporate citizenship in developing countries: New partnership perspectives* (pp. 29–56). Copenhagen: Copenhagen Business School Press.

Visser, W. (2008). Corporate social responsibility in developing countries. In A. Crane et al. (Eds.), *The Oxford handbook of corporate social responsibility* (pp. 473–479). Oxford, UK: Oxford University Press.

Visser, W. (2010). The age of responsibility: CSR 2.0 and the new DNA of business. *Journal of Business Systems. Governance and Ethics, 5*(3), 7–22.

Visser, W. (2013). *Creating shared value: Revolution or clever con?*. Retrieved from http://www.waynevisser.com/wp-content/uploads/2013/08/blog_csv_csr_wvisser.pdf

Visser, W., Matten, D., Pohl, M., & Tolhurst, N. (2007). *The A to Z of Corporate Social Responsibility*. London: Wiley.

Werner, W. (2009). Corporate social responsibility initiatives addressing social exclusion in Bangladesh. *Journal of Health, Population, and Nutrition, 27*(4), 545–562. doi:10.3329/jhpn.v27i4.3401 PMID:19761088

Werther, W. B. Jr, & Chandler, D. (2011). *Strategic corporate social responsibility: Stakeholders in a global environment*. Los Angeles, CA: Sage.

Wheeler, D., Colbert, B., & Freeman, R. E. (2003). Focusing on value: Reconciling corporate social responsibility, sustainability and a stakeholder approach in a network world. *Journal of General Management, 28*(3), 1–28. doi:10.1177/030630700302800301

Whelan, G. (2012). The political perspective of corporate social responsibility: A critical research agenda. *Business Ethics Quarterly, 22*(4), 709–737. doi:10.5840/beq201222445

Whelan, G. (2013). Political corporate social responsibility: Some clarifications. *Business Ethics Journal Review, 1*(10), 63–68. doi:10.12747/bejr2013.01.10

Wilburn, K., & Wilburn, R. (2014). Demonstrating a commitment to corporate social responsibility not simply shared value. *Business & Professional Ethics Journal, 33*(1), 1–15. doi:10.5840/bpej20144216

Windsor, D. (2013). Corporate social responsibility and irresponsibility: A positive theory approach. *Journal of Business Research, 66*(10), 1937–1944. doi:10.1016/j.jbusres.2013.02.016

Young, G. (2012). *Strategic corporate social responsibility and small to medium businesses in Australia*. Creative Commons.

KEY TERMS AND DEFINITIONS

Corporate Social Responsibility: This refers to the continuing commitment by business to contribute to economic development while improving the quality of life of the workforce and their families as well as of the community and society at large.

Created Share Value: This is a paradigm shift in corporate social responsibility and sustainability strategy where business create economic values and values for societies through the simultaneous pursuit of economic, social and societal goals. Companies can create shared values through re-conceiving products and markets, redefining productivity in the value chain and building supportive industry clusters at the company's locations.

Shared Value: This can be defined as policies and operating practices that enhance the competitiveness of a company while simultaneously advancing the economic and social conditions in the community in which it operates.

Sustainable Development: This refers to development that meets the needs of the present generation without compromising the ability of the future generations to meet their needs.

Section 2
Sharing Values and Local Experiences

Chapter 7
Creating Shared Value in the 21st Century:
The Case of Toyota Motor Company

Sorin-George Toma
University of Bucharest, Romania

Paul Marinescu
University of Bucharest, Romania

Cătălin Grădinaru
University of Bucharest, Romania

ABSTRACT

Companies benefit society by supplying products and services to customers, creating jobs for people, providing incomes for their employees, investing in knowledge or developing communities. The last decades have witnessed significant developments in re-conceptualizing the role of companies in society. By creating shared value, companies consider society as an integral part of their businesses and link economic performance with societal progress. In order to meet this challenge one of their most valuable options is the implementation of the lean management approach. The chapter aims to explore the theoretical foundation of the shared value concept and to exemplify the case of Toyota Motor Company. The research method is the case study. The study shows that there is a Toyota Way in creating shared value.

INTRODUCTION

Most economic activities today are organized around companies, either public or private. They are among the most important inventions in history that have successfully passed the test of time (Butler, 1989) and some of the dominant institutions in society. Companies benefit society by supplying products and services to customers, creating jobs for people, providing incomes for their employees, investing in knowledge or developing communities. Therefore, they act as change agents that contribute to economic growth and social development (Costa & Martí, 2012). As businesses constitute the economic basis of

DOI: 10.4018/978-1-5225-3147-0.ch007

our society and its cornerstone of prosperity, we should all have an interest in their goals and the rules they have to follow (Shaw & Barry, 2016, p. 14). Moreover, there is a continuing debate and a growing focus on the role of businesses in today's society.

Businesses and society are not separated parts but highly interdependent (Lawrence & Weber, 2008, pp. 4-5). There are two visages of business organizations within society as the two faces of Janus: the good and the bad company. Sometimes a company looks a good character (e.g., corporate donations), sometimes looks a bad character (e.g., corporate fraud). The plethora of testimonies on the rational and irrational behaviors exhibited by companies show that the starting point is the antagonism between the shareholder theory and the stakeholder theory. These theories reflect the character of two types of capitalism: the Anglo-Saxon market capitalism or the shareholder model and the Rhenish capitalism or the stakeholder model (Piketty, 2014, pp. 145-146). The United States of America (USA) and Great Britain epitomize the Anglo-Saxon capitalism whereas Germany and Japan portray the Rhenish capitalism (Albert, 1993).

On the one hand, there are scholars and practitioners who argue that a company represents a social organism comprising of a mixture of connected virtues and vices that exists to generate economic outcomes such as wealth, not to resolve societal issues (Devinney, 2009). The company serves the interests of whoever controls it: the shareholder (Dugger, 1989). According to shareholder theory companies aim at shareholder value maximization. Businesses use their resources in order to increase their profits and generate wealth (Friedman, 1970) because they are created to make money. The objective function of a company aims to maximize its total market value through profit maximization (Jensen, 2001). In other words, the purpose of a company is to obtain the highest profit as it operates for the welfare of its shareholders or value maximization.

On the other hand, corporations exist to benefit the whole society (Wallman, 1999). Since their emergence business organizations have brought much good to society. As society is a complex and dynamic organism the analysis of the role of business in society should take into account both the activities performed by companies and the social context within which they activate (Fitzgerald & Cormack, 2006). Most of great companies believe that businesses are an intrinsic part of society (Kanter, 2011) and are aware of the need to be socially responsible. Stakeholder theory asserts that companies should focus not only on their financial achievement but also on their social performance (Miles, 2012). This means that companies have to pay attention to build strong and positive relationships with their stakeholders.

However, many business organizations, especially multinational and transnational corporations, have been blamed for the negative impact their operations provoked all over the world. In recent times, the increased power of the corporations and the weakening of the state's authority over economic activities have led to "higher levels of private profit at the expense of society" as underlined by Mohammed (2013, p. 245). Several researches have pointed out that companies are seen as a major cause of social, environmental, and economic problems (Greenwood, 2007, pp. 315-316; Toma & Marinescu, 2013, pp. 109-110). Corporate greed and irresponsibility are two of the main factors that should be taken into consideration by businesses in order to address the sustainability challenges (Zadek, 2004).

More than ever companies have been undergoing increased scrutiny in the light of their bad behavior that led to business scandals (e.g., Enron collapse). Companies should not encourage and promote the development of unhealthy practices such as cheating and fraud (Friedland, 2009). This is why company accountability to its various stakeholders, such as employees and/or unions, consumers and consumers' associations (Craig-Smith, 1990), environmental groups, shareholders, government or society, reflects corporate responses to changes in today's society.

The last decades have witnessed significant developments in re-conceptualizing the role of companies in society. By overcoming the dichotomist approach about business and society, concepts like "capitalism with a human face", "conscious capitalism", "humanizing the company", "value co-creation", "stakeholder responsiveness" or "shared value" stress the idea that companies have understood the need to be good to their multiple stakeholders in order to succeed (Bassi, Frauenheim, McMurrer, & Costello, 2011). Thus, companies should identify its stakeholders and deliver value to all of them since it is morally to do so. In order to meet this challenge one of the most valuable options is the implementation of lean management (LM) at the company level because lean not only eliminates all types of waste but also creates and provides value (Murman et al., 2002) to stakeholders.

This study builds on a growing body of business literature that emphasizes the popularity of the shared value concept. This rather novel notion that differs from corporate social responsibility reveals the need to re-connect companies with the society within they act (Porter & Kramer, 2011, pp. 4-6). By creating shared value (CSV), companies consider society as an integral part of their businesses and link economic performance with societal progress.

The chapter aims to explore the theoretical foundation of the shared value concept and to exemplify the case of Toyota Motor Company (TMC) that represents the focus of the study. The research method is the case study, a method that covers a broad variety of subjects, such as social and societal problems, management or businesses (Gomm, Hammersley, & Foster, 2000; Gerring, 2007; Dul & Hak, 2008; Yin, 2012; Farquhar, 2012; Bryman & Bell, 2015). In order to set the context, the next section analyzes the shared value concept by mixing the economic perspective with the societal perspective and identifies its different sources found in the business literature. It is followed by a presentation of the research methodology. Thereafter, the study investigates the way the Japanese automaker is CSV and outlines the importance of LM in this process. The chapter ends with conclusion.

The research question is the following: How has TMC succeeded in CSV?

The paper attempts to make three contributions to the business literature. The first is to present the differences between the traditional and the new view on value creation. The second aims at providing a theoretical model of linking LM and CSV at TMC. The third is to identify and emphasize the societal benefits of CSV at TMC.

THEORETICAL FRAMEWORK

Defining the main concepts and their relationships is beneficial for what is to come within the chapter. Secondary data were collected through desk research based on a significant literature review. The sources were books and journal articles mainly from the areas of operations and production management, quality management, marketing and business ethics, and were found in libraries and electronic databases (e.g., Emerald Insight, Springer).

The authors propose the analysis of the concept of shared value from two perspectives. The economic approach focuses on value and value creation whereas the societal approach concentrates mostly on social and environmental issues.

The value concept has always been at the core of business organizations. According to Liberman and Balasubramanian (2007), a company creates value by "producing and delivering goods/services at a cost that is lower than what the consumer is willing to pay for that good/service" (p. 7). Companies that do not deliver valuable products and/or services do not make money and go out of business. A broader definition that links market and nonmarket issues considers value as "the capacity of a good, service, or activity to satisfy a need or provide a benefit to a person or legal entity", as shown by Haksever, Chaganti and Cook (2004, p. 292).

As a multifaceted and complicated phenomenon (Ravald & Grönroos, 1996), value has different meanings for different people. This is why a distinction between use value and exchange value has to be made. Bowman and Ambrosini (2010) asserted that use values are "properties of products and services that provide utility" and exchange values are monetary amounts "exchanged between the firm and its customers or suppliers when use values are traded" (p. 480).

In order to provide a practical framework to conceptualize value Smith and Colgate (2007) found five major sources of value (information, products, interactions, environment, and ownership) and four main types of value that can be created by organizations (functional/instrumental value, experiential/hedonic value, symbolic/expressive value, and cost/sacrifice value). These categories show the extent to which:

- A product or service is useful (functional/instrumental value),
- A product or service generates appropriates experiences for the customer (experiential/hedonic value),
- Customers attach or associate psychological meaning to a product or service (symbolic/expressive value),

and the relation with transaction costs, such as search costs or operating costs (cost/sacrifice value). More recently, Almquist, Senior and Bloch (2016) identified four categories of fundamental attributes of value as follows: functional (e.g., quality), emotional (e.g., attractiveness), life changing (e.g., self-actualization) and social impact (e.g., self-transcendence).

Value has been traditionally analyzed from the supply side (Priem, 2007) but in the knowledge-based economy it has shifted from a firm centric view to a multilevel experience involving various interacting socioeconomic actors such as producers or customers. In fact, stakeholders are the most important actors for a company because they can affect, or are affected, by its actions and results (Freeman, 1984). Thus, the company should be managed for their benefit (Langtry, 1994) because "the organizational wealth can be created (or destroyed) through relationships with stakeholders of all kind" as underlined by Post, Preston and Sauter-Sachs (2002, p. 1). Primary stakeholders (e.g., employees, suppliers, consumers, shareholders) have a major impact on the company's performance whereas secondary stakeholders (e.g., media, non-governmental organizations) exert less influence on it (Biggemann, Williams, & Kro, 2014). Starting from the distinctive types of value that are present in all relations between companies and their stakeholders, Argandoña (2011) identified economic extrinsic value (e.g., remuneration), intangible extrinsic value (e.g., recognition), psychological intrinsic value (e.g., work satisfaction), intrinsic value (e.g., operational learning), transcendent value (e.g., evaluative learning), and value that consists of positive or negative externalities (e.g., harm to the environment).

Building, maintaining and developing good relationships with its stakeholders should be on the top of the agenda of any company. In this respect, companies should not forget to take into consideration that value means different things for each stakeholder and that they might have competing and even conflicting interests. So, customers are interested in optimizing "value for money", suppliers are searching to optimize the exchange value received for the use value supplied, shareholders are aiming at optimizing the exchange value returned for the exchange value invested (Bowman & Ambrosini, 2010), employees are interested in gaining higher wages and other benefits (e.g., pensions), and communities are expecting to obtain charitable contributions or local investments. As a result, the way value is created has become a central issue within companies in spite of the fact that there is little consensus in the business literature on what it is or how it can be achieved (Lepak, Smith, & Taylor, 2007).

Customers were the first stakeholders which highly contributed to the birth of value co-creation. Until recent years, companies focused especially on proactive and responsive market orientation in order to learn from customers and competitors, to understand and satisfy customers' expressed and latent needs, and to improve their business profitability (Narver & Slater, 1990; Slater & Narver, 1995; Slater & Narver, 1998; Hong, Doll, Nahm, & Li, 2004; Narver, Slater, & MacLachlan, 2004; Blocker, Flint, Myers, & Slater, 2011). Since the transformation of customers from "passive audiences" to "active players" (Prahalad & Ramaswamy, 2000) a new logic for value creation has appeared in the business world: they want "to interact with firms and thereby co-create value", as pointed out by Prahalad and Ramaswamy (2004a, p. 5). As today's customers are more informed and connected than in the past they are increasingly sharing their interactions and experiences that range from ideas to feelings. Whether as individuals or as members of physical and/or virtual communities (e.g., blogs, chatrooms), customers and other stakeholders can and want to be involved in the co-creation of value (Ramaswamy, 2008). The field of co-creation has developed because of the continuous expansion of mobile technology, online communities, Internet connectivity, convergence of technologies, etc. Consequently, companies have understood the need to engage their stakeholders in value creation.

Three main processes were identified as forming the foundation for value co-creation as follows: customer value-creating processes, supplier value-creating processes, and encounter processes (Payne, Storbacka, & Frow, 2008). The customer value-creating process comprises customer learning and relationship experience (e.g., cognition, emotion) whereas the supplier value-creating process includes organizational leaning and co-creation and relationship experience design (e.g., co-creating opportunities, planning). On its turn, the encounter process relates to the two-way interactions between customer and supplier (e.g., direct mailings, complaints).

All these processes reveal three hierarchical levels of value creation for all companies: core business, enlarged enterprise, and business ecosystem (Letaifa, 2014). The first level, core business, encompasses the core competencies of the company, its distribution channels and direct suppliers. The second level, the enlarged enterprises, refers to direct customers and their customers, suppliers of suppliers and of complementary products and services. The third level, the business ecosystem, includes other actors such as competitors, investors, governmental organizations, unions. As networks organizations, business ecosystem relates to "intentional communities of economic actors whose individual business activities share in some large measures the fate of the whole community" as shown by Moore (2006, p. 33). The spread of knowledge as the most important resource used by the ecosystem participants has led to the advent of the so-called "knowledge-based ecosystem", defined by Van der Borgh, Cloodt and Romme (2012) as "a social and economic environment providing specific value sources that individual companies seek in their continuous quest for performance improvement" (p. 152).

The fierce competition within knowledge-based ecosystems forces business organizations to unceasing innovation. Knowledge necessitates an increased contribution of social capital to company's ability to innovate and create value (Tsai & Ghoshal, 1998). However, companies are aware that they do not possess all the required resources, especially knowledge, to keep the pace of innovation and they join their forces with other economic actors (e.g., competitors, suppliers). Strategic alliances have proved to be a logical response to the innovation challenge. Doz and Hamel (1998) demonstrated that co-specialization, a specific purpose of alliances, represents "the synergistic value creation that results from the combining of previously separate resources, positions, skills, and knowledge sources" (p. 5). This means that value creation starts from the connectivity established among a wide variety of actors because "strategic resources and knowledge come not only from within the organization's boundaries, but also from outside", as underlined by Lai, Zhang, Lee and Zhao (2012, p. 445).

Value is not created anymore by companies themselves but through intense relationships with their stakeholders (Busco, Frigo, Riccaboni, & Quattrone, 2013). Stakeholders are increasingly playing an active role in the value creation process (Frigo & Ramaswamy, 2009; Freeman, 2010). This suggests that the old concept of value creation is no longer available (Table 1). Instead, co-creation becomes the new business thrust, imposing companies to establish and develop long-term relationships with their stakeholders, either internal (Grace & Lo Iacono, 2015) or external (Prahalad & Ramaswamy, 2004c). Companies have begun to abandon the outdated approach to value creation and increasingly embraced co-creation by taking into account not only the social and environmental issues, but also other societal needs (e.g., education).

The knowledge-based society has brought a different meaning of the notion of value. Since the end of the last century a series of articles written by M. E. Porter and M. R. Kramer and published by Harvard Business Review have led to the emergence of the shared value concept, one of the most debated subjects in the business literature in the past decade (Porter & Kramer, 1999; Porter & Kramer, 2002; Porter & Kramer, 2006). Shared value was defined by Porter and Kramer (2011) as "policies and operating practices that enhance the competitiveness of a company while simultaneously advancing the economic and social conditions in the communities in which it operates" (p. 66). Pirson (2012) showed that the concept states that "economic value can only be created in a sustainable fashion when all stakeholders including society can appreciate the value created" (p. 32). Companies can create shared value by re-conceiving products and markets, redefining productivity in their value chains, and building supportive clusters at their locations. In order to implement this approach, companies rely on the following five interconnected elements: embedding a social purpose, defining the social need, measuring shared value, creating the optimal innovation structure, and co-creating with external stakeholders (Pfitzer, Bockstette, & Stamp, 2013).

Table 1. Old versus new in value creation

Traditional/Old View on Value Creation	New View on Value Creation (Co-Creation)
• Companies create value unilaterally • Companies are focusing on products and/or services • Value resides in product and/or service • The dominant model is a "firm and product centric" view of value • Companies and consumers have distinct identities and roles • Product and/or service innovations • Managers are reactive and responsive • Supply networks are deterministic • The boundaries of the company are clearly defined • Focus on value chains, co-operation and competition	• Companies engage consumers and other stakeholders in value creation as co-creators • Companies are focusing on experience as the basis of value • Connected consumers and thematic consumer communities are key drivers of co-creation • Companies share with their stakeholders the convergence of their roles through dialogue and transparency • Companies and their stakeholders are co-evolving and are joint problem solvers creating unique value • Experience innovations • Managers are anticipative • Supply networks are not predetermined • The boundaries of the company are evasive • Focus on value networks and co-opetition

Sources: Adapted from Prahalad & Ramaswamy, 2004b; Hearn & Pace, 2006; Leavy & Moitra, 2006; Saarijärvi, Kannan, & Kuusela, 2013

The concept of shared value helps today's companies to better understand the business-society relationship. In essence, it appears to "merely advance a conventional rhetoric about business and society that what is good for business is good for society", as pointed out by Aakhus and Bzdak (2012, p. 233). From a societal point of view, Hartman and Werhane (2013, p. 42) considered that shared value represents a viable concept for reconstructing "a corporate worldview to tackle new-world social, environmental and economic problems" that provides the framework for partnership between business and society.

The idea of balancing the economic and social goals of value creation process is not new. Attempts that promoted the social mission of a company emerged at the end of the Second World War. P. F. Drucker (1946), the father of modern management, emphasized that any corporation should be a social institution and a community for all employees: "...the essence of the corporation is social, that is human organization" (p. 31). As a representative institution of the society of which is a part, the corporation has to be analyzed "in terms of the society it serves and in its relation to the individuals who constitute the society", according to Drucker (1946, p. 30). In Drucker's view a harmonious relationship between society and corporation is mandatory within a democratic society. Later, the stakeholder approach highlighted once again the idea of balanced goals of a company (Freeman, 1984). More recently, Hart & Milstein (2003) asserted that a company can create sustainable value by reducing the level of material consumption and pollution, operating at higher levels of transparency and developing eco-technologies.

The shared value concept presents several key characteristics. Firstly, the concept stresses the way companies try to maintain their social legitimacy (Grant, 2013) as Porter and Kramer "present a model of integral profit maximization and social engagement of businesses" as showed by Von Liel (2016, p. 13). Secondly, CSV does not represent a synonym for corporate philanthropy or corporate social responsibility (Krzyżanowska & Tkaczyk, 2014). Thirdly, shared value creation relates both to the internal and external environment of a company. The sharing imperative made companies to reaffirm their openness towards their employees and customers (Chakravarthy, 2010), and society at large. Fourthly, the concept involves the designing and implementation of a business model that links economic performance with social progress. The employees of a company that understand social problems more thoroughly are deeply involved in the achievement of its social purpose (Pfitzer, Bockstette, & Stamp, 2013). Fifthly, shared value recognizes the importance of societal needs within today's business philosophy. Sixthly, CSV enhances the competitiveness of a company through the alignment of its stakeholders with the goal and objectives of the company. Seventhly, the concept has many strengths (e.g., a helpful concept for scholars and practitioners), but also some weaknesses (e.g., the tensions between economic and social aims) that "threaten the potential of CSV to achieve its aims of re-legitimizing business and reshaping capitalism", as presented by Crane, Palazzo, Spence and Matten (2014, p. 132).

Today's companies are increasingly aware of the need to conciliate their economic purpose with their social obligations. The creation of shared value imposes companies to generate economic value by taking into account the societal needs and challenges. This is why the so-called "shared value approach" has gained prominence both in the business and academic world. The proof is the increasing involvement of companies in environmental and social issues (Serafeim, 2014, pp. 2-4). All in all, there is a mutual dependence between two fundamental institutions- society and corporation (Michelini & Fiorentino, 2012)-, which implies that current companies should incorporate a more humanistic philosophy in their business activities.

By redesigning the relationships between businesses and society, CSV requires corporate management to develop a new understanding of the interdependence between social and business results and to acquire new knowledge in order to create societal value. Consequently, CSV becomes the main goal

(Figure 1) of the company (Porter & Kramer, 2011). This is why management approaches that address both business and societal needs have been generated and implemented especially in big companies. One of them is illustrated by LM, a new paradigm of management launched by the Japanese (Liker & Ross, 2017) and a management philosophy that affects the way companies are organized internally and externally (Shah & Ward, 2007) as it is going far beyond the workplace.

The meaning and interpretation of lean has constantly evolved over time and its development is still going on (Ingelsson & Mårtensson, 2014). For example, the last decade has witnessed a hybridization of lean all over the world (Abo, 2014). Lean represents not only a "tremendously powerful production system leading to major leaps in quality, productivity, and delivery performance and to improvements in employee health, safety, and morale as well", according to Liker (1998, p. 498), an integrated system aimed at eliminating waste, but also a different way of thinking about making business by adding value for all supply chain participants (Shamah, 2013). A company that embraces lean personifies "an adaptive organization that consistently generates the most value possible for all stakeholders from all of the resources it can bring to bear", as showed by Jacquemont (2014, p. 11), and demonstrates a passion for continuous improvement, mentoring and learning, and disciplined execution (Koenigsaecker, 2013).

On its turn, LM is seen by Charron, Harrington, Voehl and Wiggin (2015) as "a systematic and very focused approach for guiding employee learning, education, and practice of Lean principles and philosophies across an enterprise" (p. 3). LM was considered by Krafcik (1988) as "most conducive to improved productivity and quality performance" (p. 51). Initially, its essence was codified into five principles (Womack & Jones, 2003):

- Specify value.
- Identify the value stream for each product.
- Avoid interruptions in value flow.
- Let the customer pull value from the producer.
- Pursue perfection.

Later, other principles were added such as (Soriano-Meier & Forrester, 2002; Shah & Ward, 2007):

- Committed management.
- Involve supply chain management.

Lean production is "an integrated socio-technical system whose main objective is to eliminate waste by concurrently reducing or minimizing supplier, customer, and internal variability", as pointed out by Shah and Ward (2007, p. 791), or "an approach to or a strategy for managing operations and thus an overarching concept that includes company culture, values, basic principles, methods, leadership, and employee-ship", as exposed by Stålberg and Fundin (2016, p. 268). It encompasses several key elements (Figure 2) that provides companies the possibility to do more and more with less and less (Womack & Jones, 2003) by carrying out a continuous battle against waste (Lewis, 2000; George, 2003).

Thus, the relevance of LM to CSV is clearly shown by several elements. Firstly, LM symbolizes a new path to offer more benefits to society through waste elimination. Secondly, LM explicitly specifies what creates value from a multiple perspective (e.g., company, customer). Thirdly, LM supports companies to generate the most value possible for all their stakeholders as value is always the central focus of LM. Fourthly, LM provides the entire flow of value-creating activities and, therefore, identifies the

Figure 1. The relationship between CSV and corporate management

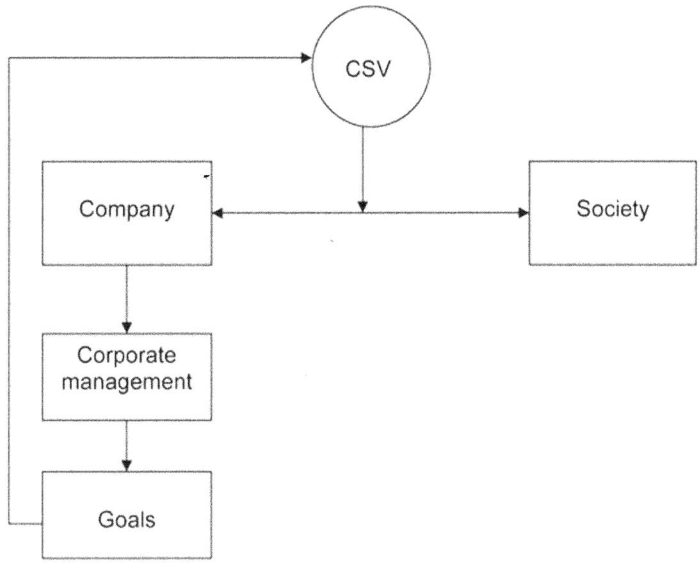

Figure 2. The key elements of lean production
Source: adapted from Katayama and Benett, 1996

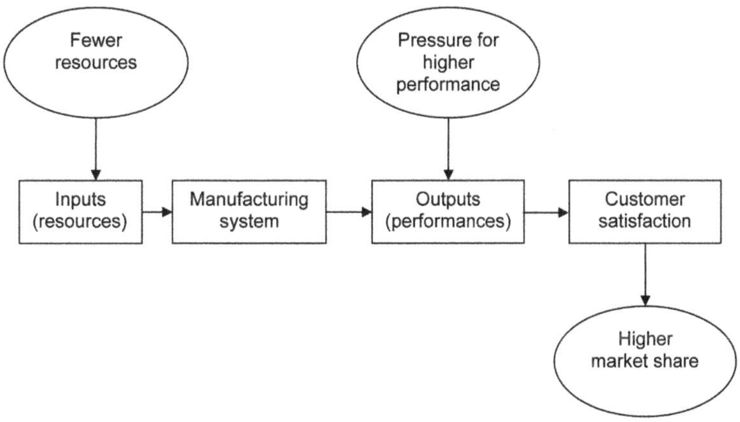

contribution of all the interested parties in the process. Fifthly, LM imposes the full involvement of the supply chain parties (e.g., several stakeholders) in value co-creation. Sixthly, LM highly contributes to adding value at each step along the value stream. From this point of view the case of TMC has proved to be a useful example.

RESEARCH METHODOLOGY

In order to answer the research question, an empirical research methodology is required. Several reasons explain the selection of the case study method as a research method within this chapter. First, the case study represents "the preferred method when "how" or „why" questions are being posed, the investigator has little control over events, and the focus is on a contemporary phenomenon within a real-life context", as showed by Yin (2009, p. 2), and facilitates the examination of a phenomenon by employing a variety of data sources (Baxter & Jack, 2008). It has been defined as "an empirical inquiry that investigates a contemporary phenomenon within its real-life context; when the boundaries between phenomenon and context are not clearly evident; and in which multiple sources of evidence are used", as pointed out by Yin (1984, p. 23), "an in-depth, multifaceted investigation, using qualitative research methods, of a single social phenomenon", as presented by Feagin, Orum and Sjoberg (1991, p. 2), or "the study of the particularity and complexity of a single case", as exposed by Stake (1995, p. xi). Second, the case study plays a prominent role in business research as it produces rich descriptions concerning singular topics and generates findings of relevance about specific cases such as individuals, processes, groups, organizations, communities or nations (Dul & Hak, 2008; Farquhar, 2012; Bryman & Bell, 2015). Also, it can explore, describe, explain, and compare single or numerous cases, and involve different levels of analysis (Yin, 1984). Third, the diversity of case studies contributes to the knowledge of diverse phenomena and fulfills a positive role in both human and organizational learning (Flyvbjerg, 2006). Three main types have been identified starting from the purposes of a case study as follows (Stake, 1994):

- The intrinsic case study that tries to better understand a particular case;
- The instrumental case study that seeks to gain insight into an issue, to apply the findings beyond a particular case or to build and/or refine a theory (Eisenhardt, 1989);
- The collective case study that extends the instrumental case to cover several cases.

The first two types are portrayed by the case of TMC. This is a single case study, a case study in which data from one company is enough to answer the research question.

CREATING SHARED VALUE THROUGH LEAN MANAGEMENT: THE CASE OF TOYOTA MOTOR COMPANY

The authors consider that CSV at TMC expresses the deployment of an ongoing process as continuous improvement is endless and has been determined by the successful foundation and implementation of its LM. LM is not just a set of guiding principles, methods, practices and techniques, but a holistic management philosophy developed by the Japanese automaker that is described through 14 principles divided into the four parts of the "4P" model specific to Toyota Way- philosophy (long-term thinking), process (eliminate waste), people and partners (respect, challenge and grow them), problem solving (continuous improvement and learning) (Liker, 2004).

Therefore, the emergence and development of LM has represented the aggregate result of several factors from both the external and internal environment of TMC during its historical evolution. These two types of environment proved to be strongly interconnected in Japan. On the one hand, TMC is CSV through LM with the stakeholders' engagement. On the other hand, TMC influences its external and internal environment by CSV. This is why the research proposes a theoretical model that aims to linking LM and CSV at TMC (Figure 3).

Figure 3. A theoretical model of linking LM and CSV at TMC

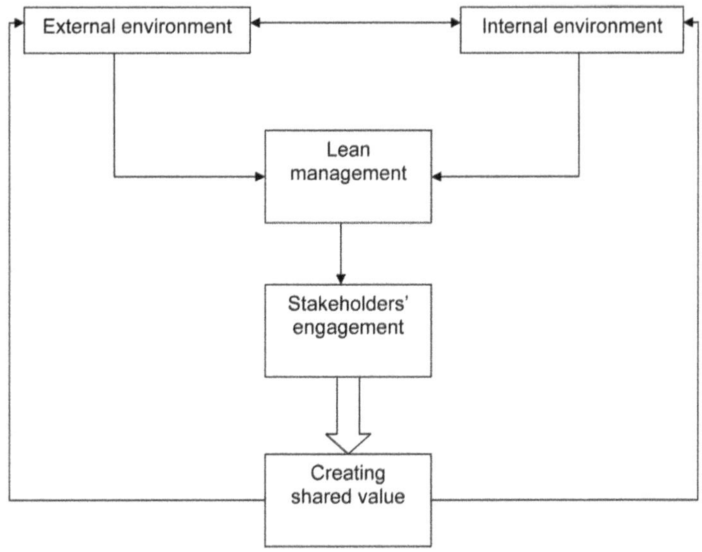

Factors of the External Environment

Some of the most important factors of the external environment were the following:

Japanese History and Society

For a relatively long period of time, Japan was isolated from the rest of the world. During the Edo period (1603-1867) the social organization of Japan consisted on several castes/classes (e.g., merchants, farmers, artisans) in which the *samurai* (one who serves) was powerful. The *Bushido* (the "way of the warrior") Code or the *samurai* code of behavior emphasized eight virtues: rectitude or justice, courage, benevolence or mercy, politeness, honesty and sincerity, honor, loyalty, character and self-control (Nitobé, 2002). The *ie* (house/family as a whole) was an ethical and socio-economic unit and included both *ko* (duty to parents) and *on* (reciprocal obligations between family members). As the family represented the smallest human community and the state the largest one, values such as harmony, communitarianism, solidarity, group consciousness, paternalism, filial piety, loyalty, and obedience were highly appreciated and promoted within a so-called "relational capitalism" (Okimoto & Rohlen, 1988, p. 266). This is why the Japanese family provided an institutional logic for both the Japanese corporate networks and management (Bhappu, 2000). After the collapse of the Tokugawa Shogunate, the Meiji Restoration (1868-1912) brought an era of major changes. Japan opened its doors to the Western countries, and became an industrial state and a modern society in the twentieth century. However, the Japanese society has remained highly homogeneous (Nakane, 1972, p. 141) and collectivist (Hofstede, Hofstede, & Minkow, 2010, pp. 111-112).

Human and Relational Capitalism

The Japanese economic philosophy is characterized by three principles: (1) human resources are the most valuable factor of production; (2) people are intellectual beings; (3) people are psychological beings (Ozaki, 1991, p. 10). Unlike many other countries, Japan advocates a human/people oriented capitalism taking into account that the lack of natural resources has imposed the people to live with scarcity. There is also a relational capitalism because employees, shareholders, suppliers, customers, members of the business groups and (local) government are all considered as stakeholders (Groenewegen, 1997) and parts of the business networks.

Japanese Economy

Until the end of the Second World War, the economy was highly concentrated, being dominated by *zaibatsu* (huge oligopolistic financial or industrial trusts). After the war, the Allied occupation decided to dissolve the old *zaibats*u, but new powerful groups appeared under the name of *keiretsu* (industrial and business groups) The three consecutive postwar decades constituted a period of rapid economic growth that transformed Japan in the second economic superpower of the world in the beginning of the 1970s (Kosai, 1986).

Japanese Institutions

The revival of the Japanese economy after the Second World War owed much to the government. The Japanese government in close collaboration with the Ministry of International Trade and Industry (MITI), the Economic Planning Agency, the Supreme Export Council and several Japanese business associations (e.g., the Federation of Economic Organizations, the Federation of Employers' Associations) designed, coordinated and implemented industrial, financial and commercial policies that highly stimulated the development of Japanese companies (Johnson, 1982). There are still tight government-business connections in today's Japanese economy.

Japanese Culture

Shintoism, Confucianism, Buddhism, and Taoism are seen as the formative elements of the Japanese culture (Table 2). The interaction among these religions led to a multilayered and eclectic cultural milieu (Davies, 2016). The term *amae* (a feeling of dependence) defines the Japanese psyche and describes the desire to be loved and protected (Namiki & Sethi, 1988). Other significant Japanese culture themes include the *ringi* (consensus) system, long-termism, domination and *karma* (the results of a person's actions in one life that influence what will happen in his future lives), sensitivity and tactfulness (Bjerke, 1999).

Quality Movement

The 1950s witnessed several visits made to Japan by two American quality gurus, W. E. Deming and J. M. Juran. They were invited by the Union of Japanese Scientists and Engineers to teach the Japanese quality control. Their lectures created a favorable atmosphere to quality in the Japanese companies and quality control became a managerial tool (Ishikawa, 1985, pp. 17-19). As the quality concept penetrated

Table 2. Characteristics of the main religions in Japan

Shintoism	Buddhism	Confucianism	Taoism
The "inside" is pure. There is an intimate connection between men and *kami* (spirits/gods). There is not a clear line of demarcation between man and nature. The man is an integral part of the whole.	Truth lies beyond rational analysis. Human desires cause suffering. Zen meditation and self-discipline, compassion, charity, hospitality, detachment, and internal purification are important. Zen states that people can achieve enlightenment.	There are four principles of right conduct: 1. *jen* (humanism); 2. *li* (faithfulness, loyalty, justice); 3. *li* (propriety, ritual, respect for social norms); 4. *chih* (wisdom).	The human being is a small universe corresponding to the large universe. Introspection, meditation, and reflection are important.

Source: Davies, 2016

most industries, Japan designed and implemented strategies needed for a true quality revolution in the whole economy. According to Juran (1989), some of them were decisive as follows:

- *"The upper managers personally took charge of leading the revolution.*
- *All levels and functions underwent training in managing for quality.*
- *Quality improvement was undertaken at a continuing, revolutionary pace.*
- *The work force was enlisted in quality improvement through the QC-circle concept." (p. 8)*

In fact, there was a holistic Japanese understanding of quality related to quality of the product/service, quality of management, quality of the community relations, quality of the company's performance, quality of the work environment, and quality of the company image in society (Nadler, 1984).

Factors of the Internal Environment

Also, some of the main factors from the internal environment were the following:

TMC History

Toyota started as a small Japanese family-controlled enterprise, Toyoda Loom Works, in 1894. The founder, Sakichi Toyoda (1867-1930), began to design and build wooden spinning machines in order to make easier the weaving job of his mother. His son, Kiichiro (1894-1952) set up TMC, Ltd., in 1937. The pre-war beginning was rather difficult as the manufacturing process was rudimentary, but TMC succeeded in launching its first car, the Model AA Sedan, that combined the body shape of a Chrysler with the engine of a Chevrolet (Magee, 2008, p. 16). In 2008, after a long dominance of the American companies, TMC became the largest automaker of the world. In the period 2014-2015, the Japanese company held the first position (Table 3). At the heart of its success story are the TPS and LM.

Business Philosophy

Sakichi was not only a persevering entrepreneur, a creative machinist and a fast learner, but also a mindful, visionary and assertive industrialist engaged in applying a humanitarian business philosophy to his inventions and promoting a contributive business in society (Table 4). Later, he convinced Kiichiro that

Table 3. The world's largest automakers in the period 2014-2015

Rank	Company	Sales (Number of Cars)	
		2015	2014
1	Toyota (Japan)	10,083,783	10,285,546
2	Volkswagen (Germany)	9,930,600	10,137,400
3	General Motors (USA)	9,800,000	9,924,880

Source: Schmitt, 2016, after company data. GM, VW: Deliveries. Toyota: Production.

it was his turn to make an effort to give something that will benefit the Japanese society (Reingold, 1999). In developing an automobile, Kiichiro succeeded in pursuing one of his father's business ideal: "the betterment of people through creative enterprise", as Magee noticed (2008, p. 15). Sakichi taught Kiichiro many useful things such as the fact that the ability of people to solve problems is unlimited or the need to continuously make improvements in order to reduce waste.

Kiichiro's thinking was also influenced by Shotaro Kamiya (1898-1980). Kamiya's motto "Customer first, dealer second, manufacturer third" guided the company during the time. In this respect, he created new channels of distribution according to the different models of automobiles produced by Toyota, making the purchasing experience easier for its customers. It was possible due to his superior understanding of the necessity of creating co-existence and co-prosperity with dealers and, therefore, offering true customer satisfaction (Kamiya, 1976). According to Hino (2006), three key ideas of Kamiya's thinking are still actually at TMC: "emphasis on the customer, a long-term perspective, and an orientation toward information" (p. 10). At the end of last century, TMC established its guiding principles (Table 5).

Table 4. Toyota precepts (established in 1935)

1. Be contributive to the development and welfare of the country by working together, regardless of position, in faithfully fulfilling your duties.
2. Be at the vanguard of the times through endless creativity, inquisitiveness and pursuit of improvement.
3. Be practical and avoid frivolity.
4. Be kind and generous, strive to create a warm, homelike atmosphere.
5. Be reverent, and show gratitude for things great and small in thought and deed.

Source: Toyota Motor Company, 2016 a

Table 5. Guiding principles at Toyota (established in 1992, revised in 1997)

8. Honor the language and spirit of the law of every nation and undertake open and fair business activities to be a good corporate citizen of the world.
9. Respect the culture and customs of every nation and contribute to economic and social development through corporate activities in their respective communities.
10. Dedicate our business to providing clean and safe products and to enhancing the quality of life everywhere through all of our activities.
11. Create and develop advanced technologies and provide outstanding products and services that fulfill the needs of customers worldwide.
12. Foster a corporate culture that enhances both individual creativity and the value of teamwork, while honoring mutual trust and respect between labor and management.
13. Pursue growth through harmony with the global community via innovative management.
14. Work with business partners in research and manufacture to achieve stable, long-term growth and mutual benefits, while keeping ourselves open to new partnerships.

Source: Toyota Motor Company, 2016b

Leadership

One of the key successful elements of TMC has been the continuity of leadership during its history that comprises three main periods: struggle, growth, and the leap forward (Sato, 2008, p. 334). In each period TMC enjoyed the presence of great leaders such as Sakichi, Kiichiro or Eiji Toyoda. In Eiji's view, the main features of a leader are creativity, resourcefulness, wisdom, and hard work (Magee, 2007, p. 35). In fact, most of the presidents and managers of Toyota have proved to be visionary leaders who have set and realized ambitious *hoshin* (goals), strongly believed in *nemawashi* (a consensus-based process for discussing problems and identifying potential solutions together with all affected people), and constituted enduring examples for all the employees.

Learning Organization

TMC has created a favorable work environment for learning and knowledge sharing. Its leaders have endlessly expressed their commitment for lifelong learning. By continually seeking technical improvements, Sakichi traveled to Europe and studied the British machineries produced by Platt Brothers & Co., Ltd. There, he acquired new knowledge, including the Western business principles. Also, Sakichi bought and read Samuel Smiles' motivational book *Self-Help* that promoted the virtues of self-improvement and thrift (Liker, 2004, p. 17). On his turn, Kiichiro traveled to Detroit in the USA, where he meticulously analyzed the assembly line designed by Henry Ford. After stepping up the automobile research and production activities within Toyoda Automatic Loom Works in 1934, he dispatched an engine-casting specialist, Suda Takatoshi, to the USA in order to study the manufacturing of components in the automotive industry. After the war, TMC chose "to learn by doing rather than buy in ready-made equipment and designs, copying Western machines in their own workshops and adapting them to the smaller volumes demanded by the Japanese market", as showed by Tolliday and Zeitlin (1986, p. 14), and participated in the American training programs (e.g., process improvement). In the early 1950s, Eiji Toyoda (1913-2013), Kiichiro's cousin, visited the Ford's Rouge Plant in Detroit. He worked together with Taiichi Ohno (1912-1990), as they both were disciples of "learning by doing" philosophy, and developed some important concepts such as *kaizen* (continuous improvement).

People

A Toyota saying, *mono zukuri wa hito zukuri* (making things is about making people), synthesizes the fact that people are company's treasure. Since its establishment, TMC has always made appreciable efforts to carefully select, recruit, train, develop and motivate people, and to fully integrate them into the lean work environment. For example, Kiichiro recruited Japanese automobile experts and succeeded together in completing a prototype motorcycle engine by the end of 1933. Also, he rapidly understood the importance of marketing in creating and developing a successful business and appointed Kamiya, a businessman, to begin Toyota's sales and marketing operations in 1935.

TPS

The roots of LM are to be found in the TPS, a system that has continuously evolved during the time. A self-made man, Sakichi learned from practice and invented manual and power looms that were cheaper and better than the old looms. His approach based on trial and errors led to the appearance of *genchi genbutsu* (going to the source in order to solve problems and improve processes). He also thought to automatically stop the loom whenever something was wrong through a mechanism that evolved into *jidoka* (autonomation/automation with a human touch), one of the pillars of TPS. Following his father's legacy, Kiichiro made an important contribution to the future Toyota's *kanban* (small card) system which was similar to the American supermarket system. As the successor of the Fordist system, TPS proved to be initially the proper system for a smaller market as the Japanese market, and later, the best solution for the whole global automotive industry. In Liker's view (2004), Toyota leaders understood the need to adapt Ford's manufacturing system "to achieve simultaneously high quality, low cost, short lead times, and flexibility" (p. 21) and launched a production system that incorporates key stakeholders according to the principle "customer first, employee satisfaction, and company stability", as pointed out by Magee (2008, p. 27). The goal of the TPS is the absolute elimination of *muda* (waste). Starting from this goal derive the following three subordinate objectives: highest quality, lowest cost, and shortest lead time (Magee, 2008, p. 31). As waste absorbs resources without creating value (Basu & Wright, 2004), the first step in implementing the TPS is to identify all types of waste (e.g., waste of overproduction, waste of stock on hand (inventory), waste of making defective products, etc.). Each type of waste corresponds to a specific form of loss in value such as loss in material or equipment utilization (Ruffa, 2008). Finally, by the elimination of *muda* TMC is improving its operating efficiency. The two main pillars of the TPS are:

- **Just-In-Time (JIT):** According to Ohno (1988), JIT means that "the right parts needed in assembly reach the assembly line at the time they are needed and only in the amount needed" (p. 4), and imposes hard work, dedication, harmony, cooperation and discipline within a flow process (Schonberger, 1982).
- Autonomation, which is related to the fact that machines are equipped with a special device that stops them instantly when defective products appear.

These pillars are supported by other concepts of the TPS such as *monozukuri* (the spirit of manufacturing), *shojinka* (flexible work force), and *soikufu* (creative thinking/inventive ideas). Putting all these concepts and principles in practice has required the establishment of specific systems (e.g., *kanban*, visual control, etc.) and methods (e.g., production smoothing, standardization of operations, etc.) (Monden, 1988, pp. 1-13).

Basically, LM changes the way TMC is organized internally and externally, and provides an adequate framework for CSV. Thus, LM stimulates and promotes stakeholders' engagement in the value creation process. The Japanese automaker has succeeded in CSV by actively involving its main stakeholders through various methods, tools, techniques and practices, mostly specific to LM (Table 6), as follows:

1. Employees:

Since its establishment, TMC has realized that human resources are its most important asset. The employees themselves consider that the company is a community (Womack, Jones, & Roos, 1991) or a family in which "one lives within and should identify with and belong to", as Pascale and Athos noticed (1986, p. 179), because Toyota provides jobs and training, contributes to the well being of its work force, creates a friendly work environment based on respect for people, encourages learning, stimulates participation and working in teams, offers access to numerous facilities (housing, recreation), etc. This is why Toyota people are loyal to their company and think that they share together the same destiny (Yoneyama, 2007, p. 213).

Learning-by-doing, learning in teams, training and work experience show that Toyota's employees are both lifelong learning and knowledge workers. As a consequence, Osono, Shimizu and Takeuchi (2008) considered TMC as "a quintessential exemplar of the knowledge-driven approach to growth thus far" (p. 209) and Hines, Holweg and Rich (2004) saw it as a learning organization that seeks to "maximize the learning opportunities of employees, suppliers, customers and even competitors" (p. 1005). This means that Toyota exhibits a total dedication to developing people (Liker & Meier, 2007, pp. 6-7).

In comparison with the traditional model of work organization, Toyota proposes a more humanistic and integrated work system that puts on the first place the understanding of people and human motivation (Jönsson & Schölin, 2014, p. 1005). Employees' integration is facilitated through social relations both inside and outside the company (e.g., using *senseis* as master teachers and mentors). In this light, quality circles are designed to "address not only quality issues but also such issues as cost, safety, and productivity", as showed by Imai (1997, p. 10). Suggestion boxes are also used to gather ideas from quality circles and individuals.

In order to minimize employee turnover, to support organizational cohesion, to increase organizational flexibility and to strengthen its operational efficiency and maintenance capability, TMC provides on-the-job and off-the-job training to its employees (Matsuo, 2015, p. 1186). For example, Toyota Motor Manufacturing (UK) implemented a three-year, in-house adult-apprenticeship program designed for workers with no technical qualification. Another tool, *Hoshin Kanri*, allows the negotiation of each work unit's objectives and the establishment of periodic cycles of reflection and learning (Sagalovsky, 2015, p. 973-974).

TMC has made significant efforts to change management and workers into *Kaizen*-conscious people. In Imai's (1986) view, *Kaizen* constitutes a "customer-driven strategy for improvement" (p. xxxii) that leads to increased customer satisfaction.

2. Customers:

TMC has understood that customers are interested in buying products that "are accompanied by good after-sales services, are of reliable quality, and have good compatibility and long lifetimes with little dispersion", as Ishikawa noticed (1993, p. 18). Also, Toyota's culture focuses on building long-term relationships with customers and providing the value they desire by working closely together (Womack & Jones, 2007; Liker & Hoseus, 2008). The "voice of the customers" is heard and incorporated into the product through the quality function deployment, a quality tool that facilitates systematic co-operation between Toyota's departments.

3. Suppliers:

TMC has established long-term partnerships with its suppliers by sharing with them the value pie in a higher proportion. This leads to better quality relationships characterized by trust and commitment (Wagner & Lindemann, 2008, pp. 545-546), but supplier partnering means much more for Toyota: learning and joint improvement activities, consulting assistance, information sharing, control systems, etc. (Liker & Meier, 2006, pp. 273-290). For example, TMC dispatches *shukko* (original equipment manufacturer (OEM) purchasing managers) to monitor the suppliers' performance. As suppliers are seen as business partners, TMC support them through various groups such as Toyota's Supplier Commodity Engineering, Operations Management Consulting Division or Toyota Supplier Support Center (Marksberry, 2012, pp. 281-282).

4. Competitors:

Interesting enough is the fact that Toyota has collaborated with its competitors. In 1984, TMC created New United Motor Manufacturing (NUMMI), a joint-venture with General Motors. Toyota sought to open its first manufacturing base in the USA whereas General Motors had the opportunity to assimilate the TPS. NUMMI was an example of knowledge transfer between TMC and General Motors. Toyota tested its capacity to implement the TPS in an American factory whereas the American automaker learned how to use Toyota's lean approach.

The roots of CSV at TMC are to be found in its "respect for humanity" philosophy. From this point of view, Toyota has always sought harmony among people, society and the environment, and continuously strived to contribute to the social progress of society. Thus, Toyota "will lead the way to the future of mobility, enriching lives around the world with the safest and most responsible ways of moving people", according to its vision (TMC, 2017a, para. 1). In this way, the Japanese automaker has declared its long-term commitment towards CSV. Consequently, TMC is CSV together with its stakeholders as follows (Toyota Foundation, 1974; Toyota Motor Corporation, 2006: Toyota Mobility Foundation, 2016; Toyota Motor Company, 2017b):

- In connection with its Board of Directors, and in collaboration with universities and other companies, TMC established the Toyota Foundation in 1971 to promote and finance activities that bring benefits to society (Table 7). As a grant-making foundation, it aims to protect human and natural environments, and to support education, culture and social welfare.
- In connection with its Board of Directors, and in collaboration with governments, universities, non-profit organizations, and research institutions, TMC created the Toyota Mobility Foundation in 2014 to develop a better mobile society and enrich the lives of communities. The company helps to improve the quality of life of local residents from various areas (e.g., rural communities, mountainous regions, populous cities) through mobility.
- TMC carries forward its core belief of creating ever-better cars for its customers all over the world. By highly involving its employees and suppliers, and by continuously seeking to understand the customers' needs, the company has unrelentingly faced the challenges of contributing to society by producing ever-better cars. In order to provide well-built and low-emission cars (Table 7) TMC promotes smart and innovative *monozukuri* in working together with its suppliers.
- TMC has created a harmonious, safe and lively work environment together with its employees. The company provides equal employment opportunities for all people, respects employee rights, and complies with all labor laws and regulations of the countries where it operates. Also, TMC supports and stimulates the personal development of employees worldwide.
- In close cooperation with the communities within it acts, TMC has deployed environmental preservation activities. The company understands the necessity of environmental conservation, embraces a proactive policy, and seriously takes environmental impacts into consideration.

Table 6. Methods, tools, techniques and practices used by TMC in order to involve its main stakeholders in CSV

Stakeholder	Methods and Practices
Employees	• Job security • On-the-job and off-the-job training • Job rotation • Job variety • Cross training • Organizational, team and individual learning • Quality circles (QC) • *Kaizen* groups • Quality function deployment • Teamwork • Empowerment • Team based problem solving • Cause and effect diagrams • Suggestion system • Fast feedback • Five whys • Standardized and simplified work • *Poka yoke* (mistake proofing) • Cross functional management • Compensation and rewards, etc.
Customers	• Innovative and reliable products • Ongoing communication • Voice of the Customer (VOC) • Customer support • After-sales service, etc.
Suppliers	• Long-term partnerships • Monitoring supplier activity • Joint problem solving and improvement activities • Training • Ongoing communication • Building networks of suppliers and supplier associations • Financial assistance • Technology transfer • Joint ventures, etc.
Competitors	• Strategic alliances • Joint ventures, etc.

- TMC has worked closely with its employees and suppliers to comply with the national and international legislation and to take appropriate measures against any illegal or criminal acts. So, the company contributes to the realization of a secure global society.

In sum, there is a Toyota Way in CSV. Firstly, TMC is CSV according to the Toyoda precepts and its guiding principles. Secondly, the Japanese company proves to represent a valuable example for other automakers by redefining its goal as providing low-emission mobility. Thirdly, value creation at TMC is shared with its multiple stakeholders because of its LM approach. Fourthly, TMC has enhanced its corporate values, gained competitive advantages, and obtained environmental sustainability by embedding societal needs in its way of doing businesses.

Table 7. Societal benefits of CSV at TMC

Levels of CSV	Societal Benefits
Reconceiving products and markets	• Designing and producing well-built and eco-friendly cars • Providing smart, affordable, distinctive, and fun to drive cars to ensure safety, peace of mind, and *Waku-doki* (excitement and exhilaration that wows people) • Creating and producing automated driving technologies which lead to the emergence and implementation of the mobility teammate concept (people and cars are partners) • Providing special cars for people with disabilities and older persons • Developing solutions for next generation mobility • Providing traffic safety campaigns • Develop solutions to meet critical mobility needs through design thinking, etc.
Redefining productivity in the value chain	• Enriching lives communities and societies • Providing low-emission mobility • Adopting more low CO2 emission materials and reducing carbon footprint • Improving job skills • Increasing employees' incomes • Providing a better work environment • Reducing raw materials consumption • Reducing energy use • Promoting use of renewable energy • Optimizing water usage • Adopting more recycled biomaterials, etc.
Enabling local cluster development	• Supporting the revival and reconstruction of communities • Developing human relationships and encouraging mutual support • Increasing human happiness • Increasing social welfare • Promoting educational programs • Creating, developing and transmitting culture • Collaborating to multigenerational and multicultural inclusion in communities • Contributing to a safer and more secure society • Increasing job creation • Involving in charitable activities, etc.

CONCLUSION

CSV represents a challenging attempt for today's companies all over the world. Putting together corporate interests and societal needs still remains a difficult task for them. However, more and more companies have demonstrated a greater involvement in social and environmental issues in recent years.

This study aims to make a number of contributions both from a theoretical and practical perspective. From a theoretical standpoint, it brings some clarifications related to the shared value concept which has become a popular topic in the business literature in the past decade. The results show that in comparison with the old view on value creation, co-creation imposes companies to take into account a broad spectrum of societal needs. Also, they demonstrate that value is increasingly created by companies through the engagement of their multiple stakeholders and implies, therefore, the connectivity between several economic actors as shown in other researches (Freeman, 2010). This means that CSV imposes companies to embed a social purpose in their business philosophy as they exist to serve society within they function as it is illustrated by the LM paradigm. This is why the chapter provides a theoretical model of linking LM and CSV at TMC.

From a practical point of view, TMC constitutes a valuable case study in which the Japanese automaker is CSV through LM. The results show that LM stimulates the active involvement of Toyota's stakeholder in the value creation process. Also, the study concludes that there is a specific Toyota Way in CSV based on the fact that TMC has made continuous efforts to contribute to society by producing ever-better cars and offering low-emission mobility. As the current case study is limited to TMC, future research should focus on expanding the analysis to other companies for further validation.

REFERENCES

Aakhus, M., & Bzdak, M. (2012). Revisiting the Role of Shared Value in the Business-Society Relationship. *Business & Professional Ethics Journal*, *31*(2), 231–246. doi:10.5840/bpej201231211

Abo, T. (2014). Researching international transfer of the Japanese-style management and production system: Hybrid factories in six continents. *Asian Business & Management*, *14*(1), 5–35. doi:10.1057/abm.2014.13

Albert, M. (1993). *Capitalism Against Capitalism*. London: Whurr.

Almquist, E., Senior, J., & Bloch, N. (2016). The Elements of Value. *Harvard Business Review*, *94*(9), 47–53.

Argandoña, A. (2011). *Stakeholder theory and value creation*. IESE Business School- University of Navarra, WP-922. Retrieved May 29, 2016, from http://www.iese.edu/research/pdfs/di-0922-e.pdf

Bassi, L., Frauenheim, E., McMurrer, D., & Costello, L. (2011). *Good Company: Business Success in the Worthiness Era*. San Francisco, CA: Berrett-Koehler Publishers.

Basu, R., & Wright, N. (2004). *Quality Beyond Six Sigma*. Oxford, UK: Elsevier Butterworth-Heinemann.

Baxter, P., & Jack, S. (2008). Qualitative Case Study Methodology: Study Design and Implementation for Novice Researchers. *Qualitative Report*, *13*(4), 544–559.

Bhappu, A. D. (2000). The Japanese family: An institutional logic for Japanese corporate networks and Japanese management. *Academy of Management Review*, *25*(2), 409–415.

Biggemann, S., Williams, M., & Kro, G. (2014). Building in sustainability, social responsibility and value co-creation. *Journal of Business and Industrial Marketing*, *29*(4), 304–312. doi:10.1108/JBIM-08-2013-0161

Bjerke, B. (1999). *Business Leadership and Culture*. Cheltenham, UK: Edward Elgar. doi:10.4337/9781840647600

Blocker, C. P., Flint, D. J., Myers, M. B., & Slater, S. F. (2011). Proactive customer orientation and its role for creating customer value in global markets. *Journal of the Academy of Marketing Science*, *39*(2), 216–233. doi:10.1007/s11747-010-0202-9

Bowman, C., & Ambrosini, V. (2010). How value is created, captured and destroyed. *European Business Review*, *22*(5), 479–495. doi:10.1108/09555341011068903

Bryman, A., & Bell, E. (2015). *Business Research Methods* (4th ed.). Oxford, UK: Oxford University Press.

Burton, N. (2015). *Toyota MR2: The Complete Story*. Wiltshire, UK: Crowood Press.

Busco, C., Frigo, M. L., Riccaboni, A., & Quattrone, P. (Eds.). (2013). *Integrated Reporting: Concepts and Cases that Redefine Corporate Accountability*. New York, NY: Springer-Verlag GmbH. doi:10.1007/978-3-319-02168-3

Butler, H. N. (1989). The contractual theory of the corporation. *George Mason University Law Review*, *11*(4), 99–123.

Chakravarthy, B. (2010). The sharing imperative. *Strategy and Leadership*, *38*(1), 37–41. doi:10.1108/10878571011009877

Charron, R., Harrington, H. J., Voehl, F., & Wiggin, H. (2015). *The Lean Management Systems Handbook*. Boca Raton, FL: CRC Press.

Costa, J. E. R., & Martí, J. M. R. (Eds.). (2012). *Towards a New Theory of the Firm: Humanizing the Firm and the Management Profession*. Bilbao: Fundación BBVA.

Craig-Smith, N. (1990). *Morality and the Market: Consumer Pressure for Corporate Responsibility*. London: Routledge.

Crane, A., Palazzo, G., Spence, L. J., & Matten, D. (2014). Contesting the Value of Creating Shared Value. *California Management Review*, *56*(2), 130–153. doi:10.1525/cmr.2014.56.2.130

Davies, R. J. (2016). *Japanese Culture: The Religious and Philosophical Foundations*. Rutland, VT: Tuttle Publishing.

Devinney, T. M. (2009). Is the Socially Responsible Corporation a Myth? The Good, the Bad, and the Ugly of Corporate Social Responsibility. *The Academy of Management Perspectives*, *23*(2), 44–56. doi:10.5465/AMP.2009.39985540

Doz, Y. L., & Hamel, G. (1998). *Alliance Advantage: The Art of Creating Value through Partnering*. Boston, MA: Harvard Business School.

Drucker, P. F. (1946). *The Concept of the Corporation*. New York, NY: Harper Collins Publishers.

Dugger, W. M. (1989). *Corporate Hegemony*. Westport, CT: Greenwood Press.

Dul, J., & Hak, T. (2008). *Case Study Methodology in Business Research*. Oxford: Butterworth-Heinemann.

Eisenhardt, K. M. (1989). Building Theories from Case Study Research. *Academy of Management Review*, *14*(4), 532–550.

Farquhar, J. D. (2012). *Case Studies Research for Business*. Thousand Oaks, CA: Sage Publications. doi:10.4135/9781446287910

Feagin, J. R., Orum, A. M., & Sjoberg, G. (Eds.). (1991). *A Case for the Case Study*. Chapel Hill, NC: The University of North Carolina Press.

Fitzgerald, N., & Cormack, M. (2006). *The Role of Business in Society: An Agenda for Action*. Retrieved May 26, 2016, from https://www.hks.harvard.edu/m-rcbg/CSRI/publications/report_12_CGI%20Role%20of%20Business%20in%20Society%20Report%20FINAL%2010-03-06.pdf

Flyvbjerg, B. (2006). Five Misunderstandings About Case-Study Research. *Qualitative Inquiry*, *12*(2), 219–245. doi:10.1177/1077800405284363

Freeman, R. E. (1984). *Strategic Management – A Stakeholder Approach*. Boston, MA: Pitman.

Freeman, R. E. (2010). Managing for Stakeholders: Trade-offs or Value Creation. *Journal of Business Ethics*, *96*(1), 7–9. doi:10.1007/s10551-011-0935-5

Friedland, J. (Ed.). (2009). *Doing Well and Good: The Human Face of the New Capitalism*. Charlotte, NC: Information Age Publishing.

Friedman, M. (1970). The social responsibility of business is to increase its profits. In T. Beauchamp & N. Bowie (Eds.), Ethical Theory and Business (pp. 50–55). Upper Saddle River, NJ: Prentice Hall.

Frigo, M. L., & Ramaswamy, V. (2009). Co-creating strategic risk-return management. *Strategic Finance*, *5*(May), 25–33.

George, M. L. (2003). *Lean Six Sigma for Service: How to Use Lean Speed and Six Sigma Quality to Improve Services and Transactions*. New York, NY: McGraw-Hill.

Gerring, J. (2007). *Case Study Research: Principles and Practices*. New York, NY: Cambridge University Press.

Gomm, R., Hammersley, M., & Foster, P. (2000). *Case Study Method: Key Issues, Key Texts*. Thousand Oaks, CA: Sage Publications.

Grace, D., & Lo Iacono, J. (2015). Value creation: An internal customers perspective. *Journal of Services Marketing*, *29*(6/7), 560–570. doi:10.1108/JSM-09-2014-0311

Grant, R. M. (2013). *Contemporary Strategy Analysis*. Chichester, UK: Wiley.

Greenwood, M. (2007). Stakeholder engagement: Beyond the myth of corporate responsibility. *Journal of Business Ethics*, *74*(4), 315–327. doi:10.1007/s10551-007-9509-y

Groenewegen, J. (1997). Institutions of capitalisms: American, European, and Japanese systems compared. *Journal of Economic Issues*, *31*(2), 333–347. doi:10.1080/00213624.1997.11505921

Haksever, C., Chaganti, R., & Cook, R. G. (2004). A Model of Value Creation: Strategic View. *Journal of Business Ethics*, *49*(3), 291–305. doi:10.1023/B:BUSI.0000017968.21563.05

Hart, S. L., & Milstein, M. B. (2003). Creating sustainable value. *The Academy of Management Executive*, *17*(2), 56–67. doi:10.5465/AME.2003.10025194

Hartman, L. P., & Werhane, P. H. (2013). Proposition: Shared Value as an Incomplete Mental Model. *Business Ethics Journal Review*, *1*(6), 36–43. doi:10.12747/bejr2013.01.02

Hearn, G., & Pace, C. (2006). Value-creating ecologies: Understanding next generation business systems. *Foresight*, *8*(1), 55–65. doi:10.1108/14636680610647147

Hines, P., Holweg, M., & Rich, N. (2004). Learning to evolve. *International Journal of Operations & Production Management*, *24*(10), 994–1011. doi:10.1108/01443570410558049

Hino, S. (2006). *Inside the Mind of Toyota: Management Principles for Enduring Growth*. New York, NY: Productivity Press.

Hofstede, G., Hofstede, G. J., & Minkow, M. (2010). *Cultures and Organizations: Software of the Mind* (3rd ed.). New York, NY: McGraw-Hill.

Hong, P., Doll, W. J., Nahm, A. Y., & Li, X. (2004). Knowledge sharing in integrated product development. *European Journal of Innovation Management*, *7*(2), 102–112. doi:10.1108/14601060410534393

Imai, M. (1986). *Kaizen: The Key to Japan's Competitive Success*. New York, NY: McGraw-Hill.

Imai, M. (1997). *Gemba Kaizen: A Commonsense, Low-Cost Approach to Management*. New York, NY: McGraw-Hill.

Ingelsson, P., & Mårtensson, A. (2014). Measuring the importance and practices of Lean values. *The TQM Journal*, *26*(5), 463–474. doi:10.1108/TQM-07-2012-0047

Ishikawa, K. (1985). *What is Quality Control? The Japanese Way*. Englewood Cliffs, NJ: Prentice-Hall.

Ishikawa, K. (1993). *Introduction to Quality Control*. Tokyo: 3A Corporation.

Jacquemont, D. (2014) The organization that renews itself: Lasting value from lean management. In C. Johnson (Ed.), *The Lean Management Enterprise* (pp. 8-15). Retrieved December 12, 2016, from www.mckinsey.com/leanmanagement/2014_lean_management_enterprise_compendium.ashx

Jensen, M. C. (2001). Value Maximisation, Stakeholder Theory, and the Corporate Objective Function. *European Financial Management*, *7*(3), 297–317. doi:10.1111/1468-036X.00158

Johnson, C. (1982). *MITI and the Japanese Miracle: The Growth of Industrial Policy, 1925-1975*. Stanford, CA: Stanford University Press.

Jönsson, S., & Schölin, T. (2014). Potentials facilitators of workplace learning in a TPS based company. *Journal of Management Development*, *33*(10), 1004–1018. doi:10.1108/JMD-10-2012-0130

Juran, J. M. (1989). *Juran on Leadership for Quality: An Executive Handbook*. New York, NY: The Free Press.

Kamiya, S. (1976). *My Life with Toyota*. Toyota Motor Sales Company, Ltd.

Kanter, R. M. (2011). How Great Companies Think Differently. *Harvard Business Review*, *89*(11), 66–78.

Katayama, H., & Benett, D. (1996). Lean production in a changing competitive world: A Japanese perspective. *Journal of Operations & Production Management*, *16*(2), 8–23. doi:10.1108/01443579610109811

Koenigsaecker, G. (2013). *Leading the Lean Enterprise Transformation* (2nd ed.). Boca Raton, FL: CRC Press.

Kosai, Y. (1986). *The Era of High-Speed Growth. Notes on the Postwar Japanese Economy*. Tokyo: University of Tokyo Press.

Krafcik, J. F. (1988). Triumph of the lean production system. *Sloan Management Review*, *30*(1), 41–52.

Krzyżanowska, M., & Tkaczyk, J. (2014). Shared Value Creation and Marketing. *Management and Business Administration. Central Europe*, *22*(4), 153–167.

Lai, F., Zhang, M., Lee, D. M. S., & Zhao, X. (2012). The Impact of Supply Chain Integration on Mass Customization Capability: An Extended Resource-Based View. *IEEE Transactions on Engineering Management*, *59*(3), 443–456. doi:10.1109/TEM.2012.2189009

Langtry, B. (1994). Stakeholders and the moral responsibilities of businesses. *Business Ethics Quarterly*, *4*(4), 431–443. doi:10.2307/3857342

Lawrence, A. T., & Weber, J. (2008). *Business and Society*. New York, NY: McGraw-Hill Irwin.

Leavy, B., & Moitra, D. (2006). The practice of co-creating unique value with customers: An interview with C. K. Prahalad. *Strategy and Leadership*, *34*(2), 4–9. doi:10.1108/10878570610652581

Lepak, D. P., Smith, K. G., & Taylor, M. S. (2007). Value creation and value capture: A multilevel perspective. *Academy of Management Review*, *32*(1), 180–194. doi:10.5465/AMR.2007.23464011

Letaifa, S. B. (2014). The uneasy transition from supply chains to ecosystems. *Management Decision*, *52*(2), 278–295. doi:10.1108/MD-06-2013-0329

Lewis, M. A. (2000). Lean production and sustainable competitive advantage. *International Journal of Operations & Production Management*, *20*(8), 959–978. doi:10.1108/01443570010332971

Liberman, M. B., & Balasubramanian, N. (2007). *Measuring Value Creation and Its Distribution Among Stakeholders of the Firm*. Retrieved May 29, 2016, from http://www.anderson.ucla.edu/faculty/marvin.lieberman/docs/LiebermanSubra_VCD.pdf

Liker, J. K. (Ed.). (1998). *Becoming Lean: Inside Stories of U.S. Manufacturers*. Portland, OR: Productivity Press.

Liker, J. K. (2004). *The Toyota Way: 14 Management Principles from the World's Greatest Manufacturer*. New York, NY: McGraw-Hill.

Liker, J. K., & Hoseus, M. (2008). *Toyota Culture: The Heart and Soul of the Toyota Way*. New York, NY: McGraw-Hill.

Liker, J. K., & Meier, D. P. (2006). *The Toyota Way Fieldbook: A Practical Guide for Implementing Toyota's 4Ps*. New York, NY: McGraw-Hill.

Liker, J. K., & Meier, D. P. (2007). *Toyota Talent: Developing your People the Toyota Way*. New York, NY: McGraw-Hill.

Liker, J. K., & Ross, K. (2017). *The Toyota Way to Service Excellence*. New York, NY: McGraw-Hill.

Magee, D. (2008). *How Toyota Became #1: Leadership Lessons from the World's Greatest Car Company*. New York, NY: Portfolio.

Marksberry, P. (2012). Investigating The Way for Toyota suppliers. A quantitative outlook on Toyota replicating efforts for supplier development. *Benchmarking: An International Journal*, *19*(2), 277–298. doi:10.1108/14635771211224572

Matsuo, M. (2015). Human resource development programs for knowledge transfer and creation: The case of the Toyota Technical Development Corporation. *Journal of Knowledge Management*, *19*(6), 1186–1203. doi:10.1108/JKM-03-2015-0108

May, M. E. (2007). *The Elegant Solution: Toyota's Formula for Mastering Innovation*. New York, NY: The Free Press.

Michelini, L., & Fiorentino, D. (2012). New business models for creating shared value. *Social Responsibility Journal*, *8*(4), 561–577. doi:10.1108/17471111211272129

Miles, J. A. (2012). *Management and Organization Theory*. San Francisco, CA: Jossey-Bass.

Mohammed, M. (2013). Corporate accountability in the context of sustainability- a conceptual framework. *EuroMed Journal of Business*, *8*(3), 243–254. doi:10.1108/EMJB-05-2013-0026

Monden, Y. (1998). *Toyota Production System: An Integrated Approach to Just-In-Time*. Norcross, GA: Engineering & Management Press.

Moore, J. F. (2006). Business ecosystems and the view from the firm. *Antitrust Bulletin*, *51*(1), 31-75. Retrieved May 27, 2016, from http://www.antitrustinstitute.org/files/Business%20ecosystems%20and%20the%20view%20from%20the%20firm,%20antitrust%20bu_081320081450.pdf

Murman, M. E., Allen, T., Bozdogan, K., Cutcher-Gershenfeld, J., McManus, H., Nightingale, D., & Widnall, S. et al. (2002). *Lean Enterprise Value: Insights from MIT's Lean Aerospace Initiative*. New York, NY: Palgrave. doi:10.1057/9781403907509

Nadler, L. (1984). What Japan learned from the U.S.- that we forgot to remember. *California Management Review*, *26*(4), 46-61.

Nakane, C. (1972). *Japanese Society*. Berkeley, CA: University of California Press.

Namiki, N., & Sethi, S. P. (1988). Japan. In R. Nath (Ed.), *Comparative Management* (pp. 55–96). Pensacola, FL: Ballinger Publishing Company.

Narver, J. C., & Slater, S. F. (1990). The Effect of a Market Orientation on Business Profitability. *Journal of Marketing*, *54*(4), 20–35. doi:10.2307/1251757

Narver, J. C., Slater, S. F., & MacLachlan, D. (2004). Responsive and proactive market orientation and new-product success. *Journal of Product Innovation Management*, *21*(5), 334–347. doi:10.1111/j.0737-6782.2004.00086.x

Nitobé, I. (2002). *Bushido: The Soul of Japan*. Tokyo: Kodansha International.

Ohno, T. (1988). *Toyota Production System Beyond Large-Scale Production*. Portland, OR: Productivity Press.

Okimoto, D. I., & Rohlen, T. P. (Eds.). (1988). *Inside the Japanese System*. Stanford, CA: Stanford University Press.

Osono, E., Shimizu, N., Takeuchi, H., & Dorton, J. K. (2008). *Extreme Toyota: Radical Contradictions That Drive Success at the World's Best Manufacturer*. Hoboken, NJ: John Wiley & Sons.

Ozaki, R. S. (1991). *Human Capitalism. The Japanese Enterprise System as World Model*. Tokyo: Kodansha International.

Pascale, R. T., & Athos, A. G. (1986). *The Art of Japanese Management*. London: Penguin Books.

Payne, A. F., Storbacka, K., & Frow, P. (2008). Managing the co-creation of value. *Academy of Marketing Science Journal, 36*(1), 83–96. doi:10.1007/s11747-007-0070-0

Pfitzer, M., Bockstette, V., & Stamp, M. (2013). Innovating for Shared Value. *Harvard Business Review, 91*(7), 100–107.

Piketty, T. (2014). *Capital in the Twenty-First Century*. Cambridge, MA: The Belknap Press of Harvard University Press. doi:10.4159/9780674369542

Pirson, M. (2012). Social entrepreneurs as the paragons of shared value creation? A critical perspective. *Social Enterprise Journal, 8*(1), 31–48. doi:10.1108/17508611211226575

Porter, M. E., Hills, G., Pfitzer, M., Patscheke, S., & Hawkins, E. (2012). *Measuring Shared Value: How to Unlock Value by Linking Social and Business Results*. Retrieved January 3, 2017, from http://animus-csr.com/docs/Measuring_Shared_Value.pdf

Porter, M. E., & Kramer, M. R. (1999). Philanthropy's New Agenda: Creating Value. *Harvard Business Review, 77*(6), 121–131. PMID:10662001

Porter, M. E., & Kramer, M. R. (2002). The Competitive Advantage of Corporate Philanthropy. *Harvard Business Review, 80*(12), 56–68. PMID:12510538

Porter, M. E., & Kramer, M. R. (2006). Strategy and Society: The Link between Competitive Advantage and Corporate Social Responsibility. *Harvard Business Review, 84*(12), 78–92. PMID:17183795

Porter, M. E., & Kramer, M. R. (2011). Creating Shared Value. *Harvard Business Review, 89*(1/2), 62–77.

Post, J. E., Preston, L. E., & Sauter-Sachs, S. (2002). *Redefining the Corporation: Stakeholder Management and Organizational Wealth*. Stanford, CA: Stanford University Press.

Prahalad, C. K., & Ramaswamy, V. (2000). Co-opting customer competence. *Harvard Business Review, 78*(1), 79–90.

Prahalad, C. K., & Ramaswamy, V. (2004a). *The Future of Competition: Co-Creating Unique Value with Customers*. Boston, MA: Harvard Business School.

Prahalad, C. K., & Ramaswamy, V. (2004b). Co-creation experiences: The next practice in value creation. *Journal of Interactive Marketing, 18*(3), 5–14. doi:10.1002/dir.20015

Prahalad, C. K., & Ramaswamy, V. (2004c). Co-creating unique value with customers. *Strategy and Leadership, 32*(3), 4–9. doi:10.1108/10878570410699249

Priem, R. L. (2007). A consumer perspective on value creation. *Academy of Management Review*, *32*(1), 219–235. doi:10.5465/AMR.2007.23464055

Ramaswamy, V. (2008). Co-creating value through customers experiences: The Nike case. *Strategy and Leadership*, *36*(5), 9–14. doi:10.1108/10878570810902068

Ravald, A., & Grönroos, C. (1996). The value concept and relationship marketing. *European Journal of Marketing*, *30*(2), 19–30. doi:10.1108/03090569610106626

Reingold, E. (1999). *Toyota: People, Ideas, and the Challenge of the New*. London: Penguin Books.

Ruffa, S. A. (2008). *Going Lean: How the Best Companies Apply Lean Manufacturing Principles to Shatter Uncertainty, Drive Innovation, and Maximize Profits*. New York, NY: AMACOM.

Saarijärvi, H., Kannan, P. K., & Kuusela, H. (2013). Value co-creation: Theoretical approaches and practical implications. *European Business Review*, *25*(1), 6–19. doi:10.1108/09555341311287718

Sagalovsky, B. (2015). Organizing for Lean: Autonomy, recursion and cohesion. *Kybernetes*, *44*(6/7), 970–983. doi:10.1108/K-01-2015-0020

Sato, M. (2008). *The Toyota Leaders*. New York, NY: Vertical.

Schmitt, B. (2016). *Nice Try VW: Toyota Again World's Largest Automaker*. Retrieved May 10, 2016, from https://dailykanban.com/2016/01/nice-try-vw-toyota-again-worlds-largest-automaker/

Schonberger, R. J. (1982). *Japanese Manufacturing Techniques: Nine Hidden Lessons in Simplicity*. New York, NY: The Free Press.

Serafeim, G. (2014). *The Role of the Corporation in Society: An Alternative View and Opportunities for Future Research*. Harvard Business School, Working paper 14-110. Retrieved May 21, 2016, from http://www.hbs.edu/faculty/Publication%20Files/14-110_e7a7f1b3-be0d-4992-93cc-7a4834daebf1.pdf

Shah, R., & Ward, P. T. (2007). Defining and developing measures of lean production. *Journal of Operations Management*, *25*(4), 785–805. doi:10.1016/j.jom.2007.01.019

Shamah, R. A. M. (2013). Measuring and building lean thinking for value creation in supply chains. *International Journal of Lean Six Sigma*, *4*(1), 17–35. doi:10.1108/20401461311310490

Shaw, W. H., & Barry, V. (2016). *Moral Issues in Business*. Boston, MA: Cengage Learning.

Slater, S. F., & Narver, J. C. (1995). Market Orientation and the Learning Organization. *Journal of Marketing*, *59*(3), 63–74. doi:10.2307/1252120

Slater, S. F., & Narver, J. C. (1998). Customer led and market-oriented: Lets not confuse the two. *Strategic Management Journal*, *19*(10), 1001–1006. doi:10.1002/(SICI)1097-0266(199810)19:10<1001::AID-SMJ996>3.0.CO;2-4

Smith, J. B., & Colgate, M. (2007). Customer value creation: A practical framework. *Journal of Marketing Theory and Practice*, *15*(1), 7–23. doi:10.2753/MTP1069-6679150101

Soriano-Meier, H., & Forrester, P. L. (2002). A model for evaluate the degree of the leanness of manufacturing firms. *Integrated Manufacturing Systems*, *13*(2), 104–109. doi:10.1108/09576060210415437

Stake, R. E. (1994). Case studies. In N. K. Denzin & Y. S. Lincoln (Eds.), *Handbook of Qualitative Research* (pp. 236–247). Thousand Oaks, CA: Sage Publications.

Stake, R. E. (1995). *The Art of Case Study Research*. Thousand Oaks, CA: Sage Publications.

Stålberg, L., & Fundin, A. (2016). Exploring a holistic perspective on production system improvement. *International Journal of Quality & Reliability Management*, *33*(2), 267–283. doi:10.1108/IJQRM-11-2013-0187

Tolliday, S., & Zeitlin, J. (Eds.). (1986). *The Automobile Industry and its Workers: between Fordism and Flexibility*. Cambridge, UK: Polity Press.

Toma, S.-G., & Marinescu, P. (2013). Social responsibility versus corporate social irresponsibility. *Economy & Business*, *7*(3), 109–115.

Toyota Foundation. (1974). *Prospectus and History*. Retrieved March 31, 2016, from https://www.toyotafound.or.jp/english/profile/history.html

Toyota Mobility Foundation. (2016). *Mobility Issues*. Retrieved December 29, 2016, from http://www.toyotamobilityfoundation.org/en/ projects/

Toyota Motor Company. (2016a). *Toyota Precepts: The Base of the Global Vision*. Retrieved March 31, 2016, from http://www.toyota-global.com/company/toyota_traditions/company/apr_2012.html

Toyota Motor Company. (2016b). *Guiding Principles at Toyota*. Retrieved March 29, 2016, from http://www.toyota-global.com/company/ vision_philosophy/guiding_principles.html

Toyota Motor Company. (2017a). *Toyota Global Vision*. Retrieved January 3, 2017, from http://www.toyota-global.com/company/vision_philosophy/toyota_global_vision_2020.html

Toyota Motor Company. (2017b). *Sustainable Management Report*. Retrieved January 3, 2017, from http://www.toyota-global.com/sustainability/report/ar-smr/pdf/sustainable_management_report16_fe.pdf

Toyota Motor Corporation. (2006). *Toyota Code of Conduct*. Retrieved March 31, 2016, from http://www.toyota-global.com/company/history_of_toyota/75years/common/pdf/code_of_conduct.pdf

Tsai, W., & Ghoshal, S. (1998). Social capital and value creation: The role of intrafirm networks. *Academy of Management Journal*, *41*(4), 464–476. doi:10.2307/257085

Van der Borgh, M., Cloodt, M., & Romme, A. G. L. (2012). Value creation by knowledge-based ecosystems: Evidence from a field study. *R & D Management*, *42*(2), 150–169. doi:10.1111/j.1467-9310.2011.00673.x

Von Liel, B. (2016). *Creating Shared Value as Future Factor of Competition: Analysis and Empirical Evidence*. Wiesbaden: Springer Fachmedien. doi:10.1007/978-3-658-12603-2

Wagner, S. M., & Lindemann, E. (2008). Determinants of value sharing in channel relationships. *Journal of Business and Industrial Marketing*, *23*(8), 544–533. doi:10.1108/08858620810913353

Wallman, S. M. H. (1999). Understanding the Purpose of a Corporation: An Introduction. *The Journal of Corporation Law*, *24*(4), 807–818.

Womack, J. P., & Jones, D. T. (2003). *Lean Thinking. Banish Waste and Create Wealth in Your Corporation*. New York, NY: Free Press.

Womack, J. P., & Jones, D. T. (2007). *Lean Solutions: How Companies and Customers Can Create Value and Wealth Together*. London: Simon & Schuster.

Womack, J. P., Jones, D. T., & Roos, D. (1991). *The Machine that Changed the World: The Story of Lean Production*. New York, NY: Harper Perennial.

Yin, R. K. (1984). *Case Study Research: Design and Methods*. Beverly Hills, CA: Sage Publications.

Yin, R. K. (2009). *Case Study Research: Design and Methods* (4th ed.). Thousand Oaks, CA: Sage Publications.

Yin, R. K. (2012). *Applications of Case Study Research* (3rd ed.). Thousand Oaks, CA: Sage Publications.

Yoneyama, E. (2007). Phenomenology of life, Zen and management. *Society and Business Review*, *2*(2), 204–217. doi:10.1108/17465680710757411

Zadek, S. (2004). The path to corporate responsibility. *Harvard Business Review*, *82*(12), 125–132. PMID:15605571

Chapter 8
The Impact of Events:
To Which Extent Are They Sustainable for Tourist Destinations? Some Evidences From Expo Milano 2015

Patrizia Silvestrelli
University of Macerata, Italy

ABSTRACT

This chapter argues about some of the main effects generated by cultural events on the host territory with the aim at verifying under which conditions an event creates value for all stakeholders and is sustainable. Sustainability is not a static condition but an ever-changing process, which should lead to enhanced life conditions from an economic, social and environmental point of view. This requires that all stakeholders not only participate but also deeply share values as well as local resources, take part in common projects and act to achieve mutual goals. In this regard, Expo Milano 2015 is analyzed as a significant example, because not only it promotes a virtuous theme but also it represents the product of intents and values shared by different organizations. However, despite the undisputed value generated by the event, the aim is to call into question its degree of sustainability, in relation to the policies implemented for promoting the event, the firms' strategy, as well as the social and economic effects in Milan and in Italy.

INTRODUCTION

Coherently to the book's theme, this chapter aims at presenting some critical issues about sustainable development in case of events performing. The goal is to analyze the effects of an event in the host territory and evaluate if the value generated is sustainable for *all* stakeholders from an economic, social and environmental point of view.

The Expo Milano 2015 is a significant example of event and definitely suitable for our aim at least for two reasons. First of all, it is an exceptional event able to *attract* people from all over the world, so it has presumably a deep impact over the host territory. Secondly, it promotes a particular *theme* that is «Feeding the Planet. Energy for Life». Sustainability is addressed to food sector development, in terms

DOI: 10.4018/978-1-5225-3147-0.ch008

of providing sufficient and healthy food for all the world inhabitants, finding sustainable solutions for production and consumption and sharing best practices and guidelines for the future. It is clear that this theme makes the event very interesting for many organizations, which operate in different sectors but share the urgency to face the problem of how to "feed the planet" and prevent hunger, especially in consideration of the rapid depletion of agricultural resources.

In these terms, the exposition becomes, on one side, a *social meeting place* for people directly involved in the fair and, on the other side, one among the most powerful *cultural attractions* for tourists in Milan. This double feature enhances the destination's value from both a social and tourist point of view and increases the destination attractiveness.

However, more attractiveness does not necessary imply sustainable development. Certainly, cultural events make destinations more attractive but we cannot take for granted that sustainability is improved because the tourist flow increases. In fact, the tourism incoming can alter the equilibrium of local communities as well as the activities promoted to perform the event can damage other local businesses. In the article published by The Guardian in May 12th 2015, Oliver Wainwright, one of the most famous art critic in the world, not only criticizes the event, but also calls into question the effectiveness of all universal exhibitions, because of high costs, incongruity between intentions and actions and controversial effects in the territories.

The role of governance is certainly crucial to develop initiatives aimed at improving sustainability. Governance should involve organizations from both public and private sectors as well as civil society, working all together within a set of values and principles. This requires trust between stakeholders, who share knowledge, rules and responsibilities, including co-funding. In other words, it means to act as a *network*, which implies not only *participation* but also *profound sharing*.

This is stated in the main document of UNWTO Algarve Forum, held in Portugal in 2011, according to which we should consider new ways to ensure innovation and sustainable development by means of governance through *networking*, which can foster cooperation among a large range of stakeholders, in order to transform collective intelligence into decisions and actions.

All these issues direct our attention to the need of verifying the degree of sustainability of the event. This means to assure that Expo would be able to create sustainable value not only in the short but also in the medium and long term for Milan as well as the whole country, from an economic, social and environmental point of view.

BACKGROUND

Organizing cultural events with high tourist potential requires a noteworthy effort to the host territory, local institutions, firms and citizens in terms of resources consumption, local investments and coordination of all activities, aimed at both planning and implementing the event. However, in considering the advantages that these events can carry along, a number of cities have followed a strategy of hosting mega-events in order to boost their reputation and economies (Roche, 1994; Burbank, Andranovick & Heying, 2001).

Events can be seen as "tourist products", arising from creativity (individual and collective) and able to generate cultural innovation and enhance the destination attractiveness. Several scholars of *event management* focus on the event development to increase destination competitiveness. Getz (2008) claims that territories should plan and develop events like firms invest for their new products, because they contribute consistently to the place's growth. Moreover, events create new business spaces that allow entrepreneurs within the community to leverage or change existing institutional arrangements (Essex & Chalkley, 1998; Meyer, Brooks & Goes, 1990).

From a tourist point of view, events allow people to live fulfill experiences and, for this reason, they have to be unique and able to involve tourists and inhabitants emotively and physically (Pine & Gilmore, 1999). Clearly, every event acquires specific features in relation to the place where is performed. Even more, specific local resources make a field suitable for particular events (Law, 1996). According to Resciniti (2008), three are the basic factors of event management required to enhance tourist experience: a) *Program* (the core of tourist offering), b) *Location* (the place where the event is performed) and c) *Services* (to make the event feasible).

However, we cannot assume that the event's impact in the host field always leads to a real growth, particularly in the long term. In fact, an event can alter in different ways the economic, social and natural environment and this puts seriously in question the value of the *whole* happening (Baade & Matheson, 2004; Cherubini, Bonetti, Iasevoli & Resciniti, 2009; Fourie & Santana-Gallego, 2011; Zimbalist, 2015).

Regardless the fact that organizations may be permanent or temporary, events are the result of networking, involving different actors through "cooperation chains" (Sedita, 2009). Among those actors, tourist plays an important role as a protagonist and co-producer of the tourist experience (Pine & Gilmore, 1999). If tourists participate in the event is plausible to believe that the event will be successful. At the same time, the way in which people participate in the event determines the level of its performance (Gregori, Pencarelli, Splendiani & Temperini, 2013).

Networking requires an appropriate governance, though. One of the first challenge to make an event successful lies in the ability of governance (local administrators and/or private firms) to meet the interests of all stakeholders who participate directly or indirectly in the event. Indeed, stakeholders have usually different degree of importance in territorial and urban development (De Nisco, Riviezzo & Napolitano, 2008) and, therefore, it is crucial to identify which ones are more prevalent in terms of degree of commitment, interests and power in affecting decisions and results.

Moreover, it is important to qualify the type of interrelations between firms and environmental factors within the destination and comprehend how these relationships generate value and sustainability for all stakeholders, increasing the destination competitiveness (Dredge, 2006, 2010; Halme & Fadeeva, 2000; Pavlovich, 2001; Tinsley & Lynch, 2001; Tyler & Dinan, 2001).

Destination governance is thus crucial in terms of planning, coordination and integration and for that reason it requires to be "participated", which means *unanimously shared* by all stakeholders. This implies to embrace disparate interests, enhance the projects promoted, and integrate all activities, in order to create an event that is heterogeneous in the inside and congruent in the outside towards the audience.

The role of governance becomes more complex when the event has an international dimension, like great expositions, and thus involves both local operators and foreign organizations. The event's site becomes the center of a complex network of relationships that transcends national boundaries, involving actors who are somehow different in size, notoriety and *modus operandi* but share values and purposes inspiring the whole event. Consequently, the success of these initiatives depends on the ability of the organizations to operate as a "system" not only to plan and implement the activities aimed at performing the event, but also to verify and measure the impact that the event generates over the host territory. Clearly, it is more difficult to deal with numerous stakeholders, but if they partake of projects improving the *community well-being* it is likely that a more profuse degree of sustainability can be reached (Henderson, 2005; Pechlaner, Bachinger, Volgger & Anzengruber-Fischer, 2014).

The definition of sustainability has been formalized by the *World Commission on Environment and Development* (Brundtland Commission) in 1987. The report defined sustainable development as «development which meets the needs of current generations without compromising the ability of future generations to meet their own needs». This implies to combine economic growth with social development and environmental resources safeguard. In this regard, we mention the three pillars of sustainable development that organizations should take in consideration:

- **Economic Effectiveness:** It is related to organization *well-acting*, which implies pursuing company mission, obtaining adequate economic returns, and generating wealth for the community. In other words, to remain effective and efficient in the long term.
- **Social Effectiveness:** It concerns the ability of maintaining fair relationships not only with employees but also with all other stakeholders, primarily the local actors sited where the company is rooted, respecting their needs and expectations.
- **Environmental Effectiveness:** It is associated to the respect of natural heritage, which implies to employ resources rationally and avoid damages in order to maintain the natural equilibrium of the environment.

These three dimensions should inspire all entrepreneurial and managerial actions; at the same time, they can be also guidelines for every human behavior and the whole society, including citizens as well as public and private policy makers.

In base of what previously stated, we wonder which kind of *impacts* in the host filed occur. Specifically, does the event generate value for *all* stakeholders? Moreover, is that *value sustainable in the long term* that means to be effective from an economic, social and environmental point of view?

In order to investigate about the abovementioned issues, we take into consideration the event Expo Milan 2015, which is analyzed by adopting a *qualitative* approach. This method is well suited for our aim, since it allows us to investigate a contemporary phenomenon within its real-life context, having not clear both multiple sources of evidence and boundaries between phenomenon and context. This type of approach leads to identify facts, actors and their interactions, and extrapolate significant implications useful to explain economic and social phenomena (Edmondson & McManus, 2007).

Concerning tools to measure the impact of Expo Milano 2015, the model edited by the World Tourism Organization (UNWTO) to estimate the level of sustainable development in tourist destinations is appropriate.

In relation to the *economic* dimension, the indicators are *economic-financial* and *strategic-competitive*. While the first one concerns to *quantitative* elements (number of participants, ticket revenues and resources invested for the event), the second one provides *qualitative* hints (event's notoriety, synergies coming from the interaction among different actors, and opportunity to develop employment and entrepreneurship).

For evaluating the *social* dimension, it is important to identify tangible and intangible aspects of the benefits arising from the event and any possible change in the residents' quality of life. Some examples are investments in infrastructures, increase of social cohesion, satisfaction and participation in the event, job opportunities and tourist development.

Finally, with regard to the *environmental* dimension, performing the event should not provoke alteration in the natural equilibrium of the host territory, like modifying landscape, producing noise and air pollution, increasing waste, and overusing energy and water resources.

We can therefore assume that an event is sustainable when it satisfies the economic purposes of the operators involved, meet the social and cultural needs of residents and tourists and, finally, preserves the natural environment where the event is performed (the destination).

From a tourism development point of view, all those aspects are the prerequisites to make a destination competitive. In this regard, we agree with the model of Weaver (2000; 2005; 2012), who emphasizes the fact that tourism destination development can be reached if two specific conditions take place together:

- **Tourism Intensity:** It indicates tourists-residents ratio, number of employees in tourist activities and accommodation capacity.
- **Regulation:** It refers to tourism legislation, environmental law, community wellness, integration policies and cultural heritage safeguard.

The two conditions should be taken as primary factors to measure the tourism destination competitiveness and they cannot be analyzed separately. In fact, it is within the combination between tourist intensity and regulation that it is possible to evaluate the destination competitiveness, because tourism incoming is important but not sustainable if not disciplined by regulation policies. In the following sections, we will try to verify these issues in relation to Expo Milano 2015.

THE EXPO 2015: PLANNING AND MANAGING THE EVENT

World Expositions are huge international events aimed at providing a cultural, educational and commercial experience to visitors and countries taking part in the event. They give the opportunity to people from around the world to meet and talk, reinforcing cooperation and integration between the different populations.

World Expositions take place every five years, every time in a different country, and gather communities, organizations, operators and citizens towards topics of great interest. These events are managed by the *Bureau International des Expositions* (BIE), established in Paris in 1928, which defines every time the Expo's objective as well as oversees and regulates calendar, biddings, participation rules and event management.

In order to analyze the impact of the event in the host territory, it can be useful to explain some important characteristics of this type of event.

World Expositions can be classified in two categories:

- **Registered:** They are the biggest category events, also called "major".
- **Recognized:** They are somehow unofficially fairs, named "minor".

Registered expositions were called also "Universal Expositions", even though this name is no longer in use as an official term. In this type of events, participants generally build their own pavilions for promoting products, culture, business and values. As a result, nations compete for the most outstanding or memorable structures. This makes registered expositions more extravagant and expensive than recognized expositions.

The first World Expo was held in *The Crystal Palace* in Hyde Park, London, United Kingdom, in 1851, under the title "Great Exhibition of the Works of Industry of All Nations". Other famous recent Registered Expositions include Brussels Expo in 1958, Montreal Expo in 1967, Osaka Expo in 1970, and Seville Expo in 1992.

On the other side, recognized expositions – called also *International* or *Specialized Expositions* – are smaller in scope and investments and generally shorter in duration (between three weeks and three months) and they usually take place between two registered exhibitions. Compared to registered exhibitions, they require minor investments since the architectural fees are lower. Participants have only to rent the space from the host committee and use prefabricated structures that are adjusted with the nation's colors, design and brands (*country identity*) and equipped to exhibit products and services (Jackson, 2008).

With regard to registered World Expositions, they have become an important place for international dialogue, public diplomacy and cooperation among countries, in regard of crucial issues challenging the global community. The 2015 edition was located in Milan and promoted the theme «Feeding the Planet. Energy for Life» from May 1st to October 31st 2015. The city became a global showcase where more than 140 countries promoted their technologies and solutions to respond to a serious challenge: being able to guarantee healthy, safe and sufficient food for everyone, while respecting the Planet and its resources.

Therefore, this edition embraces technology, innovation, culture, traditions and creativity, connecting them to food and diet. The aim is to increase awareness on the need of creating the right conditions under which all people of the world can have enough and healthy food.

Within the main issue promoted by the exhibition, there are seven sub-themes:

1. Science for Food Safety, Security and Quality.
2. Innovation in Agro Food Supply Chain.
3. Technology for Agriculture and Biodiversity.
4. Dietary Education.
5. Solidarity and Cooperation on Food.
6. Food for Better Lifestyles.
7. Food in the World's Cultures and Ethnic Groups.

Notwithstanding the value of Expo Milano 2015 and its noble purpose, our goal is to analyze the impacts – positive as well as negative – in the host city. Moreover, our concern is about the *degree of persistence* of those effects. In fact, it is misleading to consider only the effects while the event was performing, like tickets revenues and hotel occupancy. It is important to evaluate also the effects coming up after the event has quit and look at those from a long time perspective.

Although today is not possible yet to assess exhaustively all impacts of the event, it is possible in any case to argue about some topics useful to our analysis. These issues are indicated below and described in the following sessions:

- Choice of Milan as event location.
- Economic impact and effects on tourism sector.
- Variety of stakeholders participating in the event, particularly multinational companies operating in the food industry.
- Employment development and social growth.

Choosing the Event Location

The location for world exhibitions is chosen through a candidacy process, which takes into account place reputation, accommodation capacity and skills in organizing and managing cultural activities, social events and tourist flows. It is obvious that the location should be advanced, so the choice usually falls among selected tourist destinations, which are well developed and known at international level. For the host country, the Exposition is a unique opportunity to show off national culture, traditions, innovations, lifestyle and cultural heritage as well as to build strong international relationships. The Expo Milano 2015 has involved 145 exhibitors, 4 international organizations and some non-government organizations as well as companies as key stakeholders in the global debate on nutrition and food. The event welcomed over 21 million visitors, which visited the 1.1 million square meters exhibition area.

The choice to perform the Expo 2015 in Milan derives from several factors that confirm the important worldwide role of the city from both cultural and economic point of view.

The authority in charge of selecting the location is the *International Exhibition Office* of the *Bureau of International Expositions*, which establishes if a site has some specific prerequisites, like geographical position, availability of an equipped area where to perform the event, number of visitors estimated and support of local authorities. In this regard, Milan met those requirements for several reasons, which are listed below:

1. It is placed in a favorable geographic position, well connected to other cities both at national and international level thanks to the network of infrastructures available.
2. It is one of the most important capitals of fashion and design, representing the *Made in Italy* brand worldwide.
3. It enhances the Italian food traditions through promoting both agricultural production and food industry.
4. It plays an active role in implementing initiatives aimed at enhancing the social context and cooperates with other organizations at international level to improve the people quality of life.
5. It is plentiful of great cultural goods, which attract tourists from all over the world.
6. It represents the strategic center for the Italian economy (specifically for finance, publishing and innovation) and one of the most important economic hub at European level.

Milan is a perfect example of *community destination*, where the munificence of its territory is due to both environmental attractions and policies promoted by local organizations (Pearce, 1999; Pechlaner, Raich & Beritelli, 2010). The city becomes a platform to exchange ideas, share solutions concerning food issues and stimulate each country in promoting innovation with the aim of achieving a more sustainable future.

The Expo has certainly brought several advantages to Milan and its important legacy can be measure in base of both *tangible* and *intangible* factors.

Among *tangible* aspects, we can mention the following ones:

- **Pavilions and Buildings:** Structures specifically built for the event, like the Tree of Life. Concerning previous Expositions, we can cite the well knows *Eiffel Tower* in Paris (1889), *Atomium* in Brussels (1958) or *Space Needle* in Seattle (1962)).

- **Infrastructures and Drivability:** This refers to feasibility improvement of the city.
- **Place Requalification:** It concerns restoration projects for buildings, monuments and stores that enhance the image of Milan.
- **Wellness:** The improvement of citizens' quality of life.
- **Attractiveness:** City appeal upgrading and increase in tourist flow.

Concerning the *intangible* elements, we can say that just the fact that Milan hosted an event promoting a so important theme makes the place remarkable and memorable. The noble nature of the topic is not new for the global community, though. Also previous Expositions have dealt with issues concerning human well-being, like «water safeguard» in Zaragoza (Spain, 1988), «oceans protection» in Yeosu (Korea, 2012) and «quality of life in the cities» in Shanghai (China, 2010).

Humankind and its history are the central themes of Universal Expositions. The human history is told through economic, cultural and political events, like industrial growth, innovations, countries development and social changes. Ever since the first edition in 1851 in The Crystal Palace of London, Universal Expositions have been the perfect stage to show off the most ambitious successes that the humanity has achieved over time. It is a unique occasion not only to share technologies and discoveries, but also to bring to life architectural projects and artistic trends. In the last edition, the topic reflects the huge challenge that global community has to face in finding the right (sustainable) balance between producing food and respecting the planet.

Therefore, the place (destination) becomes representative for the event all over the world and its landscapes and cultural symbols characterize the specific Expo edition, like the Eiffel Tower built in Paris when the city hosted the Exposition in 1889. This usually happens also for other mega-events like Olympics, where – just like Expo – event and place are strongly interconnected. In this regard, Glynn (2008, pp. 1137) highlights that "most cities that host games actively seek to enhance their images and reputation by staging this event; they aspire to legitimately claim the world-class status that is associated with an Olympic city and generally succeed in doing so. And, the very act of staging events in local geographic fields tends to imprint particular events with the character and traditions of the host cities".

The city becomes the *hub* of local, national and international relationships where people coming from different background and culture can share ideas and experiences. Event ideology merges with the place, which is the center of common channels of dialogue and discussion. Moreover, events performing can affect the way institutions and firms interact locally. Events requires to be planned, organized and implemented and, therefore, as underlined by Glynn (2008, pp. 1119) "such institutionalized meanings around events can fortify or change the relationships that structure a filed". In these terms, Milan is not only the territory where the event takes place, but also the *cradle of innovation* (Amato, Varaldo & Lazzeroni, 2006, pp. 25), as it creates knowledge aimed at both improving the people quality of life and making organizations more sustainable in their way of doing business. Knowledge, innovations and solutions are pursued in name of the universal human right to have food and the need to respect natural resources worldwide. In this regard, we can cite some interesting issues that have been discussed in Expo 2015:

- Learn the meaning of sustainability and its dimensions, in order to create a common language and feeling.
- Waste reduction and management (especially for those not biodegradable materials like plastics and chemicals).

- People education to be more eco-friendly and make healthy choices when producing and consuming food.
- Exploit economic and social sciences models to find solutions aimed at improving the degree of sustainability for the global community.

These important issues regard not only today world inhabitants, but also future generations, which will have to face undoubtedly the environmental conditions that *today* we decide to leave them.

This lead to highlight the risks of hosting a mega event (Fourie & Santana-Gallego, 2011; Zimbalist, 2015). We cannot disregard the fact that events like Expo alter the natural spaces in which they occur, because they require greater use of natural resources, development of specific goods and services and improvement of structures and infrastructures that might change the landscape. For the locals, the event can jeopardize their every-day life as well as city livability and places accessibility. A survey conducted before Expo staging by "Voice from the Blog" highlights that residents doubt if the event can have a positive impact on Milan. The major risk they mention concerns delay and deferments as well as deterioration of air pollution, traffic and security, which are the biggest problems affecting the city.

These problems certainly worsened during the event and, in any case, it is quite difficult to estimate in the pre-event phase to which extent they would have really aggravated. It would be useful to evaluate – when possible – *a plan of actions aimed at limiting disadvantages for the host city and making the event's benefits persist in the medium and long term.* This means reestablishing the internal equilibrium of local community after the event ran out, restoring any change occurred in the natural environment, maintaining the economic growth generated and, not least, making plans aimed at dismantling or converting pavilions and structures created on purpose for the event. This last aspect is currently a discussion topic of great attention by local government, private firms and the whole community in Milan.

The Economic Impact and the Effect on Tourism Sector

Involving different operators, the event assumes a multifaceted dimension and its effects in the territory can be quite significant, in terms of both economic development and respect of social and environmental issues (Andranovich, Burbank & Heying, 2001; Williams & Bowdin, 2007; Cherubini *et al.*, 2009).

In this regard, Della Lucia (2013) argues that the impact of an event on the economic system lies in the sum of the activities linked to

- **Direct Costs:** They are related to services production and delivery (e.g. facilities, equipment, advertising).
- **Visitors:** They concern costs related to ticket purchase, accommodation, meals, ecc.
- **Indirect Costs:** They involve cost to provide the resources necessary to create goods and services (e.g. catering, transportation and trading).

Regarding the Expo Milano 2015, SDA Bocconi School of Management in cooperation with the Chamber of Commerce of Milan carried out an interesting study in 2013, which estimated that the event would be able to generate an economic value of 23.6 billion of euro between 2012 and 2020 (Dell'Acqua, Morri & Quaini, 2013). The model for estimating the income of Expo 2015 is based on four different levels of impacts that are listed below:

1. **Direct Economic Impact:** Direct investments made by Expo Ltd. to set up the exhibition site and by foreign organizations to participate in the event; tourist incoming.
2. **Indirect and Induced Economic Impact:** Products and services supplying, activities management and coordination, tourist purchases.
3. **Event Legacy:** Entrepreneurship development, real estate assets improvement, foreign investment increase and tourism sector enhancement.
4. **Technological Infrastructures Improvement and International Relationships Enhancement:** International business development as new contract with foreign partners, economic value, enhancement of Italian products and tourism improvement.

The research highlights that the event's effects would be positive for the territory and we agree with this point. However, at that time the study could not obviously consider the changes occurred both during the event outfitting and while the event was performing, as well as the problems related to ex-post event management. Moreover, costs and revenues estimate are not always realistic: the analysis ex-post about big events often highlights that costs were underestimated while revenues overestimated (Fourie & Santana-Gallego, 2011; Perrotti, 2014; Massiani, 2015). For instance, according to the initial project, the costs for building pavilions have expected to be about 3.2 billion euro, but they have increased considerably over time. As an example, 63 million calculated to create the Italian pavilion increased up to 92 million, a part of which employed to use temporary upholsteries to cover unfinished parts of the pavilion.

Data indicated in the Expo Ltd. final balance (December 31st 2015) show that there is a financial and economic discrepancy between previous budget and financial statement. This situation is not unusual but common in most mega events. In this regard, several scholars and economic operators are sceptical about the economic benefits generated by big events, since the real extent of costs and revenues is not completely clear and it is complicated to evaluate concretely their impact in the host city (Siegfried & Zimbalist, 2002; Baade, 2006; Matheson, 2006).

Concerning the effect on tourism sector, we can undoubtedly assert that in general the Exposition had a positive impact on the territory both a local and national level. However, it is necessary to analyze in detail *where* and *how* the improvement took place and the extent to which tourism development is really sustainable.

Firstly, we wonder if the event has been able to enhance so much the attractiveness of the territory that it became the main motivation for people to go to Milan.

It is clear that Expo Milano 2015 attracted operators from different parts of the world interested in different ways in the theme «Feeding the planet, Energy for Life». At the same time, several tourists went to Milan to participate in the event, visit the site and explore pavilions, even though they were *not directly* involved in the event because more interested in other cultural attractions of the city. In these terms, Expo can be considered a powerful *tourist product*, which enriches tourist offer and attracts visitors, involving them through unique and fulfilling experiences (Gets, 2008; Resciniti, 2008; Pine & Gilmore, 1999).

The increase in hotel booking confirms this view. According to the survey conducted by HRS Hotel Reservation, hotels located both in Milan and in suburban areas have recorded a noteworthy increase in room occupancy rate: in the first three months of Expo (May, June and July) tourists have booked 77% more than in the same period in 2014. Indeed, in those three months, 81% of visitors (59% of which coming from the European countries) declared that the motivation for travelling to Milan was for tourism and their permanence was almost two nights on average, which is more or less the time needed to visit Expo. Based on this survey, it is plausible to affirm that the event could be the main motivation of travelling.

Even though data show a significant increase of tourists between May and September 2015, we have to consider that Expo is an exceptional circumstance. This event is not permanent at all in the city, but strictly temporary because the International Exhibition Office chooses every time a different location. Therefore, all benefits arising from the event have to be evaluated not only during the exhibition but also when the event comes to end and the tourist flow quits moving to the site (Smith, 2006). This implies to measure both costs/benefits for operators and overall effectiveness of the event in the *long term*. On the other hand, the increase of tourist incoming is not sufficient to argue that the *whole* tourist sector has grown. In fact, beyond hotel booking, there are other factors contributing to improve tourism development.

In general, tourism development can take place when all stakeholders share a common project, satisfy their interests and generate economic and social benefits for the entire territory, improving the destination's competitiveness (Glynn, 2008). For Expo, this did not happen in some cases. Some cultural and catering firms, for example, benefited partially from the event and some of those noticed even a decrease in their business. The reason lies in the fact that the tourists interested in the event presumably did not go to visit other historical and cultural sites in Milan, like museums, art galleries and shopping malls (Perrotti, 2014). Even restaurants and bars in downtown did not measure a relevant increase of the number of clients, who probably found more attractive the ones located inside the Expo area. In other words, what happened is related to a *qualitative change in tourist's preferences* and it does not concern a quantitative increase of the activities in which tourists participate.

Another contradictory aspect regards hospitality management in the city. We wonder if it is correct to talk about tourist development, in considering the increase of hotel price occurred from Spring to Autumn 2015. According to a research carried out by Hotel.com on Hotel Price Index, this increase oscillated between 17% and 30%. Certainly, this is a very lucrative policy for hotels, but only in the short time. In fact, significant price modifications can be even counterproductive in the medium and long term, damaging image and degree of attractiveness of the destination Milano. Moreover, this kind of price strategy can seriously compromise tourist experience, who feel betrayed and cheated, especially if room rate is perceived too high in relation to the quality level of the services offered by hotels. This condition cannot be defined fully sustainable.

The Presence of Multinationals: Is It Coherent With Expo Milano 2015?

One of the main criticism to Expo regards the presence of some multinationals belonging to the food sector, like McDonald's and Coca Cola. These companies have invested more than 20 million of euro to build their exhibition stands, which occupied big areas of exposition.

The controversy arises from the fact that these companies are not coherent for mission and market competitive strategies with Expo theme and the message that this event intends to convey. «Feeding the planet. Energy for Life» is addressed to find more sustainable models to cultivate and use food resources, enhance local products and distribute food more equitably among all populations in the world. This is somehow consistent to the *slow food* philosophy, aimed at developing people awareness about the need to market safe products as well as respect traditions, communities and human rights rather than the interest towards performance, profit and company image.

On the contrary, McDonald's and Coca Cola represent multinationals producing for mass markets worldwide. They do not promote slow food beliefs, since they offer to consumers standardized products that, in addition, have been often criticized because of their questionable quality.

Another disapproval comes from the fact these companies take care more of reaching economies of scale through efficient manufacturing systems, delocalization and distribution networks than respecting local communities, improving employment and producing healthy food.

It is reasonable to believe that these multinationals have a "speculative" purpose that leads them to participate in the event. On the other hand, Expo represents an important opportunity for all firms involved not only to promote their brand and expand their international visibility, but also to improve company image. This certainly affects positively customer perception and stakeholders opinion.

The majority of firms are in fact aware about the importance of implementing business actions that are sustainable, because they represent the requisites to reach "legitimateness" in both the task and general environment. In this regard, Cafferata (2014, pp. 18) states that the firm has also a "social" role in the community, which means that it is born to *serve* markets as well as people, to be functional not only to reach the goals of its founder, but also to meet the people and community needs. That is to *satisfy social needs*.

Therefore, is the presence of McDonald's and Coca Cola appropriate in the event? It is not easy to give an answer and, in any case, we would risk to fall into an endless debate about what is "ethically correct" and what is not.

In our opinion, the matter is another. Do McDonald's and Coca Cola generate value for Expo? They probably do. Yet, is this value shared among all firms participating in the event? In our opinion, certainly it is.

The presence of these famous multinationals is able to generate value for both single organizations and the whole event, thanks to the reliability of their global brands (Miyazaki & Morgan, 2001). These brands contribute to strengthen the overall image of the event at least for three reasons:

1. They are well known to all customers worldwide and thus make more "familiar" an heterogeneous event like Expo.
2. Mass products are able to join consumers who are usually different in culture but similar in needs and lifestyle.
3. Communication strategy of these companies merges with the event, reinforcing the final message and attractiveness.

Beyond the possible differences among operators, an event is naturally the result of a *creative process* involving many organizations, which cooperate and share goals, expectations and interests. It is within the network of relationships that the value of the event can be searched (Gregori *et al.* 2013, pp. 222).

From our point of view, multinational companies are not incompatible with Expo, even if they are far away from the principles inspiring the event and the strategies promoted by small firms presenting in the event. More than size and different marketing strategies, it should be useful to focus on the *synergies arising from cooperation through sharing different but complementary knowledge and skills.* This can generate real value. In fact, small enterprises of food sector usually produce high quality goods, but they often lack the skills to promote them successfully, especially at global level. On the contrary, big companies usually produce mass-market goods and know how to deal with the international markets. The opportunity to interact and cooperate can lead these firms to acquire reciprocally knowledge and develop competences to face the worldwide economic challenges.

Moreover, Expo Milano 2015 gave firms the possibility to find out about food production in base of two different factors: traditional cultural values and use of new technologies. These two aspects do not stand apart, but are very much interconnected. Besides being an opportunity for industry players, Great Expositions are firstly part of a *cultural journey* aimed at highlighting the changes that population of the planet is currently facing, and these changes involve seriously large as well as small firms.

Therefore, it is beneficial that all organizations give their contribution in searching new sustainable ways to manage food resources in the planet. In this way, the event acquires a double meaning: it is the *context* for a constructive dialogue and the *tool* to promote successful policies for developing the agri-food sector worldwide.

Employment Development

All activities aimed at building structures and managing initiatives have generated a discrete increase of local employment, although not significantly as supposed. According to the mentioned study by SDA Bocconi and the Chamber of Commerce of Milan, Expo would be able to create 191,000 jobs in the period between 2012 and 2020, the majority of which (about 102,000) regarding people resident in Milan and its province, 26,000 in Lombardia Region and 62,000 in the rest of Italy. The employment of these human resources should have articulated in 35,000 work units in the pre-event phase, 67,000 while the even would have performed and 89,000 in the following five years. According to these forecasts, the event should have affected positively labor market in the long term both at local and national level.

Indeed, the survey identifies the business sectors where a major number of hiring could have taken place, like building construction, tourism and catering, highlighting some differences in relation to different phases of the event (planning, managing and post-event analysis). In the planning stage, the major increase in employment is estimated to be in construction, services and other industrial sector like interior design, food and distribution; during the event, tourism sector, catering and services (for firms and people) involve most of the employees; and finally, in the following years, employment regards mainly business services and commercial activities.

However, despite the undoubted value of this interesting study, the analysis does not take into account that the people hired for Expo may have already a job. This means that it concerns not an increase of the employment as a whole, but an *additional* employment, as highlighted by Perrotti (2014). In other words, it is difficult to distinguish between those people already hired for other business projects and temporary employed in Expo and those ones who was newly hired for the event.

Another problem concerns the type of contracts through which workers have been hired. In many cases, they were short-term contracts, part-time jobs and even stages. This suggest that many people was engaged for the event and there is no guarantee that they will become stable workforce in the future.

The Measurement Centre for Labor Market of the Milan Province carried out a study by comparing the number of employees estimated with the one truly calculated until today. The study highlights that local businesses have hired about 4,700 workers between 2012 and January 2015 (pre-event phase). This is far away from the numbers forecasted in the study previously mentioned, although the 35,000 employees estimated were supposed to come from not only Milan, but also Lombardia Region and the rest of Italy.

Furthermore, the impact of Expo on employment could be marginal, since, according to an Istat survey, labor market in the province of Milan had already improved since 2011, maintaining this positive trend even in the following years. This signifies that employment development does not strictly depend on the event.

In any case, we need to recognize that it is difficult to define the workforce directly or indirectly involved in Expo performing from both a quantitative and qualitative point of view. A deeper analysis about hiring, employment contracts and tasks performed should be done in order to measure to which extent the event has truly affected labor market in Milan, Lombardia Region and Italy.

MEASURING SUSTAINABILITY THROUGH IMPROVING "REGULATION"

From the sustainability point of view, tourism development able to make destinations competitive takes place not only because of an increase in tourist flows, but also thanks to control and regulation over all initiatives, like legal norms, consumer safeguard and respect of residents and communities. In this regard, Weaver (2000) proposes a model that can be useful to measure the sustainability of tourism destinations. The scholar claims that tourist flow alone is not sufficient to create sustainability; instead, a tourist destination becomes sustainable when specific norms regulate all tourist activities with the aim at protecting interests of both people and organizations.

The model is useful from a *static* view because it shows a context of destination development scenarios, which depicts four inclusive tourism ideal types defined by scale and sustainability-conducive regulation (see Figure 1). At the same time, it is even more meaningful if we consider it from a *dynamic* point of view (Weaver, 2000; 2012).

Despite the undisputed value of the "intensity" variable in terms of tourist flow and economic returns, it is advisable that a destination evolved towards sustainable conditions, which takes into account the "regulation" of tourist activities. *Circumstantial alternative tourism* (CAT) is unregulated tourism, which can indicate destinations either living initial stage of life or not involved in high tourist flow (like *tourism niche*). This condition can advance to *unsustainable mass tourism* (UMT) involving more tourist intensity with poor regulation. This evolution is not always beneficial, though. On the contrary, the CAT transition to *deliberate alternative tourism* (DAT) entails more regulation, which implies an improvement from the sustainability point of view, because regulations ensure the preservation of small-scale alternative tourism practices characterizing the CAT destination. Finally, moving to attain *sustainable mass tourism* (SMT) means to build regulations more relevant to large-scale modes of tourism activity.

These paths show a *virtuous cycle* of destination evolution (indicated with black arrows in Figure 1). We have to consider, however, that destination condition can change towards worst scenarios characterizing by low regulation where environmental and social conditions are scarcely sustainable (signed by dotted black arrows in Figure 1).

The dynamic view of the model shows that planning and management of sustainable destinations require the proactive implementation of measures, which better ensure environmentally and socio-culturally sustainable outcomes for large- or small-scale tourism.

If we apply the model to Milano destination, we can say that the city attracts millions of people every year, which are interested not only in cultural local goods but also in events, conferences and shows that the city is used to organize and host. So the *intensity* variable is surely satisfied. What is not fully developed concerns *regulation*, which can be connected to the critical issues argued in the previous sections, like resources exploitation, traffic, security, costs and employment development. These factors did not certainly improve during the event; on the contrary, they showed a certain degree of deterioration.

In base of what stated above, what can we say about the impact of Expo in Milan in terms of sustainable development? Certainly, intensity increased significantly, leading to local growth, in terms of economic returns, tourism development, business improvement and international prestige coming from hosting the event. All of these affect positively destination competitiveness and make the destination

Figure 1. Tourism destination development scenarios
Source: Weaver, 2000.

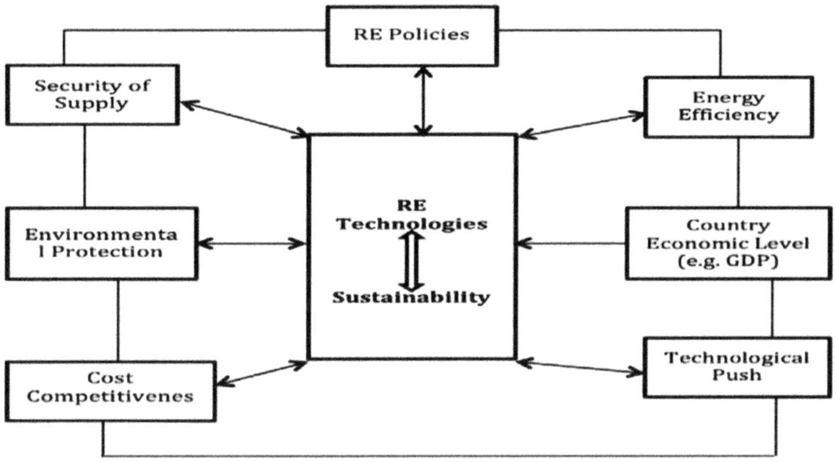

move to a better condition in terms of regulation and, therefore, of sustainability (see Figure 2). However, following what we have argued in the previous sections, those positive effects are maybe not sufficient for reaching sustainable development, since some prerequisites were not – or only partially – satisfied.

CONCLUSION

The Expo theme "Feeding the Planet, Energy for Life" leads to reflect on issues of humanitarian concern, relating not only to sustainable development of agricultural sector and food industry, but also to wellness of the entire world population.

Figure 2. The destination "Milano" and its evolution in Weaver Model
Source: Adapted in Weaver, 2000.

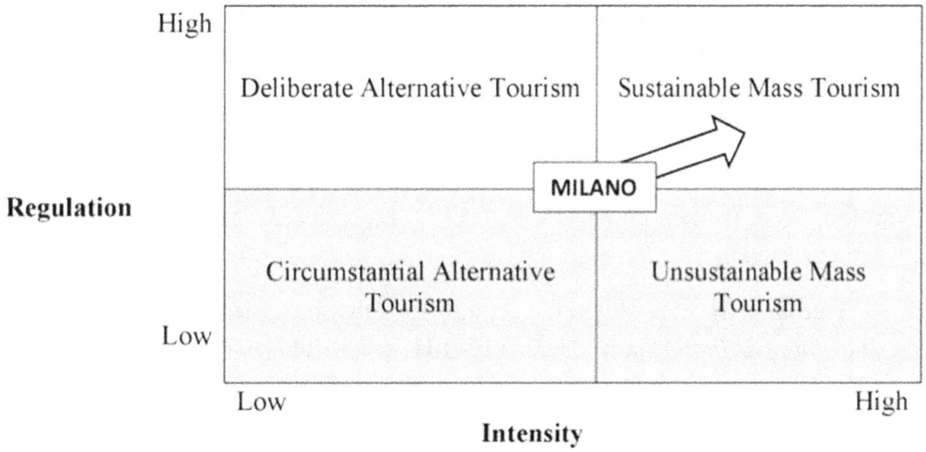

The event had a significant impact in Milan as well as in other neighboring regional and national areas. However, it seems quite difficult to assess the extent to which the event generated economic development and social growth for the local community so far.

We cannot deny that, for host cities, mega-events like Expo bequeath many assets, including the reputation in organizing and managing events of global impact as well as the ability of combining local with international culture, generating economic value and improving community social life. The event becomes the *context* and *tool* to develop sets of relationships and symbolic links among actors who participate in projects and share ideals. At the same time, the field is decisive for Expo success, since it outlines spaces, norms and resources, giving the event the features and symbols of the hosting city. Therefore, event staging requires territorial policies that pursue economic principles, preserve cultural assets of communities and safeguard natural and social environment where communities are located. From this perspective, shared governance is crucial. Policy makers, firms and individuals have to take part in common projects, share values and beliefs with the aim at making economic and social initiatives sustainable.

However, it is not possible to measure precisely the impact of Expo in terms of economic returns for firms, institutions and individuals. The economic impact cannot be evaluated only in relation to infrastructures construction and total commercial activities, because there are other factors affecting the event's result. Partial estimates in ex-ante studies, distortions in analyzing tourist flows and locals participation, alteration of the normal supply-chain activities, misreading employment development and several hidden costs call into question the benefits of hosting a mega event. Therefore, evaluating the impact of Universal Expositions requires a multidimensional approach and complementary tools, which can measure the huge amount of activities and interests involved in the event and clarify their economic links affecting the hosting territory.

Moreover, Expo generated a significant degree of economic growth in the *short* term, but *it seems quite difficult to evaluate such growth and its effects in the medium and long term*. Our analysis shows that what is maybe missing – or not clearly expressed yet – is stakeholders participation and sharing after the event ran out, because *sustainable development acquires a real significance when sought in the medium and long perspective*.

From the tourism point of view, any innovation – including mega-events performing – requires entrepreneurial and institutional behavior accountable for people and territories, which should lead to sharing and collective learning without compromising environmental and cultural assets. The critical task for policy makers is to assess different development paths in terms of their likelihood and desirability. This requires to identifying specific scenarios and, accordingly, designing appropriate strategies.

REFERENCES

Amato, G., Varaldo, R., & Lazzeroni, M. (Eds.). (2006). La città della conoscenza e dell'innovazione. Milano, Italy: Franco Angeli.

Andranovich, G., Burbank, M. J., & Heying, C. H. (2001). Olympic cities: Lessons learned from mega-event politics. *Journal of Urban Affairs*, *23*(2), 113–131. doi:10.1111/0735-2166.00079

Baade, R. (2006). The Economic Impact of Mega-sporting Events. In W. Andreff & S. Szymansky (Eds.), *Handbook on the Economics of Sport*. Cheltenham, UK: Edward Elgar. doi:10.4337/9781847204073.00024

Baade, R., & Matheson, V. (2004). The quest for the Cup: Assessing the Economic Impact of the World Cup. *Regional Studies*, *38*(4), 343–354. doi:10.1080/03434002000213888

Burbank, M. J., Andranovick, G. D., & Heying, C. H. (2001). *Olympic Dreams: The Impact of Mega-Events on Local Politics*. Boulder, CO: Lynne Rienner Publisher.

Cafferata, R. (2014). *Management in adattamento. Tra razionalità economica, evoluzione e imperfezione dei sistemi*. Bologna: Il Mulino.

Cherubini S., Bonetti E., Iasevoli G., & Resciniti R. (2009). *Il valore degli eventi. Valutare ex ante ed ex post gli effetti socio-economici, esperenziali e territoriali*. Milano, Italy: Franco Angeli.

De Nisco, A., Riviezzo, A., & Napolitano, M. R. (2008). The role of stakeholders in town centre management: Guidelines for identification and analysis. *Journal of Place Management and Development*, *1*(2), 166–176. doi:10.1108/17538330810889998

Dell'Acqua A., Morri G. & Quaini E. (2013). *L'indotto di Expo 2015. Analisi di impatto economico*. Milano, Italy: SDA Bocconi.

Della Lucia, M. (2013). Economic performance measurement system for event planning and investment decision making. *Tourism Management*, *34*, 91–100. doi:10.1016/j.tourman.2012.03.016

Dredge, D. (2006). Policy networks and the local organizations of tourism. *Tourism Management*, *27*(2), 269–280. doi:10.1016/j.tourman.2004.10.003

Dredge, D. (2010). Place Change and Tourism Development Conflicts: Evaluating Public Interest. *Tourism Management*, *31*(1), 104–112. doi:10.1016/j.tourman.2009.01.004

Edmonson, A., & McManus, S. (2007). Methodological fit in management field research. *Academy of Management Review*, *4*(4), 1155–1179. doi:10.5465/AMR.2007.26586086

Essex, S. J., & Chalkley, B. (1998). Olympics Games: Catalyst of urban change. *Leisure Studies*, *17*(3), 187–206. doi:10.1080/026143698375123

Fourie, J., & Santana-Gallego, M. (2011). The impact of mega-sport events on tourist arrivals. *Tourism Management*, *32*(6), 1364–1370. doi:10.1016/j.tourman.2011.01.011

Getz, D. (2008). Event Tourism: Definition, Evolution, and Research. *Tourism Management*, *29*(3), 403–418. doi:10.1016/j.tourman.2007.07.017

Glynn, M. A. (2008). Configuring the Field of Play: Hao Hosting the Olympics Games Impacts Civil Community. *Journal of Management Studies*, *45*(6), 1117–1146. doi:10.1111/j.1467-6486.2008.00785.x

Gregori, G. L., Pencarelli, T., Splendiani, S., & Temperini, V. (2013). Sustainable Tourism and Value Creation for the Territory: Towards a Holistic Model of Event Impact Measurement. *Calitatea-Acces to Succes*, *14*(135), 97–102.

Halme, M., & Fadeeva, Z. (2000). Small and medium-size tourism enterprises in sustainable development networks. *Greener Management International*, *30*(Summer), 97–113.

Henderson, J. C. (2005). Planning, changing landscapes and tourism in Singapore. *Journal of Sustainable Tourism*, *13*(2), 123–136. doi:10.1080/09669580508668482

Jackson, A. (2008). *EXPO International Expositions 1851–2010*. London, UK: V&A Publishing.

Law, C. (Ed.). (1996). *Tourism in Major Cities*. London: International Thompson Business Press.

Massiani J. (2015). L'impatto economico dell'Expo, dal sogno alla realtà. *EyesReg*, *5*(4).

Matheson, V. (2006). Economic Impact Analysis. In W. Andreff & S. Szymansky (Eds.), *Handbook on the Economics of Sport*. Cheltenham, UK: Edward Elgar. doi:10.4337/9781847204073.00020

Meyer, A. D., Brooks, G. R., & Goes, J. B. (1990). Environmental jolts and industry revolutions: Organizational response to discontinuous change. *Strategic Management Journal*, *11*, 93–110.

Miyazaki, A. D., & Morgan, A. G. (2001). Assessing market value of event sponsoring: Corporate Olympic sponsorship. *Journal of Business Research*, *41*(Jan-Feb), 9–15.

Nutrire il Pianeta. Energia per la Vita! (2015). Retrieved from http://www.expo2015.org/

Pavlovich, K. (2001). The twin landscapes of Waitamo: Tourism network and sustainability through the Landscape Group. *Journal of Sustainable Tourism*, *9*(6), 491–504. doi:10.1080/09669580108667416

Pearce, D. (1999). Tourism in Paris: Studies at the microscale. *Annals of Tourism Research*, *26*(1), 77–97. doi:10.1016/S0160-7383(98)00051-6

Pechlaner, H., Bachinger, M., Volgger, M., & Anzengruber-Fischer, E. (2014). Cooperative core competencies in tourism: Combining resource-based and relational approaches in destination governance. *European Journal of Tourism Research*, *8*, 5–19.

Pechlaner, H., Raich, F., & Beritelli, P. (2010). *Destination Governance. Tourism Review*, 65(4), 4–85.

Perrotti, R. (2014). *Perché l'Expo è un grande errore*. Retrieved May 3, 2016, from http://www.lavoce.info/wp-content/uploads/2014/05/Perch%C3%A9-lExpo-%C3%A8-un-grande-errore.pdf

Pine, B. J., & Gilmore, J. H. (1999). *The Experience Economy*. Boston, MA: Harvard Business School.

Resciniti, R. (2008). L'event experience per orientare il sistema di offerta. In R. Resciniti & G. Maggiore (Eds.), *Event experience. Progettare e gestire eventi da ricordare*. Napoli: Edizioni Scientifiche Italiane.

Roche, M. (1994). Mega-events and urban policy. *Annals of Tourism Research*, *21*(1), 1–19. doi:10.1016/0160-7383(94)90002-7

Sarti, M. (2015). *Tutti I numeri di Expo 2015*. Retrieved July 12, 2016, from http://www.jobintourism.it/job/articolo.php?id_articoli=24040

Sedita, S. R. (2009). Le organizzazioni project-based. In S. R. Sedita & M. Paiola (Eds.), *Il management della creatività. Reti, comunità e territori*. Roma: Carocci Editore.

Siegfried, J., & Zimbalist, A. (2002). A Note on the Local Economic Impact of Sports Expenditures. *Journal of Sports Economics*, *3*(4), 361–366. doi:10.1177/152700202237501

Smith, A. (2006). After the Circus Leaves Town: The Relationship between Sports Events, Tourism and Urban Regeneration. In K. Smith (Ed.), *Tourism, Culture and Regeneration* (pp. 69–84). Oxon, UK: CABI Publishing. doi:10.1079/9781845931308.0085

The BIE and the Universal Expositions I Expo Milano 2015. (2015) Retrieved on March 7th 2016 from http://www.expo2015.org/archive/en/learn-more/the-history-/the-bie-and-the-universal-expositions.html

The meaning of EXPO Milan 2015. (2015) Retrieved January 14, 2016, from http://www.expo2015.org/archive/en/learn-more/the-history-/the-meaning-of-expo.html

Tinsley, R., & Lynch, P. (2001). Small tourism business network and destination development. *International Journal of Hospitality Management*, *20*(4), 367–378. doi:10.1016/S0278-4319(01)00024-X

Transforming our world: the 2030 Agenda for Sustainable Development (Resolution adopted by the General Assembly on 25 September 2015). (2015). Retrieved November 28, 2015, from http://www.un.org/ga/search/view_doc.asp?symbol=A/RES/70/1&Lang=E

Tyler, D., & Dinan, C. (2001). The role of interest groups in England's emerging tourism policy network. *Current Issue in Tourism*, *4*(2-4), 210–252.

United Nations. (n.d.). *Home. Sustainable Development Knowledge Platform*. Retrieved from https://sustainabledevelopment.un.org/

Wainwright, O. (2015). *Expo 2015: what does Milan gain by hosting this bloated global extravaganza?*. Retrieved October 20, 2016, from http://www.theguardian.com/cities/2015/may/12/expo-2015-what-does-milan-gain-by-hosting-this-bloated-global-extravaganza

Weaver, D. B. (2000). A broad context model of destination development scenarios. *Tourism Management*, *21*(3), 217–224. doi:10.1016/S0261-5177(99)00054-0

Weaver, D. B. (2005). The distinctive dynamics of exurban tourism. *International Journal of Tourism Research*, *7*(1), 23–33. doi:10.1002/jtr.521

Weaver, D. B. (2012). Organic, incremental and induced paths to sustainable mass tourism convergence. *Tourism Management*, *33*(5), 1030–1037. doi:10.1016/j.tourman.2011.08.011

Williams, M., & Bowdin, G. A. J. (2007). Festival evaluation: An explanatory of seven UK arts festivals. *Managing Leisure*, *12*(2-3), 187–203. doi:10.1080/13606710701339520

Zimbalist, A. (2015). *Circus maximus: The Economic Gamble behind Hosting the Olympics and the World Cup*. Washington, DC: Brookings Institution Press.

KEY TERMS AND DEFINITIONS

Economic Impact: The effect that a certain human activity generates in a territory or within a society. From a tourist point of view, hotel management, events and tourist incoming usually affect the economic development of a place.

Expositions: Global fairs aimed at promoting important issues of great interest like innovation technology, social development and human right enhancement. Expo Milan 2015 calls people attention to the urgent need to develop more healthy food and create the requisites to reduce world hunger.

Hospitality: It concerns the ability of a place to welcome gusts and tourists who can enjoy a wide range of services like hotels, restaurants, shops, entertainments, etc.

Sustainable Tourism: The kind of tourism that does not compromise the environmental conditions where tourist activities are developed. It regards firms as well as tourists' behavior in respecting the natural, social and economic environment of a specific place.

Tourist Destination: A city, an area or a country offering differentiated services and products for tourist entertainment. A destination can be considered as a tourist product since it is built up to satisfy tourist needs. Sometimes, just landscapes and natural resources make a place interesting and unique so suitable for tourists wants.

Tourist Event: Any activity, like local fairs, exhibitions and shows, aimed at enhancing tourist destinations and improving tourist offer. It can involve locals as well as foreign people.

Tourist Regulation: All those norms and laws aimed at controlling tourist activities, like hotel policies, safety, waste management, tourist assistance, etc. Tourist intensity – in terms of incoming – is certainly important from an economic point of view, but tourist intensity without regulation can damage the natural environment, compromise tourist loyalty and jeopardize locals' lifestyle.

Tourist Value: The value generated within the tourist sector in relation to both a specific place and an entire country. The value is not only economic but also cultural and social because it enhances people as well as firms' activities. Therefore, tourist value should be holistic that is the result coming from the interaction and synergies among different actors in the territory.

Chapter 9
Managing the Recycling Business in Istanbul:
Inclusion or Exclusion of Waste Pickers?

Nuray Cakirli
University of Goettingen, Germany

Aytug Sozuer
University of Yalova, Turkey

ABSTRACT

The global waste market is estimated at US$410 billion a year and growing, while only 25 per cent of total waste is known as recovered and recycled. Besides, this figure does not include the informal segment in which around 20 million people work as waste pickers in developing countries. Solid waste management policy and recycling practices differ among certain parts of the world to a large extent. Industrialized countries generally have formal and automated waste management systems, whereas developing countries rely on the informal sector. In Istanbul, which is one of the few megacities in the world appear to be at the crossroad of a policy choice. Authorities will either privatize the recycling business for large firms or try to follow more inclusive approach for more than 100,000 waste pickers in the city. Based on the literature, this study will review the formal waste management systems and describe the integration of informal recycling sector in particular world regions that may have policy implications for Istanbul.

INTRODUCTION

Municipal solid waste (MSW) has become a complex problem in major cities of the developing world, mostly due to rapid industrialization and increased urbanization. Particularly, municipalities of the growing cities struggle to handle MSW because of poor collection and disposal systems. Inadequate waste removal and management facilities, as well as continuing population growth and higher consumption levels make MSW management issue much tougher to solve today. Furthermore, if not managed properly, MSW is likely to pollute air, water, and land, which will risk residents' health and environment (Medina, 2005).

DOI: 10.4018/978-1-5225-3147-0.ch009

In order to tackle challenges of managing solid waste, cities respond by improving their MSW management policy, such as installing new waste collection and recycling programs. Although the practices have evolved in recent years, MSW is not being suitably managed and material recovery is still inefficient. Many big city municipalities in developing countries' lack the resources to comply with the growing demand for MSW management services. Thus, many individuals engage in informal waste picking and recycling activities to make a living (Marello & Helwege, 2014).

Informal waste pickers, who are also known as scavengers, collect and commercialize solid waste informally in cities. They perform similar to formal agents in the waste stream. Waste pickers collect recyclable and reusable materials from the generated waste and push forward through the recycling value chain, as do the official or authorized waste collectors (Moreno-Sanchez & Maldonado, 2006). Scavenging contributes to material recovery from the garbage that has already been disposed, yet probably will be lost in dumpsites and landfills unless collected. Moreover, this activity reduces the costs of city's waste management programs by collecting the recyclable material. Besides the quantity of recovered waste, informal waste picking generates income for disadvantaged parts of the community. The studies which point out the economic and environmental benefits of waste pickers suggest that, system improvements without consideration of waste pickers could be highly counter-efficient (Wilson, Velis, & Cheeseman, 2006). Therefore, the recognition of the role that waste pickers could play in MSW programs deems necessary.

Istanbul, a megacity with around 15 million inhabitants, faces MSW management issues as well. Currently, land filling, which is an environmentally unfriendly practice, is the main method for MSW management in the city. However, only half of the 17.000 tons of MSW produced daily in Istanbul could be recycled (ISTAC, 2016). The shortage in services and increase of the needy naturally leads to scavenging activity in this metropolis. The total number of waste pickers is estimated at more than half a million around the country, where approximately one fifth is active in Istanbul. Moreover, the community has been significantly expanded in the last few years due to more than 3 million refugee inflows from war zones in the Middle East (EC, 2016). Although they perform a valuable activity for the ecosystem, a challenge appeared for waste pickers from the local and national authorities restricting their work and permitting only licensed institutions for waste collection. Based on media resources, it is inferred that the formal waste management community tries to eliminate the informal sector in order to collect the complete recycling rent, especially in major cities of Turkey. Recent developments also show that the authorities are drawing regulations in favour of formal enterprises. Despite many initiatives and researches around the world signal the integration of waste pickers in the formal network as a viable option for inclusive development, the approach taken in Istanbul appears to the contrary.

Apparently, there are pros and cons of granting exclusivity to public and private enterprises for recycling business compared to formalizing and organizing waste pickers as an inclusive policy option. The purpose of this study is to present the examples of recycling management in highly industrialized nations and developing countries in order to understand the materialization of both systems. Therefore, the context and actions in different parts of the world will be reviewed to evaluate their relevance for MSW management in Istanbul.

The study first describes the MSW management and the informal recycling sector in general and then presents those issues in the context of Istanbul. The interpretations of the study would likely have policy implications for the emerging metropolis.

MUNICIPAL SOLID WASTE MANAGEMENT

Overview

The term "waste" is any substance which is discarded after primary use, including solid, semi-solid or contained gaseous materials, originating from various industries, commercial operations, and from community activities (USEPA, undated). Urban waste differs from waste in that it consists of organic and inorganic components. The heterogeneous collection of urban waste, the nature of which differs region to region, is known as municipal solid waste (UNEP, 2005). The definition of municipal solid waste differs from one country to another. Further, it has changed over time and some reported the MSW as the amount collected rather than generated (EEA, 2015). OECD (2008) defines municipal waste, as type of waste collected and treated by, or for municipalities and consists of predominantly household waste, and bulky and commercial waste, as well as similar waste handled at the institutions and small business, commerce and trade, office buildings, street sweepings. Waste generated from sewage networks and treatment, from municipal construction and demolition is excluded from the definition.

Waste management is one of the important issues of concern that the priority is given especially in industrialized nations. Waste generation rates differ widely within and between countries. It usually depends on sociocultural characteristics, income levels, as well as climatic factors. Similarly, MSW collection, composition, disposal, and recycling practices also vary from developed and developing countries, from urban and rural areas, and from industrial and household producers. There is a strong positive relationship between the waste generation rates and income levels. For instance, one of the latest available data within the period 2005-2012 show that, the median generation rates of high-income countries are about six times higher than in low-income countries (UNEP, 2015). Another projection in Figure 1, illustrates that the higher income level and higher rates in urbanization cause higher amount of solid waste production.

According to the World Bank (2012), countries are classified into four income levels. The classification of the countries is countrywide, besides, it should be noted that, in several countries the average national affluence can be very different from the average affluence of the urban populations. Therefore, urban residence is important for projecting waste. In addition, since China has been included in the lower middle income group, compared to upper-middle income group, the average per capita waste generation amount for this group increased. Overall, the figure shows that the amount of urban waste will be much more in high-income countries than upper and lower middle income countries in 2025.

In high-income countries, recyclable material collection services are usually undertaken formally. Facilities with respect to sorting and processing are also common and regulated. There is an increasing attention towards long-term markets. In middle-income countries, there has been high technology sorting and processing facilities, thus recycling rates are relatively high. In respect, recycling markets in these countries are more regulated. There have been almost no organized programs regarding recycling in low-income countries. Recyclable materials often contain odd and ends of different items such as e-waste and ship-breaking. The large price fluctuations also appear in these markets due to unregulated operations. In addition, recycling activities exist through the informal sector and include a number of middlemen, who purchase recyclables collected through the informal waste picking and sells to scrap dealers, who in turn sell them to the industry (UNEP, 2015).

Figure 1. Urban waste generation by income level and year (World Bank, 2012)
Source: World Bank, 2012

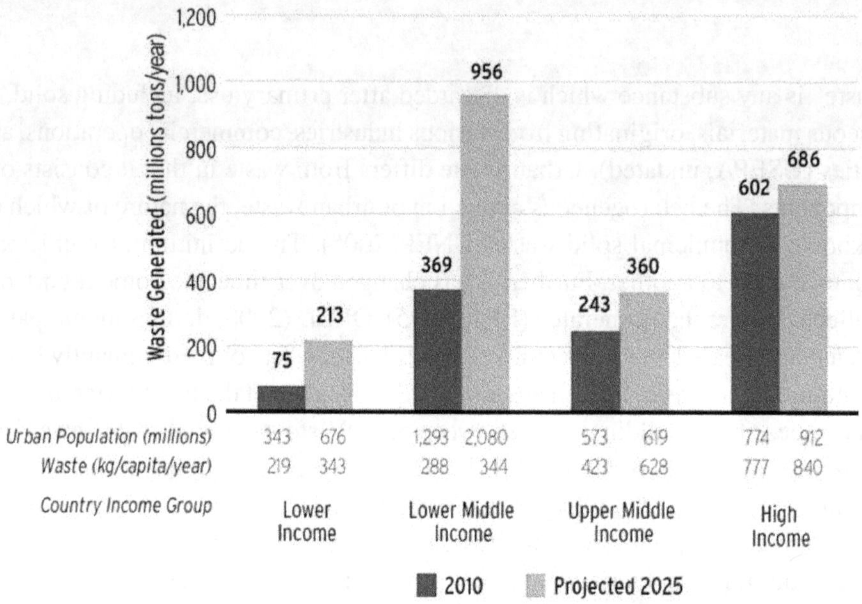

Solid wastes generated in developing countries are primarily disposed of to landfill, since this option has been the simplest, cheapest and most cost-effective method for waste disposal (Barrett & Lawler, 1995; Palmer, Sigman, & Walls, 1997). However, MSW is a complex and multi-dimensional issue. In recent years, a vast number of studies have been done to determine the factors influencing waste management systems in cities in developing countries. Understanding of the factors related to solid waste problems enables governors to plan municipal solid waste management and taking action to control of accelerated rate of the waste in developing countries (Minghua et al., 2009; Othman, Noor, Abba, Yusuf, & Hassan, 2013; Guerrero, Maas, & Hogland, 2013). One important element is resulted as the supply of waste facilities; the number of and distance to the containers increase likelihood of dumping waste into the unregulated areas (Tadesse, Ruijs, & Hagos, 2008). Pokhrel and Viraraghavan (2005) note that the lack of financial resources negatively affects proper waste disposal. Financial constraints as well as the absence of legislation prevent governments constructing well-equipped sanitary landfills.

A clear example of formal recycling management in the world can be found in the practices of the European Union (EU) (Stokes, Köster, & Sambrook, 2013). The following section will outline MSW and recycling management in the area.

MSW and Recycling in the EU

Recycling is the third best option, as the waste hierarchy indicates, after prevention (source reduction and reduce) and reuse, the recycling industry has become an important sector. The EU waste policy aims to ensure that, through recycling, waste is used as a raw material wherever possible to produce new products. Therefore, the EU actively drives member states to recycle economically valuable materials which are used in household and industry levels.

Municipal waste handling practices in the EU have progressed over the last two decades from proper disposal methods to a greater focus on prevention at source and recycling. An efficient municipal waste management, advancing the top level in the waste hierarchy does not only contribute to higher value extracting from resources but also reduces the pressures on the environment (EEA, 2015). In addition, it generates a higher quality of life, especially in metropolitan areas, by potentially mitigating climate change and creating jobs (Girard, 2006; Marello & Helwege, 2014).

MSW in the EU only represents about 10% of total generated waste. However, waste generated by municipality is important as it has a diverse composition linked to consumption patterns. Furthermore, environmentally sound management of MSW is always challenging, since it has a complex character. Thus, having more efficient MSW systems indicates better performance in the overall waste management. In other words, by increasing municipal waste recycling rates, countries decrease the amount of land filling (EEA, 2013).

There has been 16 tons of used material per capita per year, of which 6 tons become waste. This number infers that the economy of the EU loses a significant amount of potential secondary raw materials, such as glass, paper, and plastics in waste streams. In 2010, approximately 2.5 billion tons of waste was generated in the EU, yet only 40% of it was reused or recycled. In developing countries, more than 80% becomes a landfill waste (Eurostat, 2016). The volume of the recyclable materials sorted and placed on the market increased to 36% of this total waste production (EC, 2010), however some 600 million tons could also be served by reusing or recycling.

In order to sustain material use and to increase recycling rates, a variety of policies have been introduced. The Waste Framework Directive 2008/98 particularly puts high standards and norms for waste management in member states. The Directive, as one of the main movers, has contributed to increase recycling and recover percentages of waste (EEA, 2011). In accordance with directive, individual countries have targeted for 50% of their municipal waste (more precisely specific types of household and similar wastes) to be recycled by 2020 (EEA, 2013). Consequently, most of the member states reduced land filling between 10% and 20% in the period of 2001-2010 (Eurostat, 2012). Similarly, generation of MSW per capita in Europe has clearly improved every year in the last decade. The amount of municipal solid waste per capita decreased, however wealthier countries generated more per capita, such as 668 kg. in Denmark, but only 271 kg. in Romania (EEA, 2015). The academic literature also supports the phenomenon by exploring the ways to increase recycling performance (Dijkgraaf & Gradus, 2016).

As a candidate member of the Union, Turkey will not be exempt from the EU regulations in the middle term. Thus, in terms of solid waste management, the current situation of Turkey and its major city Istanbul is represented in the following sections.

MSW in Turkey

In Turkey, where the amount of MSW per capita is 394.2 kg (TUIK, 2014), land filling is the main method for disposing municipal waste. Although MSW management in the country has improved because of strong governance in big cities, most of solid wastes are not disposed properly (TMEF 2008). In order to enable better management of municipal waste, the regulations known as Municipalities Law (No. 1580) and the Metropolitan Municipalities Laws (No. 5216 and No. 3030) state the responsibilities of the metropolitan district municipalities in the collection and transportation of urban solid waste from the cities to the transfer stations. In other words, according to the national legislation on waste management, metropolitan municipalities and metropolitan district municipalities are responsible for the construction and operation of separation, disposal, and composting facilities.

The solid-waste control regulation in Turkey, which was formed in March 1991 and amended in 2005 covers management of municipal solid waste and aims to control the impacts of urban solid waste on the natural environment. One of the main focuses of the regulation laid on the minimization of plastic waste. In harmony with this regulation, to increase the rate of recycling, an allotment has implemented for packaging materials to be collected and recycled separately by the producers. However, this requirement could not be monitored sufficiently and therefore, failed (Kocasoy, 2003). In 2007, a new regulation on packaging (No. 26562) set some rules to prevent formation of packaging waste and to reduce the amount by reusing, recovering, and recycling (Kanat, 2010).

Although there has been no legal obligation to meet the targets set by the EU yet, Turkey sets several goals for municipal solid waste management. The ministry of Environment and Forestry has set five-year action plan between the years 2008 and 2012. In order to increase rates of recycled materials, "Waste Management Action Plan" was adopted. According to the plan, 25.9 million tons of municipal solid waste has been disposed in 2012 (TUIK, 2012). In the same year, average daily municipal solid waste has been calculated as 1.12 kg. per capita. 60.5% of disposed waste was either separated and sent to the licensed stock sites or composted, whereas 37.8% was directly disposed in the landfills. Compared to 2008, the amount of municipal waste disposal decreased about 22.9% and the waste collected at licensed stock sites and recycling locations was increased about 41.4% (TUIK, 2014).

The results from the waste management action plan suggested several courses of action for the development of long-term waste management and recycling plans in Turkey. In order to increase the total recycling rates, Turkey set the vision plan for 2023. "National Recycling Strategy and Action Plan", which is prepared by Turkish Ministry of Science, Industry and Technology for the years between 2014 and 2017. The plan is considered as an important point to reach the vision of 2023, since it has been prepared to find solutions to the recycling problems and reach sustainable recycling systems. The plan mainly focuses on increasing public awareness, revision and full implementation of recycling legislation, and development of infrastructure for maintaining recycling mechanisms (TMSIT, 2014).

MSW in Istanbul

Istanbul, where the population is estimated around 15 million people (TUIK, 2013), is the largest city of Turkey and it is the main centre of industrial, financial, and further economic activities. Municipal waste generation per capita in the city is approximately 470 kg. (TMEF, 2008). The solid waste in Istanbul is collected by 39 district municipalities under the Metropolitan Municipality. With regard to regulations, district municipalities collect and transport regional urban waste to the transfer stations, whereas the central municipality operates solid waste collection from the main venues and public parks. The central metropolitan municipality is also responsible for the process of all solid waste that are brought to the transfer stations, as well as construction and operation of the final disposal sites (Kanat, 2010). Currently, the common method in MSW in Istanbul is the collection, transportation, and land filling, therefore, major part of the waste is collected from curbside collection points and taken to the unregulated dumping sites.

Istanbul Metropolitan Municipality has invested and now operates diverse disposal facilities including sanitary landfills, composting, and medical waste disposal facilities. In order to address municipal solid waste issues, Istanbul Environmental Management Industry and Trading Company (ISTAC) was established in 1994. As a responsible municipal service company for collecting and disposing solid waste in Istanbul, ISTAC has established sanitary landfills, which are designed to produce solutions for waste problems and operates sanitary landfills that meet international standards. However, daily solid waste generation used to be around 8,000 tons in 1995 and it is more than doubled in less than two decades (Yildiz, Balahorli, Hosoglu, & Sezer, 2014). In 2013, 17,000 tons of total waste was collected from the districts, transported to transfer stations, and then moved to sanitary landfills on a daily basis. This brings increasing costs to the city of Istanbul. For instance, the transportation of municipal wastes from districts to landfill locations and the payment of garbage collectors generate high operation costs for the district municipalities (Turan, Coruh, Akdemir, & Ergun, 2009). One advantage of land filling is the gas produced at the landfills can be used to produce energy. The production of 34 megawatts of energy per hour from the landfills is equivalent to the electricity consumption of about 800,000 inhabitants (ISTAC, 2016). On the other hand, the Istanbul Municipal Infrastructure Project aims to improve environmental management and strengthen the municipal services and infrastructure (Aqwadem, 2007). With the project, government proposes new solutions to replace land filling in order to minimize the environmental damage and develop economical aspects of the waste stream.

After above-mentioned formal means of MSW management, the following section will describe the informal waste picking and recycling activity, which occurs especially in growing urban areas where formal services are insufficient.

THE INFORMAL SECTOR OF RECYCLING

Overview

The informal recycling sector refers to unrecorded and unregulated recycling activities of waste pickers who are also known as scavengers. Their basic work includes the collection of recyclable and reusable materials from municipal waste, sorting, and bringing them to relevant shops or warehouses. The materials that are mostly picked are paper, cardboard, glass, plastics, metals, fabric for industrial use and organic waste, which has value for agriculture (Wilson et al., 2006).

In the context of municipal solid waste, at least four types of waste picking activities can be mentioned (Wilson, Araba, Chniwah, & Cheeseman, 2009):

1. **Itinerant Waste Buying:** Collecting of particular recyclable materials or reusable waste from households in return for money or other material.
2. **Street Waste Picking:** Recovering secondary materials from mixed waste or communal containers.
3. **Municipal Waste Collection:** Recovering secondary materials on route from communal collection to disposal sites.
4. **Waste Picking From Dumps:** Sorting through waste before it is filled at open dump sites.

The collected recyclables are sold to small-scale dealers where they are piled and re-sold to intermediaries who process and bundle them for industrial buying (Scheinberg, 2011). A model for the informal recycling sector is illustrated in Figure 2.

Medina (2007) underlines the following differences between industrialized nations and economically developing countries in terms of waste generation and recycling, which eventually separate the MSW management approaches:

Figure 2. A model for waste picking sector (Scheinberg, 2011)
Source: Scheinberg, 2011

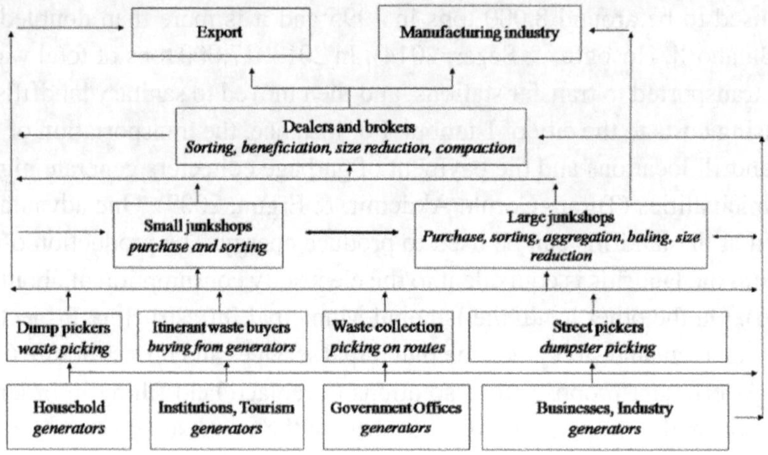

1. Industrialized countries have relatively higher capital and labour costs, so they form capital-intensive waste management services. On the other hand, labour-intensive systems are more reasonable for developing countries, since that means work opportunities for the unemployed.
2. The lack of transportation structure as in improper roads or streets hampers widely use of regular collection vehicles in the developing countries.
3. In industrialized countries, the quantity of waste is relatively higher due to consumption level. Besides, the significant amount of waste composition includes packaging material such as cans, bottles or plastic, which are basic recycling items. On the other hand, the solid waste in developing countries has more organic content such as fruits, vegetables, and unpacked food, which has less potential for reuse.

In regard to those conditions, solid waste is not adequately managed formally in developing countries. Besides, informal sector is highly dependent on collecting reusable material from waste streams to earn their living and that's why, waste pickers can achieve higher recycling rates than the formal sector (ILO, 2012). By using the power of the waste pickers, recycling rates can be increased and landfill diversion rates can be decreased without the need for expensive, high technology solutions.

In terms of waste pickers, this sector is characterized as low-paid, labour-intensive, and low technology (Wilson et al., 2006). Considering 20 million is found as a reasonable estimate for the number of waste pickers around the world (ILO, 2012), the sector implies a huge community with its economic impact of several billion US dollars a year (Medina, 2007).

Waste picking is generally associated with the developing world since several socioeconomic conditions are commonly found. The fundamental causes are depicted as the rapid urbanization due to population growth or migration, and the shortage of municipal resources to provide good waste management services (Moreno-Sanchez & Maldonado, 2006).

The positive aspects of the informal waste picking activities indicate economic, social, and ecological impacts, those which have direct and indirect positive effects on the municipalities' economies. There have been several empirical studies emphasize the importance of the informal sector in the economies of developing countries. For example, in terms of recruitment, informal employment has accounted for 48% of non-agricultural employment in North Africa, 51% in Latin America, 65% in Asia, and 72% in sub-Saharan Africa. When the agricultural employment is included, these numbers go beyond 90% in India and many sub-Saharan African countries (WIEGO, 2000).

Informal waste sector, a term which has recently replaced with "informal economy", refers to a broad concept that includes enterprises with employments in developing, transition, and advanced developed economies (Medina, 2011). The contributions of the informal waste sector to the formal activities propose factoring of these activities into the official waste management systems. Despite of its unofficial situation, comparing to the formal sector, the informal recycling management has no or negligible cost to the other stakeholders such as central governments, local municipalities, and residents. Therefore, the informal sector reduces overall solid waste management costs. The informal recycling, which recovers up to one third of the waste in a self-financing way, economically supplements the formal waste management system in many aspects. For instance, it contributes to the resource economy. The high and unstable prices in primary resources constrain stakeholders to look for alternatives in improving the efficiency of material use. Accordingly, sustainable integration of the informal recycling sector into the waste management cycles enhances avoidance of waste generation, reduction of the quantity in landfills, as well as reuse and recycling of secondary resources. By transforming waste into tradable commodities, new enterprises and networks evolve, investments realize, hence recruitment and labour generation increase (Medina, 2011).

The informal waste sector recovers much larger rates than the formal sector. Since the revenues derived from selling recovered materials are vital for the livelihoods of the pickers involved, achieved recovery rates are known as 80% in the developing countries. Even though the process is undertaken outside official channels, untaxed and unlicensed, it saves the formal sector finances by reducing the waste quantities and overall costs of waste management (Wilson et al., 2009).

The informal sector influences various levels in the complex economic networks. The activities often take place within unofficial and informal channels. Thus, even though the positive effects of the informal recycling sector are recognized, it cannot be easily quantified. However, recent studies concerning recycling rates on the informal waste collection and profitability of the informal sector show important findings. In their study, Salau, Sen, and Osho (2016) measure and compare the recycling rates between the formal and informal sectors in order to identify their impacts on the recycling rates. They investigate the influence of the two sectors on the recycling rate of Lagos State and imply that the informal recycling activities contribute more to the recycling rate of the state than the formal sector. A study by Scheinberg, Simpson, and Gupt (2010) compare the material recovery by formal and informal sectors in six different cities, and reveal that informal sector activities are profitable without service returns and tend to be discrete earning business. According to their study, which focuses on analyzing informal economic activities in the informal service sectors and the informal valorization (recovery) sector, in many cities, the formal sector mainly has responsibility to provide the collection and disposal services. This provision brings financial burdens which have to be provided by local governments. Moreover, it does not achieve high recycling rates and causes high operational costs. In addition, the formal activities in the service sector and material returns are tend to be just a small part of their income. Conversely, the informal sector labour works directly for recovering and recycling of valuable materials, and contributes to these activities against tips and voluntary fees, as the main source of income is returns of selling the collected materials. This causes significantly lower net costs in the informal collection. In the end, the informal sector saves a considerable amount of money, which is allocated for collection and disposal costs by the formal authorities. In another study, Burcea (2015) analyzes the informal waste recycling activities of waste pickers and enterprises from the economic, social and environmental perspectives. He emphasizes that, compared with formal waste activities, the benefits from waste valorization possibilities can be more increased by organizing the informal waste sector.

Organizing well-managed informal recycling systems generates environmental and social benefits. Informal recycling activities have positive effects on the natural environment by saving large amounts of materials out of landfills, thereby increasing the total amount of recyclable materials. The positive effect also seen in the mitigation of greenhouse gases, since the reduction of the waste ended up in the dumpsites and landfills lessens greenhouse gas emissions. Emission reduction contributes potentially to climate protection (Scheinberg et al., 2010).

The advantages of the informal sector concerning monetary and environmental issues for the municipalities and communities do not overcome social disadvantages for the informal recyclers. (Burcea, 2015). The majority of the informal workers and their families usually constitute the lowest income level of society and are in marginalized position. The lack of sanitary services, social and health care benefits, poor living and working conditions, social exclusion, child labour, stigmatization and harassment, lower life expectancy, as well as a limited access to the social security system are the facts for informal sector (Gutberlet, 2008; Ezeah, Fazakerley, & Roberts, 2013; Wilson et al., 2006).

In order to impede present social paradigms, increase the economic and environmental advantages of the informal sector, and serve better health and hygiene conditions to the waste pickers, integration of the informal sector to the formal system is a viable option. To communicate knowledge to the future policies and decision-making processes, it is crucial to understand and analyse the experiences of informal sector in the context of different countries and regions (Gerdes & Gunsilius, 2010).

Current Issues in Waste Picking

The recognition of the informal solid waste and recycling sector has existed since the beginning of the urbanization and industrialization in Europe and North America. In North America, the informal waste pickers are named as rag pickers who serve as itinerant workers and excluded from the social system without accessing to the formal labour market. They were usually the members of the lower castes, specific social or ethnic groups. Although waste picking still has a low social status universally, the attention has gradually shifted to exploring the efficiency and technical identity of the sector, as well as the contribution of the informal segment to the sustainable local waste management solutions (Scheinberg, undated).

The informal waste picking is confronted with several issues which also exist for the formal sector. Solid waste management, particularly in developing and emerging countries, appears as a growing financial and environmental problem. In order to enhance a proper waste collection, some countries choose the privatization option. Privatizing the services of collection, disposal or treatment of solid waste, and involving international companies to the value chain occurred as an important tool to modernize and improve urban waste management systems. Local authorities tended to follow the modernization process, as it supposedly decreases the labour costs for the formal sector (Marello & Helwege, 2014).

However, privatization to modernize solid waste management systems in several countries failed to succeed in its effort to improve the municipal solid waste management. The multinational companies which provided 'systematic' or 'methodical' tools to manage waste collection, ignored national private or public sector that were not quite receptive for understanding the dynamics and practices of the new techniques. In addition, operational costs increased much more (Scheinberg, undated). Furthermore, the possibilities to integrate the informal waste pickers into the modernization process were neglected. In the end, both privatization and modernization undermined the typical scavenging activity and drove waste pickers out of the recycling value chain (ILO, 2012; Scheinberg 2011).

Concurrent with privatization as well as modernization issues concerning the waste picking, there are some other insufficiencies that have to be overcome by the municipalities in developing countries. An important output emerges about the initiatives taken by different organizations and corporations such as International Labour Organization (ILO), which shows the most consistent history of working in the informal sector. Studies of the privatization and modernization particularly indicate that to involve the informal sector in solid waste management support considerable amount of jobs, generate and sustain income, and provide a beneficial input for the local waste picking activities for the sake of recycling (Scheinberg, undated). On the other hand, reports by ILO also underline an increase in child labour. As income levels in the informal segment are subjective to age and gender, children and women as the least sophisticated forms of labour, form a significant portion of the waste pickers and participate in collecting of waste from dumps and streets, waste handling or sorting (Cointreau, 2006). Since 2003, ILO has been focusing on thematic evaluation of the recycling activities to eradicate child labour in order to stop child labour and support the under-aged pickers to recover from this work. The Organization has taken protective and preventive measures which address several issues related to child labour in waste picking; from legal protection and capacity-building to education, awareness, and income generation (ILO, 2011).

Occupational health and safety hazards and injury issues due to lack of education, awareness, and hygienic conditions are other key challenges appear to the informal waste pickers. High occupational hazards, especially from electronic wastes, require prevention of waste collection within sanitary landfills, since the existing landfills in many developing countries are in improper health and safety conditions. Only improved waste collection processes can reduce health risks of the informal pickers and their families who are prone to social insecurity and incapable to access to proper healthcare, as well as the surrounding populations which are also exposed to the risks (Moreno-Sanchez & Maldonado, 2006). Since the informal waste pickers usually underestimate the dangerous character of their everyday scavenging activity, it is important to inform and train them in health and safety issues. To do this, ILO has developed a collaborative work with the Japan International Cooperation Agency (JICA) in 2010, and published a training manual to support improvements in the working conditions of the workers of waste collection. The manual actually focuses on the formal collectors, however in most cases it could be applied to all related practices for significantly reducing occupational impacts of the informal segment (Medina, 2011).

In response to alienation and above mentioned challenges, waste pickers began networking and formed supportive organizations to seek recognition in the recycling ecosystem. Organizations occurred in different forms such as negotiating collective rights, engaging existing regional or national network, organizing activities under apolitical, non-governmental organizations (NGOs) or church organizations (Tuttle, 2009). Among those, microenterprises, cooperatives, and public-private partnerships are seen as the most successful models for organizing the waste pickers (Medina, 2008). In 1990s, the burgeoning movement of the pickers occurred in different lands simultaneously, especially in the South America. National meetings were held in Brazil and Columbia. The motivation was to make demands and deals as formal institutions. The first Latin American congress of waste pickers was held in 2003 and the second one organized in 2005, again in Brazil with participants around 1,000. In 2008, the first world conference of waste pickers took place in Columbia and participants came from 34 countries. Eventually, the Global Alliance of Waste Pickers was formed and declared that waste picker organizations around the world would collaborate for social and economic inclusion. Since then, along with South America, further movements have taken place in Asia and Africa pursuing claims towards governments to improve livelihood and welfare of waste pickers (WIEGO, 2014; van Zeeland, 2014).

Waste Pickers in Istanbul

Shortage in MSW management systems in the metropolitans, as well as in Istanbul, creates a job area for informal waste pickers. Waste pickers make their living by collecting, sorting, and selling of reusable and recyclable materials which are thrown away by households. As a megacity, Istanbul's population continuously increases. Besides, industrialization and consumption patterns have contributed to an increasing amount of municipal solid waste. Similar to other metropolitan areas, waste pickers took the advantage of insufficient formal waste management programs by collecting reusable and renewable materials from the streets of Istanbul until recent times (Yigit, 2015). However, in Turkey, waste picking is widely considered illegal, worthless albeit strenuous, and because of their low status, they have a negative impact on the middle and higher social status of society (Ozgen, 2001). As the beginning of 2016, with the directive of Ministry of Environment and Urbanization, Municipality of Istanbul has started actions to eradicate informal collection activities. The Municipality banned waste pickers from waste collection and began to fine firms that buy material from the informal sector (HaberTurk, 2016). Actually, the legislation prohibiting informal the scavenging activity has been valid since 2005, however, it was not the authorities' decision to implement it thoroughly until the beginning of 2016.

In Istanbul, waste picking has been formed as an informal sector, which is interrelated to the formal segment. For instance, waste pickers, as private collectors, usually collect and sell materials to the warehouse owners who are working as middlemen. An average work day lasts around 12 hours and some 200-250 kg. of weight is collected, which returns around 10-15 USD for a picker. Although waste pickers hold a verbal contract with the warehouse owners, they are not secured by their "boss" in case of health problems or other incidents. Further, waste pickers in Istanbul occasionally supply their working equipment on their own.

Since 2010, the number of waste pickers boosted in Turkey partly due to incoming refugees especially from Syria. It is estimated that there are more than 500,000 waste pickers around Turkey of which roughly 100,000 are located in Istanbul. Most likely, the increasing number of informal sector waste pickers and the spreading scavenging activity prompted officials to take action and implement the current law on waste collection. Besides, the lobbying of private firms which are licensed to collect waste might also have a role in this recent development. Currently, the number of licensed collection and separation facilities increased to 1,000 approximately. Due to this challenge, which jeopardizes the scavenging work, waste pickers started to get organized through associations such as the Recycling Workers Association, Street Waste Collectors Association, and Waste Pickers Association in recent years to protect their rights. Those have several thousands of members from major Turkish cities like Ankara, Adana, Istanbul, and Izmir. However, because of economic constraints and dispersed settlement, waste pickers of Istanbul are not well coordinated. Another initiation of waste pickers in Istanbul to gain recognition is a magazine called "Katik", which is published since 2007. It appeals to the general audience with content depicting waste pickers' living conditions, social life, views, problems, and challenges they face in daily life (Ozsoy, 2012).

There are plenty of studies about waste pickers worldwide, which address the challenges and opportunities of scavenging activity in developing countries. However, studies in Turkish context are very limited. Thus, there is a scant knowledge on waste pickers of the country. Apart from academic research, the media provides the majority of information about scavengers in Istanbul. These resources mainly give information about the living conditions of the informal waste pickers and explain how they contribute to the local economy and environmental sustainability. However, they rather perform retrospective analysis, describing the problems and addressing possibilities and the rights to be recognized as formal workers. Similarly, the current literature only provides information about waste pickers' working conditions in a systematic way. For example, a yearlong fieldwork project among waste paper pickers in Istanbul by Yigit (2015) reports their profiles and occupational dynamics by exploring the intersection of subjects such as ethnicity, migration, and the informal economy based on ethnographic evidence. In another study, Deniz (2010) makes a field research about scavengers in Ankara with an aim to examine the organization of waste pickers and inner mechanisms of the informal waste sector for her master thesis. In regard to the literature review, she argues that studies related to informal waste collectors in Turkey either form a concept of waste pickers as a category of urban poor or advance the analysis of scavenging as an instrument to explain characteristics of urban poverty (Deniz 2010). Indeed, there are a considerable amount of studies, which relate urban poverty to the informal recycling sector (Ergun, 2005; Ozgen, 2001; Yardimci & Saltan, 2007). In their works, researchers acknowledge that urban waste pickers are among the poorest people facing strenuous working conditions in Turkey. They also argue that the causes of poverty increase social inequality and this generates social stigma and harassment towards waste pickers.

Yigit (2015) notes that one of the most important characteristics of waste pickers is that they were migrants to Istanbul or was born as a child of a migrant. They usually do scavenging as a family job since the families previously migrated to Istanbul from rural areas for work and could survive through waste picking. He argues that, the strength of kin ties in Istanbul is the most important factor determining the place where immigrants settle and find jobs. The relationships that waste pickers maintained over time are important. Thereby, as immigrants, they could pursue waste picking work together with the family members. Another important characteristic of scavenging is the easiness of entry. Waste picking is a kind of job that one can quickly understand and once knowing which waste is valuable, anyone can start doing it without any education. Therefore, low skills, minimum previous work experience, little capital and equipment requirements to start are the basic impediments of waste picking to enter (Yigit, 2015).

Although this limited knowledge about the informal segment in Istanbul hampers a healthy discussion of inclusive policies in waste management, several experiences worldwide could shed light on the topic.

DISCUSSION

First of all, it can be suggested that waste pickers are beneficial to the environment and the economy. As solid waste recycling reduces pollution, use of virgin materials, and saves energy; so do the waste picker activities. Besides, informal recycling sector decreases the municipal expenses for solid waste management by saving the effort for waste collection, transportation, disposal, and extends the life of dumpsites and landfills. In areas where there are no formal solid waste management structures, waste pickers can be the only source of action in recycling flow. Moreover, waste pickers contribute to the system by recovering materials from mixed waste that is already lost in the disposal stream (Moreno-Sanchez &

Maldonado, 2006). Furthermore, waste picking activities reflect an income opportunity for many parts of the society such as women, migrants, handicapped individuals as well as unskilled labour. In the fact that there are very limited statistic data reflecting on this phenomenon (Gunsilius et al., 2011), an oft cited figure is that more than two per cent of the urban population in Asia and Latin America make a living from scavenging (Medina, 2008).

Recently, almost all stakeholders in solid waste management system agree that, informal recycling sector provides some economic, social, and environmental benefits in developing countries (UN-HABITAT, 2010). In respect to their fight for recognition, it may be plausible for authorities to adopt inclusive policies and embrace the opportunity for further value creation (Dias, 2012). To begin with, the circumstances for waste pickers can be improved by a certain degree of formalization, training and securing a level of health and safety (ILO, 2012). Initiatives to regulate the informal sector would also help a decline in illegal activities (Medina, 2007).

However, Scheinberg (2011) criticizes development programs, which see waste pickers as decontextualized entities to be cured for maintaining the system. She urges researchers, practitioners, and officers to acknowledge the phenomenon more systemically and accept the fact that waste pickers are significant economic and environmental agents. The three common development approaches, namely; i) the welfare-based approach, ii) the development-oriented approach, and iii) the rights-based approach are said to be far from fixing the issue. The first approach assumes waste pickers as the "victims of society" and deals with improving the standard livelihood of waste pickers and their families without considering the overall framework they are embedded. The second approach, which resembles to the former, focuses on the capacity building of people engaged in waste picking through education or microcredits in order to pave the way for "better" careers. This one too lacks a proper view of waste pickers' position in the recycling ecosystem. The third one appreciates the existence of waste pickers as social actors and recognizes their political being. In this approach, the role of waste pickers in the institutional environment is supported; however their economic contributions in the solid waste management structure are not really addressed. Therefore, any development projects, which do not take account of the interconnectedness of different forces in the system and underestimate waste picking as a legitimate economic activity, may fail to reach the targets (Scheinberg, 2011).

On the other hand, Fergutz, Dias, and Mitlin (2011) list several corporate social responsibility practices that actually help scavenging activity. Although being limited, these actions include; promoting the direct exchange of households and buyers with waste picker cooperatives, training waste pickers for proper material handling, and providing tools and gears for work efficiency. However, current regulations in Turkey take waste picking as an illegal activity and apply monetary penalties for exchanges with waste pickers (HaberTurk, 2016). Thus, corporate social responsibility practices are not applicable, at least for the time being in Turkey.

Around the world, researchers also investigate different solid waste management systems and try to derive lessons for more inclusive policy options. For example, Nzeadibe (2009) in Nigeria, Sembiring and Nitivattananon (2010) in Indonesia, Schenck and Blaauw (2011) in South Africa, Hayami, Dikshit, and Mishra (2006) in India make profiles of the particular informal recycling sectors, underline their significance, and stress the importance of an integrative approach. However, it appears that getting involved in the system is not taken for granted. Studies show that, it requires waste pickers' persevering struggle with the officials to gain rights and recognition by law (Chikarmane, 2012; Dias, 2010). For example, Betancourt (2010) depicts the long lasting efforts of waste pickers in Bogota, Columbia in order to gain recognition and inclusion in the recycling process despite the little initial concerns from local authorities. Marello and Helwege (2014) demonstrate several cases of collaborative models between municipal solid waste systems and waste picker cooperatives at varying degrees of success in Nicaragua, Brazil, and Mexico.

A typical conflict case starts with a government's or local authority's decision for an exclusive policy in a developing region and privatize the solid was management system. Despite the fact that many people are engaged in scavenging as a "permanent job" for survival, waste pickers are restricted from the waste stream and their activity is criminalized. However, the livelihood of waste pickers depends on recycling and this sort of action, which overlooks their existence, urge them to resist by activism. Through cooperatives and generally backed up by non-governmental organizations; social mobilization, lobbying, and legal cases start. Where organizations are strong such as in Brazil, Columbia, and India, consequences occur in favour of waste pickers and more integrative approaches are followed in many cases. Otherwise, waste pickers' vulnerability escalates for the sake of private firms. Therefore, in regions where there's a significant stratum of waste pickers, exclusive policies would either face heavy resistance and institutional fight back or a repression, which may lead to disengagement of many people from society for worse. In order to avoid those inefficient and unsatisfactory conditions from the beginning, inclusive policies in municipal solid waste management in developing countries emerge as a rational option even merely in terms of decision making logic.

Concerning the recycling system in Istanbul, conventional methods such as separated bins on sites or licensing certain firms for reusable waste collection do not explicitly represent an inclusion for waste pickers. On the contrary, they reduce the chances of survival and frustrate significant number of people. With respect to this reality, authorities should consider the consequences if they choose to cut scavenging away with punitive measures. With this in mind, there is a case in which a district municipality of Istanbul promotes licensed firms to integrate waste pickers in their organizations (Sultangazi, 2015). However, it is known that the majority of waste pickers, rather than hope or qualify for being a company worker, prefer to work independently. Besides, the potential number of employment is not expected to cover most of the active waste pickers in the area. Another case appeared in the city of Adana, south of Turkey, where the regional waste picker association established a private firm and received a license of waste collection (Hurriyet, 2016). This could be a fine exemplar, but it may not suffice to be a promising model per se because it might pertain to just a successful initiation of a particular group of people.

The importance of organizational activity such as cooperatives is emphasized as a key solution to progress with regard to waste pickers' problems. In two relevant workshops held in 2016, one organized by Street Waste Collectors Association (Satder, 2016) and the other co-organized by the Ministry of Labour and Social Security and International Labour Organization (GTB/ILO, 2016), cooperative type of firms are recognized as a viable option. Above mentioned cases around the world also suggest the same path. Besides, the legislation in Turkey is available for waste pickers to form cooperative firms. On the other hand, the question would be whether it is realistic to expect waste pickers organize by themselves in the short term and set up cooperatives, which they probably know little about, especially in the megacity of Istanbul. However, current networks do not signal that such a development can take off easily. Here, a policy is required to expedite the formation of cooperatives, if an inclusion is intended by the authorities. This relates to the licensing arrangements of the municipalities. A possible way of integration through policy would be to regulate the collection and separation facilities to become cooperatives. Within active legislation, which determines the facilities' physical requirements, it may be added that a facility's formal organization type has to be a cooperative with a certain number of members. As anticipated, the members of the cooperatives would be waste pickers and municipalities will only need to audit the cooperatives whether they keep certain working standards. The scheme may twist the entities at first, but the market is likely to arrange itself suitably in the short term because this type of regulation counts all actors of the recycling ecosystem.

CONCLUSION

In recent times, there has been varying degrees of developments in municipal solid waste management and recycling concept around the world. Although, the impact of extant MSW and the importance of recycling for the environment and the health are acknowledged, not all countries are able to cope with the phenomenon in the same way. For instance, recycling industry has become an important sector of the economy in industrialized nations. It is regarded as the third best option after prevention and reuse as the waste hierarchy indicates. Through recycling, waste is used wherever possible as a raw material to produce new products. In the European Union, member states are driven to recycle economically valuable materials which are used in households and industry. Eventually, more technology-intensive systems are installed in the region to achieve high efficiency rates. On the other hand, waste management practices are different in the developing countries. They tend to rely more on informal sector due to lack of adequate capital and infrastructure for modernization and the availability of cheap labour. However, sometimes there may be a conflict of interests between formal and informal parties where waste collection services are privatized. Thanks to initiatives to enhance communication between informal recyclers and the formal solid waste establishments, there are successful cases of integrating the informal sector into the formal solid waste management domain. This is also in respect to spreading recognition of waste pickers as important economic and environmental agents in the developing world. It has been acknowledged that informal recycling has multiple benefits for many areas of the local economy by contributing to the local business, as well as public health and environmental sustainability.

Similar to developing world, a megacity like Istanbul also faces MSW management issues because of administrative, financial, and technical shortages. Naturally, more than 6 million tons/year amount of waste disposed in the city is not easy to handle. Typically, this also creates a job opportunity for the waste pickers of the city. An estimation of 100,000 waste pickers in Istanbul roughly represents about half a million people including families. On the other hand, waste picking is generally viewed as a problem in the formal MSW management system in Turkey. Instead of proper integration of the informal workers, whose livelihood is dependent on recycling, there appears a restrictive approach for scavenging. Especially new regulations of the municipalities aim to exclude waste pickers from the ecosystem without any substituting programs. Furthermore, waste picker community and the relevant NGOs in Istanbul do not appear strongly organized to fight against this trend. Although there have been few formal movements to organize recycling in the city, more initiatives and applied research should be undertaken to recover more from solid waste. There are evident cases around the world that affirm inclusive policies lead to favourable results for all stakeholders. Therefore, this study stresses a new action for authorities to reconsider the priorities in Istanbul with a holistic view in order to figure out sustainable arrangements for all parties in the waste stream. A possible way could be to regulate the market in a way that requires waste collection and separation facilities to be cooperative type of organizations partnering with waste pickers.

Finally, it is expected that this exploration of an informal recycling sector, which recently gains academic interest, in a less known context, such as Istanbul, will contribute to the value sharing research.

REFERENCES

Aqwadem (Consultancy). (2007). *Istanbul municipal infrastructure project: Closure of existing illegal waste sites.* Environmental Assessment Report and Management Plan. Retrieved May 20, 2016, from http://www-wds.worldbank.org/external/default/WDSContentServer/WDSP/IB/2007/04/04/000020439_20070404155958/Rendered/PDF/E16170EMP0IstanbulEnglish.pdf

Barrett, A., & Lawler, J. (1995). *The Economics of Solid Waste Management in Ireland.* Retrieved May 15, 2016, from https://www.esri.ie/pubs/PRS26.pdf

Betancourt, A. A. (2010). *Waste Pickers in Bogota: From Informal Practice to Policy* (Unpublished master's thesis). Massachusetts Institute of Technology, Cambridge, MA.

Burcea, G. Ş. (2015). The economical, social and environmental implications of informal waste collection and recycling. *Theoretical and Empirical Researches in Urban Management, 10*(3), 14–24.

Chikarmane, P. (2012). *Integrating waste pickers into municipal solid waste management in Pune, India.* WIEGO Policy Brief No 8. Retrieved March 5, 2016, from http://www.inclusivecities.org/wp-content/uploads/2012/10/Chikarmane_WIEGO_PB8.pdf

Cointreau, S. (2006). *Occupational and environmental health issues of solid waste management- Special emphasis on Middle-and Lower-Income countries.* The World Bank Group Urban Papers, UP-2. Retrieved January 5, 2017, from http://siteresources.worldbank.org/INTUSWM/ Resources/up-2.pdf

Deniz, G. C. (2010). *The Informal Waste Collection Sector and the Waste Pickers; A Case Study in Ankara* (Unpublished master's thesis). Bogazici University, Istanbul, Turkey.

Dias, S. (2010). *Overview of legal framework for social inclusion in solid waste management in Brazil.* WIEGO Research Paper. Retrieved March 5, 2016, from http://wiego.org/sites/wiego.org/ files/publications/files/Dias_Brazil_Legal_framework_social_inclusion_waste_0.pdf

Dias, S. (2012). Not to be taken for granted: what informal waste pickers offer the urban economy. *The Global Urbanist.* Retrieved April 4, 2016, from http://globalurbanist.com/2012/11/27/waste-pickers

Dijkgraaf, E., & Gradus, R. (2016). *Post separation of plastic waste: Better for the environment and lower collection costs.* Tinbergen Institute Discussion Paper 16-103/VI. Retrieved January 5, 2017 from https://ssrn.com/abstract=2875279

EC (European Commission). (2010). *Being Wise with Waste: The EU's Approach to Waste Management.* Retrieved May 15, 2016, from http://ec.europa.eu/environment/waste/pdf/WASTE%20 BROCHURE.pdf

EC (European Commission). (2016). *Turkiye Multeci Krizi.* Retrieved June 30, 2016, from http://ec.europa.eu/echo/files/aid/countries/factsheets/turkey_syrian_crisis_tr.pdf

EEA (European Environment Agency). (2011). *Recycling Industry Can Boost the European Economy.* Retrieved May 21, 2016, from http://www.eea.europa.eu/downloads/96d2c164-96d6-47d8-bda4-3b856a32747e/1332497451/recycling-industry-can-boost-the.pdf

EEA (European Environment Agency). (2013). *Managing Municipal Solid Waste — A review of Achievements in 32 European countries. Report No. 2.2013*. Retrieved May 12, 2016, from file:///C:/Users/pc/Downloads/Managing%20municipal%20solid%20waste%20(2).pdf

EEA (European Environment Agency). (2015). *SOER - Cross-Country Comparisons. Waste. Municipal Solid Waste Generation and Management*. Retrieved May 12, 2016, from http://www. eea.europa.eu/soer-2015/countries-comparison/waste

Ergun, C. (2005). *Yoksulluk ve Enformel Sektor: Cop Toplayicilari Ornegi (Isparta-Izmir Karsilastirmasi)* (Unpublished master's thesis). Süleyman Demirel University, Isparta.

Eurostat. (2012). *Municipal Waste*. Retrieved May 11, 2016, from http://epp.eurostat. ec.europa.eu/portal-page-porta./statistics/search_database

Eurostat. (2016). *European Statistics*. Retrieved May 11, 2016, from http://ec.europa.eu/ eurostat/statistics-explained/index.php/Municipal_waste_statistics

Ezeah, C., Fazakerley, J. A., & Roberts, C. L. (2013). Emerging trends in informal sector recycling in developing and transition countries. *Waste Management (New York, N.Y.)*, *33*(11), 2509–2519. doi:10.1016/j.wasman.2013.06.020 PMID:23886489

Fergutz, O., Dias, S., & Mitlin, D. (2011). Developing urban waste management in Brazil with waste picker organizations. *Environment and Urbanization*, *23*(2), 597–608. doi:10.1177/0956247811418742

Gerdes, P., & Gunsilius, E. (2010). *The waste experts: Enabling conditions for informal sector integration in solid waste management. Lessons learned from Brazil, Egypt and India*. GTZ Deutsche Gesellschaft für Technische Zusammenarbeit GmbH. Retrieved January 10, 2017, from https://www.giz.de/en/downloads/gtz2010-waste-experts-conditions-is-integration.pdf

Girard, L. F. (2006). Celebrating our urban heritage - Innovative strategies for urban heritage conservations, sustainable development, and renewable energy. *Global Urban Development.*, *2*(1), 1–10.

GTB/ILO (Turkish Ministry of Labour and Social Security/International Labour Organization). (2016). *Geri Dönüşüm Sektöründe Kooperatifçilik Potansiyeli Çalıştayı*, Retrieved January 15, 2017, from http://koop.gtb.gov.tr/haberler/turkiyedeki-atik-toplayicilarinin-kooperatiflesmesine-yonelik-cok-onemli-adimlar-atildi

Guerrero, L. A., Maas, G., & Hogland, W. (2013). Solid waste management challenges for cities in developing countries. *Waste Management (New York, N.Y.)*, *30*(1), 220–232. doi:10.1016/j.wasman.2012.09.008 PMID:23098815

Gunsilius, E., Spies, S., Garcia-Cortez, S., Medina, M., Dias, S., & Scheinberg, A. (2011). *Recovering Resources, Creating Opportunities. Integrating the Informal Sector into Solid Waste Management*. Retrieved January 7, 2017, from https://www.giz.de/en/downloads/giz2011-en-recycling-partnerships-informal-sector-final-report.pdf

Gutberlet, J. (2008). Empowering collective recycling initiatives: Video documentation and action research with a recycling co-op in Brazil. *Resources, Conservation and Recycling*, *52*(4), 659–670. doi:10.1016/j.resconrec.2007.08.006

HaberTurk. (2016). *A'dan Z'ye Kagit Toplama Krizi*. Retrieved June 30, 2016, from http://www.haberturk.com/gundem/haber/1187912-adan-zye-kagit-toplama-krizi

Hayami, Y., Dikshit, A. K., & Mishra, S. N. (2006). Waste pickers and collectors in Delhi: Poverty and environment in an urban informal sector. *The Journal of Development Studies*, *42*(1), 41–69. doi:10.1080/00220380500356662

Hurriyet. (2016). *Atik Toplayicilar Sirketlesti*. Retrieved January 15, 2017, from http://www. hurriyet.com.tr/atik-toplayicilar-sirketlesti-37290120

ILO (International Labour Organization). (2011). *Children in hazardous work: what we know what we need to do*. International Programme on Elimination of Child Labour (IPEC). ILO. Retrieved 7 January, from http://www.ilo.org/wcmsp5/groups/public/@dgreports/@dcomm/@publ/documents/ publication/wcms_155428.pdf

ILO (International Labour Organization). (2012). *Working Towards Sustainable Development: Opportunities for Decent Work and Social Inclusion in a Green Economy*. Retrieved February 13, 2015, from http://www.ilo.org/global/publications/ilo-bookstore/order-online/books/WCMS181836/ lang--en/index.htm

ISTAC (Istanbul Environmental Management Industry and Trading Inc.). (2015). *Integrated Solid Waste Management - Strategic Plan 2015-2019*. Retrieved May 28, 2016, from http://www.istac.istanbul/contents/15/WEB_ISTAC_STRATEJI.pdf

ISTAC (Istanbul Environmental Management Industry and Trading Inc.). (2016). *IBB 100 Milyonu Cope Gitmekten Kurtardi*. Retrieved May 28, 2016, from http://www.ibb.istanbul/tr-TR/ Pages/Haber.aspx?NewsID=23017#.V3JR0riLTIU

Kanat, G. (2010). Country report. Municipal solid waste management in Istanbul. *Waste Management (New York, N.Y.)*, *30*(8-9), 1737–1745. doi:10.1016/j.wasman.2010.01.036 PMID:20185290

Kocasoy, G. (2003). *Institutional Structure of the Solid Waste and Landfill Management in Developing Countries*. Paper presented at 9th International Waste Management and Landfill Symposium, Sardinia, Italy.

Marello, M., & Helwege, A. (2014). *Solid waste management and social inclusion of waste pickers: Opportunities and challenges*. GEGI (Global Economic Governance Initiative) working paper. Retrieved March 3, 2016, from https://www.bu.edu/pardeeschool/files/2014/11/Social-Inclusion-Working-Paper.pdf

Medina, M. (2005). Serving the unserved: Informal refuse collection in Mexico. *Waste Management & Research*, *23*(5), 390–397. doi:10.1177/0734242X05057698 PMID:16273947

Medina, M. (2008). The informal recycling sector in developing countries- Organizing waste pickers to enhance their impact. *Gridlines*. Retrieved March 1, 2016, from https://www.ppiaf.org/ sites/ppiaf.org/files/publication/Gridlines-44-Informal%20Recycling%20-%20MMedina.pdf

Medina, M. (2011). *The informal sector – a driving force for recycling management. Recovering resources, creating opportunities: Integrating the informal sector into solid waste management*. GIZ GmbH (German International Cooperation), Partnership for Recycling Management. Retrieved January 10, 2017, from https://www.giz.de/en/downloads/giz2011-en-recycling-partnerships-informal-sector-final-report.pdf

Minghua, Z., Xiumin, F., Rovetta, A., Qichang, H., Vicentini, F., Bingkai, L., & Yi, L. et al. (2009). Municipal solid waste management in Pudong New Area, China. *Journal of Waste Management*, *29*(3), 1227–1233. doi:10.1016/j.wasman.2008.07.016 PMID:18951780

Moreno-Sanchez, R. D. P., & Maldonado, J. H. (2006). Dynamic model of solid waste management in developing countries. *Environment and Development Economics*, *3*(03), 371–391. doi:10.1017/S1355770X06002853

Nzeadibe, T. C. (2009). Solid waste reforms and informal recycling in Enugu urban area, Nigeria. *Habitat International*, *33*(1), 93–99. doi:10.1016/j.habitatint.2008.05.006

OECD (Organisation for Economic Co-operation and Development). (2008). *Environmental Performance Reviews: Turkey*. Retrieved March 3, 2016, from http://www.oecd.org/environment/ country-reviews/environmentalperformancereviewsturkey2008.htm

Othman, S. N., Noor, Z. Z., Abba, A. H., Yusuf, R. O., & Hassan, A. A. (2013). Review of life cycle assessment of integrated solid waste management in some Asian countries. *Journal of Cleaner Production*, *41*, 251–262. doi:10.1016/j.jclepro.2012.09.043

Ozgen, H. N. (2001). Kentte yeni yoksulluk ve cop insanlari. *Toplum ve Bilim*, *89*, 88–101.

Ozsoy, D. (2012). Yeni kent yoksullugu, atik toplayicilari ve temsil sorunsali: Katik dergisi uzerine bir inceleme. *Istanbul Universitesi Iletisim Fakultesi Dergisi*, *43*, 105–121.

Palmer, K., Sigman, H., & Walls, M. (1997). The cost of reducing municipal solid waste. *Journal of Environmental Economics and Management*, *33*(2), 128–150. doi:10.1006/jeem.1997.0986

Pokhrel, D., & Viraraghavan, T. (2005). Municipal solid waste management in Nepal: Practices and challenges. *Journal of Waste Management*, *25*(5), 555–562. doi:10.1016/j.wasman.2005.01.020 PMID:15925764

Salau, O., Sen, L., Osho, S., & Adejonwo-Osho, O. (2016). Empirical investigation of formal and informal sectors in waste recycling of the municipal waste management system of developing countries. *Journal of Environment and Ecology.*, *7*(2), 21–33. doi:10.5296/jee.v7i2.10007

Satder (Street Waste Collectors Association). (2016). *Geri Donusum Emekcilerinin Sorunlari ve Cozum Onerileri Clistayi.* Retrieved December 20, 2016, from https://www.sokakatik toplayicilari.com/category/calistay/

Scheinberg, A. (2011). *Value Added: Modes of Sustainable Recycling in the Modernisation of Water Management Systems*. Wageningen, The Netherlands: Wageningen University.

Scheinberg, A. (n.d.). *Privatisation and the informal sector: Thinking locally, acting globally?*. WASTE, Advisors on Urban Environment and Development, and Wageningen University, Environmental Policy Department. Retrieved January 5, 2017, from http://www.iswa.org/uploads/ txiswaknowledgebase/620431Paper.pdf

Scheinberg, A., Simpson, M., & Gupt, Y. (2010). *Economic aspects of the informal sector in solid waste.* Research report for GTZ (German Technical Cooperation). Retrieved January 6, 2017, from https://www.giz.de/expertise/downloads/gtz2010-en-Economic-Aspects-WASTE.pdf

Schenk, R., & Blaauw, P. F. (2011). The work and lives of street waste pickers in Pretoria- a case study of recycling in South Africa's urban informal economy. *Urban Forum, 22*, 411-430.

Sembiring, E., & Nitivattananon, V. (2010). Sustainable solid waste management toward an inclusive society: Integration of the informal sector. *Resources, Conservation and Recycling*, *54*(11), 802–809. doi:10.1016/j.resconrec.2009.12.010

Stokes, R. G., Köster, R., & Sambrook, S. C. (2013). *The Business of Waste: Great Britain and Germany, 1945 to the Present*. Cambridge, UK: Cambridge University Press. doi:10.1017/CBO9781139225663

Sultangazi (District municipality). (2015). *Sokak Toplayıcılari Geri Donusum Sistemine Kazandirildi*. Retrieved January 10, 2017, from http://www.sultangazi.bel.tr/tr/guncel-haberler/sokak-toplayicilari-geri-donusum-sistemine-kazandirildi_231

Tadesse, T., Ruijs, A., & Hagos, F. (2008). Household waste disposal in Mekelle city. Northern Ethiopia. *Journal of Waste Management*, *28*(10), 2003–2012. doi:10.1016/j.wasman.2007.08.015 PMID:17936609

TMEF (Turkish Ministry of Environment and Forestry). (2008). *Waste Management Action Plan 2008-2012*. Retrieved February 20, 2016, from http://www.cygm.gov.tr/cygm/files/eylemplan/ atikeylemplani.pdf

TMSIT (Turkish Ministry of Science, Industry and Technology). (2014). *National Recycling Strategy Document and Action Plan 2014-2017*. Retrieved February 20, 2016, from http://www.resmigazete. gov. tr/eskiler/2014/12/20141230M1-12-1.pdf

TUIK (Turkish Statistical Institute). (2012). *Municipal Solid Waste Statistics*. Retrieved March 1, 2016, from http://www.tuik.gov.tr/PreHaberBultenleri.do?id=16170

TUIK (Turkish Statistical Institute). (2013). *Municipal Solid Waste Statistics*. Retrieved March 1, 2016, from http://www.turkstat.gov.tr/PreHaberBultenleri.do?id=15844

TUIK (Turkish Statistical Institute). (2014). *Municipal Solid Waste Statistics*. Retrieved March 1, 2016, from http://www.tuik.gov.tr/PreHaberBultenleri.do?id=18777

Turan, N. G., Coruh, S., Akdemir, A., & Ergun, O. N. (2009). Municipal solid waste management strategies in Turkey. *Waste Management (New York, N.Y.)*, *29*(1), 465–469. doi:10.1016/j.wasman.2008.06.004 PMID:18644708

Tuttle, L. (2009). Ankara Recycling Association, Turkey. In M. Samson (Ed.), Refusing to be Cast Aside: Waste Pickers Organizing Around the World (pp. 15-16). Cambridge, MA: Women in Informal Employment: Globalizing and Organizing (WIEGO).

UN-HABITAT (United Nations Human Settlements Programme). (2010). *Solid Waste Management in the World's Cities*. Retrieved February 5, 2016, from http://unhabitat.org/books/solid-waste-management-in-the-worlds-cities-water-and-sanitation-in-the-worlds-cities-2010-2

UNEP (United Nations Environment Program). (2005). *Solid Waste Management*. Retrieved May 25, 2016, from http://www.unep.org/ietc/Portals/136/SWM-Vol1-Part1-Chapters1to3.pdf

UNEP (United Nations Environment Program). (2015). *Global Waste Management Outlook*. Retrieved May 25, 2016, from http://www.unep.org/ietc/Portals/136/Publications/Waste%20 Management/GWMO%20 report/GWMO%20full%20report.pdf

USEPA (United Stated Environmental Protection Agency). (n.d.). *Wastes - Non-hazardous Waste – Municipal Solid Waste*. Retrieved February 5, 2016, from https://archive.epa.gov/epawaste/nonhaz/ municipal/web/html/index.html

Van Zeeland, A. J. W. M. (2014). *The Interaction between Popular Economy, Social Movements and Public Policies: A Case Study of the Waste Pickers' Movement*. Geneva, Switzerland: United Nations Research Institute for Social Development.

WIEGO (Women in the Informal Economy Organising and Globalising). (2000). *Women in the Informal Economy*. Cambridge, MA: WIEGO.

WIEGO (Women in the Informal Economy Organising and Globalising). (2014). *The Urban Informal Workforce: Waste Pickers/Recyclers*. Retrieved March 3, 2016, from http://wiego.org/sites/ wiego.org/ files/publications/files/IEMS-waste-picker-report.pdf

Wilson, D. C., Araba, A. O., Chinwah, K., & Cheeseman, C. R. (2009). Building recycling rates through the informal sector. *Waste Management (New York, N.Y.)*, *29*(2), 629–635. doi:10.1016/j.wasman.2008.06.016 PMID:18701272

Wilson, D. C., Velis, C., & Cheeseman, C. (2006). Role of informal sector recycling in waste management in developing countries. *Habitat International*, *30*(4), 797–808. doi:10.1016/j.habitatint.2005.09.005

World Bank. (2012). *Urban Development Series. What a Waste. A Global Review of Solid Waste Management*. Retrieved April 5, 2016, from http://siteresources.worldbank.org/INTURBAN DEVELOPMENT/ Resources/336387-1334852610766/What_a_Waste2012_Final.pdf

Yardimci, S., & Saltan, A. (2007). Geri donusumun gorunmeyen yuzu. *Toplum ve Bilim*, *108*, 206–238.

Yigit, I. (2015). Survival tactics of waste paper pickers in Istanbul. *Journal of Ethnic and Cultural Studies*, *2*(1), 1–14.

Yildiz, S., Balahorli, V., Hosoglu, F., & Sezer, K. (2014). Waste management in the metropolis of Istanbul - Waste incineration and energy production facility in Istanbul Waste Management. *Vivis*, *3*, 265–275.

KEY TERMS AND DEFINITIONS

Municipal Solid Waste: Waste generated in the households, commercial institutions, and streets such as glass, paper, plastics, fabric, and organic material within the territories of municipalities.

Recycling: Recovering waste in a way that it becomes reusable.

Scavenging: An activity of informal collection and commercializing the solid waste.

Solid Waste Management: A system of collection, transfer, recycling, and disposal of solid waste generated in the urban areas.

Waste Picker: An individual who collect and commercialize urban solid waste informally.

Chapter 10
Smart Cities and Internet Technology Research for Sustainable and Inclusive Development:
An Integrated Approach of Best Practices for Policy Makers and Educators

Christina Marouli
The American College of Greece, Greece

Miltiadis Lytras
The American College of Greece, Greece

ABSTRACT

The concept of smart cities has recently emerged to highlight the significance of innovation and information technologies in urban planning. In this chapter, after a discussion of different conceptions and important dimensions of smart cities, a wealth of information technologies that have been used in cities for a variety of services is presented. The authors advocate that smart urban solutions should be designed within a smart cities vision and strategic plan, defined by people's needs. They propose an integrated strategic policy making model for smart, sustainable and inclusive cities and they make recommendations for policies and education for smart cities. The special character of public and private spaces, the significance of everyday life, the pivotal role of open governance and meaningful citizen participation, as well as the balance between the desired surveillance for efficient resource management and freedom and creativity have been highlighted as challenges that should inform the design of smart urban solutions and future research on smart cities.

DOI: 10.4018/978-1-5225-3147-0.ch010

INTRODUCTION

"Where do you live? In the city of …." This is the answer of most of the people on Earth in our days. More than half of the Earth's human population lives in cities. So do Maria, John and Mike.

"How is your life?" John asked Maria who lives in Athens. "I wake up in the morning, I take my car and I rush to work; work is not in walking distance from home. Maybe I could consider walking some day, but I am always in a hurry. It would be good exercise and the truth is I am sitting most of the day. I finish work sometime in the late afternoon and I go by the super market or do other chores before going home. When I arrive, I change clothes, I check if I need to cook, I do some housework and I take my kids to their activities. They have different lessons – music, tennis, English lessons, and French. Every evening we have something. I am a taxi driver. They are also very busy – from very early on in their lives. I also call my mom, who is old now and has several health problems. She lives with a caretaker. Unfortunately, I cannot go every day. She lives at the other end of the city. We do not have the capacity to live together. We say a few words with my husband at the end of the day and he goes to sleep. I sleep later and sometimes well after midnight, as I often need to prepare for the next day's work. The bad thing is that we have considerable noise from the street and sometimes I don't sleep well. I am often tired. Weekends are less packed with "must do" activities. We see friends during the weekend and we may go to a movie, a music event, or simply take a walk somewhere in the city or the mountain close to us. They live mostly in other parts of the city. Our neighbors, we see in passing as we walk up and down the stairs of our apartment building. How about you? How is your life in … in Massachusetts, John?"

"Similar in many respects. I wake up, get prepared, take my car and drive to work. I am always prepared for a long commute and possibly even traffic at parts of the trip. I finish work and return home in the evening. I take supper with my girlfriend and then, we relax for 2-3 hours. If she is busy, I watch TV. I also talk with friends over Facebook. I also like posting photos on instagram. I like communicating with friends. But, we also end up doing it only in the weekends. I read a book and maybe write something; I like writing. But I have to say that oftentimes, I get a message from my boss for an urgent issue or a work that needs to be done. So, I spend some time thinking about that too. And then I sleep, at around midnight. I take care of the garden, the cars etc. in the weekend and I go to the supermarket, usually on the way back from work on Friday. I want more contact with friends." John replies.

Maria says: "And I want more time for relaxation, for myself!".

Mike, who sits nearby, has followed the conversation. He is sitting at the bench near their table. He jumps in. "Hm… I have ample time! I sleep wherever I find on the streets. Generally, I sleep around here but when it is cold I try to find a warmer place. It is not easy. I have adjusted to the noise. I can sleep anywhere. When I wake up, I think of how I will get food today, where I should go to get some water and if I could manage to take a shower. I sometimes go the homeless shelter, but not everyday because it is a hard and sad place. But I have to say, I have made some friends there. And I like going for that. Being on the street like me makes people scared. They may give me some money sometimes – I am thankful – but this is no connection, real connection. Some smile at me… I wish I had a job of sorts so that I could earn a living. But I admit that I would prefer a job that allows me to live and be free too."

Maria and John looked at him and remained silent. They looked into his eyes and so the human being who was like themselves.

Cities ... people – similar and different; buildings of all sorts and quality, streets, parks; lands of economic and cultural opportunity; flashy, noisy, harsh places. Not the same for all.

(Marouli, 2016)

Cities imply a high density of people living together, sharing space and resources for the fulfillment of their basic needs, for security, commercial and civic activity, with communal - public spaces to mingle and socialize and private spaces for personal and family life. High concentrations facilitate interaction between people and businesses; thus, cities offer more job and educational opportunities, and usually a greater variety of services. However, high density urban populations also imply increased strain on natural resources, energy and nature often surpassing local ecosystem's carrying capacity, and thus causing environmental problems which in turn negatively impact human societies, individuals and economic opportunities.

The conception of the city has evolved over time. In the ancient polis, cities were city-states, relatively autonomous, with public spaces (agora) for civic and commercial activities aiming to cultivate the sense of community and discuss community affairs. In recent times, the conception of the city has developed from a mechanistic view of the city which characterized urban planning in the 1960s and 1970s, to the city as an organism (input – metabolism – output), and later to the need to incorporate economic and social sustainability to the physical environmental considerations of urban design. Recently, the term smart cities has been adopted in scientific and policy circles.

In this paper, we will explore what smart cities aim to do, how information and communication technologies (ICTs) have been used for the enhancement of urban life, the challenges posed by this new theoretical direction and the adoption of innovative technologies in urban planning. We will conclude with a proposed model for the introduction of innovations in the cities in order to promote quality of life for all. We will start with a discussion of the basic concepts - smart cities and quality of life, followed by a review of innovative technologies used in smart cities, their benefits and challenges. We will then try to connect the needs of modern cities with the benefits and challenges of ICT applications in urban contexts, and we will conclude with suggestions for policy, education and research.

SMART CITIES: HISTORY AND CONTROVERSIES

There is no agreement on a single description of smart cities. Several definitions have been proposed giving different emphasis on different aspects of it. As Angelidou (2015) indicates, the roots of smart cities can be found in the 19th century with theories that focus on future visions of the city. Some view the city as a healthy and functional entity. The futurist movement focuses on the "technological triumph" of humanity over nature and the environment; the notion that "houses and cities ought to encompass modern industrial methods and work as effortlessly as machines" (p. 96). Planned cities address the increasing need for shelter and healthy living conditions. As we moved from the industrial society to the knowledge economy – an economy that is knowledge rather than labor intensive, cities were reconceived as urban communities that use technology to facilitate knowledge and innovation. As Komninos

(2011) indicated, the first such smart city (i.e. knowledge and innovative city) was Bletchley Park in the UK in 1939; it housed in isolation mainly cryptography scientists and experts for war-related purposes. "Here for the first time, individual, collective, and machine intelligence were concerted on a community-wide level, endowing a physical settlement with higher problem-solving capacity, quicker responses, better quality procedures and lower operation costs." (Angelidou, 2015, p.99)

In the 1960s, communications have started being an issue of concern within the urban context. By the 1990s, ICTs have been proposed by many as the main enabler of democracy and efficient city management. Distance is no longer a limiting factor in communications and market transactions.

Given this history, most often smart cities are conceived either as cities that utilize innovative technologies for efficient use of resources - digital technologies play a pivotal role in this approach; or as urban communities that use creative approaches to the management of resources and urban problems in general (Robinson, 2015). In both cases, the proposed goal is comfortable, healthy and sustainable living. The difference appears to lie in the means towards that goal: more efficient management, knowledge development and innovation (mainly technological and environmental), and more rarely social innovations.

There is also no agreement about the conception of smart versus intelligent cities. For some, intelligent cities are those that hold a high capacity for learning and innovation, while for others they imply high use of digital technologies and innovation and constitute a part of the smart city concept (Jusevicius, & Liugailaite, 2013). Marshal-Llacuna and Segal (2016) suggest that intelligent cities constitute a broader concept than smart cities. For them, the concept of intelligent cities imply more educated, collaborative and complex multi-system approaches. In all cases, smartness in cities implies effective use of knowledge and innovations for solutions to social problems and better quality of life; it involves technology and innovation. The main goals of different approaches to smart cities may differ: some emphasize the efficient management and use of resources in cities, while others aim for a good quality of life for urban inhabitants within the carrying capacity of the environment.

The approach to smart cities differs from country to country, region to region, as it is context specific, reflecting the aspirations and realities of local societies (Manville et al., 2014; Arku, 2009; Ministry of Urban Development – India, 2015). The concept of smart cities has now a prominent role in the policy making of the European Union. Smart cities, as defined in several documents of the European Commission (Manville et al., 2014; European Innovation Partnership on Smart Cities and Communities, 2013; European Commission, 2015), emphasize the use of digital and telecommunication technologies for more efficient networks and services and more efficient use of financial resources, for the benefit of city inhabitants and businesses. The Indian conception of smart cities is different (Ministry of Urban Development – India, 2015): smart cities apply technology, information and data to improve core infrastructure and services for a decent quality of life for all their citizens. This implies comprehensive development that will improve everyday life and employment opportunities for all, especially the poor and the disadvantaged, leading to inclusive urban societies.

These two approaches to smart cities imply a different conception of "quality of life". In the European conception of smart cities, there is an emphasis on economic activities and opportunities, and thus, an implicit emphasis on the individual, individual rights and comforts. The emphasis in the Indian context is inclusive cities, for better quality of life for all. Implicit in this conception is a more community-based understating of quality of life: all should be able to live a sufficiently good life.

SMART CITIES: ENABLERS AND IMPORTANT DIMENSIONS

In this paper, we use the term smart cities to refer to cities that provide good quality of life to all its citizens with effective infrastructure and services and efficient management of resources, via the use of innovative technologies and knowledge flows. Such cities are on the one hand, forward looking – looking to cities that will operate within the carrying capacity of local ecosystems and thus can provide good quality of life for future generations of city inhabitants as well (i.e. sustainable communities) – and on the other, inclusive - ensuring a good quality of life for all its citizens (i.e. inclusive processes and development). This chapter aspires to contribute some insights to the discussion of how the vision/concept of smart (sustainable and inclusive too) cities can become real city contexts.

Cities are both physical environments on the one hand and communities on the other: spaces and people. Both should be addressed in order to make our cities smart, conducive to happy and creative communities and individuals, inclusive, and environmentally friendly and sustainable. Modern smart cities have the following main dimensions (not an exhaustive list) that constitute the reality of the city, and need to be addressed in urban planning and urban life:

1. **Housing:** Housing is the space where private life occurs and family lives are based. Given the high density of many cities, housing is a main challenge of modern cities, in terms of its quality (i.e. many people do not have sufficient housing while others enjoy luxurious abodes), functionality (for everyday living needs), and environmental impacts (e.g. energy consumption, air quality, use of natural resources).
2. **Food:** Food is a basic survival need of all people, which constitutes a challenge in the cities with the high population concentrations that characterize them. Food availability, transport and quality constitute important challenges for modern cities.
3. **Energy:** Urban life assumes energy use. Cities in "developed" economies are highly energy-dependent. Energy consumption today, as it is based on fossil fuels, has significant impacts on the environment. A main challenge of modern smart cities is the limitation of energy waste - via energy efficiency - and of energy consumption, as well as the clean production of energy via the use of renewable energy sources.
4. **Transportation / Mobility:** Transportation is essential for the transfer of goods and services that are essential in cities. Mobility for people is a fundamental prerequisite for access to existing opportunities in cities. In the increasingly digital world where the meaning of distance changes, the significance of mobility and transportation is altered but does not disappear.
5. **Services:** Social, cultural, economic services are a fundamental constituent element of urban life; the human-made urban physical space, the size and density of cities, the distance of urban life from life in nature, environmental problems, the intense economic activity, and time organization in cities make the satisfaction of human – individual and communal - needs more challenging. The provision of services becomes a significant parameter of urban planning and quality of life in cities.
6. **Community and Neighborhoods:** Everyday life takes place in buildings (housing and workplaces) and in neighborhoods (public spaces for interaction). Private activities and close community (i.e. family) life occurs in housing and the workplace. Community building happens in the public areas around the house and the workplace. In neighborhoods, no matter how defined, everyday interactions and community building activities take place.

7. **Governance:** Decision making and power distribution is an essential component of city life, with added significance in the huge cities of today as direct interactions have become more limited and circumscribed. Public participation in decision making is greatly discussed but inclusive cities remain a challenge.
8. **Economic Opportunities:** Cities provide economic development and job opportunities, something that has attracted many people to urban life. Their design and regulation so that economic, social and environmental aspects get effectively integrated for good quality of life for all remains a challenge and the object of many discussions.

These are important dimensions that circumscribe everyday life, which is closely related with quality of life. Everyday life is where life takes place and relations take root; where challenges and social inequalities are experienced and new ideas and solutions are formed; where obstacles to/opportunities for a sustainable community materialize (Lefebrvre, 1971).

The transition of modern cities to smart ones cannot be seen without an integration of the previously discussed dimensions with a set of enablers that provide the constitutional ingredients for a successful outcome. Dimensions and enablers should be considered as an integral value space for the design and implementation of smart urban solutions. This is critical for planning policy making and implementation.

Important components of the smart cities concept / vision, which also constitute important enablers for the vision of smart cities to become a reality include strategic goals, technologies, participation, governance – decision-making process, as well as the definition of smartness/intelligence and quality of life. Below, we present a diagram indicating the connections we see between these enablers for the materialization of smart cities.

As Figure 1 indicates when a city claims that is it or aims to become a smart city, several forces are at work together:

- There is a set of goals that urban planners wish to achieve with the use of available technologies. Without goals, there cannot be any visionary and/or effective urban policy. Specific goals should

Figure 1. Smart cities inner context
Source: our elaboration

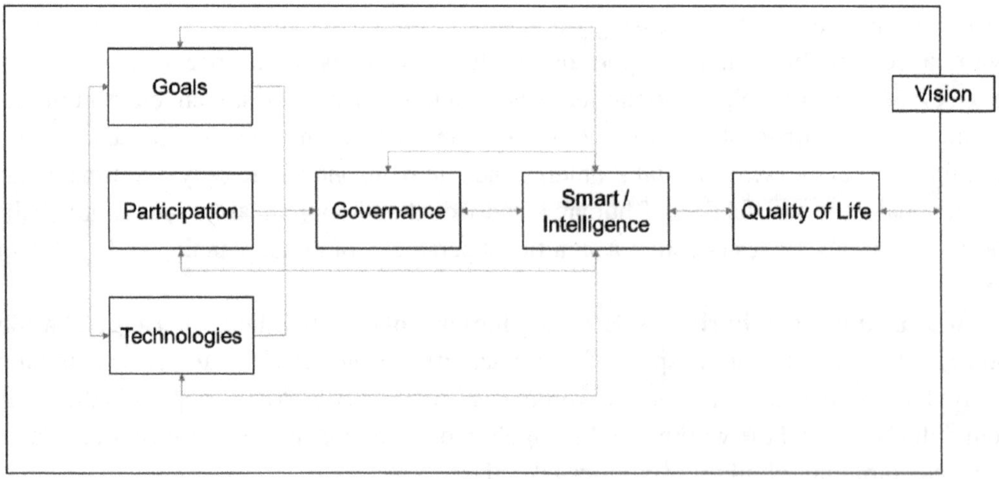

be established for the different dimensions of the city (e.g. housing, food, energy, transportation, etc) and these should reveal the close integration of all of them.

- For the decision of both the goals on the one hand and the means and technologies to be adopted on the other, participation of all the stakeholders is required, ideally at all stages of the planning process. Top-down approaches are almost certain to face obstacles and reaction from the people, leading to unsuccessful implementation.
- The goals, the processes of decision making and participation, the technologies and means used to connect the stakeholders and to take into account all relevant information and scientific data in the planning, implementation and evaluation phases constitute the governance of the city. Governance is a set of structures and processes and it involves decision-making, administration and power balances. Without careful consideration of the governance of a city, organized in line with its goals, there cannot be a smart city.
- Governance should be coupled with smart decisions and intelligence. This implies both use of ICTs but also appropriate and clever thinking that inform decision-making and aim for the integration of the different urban dimensions.
- In order to achieve effective and smart (as intelligent problem solving) use of appropriate ICTS, a vision for quality of life should inform all previous components: goals, use of technologies, governance with participation, informed by scientific and technological knowledge.

As the figure indicates, the relations between its different components are not one-way or linear. Instead, they all interrelate and affect each other, forming an integrated system of interrelations. The whole urban system interrelates with other cities and other areas at the global level.

This is the context in which information technologies should be exploited and strategically justified. The efficacy is a complicated construct and requires an interdisciplinary approach. In the next section, we present our own interpretation of the technological challenges of our times and we analyze how Smart Cities Vision can be enlightened further. The basic message we try to communicate is that technologies always provide a gallery of options and policy makers and stakeholders have to decide on their strategic fit to greater social challenges.

INFORMATION TECHNOLOGIES FOR SMART CITIES

The integration of information technologies to a smart cities agenda is one of the most interesting discussions of our times. Not only because currently we are facing a revolution in constitutional technologies for the provision of smart services like Internet of Things or Cloud Computing, but mostly because technology offers amazing capabilities for citizen-centric autonomous and collaborative services cultivating a sharing culture in isolated urban areas.

A new era of Smart Cities applications is promoted with the integration of various technologies. Lytras, García-Peñalvo and Ordóñez de Pablos (2013) discuss the role of Advanced human-computer interaction towards context-aware pervasive information systems. The successful implementation though of Urban Computing solutions requires novel ideas and new business models for collaborative learning systems capable of visioning the Knowledge Society, and its social interactions (Lytras et.al., 2015a; Lytras et.al., 2015b). Social media in the Smart City context can promote this vision significantly. The emphasis on Human Capital development (Lytras & Kurilovas, 2014a) and the integration of Social

Networks research with Innovation and Sustainability ideas can result to holistic frameworks for the integration of emerging technologies in smart cities research (Lytras et.al., 2014b; Lytras, Zhuhadar, Zhang, & Kurilovas, 2014c).

Moreover, there is a critical debate about the key aspects of technology-enabled innovation as a key response to the challenges of our times; this debate has a great impact also on the value propositions of smart cities. Hall and Landry (1997) proposed their taxonomy of types of production of innovations in the cities:

- Mega-paradigm shifts (e.g. city from a machine to a living organism to a sustainable city and now a smart city)
- Paradigm shift (the objective of the policy itself is changed)
- Basic innovation (fine tuning the problem definition)
- Best practice (outstanding example of realization)
- Good practice (realization becomes a standard benchmark)

This taxonomy provides an interesting context for further elaboration. A number of questions require a strategic interpretation for the future character of modern cities.

- Are there any emerging meta-paradigm shifts capable of transforming cities to intelligent, sustainable and inclusive living organizations?
- Should technology be kept transparent and integrated to key urban infrastructures or should technology be the catalyst of change to the current dominant paradigm?
- Is intelligence a new, integrative component of modern cities? And which are the key enabling technologies?
- Which are the required transformations in traditional learning capabilities of modern cities towards the realization of a new paradigm?
- Should policy makers of urban areas focus on functional basic innovations accompanied by the crafting of new strategic models for the integration of socio-technical components and infrastructures of modern cities?
- Which is the typical standardization workflow that permits the modeling and codification of best practices related to key processes of the daily operation of a city?
- Which are the required collaborative filtering mechanisms for the adoption of basic innovation into action in modern cities?
- Is there a way to develop a collaborative, adoptive, hub of human interactions with data and technology in order to enhance the capacity of modern cities to evolve on their own?
- What about exclusion and discrimination? How technology can promote democracy, participation and justice in the context of modern cities?

The above questions unveil a number of inefficiencies associated to modern cities related to bureaucracy, limited access to resources, critical information and communication gaps, obsolescence of technological infrastructures due to high cost, isolation of humans, weak performance of socio-technical systems, unemployment and discouraging of entrepreneurship, difficulty to promote knowledge and know-how transfer to problem solving capabilities of modern cities.

In order to answer some of these questions and to elaborate on the capacities of modern ICTs to play a critical role in the vision of smart cities, in the next section we provide our understanding for the variety of technological components of our times. It is rather a very challenging era, since a number of key technologies have entered to a new stage of maturity that expands further their value propositions. Before discussing with details the various technologies we provide eight realistic use cases in order to highlight the new challenging era of computing for smart cities research.

- **Scenario 1 - Personalized Services:** Maria is living in New York. She is using an Intelligent Agent through a portal for the selection of medical services. Doctor Locator is a social network enabled infrastructure allowing citizens to review quality of services of medical staff, rate services and planning meetings with experts. The system is exploiting the data profile of Maria and information from her Medical Portfolio, in order to recommend the doctors that fit better with her open issues. Maria and million other users exploit this infrastructure. Through collaborative filtering millions of people are rating medical services and contribute with recommendations for further evolution of services.
- **Scenario 2 - Social Responsibility:** Christina and Miltos live in Athens Greece. Last year more than 200.000 refugees arrived to Greece from Syria through Turkey and the Mediterranean Sea. They envision a system powered by wearable technologies, sensor networks and mobile networks for tracking refugees and their needs. Through wearable technologies, and smart bracelets refugees are monitored for social purposes. Additionally, the same system has the capacity to inform multilingual refugees about Greece and Europe and about procedures and information related to their lives. Though this system, every day millions of entries related to inquiries, housing, and medical services are updated and they facilitate a sufficient quality of life for refugees and the communities that accommodate them.
- **Scenario 3 - Community Building:** Patricia is living in Madrid Spain. She is using a GPS system to inform a community application about her activities. Every day she records her volunteer work in a volunteer's network. Thousands of Spanish people offer for free social services for non-educated young people. They are exploiting blended learning where local municipalities provide blended learning through Massive Open Online Courses infrastructures are used in order to support an Open Flexible Municipal University. The learners are enthusiastic about this because they develop new skills and gain knowledge that increases their employability. The local authorities are thinking about integrating this learning system with an e-marketplace where businesses will ask for employees at a pilot base.
- **Scenario 4 - Fraud Detection, Sentiment Analysis, and Anti Bullying Services:** In Chicago, two graduates from a Computer Science PhD Program, combined Machine Learning, Semantic Web and Neural Networks technologies and they built a system for data extraction in famous social networks. The purpose of the system is to monitor the behavior of users and to alert about behaviors related to bullying, fraud and terrorism. The system is real time and offers different options for filtering information.
- **Scenario 5 - People with Special Needs:** The new Mayor of Toronto decided to invest in Haptic and Wearable Technologies to promote the accessibility of blind people to key governmental offices. They decided to adopt Talking Shoes, equipped with cameras and navigation capabilities. The new system increased the access of blind people to the most relevant offices as well as their

satisfaction. The next step is to integrate natural speech recognition technologies and voice navigation to most of the key public web sites of Toronto.

- **Scenario 6 - Cultural Heritage:** In Paris, there is a strategic decision to promote the tourist experiences. For this purpose, they decided to run a big project called Open Culture with the exploitation of Virtual and Immersive Reality. The idea is simple. Louvre Museum exhibitions will be offered through Virtual Rooms to the world through a Cloud Service. Millions of people will be connected exploiting the capabilities of Virtual Reality and Artifacts digital annotation.
- **Scenario 7 - Antipoverty Networks:** In Nigeria, a local Mayor decided to develop an antipoverty network. His idea is really simple. Through crowd sourcing technologies, he developed an advanced system to ask for funding and services from millions of people worldwide in order to deliver an antipoverty network with various different services: medical services, materials collection, training offering,
- **Scenario 8 - Geriatrics:** In Sweden, an NGO related to quality of life for the elderly decided to promote a smart service for older people aiming to motivate them to participate in community activities over the network. Based on the findings of various scientific surveys that lonely older people suffer from melancholy and mental distortions, they offer varied forms of interaction through a community portal using video-conferencing, access to medical consultation, training and entertainment.
- **Scenario 9 - Personalized Billing:** In Tokyo, local authorities decided to promote a sophisticated system for personalized billing and payments of public services taking into account critical data related to income, unemployment and other factors associated to citizens. The system has the capacity to optimize the overall contributions and to minimize the unpaid accounts as well as to increase the social responsibility of the municipality.

The previous realistic scenarios are few examples of use cases related to the exploitation of the current emerging technologies in the context of smart cities. It is interesting in the next section to provide few more details for some of the most promising technologies of our times. This according to our perception and our analysis can be significant enablers of sustainability and inclusion.

The Smart Components

Technology is always evolving. The pace of technological change is also rapid. Thus, there is always a race between the adoption of the technology and its exploitation before it becomes obsolete. Nowadays, computer science and data science are in an era of transition. Sophisticated approaches to the management of Big Data, smart systems powered by Machine Learning and Cognitive Computing, methods, ubiquitous and pervasive mobile information systems, as well as mixed reality and robotics enlarge the perceived sphere of applications. It is undoubtedly a critical momentum for the humanity to investigate and to justify the role of all these promising technologies towards humanistic visions for the entire humanity and for the urban computing more specifically (Mitchell, Agle, & Wood, 1997; Parr, 2007; Yusuf, 2009).

The following is a short list of components that, when integrated, provide the context for the smart components of systems and applications for urban computing. Policy makers, educators as well as students should understand the building blocks of these systems as well as have the capability of understanding their full potential. Currently, there is a critical gap in the technology transfer because key policy makers require more time and more effort in absorbing internally the potential of these technologies. The

Figure 2. The Smart Cities Research core enabling technologies
Source: our elaboration

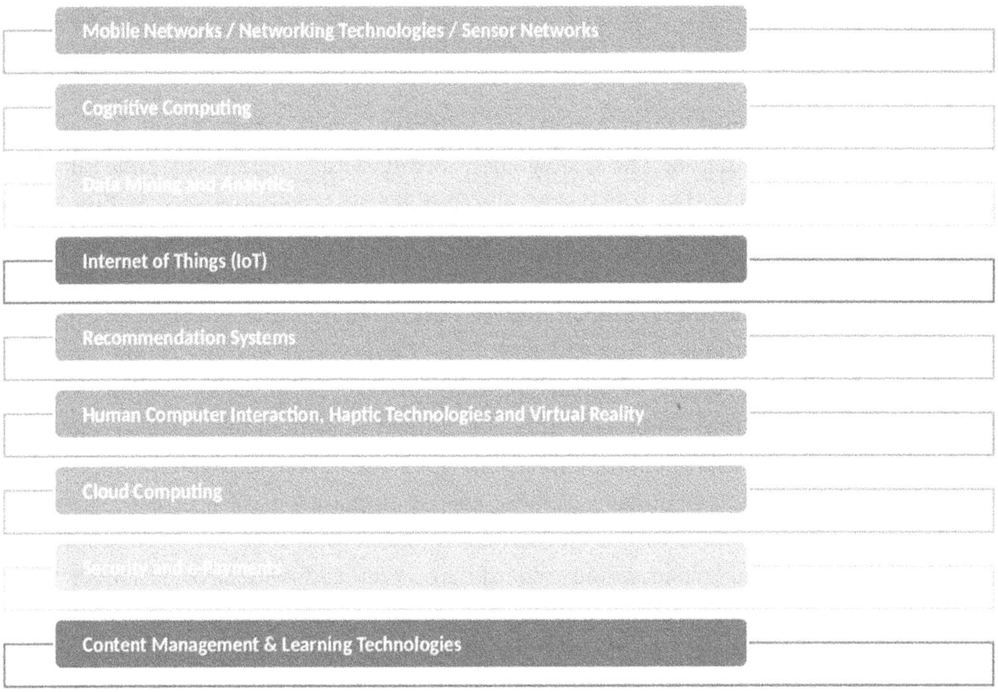

strategic vision of smart cities, even though it should not be a technological vision, it has to integrate a clear strategy on technology-enabled innovation. Even if the purpose is not from the beginning a meta-paradigm shift, approaches related to best practices or basic innovations should critically respond to the requirement to use the technology as a value carrier. In another way, the value mix of smart urban services should combine several of these technological components with a clear emphasis on the promotion of Sustainability and Inclusion.

- **Mobile Networks / Networking Technologies / Sensor Networks:** The evolution of Mobile Networks, the 5G generation is a brand new era for potential applications ranging from: Monitoring of Sensor Networks, Disaster Alerts, Personal and Wireless Cloud, Real Time Gaming, Multi-person video call, Autonomous driving, Augmented Virtual Reality, Tactile Internet, etc. For the realization of these promising technologies, there will be a necessity to promote cross-industry collaborations and shared business models. An additional key feature of these technologies related to smart cities is the application of the Sensor Networks capable of tracking, navigating and managing micro-environments. Consider for example systems capable of analyzing with sensor networks data received from thousands of wearable gadgets within a hospital.
- **Cognitive Computing:** In recent years, we realized a significant evolution in cognitive computing. Open Artificial Intelligence and many commercial solutions like IBM Watson, etc, provide a new range of sophisticated applications. The integration of advanced reasoning and querying capabilities to pervasive information systems expands further the value proposition of smart urban applications. The codification of Domain Knowledge, like for Taxation, Entrepreneurship, etc., and the

provision of smart services to citizens is a key challenge for urban computing. Additionally, the promotion of a collaborative authoring culture for the citizens secures the update of knowledge in flexible dynamic public information systems. The latest developments also in Social Networks like the Bot technology in Facebook will permit a number of intelligent questioning and answering systems.

- **Data Mining and Analytics:** Data Analytics combined with Big Data technologies constitute a new landscape for exploitation. The management of big data generated by smart urban applications is a strategic inquiry. There are several examples that potentially fit within this context. Initiatives related to Sentiment Analysis in social networks for smart cities, the application of association rules, or clustering to citizens' profiles, the identification of hidden patterns in data can boost the performance of services offered to citizens. Policy makers should be aware of these options especially for socially sensitive issues like Social Services, or for targeting services to excluded people. There is always a critical question: How can public or community services maintain sustainable information systems for the management of critical information related to people in poverty, need or exclusion? And to what extent is it feasible to use advanced approaches for the improvement of the computer literacy of these special target groups? A critical shift should also be made in the administration with a multimodal refinement of their knowledge related to these technologies, with critical considerations regarding privacy and justice. One more critical area for Data Analytics is definitely emergency systems related to Security or Anti-Terrorism.
- **Internet of Things (IoT):** Very shortly, billions of devices will be connected to the internet providing amazing capabilities for new-targeted services and business models. Especially for smart cities research, sectors like Transportation, Energy and Housing will benefit from this shift. Several brilliant ideas can promote sustainability visions related to the optimization of energy consumption, traffic control in city centers, smart automations in houses and many others. Neighborhood and community applications can integrate IoT considerations. One can think of a service capable of locating children leaving school on an interactive map; or, of services related to unwanted food in houses that can be forwarded to electronic services for anti-poverty networks. Or, one can conceive of drone services capable of delivering this food to people in need. Another example could be alarm systems integrated to smart shoes of children.
- **Recommendation Systems:** Recommendation systems or Recommender systems provide another significant constitutional technology for strategic smart cities initiatives. The provision of recommendations through advanced scenarios for the data processing and service selection is critical for different types of application domains. Recommender systems for energy consumption, customization of cultural content in events, systems related to medical services provision or identity matching are a few examples of visioning scenarios for smart cities. Consider for example a Recommender system that connects citizens with similar attitudes to societal issues, brings together experts for collective intelligence solutions, or creates collaborative work spaces for policy makers or opinion leaders etc.
- **Human Computer Interaction, Haptic Technologies and Virtual Reality:** In recent years, we also have a tremendous evolution in Human Computer Interaction. Great research on context awareness systems, haptic and wearable technologies, augmented and Immersive Virtual or Mixed Reality and Kinesthetic Research provide a brand new landscape for exploitation. Applications related to the use of Holograms technology in virtual labs in cities or the use of haptic technologies

for disabled people, are some fresh insights in smart urban services and applications. Certainly, voice recognition and Biometrics technologies will be among the "musts" in the next decade.

- **Cloud Computing:** Cloud Computing permits cost effective solutions for data, applications, software, infrastructures and services. It certainly provides a well-justified alternative strategic choice for public state or local authorities to build their services using the Cloud. Beyond some security concerns, it is evident that the Cloud will speed the adoption of the Smart Cities Vision. From this point of view, it is extremely important to analyze the strategic impact of cloud technologies for traditional services or innovative services of smart cities. Consider for example distributed databases on the cloud, or citizens' digital portfolios that are embedded to specific contexts for exploitation under Smart Cities solutions. It is obvious that all these technological capabilities require an integrated approach based on a social perspective. Ethical issues or issues related to security and privacy – ultimately related with personal freedom - must be analyzed in depth.
- **Security and E-Payments:** Electronic payments and handling of financial transactions in the context of smart cities will increasingly attract interest in the near future. The advancement of research and industrial solutions in this domain is adequate for supporting a very good quality of services.
- **Content Management Learning Technologies:** One of the most important challenges will be the need to integrate advanced knowledge and learning management capabilities in social information systems. Management of content creation, delivery and use will be a critical factor for the success of any implementations. Content is quintessential in the context of smart cities and the establishment of active and experiential learning capabilities will boost the release of unexploited capacities of intellectual and human capital in modern cities.

The previous short discussion of technological enablers shows that technology is not a panacea. There is no magic way to mix or integrate these services to meaningful solutions for smart cities. There are critical questions related to access to technology and skills required, as well as to the issue of control and personal freedom. Massive campaigns for enhancing the computer literacy of people will be required and a sustainable plan for the operation and maintenance of infrastructure. It is rather disappointing that in most funded projects relating to smart cities, most of the services are discontinued at the end of the pilot implementation phase.

A number of additional concerns highlight the necessity to develop strategic plans for the adoption of technology in a smart cities vision:

- *Need for more comprehensive and integrative approaches, rather than simply projects or isolated initiatives.* It seems that we have a lack of an integrated strategy at a governmental and urban context. There is a lot of funding for projects without any emphasis on their integration to a greater hub or to "one-stop-shop" approaches. This is a great problem since we have waste of resources, isolated systems, and duplicated efforts. It is also evident that different technologies or vendors are providing alternative solutions for the same enabling technologies and systems. This implies that well justified strategies for technology integration are required in order to promote the sustainability of smart urban solutions.
- *Discussion and databases of failures as failures are important sources of information.* Lessons learnt and Best Practices systems constitute a smart way to exploit the cumulative knowledge from smart urban projects. The collective wisdom and the know-how should be codified and dis-

seminated to various stakeholders. This could form an Observatory of lessons-learnt and Best Practices, functioning at country or continent level.

- *Data Integration in distributed Databases. What information should be included in the databases, with what criteria, decided by whom?* To this purpose, novel approaches related to Semantic Web and Resource Description Framework can offer significant services. Data management in the context of smart cities is a very complicated issue. A number of key questions beg an answer. A continuous process for the establishment of Quality Assurance mechanisms is required. Semi-automatic or automatic annotation of profiles with metadata and electronic Help Desks are also good practices.
- *Security concerns and freedom* constitute a challenging pair for Smart Cities. Should smart urban services be considered as spaces of freedom or of social control? This is a very delicate area and while a lot of scientific research provides interesting insights for the right compromise, it is still true that much should be thought and done for the development of a new culture related to regulations in the virtual or electronic landscape.

Below, we provide our own recommendation about some key areas for the exploitation of all these technologies towards quality of life and connectivity in smart cities.

The Smart Integration for Connectivity and Quality of Life

The implementation of Smart Cities Projects requires an in-depth analysis of social and technological factors. Policy making related to technology-enhanced innovation relevant to social aspects of human life is more demanding. The previous discussion on the current state-of-the-art approaches to technology provides critical insights on how these can promote the quality of life and connectivity aspects of smart cities. Table 1 is a summary of ideas and a compilation of industry-based evidence for some of the good things that are happening in smart cities research due to the merits of technology and the creative thinking of humans. In our future project, a research monograph entitled "Smart Urban Solutions for Innovation and Sustainability: Emerging Research and Opportunities" scheduled to be published in mid-2017 by IGI-Global, we are elaborating further on the key propositions.

All the examples in the previous table are indicative promising areas for applications toward the vision of Smart Cities. It is true that most of the applicable scenarios require integration of technologies, so the classification is not very strict. It is just a reference table to highlight some of the most promising areas. For sure, a more elaborated version of this table can be generated, especially in relevance to the areas of Housing, Food, Energy, Transportation / Mobility, Services, Community and neighborhoods, Governance and Economic Opportunities.

AN INTEGRATED FRAMEWORK FOR SMART, SUSTAINABLE AND INCLUSIVE CITIES

Design Challenges for Smart Cities and Indicative Case Studies

The vision of smart cities is a grand vision. As such, it is also complicated, refers to many disciplines, and integrates human and social aspects. From this perspective, any strategic policy making procedure related

Table 1. Visioning Scenarios of Smart Cities

Technologies	Smart Cities Focus	
	Quality of Life	**Connectivity**
Mobile Networks / Networking Technologies / Sensor Networks	• Tracking systems of Disabled • Smart Applications for sharing resources • Anti-poverty Networks • Personalized Services in Health, Education • Medical Management • Sensoring, Cloud, GIS applications at micro and wide levels • Protocols and Standardization of Internet Technology for Smart Cities • Intelligent services for energy and traffic monitoring	• Rapid development of active citizens communities • Micro-area networking • Disaster Management Systems • Mentoring and Counseling Services • Open Platforms for volunteer networks
Cognitive Computing	• Disease Prediction Systems • Smart Clustering of citizens • Development of Expert Systems for Advising • Anti-Fraud systems • Cognitive Behavior Treatments • Open Government, Open Data, Linked Data for Smart Cities	• Matching of peers in humanistic networks • Citizens Profile Big Data Management • Automatic Extraction of Profiles and allocation • Dynamic composition of social-related networks for active citizenship • Sentiment analysis in Social Networks • Opinion Networks composition • Energy Patterns analysis
Data Mining and Analytics	• Patterns Detection in Open Linked Data for entrepreneurship and Innovation • Automatic Selection of services based on data profiles • Data Science for Smart Cities • Visualization Techniques • Neural Networks applications for advanced probabilistic services • Patterns Recognition, clustering, classification, machine learning, fuzzy logics for Smart City Data Analysis	• Social Networks integration in Smart Cities strategies • Web applications for smart communities; • Automatic Profiling • Connectivity Analysis of Peers in Smart Cities Networks • Dynamic integration of distributed networks • Transportation, traffic and logistics optimization
Recommendation Systems	• Anti-bureaucracy applications in public sector • Rating systems and collaborative filtering platforms a local and global scale • Urban Innovation Applications • Urban Growth, Value adding Urban Services •	• Dynamic Annotation of profiles and communities • Group / community based innovation networks • Experts Matching systems • Waste Food Management in community level
Human Computer Interaction, Haptic Technologies and Virtual Reality	• Haptic Technologies for disabled • Virtual Labs for therapeutic purposes • Voice Recognition for disabled • Navigation and Tracking • Wearable and Immersive Technologies for Smart Cities • Smart Visualization systems for Energy consumption monitoring •	• Advanced visualization networks for neighborhoods • Visualization of Community services • Community based infrastructures for culture • Virtual Worlds integration in different domains • Exploitation of Internet of Things information
Cloud Computing	• Distributed applications as services • Distributed open repositories • Component based Management • Re-use of resources	• Community based collaborative storage in contexts • Cost Effective governance of Smart Cities infrastructures
Security and ePayments	• Security and Privacy Issues in Smart Cities services provision • Electronic Payment systems for government and local authorities	• Crowdfunding systems
Content Management and Learning Technologies	• Open Knowledge Platforms • Distributed Archives • Best Practices Hubs • Distance Learning applications for sensitive categories • Massive Open Online Cources Infrastructures	• Case Studies of Smart Cities Research in Education, Poverty, Disability, Water Management, Energy, Transportation, Research, Business, Tourism, Leisure, Living, Security, Economy, and Governance • Open Access to Knowledge, Open Services for Smart Cities • Virtual Universities • Informal Learning networks etc

Source: Our elaboration

to smart cities should be detailed, in-depth, flexible and functional. A strategy must be accompanied by a workflow that permits the operationalization at the everyday level. A lot of work can be done within this context. Several cluster-based strategies can be designed. However, on top of any procedure, we need to implement an Integrated Framework. In this chapter, we communicate the basic aspects of this framework, while in the near future we will publish a detailed policy making guide on the same matter.

Some of the challenges the design and development of smart cities for quality of life for all, present and future inhabitants, faces include:

- What is often missing from the discussions on smart cities, which originated from engineering and technological fields until recently when social sciences came into the discussion as well, is the discussion of social dimensions and especially of social inequalities and power differentials.
- In the effort to design and build smart cities, an apparent contradiction exists: urban planning wishes to control - at least for the sake of efficiency - and manage uncertainty, while good urban life implies also freedom, creativity, the unpredictable, connection.
- Another omission in the discussions and design of smart cities relates with the significance of everyday life – where caring and forming intimate relations primarily take place – and private space, which provides the physical context in which everydayness occurs.
- In most of the cases, policy makers overlook the fact that technology is not a panacea.
- Technology is fast moving, changing rapidly, and from this perspective, no technological component is capable of maintaining a sustainable competitive advantage for a long time. Thus, it is more important to establish frameworks for the strategic management of smart cities guiding technologies and not policies with technologies as the main focus.
- There is always a learning process incorporated in the workflow of delivering the value of smart cities. Stakeholders should be aware of it and should be motivated to form a community where problems, issues and controversies are discussed and promoted to real world solutions that address critical problems that citizens, the local community, the city or even the global society face.

Based on these challenges, we list some questions that need to be considered in the design of smart solutions.

- **Strategic Goals:** These should guide all the rest. But how should they be decided? What (e.g. public and private space, everyday life, individual and community) should they include and how should they be integrated? Which goal-setting process can facilitate efficiency (control), social inclusion, needed change and creativity for more sustainable and happier societies? Can information technologies facilitate the balance between control and efficiency on the one hand and creativity and social change on the other?
- **Technologies:** They nowadays constitute an important tool that can propose many technical solutions, surpassing space and time limitations. How can we ensure technologies that also promote freedom, creativity, connection, good quality of life for all? In which spaces / arenas should they best be applied?
- **Participation:** For quality life for all and for new forward-looking and effective and holistic approaches, participation of all involved is essential. But what is an effective participation process in modern cities? How should the public/private space-time be organized to be conducive for participation? How can technologies facilitate this process?

- **Governance – Decision Making Process:** What constitutes effective governance for smart inclusive cities? How can technologies facilitate effective decision making for the good of all humans and for healthy ecosystems in years to come?
- **Smartness / Intelligence:** How should these concepts materialize in a sustainable and inclusive city? How should technologies be used to promote both efficiency and freedom – creativity?
- **Quality of Life:** This constitutes the essence of the whole effort of smart cities as we defined them. What types of information technologies can contribute to quality of life of all? What characteristics should they have?

Currently a number of smart urban solutions and projects are ongoing worldwide. Their discussion in depth is out of the scope of this chapter. We decided to briefly discuss two interesting case studies just to highlight the complexity of the phenomenon and the complementarity of enablers and dimensions.

The first case study is SynAthina: SynAthina is an initiative of the Municipality of Athens - Greece, coordinated by the Vice-Mayor of the Civil Society and Municipal Decentralization, which aims to facilitate the connection of citizens' groups with the Municipality, and of people with different citizens' initiatives for the improvement of quality of life in the city. It reflects the vision of the Municipality of Athens to establish "a new innovative cooperative model" in the city. SynAthina uses several tools towards this goal: a web-based platform, a Facebook page, a blog, radio, youtube videos, and a municipal space in the center of Athens where different activities are housed. On the web-based platform, citizens' groups can share information about their activities and invite participation, while people can find out about a great variety of activities - social, cultural, solidarity, sports and fun, environment, education, children, neighborhood interventions - taking place in Athens. The site also includes a list of many citizens' initiatives that organize activities. According to the Mayor's – Mr. Kaminis' – introduction, the intention is to create a platform for communication with the active citizens of Athens. On the SynAthina Facebook page, announcements are made for different initiatives and invitations are extended for public participation in different decisions. One such recent announcement invites interested people and organizations to submit proposals for the integrated management of the trade and cultural areas of the Municipal Market of Kypseli. So, SynAthina aims to involve active and creative citizens in the management of urban space. This initiative of the Municipality of Athens proposes a new conception of the relation of citizens and the Municipality, a new form and forum of citizens' involvement in decision-making and management of the resources of the city. It strives to provide a forum for a more effective networking amongst grassroots groups and a more effective connection between citizens' groups, interested individuals and the Municipality itself. Indeed, it introduces a paradigm shift in the conception of municipal decision making towards a more grassroots, participatory model. At the same time, it provides innovative technology-based and traditional (i.e. space) tools and resources for this to become more feasible. In this effort, what appears to have played a catalytic role includes among others: a new and promising vision of the city and active citizens, charismatic and passionate individuals in the Municipality, and knowledge of new technologies, availability of information technologies and required funds, and good communication skills.

Another case study focusing on citizens' involvement and change of behavior is the "GREENCIT - Green citizens of Europe - Innovative tools and methods for interactive and co-creative citizens" project (funded by the LIFE funding instrument of the European Commission) which comes from Sweden. The main objective of the initiative is "how environmental policy can be interpreted and implemented into concrete citizen-oriented actions, which motivate and help citizens to change their behavior" (Green

Citizens of Europe, http://en.greencit.se/). It includes a diversity of actions: a mobile communication unit for motivation and awareness raising; "clean neighborhood" activities to increase recycling and source separation, using interactive garbage bins; joint commuting services (planned and spontaneous) using IT-services, mobile devices, SMS and GPS; new interactive energy-saving systems in residential areas using meters in apartments along with energy and water use displays with flexible interface; and screens demonstrating air quality in the city. In this project, technology is primarily used for communication of information to the public for awareness raising purposes and for change of behaviors. An interesting mix of technology-based methods and face-to-face interactions characterizes this effort. This initiative can be considered a best practice for efforts that try to translate policy into practice and behavioral change.

Policy Making for Smart Cities

All smart components of a smart city should be considered and evaluated in light of these questions, but they should also be designed in the context of a broader policy making and strategic vision, defined by people's needs. The conception of inclusive smart cities and urban life is significant as it underlines the way issues are framed and which solutions are proposed and it influences the distribution of resources (see also Bullard, 2007). A smart city policy making process would benefit if it aimed to integrate visioning, strategizing, acting, technology use, and people participation in decision making and social inclusion in a holistically innovative process. We propose the *Sustainable and Inclusive Smart Cities Strategic Policy Making Model*, desiring to incorporate social and technological innovations, for specific problems or services but also for a new conception of goals, policies and processes.

Figure 3. Sustainable and Inclusive Smart Cities Strategic Policy Making Model
Source: Our elaboration

Step 1 - Develop a Vision for the City: This is a long term strategic vision, citizen-centric, where technologies act as the vehicle of innovation, quality of life and connectivity. It should be collaborative developed and diffused to all stakeholders. It should inspire minds, behaviors and dreams for a better life in a beautiful city.

Step 2 - Develop Forums/Platforms (Using Technologies) to Involve the Community: The Community has to play a critical role in the design of strategies. It should be involved from the beginning of any initiative exploiting face to face and technologically supported interactions, while community contribution should be documented and shared. The learning process should be also flexible permitting mental and intellectual enhancements in the members of the community.

Step 3 - Set Strategic Goals: Strategic goals should be always related to quality of life and connectivity with an emphasis on humanitarian visions for wellbeing for all and for improving the quality of life and conditions of life for the people in need. Goals should also incorporate the young generation; the ultimate vision should be to give to the next generation a better world and a supporting culture.

Step 4 - Design Action Plans: The transformation of vision to solutions for smart cities requires the development of informative, detailed, measurable and feasible action plans. Due to the complexity of the phenomenon of smart cities and the variety of possible actions, the Action Plans should be developed with the greatest involvement of the community and should have the administrative commitment at all the levels of control and hierarchy. Action plans should include also updating mechanisms, while authorities or stakeholders should maintain flexible mechanisms for the realization of action plans. They should not be treated as monolithic reference documents, not even as single elements for executing control.

Step 5 - Utilize Technologies: The utilization of the technology in a cost effective way is a key prerequisite of any success in smart cities. With the revolution of Open Source Software, several viable applications are possible. Inclusive and sustainable development needs to anchor value propositions in a variety of technologies. A good practice is always to invest in technologies that are supported from well maintained vendors in the market and also to give opportunity to start up companies with innovative propositions for services and problem solving applications. This mix can secure a smooth transition from monolithic basic applications to innovations.

Step 6 - Develop a Smart City Hub Strategy: The idea of a Smart City Hub is critical. The basic objective is to have a single access holistic entrance point to all the services related to the Smart City, including all the community services and all the tools available to citizens. Currently, many isolated, dispersed information systems have limited effectiveness just because of the inability of the systems to communicate with each other and to support greater coalitions at the information-systems level. Data and application integration within Data Warehouses and Smart Cities Hubs should be a key strategic choice for policy makers. For sure, this does not imply that small, flexible and unique applications cannot run as standalone systems outside of the main hub.

Step 7 - Implement Services: The implementation of smart urban services based on Vision, Strategies and Action Plans, must follow the latest guidelines of Software Engineering and Programming. Due to the fact that we have very different methods, programming languages and tools, another critical decision is the selection of development environments. Outsourcing and in-house developments are both good practices. Cloud services are also excellent strategic choices and should be considered seriously.

Step 8 - Develop a Smart City Sustainable and Inclusive Integrative Center: The Sustainable and Inclusive Center is a socio-technical entity. It provides an infrastructure for continuous insights for the present and the future of the smart city as an evolving organization.

Step 9 - Integrate Community Feedback to Strategies and Action Plans: Community is one of the most important components of the Integrated Strategic Policy Making Model. The community is fine tuning the strategic fit and updates relevant policies. For this reason, the collective wisdom of the community should be gathered with the use of technologies but also with an expansion of option for participatory design, brainstorming and crafting of synergies. Community-based evaluation of smart urban policies should always be a priority in any evaluation program.

The Sustainable and Inclusive Smart Cities Strategic Policy Making Model presented in this section requires further elaboration. In our next book planned for publication from IGI-Global as a Research Insights edition, we provide more technical details about its implementation.

RECOMMENDATIONS FOR POLICY AND EDUCATION

Mumford (1961) argued for a complementary development of the urban environment / space and of technology. This still constitutes an important insight. Communities should formulate a common vision for their future and develop the policies, strategies and tools that will pave the way towards this vision. Given the urgency to move towards sustainable cities and the needed shifts in worldviews and in social and individual practices, participatory and inclusive but also efficient and effective processes are required for decision-making, implementation and action. The marriage of real life with virtual connections, of spaces conducive to relations, caring connections and freedom with innovative technologies, in order to develop active citizenry is a main challenge.

The use and contribution of technology to urban life should also be informed by the following observations.

- Social inequalities in a city (including inequalities in investment choices) need to be addressed by themselves and should not be assumed that will disappear / get resolved with the "smartness" of a city, as these inequalities are inscribed in space and the city (Tretter, 2013; Marouli, 1995). In addition, social innovations to help with social fragmentation and social exclusion are needed.
- Given the need for both planning / control for efficiency and freedom for good quality of life, a tenuous balance should be aimed for between urban planning and urban everyday life. This implies careful thinking about what initiatives, technologies etc. should – or should not - be applied to which aspects of urban life (e.g. public – private). Attention should be paid to both the "home economy" – which involves unpaid labor, caring etc. – and the formal economy, maybe with different goals and strategies for each.
- Smart inclusive cities design should aim for a balanced approach to the public and private spaces, with careful thought about the appropriate balance between control (planning) and freedom (creativity, flexibility, unpredictability) for each.
- Open governance with meaningful participation can further ensure citizens' "choice of choices" – ability to choose what reflects their needs and aspirations, rather than select from a preselected list of initiatives or approaches – spaces of freedom as Papadolambakis (1988) called them.

- Public participation in decision making should be supported with appropriate mechanisms – e.g. a forum / internet-based platform like the one proposed by SynAthina – that facilitate meaningful and informed participation of different social groups.
- Integration of different aspects of city life, of different urban initiatives and of different data bases, for more effective citizens' action and for more efficient policy making, e.g. via a Smart City Hub.
- Cities need to bridge the gap between the "creative stage" (creation of new ideas and innovative solutions) and "non-creative" (execution) stage, addressing both as equally important. This synthesis will provide new innovative solutions for "organization-wide innovation cultures and 'empowered' individuals" as Rickards indicated (Hall, & Landry, 1997, p.4). The hub that we proposed above and the forum that SynAthina created may facilitate this city-wide innovation culture.

Such a change in urban planning and policy making implies changes in education as well. Since a paradigm shift is needed in urban policy making, urban life and citizens' conception of the city, decision makers' but also citizens' perceptions of city life, innovations and engagement in community affairs need to be altered too. Education has a significant role to play in a transition towards smart sustainable cities. But education should be adjusted too to promote the required new values and skills. What is urgently needed in the complex urban reality of modern cities is the ability and practice of connecting – synthesizing – integrative understanding of impacts. This implies integrative innovations and a new engineering and science education. As Landry and Bianchini indicated,

...[W]e need a completely different type of creativity and innovation, in particular the creativity of being able to synthesize, to connect, to gauge impacts across different spheres of life, to see holistically.... to grasp the subtle ecologies of our systems of life and how to them sustainable (Hall, & Landry, 1997, p.4).

All education, including engineering and science education, should aim to make knowledge relevant to everyday life. Education should make transparent to learners the inseparable connection between individual action and social problems, aside of the knowledge they should impart to the students. Individual issues are social problems, and social problems result from individual choices and actions.

FUTURE RESEARCH DIRECTIONS

There is a wealth of technological innovations that have been applied to cities in order to provide better quality information, access to a wealth of knowledge, better services, more efficient decision making, and better quality of life for selected social groups. ICTs are very much integrated in the everyday life of Western cities. Future research on smart cities is challenging and there are several indications that it will receive extensive attention from different communities, including academic scholars, industry and business innovators. The fast-paced changes in technologies and the increasing concern for the future of our planet as well as for an inclusive and sustainable development can promote several research strategies.

A main wave of research will be related to social innovations and smart social solutions capable of promoting the role of community contributions to humanistic visions of modern cities.

Another critical line of research includes the integration of the home/private domain and the economy/public space, using information technologies in order to balance control for efficient management of resources and freedom, caring and creativity in the city. The ways ICTs can support the complicated smart cities decision making process are a great development for the near future.

In addition, the investigation and provision of think-tanks and spaces of freedom will be another key priority of future research. The unleashing of hidden creativity and the community involvement in decision making will require critical multidisciplinary research in various aspects. Toward this goal, the role of information technologies as a catalyst of change will be evident as ICTs are not easily or fully controllable and remain creative.

Related to policy making, research is needed regarding which information technologies can most effectively support open governance, with extensive and meaningful citizen engagement for transforming cities into smart, sustainable and inclusive urban communities.

Finally, private-public domain coalitions and joint business plans can offer the flexible financial and managerial means for the provision of many smart cities services, which we hope - with appropriate community guidance - will provide services for people in need.

CONCLUSION

What is often missing from the smart cities discussions is the integration of social dimensions and especially of social inequalities and power differentials that underlie the use of information technologies and undermine their positive impact on communities. These need to be addressed before information technologies can effectively promote happy and environmentally sustainable cities for all. We advocate that smart urban components should be designed and evaluated in light of a strategic vision for the city, a vision that reflects people's needs and aspirations. Furthermore, a holistically innovative process should be adopted leading to organizational innovation of the city – i.e. innovation not only in the conception of an idea but also related to the decision-making and the implementation of a proposal. We have proposed a range of issues that are worthy of attention so that the use of ICTs can serve the vision of smart, sustainable and inclusive cities. The special character and complementarity of public and private spaces, the significance of everyday life (where caring, relations, creativity are primarily "housed"), the pivotal role of open governance and meaningful citizen participation, as well as the balance between the desired surveillance for efficient resource management on the one hand, and freedom and creativity on the other – all have been highlighted as challenges that should inform the design and adoption of smart urban solutions. These issues beg for innovative research that can propose fruitful collaborations between engineering, social sciences and ICTs and integrative approaches. As Marshal-Llacuna and Segal (2016) suggest modern smart cities require more educated, collaborative and complex multi-system approaches, with the participation of multiple stakeholders, aiming to mutual benefit and efficiency.

Our concluding remark is that humans do still have the power to envision and create a better world for all: better quality of life and sustainable and inclusive communities. The smart cities vision is an excellent opportunity to refer again to the origins of cities: we must make sure that smart cities offer satisfaction of basic needs, security, freedom, equal opportunities for creativity, well-being, and prosperity for all.

In our authored book *Smart Urban Solutions for Innovation and Sustainability: Emerging Research and Opportunities* scheduled for publication in 2017 from IGI-Global we are further promoting our commitment to this humanistic vision.

REFERENCES

Angelidou, M. (2015). Smart cities: A conjuncture of four forces. *Cities (London, England)*, *47*, 95–106. doi:10.1016/j.cities.2015.05.004

Arku, G. (2009). Rapidly Growing African Cities Need to Adopt Smart Growth Policies to Solve Urban Development Concerns. *Urban Forum, 20*, 253-270.

Bullard, R. D. (2007). *Growing Smarter: Achieving Livable Communities, Environmental Justice, and Regional Equity*. Cambridge, MA: The MIT Press.

European Commission. (2015). *Smart cities*. Retrieved June, 8, 2016, from https://ec.europa.eu/digital-single-market/en/smart-cities

European Innovation Partnership on Smart Cities and Communities. (2013). *Strategic Implementation Plan*. Retrieved April 24, 2016 from http://ec.europa.eu/eip/smartcities/files/sip_final_en.pdf

Hall, P., & Landry, C. (1997). *Innovative and Sustainable Cities*. European Foundation for the Improvement of Living and Working Conditions.

International Union for Conservation of Nature. (n.d.). *IUCN definitions – English*. Retrieved 2, January, 2017, from https://www.iucn.org/downloads/en_iucn__glossary_definitions.pdf

Jusevicius, R., & Liugailaite, L. (2013). Smart Development: A Conceptual Framework. *Proceedings of the International Conference on Intellectual Capital, Knowledge Management & Organizational Learning* (pp. 212-219). Retrieved April 10, 2016, from http://web.a.ebscohost.com/ehost/pdfviewer/pdfviewer?vid=3&sid=a7eed2ab-4453-4beb-bbee-cb7a81961fe8%40sessionmgr4003&hid=4109

Komninos, N. (2011). Intelligent cities: Variable geometries of spatial intelligence. *Intelligent Buildings International*, *3*(3), 172–188. doi:10.1080/17508975.2011.579339

Lefebvre, H. (1971). *Everyday Life in the Modern World*. London: The Whitefriers Press.

Lytras, M. D., Al-Halabi, W., Xi Zhang, J., Masud, M., & Haraty, R. A. (2015a). Enabling Technologies and Business Infrastructures for Next Generation Social Media: Big Data, Cloud Computing, Internet of Things and Virtual Reality. *Journal of Universal Computer Science*, *21*(11), 1379–1384.

Lytras, M. D., García-Peñalvo, F. J., & Ordóñez de Pablos, P. (2013). Advanced human-computer interaction. *Computers in Human Behavior*, *29*(2), 305–306. doi:10.1016/j.chb.2012.11.018

Lytras, M. D., & Kurilovas, E. (2014a). Special issue on Information and communication technologies for human capital development. *Computers in Human Behavior*, *30*, 361. doi:10.1016/j.chb.2013.11.002

Lytras, M. D., Mathkour, H., Abdalla, H. I., Yáñez-Márquez, C., & Ordóñez de Pablos, P. (2014b). The Social Media in Academia and Education: Research R-evolutions and a Paradox: Advanced Next Generation Social Learning Innovation. *Journal of Universal Computer Science*, *20*(15), 1987–1994.

Lytras, M. D., Mathkour, H. I., Abdalla, H. I., Al-Halabi, W., Yáñez-Márquez, C., Wolfgand, S., & Siqueira, M. (2015b). An emerging - Social and emerging computing enabled philosophical paradigm for collaborative learning systems: Toward high effective next generation learning systems for the knowledge society. *Computers in Human Behavior*, *51*, 557–561. doi:10.1016/j.chb.2015.06.004

Lytras, M. D., Zhuhadar, L., Zhang, J. X., & Kurilovas, E. (2014c). Advances of Scientific Research on Technology Enhanced Learning in Social Networks and Mobile Contexts: Towards High Effective Educational Platforms for Next Generation Education. *Journal of Universal Computer Science*, *20*(10), 1402–1406.

Manville, C., et al. (2014). *Mapping Smart Cities in the EU.* European Commission, Directorate General for Internal Policies – Policy Department A: Economic and Scientific Policy.

Marouli, C. (1995). Women resisting (in) the city: Struggles, gender, class and space in Athens. *International Journal of Urban and Regional Research*, *19*(4), 534–548. doi:10.1111/j.1468-2427.1995.tb00527.x

Marshal-Llacuna, L. L., & Segal, M. E. (2016). The Intelligenter Method (I) for making smarter city projects and plans. *Cities (London, England)*, *55*, 127–138. doi:10.1016/j.cities.2016.02.006

Ministry of Urban Development - India. (2015). *Smart Cities Mission.* Retrieved June, 6, 2016, from http://smartcities.gov.in/

Mitchell, R., Agle, B., & Wood, J. (1997). Toward a Theory of Stakeholder Identification and Salience: Defining the Principle of Who and What Really Counts. *Academy of Management Review*, *22*(4), 853–886.

Mumford, L. (1961). *The City in History*. New York: Harcourt, Brace and World.

Papadolambakis, M. (1988). *Spaces of Freedom: Essays for a Dialectic of Space-making*. Athens: Exantas. (in Greek)

Parr, J. (2007). Spatial definition of the city: Four perspectives. *Urban Studies (Edinburgh, Scotland)*, *44*(2), 381–392. doi:10.1080/00420980601075059

Robinson, R. (2015). 6 inconvenient truths about Smart Cities. *The Urban Technologist*. Retrieved June, 15, 2016, from https://theurbantechnologist.com/2015/02/15/6-inconvenient-truths-about-smart-cities/

Yusuf, S. (2009). From Creativity to Innovation. *Technology in Society*, *31*(1), 1–8. doi:10.1016/j.techsoc.2008.10.007

KEY TERMS AND DEFINITIONS

Big Data: Big Data refers to the new era of Data Warehouses and Data Bases technologies. It is about Distributed Information Systems that generate huge data in terms of Volume, Variety and Velocity. The great challenge related to Big Data is the design of sophisticated systems capable of collecting, organizing and analyzing data real time for a number of personalized services and recommendations.

Business Intelligence: It is the new era of Decision Support Systems and computer-enabled intelligence. Nowadays a variety of applications and constitutional technologies, integrating Computer Science, Enterprise Computing, Statistics, Mathematics and Econometrics provide advanced services for reporting, analytical services and predicting.

Cognitive Computing: Cognitive Computing refers to the new exciting era of Artificial Intelligence in modern computing. Several emerging sophisticated approaches expand the limits of information systems and increase their capacities for autonomous decision making. Robotics, Deep Learning and Reinforcement Algorithms, approaches to crafting, evaluating and intervening upon immersive, networked, user experiences, Cognitive Computing for Smart Cities, Stimulated Social Activities and Critical Thinking within an Immersive Cognitive Environment, Integrating Analytics with Online Texts, Courseware, and Learning Environments to Measure Student Progress and Interaction, Data Analytics Platform for Detailed Reporting, Assessment, and Collaboration, Visual Analytics to Identify Patterns and Processes for Mining Large Educational Datasets and New Business Models for Next Generation Cognitive WWW are only a few aspects of a new Revolution in Computing.

Inclusive Cities: An inclusive city is one that values all people and strives to meet all citizens' basic needs equally. This also implies participatory decision making practices.

Internet Technologies: Internet Technologies are related to the services over the internet backbone, permitting content sharing, transactions and linking of entities and peers. It is the required technical backbone for the design and implementation of value adding services. Voice over IP, FTP, WWW, Video Conferencing, Instant Messaging, Cognitive apps and many others constitute a gallery of technologies for integrated solutions.

Quality of Life: It refers to the general well-being of individuals and communities. It reflects life satisfaction, including among others physical health, family, community, employment, education, wealth, religious beliefs and the environment.

Smart Cities: Smart cities are cities that provide good quality of life to all its citizens with effective infrastructure and services and efficient management of resources, via the use of innovative technologies and knowledge flows.

Sustainability: It refers to the adequate access, use and management of the natural resources, to ensure that the men and women of present and future generations are able to meet their basic needs on an uninterrupted basis. Pattern of behaviors that guarantees for each of the future generations, the option to enjoy, at the very least, the same level of welfare enjoyed by the preceding generation. Emphasis is placed on the intergenerational equity of development. (IUCN, n.d.)

Urban Computing: The use of Information and Communication Technologies for advanced applications related to networking, provision of services in urban areas. It is an alternative way to refer to the Smart Cities Applications, with an emphasis in the developmental aspects of computer based interventions. In fact, Urban Computing refers to the integration of value adding services to daily life of citizens.

Chapter 11
Increased Value Through Sharing in Multi-Sided Markets: Sustainability With Ridesharing

Nina Tura
Lappeenranta University of Technology, Finland

Aino Kuitunen
Lappeenranta University of Technology, Finland

Lauri Lättilä
SimAnalytics, Finland

Samuli Kortelainen
Lappeenranta University of Technology, Finland

ABSTRACT

The demand for more sustainable business models is increasing the need for current businesses to develop their business processes and value creation mechanisms. One way to improve sustainability is sharing resources and services in a new sharing economy paradigm. This chapter builds a conceptual model for taxi ridesharing to describe the value potential that is born by increasing the efficiency of taxi businesses. First, a framework for multisided markets is built to understand the different value elements of taxi ridesharing. Then, a conceptual mathematical model is introduced to understand the value symmetries including the cost saving potential and allocation from the perspectives of the customer and the supplier. The model shows that it is possible to have a system that creates value for both the taxi driver and the passenger, while simultaneously leading to significant reduction in CO2 emissions.

DOI: 10.4018/978-1-5225-3147-0.ch011

INTRODUCTION

The increasing awareness and interest in sustainable innovation (Boons et al., 2013) have led companies to start looking for opportunities beyond their traditional business areas. Global demand (see, e.g., United Nations, 2015), changing customer behavior and market conditions, together with the development of digital technologies have resulted in the birth of interesting new business models. One example is the emergence of the sharing economy where people have started to look for options for the consumption and ownership of resources. Shared services and so called peer-to-peer (P2P) rental markets are growing fast –their value reached $26 billion already in 2013 (Botsman, 2013). Today, sharing business models include a wide range of examples of sharing goods (eBay), services, transportation (Uber), accommodation (AirBnB), and money (crowdfunding) (Owyang, Samuel, & Grenville, 2014; Cohen & Kietzmann, 2014).

This relatively new business field has recently attracted the attention of both academic and managerial audiences (Botsman, 2013; Schor & Fitzmaurice, 2015; Cohen & Kietzmann, 2014; Belk, 2014). Due to urbanization challenges, people have started to look for options for non-satisfactory public transport and technologies, and digitalization has enabled new sharing mobility services to expand (Firnkorn & Mueller, 2011). The main characteristics of the sharing economy include the ability to facilitate sharing between strangers and rely upon impersonal trust. Especially ridesharing has grown in popularity as people want to travel fast, efficiently and at low cost (Kriston, Szabo & Inzelt, 2010).

One interesting sharing application is taxi ridesharing. There are several empirical modeling examples of the potential benefits of taxi ridesharing that show significant cost efficiency potential and positive environmental outcomes. (Santi et al. 2014a; d'Orey, Fernandes & Ferreira, 2012). Santi et al. (2014a; 2014b) have shown that ride combining could result in a 40% cut in cumulative trip length in New York taxi service – a significant benefit in terms of traveled distance versus additional travel time. d'Orey, Fernandes and Ferreira (2012) have estimated a potential of a 48% increase in the average occupancy per traveled kilometer. If passengers accept on average a 5-minute delay, it could be possible to share over 70% of the taxi rides in New York (Shmueli et al. 2015). Despite these examples, so far no many commercially viable services exist for taxi ridesharing.

In this chapter the focus is on understanding the potential for wide market acceptation of taxi ridesharing. There are two sides on the market: taxi drivers and passengers who share rides. In order to build a successful marketplace for sharing taxi rides, both sides of these markets need to have a sufficient number of entities. The second necessary perspective is the perceived value. In order to succeed in significant market penetration, both the buyers and sellers need to accept the new system. The necessary requirement for acceptance is that both sides need to get value from the system - the system needs to create a situation where both the buyers and the sellers feel that they benefit from it.

The challenge is to understand how this system should be built and where the value for the users would be. Introducing a sharing option might increase the level of passengers' discomfort, but as there are other benefits, such as reductions in service costs, the overall utility may rise (Ma, Zheng & Wolfson, 2013). To ensure the implementation of new business in two- and multi-sided markets, the value needs to be addressed from the perspectives of all involved parties (Adner & Kapoor, 2010). The objective of this chapter is to contribute to the literature by offering an analytical framework for understanding the limits for value creation when implementing sharing into an existing taxi company business model. The analysis of this problem requires two significant perspectives: 1) multi-sided markets and 2) value creation for both sides and between the markets. Multi-sided markets describe a business context where value is based on interaction between different types of actors (Adner & Kapoor, 2010; Ethiraj & Posen,

2013). Value can be created by direct network effects where value is created by the interaction of similar actors operating in the same markets or by indirect network effects where value is created by interactions between actors in different markets (Eisenmann, Parker &Van Alstyne, 2006).

The research question in this chapter is *How to create a sustainable business model for a taxi sharing service?* To answer this question, a conceptual framework and a mathematical model are introduced. These combine the value perspectives of both the passengers and drivers and aim at increasing understanding of the acceptance conditions for taxi pairing service. Individual taxi ridesharing is treated as a point-like transaction, and no indirect sustainability effects are taken into account. The model shows that both the driver and the passenger gain perceived benefits but also perceived losses in the pairing of taxi rides. The model also shows that the gained efficiency benefits can be turned into monetary gains, but the division of these gains is a matter of negotiation. Effectively, the division of benefits is a zero sum game between the driver and the passenger. In this chapter value is understood as additional benefits experienced by the implementation of the service, the difference between the evaluation of benefits and costs. Besides market value, value is understood to include intangible value (e.g. soft value elements such as customer satisfaction or societal value) that may not be directly measured in monetary terms. The outcome of the study is a detailed description of how value can be determined in a multi-sided market. Understanding this market is critical in order to get a new service successfully into the market. An important aspect of multi-sided markets is that all sides of the market need to accept the new product. If either side declines adaptation, the new product will not penetrate the market.

The chapter is organized as follows: first there is an overlook to existing literature on two-sided markets and value creation. The theoretical framework is followed by an in-depth description of a taxi-sharing case. After these, the final framework for calculating the value of using a taxi sharing service is introduced, which is followed by solutions, recommendations for future research, and conclusion.

BACKGROUND

Motivation Towards Sharing Business Models

Today, sustainability is strongly present in the development of new products and services. In addition to creating sustainable value by products, technologies and processes, recent literature has paid particular attention to the creation of sustainable business models (e.g. Abdelkafi & Täuscher, 2016; Gauthier & Gilomen, 2016). In these business models the focus is on adding value to the company and stakeholders, but also to the environment and the society (Boons & Lüdeke-Freund, 2013). The practical implication of this is that monetary measurements, such as revenue or profit, are no longer necessarily the main drivers for development (Schaltegger & Wagner, 2011; Porter & Kramer 2011). Instead, sustainability-oriented measurements, such as carbon performance (Hoffmann & Busch, 2008) and resource efficiency (Chee Tahir & Darton, 2010) have become part of business and innovation development (Nidumolu, Prahalad & Rangaswami, 2009; Seebode, Jeanrenaud & Bessant, 2012). In customer markets this can be seen in the emergence of multiple examples of services based on sharing. These examples, such as transportation (Uber) and accommodation (e.g. Airbnb) demonstrate new economic thinking in which otherwise private resources (car or home) are shared by other, often anonymous, users of the same system. Both these services have been widely adopted by users around the globe, which has led to major commercial success evident in the valuation of companies such as Uber (51B$) and AirBnB (21,5B$)

(Austin, Canibe & Slobin, 2015). These business models are successful examples of a sharing economy (Hamari, Sjöklint & Ukkonen, 2013).

Sharing business models rely on the idea of sharing and collaborative consumption (Botsmann & Rogers, 2010b) and P2P activities where people give, obtain and share resources (both human and physical). Value is created in many forms, including financial value (monetary rewards) and so called soft value streams of ecological and social rewards. Different types of services are emerging (e.g. bike and car sharing services) and increasing in importance (for example in AirBnB there were 10 million overnight stays by 2012). The sharing economy has also strong reliance on digital technologies and it involves the participation of so called high cultural capital consumers, who, instead of sharing out of necessity, elect to share (Schor & Fitzmaurice, 2015). According to Schor and Fitzmaurice (ibid.), the main motivations for participation in the sharing economy include positive economic impacts, reduced ecological impacts, increase in social connections and building social networks, as well as ideological commitment to the concepts of sharing and collaborating. The value creation activities are usually co-ordinated through community-based online services (Albinsson & Perera, 2012; Belk, 2010; Botsman & Rogers, 2010a; Hamari et al., 2015) or platforms that aim at facilitating exchanges between groups of people, establishing so called circuits of commerce (Zelizer, 2010). Platforms give common rules and build mutual trust among relative strangers taking part in sharing activities (Zelizer 2010; Belk 2014).

The motivation towards the sharing economy can arise from social, economic or technological premises. A key social driver is the increased population density that necessitates new urban solutions (Kriston, Szabo & Inzelt, 2010). The economic drivers include financial flexibility, monetizing excess or idle inventory, valuating access over ownership, or reduced transaction costs (Chui et al. 2012; Henten & Windekilde, 2016). Technological drivers are the enabling techniques, such as the increase of mobile devices, platforms and enabling payment systems (Black & Lych, 2004). Some criticism has risen concerning the complexity related to the sustainability of the sharing economy, such as deterioration of workers' rights, the sustainability benefits becoming captured into existing non-sustainable business models, or an undesirable substitution effect, such as a rebound effect resulting from increased total consumption of resources (Martin, 2016; Lopez et al.2014; Schor & Fitzmaurice, 2015; Henten & Windekilde, 2016).

Paying attention to the value proposition is crucial in establishing a functioning business model (Osterwalder & Pigneur, 2010). The interest towards sharing options is increasing, which means that companies need to pay attention to the characteristics of sharing business models. These include creating understanding of the involved stakeholders and their impact on the overall value creation and the acceptance of the business. In the following, particular attention is payed to the features of value creation in multi-sided markets.

Value Creation in Multi-Sided Markets

Value creation is a complex concept which has been studied by multiple researchers. Due to its subjective nature and multiple levels of analysis, no ultimate definition exists (Lepak, Smith & Taylor, 2007). Many sharing economy business models rely on so called two- or multi-sided markets (Adner and Kapoor, 2010; Ethiraj & Posen, 2013). According to Eisenmann, Parker and Van Alstyne (2006), in traditional value chains value is understood as flow from costs to revenue (moving from left to right). In two- (or multi-) sided markets the costs and revenue are allocated for both sides instead. This is due to distinct groups of stakeholders (such as customers and suppliers) on each side.

The literature on two- or multi-sided markets pays attention to the use of platforms to connect different consumers or consumer groups in order to internalize indirect network externalities and share their value via a functioning pricing system (e.g. Evans 2003; Eisenmann et al. 2006; Ambrus & Argenziano 2009). Network externalities are born when the utility of a consumer depends on the purchase decision of another consumer (Ambrus & Argenziano 2009). Realized positive network externalities can be seen as value appropriation. In the case of sharing the extra capacity of taxi rides, multiple positive and negative externalities are born.

In order to establish successful business models for the sharing economy, we need to create more clear understanding of how value is created and divided among the participating groups (suppliers and customers). From the business perspective, the focus is more or less in earning profits. However, understanding value from the customer perspective is more complex. Generally, the marketing literature sees customer value as a trade-off between benefits and costs that result from an exchange (see e.g. Ulaga & Eggert, 2006). Furthermore, it can also be seen as a trade-off between quality and price (e.g., Bolton & Drew, 1991; Grewal et al, 1998). The consumer behavior literature goes beyond monetary costs to include understanding psychological, emotional and cognitive factors through benefits and sacrifices (e.g. Cronin et al., 2000; Graf & Maas, 2008). Besides monetary benefits and costs, in this chapter value is seen to include also intangible factors – the additional benefits and sacrifices (i.e. value reducing elements) experienced by the taxi ridesharing service implementation. These value elements are discussed below.

Customer Perspective on Value Creation in Sharing Economy

From the perspective of the customer (taxi passenger), sharing offers an opportunity for *immediate economic impacts,* i.e. *money savings* (Schor & Fitzmaurice, 2015), as customers may *split the fares* of the service (Santi et al. 2014b). Splitting fares aims at covering the possible drawbacks of the service (e.g. the loss of privacy and extra time), with the goal of achieving wider passenger acceptance for shared services (ibid.). Furthermore, the possible benefits include *higher flexibility*, *practicality* and *better access to services*. In the sharing economy, in addition to rational value elements (such as the usefulness and quality of a product or service), we need to consider also emotional elements (Elster, 1998). These elements include *enjoyment of the activity* (Hamari et al. 2015) and the so called *"feel-good factor",* as well as other *psychological benefits* (e.g. promoting sustainability, or in rideharing fulfilling a request for help) (Schor & Fitzmaurice, 2015), as ideological issues (e.g. lifestyle, generosity, feelings and cultural issues) are strongly related to the driving motivations of the sharing economy. According to Hamari and Ukkonen (2013) the emergence of the sharing economy may help people in learning the social norms of sharing and collaboration. Furthermore, the benefits include also longer-term rewards such as *community experience* and *gift-exchange systems* (Schor & Fitzmaurice, 2015).

Although benefits exist, we should not underestimate the possible drawbacks of shared services. These drawbacks include *requirements for extra time* and *loss of privacy* (Santi et al., 2014b; Teal, 1987). For example, in the case of taxi sharing this means *passenger discomfort* quantifiable in terms of a longer travel time (Santi et al. 2014b) or sharing the ride with a stranger. In addition to emotional benefits, there might exist emotional factors hindering the development of shared business models. These could be *cognitive costs,* as there may be *perceptions of possible discomfort, risk* and *embarrassment* (Schor & Fitzmaurice, 2015). Although sharing services are argued to provide economic benefits for the customer, they may also involve *unexpected costs,* as more time and effort is needed in searching and coordination (Hamari et al. 2015).

Supplier Perspective on Value Creation in Sharing Economy

From the supplier perspective, value creation is often understood via profit – monetary revenue earned from the customer minus costs. However, from the supplier perspective, the sharing business involves also other, intangible value elements, which are not always possible to measure in monetary terms.

From the economic perspective, the sharing economy provides opportunities to deliver more value to the consumer, but also create new opportunities for the producers to *earn income*. According to Schor and Fitzmaurice (2015, pp. 12), this is because "these sites are peer-to-peer and able to re-distribute value across the supply chain, to producers and consumers, and away from middlemen." However, this can also have a negative impact on old business areas (e.g. the emergence of AirBnB has reduced the number of rented hotel rooms), and the development of internet-based platforms has created new markets that do not only complement but substitute existing markets (e.g. transportation) (Henten & Windekilde, 2016). The emergence of shared services can thus *decrease the need for the number of service providers* (e.g. reduce the need of taxi service providers / individual taxis) and *reduce the use of existing services.*

In theory, the sharing economy reduces ecological impacts (e.g. lowers greenhouse gas emissions) by circulating goods (e.g. Martin & Shaheen, 2010). For example, ridesharing is argued to help in solving traffic problems, lowering the environmental load and allowing more efficient use of all kinds of resources (Kriston, Szabo & Inzelt, 2010). From the supplier perspective, the increased efficiency can help in *reducing costs* such *as fuel and production costs* (Santi et al. 2014b). However, little research has been done on whether these benefits are actually realized or whether they are largely assumed (Schor & Fitzmaurice, 2015). *Economic rationalization* (including institutional dependencies and development realism) is seen as one of the most important barriers for companies implementing sustainability actions (Eckhardt, Belk & Devinney, 2010), which may also be relevant for the implementation of sharing models. As sharing services usually means splits in fares (Santi et al. 2014b), it is uncertain whether the incomes of executing P2P business will cover the additional costs (e.g. fuel and depreciation). Furthermore, little is known about possible *unexpected costs* (such as maintaining technologies, coordination) (Hamari et al. 2015).

The motivation for participating in sharing economy activities may also arise from the desire to increase social connections and build social networks. This may offer community experience for the customer but also allow the suppliers to *market their services, increase the awareness of the company and create new partnerships.* However, according to Schor and Fitzmaurice (2015, pp. 13): "number of platforms advertising this feature of business fail to deliver durable ties". Many shared models are highly *dependent on technologies and platforms* and require learning and adoption efforts, which may involve significant *investments* (time and monetary efforts). Also *technological risks* need to be taken into account.

Framework of the Value Impacts of Sharing Economy

In general, ridesharing business is based on sharing vehicles by passengers, including different transportation models such as carpooling and public transportation. Furthermore, dynamic (or real-time) ridesharing refers to services or systems that arranges matching rides in short notice (Agatz et al., 2012). This business of dynamic ridesharing has increased significantly over the past few years including hundreds of thousands of riders and millions of customers (Helling & Ajmal, 2017). This is an example of a new, growing industry within sharing economy (Kriston, Szabo & Inzelt, 2010) with the possibilities to provide multiple sustainability-related benefits such as reducing the number of vehicle trips and thus lowering emissions. One application of ridesharing is taxi ridesharing. This refers to model where passengers share their taxi-rides instead of taking individual rides. Figure 1 demonstrates two taxi rides that have synergies. The rides do not need to overlap fully to provide efficient pairing. The biggest benefit of pairing the rides is the decrease of the total driven distance. When combining the rides, the total distance is reduced significantly, which creates financial benefit potential and leads directly to CO_2 emission savings.

The sharing economy has been argued to bring multiple benefits by reducing the environmental load, increasing social well-being, and providing possibilities to gain profits (e.g. Schor & Fitzmaurice, 2015), and to work as a potential driver for radical sustainability improvements at local and global levels. As urbanization is increasing fast globally, the new forms of business are more than welcome to address the challenges of people accumulating to live in certain areas (Cohen & Kietzmann, 2014). Despite the rapid emergence of the sharing economy, little research has been done regarding value creation in the sharing economy and whether the benefits are actually realized or are just largely assumed (Schor & Fitzmaurice, 2015). In the sharing economy, the value creation of many business models is dependent on two or more independent stakeholder groups, being examples of two- or multi-sided markets (Evans, 2003). In order to take advantage on sustainability and the emerging sharing models of business we need to understand how value is created for the wide range of actors involved. Successful establishment of business in the two-sided market requires understanding of value creation and capturing activities for both stakeholder groups, as all sides of the market need to accept the new product or service.

The potential of taxi ridesharing is estimated to be huge with multiple monetary and non-monetary benefits (Santi et al. 2014a; d'Orey et al., 2012). Figure 2 summarizes the value elements of the taxi ridesharing in a two-sided market as a theoretical framework. Value is divided between the customer (passenger) and supplier, including both positive and negative value elements (i.e. benefits and sacrifices).

Figure 1. Example of combining two rides

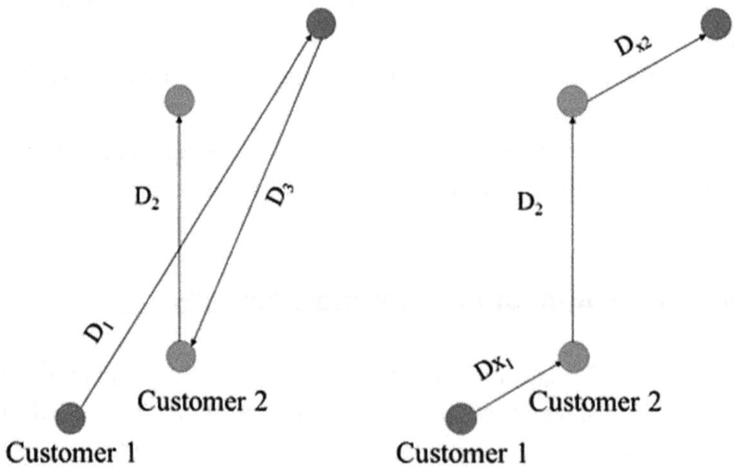

Figure 2. Framework of the value impacts of taxi ridesharing

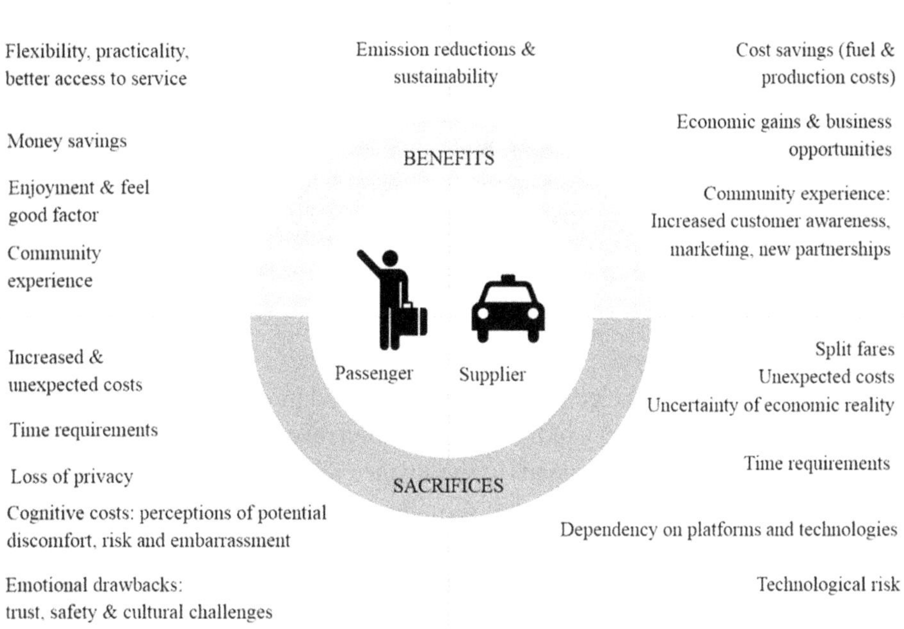

DESCRIPTION OF THE MODEL

In this part, a conceptual mathematical model describing the value creation in taxi sharing is presented. The model describes the allocation of different elements of value in a single sharing transaction. Value is presented as the net benefits of the monetary and non-monetary values described in the framework.

The core of understanding both driver and passenger acceptance is in understanding the logic of how value is created for both the taxi driver and the customer. The decision to adopt is a simple yes or no situation. It is assumed that the customers and the driver will accept the pairing option when their net benefits exceed zero (1, 2), i.e. acceptance is likely if they both benefits from the pairing.

Acceptance functions (1)

$$a_c = \begin{cases} 1; NB_{c,n} > 0 \\ 0; NB_{c,n} \leq 0 \end{cases} \tag{1}$$

$$a_d = \begin{cases} 1; NB_d > 0 \\ 0; NB_d \leq 0 \end{cases} \tag{2}$$

The first part of the model is the calculation of an individual customer's net benefit (3). The two sources of value for the customer are created by monetary savings that are dependent on the price without pairing ($R_{n,a}$) and the price of a paired ride ($R_{n,s}$). In addition to monetary value, there are also various perceived non-monetary benefits (PB_n) and losses (i.e. sacrifices) (PL_n) that are created due to pairing. These components are described in the framework above. Evaluation of the size of these value components at the general level is challenging, because their relative value compared to the monetary value is highly individual, as they are based on personal preferences. They can thus be argued to exists, but in our model we describe these components as compound variables.

$$NB_{c,n} = R_{n,a} - R_{n,s} + PB_n - PL_n \tag{3}$$

For the drivers, the net benefits can be argued to be composed mostly from monetary value (4). From the revenue perspective, pairing the rides reduces the expected revenue, depending on the unpaired price ($S_{n,a}$) and paired prices ($S_{n,s}$). Pairing also leads to diminished driving costs, which are dependent on the total costs of unpaired rides (c_n) and the distance of paired rides (c_s). In addition to direct cost savings, drivers also get other, indirect benefits from pairing (PB_d). These benefits are created e.g. through good publicity due to green awareness and increased revenue enabled by opportunity revenues, as cars are available for additional rides.

$$NB_d = \sum_{1}^{n=c} \left(R_{n,s} - R_{n,a}\right) + \sum_{1}^{n=c} c_n - c_s + PB_d \tag{4}$$

The true value of the system can be evaluated by looking more closely at the value addition and reduction from combining value creation and perceived losses. (5,6,7). In the end, the added value of the system is created from driver's perceived benefits, cost savings from more efficient use of taxies, and each customer's perceived benefits from pairing. The only negative side at the system level is the customer's perceived loss.

$$NB_s = \sum_{1}^{n=c} NB_{c,n} + NB_d \tag{5}$$

$$NB_s = \sum_{1}^{n=c} \left(R_{n,a} - R_{n,s} + PB_n - PL_n\right) + \sum_{1}^{n=c} \left(R_{n,s} - R_{n,a}\right) + \sum_{1}^{n=c} c_n - c_s + PB_d \tag{6}$$

$$NB_s = PB_d + \sum_{1}^{n=c} \left(c_n + PB_n - PL_n\right) - c_s, \begin{matrix} \forall a_c = 1 \\ \forall a_d = 1 \end{matrix} \tag{7}$$

Pricing has a significant role when looking at the decision at the individual level. At the system level, pricing is not an issue as the total system benefit remains the same, independent of the prices. However, price is critical in defining the balance of benefits between customer and driver as these benefits from a zero-sum game (Figure 3). The more these pricing benefits are moved to the customer side (implies a low price for a combined ride), the higher levels of PLn are allowed, while the driver needs more benefits from PB_d. The opposite is true when pricing is moved to benefit the drivers more.

Non-monetary value components have a significant effect on the system level value creation. If the positive non-monetary variables are higher than the negative aspects, the overall value increases (Figure 3, right). The practical outcome of additional value creation is that it is easier to find a pricing combinations that will lead to joint value creation. The effect is reversed, if the negative non-monetary components are larger, making the creation of joint value combinations harder. This also implies that if the non-monetary benefits are extremely high, there is no opportunity for joint value creation. This may be the case when e.g. the customer finds significant discomfort from sharing a taxi and there is no monetary compensation that will negate this inconvenience.

SOLUTIONS AND RECOMMENDATIONS

This study has focused on understanding the value potential of taxi ridesharing. Taxi sharing has been found to create direct benefits for the society, such as reduced CO_2 emissions (d'Orey et al., 2012) and providing a pathway to sustainability (Heinrichs, 2013; Cohen & Kietzmann, 2014). Although the viability and benefits of taxi sharing have been identified empirically (Santi et al. 2014a; d'Orey et al. 2012; Shmueli et al., 2015), these models have not yet achieved a substantial place in the market. This raises the question of why these models have not yet become a common practice.

In order to answer the question presented above, the focus needs to be turned from system level analysis to understanding value creation for the customers and drivers. In this study, a model describing value creation for the driver and the passenger from sharing taxies has been created. The chapter presented a conceptual model for defining the conditions for the creation of a fair system for each participant. From

Figure 3. Perceived passenger and driver value

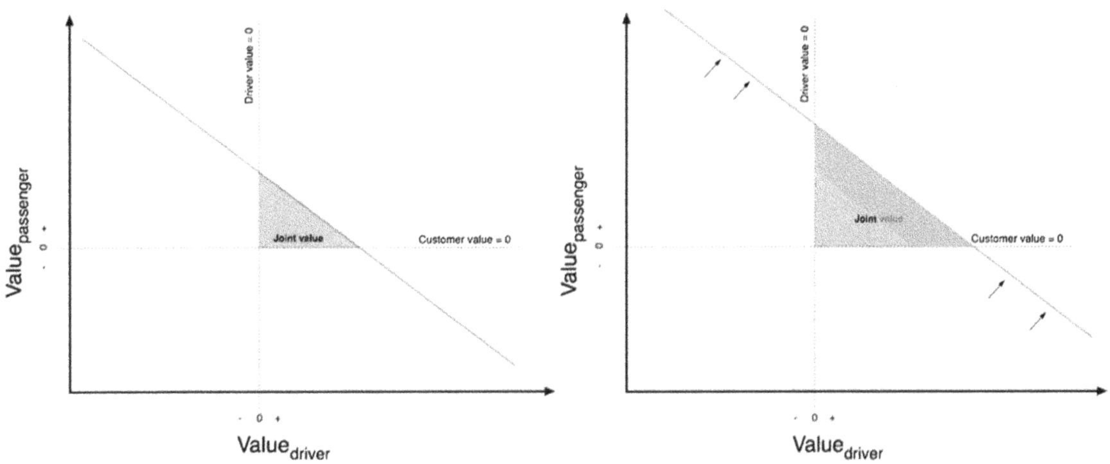

the supplier perspective, the benefits can be defined relatively simply as the value created directly from increased revenue potential and more efficient use of resources. These value components have also been confirmed by previous studies on the topic (d'Orey et al. 2012). The customer perspective is more complex, as value from sharing is created as a combination of monetary and social value. The measurement of monetary value is relatively straightforward, but the measurement of the more abstract social value is challenging, as the comparison of these value components is hard and highly individual.

The goal for creating the model was to understand how a situation where all the participating actors would benefit could be constructed in taxi sharing. All combinations were found to be extremely good for the whole system, but they may not necessarily provide additional value for the participants involved. There is significant value potential in combining taxi rides, but how this value should be divided between the driver and the passenger is not self-evident. Although value is created from both monetary and social value components, value appropriation is done with the monetary component.

On the basis of the conceptual model, it is clear that an optimal value allocation scenario can be built for sharing taxies. In order to operationalize this kind of a concept for wide use, a platform is needed to facilitate ride pairing and value appropriation. As there are no current widely implemented solutions on the market, this means that a platform needs to be created for this purpose. As two-sided markets are highly dependent on a wide acceptance of the service, without sufficient density (number of necessary passengers and taxi drivers), the chance of finding a ride decreases and may also outweigh especially the financial benefits (Agatz et al., 2012). Therefore, any new system should be done initially on a large scale or the benefits from the system might be significantly decreased.

Practical examples of ridesharing are now starting to rise. Modern alternatives to traditional taxies, like Uber and Lyft have started their ride sharing services (Uber: uberPOOL and Lyft: Lyft line). Both services are still relatively new on market, but they have been steadily growing. E.g. uberPOOL service has grown from a single city pilot to cover 45 cities in the world (Uber, 2017). So far no extensive independent study on the performance level of these services and their potential social impact exist.

Another perspective to the future of ridesharing is the role of governments. Agatz et al. (2012) suggest an establishment of subsidized rideshare system (supported by the government and local businesses, such as taxis), to increase the capacity and efficiency of the urban transportation system relatively inexpensively. Some experiments on so called "hybrid" business models have also already been executed. For example, in 2012 the city of Helsinki adopted a pilot model of on-demand bus service, Kutsuplus, which combined characteristics of public transport and taxi. As an emerging service, Kutsuplus was argued to be one of the world's most highly developed trip-combining hardware using new technology and providing a solution to congestion problems (see e.g. Brustein, 2014), and it grew fast in popularity among consumers. Despite these factors, after two and half years of working, the test is now in hold, as the necessary economic and technical conditions to move the service to the hands of private actors do not exist (Sulopuisto, 2016).

The example above highlights the importance of the impact of public sector support. The society can have an effect on the birth of these models by supporting their development (for example by taxation) and encouraging the use of the systems. On the other hand, the decision makers have the power to slow down the development. Policy makers should thus provide support for the emergence of the types of platforms that make sense from economic, environmental and social perspectives. This is in line with the notion of Cohen and Kietzmann (2014) of the importance of economic and non-economic incentives by agencies in improving overall system performance and reducing conflicts between the private and the public sector. According to Demailly and Novel (2014), making the sharing economy into a sustainable economy is much dependent on public authorities and their support (i.e. ecological taxation and regulations, efficient public transportation) to reinforce the value and environmental benefits of sharing.

FUTURE RESEARCH DIRECTIONS

This chapter has presented a model that describes the value components for drivers and customers, but so far there is little to no information about the numerical sizes of these components or their priorities. First, this sets a clear need for future research to understand the different customer preferences in sharing taxi rides. One example of value asymmetry is that some customers might value the reduced CO_2 emissions as positive compared to a regular taxi ride, whereas other users would value the reduced personal space while traveling in a negative way. Even though there are several challenges in the incommensurability of different value types, the utilization of a numerical valuation method could offer interesting insights into how different customers perceive value in this context. Thus, the intangible cultural and behavioral factors that affect the value perceived by individuals could be further incorporated into the model. These could be e.g. the variables tested by Möhlman (2015), such as 'trust', that have an effect on the satisfaction experienced by the customer when choosing the sharing option.

Second, better understanding on the long-term effects of such a model to taxi markets is needed. Increasing the potential profit of a taxi car and potentially lower user prices can have a significant effect on both the supplier and customer markets. If sharing rides lowers prices significantly, it is likely that the total number of passengers will increase, thus increasing the need for more taxi services. On the driver side of the market, increasing the profit potential should also lead to an increasing interest in offering taxi services. However, for example if the increasing effect of lowering prices is not very significant, the effect from sharing might be negative to the supplier side of the market. These long-term effects need to be thoroughly analyzed in order to understand the long-term effects of taxi sharing service on the market. Understanding these dynamics may also be necessary to get drivers to accept this new service concept.

Thirdly, creating a platform for sharing taxi rides offers interesting possibilities for both drivers and passengers. This value creation ability will also create opportunities for new businesses. Finding a good way to organize such a business and the appropriate business model for the platform is a clear follow-up question for future research.

In order to create successful innovations within the sharing economy and ensure their diffusion, we need to create scenarios where all the parties involved accept the conditions and the value created. Although this chapter has shed some light on the perceptions of creating sustainable sharing business models, more knowledge is needed on how to manage public-private partnerships (Cohen & Kietzmann, 2014) and to ensure the value creation for both sides in two- (or multi-) sided markets.

CONCLUSION

Careful design and management of the business model is crucial in order to get wide acceptance for sharing models such as taxi sharing service. Although sharing business models have been identified to have an impact on promoting sustainability (Heinrichs, 2013), research on the implementation and approval conditions for these models remains insufficient. Therefore, the main contribution of this chapter is showing the potential for wide market acceptation of sharing business models. The study contributes to the literature by focusing on the case of taxi ridesharing, illustrating an example of value creation in two-sided markets. Second, authors have introduced a conceptual mathematical framework in which the value perspectives of passengers and taxi drivers are combined. Thus the study proposes boundary conditions for building the system and creating a sustainable business model for taxi ridesharing.

Taxi sharing models are an example of business in a two-sided market (e.g. Evans, 2002) in which the successful adoption of the model is dependent on the involvement of the society. Redesigning the transportation system means a structural change to the socioeconomic system, and to facilitate both firm-level and system-level sustainability, sustainable business models are needed (Stubbs & Cocklin, 2008). The emergence of the sharing economy has already enabled the birth of new types of business models and information-based systems (such as Uber). Relying purely on these often privately owned models can, however, fail in achieving the desired environmental and social goals (Cohen & Kietzmann, 2014). According to Schor (2014), the sharing economy includes a wide potential for the creation of economic value. However, this value needs to be equally shared among the different types of actors, which requires collaboration within the private and the public sector.

From the supplier perspective, the model presented in this chapter helps in understanding the possibilities to do business in a new way. As value is usually understood through money and the price of the ride, the models helps in seeing the actual business benefits of combining rides. The tighter the margins the driver gets (e.g. if the fuel prices rises), the more willing the supplier should be to combine taxi rides (as the margin of a single ride falls, the profitability of combining rides rises).

From the passenger perspective (rational decision making), combining taxi rides involves also many soft value elements (e.g. enjoyment of the activity, enhancing sustainability) which is why some passengers may be willing to share rides without higher (monetary) benefits. On the other hand, Hamari et al. (2015) argue that although people may have a positive attitude towards collaborative consumption, it does not necessary translate into actual participation. Economic benefits, such as saving money and time, have a significant effect on behavioral intentions.

In this chapter, authors have proposed a conceptual model of value sharing, which in turn raises interesting openings for further research, including better understanding of different customer preferences and long-term effects of taxi sharing (and related) models. Furthermore, to create a sustainable business model for sharing taxi rides requires the creation of a platform and management practices. An interesting aspect about the mathematical model is that it shows how pricing questions are irrelevant at the system level. However, price contributes to value allocation between individual agents and therefore plays a major role in the decision making of an individual, and the eventual acceptance of sharing. This finding underlines the importance of this study – in sustainability issues it is important to move beyond system level value towards the level of individual decision makers. This is a challenge for future research, as it should increase understanding of individual agents and the effect of their behavior on system level sustainable value creation.

REFERENCES

Abdelkafi, N., & Täuscher, K. (2016). Business Models for Sustainability From a System Dynamics Perspective. *Organization & Environment*, *29*(1), 74–96. doi:10.1177/1086026615592930

Adner, R., & Kapoor, R. (2010). Value creation in innovation ecosystems: How the structure of technological interdependence affects firm performance in technology generations. *Strategic Management Journal*, *31*(3), 306–333. doi:10.1002/smj.821

Agatz, N., Erera, A., Savelsbergh, M., & Wang, X. (2012). Optimization for dynamic ride-sharing: A review. *European Journal of Operational Research*, *223*(2), 295–303. doi:10.1016/j.ejor.2012.05.028

Albinsson, P. A., & Perera, B. Y. (2012). Alternative marketplaces in the 21st century: Building community through sharing events. *Journal of Consumer Behaviour*, *11*(4), 303–315. doi:10.1002/cb.1389

Ambrus, A., & Argenziano, R. (2009). Asymmetric Networks in Two-Sided Markets. *American Economic Journal. Microeconomics*, *1*(1), 17–52. doi:10.1257/mic.1.1.17

Austin, S., Canibe, C., & Slobin, S. (2015). *The Billion Dollar Startup Club. Dow Jones VentureSource and The Wall Street Journal*. Retrieved March 29, 2016, from http://graphics.wsj.com/billion-dollar-club/

Belk, R. (2014). You are what you can access: Sharing and collaborative consumption online. *Journal of Business Research*, *67*(8), 1595–1600. doi:10.1016/j.jbusres.2013.10.001

Black, S. E., & Lynch, L. M. (2004). Whats driving the new economy?: The benefits of workplace innovation. *The Economic Journal*, *114*(493), 97–116. doi:10.1111/j.0013-0133.2004.00189.x

Bolton, W., & Drew, J. H. (1991). A multistage model of customers: Assessment of service quality and value. *The Journal of Consumer Research*, *17*(4), 375–384. doi:10.1086/208564

Boons, F., & Lüdeke-Freund, F. (2013). Business models for sustainable innovation: State of the art and steps towards a research agenda. *Journal of Cleaner Production*, *45*, 9–19. doi:10.1016/j.jclepro.2012.07.007

Boons, F., Montalvo, C., Quist, J., & Wagner, M. (2013). Sustainable innovation, business models and economic performance: An overview. *Journal of Cleaner Production*, *45*, 1–8. doi:10.1016/j.jclepro.2012.08.013

Botsman, R. (2013). The Rise of the Sharing Economy. *The Economist.* Retrieved April 15, 2016, from http://www.economist.com/news/leaders/21573104-internet-everything-hire-rise-sharing-economy

Botsman, R., & Rogers, R. (2010a). Beyond Zipcar: Collaborative consumption. *Harvard Business Review*, *88*(10), 30. PMID:20607961

Botsman, R., & Rogers, R. (2010b). *What's mine is yours: The rise of collaborative consumption*. New York, NY: Collins.

Brustein, J. (2014). *Helsinki's Uber for Buses Is Stuck in First Gear Bloomberg, Finland's quasi-public Kutsuplus isn't nearing a profit*. Retrieved May 10, 2016, from http://www.bloomberg.com/news/articles/2014-05-16/helsinkis-uber-for-buses-is-stuck-in-first-gear

Chee Tahir, A., & Darton, R. C. (2010). The Process Analysis Method of selecting indicators to quantify the sustainability performance of a business operation. *Journal of Cleaner Production, 18*(16-17), 1598–1607. doi:10.1016/j.jclepro.2010.07.012

Chui, M., Manyika, J., Bughin, J., Dobbs, R., Roxburgh, C., & Sarrazin, H. (2012). *The social economy: Unlocking value and productivity through social technologies.* McKinsey Global Institute.

Cohen, B., & Kietzmann, J. (2014). Ride On! Mobility Business Models for the Sharing Economy. *Organization & Environment, 27*(3), 279–296. doi:10.1177/1086026614546199

Cronin, J. J. Jr, Brady, M. K., & Hult, G. T. M. (2000). Assessing the effects of quality, value and customer satisfaction on consumer behavioral intentions in service environment. *Journal of Retailing, 76*(2), 193–218. doi:10.1016/S0022-4359(00)00028-2

D'Orey, P. M., Fernandes, R., & Ferreira, M. (2012). Empirical Evaluation of a Dynamic and Distributed Taxi-Sharing System. *Intelligent Transportation Systems (ITSC), 2012 15th International IEEE Conference on Intelligent Transportation Systems*, 140-146. doi:10.1109/ITSC.2012.6338703

Demailly, D., & Novel, A. S. (2014). *The sharing economy: make it sustainable.* Studies N°03/14. IDDRI.

Eckhardt, G. M., Belk, R., & Devinney, T. M. (2010). Why dont consumers consume ethically? *Journal of Consumer Behaviour, 9*(6), 426–436. doi:10.1002/cb.332

Eisenmann, T. R., Parker, G. G., & Van Alstyne, M. W. (2006). Strategies for Two-Sided Markets. *Harvard Business Review, 84*(10), 92. PMID:16649701

Elster, J. (1998). Emotions and Economic Theory. *Journal of Economic Literature, 36*(1), 47–74.

Ethiraj, S. K., & Posen, H. E. (2013). Do product architectures affect innovation productivity in complex product ecosystems? *Advances in Strategic Management, 30*, 127–166.

Evans, D. S. (2002). *The antitrust economics of two-sided markets.* Available at SSRN 332022

Evans, D. S. (2003). Some Empirical Aspects of Multi-Sided Platform Industries. *Review of Network Economics, 2*(3), 191–209. doi:10.2202/1446-9022.1026

Firnkorn, J., & Müller, M. (2011). What will be the environmental effects of new flee-floating carsharing systems? The case of car2go in Ulm. *Ecological Economics, 70*(8), 1519–1528. doi:10.1016/j.ecolecon.2011.03.014

Gauthier, C., & Gilomen, B. (2016). Business Models for Sustainability, Energy Efficiency in Urban Districts. *Organization & Environment, 29*(1), 124–144. doi:10.1177/1086026615592931

Graf, A., & Maas, P. (2008). Customer value from a customer perspective: A comprehensive review. *Working Papers on Risk Management and Insurance, 52*, 1-37.

Grewal, D., Monroe, K. B., & Khrisnan, R. (1998). The effects of price-comparison advertising on buyers perception on acquisition of value, transaction value, and behavioral intentions. *Journal of Marketing, 62*(2), 46–59. doi:10.2307/1252160

Hamari, J., Sjöklint, M., & Ukkonen A. (2015). The Sharing Economy: Why people participate in collaborative consumption. *Journal of the Association for Information Science and Technology*.

Heinrichs, H. (2013). Sharing economy: A potential new pathway to sustainability. *GAIA-Ecological Perspectives for Science and Society*, *22*(4), 228–231. doi:10.14512/gaia.22.4.5

Helling, B., & Ajmal, S. I. (2017). *The Year The Rideshare Industry Crushed The Taxi*. Retrieved January 17, 2017, from https://rideshareapps.com/2015-rideshare-infographic/

Henten, A. H., & Windekilde, I. M. (2016). Transaction costs and the sharing economy. *Info, 18*(1), 1-15.

Hoffmann, V. H., & Busch, T. (2008). Corporate Carbon Performance Indicators, Carbon Intensity, Dependency, Exposure, and Risk. *Journal of Industrial Ecology*, *12*(4), 505–520. doi:10.1111/j.1530-9290.2008.00066.x

Kriston, A., Szabo, T., & Inzelt, G. (2010). The marriage of car sharing and hydrogen economy: A possible solution to the main problems of urban living. *International Journal of Hydrogen Energy*, *35*(23), 12697–12708. doi:10.1016/j.ijhydene.2010.08.110

Lepak, D. P., Smith, K. G., & Taylor, M. S. (2007). Value creation and value capture: A multilevel perspective. *Academy of Management Review*, *32*(1), 180–194. doi:10.5465/AMR.2007.23464011

López, L. A., Domingos, T., Cadarso, M. Á., & Zafrilla, J. E. (2014). The smarter, the cleaner? Collaborative footprint: A further look at taxi sharing. *Proceedings of the National Academy of Sciences of the United States of America*, *111*(51), 5488–5488. doi:10.1073/pnas.1420242112 PMID:25503369

Ma, S., Zheng, Y., & Wolfson, O. (2013). T-share: A large-scale dynamic taxi ridesharing service. In *Data Engineering (ICDE), 2013 IEEE 29th International Conference,* (pp. 410-421). IEEE.

Martin, C. J. (2016). The sharing economy: A pathway to sustainability or a nightmarish form of neoliberal capitalism? *Ecological Economics*, *121*(3), 149–159. doi:10.1016/j.ecolecon.2015.11.027

Martin, E., Shaheen, S., & Lidicker, J. (2010). Impact of carsharing on household vehicle holdings: Results from North American shared-use vehicle survey. *Transportation Research Record: Journal of the Transportation Research Board*, *2143*, 150–158. doi:10.3141/2143-19

Möhlmann, M. (2015). Collaborative consumption: Determinants of satisfaction and the likelihood of using a sharing economy option again. *Journal of Consumer Behaviour*, *14*(3), 193–207. doi:10.1002/cb.1512

Nidumolu, R., Prahalad, C. K., & Rangaswami, M. R. (2009). Why sustainability is now the key driver of innovation. *Harvard Business Review*, *87*(9), 56–64.

Osterwalder, A., & Pigneur, Y. (2010). *Business Model Generation: A Handbook for Visionaries, Game Changers, and Challengers*. Hoboken, NJ: Johan Wiley & Sons.

Owyang, J., Samuel, A., & Grenville, A. (2014). *Sharing is the new buying: How to win in the collaborative economy (Report). Vision CriticalBlog*. Retrieved April 15, 2016, from http://www.web-strategist.com/blog/2014/03/03/report-sharing-is-the-new-buying-winning-in-the-collaborative-economy/

Porter, M. E., & Kramer, M. (2011). Creating shared value: Redefining capitalism and the role of the corporation in society. *Harvard Business Review*, *89*(1/2), 62–77.

Santi, P., Resta, G., Szell, M., Sobolevsky, S., Strogatz, S. H., & Ratti, C. (2014). Quantifying the benefits of vehicle pooling with shareability networks. *Proceedings of the National Academy of Sciences of the United States of America*, *111*(37), 13290–13294. doi:10.1073/pnas.1403657111 PMID:25197046

Santi, P., Resta, G., Szell, M., Sobolevsky, S., Strogatz, S. H., & Ratti, C. (2014). Reply to Lopez et al.: Sustainable implementation of taxi sharing requires understanding systemic effects. *Proceedings of the National Academy of Sciences of the United States of America*, *111*(51), 5489–5489. doi:10.1073/pnas.1421300112 PMID:25503368

Schaltegger, S., & Wagner, M. (2011). Sustainable entrepreneurship and sustainability innovation: Categories and interactions. *Business Strategy and the Environment*, *20*(4), 222–237. doi:10.1002/bse.682

Schor, J. B. (2014). *Debating the Sharing Economy. A Great Transition Initiative Essay*. Retrieved April 26, 2016, from http://greattransition.org/publication/debating-the-sharing-economy

Schor, J. B., & Fitzmaurice, C. J. (2015). *Collaborating and Connecting: The emergence of the sharing economy. In Handbook on Research on Sustainable Consumption*. Cheltenham, UK: Edward Elgar.

Seebode, D., Jeanrenaud, S., & Bessant, J. (2012). Managing innovation for sustainability. *R & D Management*, *42*(3), 195–226. doi:10.1111/j.1467-9310.2012.00678.x

Shmueli, E., Mazeh, I., Radaelli, L., Pentland, A. S., & Altshuler, Y. (2015). Ride sharing: a network perspective. In Social computing, behavioral-cultural modeling, and prediction, (pp. 434-439). Springer. doi:10.1007/978-3-319-16268-3_55

Stubbs, W., & Cocklin, C. (2008). Conceptualizing a Sustainability Business Model. *Organization & Environment*, *21*(2), 103–127. doi:10.1177/1086026608318042

Sulopuisto, O. (2016). *Why Helsinki's innovative on-demand bus service failed.* Retrieved May 15, 2016, from http://citiscope.org/story/2016/why-helsinkis-innovative-demand-bus-service-failed

Uber. (2017). *uberPOOL Share your ride and save*. Retrieved January 18, 2017, from https://www.uber.com/ride/uberpool/

Ulaga, W., & Eggert, A. (2006). Value-based differentiation in business relationships: Gaining and sustaining key supplier status, *Journal of Marketing, 70*, 119-136.

United Nations. (2015). *Global Sustainable Development Report 2015 Edition*. Advance Unedited version. Retrieved March, 2016, from https://sustainabledevelopment.un.org/content/documents/1758GSDR%202015%20Advance%20Unedited%20Version.pdf

Zelizer, V. A. (2010). *Economic Lives: How Culture Shapes the Economy*. Princeton, NJ: Princeton University Press. doi:10.1515/9781400836253

KEY TERMS AND DEFINITIONS

Business Model: Description of an organization's value creation, capturing and delivering principles and related activities.

Market Penetration: A measure of the market volume of a service (or product) compared to the total sales volume of competing services. It includes activities aiming at increasing the market share of a new or an existing service.

Monetary Value: The value of a service (or product) that is received by selling. It is the sum of money that the customer is willing to pay for the service and what is consumed in providing the service.

Multi-Sided Markets: Economic platforms that have two or more distinct user groups participating in the value creation and capturing activities. These groups provide network benefits for each other.

Sharing Economy: Collaborative consumption and peer-to-peer activities based on sharing resources (goods, services), which are usually coordinated through online platforms.

Societal Value: A concept including benefits that are addressed by the society and promote the well-being of wider areas and groups of people. The benefits include for example value elements that promote the development of transportation, healthcare, education and the environment.

Sustainability: Continued economic development without reducing natural productive capacity.

Sustainable Development: Development that aims to fulfill the needs of the present without compromising the needs of future generations. Sustainability is understood through three dimensions: ecological, economic and social.

Value: The worth of all benefits and rights experienced by ownership or participation, including both hard benefits such as money and soft benefits like enjoyment of the activity.

Value Allocation: A strategy which aims at balancing the overall amount of value between the participating actors. For example in taxi ridesharing, this includes negotiations between the taxi driver and the passenger about the price of the ride. A related term is value appropriation, in which the stakeholders involved compete to capture the value created by the business action.

Chapter 12
Investors' Reactions to the Announcement of New Constituents of BIST Sustainability Index:
An Analysis by Event Study and Mean-Median Tests

Levent Çıtak
Erciyes University, Turkey

Veli Akel
Erciyes University, Turkey

Ersan Ersoy
Nevşehir Hacıbektaş Veli University, Turkey

ABSTRACT

This study investigates the reaction of investors to the announcement of firms included in BIST Sustainability Index. Stock returns of BIST 50 firms, which are also constituents of BIST Sustainability Index, with those of BIST 50 firms that could not qualify for inclusion in BIST Sustainability Index, are compared. Based on mean/median tests, no significant difference between various returns of two groups of firms is found. Except for interval 0 to +4 days, the findings of event study indicates no significant abnormal returns for BIST Sustainability Index Constituents in the event window of 10 days surrounding the announcement day, but indicates significant positive cumulative abnormal returns for intervals 0 to +4 days, 0 to +5 days, 0 to +7 days, 0 to +8 days, 0 to +9 days and 0 to +10 days, which is an indication that investors valued the BIST Sustainability Index Constituents a few days after the announcement by investing in the stocks of these firms.

DOI: 10.4018/978-1-5225-3147-0.ch012

INTRODUCTION

Poverty, unfair distribution of income, healthcare problems, environmental pollution and technological disasters are concomitants of welfare that generate visible damages in the world. An increase in social, technological and environmental risks facing the global economy revealed that taking only financial issues into account is not enough to maintain and sustain the progress, but also social and environmental issues must be considered (Tokgöz & Önce, 2009). The concept of sustainable development emerged as a result of this necessity and was defined for the first time in 1987 in the Brundtlandt Report of World Commission on Environment and Development. According to this definition, "Development that meets the needs of the present without compromising the ability of future generations to meet their own needs is sustainable development" (World Commission on Environment and Development [WCED], 1987).

The concept of corporate sustainability refers to sustainable development at the firm level (Signitzer & Prexl, 2007). Sustainable development at the firm level can be defined as "adopting business strategies and activities that meet the needs of the enterprise and its stakeholders today while protecting, sustaining and enhancing the human and natural resources that will be needed" (International Institute for Sustainable Development [IISD], 1992)

At the macro level, the concept of sustainability refers to considering social and environmental factors, avoiding policies results of which eradicate social equity, communal living and environment. Best practices for attaining corporate sustainability can be cited as follows; making legal arrangements that decrease the harmful effects of business activities on environment and natural life, tightening public scrutiny about these arrangements, aggravating penalties for people who disobey the legal arrangements, motivating firms economically in order to popularize sustainability activities, becoming a part of international legal arrangements like Kyoto Protocol. On the other hand, abandoning the perception that considers sustainability activities as only a cost element, implementing corporate governance which is an integral part of sustainability, using eco-friendly technological devices, improving physical working conditions for employees, avoiding hazardous substances on human health in production are examples of practices to be implemented for attaining corporate sustainability at the micro level.

If environmental and other destructions, which are consequences of economic activities, continue at this speed, it is obvious that they are going to be critically harmful for both natural life and humanity in the long term. Therefore, discussions that have focused on how economic development and profitability can be achieved must be outweighed by discussions which concentrate on how healthy and sustainable life can be maintained in the near future. Therefore, before it is too late, concept of corporate sustainability must be popularized both at macro and micro levels for the sake of current and future generations. It is extremely important that firms should be aware that they are responsible for social and environmental effects of their actions on the public. Sustainability, economic development and profitability are objectives which can exist and be realized together. As a matter of fact, management's goal of maximizing the profit or maximizing the firm value has recently been evolving into a new goal that focuses on both financial issues and environmental and social issues.

Concurrently, firms have become facing increasing expectations related to environmental and social performance. Firms are motivated to develop eco–friendly business models and to contribute to the community. Moreover, not only is sustainability perceived as a subject primarily for companies, but also it is now an inseparable part of the business world. The debate about corporate sustainability has gone from "whether the firm should make investments in sustainability" to "how best this should be done." And today, most of the firms deal with corporate sustainability practices in order to increase their reputations and maintain their "social license to operate" (Robinson, Kleffner, & Bertels, 2011).

Issues about corporate sustainability have been becoming prominent among corporations and their stakeholders. Therefore, the number of corporations sharing details about their corporate sustainability practices with public has been increasing rapidly in the past years (Roca and Searcy, 2012). In addition, more firms start publishing sustainability reports and sharing news with stakeholders about their dependence on financial, social and environmental issues (Signitzer & Prexl, 2007).

Possession of competitive advantage seems vital for firms which operate in a competitive environment, because competitive advantage assists the firm to create value in the long term. In addition to this, it is believed that competitive advantage has a connection with social responsibility. As a result of rising concern about these issues, sustainability indexes in different financial markets have emerged (Lopez, Garcia, & Rodriguez, 2007). The initial sustainability indexes were generated by Dow Jones (1999) and FTSE (2001), while BIST Sustainability Index started to be calculated on the 4th of November, 2014.

In line with these developments, investors not only take firms' financial conditions into account, but also sustainability activities of them when they make investment decisions. Especially institutional investors prefer to invest in firms with high sustainability ratings (Waddock & Graves, 1997). Besides, there are plenty of studies which demonstrate that firms that pay attention to sustainability issues are preferred by investors. In addition to this, firms that do not act responsibly about social and environmental issues may lose their reputation. For instance, a giant automobile company's reputation deteriorated in 2015 because of high carbon dioxide emission.

Sustainability activities provide firms with many advantages. Corporate sustainability can foster trust between the firm and its customers by positioning the firm as a sustainable organization which produce sustainable products in the customers' eyes. Besides, corporate sustainability may result in improved ratings in financial rankings. Corporate sustainability makes sense when it contributes to the achievement of the marketing goals of sustainability management (i.e. enhancement of sales of sustainable products, creation of more sustainable production processes). Firms that primarily follow a business case view use corporate sustainability as a means to contribute to the broader organizational goals of sustainability management (i.e., image improvement, license to operate, cost saving, fulfillment of customer, and shareholder demands) (Signitzer & Prexl, 2007).

Firms that regard sustainability activities highly can also achieve savings in production costs, labor costs and costs related with occupational health and safety. For example, cost savings can be achieved with clean production systems, innovation, and energy efficiency. Safe and healthy workplace environment for employees and society can assist the firm to increase productivity, decrease compensation and legal breach, achieve savings in employees' health and safety costs. In addition, improvement in workplace environment can also increase motivation, decrease absenteeism and employee turnover rate, achieve savings in labor costs and help the firm to come up with innovative solutions. The other advantages of sustainability strategy can be cited as follows; the firm becomes less risky thereby being able to borrow at lower interest rates and to be insured at a lower cost (Tokgöz & Önce, 2009).

Firms which are sensitive to sustainability activities have many advantages. First of all, these firms may be preferred by investors who care about social and environmental issues. Secondly, these firms are perceived as more reputable by investors. In addition to these, reduction in costs, augmentation in competitive edge and being more investible especially for institutional investors are other advantages. Therefore, it is very likely that firms that place more importance on corporate sustainability are more favored by investors and they create more value for their shareholders than their rivals.

In recent years, one of the topics studied in finance literature is how investors response to firms' inclusion in or exclusion from sustainability index. The present literature reveals strong empirical evidence of positive (negative) price impacts upon inclusion (exclusion) of a firm (Cheung & Roca, 2013). Cheung and Roca (2013) state that at least five various hypotheses have been formulated in the finance literature to assert the significant price impacts. These are *the downward sloping demand curve hypothesis*, *price pressure hypothesis*, *information cost hypothesis*, *signaling hypothesis*, and *liquidity hypothesis*.

The downward sloping demand curve hypothesis and price pressure hypotheses suppose that inclusion or exclusion in the index do not contain any message so they don't have any impact on stock price. The important price impacts can be caused by changes in demand, resulting from non-information-based portfolio allocation. On the other hand, downward sloping demand curve hypothesis presumes that rise in demand is permanent, hence price and volume impacts are permanent, too (Cheung & Roca, 2013). The change in indexation status of a stock may result in excess demand and it can only be fulfilled without price change if the stock has perfect substitutes. Hence, possible explanations for an excess return based on change in indexation status can be imperfect substitutability or a downward sloping demand curve (Chen, Noronha, & Singal, 2004). After indexation of stocks, equilibrium price varies when demand curve shifts to fulfill excess demand. According to this hypothesis, stocks are not perfect substitutes for each other, and in contrast to the price pressure hypothesis, price of the stock does not revert back after indexation of the stock because the current price represents a current equilibrium distribution of shareholders (Lackmann, Ernstberger, & Stich, 2012).

The price pressure hypothesis assumes that a downward sloping demand curve is valid only for a short time period and long-term demand is purely elastic. Thus, based on the price pressure hypothesis, the excess demand caused by change in indexation status creates an increasing price pressure to convince investors to sell the stocks early. Price pressure diminishes when the temporary demand is fulfilled (Chen et al., 2004). According to the price pressure hypothesis, both increase in demand and price and volume impacts are temporary (Cheung & Roca, 2013). A sudden increase in both price and volume of the stock can be observed after indexation as well as a subsequent return of price (Lackmann et al., 2012). In conclusion, both hypotheses predict that indexation (exclusion) of stocks leads to increase (decrease) in stock returns with higher (lower) liquidity (Cheung & Roca, 2013).

The other hypotheses predict that the inclusion and exclusion of firms contain a message, and consequently have an impact on the value of stock. Mostly, the information cost hypothesis argues that indexation leads to an increase in investors' awareness toward the stock and gives more information to investors about the stock so that they can reduce information search cost and eventually information asymmetry problems. As a result, investors' awareness contributes to the existence of asymmetric price responses where a permanent change, after indexation, in the stock price of the firm but no permanent decrease in stock price of the firm excluded is expected (Chen et al., 2004).

According to the information cost hypothesis, a stock's addition to the index can increase investor awareness and decrease information search costs. Because, inclusion in the index and exclusion from the index increase the amount of information available to investors. Also, information asymmetry problems decrease, as a result. Investor awareness can increase following a stock's inclusion in the index, but awareness does not easily diminish when an exclusion event occurs. According to the hypothesis, investors expect the stock price to increase after a stock's inclusion in the sustainability index. For this reason, investors may buy such stocks and stocks' prices increase due to an increase in demand (Chen et al., 2004; Lackmann et al., 2012).

The signaling hypothesis alleged that inclusion or exclusion are perceived by investors as signals related to the future value of the stock, because private information possessed by the index publisher can be revealed by these events. All other things being equal, an expectation of increase in the future value of the stock results in an increase in the stock's current price (Cheung & Roca, 2013). According to the liquidity hypothesis, inclusion in the index leads reduction in stock volatility by enhancing the liquidity (as measured by the bid–ask spread) of the market for the underlying stock. Market makers in the stock reduce the bid–ask spread because of the flow of information-based trading to the stock market, and greater trading activities by hedgers and arbitragers. In other words, the liquidity hypothesis argues that the significant price effects caused by change in discount rate results from change in liquidity risk (Cheung & Roca, 2013).

This study aims to revisit the reaction of investors to the announcement of Sustainability Index Constituents by taking the previous study by Çıtak and Ersoy (2016), which was carried out on data when Sustainability Index was calculated for the first time with qualifying firms in BIST 30 Index, to a new level based on recent data when Sustainability Index is being calculated with qualifying firms in BIST 50 Index. In another words, this study sets out to determine whether or not the investors react differently to twenty nine BIST Sustainability Index constituents and remaining twenty one BIST 50 Index constituents that couldn't qualify for inclusion in BIST Sustainability Index. In addition, determining whether there are significant abnormal and cumulative abnormal returns around the announcement day, November 3, 2015, is aimed at.

The rest of the paper is organized as follows. The second section provides a selected literature review, while the third section discusses the characteristics of data and methodology. The fourth section presents the empirical results and the conclusion is drawn in section fifth.

LITERATURE REVIEW

Corporate sustainability, as well as corporate social responsibility has many aspects and there is a vast literature on these issues. However, investors' response to firms' inclusion in or exclusion from sustainability index is a relatively new area of research. There are not many studies on whether inclusion in or exclusion from the sustainability index affects stock prices. Therefore, in this study the literature is reviewed in a broader way to include major studies about the impact of inclusion in or exclusion from sustainability index on stock prices of the firms in question as well as the impact of corporate social responsibility and corporate sustainability on financial performance or firm value. Although there are studies suggesting the opposite, majority of the studies suggest a positive relation between corporate social responsibility/corporate sustainability and financial performance. Similarly, the number of studies, which suggest a positive impact of inclusion in a sustainability index and a negative impact of exclusion from a sustainability index on stock prices, dominate the literature.

Although Cochran and Wood (1984) find a weak evidence of positive correlation between corporate social responsibility and financial performance, studies about the impact of corporate social responsibility on performance generally find positive effects on performance, and reduction in firm risk. Mcguire et al. (1988) show that a firm's prior stock market return and accounting-based financial performance measures are more closely related to corporate social responsibility than they are related to subsequent performance. In addition, corporate social responsibility is likely to contribute to the reduction of firm risk. Waddock and Graves (1997) find that corporate social performance is positively associated with prior and future financial performance. McWilliams and Siegel (2000) document that corporate social responsibility has a neutral effect on the financial performance of firms. Orlitzky et al. (2003) find that there is a positive relation between corporate social responsibility and financial performance.

Lo and Sheu (2007) explore that corporate sustainability is positively associated with firm value for large US firms. Besides, firms with a notable sustainability progress strategy are more likely to be awarded by investors. Rossi (2009) shows that corporate sustainability practices improves the firm value for Brazilian companies. Berthelot et al. (2012) suggest that investors take into account the sustainability reports and positively value sustainability reporting. Ameer and Othman (2012) determine that the firms (the top 100 sustainable global firms selected from developed and emerging markets) which implement sustainability practices have higher financial performances measured by return on assets, profit before taxes, and cash flows from operations. Also, the relationship between corporate sustainability and financial performance is found to be bi-directional.

As far as the impact of the inclusion in and exclusion from a sustainability index on firm performance is concerned, there seems to be no clear consensus as to the existence and the direction of such an impact. There are a number of studies which find no significant impact of the inclusion in and exclusion from a sustainability index on firm performance. For example, Curran and Moran (2007) document that the announcement of an inclusion in or exclusion from the FTSE4Good UK 50 index did not cause significantly positive or negative reactions. FTSE4Good is a sustainability index which has high profile share price listing that simultaneously signals environmental and social performance for the UK. Cheung (2011) examines the effect of index inclusions in and exclusions from DJSI (Dow Jones Sustainability Index) on corporate sustainable US firms in terms of stock return, risk and liquidity. Similar to the previous one cited, this study cannot either find any strong evidence that the event announcement has a significant effect on the stock returns of index constituent stock, be they are inclusion stocks or exclusion stocks. But, it finds some temporary but significant effect on the day of change or on the days nearby. Doh et al. (2010) find evidence that the inclusion of firms in the Calvert social index does not stimulate a positive market reaction, whereas stock prices of the firms which were excluded from the index declined more than 1.5%, on the average.

On the other hand majority of studies suggest positive reactions of investors to the inclusion in a sustainability index and negative reactions to the exclusion from such an index. Dilling et al. (2008) document that investor reaction to announcements of the DJSWI inclusion has been significant for the year 2002, whereas for the whole period from 2002 to 2005 an increasingly lower average abnormal return and less significant reaction can be concluded. Becchetti et al. (2009) find that a significant upward trend in the absolute values of abnormal returns both for Domini 400 Social Index inclusions and exclusions. Consolandi et al. (2009) show that positive (negative) abnormal returns for firms included in (excluded from) the Dow Jones Sustainability Stoxx Index. Artiach et al. (2010) find that firms included in the DJSI have higher profits compared to the non-DJSI firms, and size, profitability and potential for growth are related to high levels of investment in CSP (corporate sustainability performance). They use DJSI to identify leading CSP US companies' data. Robinson et al. (2011) explore that inclusion in the DJSI causes a sustained increase for the North American firms' stock prices. On the other hand, they find some evidence that exclusion from the DJSI causes a temporary decrease in the firm values. Similarly based on DJSI, Lourenco et al. (2012) find evidence that corporate sustainability performance is positively associated with financial performance. They conclude that firm's corporate sustainability performance is important for investors. The membership of the DJSI (Dow Jones Sustainability Index) is used as a proxy of corporate sustainability performance for the largest 600 firms from Canada and the USA in this study. Lackmann et al. (2012) empirically analyze whether or not investors consider the reliability of sustainability information when determining the market value of a company. They find positive reactions to an objective external assessment of sustainability information in the form of highly significant positive abnormal returns for short time intervals surrounding the day on which a company is included in the sustainability index. The findings of this study reveals that firms that have higher risks such as systematic investment risk and financial leverage for investors react more strongly to an increase in the reliability of sustainability information.

Literature review indicates that some other studies' findings imply negative impact of both inclusion in and exclusion from a sustainability index, while there are studies, findings of which imply negative reactions to inclusion in and/or exclusion from such an index. For example, Cheung and Roca (2013) investigate the effects of risk, return and liquidity of stocks of firms in the nine Asian Pacific markets which are included in and excluded from the DJSWI. The results reveal that both index inclusion event and index exclusion event have a negative abnormal return effect after the announcement day. But there is evidence that a price reversal occurs a week after the day of change. The index inclusion and index exclusion event have increased trading volume and idiosyncratic risk, but created no change in systematic risk. Oberndorfer et al. (2013) investigate the impact of the inclusion of German firms in the DJSI STOXX and the DJSWI on the stock performance. The results show that stock markets may penalize the inclusion of a firm in sustainability indexes. The inclusions in the DJSI World have a strong negative impact. But, they don't find significant average cumulative abnormal returns for the inclusion in the DJSI STOXX. Daszyńska-Żygadlo et al. (2014) empirically examine whether investors penalize or reward firms for sustainability activities based on their inclusion in the STOXX Europe Sustainability Index and the RESPECT Index (created by Warsaw Stock Exchange). Since the results reveal that the announcement of inclusion in the STOXX Europe Sustainability Index has a negative effect the study suggests that investors may penalize the announcement of index inclusion. Besides, it finds no significant average cumulative abnormal returns for the inclusion in the RESPECT, but negative effects for the inclusion in the STOXX Europe Sustainability Index.

In Turkey, the studies generally focus on the relation between the corporate social responsibility practices and financial performance. Arsoy et al. (2012) explore a positive relationship between corporate social responsibility practices and financial performance while Başar (2014) finds a negative relationship. On the other hand Özçelik et al. (2014), and Aras et al. (2010) find no significant relation between the corporate social responsibility practices and financial performance. Alniacik et al. (2011) state that positive information about the corporate social responsibility increases the potential investor's interest. According to Dinçer (2011), the investors and the financial institutions have no interest in the firm's sustainability strategies and practices, but they have only interest in firm's financial performance.

To sum up, there is also a growing stream of research on investors' reactions to the announcement of new constituents of sustainability indexes.

METHODOLOGY

As of November 4 2014, BIST Sustainability Index was launched in Turkey encompassing selected 15 firms among BIST 30 firms that met the qualifications. The decision for firms to be included in and excluded from BIST Sustainability Index is made on an annual basis and BIST Sustainability Index constituents for the period between November 2015-October 2016 were determined by evaluating the BIST 50 Index constituents in January-March 2015 period. In November 2015, with the addition of new 14 firms, BIST Sustainability Index became to consist of 29 qualifying firms. This study aims to determine whether or not the investors react differently to BIST Sustainability Index constituents and remaining 21 BIST 50 Index constituents that couldn't qualify for inclusion in BIST Sustainability Index.

Two different methods have been used in this study. *First*, mean-median tests have been used to test whether or not stock returns of BIST 50 firms included in BIST Sustainability Index and those of BIST 50 firms that couldn't qualify for inclusion in BIST Sustainability Index are different from each other. *Second*, event study methodology has been employed to test whether the launching of BIST Sustainability Index with its new constituents resulted in statistically significant abnormal and cumulative abnormal returns. November 3, 2015 is the date when constituents of BIST Sustainability Index for the period which runs from November 2015 to October 2016 were announced (BIST 2015a). Event window was chosen as -10 and +10 days around November 3, 2015. Event study methodology will likely to answer whether or not investors place more value to firms in the sustainability index than other firms that are not included in the sustainability index (Cheung, 2011).

Mean-Median Tests

Whether or not mean/median of two independent groups is different from each other can be tested using parametric and non-parametric statistical tests. Parametric tests require the data to meet certain assumptions while non-parametric tests do not require meeting such assumptions. The means of two independent groups can be compared statistically by the Independent Samples t-Test, which is a parametric test (Field, 2009). Mann-Whitney Test and Wilcoxon Rank Sum Test are the non-parametric equivalent of the Independent Samples t-Test. Most of non-parametric tests are based on the principle of ranking the data (Field, 2009).

As a parametric statistical test, Independent Samples t-Test require the data to meet the following assumptions: 1) the sampling distribution of each group of data to be compared is normally distributed, 2) homogeneity of variance of groups to be compared, 3) data are measured at least at the interval level and 4) scores are independent (Field, 2009). Since, the first two assumptions are relevant to the data structure of this study, Shapiro-Wilk Test is used for normal distribution assumption and Levene's Test is used for homogeneity of variance assumption. Depending on whether the data meet these two assumptions, either Independent Samples t-Test or Mann Whitney Test is used on stock return data for various periods (daily, weekly and monthly).

Event Study Methodology

This study uses standard event study methodology to investigate the effect of the announcement of constituents of BIST Sustainability Index for the November 2015-October 2016 period on the stock-returns of these firms. The period between 10 trading days before and 10 trading days after November 3, 2015 comprises the event window. Abnormal returns and cumulative abnormal returns in various intervals within the event window have been calculated by taking BIST 50 Index as the benchmark index. In another words, abnormal returns have been calculated in reference to the daily returns on BIST 50 Index in various intervals within the event window of -10 days to +10 days. The objective of the event study is to test whether abnormal returns and cumulative abnormal returns in various intervals are statistically different from zero. Depending on whether abnormal returns and cumulative abnormal returns have met the normal distribution assumption, either One Sample t-Test or One Sample Wilcoxon Signed Rank Test has been used towards this end. One Sample t-Test is the one used for days and intervals in which return data are normally distributed while the latter test is used where return data are not normally distributed.

DATA

Constituents of BIST 50 Index have been broken down into two groups as qualified and non-qualified firms for inclusion in BIST Sustainability Index for the November 2015-October 2016 period. In order to test whether the stock-returns of firms within these two groups differ, closing prices have been used to calculate daily, weekly and monthly returns. As far as the event study methodology is concerned, abnormal returns and cumulative abnormal returns have been calculated based on daily stock returns.

Generating the Data Set for Mean-Median Tests

Closing prices, required for testing the difference between stock returns of 29 firms included in BIST Sustainability Index and remaining 21 BIST 50 firms which were not included in BIST Sustainability Index, have been obtained from the database of the Matriks Data Dissemination Company (Matriks). Daily, weekly and monthly stock returns of all BIST 50 firms have been calculated for the period between November 3, 2015, which marks the announcement of BIST Sustainability Index with its newcomer 21 firms, and April 18, 2016.

Geometric returns as well as arithmetic returns have been calculated for the widely accepted belief that the former might be economically more meaningful. Arithmetic stock return at time *t* is calculated by the following formula,

$$R_t = \frac{P_t - P_{t-1}}{P_{t-1}} = \frac{P_t}{P_{t-1}} - 1 \quad (1)$$

where P_t, is the closing price at time *t* and P_{t-1} is the closing price at time *t-1*.

Geometric stock return is calculated by the following formula,

$$GR_t = \ln\left(\frac{P_t}{P_{t-1}}\right) \quad (2)$$

where *ln* is the natural logarithm.

Generating the Data Set for the Event Study

In order to determine whether there are significant abnormal and cumulative abnormal returns around the announcement day, November 3, 2015, stock returns of 29 firms in BIST Sustainability Index and return on BIST 50 Index have been calculated for all days in the event window (ten trading days before and ten trading days after November 3 inclusive). Based on these daily returns, abnormal returns have been calculated for all 29 stocks and all days in the event window which led to the calculation of cumulative abnormal returns for various intervals in the event window. Abnormal returns (AR) and cumulative abnormal returns (CAR) are calculated by the following equations (Barber & Lyon, 1997):

$$AR_t = R_t - (R_{e,t}) \quad (3)$$

$$CAR_t = \sum_{t=1}^{T} [R_t - (R_{e,t})] \quad (4)$$

where,

AR_t: Abnormal return of the stock at time t,
CAR_t: Cumulative abnormal return of the stock at time t,
R_t: Daily stock return at time t,
$R_{e,t}$: Expected return on BIST 50 Index at time t.

RESEARCH HYPOTHESES AND TEST RESULTS

Research hypotheses and test results are presented under two topics, for there are two methods of analysis used in the study. The hypotheses and test results as to whether stock returns of two groups of firms differ are followed by hypotheses and test results as to whether BIST Sustainability Index constituents have significant abnormal and cumulative abnormal stock returns.

Hypotheses for the Difference Between Mean/Median of Two Groups of Firms and Test Results

In order for two independent samples *t*-test to be applied for the difference between arithmetic means of BIST Sustainability Index constituents (29 firms) and remaining non-qualifying 21 firms in BIST 50 Index above mentioned two assumptions must be met. Whether or not these two assumptions have been met is tested by the following hypotheses. The hypotheses are tested for six different return types (daily arithmetic, weekly arithmetic, monthly arithmetic, daily geometric, weekly geometric, monthly geometric)

Shapiro Wilk Test (Normality):

(H0): Sampling distribution of average returns of firm group is normally distributed.
(H1): Sampling distribution of average returns of firm group is not normally distributed.

Levene's Test (Homogeneity of Variance):

(H0): The variances of stock returns of different firm groups are equal (homogeneous)
(H1): The variances of stock returns of different firm groups are not equal (homogeneous)

Comparison of means of two independent groups via *t*-test requires the data of both groups to be normally distributed. A significance level smaller than 5% indicates that the sampling distribution is not normally distributed (Field, 2009, pp. 146-147). In Table 1 Shapiro Wilk and Levene's Test results are presented.

Table 1 indicates that all return types have normal distribution since corresponding significance levels are all above 5% for BIST Sustainability Index Constituents. On the contrary, significance levels for all return types of Non-Qualifying BIST 50 Firms are smaller than 5%, indicating a non-normal distribution. Although Levene's Test results indicate that homogeneity of variance assumption was met for arithmetic and geometric daily and weekly returns (4 return types), *t*- test cannot be applied on any of the return types, since Non-Qualifying BIST 50 Firms couldn't meet the normal distribution assumption for any of the return types. Therefore, non-parametric Mann Whitney Test has been applied for testing the difference between average stock returns of two groups of firms.

The following hypotheses are tested to determine whether or not average stock returns of BIST 50 firms included in BIST Sustainability Index and those of BIST 50 firms that couldn't qualify for inclusion in BIST Sustainability Index are different from each other.

(H0): Average stock return of BIST Sustainability Index Constituents and that of non-qualifying BIST 50 firms are equal to each other.
(H1): Average stock return of BIST Sustainability Index Constituents is greater than that of non-qualifying BIST 50 firms.

As can be seen on the last column of Table 2, one-tailed significance levels of return types are quite above 5%, which leads us to conclude that the null hypotheses cannot be rejected for any of the return types. Hence, *contrary to our expectations*, statistical evidence do not confirm that average stock returns of BIST Sustainability Index Constituents are greater than those of non-qualifying BIST 50 firms.

Table 1. Normal Distribution and Homogeneity of Variance Test Results for Average Stock Returns of BIST Sustainability Index Constituents and Non-Qualifying Firms

Rate of Return	Normal Distribution Test (Shapiro Wilk) Results		Homogeneity of Variance (Levene's Test) Results
	BIST Sustainability Index Constituent Firms (n = 29)	Non-Qualifying BIST 50 Firms (n = 21)	
Daily Return	0,910*	0,001	*0,085**
Weekly Return	0,832*	0,000	*0,062**
Monthly Return	0,211*	0,000	0,008
Daily Return (ln)	0,805*	0,024	*0,060**
Weekly Return (ln)	0,592*	0,001	*0,088**
Monthly Return (ln)	0,115*	0,002	0,014

"*" indicates validity of normal distribution and homogeneity of variance (at 5% significance level) assumptions.

Table 2. Median Stock Returns of BIST Sustainability Index Constituents and Non-Qualifying Firms and Mann Whitney Test Results

Rate of Return	Median Returns for BIST Sustainability Index Constituent Firms (n = 29)	Median Returns for Non-Qualifying BIST 50 Firms (n = 21)	Mann Whitney Test Results (One-Tailed Exact Significance)
Daily Return	0,001345	0,000798	0,356
Weekly Return	0,005767	0,004334	0,423
Monthly Return	0,007173	0,007077	0,370
Daily Return (ln)	0,001152	0,000548	0,286
Weekly Return (ln)	0,004692	0,003507	0,286
Monthly Return (ln)	0,010354	0,008814	0,469

Event Study Hypotheses and Test Results

Within the context of event study, for all BIST Sustainability Index Constituents as of November 3, 2015, either One Sample t-Test or One Sample Wilcoxon Signed Rank Test has been performed for each day in the event window in order to determine whether averages of abnormal returns (AR) and cumulative abnormal returns (CAR) are statistically different from zero. One Sample t-Tests have been performed for days on which ARs and for intervals where CARs are normally distributed, whereas One Sample Wilcoxon Signed Rank Tests have been performed for days on which ARs and for intervals where CARs are not normally distributed.

Table 3 above presents Shapiro Wilk Test results. *p*-values on the table indicate that abnormal returns (AR) on days -10, -8, -6, -5, -2, 0, +1, +2 +3, +4, +5, +6, +8 and +10 are normally distributed. Therefore, One Sample t-Tests have been performed on abnormal returns for these days. Since abnormal returns on days -9, -7, -4, -3, -1, +7 and +9 are not normally distributed, One Sample Wilcoxon Signed Rank Tests have been performed on them.

Hypotheses that test whether abnormal return average of each day within the event window is statistically different from zero are presented below.

(H0): Abnormal return average of BIST Sustainability Index Constituents on the relevant day within the event window is equal to zero ($\mu = 0$).

(H1): Abnormal return average of BIST Sustainability Index Constituents on the relevant day within the event window is different from zero ($\mu \neq 0$).

One Sample t-Test and One Sample Wilcoxon Signed Rank Test results are presented in Table 4. Significance levels of all days are greater than 5% except for day +4, whose significance level is 0,01. Therefore, for all days within the event window except day +4, abnormal return average is not statistically different from zero. This finding implies that, one year after the first launching of BIST Sustainability Index; for the most part investors are still not showing a significant reaction to BIST Sustainability Index Constituents. Although, average abnormal return (AR) on day +4 is statistically greater than zero (with a p-value of 0.01), in general investors do not seem to abruptly make buy or sell decisions by getting information prior to or after the announcement of BIST Sustainability Index with its new constituents.

Table 3. Normal Distribution Test Results for Abnormal Returns

Day	Shapiro Wilk Test Results (p-values)	Hypothesis (H0) (Accept or Reject
-10	0,194*	H0:Accept
-9	0,000	H0:Reject
-8	0,530*	H0:Accept
-7	0,013	H0:Reject
-6	0,157*	H0:Accept
-5	0,866*	H0:Accept
-4	0,005	H0:Reject
-3	0,000	H0:Reject
-2	0,360*	H0:Accept
-1	0,001	H0:Reject
0	0,779*	H0:Accept
1	0,352*	H0:Accept
2	0,598*	H0:Accept
3	0,679*	H0:Accept
4	0,100*	H0:Accept
5	0,474*	H0:Accept
6	0,278*	H0:Accept
7	0,000	H0:Reject
8	0,542*	H0:Accept
9	0,000	H0:Reject
10	0,977*	H0:Accept

"*"indicates significance at 5% significance level.

In addition to abnormal return tests, whether average cumulative abnormal return (CAR) is statistically different from zero has been tested for various intervals within the event window. Before going on with such tests, first cumulative abnormal returns have been tested for normality by Shapiro Wilk Test. Shapiro Wilk Test results are presented in Table 5. As seen on Table 5, cumulative abnormal returns within intervals "-2 to 0", "0 to +1", 0 to +2", 0 to +3", "0 to +4", 0 to +5", and "0 to +10" are normally distributed. Therefore, One Sample t-Tests have been performed on abnormal returns for these intervals. Since CARs in Intervals with p-values smaller than 5% are not normally distributed, One Sample Wilcoxon Signed Rank Tests have been performed for CARs within these intervals.

Hypotheses that test whether cumulative abnormal return average of each interval within the event window is statistically different from zero are presented below.

- (H0): Cumulative abnormal return average of BIST Sustainability Index Constituents on the relevant interval within the event window is equal to zero ($\mu = 0$).
- (H1): Cumulative abnormal return average of BIST Sustainability Index Constituents on the relevant interval within the event window is different from zero ($\mu \neq 0$).

Table 4. Daily Abnormal Return (AR) Averages and One Sample Mean/Median Test Results

Day	Abnormal Return Average	p-Value (Two-Tailed Sig.)
-10	0,003518	0,252 (t-test)
-9	0,000892	0,721 (Wilcoxon)
-8	0,001900	0,357 (t-test)
-7	-0,001487	0,456 (Wilcoxon)
-6	-0,000533	0,778 (t-test)
-5	0,001878	0,398 (t-test)
-4	-0,002611	0,721 (Wilcoxon)
-3	0,001148	0,566 (Wilcoxon)
-2	-0,002668	0,448 (t-test)
-1	-0,002315	0,596 (Wilcoxon)
0	0,002489	0,283 (t-test)
1	-0,003059	0,157 (t-test)
2	0,004310	0,189 (t-test)
3	0,000048	0,983 (t-test)
4	0,005684	0,010** (t-test)
5	0,000116	0,941 (t-test)
6	0,001579	0,352 (t-test)
7	0,000941	0,940 (Wilcoxon)
8	0,001034	0,622 (t-test)
9	0,001391	0,265 (Wilcoxon)
10	0,000627	0,831(t-test)

"**" indicates significance at 1% significance level.

The above hypotheses have been tested by either One Sample t-Test or One Sample Wilcoxon Signed Rank Test depending on whether CARs are normally distributed or not, as explained above.

Test results are presented in Table 6. As seen on Table 6, when two-tailed significance levels are considered cumulative abnormal return averages are statistically different from zero at 5% significance level only for 0 to +9 time interval and 0 to +10 time interval. However, there seems to be an increasing significance (p value decreases) from 0 to +4 time interval to 0 to +10 time interval although 0 to +6 interval distorts this pattern slightly. Moreover, in the case that one-tailed significance levels are considered, hence p-values in the last column are divided by two (for example 0,065/2 = 0,0325), all intervals after 0 to +3 days becomes significant except for CAR average for 0 to +6 days whose significance (0,127/2 = 0,0635) becomes quite close to 5%. Considering one-tailed significance levels makes sense because all CAR averages for intervals between 0 to +3 days and 0 to +10 days are positive as seen on the second column of Table 6. This pattern is statistically confirmed by one-tailed significance levels except for a negligible slight distortion in 0 to +6 days interval.

The insignificance of CAR averages for intervals -10 to -1 days, -2 to 0 days and -1 to 0 days implies that the investors do not have the ability to forecast new constituents of BIST Sustainability Index. The insignificant but negative CAR averages for intervals 0 to +1 days, 0 to +2 days imply that the inves-

Table 5. Normal Distribution Test Results for Cumulative Abnormal Returns

Day or Time Interval	Normal Distribution Test (Shapiro Wilk) Results (p-values)
-10 to +10 days	0,005
-10 to -1 days	0,000
-2 to 0 days	0,137*
-1 to 0 days	0,003
0 to+1 days	0,467*
0 to +2 days	0,989*
0 to +3 days	0,938*
0 to +4 days	0,878*
0 to +5 days	0,536*
0 to +6 days	0,044
0 to +7 days	0,000
0 to +8 days	0,030
0 to +9 days	0,006
0 to +10 days	0,197*

"*" indicates significance at 5% significance level.

tors do not value the stocks of new constituents of BIST Sustainability Index in the first two days of

Table 6. Daily Cumulative Abnormal Return Averages and One Sample Mean/Median Test Results

Day or Time Interval	Cumulative Abnormal Return Average	Two-Tailed Significance (p-value)	One-Tailed Significance (p-value)
-10 to +10 days	0,012987	0,082 (Wilcoxon)	0,041 (Wilcoxon)
-10 to -1 days	0,008102	0,689 (Wilcoxon)	0,345 (Wilcoxon)
-2 to 0 days	0,001892	0,832 (t-test)	0,416 (t-test)
-1 to 0 days	-0,002642	0,991(Wilcoxon)	0,496 (Wilcoxon)
0 to +1 days	-0,000570	0,873 (t-test)	0,437 (t-test)
0 to +2 days	-0,003740	0,406 (t-test)	0,203 (t-test)
0 to +3 days	0,003788	0,461 (t-test)	0,231 (t-test)
0 to +4 days	0,009472	0,065 (t-test)	0,033* (t-test)
0 to +5 days	0,009588	0,064 (t-test)	0,032* (t-test)
0 to +6 days	0,008449	0,127 (Wilcoxon)	0,064 (Wilcoxon)
0 to +7 days	0,011085	0,078 (Wilcoxon)	0,039* (Wilcoxon)
0 to +8 days	0,012202	0,068 (Wilcoxon)	0,034* (Wilcoxon)
0 to +9 days	0,011770	0,039* (Wilcoxon)	0,020* (Wilcoxon)
0 to +10 days	0,020147	0,013*(t-test)	0,007** (t-test)

"*"indicates statistical significance at 5% significance level and "**"indicates significance at 1% significance level.

the post-announcement period. However, following the first two days, investors seem to start valuing the constituents of BIST Sustainability Index positively by buying their stocks and generate increasing cumulative abnormal returns consistently until 10 days after the announcement day.

CONCLUSION

Becoming a constituent of the Sustainability Index on a stock exchange through an evaluation process based on attitudes and applications of firms about a wide range of issues such as environment, climate change, human rights, the structure of board of directors, etc. is not only a prestigious case, but also a means of managing risks and opportunities of firms. Similar to the role of evaluating the management of firms, capital markets may play the role of appreciating corporate sustainability efforts of firms. Investors may reflect their appreciation to sustainable firms by showing their interests to such firms through driving up their stock prices more than other firm's stock prices. In addition, the announcement of new constituents of a Sustainability Index may be appreciated by the investors, resulting in cumulative abnormal returns either in the pre-announcement period based on receiving prior information or in the post-announcement period due to spreading news. Within this context, this study investigates investors' reactions to the Announcement of New Constituents of BIST Sustainability Index on November 3, 2015, one year after the first launching of BIST Sustainability Index.

Two different methods of analysis have been used in the study. Stock returns of 29 firms listed on BIST 50 index, which are also constituents of BIST Sustainability Index, with those of rest 21 firms in BIST 50 Index that could not qualify for inclusion in BIST Sustainability Index, have been compared by appropriate Two Independent Samples Test (Mann Whitney Test). Daily, weekly and monthly returns have been calculated both arithmetically and geometrically using daily closing prices over the period of November 3, 2015 to April 18, 2016. Although for all six return types descriptive statistics reveal that average stock returns of BIST Sustainability Index Constituents are greater than those of the firms in the other group, none of these differences is statistically significant.

The second method used is event study. Results of event study indicate that within the event window covering 10 days before and 10 days after the launch of BIST Sustainability Index in November 3, 2015 with its new constituents, abnormal return average of BIST Sustainability Index Constituents is statistically significant for only 0 to +4 days interval. On the other hand, abnormal return averages of other intervals are not statistically significant, which implies that around the announcement day investors generally didn't trade stocks of BIST Sustainability Index constituents by daily sudden reactions. Event study also consisted of testing whether investors of BIST Sustainability Index Constituents generated significant cumulative abnormal returns in various intervals within the event window. The insignificance of cumulative abnormal return (CAR) averages for all three intervals covering periods prior to the announcement day, inclusive, implies that the investors do not have the ability to forecast new constituents of BIST Sustainability Index. However, in the post announcement period. CAR averages for intervals between 0 to +4 days and 0 to +10 days are statistically positive with only one exception which leads us to conclude that investors start to appreciate the BIST Sustainability Index Constituents with a lag of few days and continue their positive attitudes until 10 days after the announcement.

The findings of this study reveals that investors reactions to firms in BIST Sustainability Index have improved since the launch of the Index for the first time in 4 November, 2014, which had been taken as the announcement date in our previous study cited in the Introduction of this study. In conformance with the expectations, investors seem to have developed a more positive attitude to Sustainable Index Constituents and as consciousness about corporate sustainability becomes more acknowledged among investors the attitude may be expected to improve further. Within this context other research can be done covering new periods, new methods and cross country analyses.

REFERENCES

Alniacik, U., Alniacik, E., & Genc, N. (2011). How corporate social responsibility information influences stakeholders intentions. *Corporate Social Responsibility and Environmental Management*, *18*(4), 234–245. doi:10.1002/csr.245

Ameer, R., & Othman, R. (2012). Sustainability practices and corporate financial performance: A study based on the top global corporations. *Journal of Business Ethics*, *108*(1), 61–79. doi:10.1007/s10551-011-1063-y

Aras, G., Aybars, A., & Kutlu, Ö. (2010). Investigating the relationship between corporate social responsibility and financial performance in emerging markets. *International Journal of Productivity and Performance Management*, *59*(3), 229–254. doi:10.1108/17410401011023573

Arsoy, A. P., Arabaci, Ö., & Çiftçioğlu, A. (2012). Corporate social responsibility and financial performance relationship: The case of Turkey. *Muhasebe ve Finansman Dergisi*, *53*, 159–176.

Artiach, T., Lee, D., Nelson, D., & Walker, J. (2010). The determinants of corporate sustainability performance. *Accounting and Finance*, *50*(1), 31–51. doi:10.1111/j.1467-629X.2009.00315.x

Barber, B. M., & Lyon, J. D. (1997). Detecting long-run abnormal stock returns: The empirical power and specification of test statistics. *Journal of Financial Economics*, *43*(3), 341–372. doi:10.1016/S0304-405X(96)00890-2

Başar, B. (2014). Kurumsal sosyal sorumluluk raporlaması ve finansal performans arasındaki ilişki: Borsa istanbul'da işlem gören kimya-petrol-plastik sektörü şirketleri üzerine bir araştırma. *Yönetim ve Ekonomi Dergisi*, *21*(2), 59–72.

Becchetti, L., Ciciretti, R., & Hasan, I. (2009). Corporate social responsibility and shareholder's value: An empirical analysis. Bank of Finland Research Discussion Papers, 1, 50.

Berthelot, S., Coulmont, M., & Serret, V. (2012). Do investors value sustainability reports? A Canadian study. *Corporate Social Responsibility and Environmental Management*, *19*(6), 355–363. doi:10.1002/csr.285

Chen, H., Noronha, G., & Singal, V. (2004). The price response to S&P 500 Index additions and deletions: Evidence of asymmetry and a new explanation. *The Journal of Finance*, *59*(4), 1901–1929. doi:10.1111/j.1540-6261.2004.00683.x

Cheung, A. (2011). Do stock investors value corporate sustainability? Evidence from an event study. *Journal of Business Ethics*, *99*(2), 145–165. doi:10.1007/s10551-010-0646-3

Cheung, A., & Roca, E. (2013). The effect on price, liquidity and risk when stocks are added to and deleted from a sustainability index: Evidence from the Asia Pacific. *Journal of Asian Economics*, *24*, 51–65. doi:10.1016/j.asieco.2012.08.002

Çıtak, L., & Ersoy, E. (2016). Firmaların BIST sürdürülebilirlik endeksine alınmasına yatırımcı tepkisi: Olay çalışması ve ortalama testleri ile bir analiz. *Uluslararası Alanya İşletme Fakültesi Dergisi*, *8*(1), 43–57.

Cochran, P. L., & Wood, R. A. (1984). Corporate social responsibility and financial performance. *Academy of Management Journal*, *27*(1), 42–56. doi:10.2307/255956

Consolandi, C., Jaiswal-Dale, A., Poggiani, E., & Vercelli, A. (2009). Global standards and ethical stock indexes: The case of the Dow Jones Sustainability Stoxx Index. *Journal of Business Ethics*, *87*(1), 185–197. doi:10.1007/s10551-008-9793-1

Curran, M., & Moran, D. (2007). Impact of the FTSE4Good on firm price: An event study. *Journal of Environmental Management*, *82*(4), 529–537. doi:10.1016/j.jenvman.2006.02.010 PMID:16678334

Daszyńska-Żygadlo, K., Ryszawska, B., Słoński, T., & Zawadzki, B. M. (2014). *Investors' reactions for sustainability index inclusion –Is CSR a good news?*. Retrieved May 5, 2016, from http://hdl.handle.net/11089/14828

Dilling, P. F. A., Harris, P., & Khoo, B. (2008). The effect of corporate responsibility related information on the capital market: An event study approach. *Journal of Academy of Taiwan Business Management Review*, *5*(3), 119–127.

Dinçer, B. (2011). Do the shareholders really care about corporate social responsibility? *International Journal of Business and Social Science*, *2*(10), 71–76.

Doh, J. P., Howton, S. D., Howton, S. W., & Siegel, D. S. (2010). Does the market respond to an endorsement of social responsibility? The role of institutions, information, and legitimacy. *Journal of Management*, *36*(6), 1461–1485. doi:10.1177/0149206309337896

Field, A. (2009). *Discovering Statistics Using SPSS* (3rd ed.). London: SAGE Publications.

IISD. (1992). *Business Strategies for Sustainable Development*. Retrieved May 8, 2016, from https://www.iisd.org/business/tools/strategies.aspx

Istanbul, B. (n.d.a). *BIST Sustainability Index Ground Rules*. Retrieved May 10, 2016, from http://www.borsaistanbul.com/docs/default-source/endeksler/bist-sustainability-index-ground-rules.pdf?sfvrsn=10

Istanbul, B. (n.d.b). *BIST Sustainability Index*. Retrieved May 10, 2016, from http://www.borsaistanbul.com/en/indices/bist-stock-indices/bist-sustainability-index

Lackmann, J., Ernstberger, J., & Stich, M. (2012). Market reactions to increased reliability of sustainability information. *Journal of Business Ethics*, *107*(2), 111–128. doi:10.1007/s10551-011-1026-3

Lo, S. F., & Sheu, H. J. (2007). Is corporate sustainability a value-increasing strategy for business? *Corporate Governance: An International Review*, *15*(2), 345–358. doi:10.1111/j.1467-8683.2007.00565.x

Lopez, M. V., Garcia, A., & Rodriguez, L. (2007). Sustainable development and corporate performance: A study based on the Dow Jones Sustainability Index. *Journal of Business Ethics*, *75*(3), 285–300. doi:10.1007/s10551-006-9253-8

Lourenco, I. C., Branco, M. C., Curto, J. D., & Eugenio, T. (2012). How does the market value corporate sustainability performance? *Journal of Business Ethics*, *108*(4), 417–428. doi:10.1007/s10551-011-1102-8

Mcguire, J. B., Sundgren, A., & Schneeweis, T. (1988). Corporate social responsibility and firm financial performance. *Academy of Management Journal*, *31*(4), 854–872. doi:10.2307/256342

Mcwilliams, A., & Siegel, D. (2000). Corporate Social Responsibility and Financial Performance: Correlation or Misspecification? *Strategic Management Journal*, *21*(5), 603–609. doi:10.1002/(SICI)1097-0266(200005)21:5<603::AID-SMJ101>3.0.CO;2-3

Oberndorfer, U., Schmidt, P., Wagner, M., & Ziegler, A. (2013). Does the stock market value the inclusion in a sustainability stock index? An event study analysis for German firms. *Journal of Environmental Economics and Management*, *66*(3), 497–509. doi:10.1016/j.jeem.2013.04.005

Orlitzky, M., Schmidt, F. L., & Rynes, S. L. (2003). Corporate social and financial performance: A meta-analysis. *Organization Studies*, *24*(3), 403–441. doi:10.1177/0170840603024003910

Özçelik, F., Öztürk, B. A., & Gürsakal, S. (2014). Investigating the relationship between corporate social responsibility and financial performance in Turkey. *Atatürk Üniversitesi İktisadi ve İdari Bilimler Dergisi*, *28*(3), 189–203.

Robinson, M., Kleffner, A., & Bertels, S. (2011). Signaling sustainability leadership: Empirical evidence of the value of DJSI membership. *Journal of Business Ethics*, *101*(3), 493–505. doi:10.1007/s10551-011-0735-y

Roca, L. C., & Searcy, C. (2012). An analysis of indicators disclosed in corporate sustainability reports. *Journal of Cleaner Production*, *20*(1), 103–118. doi:10.1016/j.jclepro.2011.08.002

Rossi, J. L. (2009). *What is the value of corporate social responsibility? An answer from the Brazilian Sustainability Index*. Retrieved April 13, 2016, from http://ssrn.com/abstract=1338114

Signitzer, B., & Prexl, A. (2007). Corporate sustainability communications: Aspects of theory and professionalization. *Journal of Public Relations Research*, *20*(1), 1–19. doi:10.1080/10627260701726996

Tokgöz, N., & Önce, S. (2009). Şirket sürdürülebilirliği: Geleneksel yönetim anlayışına alternatif. *Afyon Kocatepe Üniversitesi İİBF Dergisi*, *11*(1), 249–275.

Turkishtime. (2014). Şirketlerde Sürdürülebilirlik. *Turkishtime*. Retrieved May 1, 2016, from http://www.turkishtimedergi.com/genel/sirketlerde-surdurulebilirlik/

Waddock, S. A., & Graves, S. B. (1997). The corporate social performance-financial performance link. *Strategic Management Journal*, *18*(4), 303–319. doi:10.1002/(SICI)1097-0266(199704)18:4<303::AID-SMJ869>3.0.CO;2-G

WCED. (1987). *Report of the World Commission on Environment and Development: Our Common Future*. Retrieved April 13, 2016, from http://www.un-documents.net/our-common-future.pdf

KEY TERMS AND DEFINITIONS

Borsa Istanbul (BIST) Sustainability Index: The index aims to provide a benchmark for Borsa İstanbul companies with high performance on corporate sustainability and to increase the awareness, knowledge and practice on sustainability in Turkey. Borsa İstanbul has signed a cooperation agreement with Ethical Investment Research Services Limited (EIRIS) to create BIST Sustainability Index. In accordance with this agreement, EIRIS assesses Borsa İstanbul listed companies based on the international sustainability criteria.

The Downward Sloping Demand Curve Hypothesis: It supposes that inclusion or exclusion in the index do not contain any message so they don't have any impact on stock price. This hypothesis presumes that rise in demand is permanent; hence price and volume impacts are permanent. Downward sloping demand curve pose difficulties for theories in finance that rely on the law of one price and price-takers in competitive markets.

The Price Pressure Hypothesis: It assumes that the effect of flows on current market returns is negative. Based on the price pressure hypothesis, the excess demand caused by change in indexation status creates an increasing price pressure to convince investors to sell the stocks early. When the stock market demand curve is not perfectly elastic, investors in the stock market buy (sell) shares, leading to equity flowing in and out. According to the price pressure hypothesis, there is buying (selling) pressure in the market, pushing the stock price up (down), leading to a temporary deviation from the equilibrium price, resulting in positive (negative) market returns.

Sustainable Development: It is defined as adopting business strategies and activities that meet the needs of the enterprise and its stakeholders today while protecting, sustaining and enhancing the human and natural resources that will be needed at the firm level.

Sustainability Index: The index tracks the stock performance of the leading firms in terms of economic, environmental and social criteria. The index provides an effective engagement platform for firms who want to adopt sustainable best practices. It serves as benchmarks for investors who integrate sustainability considerations into their portfolios, too.

Chapter 13
Improved Regional Entrepreneurial Ecosystems in Eastern Europe:
A Romanian Policy Approach

Roxana Voicu-Dorobanţu
Bucharest University of Economic Studies, Romania

Cătălin Ploae
Bucharest University of Economic Studies, Romania

ABSTRACT

The chapter provides a bird-eye view of Romania's position in view of its development of national and regional entrepreneurial ecosystems, before presenting a hands-on perspective of entrepreneurs in their quest for profit and impact. The methodology relies mainly on a qualitative critical description of the current situation in Romania, based on previous in-depth studies, focusing on public policies and entrepreneurial attitudes. The main objective of the chapter is to provide the reader with a clear view of the possibilities and potential of Romania in terms of developing sustainable, resilient regions, the obstacles it faces in this respect, its quest for more impact investments and its need for a holistic approach to strategic regional development.

INTRODUCTION

Value sharing is a new concept in business theory. Its creator, Michael Porter, a "Spiritus Rector" of competitiveness, introduced it for the first time in 2006 (Porter & Kramer, 2006) and redefined it in 2011 (Porter & Kramer, 2011), in an acknowledgment of the failures of the current model of capitalism. The author posits that a company cannot fully function competitively in an unhealthy community because the long-term consequences are to be considered. Porter proposes methods for measuring this shared value (Porter, Hills, Pfitzer, Patscheke, & Hawkins, 2011), building on his concept Michelini and Fiorentino (2011) propose new business models, and Bertini and Gourville (2012) introduce pricing

DOI: 10.4018/978-1-5225-3147-0.ch013

models to support the creation of the shared value. However, Crane et al. (2014) contest the concept, claiming it is unoriginal, superficial in its view of the firm and ignorant in which concerns compliance and business tensions.

This chapter provides a bridge approach to the two sides: the shared value concept is related, in reality, to the flows in a business or entrepreneurial ecosystem. For any ecosystem to perform appropriately, all its components must be in their optimal state, all flows must operate properly, and the output of the ecosystem must be evident. Thus, shared value may be considered just another element to be analyzed when looking at business or entrepreneurial ecosystems.

The chapter focuses on European and best-practice driven public policies aimed at enhancing opportunities within Romanian regions for entrepreneurs to become competitive, sustainable and innovative. The second approach to these public policies is to reduce the vulnerabilities of the knowledge sharing system, to reduce systemic constraints, to limit adverse impacts of misdirected public and private funding. The proposals and implementation of these entrepreneurial ecosystem-directed public policies are presented, underlining the advantages and disadvantages of this endeavor and best practices are revealed. It also suggests the possible future development of like policies, to enhance their impact.

Based on the concept of innovative entrepreneurial ecosystem, adapted to the specific situation of Romania, the chapter presents a variety of public policies designed to streamline the afore-mentioned ecosystem, increase its sustainability, both economic and environmental, improve the flows and enhance knowledge and value sharing.

The methodology of detection of these policies is based on two important pillars. The first pillar is represented by Romania's position regarding territorial capital; defined as the sum of economic, cultural, environmental and social assets ensuring the potential development of a particular area. The second pillar is the previously researched opinion of Romanian entrepreneurs on the facts and policies related to regional development.

Ultimately the chapter provides the reader with the following elements: a clear view of the possibilities and potential of Romania regarding developing sustainable, resilient regions, the obstacles it faces in this respect, its quest for more impact investments and its need for a holistic approach to strategic regional development.

BACKGROUND

The manner in which a business can become more competitive and provide more value for its shareholders is by no means a matter of novelty in economics research. Nor is the use of concepts from cybernetics, physics or biology to make sense of the complex systems and interactions in an economic environment. In the same vein of enabling a more profound understanding of the completely unknown, the trend nowadays in literature is to compare the business systems with biological, as suggested by Moore (1993). Value sharing becomes in this context an issue of systemic viability, rather than a matter of competitiveness (Peltoniemi, 2004). The business ecosystem, defined as "a collection of agents acting selfish or selfless, bringing added value and synergy learn from others" is nonetheless hard to identify rigorously. The boundaries of the concept are superficial (Anggraeni, Den Hartigh, & Zegveld, 2007), and often it is being used interchangeably with entrepreneurial or entrepreneurship ecosystem ((Napier & Hansen, 2011); (Malecki, 2011); (Kantis & Federico, 2012); (Isenberg, 2010)). For the latter, the authors of this chapter shall use the Mason and Brown definition (2014):

...a set of interconnected entrepreneurial actors (both potential and existing), entrepreneurial organisations (e.g. firms, venture capitalists, business angels, banks), institutions (universities, public sector agencies, financial bodies) and entrepreneurial processes (e.g. the business birth rate, numbers of high growth firms, levels of 'blockbuster entrepreneurship', number of serial entrepreneurs, degree of sellout mentality within firms and levels of entrepreneurial ambition) which formally and informally coalesce to connect, mediate and govern the performance within the local entrepreneurial environment.

According to Isenberg (2010), also quoted in the Mason and Brown (2014) OECD report, the entrepreneurship ecosystem consists of hundreds of elements which may be grouped into six categories:

...a conducive culture, enabling policies and leadership, availability of appropriate finance, quality human capital, venture-friendly markets for products, and a range of institutional and infrastructural supports.

Apart from this precise definition of the term, to be used in this chapter, the key element is the synergistic systemic operation aimed at creating value for all participants, through an optimal harnessing of creativity, existent and potential, through the reduction of externalities, and an efficient use of all factors available. These factors may be defined as the territorial capital (further on, TC) characterizing a particular area, in the case of this research, a region. The regions is defined at European Union level as an institutional division, according to NUTS 2 (Nomenclature of Territorial Units for Statistics), created to reinforce the Cohesion Policy in the Member States of the EU. Territorial capital has 9 different components, as grouped by Camagni (2008):

Private fixed capital stock; Pecuniary externalities (hard); Toll goods (excludable); Relational private services operating on: external linkages for firms, transfer of R&D results; University spin-offs; Human capital: entrepreneurship, creativity, private know-how; Pecuniary externalities (soft) Proprietary networks; Collective Goods: landscape, cultural heritage (private „ensembles"); Cooperation networks: strategic alliances in R&D and knowledge; p/p partnerships in services and schemes; Governance of land and cultural resources; Relational capital: cooperation capability (trust); collective action capability (participation); collective competencies; Resources: natural cultural (punctual); Social overhead capital: infrastructure; Agencies for R&D transfer; Receptivity enhancing tools; Connectivity; Agglomeration and district economies; Collective action: conventions; behavioral codes; representations; values.

Of particular importance in this respect are common elements: collective competencies, collective action, collective goods, cooperation networks, which relate to an intrinsic need of the region characterized by that particular territorial capital to coalesce into a functional ecosystem. Although limited (Capello, Fratesi, & Resmini, 2011), the knowledge related to TC is constantly developed, with 252,000 returns on a Google Scholar for the term used in academic documents between 2008 and 2016. Mostly, the topic is related to regional development, as researchers strive to reveal the suitable strategies to target shared growth. Also targeted is the issue of knowledge management and mismanagement, particularly in business networks and multinational corporations, as it is perceived to be disconnected to some extent from the main topic of TC ((Andriani, 2013); (Battistella, Colucci, & Nonino, 2012), (Capello, Fratesi, & Resmini, 2011)). Defined as "a set of connected relationships", business networks are the main components of an entrepreneurial ecosystem (Johanson & Vahlne, 2011), which refer to a certain extent to the relational private services mentioned in the TC components. The growth of the network (in its unit form: the business network, or in its systemic form: the entrepreneurial ecosystem) depends on knowledge sharing, learning through interaction and acquisition of new knowledge (Kogut, 2000). Apart from the overall growth of the network, the direct effect on growth at the firm level is evident (Wang, Sharma, & Cao, 2016). Knowledge sharing becomes thus essential for the competitiveness of the company (Kogut & Zander, 1996), on local and, international markets. Knowledge flows are key determinants of the overall competitiveness of the multinational company, whose mere existence depends on the skills and resources (in a nutshell, the TC, or as Andersson, Dellestrand, and Pedersen (2014) call them: country-specific advantages) of the host country.

The main component of the shared value concept is that the company cannot exist in a vacuum, it is in direct linkage to the environment in which it operates and thus, to function optimally, must work in the best environment possible. The flows between the firm as an agent of the system and the system itself are bi-directional, that is: the company benefits from the systemic advantages, but it must return to the system value, which impacts positively on the other agents.

The fact that the company exists and interacts with others, recives inflows and generates outflows is particularly relevant when we refer to the components of an entrepreneurial ecosystem: actors (agents), flows, and the dynamic between the two ((Iansiti & Levien, 2002), (Iansiti & Levien, 2004), (Iansiti & Richards, 2006)). This definition follows the main elements of any systemic map: components of the system (participants, agents, actors, members), inputs, outputs (deliverables) and the mechanism of transformation of inputs into outputs (transactions, interactions, processes). The main goal of the ecosystem is considered to be value creation (initially in (Porter & Millar, 1985), then in (Allee, 2002)), that is common welfare ((Andriani, 2013); (Battistella, Colucci, & Nonino, 2012); (Durlauf & Fafchamps, 2004)). Considering the timeline of the concept in literature, one may assume that the critiques of Porter's shared valued conceptualization are true, nonetheless the concept is not without utility. Value creation and subsequently sharing rely on the capacity of each member/participant in the ecosystem to become 'less replaceable' (Jacobides, 2013). O crucial importance in this creation of value is Social capital (a fundamental component of TC), "the institutions, relationships, and norms that shape the quality and quantity of society's social interactions". Social capital is both the coalescent factor consolidating the ecosystem as value creator or value network any web of relationships that generates tangible and intangible value through complex dynamic exchanges between two or more individuals, groups, or organizations". It becomes thus evident the reason why researchers must discuss entrepreneurial ecosystems in the context of shared value, as they represent, based on current knowledge, a possible solution for the impact involvement of companies in the communities in which take are placed.

The individuals in their social interaction, better said in their permanent approach to meet the needs, turn to the resources that constitute the capital. The term of capital has been and is usually associated with the narrowly defined economic category of monetary exchange for profit. Bourdieu offers us in terms stated above, the first systematic approach to the resources available to a person, distinguishing between economic, social and cultural capital.

Following findings of the current state of the art, it is considered that social capital is generated throughout social processes that occur between the family and society as a whole, being composed of social networks.

Among the most important functions of social capital, we could name that of being a source of social control, a guarantor of family aid, and a catalyst for social development. It is also a facilitator of access to resources through social networks to reduce transaction costs, due to its ability to be converted to other types of capital.

The most encountered in the specific literature would be the distinction between the bonding social capital and the bridging social capital. The bonding social capital characterizes the small and closed communities, based on intragroup relationships and mistrust towards other people. On the other hand, communities with high levels of bridging social capital are characterized by relationships with other and elevated levels of trust toward the alterity.

Studies conducted starting 2008 shows that, in Romania, the bridging social capital levels are lower than in the rest of Europe, Romanians having low social interactions with friends, rarely participating in the activities of associations and having less confidence in people. Romanians have few relationships outside the family, to which they attach greater importance than to friends and other groups unless they need financial aid (Voicu, 2008). Unfortunately, relations with family members provides access to similar information and resources, unlike relationships with coworkers and friends, the latter proving to be the most valuable regarding access to new information, to new contacts networks.

Romania ranks last positions in Europe also regarding active involvement in associations and relating to the trust in others, providing no surprise by this with the general trend of lower interpersonal trust and trust in institutions unique to Eastern Europe. According to EVS'99, only 10% of the Romanian trusts in others, as opposed to 62% of Nordic Europeans and 59% of the Dutch. Western Europe average is higher, somewhere around 30%, (only with French and Portuguese being distrustful, with values of 20% and 10%) (Voicu, 2010). Lack of volunteering is also a characteristic for Romanians, as 8% of all respondents carrying out activities volunteering in at least one NGO (Voicu & Voicu, 2009).Further on, the topic of valorizing the entrepreneurial ecosystem and transforming it from an academic buzz word into a real policy instrument which generates benefits in practice. In this direction, Isenberg (2010) proposes some new measures that governments or local authorities, depending on the structure of the government in a given country, should take to develop entrepreneurial ecosystems in their regions or states. These measures suggest adapting to local conditions (TC), involving all components of the ecosystem stakeholders from an early stage to encourage potential players to focus on successes (social capital and knowledge sharing), working on cultural change, focusing on organic growth. Crucial is not to create artificial structures, just for the sake of having a similar institution in the region (particularly, clusters), as they should stem from a clear need and structure of the companies present in that specific region.

Based on this theoretical background, the chapter presents in the next section the case of Romania, in its quest to create and support functional regional entrepreneurial ecosystems.

ROMANIA: A POLICY CHALLENGE FOR REGIONAL DEVELOPMENT

The Context for the Romanian Development Conundrum: A Diagnostic

A member state of the European Union since 2007, Romania ranks, at the end of 2015, on the 45th position based on the ease of doing business and on 37th position in starting a business, out of 189 economies, according to World Bank statistics. According to SBA 2014, only 0.3% of the total number of enterprises are large, which means that SMEs account for 99.7% and bring value added to 49.4%. Micro enterprises (defined as having less than nine employees and 200,000 EUR turnover) account for 87.4% of the total number of businesses, employ just 23% of the total number of employees and bring 13% of the total value added.

With almost 20 million inhabitants, it is considered one of the most significant countries in the EU and has just a few inhabitants more than the German region of Nordrhein-Westfalen. It comprises of 8 NUTS 2 regions: Bucharest-Ilfov (including the capital city of Bucharest), North-West, West, Center, South-West, South, South-East, North-East. North-East is also the largest region regarding inhabitants, with more than 3 million, while West is the smallest with almost 2 million. There is a high disparity amongst the regions, more specifically between Bucharest-Ilfov and the rest. The country is highly polarized, 6 of the eight regions being considered among the least developed regions of the EU, with 5 of them exhibiting a GDP per capita in PPS less than the critical threshold of 50% of the EU average. Overall, the country has a GDP of 54% of the EU27 average (2014 data, national indicator), with just the capital region being a transition region (with a GDP between 75% AND 90% of the EU27 average), accounting for 28% of the national GDP. The centripetal effect (targeted by the policies aimed to reduce regional disparities at European level) is evidently present in Romania. The capital city catalyzes the most investment, has a high-performance education with economic impact, is more flexible in attracting knowledge and financial flows, and may be considered a rather suitable business ecosystem, even if not a fully optimal one. Social issues influence the efficiency of this entrepreneurial ecosystem, as the human capital is affected by housing issues, urban mobility concerns, smart city, and sustainable urban area matters, quality of life externalities, a lack of sense of community. These are, however, acknowledge by the community, and more and more companies present in the capital city and its surrounding region are involved in developing a sense of growth and resilience. The capital city is also characterized by a growing entrepreneurial culture, in youth, and in areas with a low environmental impact, high social impact, or highly innovative. All the other regions are relatively similar in contribution to GDP.

In which concerns the real growth rate of gross value added, Romania does not collect data at the regional level. Therefore, a quantitative assessment of the ability to generate the value of each regional ecosystem is not possible currently. This lack of data is not a singular event at European level; most new Member States report only at national level. To be noted in this respect, that Poland, a member state of the European Union since 2004 (only three years earlier than Romania), has managed to double its absolute level of gross fixed capital as compared to Romania in the period 2011-2014.

The Romanian regions have a deficit in knowledge flows and financial flows. For instance, the number of microfinance institutions (a relevant actor in the creation of new enterprises, as experienced in other countries) varies from 7 in Center region to 1 in the South-East. The distribution at the regional level is much more uniform in which concerns the university center per region, the distribution of students at national level being balanced between the regions.

The capital region maintains its position as the most important driver of the national economy. It has

- The largest percentage of RDI average expenditure (almost 60% of all domestic funds, European Commission, 2013),
- The largest percentage of RDI employees (approximately 51% of all Romanian RDI personnel) and
- The highest allocation of funds (RDI expenditure per capita): 155 Euros as compared to a national average of 32.1 Euro/capita (2012). In comparison, Poland allocated in the same year 90.1 Euro/capita, Hungary 126.6 and the European average was of 533.1 Euro/capita. The poorest Romanian regions (South-East and South-West) allocated less than 10 Euro/capita.

Overall, Romania is facing a decline in human capital, to which the phenomena of shrinking cities and narrowing horizon of regional specialization are aggravating elements. This triad generates social issues, and companies are in the most affected areas and regions are seen as potential solutions. Faced with a crucial immigration problem, in highly specialized researchers, young specialists, medical personnel, youth from rural areas, Romania currently has more than 10% of its active population legally working abroad. To this figure, illegal workers, as well as temporary legal, must be added, estimates in this respect ranging from 4% to 10% of the active population. The decline in the social and human capital is not immediately evident when checking the unemployment rates. With a national average of 4.17% (ANOFM, March 2016) and the lowest rate in the capital region: 1.14%, Romania appears to use at maximum its labor force.

Deindustrialisation and out-migration have led to "shrinking cities" (urban areas faced with a rapid and drastic decrease of the population), and Romania is particularly affected by this phenomenon. 68% of Romanian cities have less than 20.000 inhabitants and are dependent on a single industry (Richardson & Nam, 2014). Thus, the company or companies belonging to that particular industry are the main drivers of value in that particular ecosystem, often with just the support of micro enterprises delivering non-value adding services. The natural flow of potential entrepreneurs to a more supportive environment is also proven by the high number of entrepreneurs among the Romanian immigrants (for instance, in 2011, 14% of Romanians working in Ireland were entrepreneurs). This exodus, aggravated by the lack of resources in developing startups, a deterioration in primary education, in rural areas, as well as a certain precarity of the entrepreneurial culture, paint a rather bleak image of the Romanian regions. The causes of this human and social capital decline do not reside solely in mismanaged public policies of the latter years, but rather stem from the systemic scars of the 40 years of communism, in general, and lack of private property, in particular. Romania has developed before 1989 unsustainably, the centralized approach of the socialist country, paradoxically aimed at providing the highest level of shared value, led to the creation of heavily industrialized, non-resilient regions. Heavy industries are by definition nonflexible to disruptive technologies, highly sensitive to moral aging, and highly dependent on R&D efforts. The socialist economy, structured like a centralized uber-ecosystem, did not allow for resilient measures and adaptative policies. In its autarchic model, it became heavily diversified, communicated extremely seldom regarding innovation diffusion with other countries, did not allow for spillover effects, and lacked the validation of the market for its products. Industrial monoliths dominated urban areas in various regions, without being surrounded by an ecosystem of small or medium-sized enterprises. The centralized approach also affected the relational capital, the capacity to cooperate and act collectively, as, following the December 1989 Revolution, the cultural response was reminding of the "Wild West". "Chacun pour soi," a new breed of highly independent entrepreneur emerged. Even the term "collective" has a negative connotation, as it was the name of the rural farms in which peasants were more or less forced to work, to bring value to the "community". Excessive privatization in the 90s has destroyed the monoliths, but in most regional areas (outside the capital city of Bucharest) it has left a barren ground, which should have been replaced by foreign direct investments, but that has seldom happened. The industrial monoliths have been, in most cases, closed, without being able to generate value further for the community in which they existed. The people were placed in unemployment in a rather short period, and the response of the region to such a situation was non-existent.

Thus, knowledge transfer was kept to a minimum, agencies for R&D or any other type of knowledge sharing institutions became inexistent or unfunctional, universities and research institutes lost a hight percentage of their capability to generate knowledge or disseminate the results to create value in entrepreneurial endeavors.

25 years of lack of proper entrepreneurial knowledge and skills, of dysfunctional flows of knowledge and finances (as mentioned by Isenberg, op.cit), have led to sub-optimal entrepreneurial ecosystems. Such a disparity can be credited for the initial condition of potential development, a larger population creating the potential base for a larger probability of entrepreneurial approaches and innovations. Business facilitators are also highly spread out. The country lists a total of 170 organizations of the sort (UEFISCDI, 2015): accelerators, centers for information and/or technological transfer, clusters, hubs, incubators, industrial parks, science and technology parks. The highest number is of industrial parks: 66, South listing 20, Center 17 and North West 13, all the other regions listing on average 2-3. These are followed by clusters (45 nationally), a proven solution for sharing value and fostering growth, flexibility, and resilience. These are more evenly distributed, with just Bucharest-Ilfov and Center listing more than 10. The exception is the South region with just a cluster. Accelerators may be found just in Bucharest and North-West, while Science and Technology parks just in Bucharest-Ilfov and North-East. Overall, Bucharest-Ilfov has the highest number of business facilitators (42), followed by Center (33), North-West (32), South (23), South-West (15), West (9), North-East (9) and South-East (7). The low number of Science and Technology Parks as well as of Centers for technological transfer may also be explained by the drastic decline in the number of researchers, Romania being the only country in the EU in which this is decreasing. The latest available data at European level (for the country on country comparison) is from 2012: when Romania listed a decade low of 82.8 researchers per hundred thousand inhabitants, the second lowest country in the EU (Bulgaria) accounting for nearly double: 155.2 per hundred thousand inhabitants.

In the perspective of the European Union, regions must have the capacity to generate researchers, new business majors, new courses of specialization, new specialists in applied research, highly educated and thus able to produce innovation, disseminate results and generate value. The regions which are capable of this Agent creation (in the entrepreneurial ecosystem terms) are attractive for investors, become recipients of funds as well as human resources from more disadvantaged regions, and function as optimal ecosystems. At the opposite end, there are regions which, although they have a negative balance in human capital flows, try and succeed in increasing their number of researchers, via targeted policies, the involvement of businesses and companies in the creation of courses and specialization, via citizen-private-public policies to generate more user-lead innovations. Unfortunately, Romania fits in the third category: regions with a negative balance in human capital flows and a decreasing number of researchers, still under an economic dismantling, with an acute need for targeted political will and public policies to develop and implement a suitable strategy towards a functional ecosystem.

Developing the Entrepreneurial Ecosystem at Regional Level

Entrepreneurship can be found in a national economy under a multitude of forms and with very different results not only within the framework of economic and financial welfare. Similarly, entrepreneurship is linked to technological progress, creating jobs and reducing social inequalities or environmental issues. Globalization and recent year's world crisis have determined a series of profound structural changes on entrepreneurship. Due to the constant pressure that competitiveness exercised on companies, there is clear evidence of an increase in worldwide productivity by using the latest technologies and innovation processes. Also, developments in information and communication technology have led to the creation of new markets, which have revolutionized production processes in many industrial sectors and, in particular, the tertiary sector. Advanced technology and low-cost remote transmission of information have facilitated entrepreneurs' access to knowledge and cooperation networks. Thus, they are enabled to operate on an international scale. The new opportunities have spurred entrepreneurship and creativity, considered as engines of economic development within the Horizon2020 perspective. Following empiric data in different studies, entrepreneurship generates prosperity in the society, being determinant for growth and jobs. Supporting entrepreneurship has become a priority as a way to get out of the crisis and reduce the rate of unemployment. In recent years, governments allocated financial resources to help enterprises to recover, in various forms of aid: loan guarantees, subsidies on taxation, grants for research and development designed to force innovation or encourage startups. Also becoming more common are the programs to stimulate environment investments focusing on the impact on energy efficiency and reducing carbon emissions.

There is a direct correlation between the entrepreneurial level in a country and its level of economic development. Reports of Global Entrepreneurship Monitor (GEM) confirms, through data and evaluations submitted at the global and national level, that economic development depends on the overall business activity of any region. These reports highlight the differentiations of this dependence, based on the type of economies of the assessed countries. Thus, within factors of production-oriented economies specific for poorer countries, the average rates of entrepreneurship are higher in the initial phase, which expresses the need to increase gross domestic product (GDP) by initiating new business. Within efficiency-oriented economies, the values of the GDP/capita are higher, and the rates of entrepreneurial activities in the initial phase are lower. In contrast, in economies based on innovation, these rates are higher, due to the opportunities for entrepreneurial development and innovation supplied by the business environment.

A particular case is that of Eastern European countries, including Romania, which have undergone a period of profound structural changes along with significant decreases in the population. They have fewer entrepreneurs and therefore an insufficient share of new private businesses.

Accordingly, to 2010 Country Report – "Entrepreneurship in Romania" of Global Entrepreneurship Monitor, Romania has a precarious situation, positioning 53rd among the 59 reviewed countries about the global index. The authors bring into discussion the EY 2015 Barometer of Romanian Entrepreneurship, which is a repetition of EY, G20 Entrepreneurship Barometer, being also the newest study on these issues. The mentioned study expresses problems, expectations, and needs of Romanian entrepreneurs, relying on a qualitative and quantitative analysis of Romanian business environment. Data on Romanian business environment reveals the fact that of the total number of active companies at 31 March 2015, over 64% are limited liability companies (LLC) which have on average an associate. The vast majority (91.6%) of limited liability companies are categorized as micro enterprises, averaging two employees, an average of 11.000 EUR share capital and realizing an average annual turnover of 47,000 euros. Most Romanian LLCs are registered in the capital, Bucharest and the county of Cluj.

Following the results of the study above, five pillars are supporting the development of entrepreneurship: the entrepreneurial culture, regulatory and fiscal requirements, entrepreneurship education and training, the access to finance, the coordinated assistance. Of these, only entrepreneurship teaching and training are evolving mostly positive: 62% of entrepreneurs consider this factor has improved in Romania from 2014 to 2015. Therefore, only 42% of Romanian entrepreneurs consider that the entrepreneurial culture improved in 2014, while 37% consider that the assistance provided by specialized organizations in entrepreneurship development has experienced a positive development. Only 30% of entrepreneurship environment thinks that access to finance have improved, while 20% of respondents believe that regulation and taxation experienced a positive development in 2014.

The results of this study reveal the fact that the most significant obstacles to starting and developing a business in Romania are, in the opinion of entrepreneurs, the following:

- Fiscal unpredictability, the difficult regulatory and tax system environment, the level of taxes, for 49% of respondents;
- Difficult access to finance, for 18% of interviewees;
- Lack of entrepreneurship and professional education and the entrepreneurial culture, for 14% of those surveyed;
- Lack of political stability and vision of public policies, for 7% of interviewees;
- State of local economies and the development gaps, for 6% of those surveyed;
- Corruption, for 4% of respondents.

In view of potential Romanian entrepreneurs (Voicu-Dorobanțu, 2014), the measures that government could take to support local businesses on short term are: reducing the tax burden and providing tax relief, cutting red tape and simplify legislation and the Tax Code, providing guaranteed loans, especially for start- ups, improve collaboration and communication between the public and private sectors (consistent with the need for a functional ecosystem), ensuring stability and improving the tax environment of entrepreneurship education and training.

There is a general perception that the Romanian culture is not supportive of the entrepreneurial spirit, that the cultural profile of all regions affects the entrepreneurial initiatives mainly because it discourages initiatives. Potential entrepreneurs believe that failure is a barrier for future business projects (which may constitute in one of the most damaging approaches to entrepreneurship, alongside the risk-adverse approach to most Romanians). Also, people believe that an entrepreneur is trained, and there are not academic programs in the region that promote the success stories of young entrepreneurs. The main issue is however stated to be the lack of access to funding, and yet in the short term, nobody thinks that new financial instruments will become available as mainstream on the Romanian market. Very few have the perception that between the financial instruments, the private investments are better suited to the needs of entrepreneurs in their regions. There is a lack of information regarding private investments, and a clear confusion in terms.

European Union (EU) recognizes the importance of both innovation and SMEs as growth factors. The challenge remains on how to increase the innovation potential of Small and Medium Enterprises (SMEs) and how to support them to bring innovative ideas to the market. For this, EU designed financing frameworks to support SMEs and the innovative entrepreneurship, like those provided by Horizon 2020 and COSME Programs. Horizon 2020 program introduces a new tool to support innovative SMEs ambition to exploit their ideas on international markets profitably while COSME program represents a key instrument to support internationalization, innovation and competitiveness of SMEs. Therefore, support will be provided to help to build the Innovative Management Capacity of SMEs in all regions of EU.

The European program "Horizon 2020", budgeting over 70 million for a seven years implementation period, is a financing tool that aims to strengthen the EU's position in science, but also contribute to tackling global challenges. The program seeks to finance systematically projects capable of fulfilling the technical, scientific, educational and social objectives undertaken by the Member States through the "Europe 2020" Strategy. The designed activities within H2020 framework focus on supporting SMEs that have the potential for innovation. The program is, therefore, an opportunity for Romania, for its researchers, and those working in academia or the business and, in particular, for those operating in specific areas or have developed small and medium business. The importance of H2020 is also highlighted by the reform of the way European research projects are financed through the simplifying of access to projects' funding and management. Secondly, consistency will accompany each point of the plan to ensure a smooth transition to the next stage; the last comment is to create innovative processes or products.

With a budget of 2.5 billion euros for the period 2014-2020, the Program for the Competitiveness of Enterprises and SMEs – COSME - is a funding instrument that continues the activities of the 2007-2013 programs for competitiveness and innovation. Through COSME, the authors consider that three aspects must be highlighted:

1. The entrepreneurs, especially those activating in SMEs will benefit from easier access to financing their business,
2. Citizens who wish to pursue self-employment and facing difficulties in establishing or developing their own business are supported,
3. Member State authorities will be better assisted in their efforts to design and implement effective reform policies in the field.

These new programs provide new financing tools to support the innovation activities of SMEs, covering an entire innovation cycle of a product for those companies that have the ambition to grow, develop and compete internationally. It speaks to those businesses that intend to develop a business based on an idea or concept that can compete at European or international level, which builds on a solid plan of activities that allows that concept to take shape, get mature, and progress over time.

Value Sharing in Regional Clusters: Opportunities and Challenges

Defined in the Romanian legislation (HG 918:2006 – the "Impact" Program), clusters are "groups of producers, users, and/or beneficiaries, aiming to implement best practices in the EU to increase the competitiveness of economic operators". The definition of the European Commission (COM (2008) 652/2008) introduces the regional factor: the firms forming the cluster are located near each other. It also adds an expertise element: the firms must have a sufficient scale to develop skills, suppliers, resources, services, and competencies. Thus, value generation and sharing appear to be a viable result of the cluster, in which there are no imbalances in size and skills. At European level, there is introduced another concept: the Competitiveness Pole, similar to clusters, where the firms associating in the Pole aim at implementing a joint development strategy. Currently, although financed via the 2007-2013 Structural Funds support mechanisms, the Competitiveness Poles were not a brilliant success: the first poles were funded starting with 2014, and there are currently no feedback analyses on their validity:

- **Pole 1:** Automotive industry (6 projects),
- **Pole 2:** IT (5 projects),
- **Pole 3:** Renewable energy (10 projects),
- **Pole 4:** Autonomous Systems and Robotics (6 projects),
- **Pole 5:** IT (7 projects),
- **Pole 6:** Furniture (10 projects),

- **Pole 7:** Automotive (7 projects) and
- **Pole 8:** Pharmaceuticals (4 projects) (POSCCE, 2015).

The delay in the implementation of structural funds financing for 2007-2013 (a systemic issue for Romania) has proven to be a major flaw in the plan of the Ministry of Economy, Trade and Business Environment to identify and support emerging clusters. These cluster were envisaged in poor regions, and seen as alternatives to the monolithic structures of the communist industry. The Ministry created four main actions for this: a section dedicated to clusters in the General Direction of Industrial Policy, an Inov Cluster project, meant to spread the concept and its advantages among businesses, a mapping exercise for existing clusters, and the creation of the aforementioned competitiveness poles.

Success has been met so far in the first three actions: the mapping process, the addition of the chapter in the industrial strategy and the increase in awareness of companies regarding the clustering.

In Romania, the process of identifying clusters was carried out in several stages and in several studies, as follows:

- The study coordinated by the Bucharest International Center for Entrepreneurial Studies, in 1998, which has identified three "incipient" forms of clusters in IT software, shipping and furniture industries;
- The study published in 1999 by Marco Riccardo Ferrari, assistant researcher at the Department of Economics at Bocconi University in Milan; thus identifies three so-called "proto-districts", but this time in the wood, textiles and ceramics industries (Ferrari, 1999);
- The study conducted by Valentin Ionescu (1999), which was based on earlier studies and tested their assumptions and results. The author agrees that in Romania there are no functional clusters, but argues the existence of "proto-clusters" or "emerging clusters" and reformulates his opinion by explaining the different levels of development and knowledge of the identified industrial agglomerations. Also, his assessment suggests that the ceramics industry has less potential to form clusters, although there are clear signs of progress towards the development of network-type structures.
- The VICLI Project developed within the European program INTERREG II C - CADSES. The project began in 1999 and lasted until 2001 and tried to identify and support the development of clusters. The final report of VICLI identifies for Romania four potential clusters emerged in Harghita County (Central Region of Romania) in wood, pottery, printing and switchgear industries. The emergence of these sectors is clearly linked to the area's natural resources. Also, Harghita is one of the few counties in which the input/output analysis revealed major industrial interconnections (between wood, cellulose production and printing industries).
- INCLUD project funded under the Interreg III B CADSES, European Initiative for European Regional Development Fund for 2000-2006. Using the Italian experience in identifying industrial districts, the research team has collected an impressive number of macroeconomic data on Romania's industrial structure, using international and national reports. Different potential clusters have been identified, and the study concluded that local clusters could be located in areas such as leather and footwear industry, electrical equipment and television, radio and communications equipment industry.

- Another reference for Romania is WEID project (2004). The project investigated two case studies from Romania, researching the potential existence of clusters in two areas - Banat-Crişana and Arad-Timişoara, in the sports equipment and shoe industries.
- The CURAS program (2003-2004) funded under Cooperative Agreement between the Romanian and Flemish Governments. The practical outcome of this program was the implementation of a supply chain center as a private NGO, as a first step towards institutionalizing functional clusters in the automotive sector, located in the vicinity of Dacia-Renault factory near Pitesti, Central region of Romania. This cluster could potentially be expanded in the Sibiu-Braşov regional area, where a large number of auto parts suppliers are located.

Among the latest initiatives that concentrate efforts to create innovation networks and clusters, the authors bring into discussion the following projects:

- The "Romanian Days of Innovation" FP6 project held between 2004 and 2005 that had, among other things, aimed the development of national innovation networks in the fields of ICT and biotechnology. ICT network was further supported on a national project CEEX, FP7 IST PROM.
- The FP6 project "SPRINT" (2005-2007) which aimed to develop an innovative cluster of automotive component suppliers in Romania. The novelty of this project is the importance given to research and development through the creation of joint research centers, industry research on topics agreed in the framework of joint working groups. There were also identified 12 items of interest and the working groups continue their activity in present time.
- The model called "FOUR LEAVES CLOVER" developed with the support of a FP7 project, conducted in 2008-2010, that led to the establishment of an innovative wood cluster "Pro Wood" in Braşov and Covasna region.
- The INFRATECH program - conducted in 2004-2007 by the National Authority for Scientific Research in Romania, who has targeted the creation and development of a national network of innovation and technological transfer entities (science and technology parks, business and technology incubators, information centers for technology, industry liaison offices, technology transfer centers as well as others).

Currently, there are 54 innovation and technological transfer entities accredited by the National Authority for Scientific Research in Romania according to Romanian law that are members of the National Network for Innovation and Technology Transfer. There is also a structure which unites all these entities. Many of these are members of the largest European network to support small and medium enterprises (EEN). The European connection is particularly relevant due to firstly, the position of Romania as Member State and secondly, the evident possibility of best practice transfer of know-how in the development of support of new business endeavors and the growth and scaling of existing companies. Moreover, the connection to international bodies places the Romanian enterprises and organizations in the real competitive global market.

Following national efforts to develop cluster networks in Romania in 2011 was founded the Cluster Association of Romania - CLUSTERO, with 15 clusters as founding members The aim of the association is to promote, boost and Romania's economic development by supporting the creation, development and cooperation between clusters at regional, national and international. The aim of the association is to promote and support Romania's economic development through the creation, development and cooperation between clusters at regional, national and international levels. CLUSTERO has, according to its website some 255 member companies in 42 regional clusters, with almost 7% of Romania's exports.

Whether these clusters, even in their coagulated form under CLUSTERO, represent an important component of the ecosystem remains to be seen. In theory and best practice examples, clusters, particularly regional industrial clusters, may act as lobbyist agents, may generate value and return it to the community. Value generation and sharing happens not solely via corporate social responsibility projects, but through their day to day activity: providing workforce in the area with jobs, forcing the development of the infrastructure, pushing for the creation of schools or training centers to have access to the specialists they need.

SOLUTIONS AND RECOMMENDATIONS

Regional development in Romania is a stringent need. The high disparities between regions, the polarization of the country in capital regional and the rest, the exodus of workforce abroad constitute aggravating factors in the decline of resources and potential. Solutions have been found in best practices, usually implemented based on European Union Directives. There has been no effort to leap-frog. Romania is constantly in the quest for catching up.

A few recommendations are evident:

- The acknowledgment of the need for a more active citizen-public-private partnership (C3P), or even 3P, as the businesses and citizens often perceive themselves as outside the regional ecosystem
- The acknowledgment of the need for diversified funding resources, innovative mechanisms for start-ups, and a better understanding of flaws in best-practice examples.
- The recognition of the need for better designed information and training programs, on impact investing, growth entrepreneurship
- The creation and support of more business facilitators
- The direction of funds in poor regions, in order to foster entrepreneurial endeavors, favor knowledge and financial flows, thus providing alternatives to the "factory" (the industrial monolith)
- The need to introduce in the early-age education the concept as a failure as supportive for entrepreneurship
- The need to involve businesses in the creation of custom models for the territorial capital of the region in which they activate, to foster smart specialization.
- The evident support of the collective approach, as cooperation between actors, the higher involvement of citizens and businesses in the region in which they activate, as components of the same ecosystem.

In this sense, three directions for implementation of public policy may be identified, namely:

1. **The Phased Action Plan:** None of the countries exhibiting functional entrepreneurial ecosystems (EE) have perfect EEs, and no model is perfect in its implementation. Therefore proper and sustained feedback of components/agents/actors is needed in a step-by-step approach. The creation of local action groups, free of nepotism and corruption is necessary for smart local or regional specialization. Already viable clusters may be the first stages of local action groups.

2. **The Education:** Targeted actions for the support of the knowledge flow and the creation of specialists in the fields required by the companies in that specific regional entrepreneurial ecosystem.
3. **The Financial Flow:** A proper involvement of venture funds in the development of the regional ecosystem.

FUTURE RESEARCH DIRECTIONS

The chapter presents the status quo of Romania and the entrepreneurial ecosystem it plans to develop. The main issue, however, obvious to the reader as to the researcher, relates to the reasons for failure. Instead of improving the potential regional ecosystems visibly, Romania finds itself in a flat position, plagued by the decline in human and social capital, a lack of cooperation and an extensive list of trials for development which have failed to make an impact.

Thus, the future research directions relate to several questions which have been raised during this study:

- Is the decline of human and social capital reversible?
- What are the main actions to be taken in order to overcome it?
- How knowledge management policies be more efficient in regional settings, and which are the complementary policies which may foster that impact?
- What is the proper and clear map of the regional entrepreneurial ecosystems of each of the Romanian regions?
- Which indicators must be collected at regional level in order to provide researchers and policy makers alike with proper intelligence on the ecossystems?
- What are the impact models to be used in the allocation of structural funds for the 2014-2020 Financing period and how can funds be allocated more efficiently by using these models?
- What are the most efficient smart specialization measures and policies and which of these can be implemented easily at regional level?
- Which are the main companies / successful entrepreneurs who can act as lead agent, the driver in the existing entrepreneurial ecosystem?
- Which new methods of participatory actions (such as the living lab) may be used to improve the collective approach of citizens and businesses?
- Do dynamic stochastic models, such as the RHOMOLO, proposed at EU level, be of any relevance for the policy decision maker and what are the skills needed to comprehend a similar model?
- Which Romanian regions have the highest probability to leapfrog regarding development and what are the measures to be implemented to increase that probability?
- Last, but not least, proper research must be done in which concerns the territorial capital, perceived as heterogeneous, creating centers of expertise (either emerging or intelligent).

Also important, and a large issue in the mapping of the regional ecosystem is the element of non-residents: as border regions catalyze knowledge and funds of residents from neighboring countries. This topic has not been researched in other European countries either, although Luxembourg relies mainly on non-resident knowledge.

CONCLUSION

This chapter presents the situation of Romania given its quest to develop regional entrepreneurial ecosystems. The image presented, in a birds-eye view of the system is rather bleak, the trials are few and far between, and there exists a clear lack of coagulation of efforts to make an impact.

A diagnostic based on past research, both descriptive (quantitative) and qualitative (through interviews with entrepreneurs) reveal a bleak future for the Romanian ecosystems. Without targeted measures, as presented in the Solutions and Recommendations section, the dream of having resilient regions, with reduced systemic risks, innovative and competitive is bound to remain a dream.

The chapter focuses on European and best-practice driven public policies aimed at enhancing opportunities within Romanian regions for entrepreneurs to become competitive, sustainable and innovative. These best practices are implemented at the national level through clusters, which are, according to statistics, the most numerous business facilitators in the country, apart from the obvious industrial parks. A detailed view of Romanian clusters is provided, with the caveat that their impact is still far from being commensurate.

The second approach to these public policies is to reduce the vulnerabilities of the knowledge sharing system, to reduce systemic constraints, to limit adverse impacts of misdirected public and private funding. The proposals and implementation of these entrepreneurial ecosystem-directed public policies are presented, underlining the advantages and disadvantages of this endeavor and best practices are revealed. It also suggests the possible future development of like policies, to enhance their impact.

To conclude, the title of the chapter reads as a desirable outcome, rather than a status quo. The improved regional entrepreneurial ecosystems are yet to be seen in Romania, their quantitative modeling being far from possible due to lack of data. Therefore, the only viable representation is that of ecosystemic maps, descriptions limited in insight and feedback suitable for an academic endeavor.

REFERENCES

Allee, V. (2002). *A value network approach for modeling and measuring intangibles.* Retrieved May 30, 2016, from Verna Allee: http://www.iwp.jku.at/born/mpwfst/05/Allee/05Allee_ValueNetwork_p.pdf

Andersson, U., Dellestrand, H., & Pedersen, T. (2014). The Contribution of Local Environments to Competence Creation in Multinational Enterprises. *Long Range Planning*, *47*(1–2), 87–99. doi:10.1016/j.lrp.2013.10.002

Andriani, L. (2013). *Social capital: A road map of theoretical frameworks and empirical limitations.* Retrieved from http://www.bbk.ac.uk/management/our-research/wp/WP1.pdf

Anggraeni, E., Den Hartigh, E., & Zegveld, M. (2007). *Business ecosystem as a perspective for studying the relations between firms and their business networks.* ECCON 2007 Annual Meeting.

Battistella, C., Colucci, K., & Nonino, F. (2012). Methodology of business ecosystems network analysis: a field study in Telecom Italia Future Centre. *Information systems: Crossroads for organization, management, accounting and engineering*, 239-249.

Bertini, M., & Gourville, J. T. (2012). Pricing to create shared value. *Harvard Business Review, 90*(6).

Camagni, R. (2008). Regional competitiveness: Towards a concept of territorial capital. *Modelling regional scenarios for the enlarged. Europe*, 33–47.

Capello, R., Fratesi, U., & Resmini, L. (2011). *Globalization and regional growth in Europe: past trends and future scenarios*. Springer Science & Business Media. doi:10.1007/978-3-642-19251-7

Crane, A., Palazzo, G., Spence, L. J., & Matten, D. (2014). Contesting the value of creating shared value. *California Management Review*, *56*(2), 130–153. doi:10.1525/cmr.2014.56.2.130

Durlauf, S. N., & Fafchamps, M. (2004). *Social Capital*. The Centre for The Study of African Economies (No. 214). Working Paper Series.

Ferrari, R. M. (1999). *Small enterprise clusters for local development in transition context: the case of Romania*. Milan, Italy: Bocconi University.

Iansiti, M., & Levien, R. (2002). *The New Operational Dynamics of Business Ecosystems: Implications for Policy, Operations and Technology Strategy*. Division of Research. Harvard Business School.

Iansiti, M., & Levien, R. (2004). Strategy as ecology. *Harvard Business Review*, *82*(3), 68–81. PMID:15029791

Iansiti, M., & Richards, G. L. (2006). *Information technology ecosystem: Structure, health, and performance*. Academic Press.

Ionescu, V. (1999). *Supply-Side Strategy for Productivity, Competitiveness and Convergence between the CEECs and (in) the EU-Romania Case Study*. Academic Press.

Isenberg, D. J. (2010). How to start an entrepreneurial revolution. *Harvard Business Review*, *88*(6), 40–50.

Jacobides, M. (2013). *Creating and Capturing Value in Your Business Ecosystems*. Retrieved from TedXTalk: http://www.tedxthessaloniki.com/index.php/talk_video/creating-and-capturing-value-in-your-business-ecosystems/#sthash.wUfQjlTZ.dpuf

Johanson, J., & Vahlne, J. E. (2011). Markets as networks: Implications for strategy-making. *Journal of the Academy of Marketing Science*, *39*(4), 484–491. doi:10.1007/s11747-010-0235-0

Kantis, H. D., & Federico, J. S. (2012). *Entrepreneurial Ecosystems in Latin America: The role of policies*. International Research and Policy Roundtable (Kauffman Foundation), Liverpool, UK.

Kogut, B. (2000). The network as knowledge: Generative rules and the emergence of structure. *Strategic Management Journal*, *21*(3), 405–425. doi:10.1002/(SICI)1097-0266(200003)21:3<405::AID-SMJ103>3.0.CO;2-5

Kogut, B., & Zander, U. (1996). What firms do? Coordination, identity, and learning. *Organization Science*, *7*(5), 502–518. doi:10.1287/orsc.7.5.502

Malecki, E. J. (2011). Connecting local entrepreneurial ecosystems to global innovation networks: Open innovation, double networks and knowledge integration. *International Journal of Entrepreneurship and Innovation Management*, *14*(1), 36–59. doi:10.1504/IJEIM.2011.040821

Mason, C., & Brown, R. (2014). *Entrepreneurial ecosystems and growth oriented entrepreneurship*. Paris: OECD.

Michelini, L., & Fiorentino, D. (2012). New business models for creating shared value. *Social Responsibility Journal*, *8*(4), 561–577. doi:10.1108/17471111211272129

Moore, J. F. (1993). Predators and prey: A new ecology of competition. *Harvard Business Review*, *71*(3), 75–83. PMID:10126156

Napier, G., & Hansen, C. (2011). *Ecosystems for Young Scalable Firms*. FORA Group.

Peltoniemi, M. (2004). Cluster, value network and business ecosystem: Knowledge and innovation approach. Organisations, Innovation and Complexity: New Perspectives on the Knowledge Economy, (pp. 9-10).

Porter, M. E., Hills, G., Pfitzer, M., Patscheke, S., & Hawkins, E. (2011). Measuring shared value. *How to Unlock Value by Linking Social and Business Results*, 10-11.

Porter, M. E., & Kramer, M. R. (2006). Strategy & Society. The link between competitive advantage and corporate social responsibility. *Harvard Business Review*, *84*(12), 78–92. PMID:17183795

Porter, M. E., & Kramer, M. R. (2011, January-February). The Big Idea: Creating Shared Value. How to reinvent capitalism—and unleash a wave of. *Harvard Business Review*, *89*(1), 2–17.

Porter, M. E., & Millar, V. E. (1985). How information gives you competitive advantage. *Harvard Business Review*, *63*(4), 149–152.

Richardson, H. W., & Nam, C. W. (2014). *Shrinking cities: a global perspective* (Vol. 71). Routledge.

Voicu, B. (2008). Riscurile politicilor de dezvoltare bazate pe formarea capitalului social. *Sociologie românească*, *VI*(1), 11–25.

Voicu, B. (2010). *Capital social în România începutului de Mileniu: Drumeț în țara celor fără de prieteni?*. Iași: Editura Lumen.

Voicu, B., & Voicu, M. (2009). Volunteers and Volunteering in Central and Eastern Europe. *Sociologia*, 539–563.

Voicu-Dorobanțu, R. (2014). A conceptual approach to entrepreneurial ecosystems and applied algorithms. *Advances in Applied Mathematics*, 397-406.

Wang, Z., Sharma, P. N., & Cao, J. (2016). From knowledge sharing to firm performance: A predictive model comparison. *Journal of Business Research*, *69*(10), 4650–4658. doi:10.1016/j.jbusres.2016.03.055

World Bank, Social Capital Initiative. (1998). *Social Capital Initiative Working Paper Series*. Retrieved from http://go.worldbank.org/IVEBAGOF20

KEY TERMS AND DEFINITIONS

Bucharest: The capital city of Romania, situated in the South of the country, part of the Bucharest-Ilfov region.

Business Ecosystem: A grouping of businesses, including Multinational corporations, functioning as a network, in which externalities are reduced and synergy is created.

Business Facilitators: An institution/organization providing the structure to a process enabling cooperative decision making, or to knowledge transfers.

Cluster: A group of entreprises, usually localized in a certain area, functioning as an entity in order to increase competitiveness.

Clustero: The Romanian Cluster Association, created in 2011, currently the hub for 42 clusters.

Diagnostic: An in-depth evaluation of a narrow scope of analysis, in view of identifying a certain issue or problem.

Entrepreneurship: The capacity and willingness to develop, organize and manage a business venture in view of creating value.

Public Policy: A series of activities implemented by the central public administration, with the main goal of solving a public issue, through one or several laws and regulations.

Region: A territorial unit, at NUTS 2 level, used in the European Union Cohesion Policy.

Regional Development: A general effort to reduce disparities and enhance growth in a region.

Territorial Capital: All the factors influencing the development of a region/designated area (social, environmental, cultural, economic).

Chapter 14
A Quantitative Analysis of the Impact of Renewable Energy Deployment on Sustainability:
The Turkish Case

Nurcan Kilinc-Ata
Osmaniye Korkut Ata University, Turkey

Banu Tanriover
Osmaniye Korkut Ata University, Turkey

ABSTRACT

Renewable energy sources have a large potential to contribute the sustainable development as environmentally and socioeconomically. However, the existing literature includes theoretical framework in general and there is a lack of both comprehensive theoretical and empirical framework on the relationship between sustainable development and RE technologies. This paper aims to theoretically synthesise the literature on renewable energy technologies and sustainable development for Turkey, and then classify the results by broad categories. After all, the present paper uses conceptual and quantitative analysis, which reviews each concept with conceptual framework and evaluates data with quantitative method. From this point of view, this paper attempts to make a contribution by developing a conceptual framework which allows a wide-ranging analysis of the impact of renewable energy on sustainability and which can be empirically applied to classify these benefits in Turkey.

INTRODUCTION

It is usually stated that renewable energy (RE) sources have a large potential to contribute to the sustainable development with diversification of energy supply, enriched sustainable development opportunities, discover of a domestic industry, and have a positive influence on social cohesion (Kaya & Kilic, 2015). In other words, RE creates several public advantages such as environmental development, enlarged fuel diversity, decline of energy price volatility effects on the economy, national economic security, rise

DOI: 10.4018/978-1-5225-3147-0.ch014

in economic productivity, and more efficient production procedures for GDP (Benli, 2013). They are considered an effective means for Turkey to pursue energy independence and to stimulate economic growth. This study approach will assess Turkey's RE technologies in terms of sustainability, represented in variables such as e.g., income, capital, and labor. Turkey was selected a case country because of contextual factors such as industrial institutions, RE energy consumption trends, as well as environmental and social standards. This research will shed light on the association between sustainable development and RE outcomes, the present paper develops a conceptual and methodological framework previously developed to understand the structural factors affecting the sustainable development based on RE technologies in Turkey and proposes a test of the framework empirically. The goal of the paper is to provide significant insights regarding the developing a conceptual and methodological framework previously to RE technologies in Turkey.

An emerging body of literature has investigated the contribution of RE sources to sustainability as empirically (Del Rio & Burguillo, 2009; Reddy, Uitto, Frans, & Matin, 2006). Another stream of the literature has scrutinized the aspects of the impact of RE deployment on local sustainability such as employment creation (Hillebrand, Buttermann, Behringer, & Bleuel, 2006). The renewable literature generally treats the impact of RE deployment on sustainability in conceptual framework context (Robert, 2000; Jabareen, 2008; Del Rıo & Burguillo, 2008; Musango & Brent, 2011). For instance, Robert (2000) and Jabareen (2008) investigate sustainable development within the framework a new conceptual model. They used a conceptual model to investigate various concepts and issues affecting sustainable development and the relationship between frameworks and different concepts. Jabareen (2008) point out multidisciplinary literature on sustainable development, which identifies patterns and similarities within the literature, and then sustainable development integrates the outlines to different categories and concepts. The results also showed that the conceptual analysis identifies several concepts that are synthesized the theoretical framework of sustainable development and the frameworks are relevant constitutional principles for sustainable development (Robert, 2000; Jabareen, 2008).

Del Rıo and Burguillo (2008) emphasis socioeconomic impacts of RE deployment on sustainability and they developed an amalgamated theoretical framework which lets a widespread analysis of the influence of RE on local sustainability, while Musango and Brent (2011) focus on the development of a framework which includes a technology assessment approach within the wider scope of renewable technology development for sustainability. These papers have shown that renewable policies have a positive effect on sustainability, which also have several local benefits. That is, RE polices can make a contribution on local sustainability as RE policy have obvious positive synergies on sustainability.

However, there is a lack of both comprehensive theoretical and empirical framework on the linkage between sustainable development and RE technologies in Turkey. This chapter aims to empirically analyze the sustainability influences of RE deployment by seeing a combined and comprehensive theoretical approach. This paper intends to fill this gap by incorporating value-sharing views on the form of RE technologies and sustainable development with analyzing the literature and quantitative data. A sustainable development perspective framework based on the literature developed with assessing literature review and an empirical analysis undertaken to test this framework. That is, the present manuscript builds upon current knowledge of RE technologies, develops a new conceptual framework to guide sustainability and tests the model with quantitative method. The research question that is addressed in this study is as follows: *How does evaluation of RE deployment impact on sustainability?*

This paper is organized as follows: Section 2 will discuss a brief literature review and an assessment of related studies used to understand RE sources. In section 3, the empirical study is presented. The findings and discussion will be presented in section 4. Section 5 will provide the conclusions and discuss further research areas as well as the limitations of the paper.

LITERATURE REVIEW

Turkey's demand for energy and electricity is increasing rapidly. Energy consumption has risen at an annual average rate of 4.3% considering 1990. With respect to prompt growth of energy production and consumption, environmental issues, and cost competitiveness, Turkey's RE sources are opportunity to reduce gas emissions and others (Bilgen, Keleş, Kaygusuz, Sarı, & Kaygusuz., 2008).

RE sources are recognized as a crucial source for the future, not only for Turkey, but also for the world (Balat, 2007). Turkey has mostly self-sufficient RE potential so Turkey's RE target in 2023 is 30% electricity from RE sources. For this target, the total investment required to meet the energy demand in Turkey by 2023 is anticipated at approximately $120 billion (Kolcuoglu, 2010) and Turkey is reforming its legal framework regarding European Union (EU) renewable policies (Kolcuoglu, 2010; Sirin & Ege, 2012). Turkey is also determined to decrease their dependence on non-renewable energy sources due to energy security and desire to be an energy independent country. Energy security, competitiveness, and pollution issues have made RE a driving concern. Specifically, Turkey is located in a region that has prolonged political instability affecting the price, supply, and safety of fossil resources for energy security issue.

RE sources are solar, wind, hydropower, and biogas, which are potential sources to meet global energy requirements in a sustainable approach in Turkey. In present, hydropower is the most significant kind of renewable and sustainable energy (Balat, 2007). Wind and solar energy is followed by hydropower, respectively. *Hydropower* is second largest energy source after coal. Nowadays, there are 436 sites obtainable for hydroelectric plant construction, distributed on 26 main river zones. In 2020, it is projected that around 502 new hydropower plants which will be manufactured to make use of the full available potential. *Total installed wind energy capacity* of Turkey is only 900 MW (Megawatt) in 2010. Turkey has an aim of raising the country's installed wind power capacity to 20 GW by 2023 (Benli, 2013). *Total solar energy* generation of 0.290 Mtoe (Million Tons of Oil Equivalent) in 2001 increased to 0.420 Mtoe in 2008 and is estimated to increase to 0.862 Mtoe by 2020 (Keles & Bilgen, 2012). *Biomass* is also significant because its share of total energy consumption is still high in Turkey approximately 36 Mtoe in 2008. Turkey's total geothermal heating capacity is around 31.500 MWth (Megawatt thermal) and Turkey must goal 1.2 million houses holds equivalent 7.700 MWth in 2020 (Keles & Bilgen, 2012). *Geothermal energy* use is based on hydrothermal transmission. Turkey is among the first seven countries with its potential in the world but its installed capacity is last rank. Turkey's geothermal gross theoretical, technical and obtainable heat potentials are 31500, 7500, and 2843 MWt, respectively (Bilen, 2013).

Indeed, renewables exemplify the second-largest domestic energy source after coal for Turkey and they are inevitable for Turkey because of green gas emissions (environmental protection), security of supply, cost competitiveness, economic efficiency, in a sustainable manner. For these concerns, government provides several renewable policies, which started in 1984 with third party financing, tariff, and sales tax exemptions (Bilgen et al., 2008). Several studies examined the RE policies and the European Union regulations that shaped these policies in Turkey (Erdem, 2010; Balat, 2008; Kaya, 2006). Their findings show that the policies applied by governments towards the consumption of RE have a noticeable significance on the encouragement of the consumption of renewables and policies are fosters the utilization of RE sources. In this perspective, it is considered that the growth of the consumption of RE sources strongly depends on policies by government.

The key responsibility of the increasing technologies for a sustainable global energy system is training for marketing in the developing countries that should be encouraged to participate RE sources for sustainability (Bilen et al., 2008). Turkey's energy supply must become more sustainable in the future because of above concerns. For this reason, Turkey should do more efficient use of energy and rely on RE sources (such as wind, solar, hydropower, geothermal, and biomass) for achievement (Bilen et al., 2008). While energy is the most essential input of economic sustainability it is not possible to provide sustainable deployment without caring the environment and taking economic conditions into account. Therefore, RE sources are directed towards clean energy (Baris & Kucukali, 2012).

Conceptual Framework

Relying on the relevant literature, the conceptual framework was described in the context of analyzing literature and then applied quantitative analyze with a systematic analytic approach. In other words, developing a framework is an analytical process, which includes a number of separate but highly interconnected stages. This approach comprises a systematic process of sifting, charting, and sorting materials with respect to key issues and themes, in order to demonstrate the method, and to reflect the context and variety of its applications in applied social policy research. The conceptual framework of analysis is a purely mechanical procedure, a reliable method with guaranteed results for synthesizing (Ritchie & Spencer, 2002).

A conceptual analysis on the basis of existing work on RE sources proposed to trace the main elements of sustainable development, which together build the theoretical framework of RE technologies. The conceptual model is more sophisticated for scrutinizing strategic selections for renewable technologies, which helps both as a framework for understanding this research but also as a starting point to classify encouraging approaches for further research. It is expected that arguments such as protection of property rights and ability to import materials play a role here. It also ensures a schematic picture of the proposed conceptual framework for relationships between RE technologies and sustainable development in below Figure 1, which represents sustainable development with RE technologies as a function of renewable policies, income, and technological drive. Furthermore, following conceptual framework was emerged from the literature, then, the authors will apply quantative analyze to support of this context.

Figure 1 is, more sophisticated for scrutinizing strategic selections for RE technologies which helps both as a framework for understanding this paper, as a starting point to identify encouraging approaches for quantitative methods. It also ensures a chart demonstration of the proposed conceptual framework for relationships between RE and sustainable development. The framework draws linkages between the key elements that are proposed to be of significance for increased sustainability. Furthermore, this conceptual framework gives an answer what are the main concerns to transfer from fossil based sources to RE sources. Security of supply, environmental protection, and cost competitiveness are main concerns, while technological development, energy efficiency, and increase income are profits. Combining these components facilitates the understanding of relationship between RE and sustainable development.

RE policies play crucial role to deployment renewable sources in connection with sustainable development, which relates with energy, economy, and environment (Baris & Kucukali, 2012). RE policy aiming to increase the use of renewables, to reduce the dependence on fossil based sources, to decrease

Figure 1. The conceptual framework for Turkey's RE technologies
Source: the authors elaboration

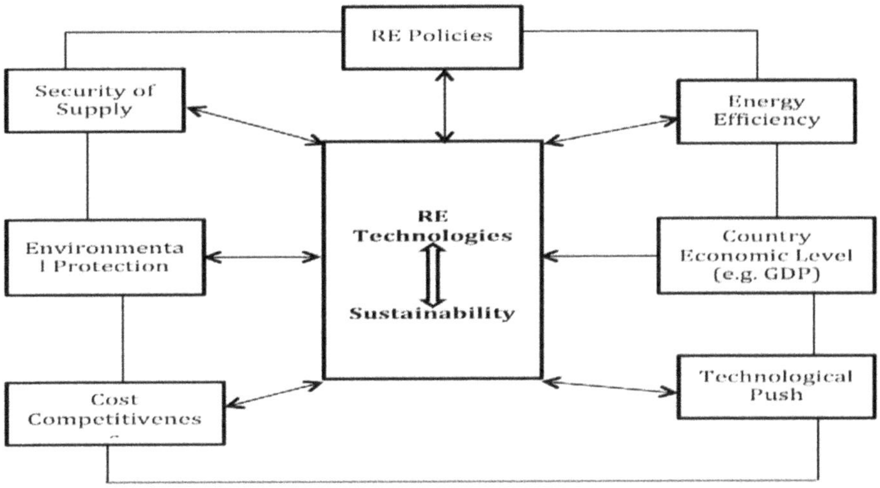

carbon emissions, to increase security of supply, to distill energy costs from oil prices, and to restrain the demand by encouraging energy efficiency.

Technology has effects on renewable investment in a certain number of manners. Musango and Brent (2011) studied the technological change as endogenous to the economy as a result of newly perceived opportunities, encouragements, thoughtful research, and improvement. According to Kowsari and Zerriffi (2011), technological dimensions are a significant feature of renewable sources. RE policies, technological push, and helping in market efficiency of renewables are all essential. However, importance of being aware of security of supply, pollution and cost effectiveness is alike. They relate to the sustainable development of a particular RE sources.

In order to be sustainable of deployment, countries need to reach energy as secure, low cost, and low environmental impact. RE technologies have much lower amounts of CO2 emissions than fossil fuel based sources. Energy sources should be limitless and not destruction the delivery of environmental goods and services comprising the climate system for sustainability. Furthermore, energy should be economically reasonable over the long term (Keles & Bilgen, 2012).

The development of a framework based on the literature, the conceptual model relates to the following propositions drawn from the literature review.

- **Proposition 1:** The country main concerns (e.g. security of supply, pollution, and cost effectiveness) are associated with sustainable development.
- **Proposition 2:** The effectiveness of renewable sources is associated with sustainable development.
- **Proposition 3:** Technological development for RE sources is associated with sustainable development.
- **Proposition 4:** Higher income is associated with a higher share of renewable investment so sustainable development.

The authors believe that each proposition have the similar level of significance to accomplish sustainable development. The effective application of RE potential in Turkey can be provided sustainable development.

DATA AND METHODS

Data

In this study, the Cobb-Douglas production function has been estimated for the purpose of investigating the importance of the increase in the RE sources in the economy of Turkey for the 1990-2014 periods. For this purpose, input-output analysis has been made with the help of Cobb-Douglas production function, and the influences of the increase in the RE sources on the total outcome have been revealed. In this case, Labor (L), Capital (C), and Renewable Energy (RE) have been used as the inputs.

In order to obtain the labor input, the annual working hours (labor force hour/year), which represented the value of the labor force as hour, and which was collected from the Turkey Statistics Institute, have been used. The value of the labor force per hour was measured by adding the worked hours according to the "Social Security and General Health Insurance and Law" with the date October 1, 2008, and number 5510, and 7,5 hours working duration per day has been accepted as the "1-day working hours". In obtaining the capital input, the real gross fixed capital formation, which was obtained from the Republic of Turkey, Central Bank, Electronic Data Distribution System, and which consists of machinery, equipment and building purchases, has been used. In order to represent the RE sources, the RE consumption, which was obtained from European Union Statistics Office (Eurostat), and which consisted of the total of the hydro power, solar thermal, wind power, biomass, renewable wastes, biogas, and geothermal energy has been used. As the last item, the real gross national product, which was obtained from the Republic of Turkey, Central Bank, Electronic Data Distribution System, was used to obtain the output.

Econometric Methodology

The hypotheses from the conceptual framework tested by using quantitative methods. The methods would apply two types of models, which are input–output approaches and more simple spreadsheets-based analytical models. The authors analyzed renewable technologies with income (GDP), capital, and labor. In order to test the influences of the increase in the RE sources on the economic growth parameters, the following production function that includes the labor and capital, which is used as the basic input in the production process in economy, has been estimated.

$$Y = f(K, L, RE) \tag{1}$$

In the production function (1), Y, K, L and RE represent the real GDP, capital, labor, and RE, respectively. The flexibility of the RE input (e_{RE}) is expressed with the help of the partial derivation and the production function (1) as follows:

$$e_{RE} = \frac{\left(\Delta Y/Y\right)}{\Delta RE/RE} = \frac{\partial Y}{\partial RE}.\frac{RE}{Y} \tag{2}$$

In this study, the Cobb-Douglas production function has been made use of to obtain the direct input flexibility of the coefficients of the inputs of the production function, in other words, the productivity levels of each input on the output. For this purpose, the following Cobb-Douglas production function has been estimated.

$$Y = AK^{\alpha}L^{\beta}RE^{\gamma} \quad A, \alpha, \beta, \gamma > 0 \tag{3}$$

In Cobb-Douglas production function (3), the $A, \alpha, \beta,$ and γ represent the fixed terms. The partial derivation of the Cobb-Douglas production function (3) according to each input gives us the Marginal Physical Productivity- MPP of the relevant input. The marginal physical productivity of the RE input (MPP_{RE}) may be expressed as follows by taking the partial derivation of the equation (3) according to the RE input:

$$MPP_{RE} = \frac{\partial Y}{\partial RE} = \gamma AK^{\alpha}L^{\beta}RE^{1-\gamma} = \gamma\frac{AK^{\alpha}L^{\beta}RE^{\gamma}}{RE} = \gamma\frac{Y}{RE}$$

If MPP_{RE}, which is the marginal physical productivity of the RE flexibility, is placed in equation (2), which is the formula of the RE flexibility, instead of ($\partial Y/\partial RE$), γ, which is on the RE input is obtained, which itself is given in Cobb-Douglas production function (3).

$$e_{RE} = \frac{\partial Y}{\partial RE}.\frac{RE}{Y} = MPP_{RE}.\frac{RE}{Y} = \gamma\frac{Y}{RE}.\frac{RE}{Y} = \gamma \tag{5}$$

In order to obtain the RE flexibility, in other words the in the equation (5) γ coefficient, the logarithmic form of the (3) Cobb-Douglas production function, which is used frequently in econometric analyses, has been formed. When the (3) Cobb-Douglas production function is converted into logarithmic form, the parameters of the relevant coefficients gives the flexibility coefficient of the relevant input (marginal physical productivity) directly.

$$\ln Y_t = a_0 + e_K \ln K_t + e_L \ln L_t + e_{RE} \ln RE_t + \varepsilon_t \tag{6}$$

The RE flexibility (e_{RE}), which will be calculated in this way, shows how much in percentage (%) the real GDP changes in the face of 1% change in the RE sources. The RE flexibility, which will be obtained with this method, will reveal the role and importance of the increase in the RE consumption in economic growth and sustainable development in the economy of Turkey.

In addition, in order to prevent fake regression problem in the (6) Cobb-Douglas production function, the stationarity tests of all the relevant variables have been realized with Augmented Dickey-Fuller (ADF) and Phillips-Peron (PP) unit root test[1]. In case of all the variables were stationary at the same level, the long-term relations between the variables have been tested. The Johansen cointegration method[2], which enables to test the multi-variable cointegrating relation, has made use of to test the long-term influences of the RE consumption on economic growth and to reveal the sustainability with this method.

Empirical Results and Discussion

This conceptual framework and the quantitative analysis will provide valuable insights into RE sources role in encouraging sustainable development to flourish and the general picture from the conceptual framework, which are aimed at contributing to the literature on sustainability in RE sources. The quantitative analysis demonstrates how to RE impact of sustainable development for Turkey.

In order to test the influences of the increase in RE use in the economy of Turkey on the economic growth and the importance of these increases in sustainable development, firstly, levels at which the real GDP (lnY), capital (lnK), labor (lnL), RE sources (lnRE) variables are stable were determined. Since the dataset is given in annual periods in unit root analyses, the maximum lag length has been defined as 3. In defining the optimal lag length, the Schwarz Information Criteria (SIC) has been made use of. The unit root tests have been estimated as constant (C), constant and trend (C+T), non-constant and non-trend (none), in three different forms. The empirical results obtained for the unit root tests of ADF and PP are summarized in Table 1.

As it seen in Table 1, all of the real GDP, capital, labor, and RE consumption variables have been found to be stable in the first difference both in the ADF and the PP unit root methods. Since all the variables have been found to be constant at the same level, Johansen cointegration method has been made use of

Table 1. Unit Root Test Results

Variables	ADF Unit Root Test			PP Unit Root Test		
	C	*C + T*	*None*	*C*	*C + T*	*None*
lnY	-1.3847	-2.3354	1.5747	-1.3653	-2.3772	1.6483
lnK	-1.8636	-3.9894[b]	0.7819	-1.8636	-2.7375	0.7966
lnL	0.1817	-0.7195	2.1873	0.0762	-0.8643	2.0729
$lnRE$	-1.8312	-2.0454	0.6081	-1.8683	-2.0875	0.6916
ΔlnY	-5.0040[a]	-4.9337[a]	-4.5844[a]	-5.0030[a]	-4.9330[a]	-4.6009[a]
ΔlnK	-4.7339[a]	-4.6222[a]	-4.7027[a]	-4.7339[a]	-4.6221[a]	-4.7027[a]
ΔlnL	-4.0653[a]	-4.2151[b]	-3.6236[a]	-4.0656[a]	-4.2117[b]	-3.6039[a]
$\Delta lnRE$	-4.8287[a]	-4.6579[a]	-4.8251[a]	-4.8287[a]	-4.6543[a]	-4.8251[a]

Note: a and b shows 1% and 5% significant level, respectively and Δ shows differences operator.

to test the long-term relation between the variables. For this purpose, first of all, the optimal lag lengths of the variables have been determined with the help of the Schwarz (SIC), Akaike (AIC), Hannan-Quinn (HQ), Log Likelihood Ratio (LR), and Final Prediction Error (FPE) criteria. Since annual dataset are used in determining the optimal lag lengths, the maximum lag length has been taken as 3. The results of the optimal lag lengths of the variables are summarized in Table 2.

As it may be observed in Table 2, the optimal lag lengths of the variables have been accepted as 1 according to all criteria. The empirical findings on the Johansen (1988) cointegration analysis, which is applied in order to test the long-term relations between the variables and to obtain the Cobb-Douglas production equation, which reveals the output flexibility of the RE input, are summarized in Table 3.

According to Table 3, it is observed that there is a long-term relation between the variables according to both trace and max-Eigen statistics. For the null hypothesis, which claims that there are no cointegrated vectors ($H_0 : r = 0$), the trace and max-Eigen statistics have been determined as 58.3058 and 32.1473, respectively. These statistical values are bigger than the critical value at 5% significance level (47.8561 and 27.5843, respectively). For this reason, the null hypothesis ($H_0 : r = 0$) in which, there are no cointegrated relations, have been rejected; and the alternative hypothesis ($H_1 : r = 1$), which claims that there is one cointegrated relation, has been accepted. The other alternative hypotheses tested for any more cointegrated relation between the series ($H_1 : r = 2$, $H_1 : r = 3$, and $H_1 : r = 4$) have been rejected. For this reason, there is a long-term relation between reel GDP, capital, labor, and

Table 2. Determining the Optimal Lag Length

Lag	*SIC*	*AIC*	*HQ*	*LR*	*FPE*
0	-2.6997	-2.7988	-2.7555	NA	0.0002
1	-4.3203*	-4.6179*	-4.5478*	41.4703*	3.40E-05*
2	-3.7981	-4.2939	-4.1771	0.6751	4.76E-05
3	-3.4468	-4.1411	-3.8776	3.1615	5.71E-05

Table 3. Johansen Cointegration Test Results

Hypothesis	Trace Statistic	Max-Eigen Statistic
$H_0 : r = 0$ $H_1 : r = 1$	58.3058[a] (47.8561)	32.1473[a] (27.5843)
$H_0 : r = 1$ $H_1 : r = 2$	26.1585 (29.7971)	17.0875 (21.1316)
$H_0 : r = 2$ $H_1 : r = 3$	9.0709 (15.4947)	9.0485 (14.2646)
$H_0 : r = 3$ $H_1 : r = 4$	0.0224 (3.8414)	0.0224 (3.8414)

Note: r is number of cointegrating vector and parenthetical are for 5% critical value.

Table 4. Normalized Cointegrating Vector - Cobb Douglas Production Function

lnY(-1)	C	lnK(-1)	lnL(-1)	lnRE(-1)
1.0000	-31.2325	-2.3059*	2.0857*	1.9905*
		(0.2680)	(1.0019)	(0.7785)
		[-8.6021]	[2.0816]	[2.5567]

Note: * means that coefficient is statistically significant.

RE consumption for both test statistics. In other words, there is at least one cointegrated vector between the series handled.

When the cointegrated vector is normalized according to the reel GDP variable (dependent variable), the Cobb-Douglas production equation summarized in Table 4 has been achieved.

According to Table 4, the marginal physical productivity of the RE, in other words, the output flexibility of the RE has been found to be positive and statistically significant. The output flexibility of the RE shows that a 1% increase in the RE sources leads to nearly 2% increase in real GDP. Based on this situation, it may be claimed that the increase in the use of RE sources in the economy of Turkey gives acceleration to the economic growth, and negative exteriority decrease with the decrease in the release of greenhouse gasses and plays an important role in ensuring sustainable development.

The paper might have implications for academia and make a contribution there e.g. by developing a framework and adding a previously ignored perspectives and additional relevant variables to a framework on RE technologies. It thus contributes filling a gap the authors identified. This framework is empirically tested with econometric model on RE consumption could emerge. The present study then also has practical implications, so makes a contribution to shaping Turkish public policy by e.g. providing policy makers with insights from relevant stakeholder and enable them to look at views from other policy makers from other country context which might also be applied to Turkey context.

CONCLUSION

This paper aimed to develop a conceptual framework for sustainability with RE technologies, policies, and economic approach. The aim of this paper was to scrutinize the experience of Turkey's RE technologies situation for sustainable development. Developing a conceptual framework based on literature and quantative analysis, this study sought to shed light on an under-researched aspect of how sustainable development is affected by RE technologies and other factors. The conceptual framework and the quantitative tests also allowed us to draw a clearer picture of the relationship between RE technologies and sustainable development.

In this paper, this chapter presented evidence from Turkey's RE technologies effects on sustainability with both conceptual and quantitative analyses. For instance, Turkey should fix the impetus in political commitment in shaping Turkey's RE policies and directives with EU collaboration. Furthermore, another striking finding presented in the quantitative analysis is that the RE technologies play a crucial role for sustainability. This study also provides some valuable further intuitions. First, this paper expands the emerging literature in the field of RE technologies and extends the validity of previous findings. Second, this study further develops the conceptual framework based on existing literature. Specifically, the RE technologies are important for encouraging sustainability.

Furthermore, this study is bridge the link between theory and practice. While the authors find out a conceptual framework to review the literature in the first section, the authors proved the conceptual framework with econometric analysis in the second section. This chapter's conceptual model relates to the some propositions, which are main concerns for Turkey, the effectiveness of renewable sources, technological development for RE sources and a higher share of renewable investment are associated with sustainable development. For this propositions evidence, the present paper used input–output approaches and more simple spreadsheets-based analytical models. The results display that there is a long-term relation between reel GDP, capital, labor, and RE consumption.

Renewables help to world energy security of supply, decreasing dependency of fossil fuel sources, and ensure carbon emission opportunities. RE technologies are also cost competitive in today's market. RE sources have a large effect on efforts to reach sustainability, which are crucial to accomplishing sustainability target of Turkey. In this way, Europe requirements for RE sources should be revised considering Turkey's situations. Turkish government should support the national RE sources and use the installed power plants cost-effectively with effective energy policies. In order to decrease the dependency, environmental pollution, and increase the improvement level of the country by raising the economic level of the country, Turkey should use and improve its RE sources efficiently and should encourage new technologies and use all its RE potential.

The conclusions that can be drawn from this study are limited because of its preliminary nature. The limitation is that it was the intention of this study to be constrained with Turkey. The findings, therefore, may not be meaningful to generalize to other country contexts. Furthermore, this study includes mainly the period 1990 to 2014. The application of the model with a reduced number of observations, despite its limitations since it was very difficult to reach wider data in Turkey. The above limitations should be considered in future research.

REFERENCES

Balat, H. (2007). A renewable perspective for sustainable energy development in Turkey: The case of small hydropower plants. *Renewable & Sustainable Energy Reviews*, *11*(9), 2152–2165. doi:10.1016/j.rser.2006.03.002

Balat, H. (2008). Contribution of green energy sources to electrical power production of Turkey: A review. *Renewable & Sustainable Energy Reviews*, *12*(6), 1652–1666. doi:10.1016/j.rser.2007.03.001

Baris, K., & Kucukali, S. (2012). Availability of renewable energy sources in Turkey: Current situation, potential, government policies and the EU perspective. *Energy Policy*, *42*, 377–391. doi:10.1016/j.enpol.2011.12.002

Benli, H. (2013). Potential of renewable energy in electrical energy production and sustainable energy development of Turkey: Performance and policies. *Renewable Energy*, *50*, 33–46. doi:10.1016/j.renene.2012.06.051

Bilen, K., Ozyurt, O., Bakırcı, K., Karslı, S., Erdogan, S., Yılmaz, M., & Comaklı, O. (2008). Energy production, consumption, and environmental pollution for sustainable development: A case study in Turkey. *Renewable & Sustainable Energy Reviews*, *12*(6), 1529–1561. doi:10.1016/j.rser.2007.03.003

Bilgen, S., Keleş, S., Kaygusuz, A., Sarı, A., & Kaygusuz, K. (2008). Global warming and renewable energy sources for sustainable development: A case study in Turkey. *Renewable & Sustainable Energy Reviews*, *12*(2), 372–396. doi:10.1016/j.rser.2006.07.016

Del Rıo, P., & Burguillo, M. (2008). Assessing the impact of renewable energy deployment on local sustainability: Towards a theoretical framework. *Renewable & Sustainable Energy Reviews*, *12*(5), 1325–1344. doi:10.1016/j.rser.2007.03.004

Del Rıo, P., & Burguillo, M. (2009). An empirical analysis of the impact of renewable energy deployment on local sustainability. *Renewable & Sustainable Energy Reviews*, *13*(6-7), 1314–1325. doi:10.1016/j.rser.2008.08.001

Dickey, D., & Fuller, W. A. (1979). Distribution of the Estimators for Autoregressive Time Series with a Unit Root. *Journal of the American Statistical Association*, *74*, 427–431.

Dickey, D., & Fuller, W. A. (1981). Likelihood Ratio Statistics for Autoregressive Time Series with A Unit Root. *Econometrica*, *49*(4), 1057–1072. doi:10.2307/1912517

Erdem, Z. K. (2010). The contribution of renewable sources in meeting Turkeys energy related challenges. *Renewable & Sustainable Energy Reviews*, *9*(9), 2710–2722. doi:10.1016/j.rser.2010.07.003

Hillebrand, B., Buttermann, H., Behringer, J., & Bleuel, M. (2006). The expansion of renewable energies and employment effects in Germany. *Energy Policy*, *34*(18), 3484–3494. doi:10.1016/j.enpol.2005.06.017

Jabareen, Y. (2006). A new conceptual framework for sustainable development. *Environment, Development and Sustainability*, *10*(2), 179–192. doi:10.1007/s10668-006-9058-z

Johansen, S. (1988). Statistical Analysis of Cointegrating Vectors. *Journal of Economic Dynamics & Control*, *12*(2-3), 231–254. doi:10.1016/0165-1889(88)90041-3

Kaya, D. (2006). Renewable energy policies in Turkey. *Renewable & Sustainable Energy Reviews*, *10*(2), 152–163. doi:10.1016/j.rser.2004.08.001

Kaya, D., & Kilic, F. C. (2015). New markets for renewable industries: Developing countries-Turkey, its potential and policies. *Journal of Energy in Southern Africa*, *26*(1), 25–35.

Keleş, S., & Bilgen, S. (2012). Renewable energy sources in Turkey for climate change mitigation and energy sustainability. *Renewable & Sustainable Energy Reviews*, *16*(7), 5199–5206. doi:10.1016/j.rser.2012.05.026

Kolcuoglu, D. (2010). *Renewable Energy: Turkey's Hope for Energy Independence*. Retrieved October 15, 2016, from http://www.hg.org/article.asp?id=24256

Kowsari, R., & Zerriffi, H. (2011). Three dimensional energy profile: A conceptual framework for assessing household energy use. *Energy Policy*, *39*(12), 7505–7517. doi:10.1016/j.enpol.2011.06.030

Musango, J. K., & Brent, A. C. (2011). A conceptual framework for energy technology sustainability assessment. *Energy for Sustainable Development*, *15*(1), 84–91. doi:10.1016/j.esd.2010.10.005

Phillips, P. C. B., & Peron, P. (1988). Testing for a Unit Root in Time Series Regression. *Biometrika*, *75*(2), 336–346. doi:10.1093/biomet/75.2.335

Reddy, V., Uitto, J., Frans, D., & Matin, N. (2006). Achieving global environmental benefits through local development of clean energy? The case of small hilly hydel in India. *Energy Policy*, *34*(18), 4069–4080. doi:10.1016/j.enpol.2005.09.026

Ritchie, J. and Spencer, L. (2002). Qualitative data analysis for applied policy research. *The Qualitative Researcher's Companion*, 305-329.

Robert, K. H. (2000). Tools and concepts for sustainable development, how do they relate to a general framework for sustainable development, and to each other? *Journal of Cleaner Production*, *8*(3), 243–254. doi:10.1016/S0959-6526(00)00011-1

Sirin, S., & Ege, A. (2012). Overcoming problems in Turkeys renewable energy policy: How can EU contribute? *Renewable & Sustainable Energy Reviews*, *16*(7), 4917–4926. doi:10.1016/j.rser.2012.03.067

KEY TERMS AND DEFINITIONS

Cobb-Douglas Production Function: It is a particular functional form of the production function, widely used to represent the technological relationship between the amounts of two or more inputs, particularly physical capital and labor, and the amount of output that can be produced by those inputs.

Conceptual Framework: The belief that it is an analytical frame with several deviations and circumstances.

Cost Competitiveness: A type of evaluating method where a business sets a comparatively low price in order to improve the demand for its product among consumers, as well as its competitive position in the market.

Energy Efficiency: A belief that it is the ratio between the valuable output and input of an energy conversion process.

Environmental Protection: It indicates to any activity to sustain or renovate the quality of environmental issues.

Input-Output Analysis: It is a method of econometric analysis based on interdependencies between economic divisions.

Renewable Energy Technologies: It means that generate clean energy from wind, solar, hydropower, geothermal and biomass resources.

Security of Supply: it is particularly related to the cross-border movement of advocacy equipment for energy sources.

ENDNOTES

1. For detail information about Augmented Dickey-Fuller and Phillips-Peron unit root test, please look at Dickey and Fuller (1979, 1981); Phillips and Peron (1988) studies.
2. For detail information about Johansen cointegration method, please look at Johansen (1988) study.

Chapter 15
Oil and Gas Discoveries in Kenya:
Important Global Exploration and Production Value Chain Lessons for the Society

Nickanor Amwata Owuor
University of Kurdistan – Hewlêr, Iraq

ABSTRACT

This chapter introduces the key constituent activities of the oil and gas industry and aims to outline the core benefits that the recent oil and gas discoveries in Kenya herald to the country's expectant population. It describes and analyzes the global oil and gas industry with a focus on its strategic, financial, and business aspects. It also identifies the opportunities for participation in the industry value chain through which the oil and gas revenues can be of benefit to the Kenyan people. However, the study's focus is on the creation of social value at the community or country level rather than on private shareholder value. Moreover, the chapter only examines upstream activities—that is, exploration and production—even though the implications might also apply to midstream and downstream activities.

INTRODUCTION

The objective of this chapter is to highlight how Oil and Gas, as a new resource bequeathed to the Kenyan society can be used to bring economic and social transformation to the country and people. Thus, the industry dynamics, key constituent activities of the Oil and Gas industry, and value chain opportunities that can benefit the country are explained.

The chapter is organized into five sections, explaining: the history of exploration in Kenya, the industry-community interface, global industry dynamics and stakeholders, the oil and gas value chain, and implications for the future.

DOI: 10.4018/978-1-5225-3147-0.ch015

HISTORY AND HIGHLIGHTS OF EXPLORATION ACTIVITIES IN KENYA

According to the National Oil Corporation of Kenya (nd) there are four principal exploration basins in Kenya: the Lamu Basin, the Anza Basin, the Mandera Basin, and the Tertiary Rift Basin. The exploration basins are split into 46 blocks, out of which 39 are licensed to 22 different operators, including one block that is reserved for the National Oil Corporation of Kenya.

Oil exploration in Kenya began in the 1950s, with the first well being drilled in 1960. British Petroleum and Shell began exploring in Kenya in 1954 in the Lamu Embayment, where they drilled 10 wells. None of the wells were fully evaluated or completed for production, despite several indications of oil staining and untested zones with gas shows. In the following decades, limited exploration yielded nothing.

There has been a renewed and intensified interest in the Kenyan upstream oil and gas (O&G) sector following discoveries of O&G deposits in the country in the last few years and further spurred by earlier similar discoveries in neighboring East African community partner states Uganda and Tanzania.

Currently, the Ministry of Energy and the National Oil Corporation of Kenya are mandated to negotiate and sign contracts on behalf of the Kenyan government with international oil exploration investors to participate in the O&G exploration in Kenya. The terms and conditions of petroleum exploration contracts are subject to negotiation and are governed by:

- The Petroleum (Exploration and Production) Act Cap 308 1986 revised edition.
- The Petroleum (Exploration and Production) Regulations.
- The Income Tax (Amendment) Act made to specify the fiscal regime applicable to petroleum operations.

In addition to the five production sharing contracts (PSCs) that the Kenyan government has entered into with Tullow Oil and its partners for exploration in the Tertiary Rift Basin, the government has also entered into PSCs under which exploration is taking place in the Lamu and Anza basins (Ministry of Energy and Petroleum, 2016). There has been a good deal of transactional activity surrounding these PSCs in recent years, with several new ones lined up. For example, in February 2016, Africa Oil ceded a part of its interest to Maersk Oil of Denmark in a transaction referred to as a "farm in," which is a positive sign, as it signals the entry of a major player in the field apart from just the independents (Maersk Oil, 2016). At the same time, Pancontinental Oil & Gas of Australia and its joint venture partner PTT Exploration and Production Company of Thailand withdrew from Block L10A in the Lamu Basin offshore, where oil had already been discovered, citing high operational costs. Pancontinental held 18.75% interest and PTT held 31.25% interest, leaving the only remaining operator, BG Group, with a 100% stake (Irungu, 2015).

Following exploration activity in recent years, the Ministry of Energy and Petroleum (2016) has indicated that the four basins- that is Lamu, Anza, Mandera and Tertiary Rift have yielded different results. In the Lamu Basin, 20 wells have been dug, out of which 10 indicated traces and out of these 2 discoveries have been made. One with gas and another one with oil. 6 wells in the basin were however declared dry wells. In Anza basin, 17 wells were dug and 9 of them had some show, but only 1 discovery has been made and in total 7 wells were regarded as dry and abandoned. The Tertiary Rift is where the largest number of wells have been dug, that is, 35 in total. Out of these, 4 wells had shown traces. There were also 9 exploration discoveries in this basin. One was found with oil and gas and another one was found dry. The Mandera Basin meanwhile has not provided any positive results. 2 wells were dug but were considered dry even though one of them has just oil seep.

THE INDUSTRY-COMMUNITY INTERFACE IN KENYA

To most Kenyans, especially those from the host communities, these discoveries were a godsend after several decades of unsuccessful exploration outcomes, where many O&G companies, including Exxon, Total, Chevron, Woodside, and CNOOC, tried their luck onshore and offshore in vain. Following Tullow Oil's announcement on 26 March 2012 that, together with its partners Africa Oil and Centric Energy, they had discovered oil in Kenya in the Tertiary Rift Basin, and Pancontinental announcing the striking of natural gas in the Lamu Basin, the chances of Kenya becoming a petroleum exporter excited many, especially in the communities where these deposits are located. While that's the good news, the bad news is that there are already signs of trouble, even before anything is lifted off the ground. Examples include the November 2013 public protests on site in Turkana County, which forced Tullow to cease its operations due to fears of disorder because of a "go-slow" by workers which was followed by a complete strike by employees at the same time (Kavanagh & Manson, 2013). A similar act recurred a year later in October 2014 (Miyungu, 2014; Reuters, 2014).

The disenchantment, however, may also extend beyond Turkana County. For example, in Lamu County, the much-anticipated gas wealth and the prospect of a pipeline and port is one of the reasons fronted for the conflict that has led to the loss of many lives in the county, leading to the declaration of a state of emergency in those areas (Vogt, 2014). Even in other areas where exploration had commenced, such as in Marakwet County and in Kisumu and Kericho counties, locals are already digging in and putting up all manner of demands (Odhiambo, 2014; Kibor, 2016; Laventure, 2016; Kipsang, 2016).

In some sense, one can feel for these locals. Turkana County, for example, is the most remote and desperate region in Kenya, left for years on end without roads, schools, health care, and other amenities. Therefore, the face of Turkana has always been its thousands of emaciated residents, including women, children, and the elderly who continually face starvation, spending days on end without food and with no help in sight every time a drought ravages the country (Human Rights Watch, 2015; Johannes, Zulu & Kalipeni, 2015). At the same time, in most far-flung areas in Northern Kenya, insecurity is an ever-present danger. It is not uncommon to see herdsmen from pastoralist communities carrying sophisticated arms like AK47s. In fact, Control Risks, a security service provider and consultancy firm, rates the security risks in Nairobi and northern and eastern areas of Kenya in the range of moderate to high (Control Risks, 2012). Therefore, for any operator, this is quite a predicament, as they are often easy targets for blame, even though, strictly speaking, any failure may in most instances have nothing to do with the firm. But if not handled properly, the firm's activities may just act as the trigger.

This presents an inherently clear and present danger that calls for all stakeholders to act meticulously, as it is what may determine whether this newfound commonwealth would lead Kenya into a Nigeria-like situation or steer it into prosperity and greatness, as in such countries as Malaysia or the Gulf countries. That is perhaps the main question for all stakeholders to ponder.

The story of how Nigeria, despite being a leading global producer of O&G, has slid into a desperate depth of conflict, corruption, bad governance, poverty, and destitution as a result of the phenomenon commonly known as a "resource curse," tells how discontentment among the impoverished population in the Niger Delta became a breeding ground for militant activities (Mähler, 2010, 2012; Musa, 2008; Sala-i-Martin & Subramanian, 2003; Watts, 2004).

The resource curse is a paradox in the O&G industry where, despite high resource prices, the living standards in many oil-producing countries are low, and the communities largely remain poor. This is unfortunately the case in most of the African O&G-producing countries, such as Nigeria, Angola, and

Chad. This condition has led to the inability of these countries, even though rich in natural resources, to use that wealth to strengthen their economies. Thus, counterintuitively, they have experienced lower economic growth than countries without such an abundance of natural resources (Auty, 1993).

Kenya stands the risk of falling into the same trap. In fact, the Kenyan discovery sites, with their remoteness and lack of development and infrastructure, almost mirror the Niger Delta.

Other African O&G producers are not fairing any better, including Angola, which suffered decades-old civil war, even though it is displaying some signs of progress since the peace treaty was signed in 2002. Even with this semblance of progress, as reflected in the massive infrastructural projects in Angola, this has increased the country's cost of living, thus creating further problems of massive inequality. In fact, Luanda, the capital city, is often categorized as one of the most expensive cities in the world (Dudley, 2011; Ovadia, 2012).

Amidst the newfound wealth the sense of inequity in Angola is demonstrated by the fact that 70% of the population live on US$2 a day or less. At the same time one in six children die before reaching the age of five and more than 150,000 children die each year – making it one of the deadliest place in the world to be a child (Transparency International, 2016).

Chad, Sudan, and South Sudan are embroiled in ongoing strife, which has prevented the O&G gains from trickling down.

In contrast, there are examples of countries, such as Malaysia, Saudi Arabia, and Qatar that have witnessed stellar growth, propelled not only by O&G revenues but also by the O&G value chain opportunities. Ideally, the O&G sector encompasses enormous linkage potential, both forward and backward, that can fuel endogenous growth in all other sectors. In fact, "the extent of the growth impact of oil and gas activities on the larger economy lies not in the growth in output of crude oil per se but the processes and the value-adding functions of factors of production" (Musa, 2008, p. 170).

THE GLOBAL OIL AND GAS INDUSTRY DYNAMICS AND STAKEHOLDERS: A PRIMER

This section offers a primer on the global industry dynamics and stakeholders, painting a picture of the nature of the industry and the typical driving force for different interest groups (e.g., the civil society, the government, and the firm).

The O&G industry is one of the world's largest and most important global industries. It encompasses a range of different activities and processes that jointly contribute to and have the potential for massive transformation of host country communities. These different activities are integrally linked with one another in different ways, either conceptually, contractually, and/or physically. These linkages might occur within or across individual firms and within or across industries or even national boundaries (Inkpen & Moffett, 2011).

The International Energy Agency (2014) predicts that energy demand will rise by an estimated 37% by 2040, and that most of the world's growing energy needs through 2030 will continue to be met by oil, gas, and coal. The industry is therefore all encompassing and touches everyone's lives with products ranging from transportation, heating, electricity fuels, asphalt, lubricants, and propane to thousands of petrochemical products from carpets to eyeglasses to clothing and the like. The industry has a bearing on other issues, including national security, elections, geopolitics, and even international conflicts.

Therefore, the price of crude oil and natural gas are invariably the two most closely observed commodity prices in the global economy.

However, O&G capital projects are becoming ever more complex. O&G firms thus continuously find themselves venturing into new frontiers and unfamiliar terrain, extracting unconventional resources, managing intricate supply chains, and complying with rigorous environmental, health, and safety regulations, all of which present huge challenges. Even the most successful companies routinely suffer cost and schedule overruns (Inkpen & Moffett, 2011).

The industry is undergoing massive disruption, even as the global population continues to be extremely reliant on these organic energy sources. This necessitates a thorough look at the emerging new macro and micro trends affecting the industry.

According to Inkpen and Moffett (2011), there are often various kinds of stakeholders in the O&G industry with wide-ranging interests, stakes, and rights in the value chain. They can be delineated as financial stakeholders, business stakeholders, social stakeholders, and internal stakeholders as well as different government organizations and regulators, equity exchanges, social and environmental interest groups, and nongovernmental organizations.

There are two primary financial stakeholders of the firm who are the providers of capital for both investment and operation: the shareholders and the creditors. Shareholders are the actual owners of the firm, holding title to the firm's assets and operations as a result of their capital investments. Creditors, who typically provide bank loans (more common in Europe and Asia) or debt markets (more common in Anglo-American markets), lend capital to the firm in exchange for promised repayment of both the principal amount and the return (interest).

The business stakeholders are comprised of the firm's suppliers and customers as well as its employees, including management and leadership, who represent the core of what business strategists term the firm's value chain of internal stakeholders.

The communities and the society represent the social stakeholders. Social stakeholders are more distant from the firm's actual operations and transactions than other stakeholders but can still have a large influence on or be influenced by the success or failure of the corporation (Inkpen & Moffett, 2011, p. 46).

Each stakeholder category has a different voice in the vision, strategy, and operation of the firm. While the government will always want to maximize resource revenues, the employees and management will always want better pay and working conditions, and the communities will always want everything ranging from sustainable livelihoods to water. The owners, financiers, regulators, and nongovernmental organizations often also have diverse stakes to claim from the firm. Therefore, balancing these various and divergent interests is very important for the firm's smooth operation.

OIL AND GAS VALUE CHAIN

According to the American Petroleum Institute (n.d.), "the oil and natural gas supply chains can be complicated and sometimes obscure systems to many who rely on their products and services." The concept of value chain analysis is a generic business analysis tool that was first proposed by Porter (1985) in his famous book Competitive Advantage, in which he suggests that, to be competitive, the firm should investigate the sequence of consecutive activities that are required to convey value to the market by delivering a product or service to the customer.

It involves a thorough study of the entire chain from conception and procurement, through the different phases of production and distribution, to the final customer. Such analysis is relevant and can be performed for individual firms or even for groups of firms whose value chains are intertwined—usually business partners, such as suppliers, distributors/sellers, and customers for selected industries (within or across national borders).

In the O&G industry, the typical major value chain stages include development, production, processing, transportation, and marketing of hydrocarbon. These are usually classified as upstream, midstream, and downstream in industry parlance.

The upstream (also known as Exploration and Production or E&P) is the aspect of the industry which deals with bringing crude oil and gas from under the ground to the surface. While the midstream deals with the wholesale marketing of the unrefined hydrocarbons, storing them in oil and gas terminals, tanks and so on for onward shipment as well as well as physically transporting them through various means like pipeline, rail, ships or tankers and even trucks from the site of production to refineries and deliver the various refined products onward to downstream distributors. The downstream on the other hand deals with refining, processing and purifying the different grades of crude oil and gas and the marketing and distribution of these together with other commercial products derived from oil and gas commonly known as petrochemicals. The petrochemicals here include literally a range of thousands of derivatives from oil and gas such as fertilizers, lubricants, plastics, asphalt, etc. The players in the industry are often characterized as integrated oil companies (IOCs), national oil companies, the independents as well as the oil service companies. The abbreviation IOC is also often used to refer to international oil companies, which basically means such kind of companies whose operations stretch over several countries, be they integrated, independents or service companies. The integrated are vertically integrated companies with global operations spanning the entire oil and gas value chain. The big five oil companies-that is, Royal Dutch/Shell, Exxon –Mobil, BP, Chevron and Total which are massive in size and have operations cutting across downstream, midstream and downstream. They are also known as the "oil majors. "The independents on the other hand are Medium-size independent companies that operate in a specific kinds of markets, region or country, or even internationally. Examples include players such as Anadarko, Tullow, etc. The national oil companies (NOCs) are majority-owned by the government, and are mostly responsible for managing production and defending their national interests in the oil and gas sector in the host countries. Many of the leading producing countries have a national oil and gas companies like Saudi Aramco in Saudi Arabia, Nigerian National Petroleum Corporation (NNPC) in Nigeria, Sonangol in Angola, Petróleos Mexicanos (PEMEX) in Mexico and Petróleos de Venezuela SA (PDVSA) in Venezuela etc. Some of the NOCs have grown so big and have operations across several countries that they can also be classified as internal oil companies (IOCs) rivaling the oil majors. Chinese NOCs represent some of the kind of firms.

Oil and gas service companies represent firms that provide products, services and technology to the O & G industry. Examples of such firms include Schlumberger, Weatherford, Halliburton, etc. They deliver specific technical expertise, such as geophysical surveys and drilling, well flow management, etc. Also in this class of firms include engineering companies such as Technip which have expertise in project management, engineering and construction for the O & G industry.

What Do Exploration and Production Companies Buy, and What Are the Value Chain Opportunities?

Procurement in exploration and production (E&P) is big business, as O&G companies buy several kinds of goods and services to support their global operations. "Activities involved in exploration and production (E&P) are seismic surveying, drilling, rig construction and land management, among others" (Kavi, 2009, p. S9). For example, see Achilles (2014) for a complete list containing hundreds of products and services, each representing tremendous opportunities for local community development.

In industry parlance, local content refers to the inclusion of local firms and communities in the value chain and is a term that has increasingly found its place not only in the O&G industry but also in other extractive industries. More precisely, the term is generally used to refer to

> *...the added value brought to a host nation (national, regional and local areas in that country...) through the activities of the oil and gas industry. This may be measured . . . and undertaken through activities such as but not limited to workforce development... investments in supplier development... [and] community development. (International Petroleum Industry Environmental Conservation Association, 2013)*

Norway has received accolades as one of the first countries to adopt local content requirements via legislation. This enabled the country to move from almost zero local content in the 1960s when it first discovered the resource to 50% within a decade. Brazil followed suit with similar arrangements (Ernst & Young, 2014). Several other O&G-producing countries have in the recent past been in a race to try to adopt local content in various ways, either through influence or via legislative regulatory frameworks. For example, efforts to boost local content have gathered momentum in countries such as Nigeria, Angola, Kazakhstan, Tanzania, Ghana, Uganda Equatorial Guinea, Indonesia, and Russia. In each of these countries, the provisions and implementation of local content varies from the very stringent ones, which carry hefty penalties for noncompliance, as in Kazakhstan, to less stringent ones, which are more lenient (Esteves, Coyne & Moreno, 2013). Therefore, local content has emerged as a priority strategy for many operators and host countries who are moving away from mere rent to seek more inclusive and sustainable growth.

Tullow Oil, one of the leading independent E&P firms in emerging markets such as Africa, works "to maximise participation of local businesses within our supply chain to ensure the oil and gas sector creates positive impacts on the economies and lives of local communities where we operate" (Tullow Oil PLC, 2016). The company reportedly spent US$309 million with local suppliers globally in 2015.

Local Content in O&G in Kenya: How "Local" Is Local?

Although the O&G sector is still nascent in Kenya and there is no primary local content legislation, even though it has been proposed, other legislation, such as the Petroleum Act, is not explicit, and it is only indicated more explicitly in the PSC signed with the company. According to a study by Adam Smith International (2015), the potential for E&P total local content spending in the country is in the range of between USD 300 million to USD 700 million just for exploration activity while the potential for construction activity ranges between USD 400 million to USD 1 billion. However that is just the potential which is obviously huge. The estimated actual local content capture is much smaller and ranges between USD 60 million to USD 120 million for exploration. While for construction activity it ranges between USD 120 million and USD 300 million for construction activity. This reflects a huge deficit.

For Tullow Oil, in their Kenyan operations, the company's total spent with Kenyan suppliers has been growing steadily over the years, in line with their increased operational activity. The total amount spent on local content stood at Kenyan Shillings (KES) 4.1 billion in 2013, up from KES2.4 billion in 2012 and KES2.1 billion in 2011 (one U.S. dollar is approximately 101 KES). This has also been due to sensitization of contractors on the need to optimize local content (Tullow Oil, 2014).

The capacity of local firms is however considered to be very limited in most of the core areas of exploration and production. According to Adam Smith International (2015) areas where local firms have proven capacity to deliver include indirect or support services such as: transport, accommodation, catering, office supplies, etc. However, when it comes to specialist, direct and core services such as the range of rig site services then their capacity to deliver, whether technical or financial is lacking or very limited. This is however understandable since it normally takes several years to develop such capacity. Therefore one of the ways of developing such capacity effectively is through local content provisions.

However, out of the KES4.1 billion Tullow Oil spent with local suppliers in 2013, only KES259 million was with local community businesses (i.e., businesses in Turkana County in Kenya), representing only 6.3%. This effort has, however, not placated everyone. This appears to have infuriated local leaders, especially Turkana parliament leaders, who recently converged and issued very strong statements at press conferences in Nairobi, suggesting that it might just be the lull before a storm (Njagi, 2016).

In its report for 2013, Tullow Oil (2014) indicated a commitment to transparency about government payments, believing this enables communities, citizens, and governments to have a constructive debate on the sustainable management of oil revenues. The total payments amounted to KES6.1 billion in 2013, with payments made to all Kenyan stakeholder groups, including taxes to the national government, expenditures with local suppliers, and discretionary investment in community projects. The distribution includes:

- **Social Investment:** 0.1 billion Kenya Shillings
- **Local Content Expenditure:** 4.1 billion Kenya Shillings
- **Payments to Government and Agencies:** 1.9 billion Kenya Shillings

After the brief unrest witnessed in 2013 that was triggered by community concerns over local employment and business opportunities which halted operations momentarily in Blocks 10BB and 13T, Tullow Oil has seemingly realized the need for a more proactive stakeholder engagement, especially with the community. Working together with the government, the company was able to establish a Memorandum of Understanding in which a way forward was set out and sought to improve both impact management and stakeholder engagement. As a result, the company has enhanced and expanded capacity-building initiatives aimed at encouraging local entrepreneurs to participate in the value chain.

In its employment of subcontractors, the company has also endeavored to align itself with community needs. Tullow Oil has employed more than 2,000 subcontractors through its network of suppliers; as a result of this realignment, the total Turkana workforce shot up to 59% among the total subcontractors employed through the company's supply chain in 2013. However, the bulk of these are in the unskilled and semiskilled categories representing 677(98%) and 380 (78%) respectively. In upper categories, the representation of Turkanas is still very small - that is, only 2 out of 72 in the management category and none at all at the director level. The figures do not include Tullow's own direct employees (Tullow Oil, 2014).

However, even though community engagement seems to have been stepped up in Turkana, the biggest operational area so far, which deserves credit, there are other indications that there may not be much of that for other exploration sites, such as Elgeyo Marakwet and Kericho/Kisumu. Therefore, at other sites like Kisumu, where Tullow Oil has set up base in Onyuongo in Nyakach, things may not be faring very well. In August 2015, I conducted some interviews with several youth in the area, which also happens to be within a 3-kilometer radius from my maternal grandparents' home.

The level of information asymmetry and apathy toward the operation was very apparent. Several youth had a lot to say, and the following sentiments captured their most pressing thoughts:

Interview Responses:

What we have been told is that the land here has a lot of potential and we may be asked to vacate soon. Should we be asked to vacate then the company will have to pay us large sums since this is our ancestral land.

The area Chief is my uncle and we were promised by him that this project will bring us jobs. But where are the jobs?

We cannot even do business with the company. They have not told us what they need so that we can supply. All we see are big cars and police escort.

This place as you can see is very dry and what we are lacking is water. When such a project is launched in our area we expect them to bring us water. The water they use is brought from Kisumu and we just watch from a distance as they consume it while we as a community go thirsty.

We have a youth group but do not understand what this company needs that we can collect our little savings and supply. It can make us money. I believe if we get the tender then even banks can give us loans.

We expect other institutions to come here. Banks and even universities will come here and we are not yet sure how to prepare ourselves for their coming.

A few were hired supposedly to provide security but they do not seem to have much to do since all the security work is already provided by the police.

This area is prone to violence because of cattle rustling from other neighboring communities around. With such a project that cuts across the border, the issue of insecurity should be addressed immediately. (Interview, August 20, 2015)

In yet another site, Kerio Valley, Elgeyo Marakwet County, where Tullow Oil indicated recently that drilling had revealed chances of significant deposits, ultimatums have been issued with aptly crafted slogans such as "no roads, no oil" or "no title deeds, no oil" (Kipsang, 2016).

Development Challenges in Kenya

Even though Kenya is touted as one of the fast-developing economies in the "Africa Rising" narrative, the reality points to a completely different picture that suggests it might only be a paper tiger, as there is quite a lot beneath the surface. The country was bedeviled by fiscal deficit equal to about 8% of GDP in 2015/2016. Public debt was Kenya Shillings (KES) 3,706 billion in 2016, equivalent to 52.7% of GDP. This continues to threaten the fiscal sustainability in the long run.

Some of the myriad identifiable challenges that the Kenyan society continues to face, and with which every oil and gas operator may have to contend, include the following:

- **Poverty, Unemployment, and Inequality:** The bifurcation of the country's society along the lines of rich and poor is worrisome. According to the 2015 United Nations Development Programme Human Development Report, 48% of the estimated Kenyan population of 45.5 million lives below the poverty line. The country ranked 145 out of 188 countries and territories surveyed and is ranked sixth among the top 10 countries in Sub-Saharan Africa, with a large percentage of the population living in extreme poverty. All the indicators for health, education and standard of living point to multidimensional deprivation for this sizeable population. In addition, upwards of 70% of the young working class—almost 10 million people—are unemployed (United Nations Development Programme, 2015). This presents a serious threat to the country's security, as a large number of these unemployed youth end up engaging in criminal activities or even becoming radicalized and joining such terrorist organizations as Alshabab, which has active cells in the country and in neighboring Somalia. It is estimated that up to 700 Kenyan youths have joined the ranks of Alshabab, and the main reason cited for this is unemployment (Schifrin& Fannin, 2016).
- **Poor Infrastructure:** Critical infrastructure, such as roads, schools, water, energy, and health care, still present a serious problem in Kenya. There are large swathes of the country that have no access to such critical infrastructure. For example, northern parts of Kenya have been so neglected by successive regimes that many people die due to lack of access to health care, and illiteracy is very high because there are no schools in expansive areas. The matter of poor road networks in Kenya is constantly in the news. Hardly a week passes without a news item about communities protesting about poor roads or even the lack of roadways. Such protests stretch the entire length and breadth of the country.
- **Climate Change:** Climate change has increasingly become a serious matter of concern for the entire world but even more so in the developing world. In Kenya, the population faces increasing danger due to climate change that has severely affected the country, particularly through rising risks of droughts and floods. According to Human Rights Watch (2015) Turkana County, for example, and other areas in northern Kenya are at the precipice.
- **Tribalism:** In a country such as Kenya, where political and ethnic competition often lead to various forms of violence as witnessed in the 2007–2008 post-election violence that raged for 3 months and claimed upwards of 1,500 lives. Sometimes the reaons for tribal conflict can be as baffling as cattle rustling, which is an outdated traditional practice by certain communities. This is something which should not even find itself in the modern age.
- **Corruption:** Corruption in its various manifestations is endemic in Kenya. It is reported that the country loses 400 billion Kenyan Shillings annually due to corruption. The country ranks 139 out of 168 with an index of 25 according to Transparency International, the Berlin based global

good governance and anticorruption crusader. (Transparency International, 2016). The bulk of the corruption taking place can be characterized as white-collar corruption—that is, the kind of corruption perpetuated by people who are enlightened and would have most likely passed through university.

The O&G discoveries present an opportunity and economic stimulus for the country to navigate through these development challenges. Other than revenues earned by the government through various taxes imposed on the sector, a greater opportunity lies in local content opportunities.

Local Content and Transparency in the Oil and Gas Sector

Although there are arguments in favor of local content in the sense that it is seen as a way of spurring development, counterarguments have also surfaced as to whether it is not just some form of neo-protectionism in an age where companies, especially O&G companies, should be seeking international competitiveness (Warner, 2011).

This presents a tough choice for the firm, especially in cases where local content requirements are anchored in regulations, given that as much as they may be willing to do business with local firms, in some cases, it may prove quite difficult to get such firms with the requisite competency to deliver on projects with precision like their more well-experienced global counterparts.

Another reason why the local content requirements are sometimes viewed with suspicion is that, in some instances, the supposed local firms awarded the contracts end up being shell companies and used only as conduits for corruption. Even employment opportunities granted as part of such requirements are often fraught with cronyism and political interference (Martini & Transparency International, 2014).

Even though the sector is still nascent in the county, an alarm has been raised by the Kenya Civil Society Platform on Oil and Gas and by Oxfam. Among the issues noted include fears for the environment, limited stakeholder engagement, and the lack of sufficient transparency, especially on the part of the government (Hubert, 2016).

In Kenya, even though Article 35 of the Constitution recognizes the right of the citizens to demand public information held by the state, the appropriate legislative framework meant to make it possible and to facilitate such access is still dragging before Parliament. This has been one of the longest-running legislative attempts in Kenya, having taken more than 14 years before Parliament (Mutahi, 2015). The Kenyan government has continued to exploit this weakness and does not reveal to the public any dealings in the O&G sector. Thus, the general public has no idea as to what may be accrued to the state in the form of state-owned company production entitlements, profits and taxes, royalties and dividends, licenses and concessions fees, or any other significant government benefits. This is contrary to the requirements of Article 35 of the Kenyan Constitution.

According to the Norway-based Extractive Industries Transparency Initiative (2016), which promotes public awareness about how countries manage their oil, gas, and mineral resources, Kenya is not among the countries declared compliant and is neither a candidate country trying to achieve desired transparency.

It is evident from the forgoing discussions that there is a lot at stake in Kenya and transparency is lacking in the O&G operations and that if this is not corrected then the industry would be facing some serious problems in the not so distant future.

IMPLICATIONS FOR THE FUTURE OF THE INDUSTRY

Energy and man can never really be separated. As long as human beings require a source of electricity, heating, and fuel, and as long as there will still be a source of supply for these, the demand for O&G cannot in the foreseeable future be discounted. The number of cars being manufactured bear witness to O&G's sustainable influence. Because of the convenience provided by O&G, and the ready availability of, previously, oil and now gas, it is not easy to fathom a world without O&G, the necessary supply.

But while the demand might have continued to ascend for many years now, the supply has not been commensurate. At the same time, the price has been shaky, making the supply countries wary. For example, the Organization of the Petroleum Exporting Countries has faced the worst fears caused by the oil price fluctuation, and the free open market has not fared much better.

A majority of the world's leading producers have had to contend with depressed prices over the years.

It was likely not thought possible that, in 2014–2015, the price of oil would plummet to as low as $30 or below per barrel. This is especially because the price of oil had rallied to as high as $100 dollars per barrel in the preceding years.

Therefore, on the demand and supply side, even though the factors still remain the same, price has never been left to demand and supply factors alone. Instead, there are a variety of geopolitical issues that have increasingly played a part in the determination of prices. For example, in recent years, the animosity among major producers in the Middle East, Iran, and the Kingdom of Saudi Arabia has been a major impediment in the stabilization of prices. At the same time, the instability that has been experienced in Iraq, Syria, and Yemen, some of the major producers in the region, has not helped matters. The security situation in Iraq, for example, has occasioned the halting of production from some of the major oil fields, while some of the oil fields have also fallen into the hands of the Islamic State terrorist group. Even the distribution side has been severely affected in Iraq in recent years due to the constant threats and attacks on the midstream and downstream infrastructures.

The emergence of the Islamic State terrorist group proves the point. Some of the major producing fields in Iraq and Syria have been cut off. Such distribution infrastructures as pipelines have been destroyed in some parts, resulting in reduced production, distribution bottlenecks, and smuggling of product.

For example, it is reported that the Islamic State might have been smuggling oil out of the territory it holds in Iraq and Syria for as low as USD$25 per barrel. Such are the events that have contributed to the distortion in the marketplace in recent years.

These threaten the future of potential new oil producers in the rest of the world like Kenya. Thus, despite having a limited potential of only 600 billion barrels in some of its discovered oil fields, Kenya stands at risk as a result of these geopolitical factors. As a result, local content policy presents the greatest opportunity for maximum impact to be felt on the ground for local communities.

CONCLUSION

The chapter initiates a descriptive but important discussion on the potential benefit of the oil and gas resource to the Kenyan society. The study's focus is on the creation of social value at the community or country level rather than on private shareholder value. Moreover, the chapter only examines upstream activities—that is, exploration and production—even though the implications might also apply to midstream and downstream activities. Therefore, it may be of interest for future research to quantify the benefits and impact of the entire industry value chain in the country.

REFERENCES

Achilles. (2014). *Achilles oil & gas product and service codes.* Retrieved June 30, 2016, from http://www.achilles.com/images/locale/en-EN/communities/east-africa-oil-and-gas/pdf/Achilles-Oil-and-Gas-Product-and-Service-Codes.pdf

Adam Smith International. (2015). *Kenya Extractive Industries Development Programme: Extractives industry local content early gap analysis summary report.* Retrieved June 30, 2016, from http://www.adamsmithinternational.com/documents/resource-uploads/Extractives_Local_Content_in_Kenya.pdf

American Petroleum Institute. (n.d.). *Oil & natural gas supply chains.* Retrieved June 30, 2016, from http://www.api.org/Policy-and-Issues/Policy-Items/Safety/Understanding-the-oil-natural-gas-supply-chains

Auty, R. M. (1993). *Sustaining development in mineral economies: The resource curse thesis.* London: Routledge.

Control Risks. (2012). *A new frontier: Oil and gas in East Africa.* Retrieved June 30, 2016, from https://www.controlrisks.com/~/media/Public%20Site/Files/Our%20Thinking/east_africa_whitepaper_LR_web.pdf

Dudley, N. (2011). Supplement: Angola - Economy - A private key to sustained growth. *The Banker.*

Ernst & Young. (2014). *Creating shared value in Africa: Local content in the oil and gas industry.* Retrieved from http://www.ey.com/Publication/vwLUAssets/EY-creating-shared-value-in-africa/$FILE/EY-creating-shared-value-in-africa.pdf

Esteves, A. M., Coyne, B., & Moreno, A. (2013). *Local Content Initiatives: Enhancing the Sub-National Benefits of the Oil, Gas, and Mining Sectors.* Retrieved June 30, 2016, from http://www.resourcegovernance.org/sites/default/files/Sub_Enhance_Benefits_20151125.pdf

Extractive Industries Transparency Initiative. (2016). *EITI Progress Report 2016- From Reports to Results.* Retrieved June 30, 2016, from https://eiti.org/files/progressreport.pdf

Hubert, D. (2016). *The Use of Tax Havens in the Ownership of Kenyan Petroleum Rights.* Retrieved June 30, 2016, from https://www.oxfam.org/sites/www.oxfam.org/files/file_attachments/rr-tax-havens-kenyan-petroleum-rights-100516-en_0.pdf

Human Rights Watch. (2015). *"There is No Time Left" Climate Change, Environmental Threats, and Human Rights in Turkana County, Kenya.* Retrieved from https://www.hrw.org/report/2015/10/15/there-no-time-left/climate-change-environmental-threats-and-human-rights-turkana

Inkpen, A. C., & Moffett, M. H. (2011). *The global oil & gas industry: Management, strategy & finance.* Tulsa, OK: PennWell.

International Energy Agency. (2014). *World energy outlook 2014.* Retrieved June 30, 2016, from https://www.iea.org/Textbase/npsum/WEO2014SUM.pdf

International Petroleum Industry Environmental Conservation Association. (2013). *Social and economic development.* Retrieved from http://www.ipieca.org/topic/social-responsibility/social-and-economic-development

Irungu, G. (2015, June 2). Australian explorer pulls out of second Lamu oil block. *Business Daily.* Retrieved June 30, 2016, from http://www.businessdailyafrica.com/Australian-explorer-pulls-out-of-second-Lamu-oil-block-/-/539552/2737918/-/br6rt7z/-/index.html

Johannes, E. M., Zulu, L. C., & Kalipeni, E. (2015). Oil discovery in Turkana County, Kenya: A source of conflict or development? *African Geographical Review*, *34*(2), 142–164. doi:10.1080/19376812.2014.884466

Kavi, K. (2009). The upstream energy value chain. *Oil & Gas Journal*, *107*(45), S9–S11.

Kibor, F. (2014, October 2). Tullow told to unveil exploration plan for Kerio Valley and Elgeyo Marakwet. *The Standard.* Retrieved June 30, 2016, from http://www.standardmedia.co.ke/article/2000136815/tullow-told-to-unveil-exploration-plan-for-kerio-valley-and-elgeyo-marakwet

Kipsang, W. (2016, March 29). Showdown as Elgeyo-Marakwet, Turkana county leaders give terms for exploration. *Daily Nation.* Retrieved June 30, 2016, from http://www.nation.co.ke/news/Leaders-want-title-deeds-before-oil-exploration/-/1056/3137222/-/4hmjhp/-/index.html

Laventure, L. (2016). *How the search for oil is inflaming tensions in Kenya.* Retrieved June 30, 2016, from http://www.aljazeera.com/indepth/features/2016/03/search-oil-inflaming-tensions-kenya-160302094606486.html

Maersk Oil. (2016, February 3). *Maersk Oil completes acquisition of East African licences* (Press release). Retrieved June 30, 2016, from http://www.maerskoil.com/media/newsroom/pages/maersk_oil_completes_acquisition_of_east_african_licences.aspx

Mahler, A. (2010). *Nigeria: A prime example of the resource curse? Revisiting the oil-violence link in the Niger Delta.* Retrieved June 30, 2016, from https://www.giga-hamburg.de/en/system/files/publications/wp120_maehler.pdf

Mahler, A. (2012). An inescapable curse? Resource management, violent conflict, and peacebuilding in the Niger Delta. In P. Lujala & S. A. Rustad (Eds.), *High-value natural resources and post-conflict peacebuilding* (pp. 391–412). London: Routledge.

Martini & Transparency International. (2014). *Local content policies and corruption in the oil and gas industry.* Retrieved June 30, 2016, from http://www.u4.no/publications/local-content-policies-and-corruption-in-the-oil-and-gas-industry/

Ministry of Energy and Petroleum. (2016). *Basinal wells.* Retrieved June 30, 2016, from http://www.energy.go.ke/index.php/petroleum-areas-of-interest/file/873-basinal-wells.html

Miyungu, J. N. (2014, October 12). Tullow faces worker unrest at Turkana exploration sites. *The Standard.* Retrieved June 30, 2016, from http://www.standardmedia.co.ke/business/article/2000137914/tullow-faces-worker-unrest-at-turkana-exploration-sites

Musa, J. I. (2008). Growth prospects of oil and gas abundant economies: The Nigerian experience (1970–2000). *Journal of Economic Studies (Glasgow, Scotland)*, *35*(2), 170–190. doi:10.1108/01443580810870155

Mutahi, P. (2015, September 29). Access to information is a fundamental right, so we need laws to make it possible. *Daily Nation.* Retrieved June 30, 2016, from http://www.nation.co.ke/oped/Opinion/Access-to-information-is-a-fundamental-right/-/440808/2888946/-/n8a9eb/-/index.html

National Oil Corporation of Kenya. (n.d.). *Oil and Gas Exploration History in Kenya*. Retrieved June 30, 2016, from http://nationaloil.co.ke/site/3.php?id=1

Njagi, J. (2016, March 24). Not so fast, say Turkana MPs as they vow to block pipeline works. *Daily Nation*. Retrieved June 30, 2016, from http://www.nation.co.ke/news/Oil-bid-suffers-fresh-hitch-as-MPs-vow-to-block-works/-/1056/3131484/-/us7i92z/-/index.html

Odhiambo, M. (2014, June 25). Company rules out payment for land in oil search. *Daily Nation*. Retrieved June 30, 2016, from http://mobile.nation.co.ke/counties/Company-rules-out-payment-for-land-in-oil-search/-/1950480/2361950/-/format/xhtml/-/dtj55d/-/index.html

Onuoha, G. (2016). *A 'rising Africa' in a resource-rich context: Change, continuity and implications for development*. Academic Press.

Ovadia, J. (2012). The dual nature of local content in Angolas oil and gas industry: Development vs. elite accumulation. *Journal of Contemporary African Studies*, *30*(3), 395–417. doi:10.1080/02589001.2012.701846

Porter, M. E. (1985). *Competitive advantage: Creating and sustaining superior performance*. New York, NY: The Free Press.

Sala-i-Martin, X., & Subramanian, A. (2003). *Addressing the natural resource curse: An illustration from Nigeria*. Cambridge, MA: National Bureau of Economic Research. doi:10.3386/w9804

Schifrin, N., & Fannin, Z. (2016). *How Al-Shabab is recruiting young men from Kenya*. Retrieved June 30, 2016, from http://www.pbs.org/newshour/bb/how-al-shabaab-is-recruiting-young-men-from-kenya/

Transparency International. (2016). *Corruption Perceptions Index 2015*. Retrieved June 30, 2016, from http://www.transparency.org/cpi2015#downloads

Tullow Oil P. L. C. (2014). *Tullow in Kenya*. Retrieved June 30, 2016, from http://www.tullowoil.com/Media/docs/default-source/operations/tullow-kenya-profile.pdf?sfvrsn=2

Tullow Oil P. L. C. (2016). *About local content*. Retrieved June 30, 2016, from http://www.tullowoil.com/suppliers/about-local-content

United Nations Development Programme. (2015). *Human Development Indicators*. Retrieved June 30, 2016, from http://hdr.undp.org/en/countries/profiles/KEN

Vogt, H. (2014, August 19). Violence Imperils Kenya Port Project: Land Disputes, Terrorism Threaten Plan to Turn Coastal Region Into Economic Hub. *The Wall Street Journal*. Retrieved June 30, 2016, from http://www.wsj.com/articles/violence-imperils-kenya-port-project-1408490217

Warner, M. (2011). *Local content in procurement: Creating local jobs and competitive domestic industries in supply chains*. Sheffield, UK: Greenleaf Pub.

Watts, M. (2004). Resource curse? Governmentality, oil and power in the Niger Delta, Nigeria. *Geopolitics*, *9*(1), 50–80. doi:10.1080/14650040412331307832

KEY TERMS AND DEFINITIONS

Downstream: The operations at the final stage of the oil and gas value chain which include the processing, storage and transportation of crude oil and natural gas, refining, distribution and retail services for final products and byproducts.

Exploration and Production: The process that involves searching and extracting oil and gas onshore or offshore. Also known as upstream.

Inclusive Development: The perspective which ensures that all marginalized and excluded groups are recognized and incorporated as stakeholders in development processes.

Local Content: The value, volume or percentage of locally sourced materials, worker, finances, goods and services rendered to the oil and gas industry.

Midstream: The operations after production of crude oil and natural gas which involve transportation of crude oil and liquid natural gas via networks of pipelines, rail, trucks, tankers and barges from the oil fields to the major markets, passing through several pumping stations.

Upstream: The operations which enables the firm to discover and produce crude oil and natural gas. Also known as exploration and production.

Value Chain: A whole set of interrelated activities that enable the firm to transform inputs into outputs which, in turn, add to the bottom line and enable the firm to create competitive advantage.

Value Sharing: Generating economic value for the firm in a way that generates value for society as well by helping the society to address its challenges.

Compilation of References

Aaker, D. (1994). Building a Brand: The Saturn Story. *California Management Review*, *36*(2), 114–121. doi:10.2307/41165748

Aakhus, M., & Bzdak, M. (2012). Revisiting the Role of Shared Value in the Business-Society Relationship. *Business & Professional Ethics Journal*, *31*(2), 231–246. doi:10.5840/bpej201231211

Abdelkafi, N., & Täuscher, K. (2016). Business Models for Sustainability From a System Dynamics Perspective. *Organization & Environment*, *29*(1), 74–96. doi:10.1177/1086026615592930

Abo, T. (2014). Researching international transfer of the Japanese-style management and production system: Hybrid factories in six continents. *Asian Business & Management*, *14*(1), 5–35. doi:10.1057/abm.2014.13

Achilles. (2014). *Achilles oil & gas product and service codes*. Retrieved June 30, 2016, from http://www.achilles.com/images/locale/en-EN/communities/east-africa-oil-and-gas/pdf/Achilles-Oil-and-Gas-Product-and-Service-Codes.pdf

Ackerman, R. W. (1973). How Companies Respond to Social Demands. *Harvard University Review*, *51*(4), 88–98.

Adam Smith International. (2015). *Kenya Extractive Industries Development Programme: Extractives industry local content early gap analysis summary report*. Retrieved June 30, 2016, from http://www.adamsmithinternational.com/documents/resource-uploads/Extractives_Local_Content_in_Kenya.pdf

Adams, R. B., Licht, A. N., & Sagiv, L. (2011). Shareholders and stakeholders: How do directors decide? *Strategic Management Journal*, *32*(12), 1331–1355. doi:10.1002/smj.940

Adner, R., & Kapoor, R. (2010). Value creation in innovation ecosystems: How the structure of technological interdependence affects firm performance in technology generations. *Strategic Management Journal*, *31*(3), 306–333. doi:10.1002/smj.821

Afrin, S. (2013). Traditional vs strategic corporate social responsibility: In pursuit of supporting sustainable development. *Journal of Economics and Sustainable Development*, *4*(20), 153–157.

Agatz, N., Erera, A., Savelsbergh, M., & Wang, X. (2012). Optimization for dynamic ride-sharing: A review. *European Journal of Operational Research*, *223*(2), 295–303. doi:10.1016/j.ejor.2012.05.028

Agle, B. R., Donaldson, T., Freeman, R. E., Jensen, M. C., Mitchell, R. K., & Wood, D. J. (2008). Dialogue: Toward superior stakeholder theory. *Business Ethics Quarterly*, *18*(2), 153–190. doi:10.5840/beq200818214

Agle, B. R., Mitchell, R. K., & Sonnenfeld, J. A. (1999). Who Matters to CEOs? An Investigation of Stakeholder Attributes and Salience, Corporate Performance and CEO Values. *Academy of Management Journal*, *42*(5), 507–526. doi:10.2307/256973

Ahmad, N. H., Nasurdin, A. M., Halim, H. A., & Taghizadeh, S. K. (2013). The Pursuit of Entrepreneurial Initiatives at the Silver Age: From the Lens of Malaysian Silver Entrepreneurs. *Procedia: Social and Behavioral Sciences*, *129*, 305–313. doi:10.1016/j.sbspro.2014.03.681

Ahmed, N. Z., Montagno, R. V., & Firenze, R. J. (1998). Organizational Performance and Environmental Consciousness: An Empirical Study. *Management Decision*, *36*(2), 57–62. doi:10.1108/00251749810204124

Airoldi, G., Brunetti, G., & Coda, V. (2005). *Economia Aziendale*. Bologna, Italy: Il Mulino.

Albert, M. (1993). *Capitalism Against Capitalism*. London: Whurr.

Albinsson, P. A., & Perera, B. Y. (2012). Alternative marketplaces in the 21st century: Building community through sharing events. *Journal of Consumer Behaviour*, *11*(4), 303–315. doi:10.1002/cb.1389

Aleandri, G., & Refrigeri, L. (2013). Lifelong Learning, Training and Education in Globaized Economic Systems: Analysis and Perspectives. *Procedia: Social and Behavioral Sciences*, *93*(21), 1242–1248. doi:10.1016/j.sbspro.2013.10.022

Alexander, C. R., & Cohen, M. A. (1999). Why do corporations become criminals? Ownership, hidden actions, and crime as an agency cost. *Journal of Corporate Finance*, *5*(1), 1–34. doi:10.1016/S0929-1199(98)00015-7

Alexander, D., & Servalli, S. (2011). Economia Aziendale and financial valuations in Italy: Some contradictions and insights. *Accounting History*, *16*(3), 291–312. doi:10.1177/1032373211407052

Allee, V. (2002). *A value network approach for modeling and measuring intangibles*. Retrieved May 30, 2016, from Verna Allee: http://www.iwp.jku.at/born/mpwfst/05/Allee/05Allee_ValueNetwork_p.pdf

Allen, W. T. (1992). Our schizophrenic conception of the business corporation. *Cardozo Law Review*, *14*, 261–281.

Almquist, E., Senior, J., & Bloch, N. (2016). The Elements of Value. *Harvard Business Review*, *94*(9), 47–53.

Alniacik, U., Alniacik, E., & Genc, N. (2011). How corporate social responsibility information influences stakeholders intentions. *Corporate Social Responsibility and Environmental Management*, *18*(4), 234–245. doi:10.1002/csr.245

Altman, D., & Berman, J. (2011). The single bottom line. *Dalberg Global Development Advisor*, 1-13.

Altman, B. W., & Vidaver-Cohen, D. (2000). Corporate Citizenship in the New Millennium: Foundation for an Architecture of Excellence. *Business and Society Review*, *105*(1), 145–169. doi:10.1111/0045-3609.00069

Amaduzzi, A. (1936). Aziende di erogazione. Primi problemi di organizzazione gestione e rilevazione. Casa editrice Giuseppe Principato.

Amaduzzi, A. (1977). Situazione e prospettive degli studi aziendali. *Rivista Italiana di Ragioneria e di Economia Aziendale*, 1.

Amaduzzi, A. (1948). *Il sistema produttivo dell'impresa nelle condizioni del suo equilibrio e nel suo andamento*. Rome, Italy: Kappa Edition.

Amaduzzi, A. (1978). *L'azienda nel suo sistema e nell'ordine delle sue rilevazioni*. Turin, Italy: Utet.

Amaeshi, K., Adi, B., Ogbechie, C., & Amao, O. (2006). *Corporate social responsibility in Nigeria: Western mimicry or indigenous practices?*. Research Paper Series, International Centre for Corporate Social Responsibility, Nottingham University.

Amato, G., Varaldo, R., & Lazzeroni, M. (Eds.). (2006). La città della conoscenza e dell'innovazione. Milano, Italy: Franco Angeli.

Ambrus, A., & Argenziano, R. (2009). Asymmetric Networks in Two-Sided Markets. *American Economic Journal. Microeconomics, 1*(1), 17–52. doi:10.1257/mic.1.1.17

Ameer, R., & Othman, R. (2012). Sustainability practices and corporate financial performance: A study based on the top global corporations. *Journal of Business Ethics, 108*(1), 61–79. doi:10.1007/s10551-011-1063-y

American Petroleum Institute. (n.d.). *Oil & natural gas supply chains.* Retrieved June 30, 2016, from http://www.api.org/Policy-and-Issues/Policy-Items/Safety/Understanding-the-oil-natural-gas-supply-chains

Amodeo, D. (1964). *Ragioneria generale delle imprese.* Naples, Italy: Giannini.

Andersson, U., Dellestrand, H., & Pedersen, T. (2014). The Contribution of Local Environments to Competence Creation in Multinational Enterprises. *Long Range Planning, 47*(1–2), 87–99. doi:10.1016/j.lrp.2013.10.002

Andranovich, G., Burbank, M. J., & Heying, C. H. (2001). Olympic cities: Lessons learned from mega-event politics. *Journal of Urban Affairs, 23*(2), 113–131. doi:10.1111/0735-2166.00079

Andriani, L. (2013). *Social capital: A road map of theoretical frameworks and empirical limitations.* Retrieved from http://www.bbk.ac.uk/management/our-research/wp/WP1.pdf

Angelidou, M. (2015). Smart cities: A conjuncture of four forces. *Cities (London, England), 47*, 95–106. doi:10.1016/j.cities.2015.05.004

Anggraeni, E., Den Hartigh, E., & Zegveld, M. (2007). *Business ecosystem as a perspective for studying the relations between firms and their business networks.* ECCON 2007 Annual Meeting.

Ansari, S., Muni, K., & Gregg, T. (2012). Impact at the Bottom of the Pyramid: The Role of Social Capital in Capability Development and Community Empowerment. *Journal of Management Studies, 49*(4), 813–842. doi:10.1111/j.1467-6486.2012.01042.x

Anselmi, L. (2014). *Percorsi aziendali per le pubbliche amministrazioni.* Turin, Italy: Giappichelli.

Aqwadem (Consultancy). (2007). *Istanbul municipal infrastructure project: Closure of existing illegal waste sites.* Environmental Assessment Report and Management Plan. Retrieved May 20, 2016, from http://www-wds.worldbank.org/external/default/WDSContentServer/WDSP/IB/2007/04/04/ 000020439_20070404155958/Rendered/PDF/E16170EMP0IstanbulEnglish.pdf

Aras, G., Aybars, A., & Kutlu, Ö. (2010). Investigating the relationship between corporate social responsibility and financial performance in emerging markets. *International Journal of Productivity and Performance Management, 59*(3), 229–254. doi:10.1108/17410401011023573

Argandoña, A. (2011). *Stakeholder theory and value creation.* IESE Business School- University of Navarra, WP-922. Retrieved May 29, 2016, from http://www.iese.edu/research/pdfs/di-0922-e.pdf

Argandoña, A. (2011). *Stakeholder theory and value creation.* Working paper, IESE Business School, 922, 1–13.

Argandoña, A. (1998). The stakeholder theory and the common good. *Journal of Business Ethics, 17*(9-10), 1093–1102. doi:10.1023/A:1006075517423

Argenti, J. (1997). Stakeholders: The case against. *Long Range Planning, 30*(3), 442–445. doi:10.1016/S0024-6301(97)00004-6

Ariely, D., & Zakay, D. (2001). A timely account of the role of duration in decision making. *Acta Psychologica, 108*(2), 187–207. doi:10.1016/S0001-6918(01)00034-8 PMID:11569762

Arku, G. (2009). Rapidly Growing African Cities Need to Adopt Smart Growth Policies to Solve Urban Development Concerns. *Urban Forum, 20*, 253-270.

Arora, B., & Puranik, R. (2004). A review of corporate social responsibility in India. *Society for International Development*, *47*(3), 93–100.

Arsoy, A. P., Arabaci, Ö., & Çiftçioğlu, A. (2012). Corporate social responsibility and financial performance relationship: The case of Turkey. *Muhasebe ve Finansman Dergisi*, *53*, 159–176.

Arthur, E. E. (1987). The ethics of corporate governance. *Journal of Business Ethics*, *6*(1), 59–70. doi:10.1007/BF00382949

Artiach, T., Lee, D., Nelson, D., & Walker, J. (2010). The determinants of corporate sustainability performance. *Accounting and Finance*, *50*(1), 31–51. doi:10.1111/j.1467-629X.2009.00315.x

Aspelund, A., Fjell, L., & Rødland, S. E. (2015). *Doing good and doing well - On the relationship between Internationalization and Social Responsibility.* Paper presented at the 18th McGill International Entrepreneurship Conference, Al-Ain, UAE.

Austin, S., Canibe, C., & Slobin, S. (2015). *The Billion Dollar Startup Club. Dow Jones VentureSource and The Wall Street Journal*. Retrieved March 29, 2016, from http://graphics.wsj.com/billion-dollar-club/

Auty, R. M. (1993). *Sustaining development in mineral economies: The resource curse thesis*. London: Routledge.

Baade, R. (2006). The Economic Impact of Mega-sporting Events. In W. Andreff & S. Szymansky (Eds.), *Handbook on the Economics of Sport*. Cheltenham, UK: Edward Elgar. doi:10.4337/9781847204073.00024

Baade, R., & Matheson, V. (2004). The quest for the Cup: Assessing the Economic Impact of the World Cup. *Regional Studies*, *38*(4), 343–354. doi:10.1080/03434002000213888

Baetz, B., & Kenneth, C. (1998). The relationship between mission statements and firm performance: An exploratory study. *Journal of Management Studies*, *35*(6), 823–853. doi:10.1111/1467-6486.00121

Balasubramanian, N. K., Kimber, D., & Siemensma, F. (2005). Emerging opportunities or traditions reinforced? An analysis of the attitudes towards CSR, and trends of thinking about CSR in India. *Journal of Corporate Citizenship*, *17*(2), 79–92. doi:10.9774/GLEAF.4700.2005.sp.00010

Balat, H. (2007). A renewable perspective for sustainable energy development in Turkey: The case of small hydropower plants. *Renewable & Sustainable Energy Reviews*, *11*(9), 2152–2165. doi:10.1016/j.rser.2006.03.002

Balat, H. (2008). Contribution of green energy sources to electrical power production of Turkey: A review. *Renewable & Sustainable Energy Reviews*, *12*(6), 1652–1666. doi:10.1016/j.rser.2007.03.001

Barber, B. M., & Lyon, J. D. (1997). Detecting long-run abnormal stock returns: The empirical power and specification of test statistics. *Journal of Financial Economics*, *43*(3), 341–372. doi:10.1016/S0304-405X(96)00890-2

Baris, K., & Kucukali, S. (2012). Availability of renewable energy sources in Turkey: Current situation, potential, government policies and the EU perspective. *Energy Policy*, *42*, 377–391. doi:10.1016/j.enpol.2011.12.002

Barney, J. B. (2001). Resource-based theories of competitive advantage: A ten-year retrospective on the resource-based view. *Journal of Management*, *27*(6), 643–650. doi:10.1177/014920630102700602

Barney, J. B., & Hansen, M. H. (1994). Trustworthiness as a Source of Competitive Advantage. *Strategic Management Journal*, *15*(S1), 175–190. doi:10.1002/smj.4250150912

Barrett, A., & Lawler, J. (1995). *The Economics of Solid Waste Management in Ireland*. Retrieved May 15, 2016, from https://www.esri.ie/pubs/PRS26.pdf

Bart, C. K. (2001). Exploring the application of mission statements on the world wide web. *Internet Research: Electronic Networking Applications and Policy*, *11*(4), 360–368. doi:10.1108/10662240110402812

Başar, B. (2014). Kurumsal sosyal sorumluluk raporlaması ve finansal performans arasındaki ilişki: Borsa istanbul'da işlem gören kimya-petrol-plastik sektörü şirketleri üzerine bir araştırma. *Yönetim ve Ekonomi Dergisi*, *21*(2), 59–72.

Baskin, J. (2006). Corporate responsibility in emerging markets. *Journal of Corporate Citizenship*, *24*(4), 29–47. doi:10.9774/GLEAF.4700.2006.wi.00006

Bassi, L., Frauenheim, E., McMurrer, D., & Costello, L. (2011). *Good Company: Business Success in the Worthiness Era*. San Francisco, CA: Berrett-Koehler Publishers.

Basu, R., & Wright, N. (2004). *Quality Beyond Six Sigma*. Oxford, UK: Elsevier Butterworth-Heinemann.

Battistella, C., Colucci, K., & Nonino, F. (2012). Methodology of business ecosystems network analysis: a field study in Telecom Italia Future Centre. *Information systems: Crossroads for organization, management, accounting and engineering*, 239-249.

Baxter, P., & Jack, S. (2008). Qualitative Case Study Methodology: Study Design and Implementation for Novice Researchers. *Qualitative Report*, *13*(4), 544–559.

Becchetti, L., Ciciretti, R., & Hasan, I. (2009). Corporate social responsibility and shareholder's value: An empirical analysis. Bank of Finland Research Discussion Papers, 1, 50.

Belk, R. (2014). You are what you can access: Sharing and collaborative consumption online. *Journal of Business Research*, *67*(8), 1595–1600. doi:10.1016/j.jbusres.2013.10.001

Bendheim, C. L., Waddock, S. A., & Graves, S. B. (1998). Determining Best Practice in Corporate-Stakeholder Relations Using Data Envelopment Analysis. *Business & Society*, *37*(3), 306–339. doi:10.1177/000765039803700304

Benli, H. (2013). Potential of renewable energy in electrical energy production and sustainable energy development of Turkey: Performance and policies. *Renewable Energy*, *50*, 33–46. doi:10.1016/j.renene.2012.06.051

Berle, A. A., & Means, G. C. (1932). *The modern corporation and private property*. New York: MacMillan.

Berman, S. L., Wicks, A. C., Kotha, S., & Jones, T. M. (1999). Does Stakeholder Orientation Matter? The Relationship between Stakeholder Management Models and the Firm Financial Performance. *Academy of Management Journal*, *42*(5), 488–509. doi:10.2307/256972

Berry, L. (2007). The Best Companies are generous Companies. *Business Horizons*, *50*(4), 263–269. doi:10.1016/j.bushor.2007.02.003

Berthelot, S., Coulmont, M., & Serret, V. (2012). Do investors value sustainability reports? A Canadian study. *Corporate Social Responsibility and Environmental Management*, *19*(6), 355–363. doi:10.1002/csr.285

Bertini, M., & Gourville, J. T. (2012). Pricing to create shared value. *Harvard Business Review, 90*(6).

Bertini, U. (2014). *La corporate governance, fattore di superamento della crisi e di sviluppo dell'economia*. Opening speech at the inauguration of the academic year of Unicusano University.

Bertini, M., & Gourville, J. T. (2012). Pricing to create shared value: Rethinking the way prices are set can expand the pie for everyone. *Harvard Business Review*, *90*(6), 96–104.

Bertini, U. (2013). *Scritti di politica aziendale. Quarta edizione riveduta e ampliata* (Vol. 33). Turin, Italy: Giappichelli.

Beschorner, T. (2013). Creating shared value: The one-trick Pony approach – A comment on Michael Porter and Mark Kramer. *Business Ethics Journal Review, 17*(1), 106–112. doi:10.12747/bcjr2013.01.17

Betancourt, A. A. (2010). *Waste Pickers in Bogota: From Informal Practice to Policy* (Unpublished master's thesis). Massachusetts Institute of Technology, Cambridge, MA.

Beugré, C. (2017). *Social Entrepreneurship. Managing the Creation of Social Value*. New York: Routledge.

Bhappu, A. D. (2000). The Japanese family: An institutional logic for Japanese corporate networks and Japanese management. *Academy of Management Review, 25*(2), 409–415.

Bhattacharya, C. B., Sen, S., & Korschun, D. (2008). Using corporate social responsibility to win the war for talent. *MIT Sloan Management Review, 49*(2), 37–44.

Bhattacharyya, S. K., & Rahman, Z. (2003). Why large local conglomerates may not work in emerging markets. *European Business Review, 15*(2), 105–115. doi:10.1108/09555340310464731

Biggemann, S., Williams, M., & Kro, G. (2014). Building in sustainability, social responsibility and value co-creation. *Journal of Business and Industrial Marketing, 29*(4), 304–312. doi:10.1108/JBIM-08-2013-0161

Bilen, K., Ozyurt, O., Bakırcı, K., Karslı, S., Erdogan, S., Yılmaz, M., & Comaklı, O. (2008). Energy production, consumption, and environmental pollution for sustainable development: A case study in Turkey. *Renewable & Sustainable Energy Reviews, 12*(6), 1529–1561. doi:10.1016/j.rser.2007.03.003

Bilgen, S., Keleş, S., Kaygusuz, A., Sarı, A., & Kaygusuz, K. (2008). Global warming and renewable energy sources for sustainable development: A case study in Turkey. *Renewable & Sustainable Energy Reviews, 12*(2), 372–396. doi:10.1016/j.rser.2006.07.016

Bisgaard, T. (2009). *Corporate social innovation, companies' participation in solving global challenges*. Retrieved July 2010, from http://samfundsansvar.dk/file/319040/csi_corporate_social_innovation_juli_2010.pdf

Bjerke, B. (1999). *Business Leadership and Culture*. Cheltenham, UK: Edward Elgar. doi:10.4337/9781840647600

Black, S. E., & Lynch, L. M. (2004). Whats driving the new economy?: The benefits of workplace innovation. *The Economic Journal, 114*(493), 97–116. doi:10.1111/j.0013-0133.2004.00189.x

Blocker, C. P., Flint, D. J., Myers, M. B., & Slater, S. F. (2011). Proactive customer orientation and its role for creating customer value in global markets. *Journal of the Academy of Marketing Science, 39*(2), 216–233. doi:10.1007/s11747-010-0202-9

Blodgett, M. S., Hoitash, R., & Markelevich, A. (2014). Sustaining the Financial Value of Global CSR: Reconciling Corporate and Stakeholder Interests in a Less Regulated Environment. *Business and Society Review, 119*(1), 95–124. doi:10.1111/basr.12026

Bocken, N., Short, S., Rana, P., & Evans, S. (2013). A value mapping tool for sustainable business modelling. *Corporate Governance, 13*(5), 482–497. doi:10.1108/CG-06-2013-0078

Bockstette, V. (2011, Nov. 16). Create shared value with a trampoline approach. *Harvard Business Review Blog Network*.

Bockstette, V., & Stamp, M. (2011). *Creating shared value: A how-to guide for the new corporate (r)evolution*. Retrieved from http://www.fsg.org/publications/creating-shared-value-how-guide-new-corporate-revolution

Bockstette, V., Pfitzer, M., Smith, D., Bhavaraju, N., Priestley, C., & Bhatt, A. (2014). *Banking on shared value: How banks profit by rethinking their business.* Retrieved from http://www.fsg.org/publications/banking-shared-value

Bockstette, V., & Stamp, M. (2011). *Creating Shared Value: A How-to Guide for the New Corporate (R)evolution.* Boston: FSG.

Bolon, D. S. (2005). Comparing mission statement content in for-profit and not-for-profit hospitals: Does mission really matter? *Hospital Topics, 83*(4), 2–9. doi:10.3200/HTPS.83.4.2-10 PMID:16425696

Bolton, W., & Drew, J. H. (1991). A multistage model of customers: Assessment of service quality and value. *The Journal of Consumer Research, 17*(4), 375–384. doi:10.1086/208564

Boons, F., & Lüdeke-Freund, F. (2013). Business models for sustainable innovation: State of the art and steps towards a research agenda. *Journal of Cleaner Production, 45*, 9–19. doi:10.1016/j.jclepro.2012.07.007

Boons, F., Montalvo, C., Quist, J., & Wagner, M. (2013). Sustainable innovation, business models and economic performance: An overview. *Journal of Cleaner Production, 45*, 1–8. doi:10.1016/j.jclepro.2012.08.013

Borgonovi, E. (2014). La rilevanza del concetto di istituto per l'economia aziendale. *Economia Aziendale Online, 5*(1), 3–10.

Bosch-Badia, M. T., Montllor-Serrats, J., & Tarrazon, M. A. (2013). Corporate social responsibility from Friedman to Porter and Kramer. *Theoretical Economic Letters, 3*(3), 11–15. doi:10.4236/tel.2013.33A003

Botsman, R. (2013). The Rise of the Sharing Economy. *The Economist.* Retrieved April 15, 2016, from http://www.economist.com/news/leaders/21573104-internet-everything-hire-rise-sharing-economy

Botsman, R., & Rogers, R. (2010). *What's Mine Is Yours: The Rise of Collaborative Consumption.* New York: Harper Business.

Botsman, R., & Rogers, R. (2010a). Beyond Zipcar: Collaborative consumption. *Harvard Business Review, 88*(10), 30. PMID:20607961

Botsman, R., & Rogers, R. (2010b). *What's mine is yours: The rise of collaborative consumption.* New York, NY: Collins.

Bowman, C., & Ambrosini, V. (2010). How value is created, captured and destroyed. *European Business Review, 22*(5), 479–495. doi:10.1108/09555341011068903

Brief, A. P., Buttram, R. T., & Dukerich, J. M. (2001). Collective corruption in the corporate world: Toward a process model. In M. E. Turner (Ed.), *Groups at Work: Theory and Research* (pp. 471–499). Mahwah, NJ: Erlbaum.

British Council, UNDP, CII, & Pricewaterhouse Coopers. (2002). Corporate Social Responsibility Survey. A Survey by British Council, UNDP, CII and Pricewaterhouse Coopers.

Bromiley, P., & Marcus, A. (1989). The Deterrent to Dubious Corporate Behavior: Profitability, Probability, and Safety Recalls. *Strategic Management Journal, 10*(3), 233–250. doi:10.1002/smj.4250100304

Brown, D., & Knudsen, J. S. (2013). *Generating value for investors and society.* The Conference Board.

Browne, J., & Nuttall, R. (2013). Beyond corporate social responsibility: Integrated external engagement. McKinsey & Company.

Brown, T. J., & Dacin, P. A. (1997). The Company and the Product: Corporate Associations and Consumer Product Responses. *Journal of Marketing, 61*(1), 68–85. doi:10.2307/1252190

Brugmann, J., & Prahalad, C. K. (2007). Co-Creating Business's New Social Compact. *Harvard Business Review*, *85*(2), 80–90. PMID:17345682

Brustein, J. (2014). *Helsinki's Uber for Buses Is Stuck in First Gear Bloomberg, Finland's quasi-public Kutsuplus isn't nearing a profit*. Retrieved May 10, 2016, from http://www.bloomberg.com/news/articles/2014-05-16/helsinkis-uber-for-buses-is-stuck-in-first-gear

Bryman, A., & Bell, E. (2015). *Business Research Methods* (4th ed.). Oxford, UK: Oxford University Press.

Bujor, A., & Avasilicai, S. (2016). The creative entrepreneur: A framework of analysis. *Procedia: Social and Behavioral Sciences*, *221*, 21–28. doi:10.1016/j.sbspro.2016.05.086

Bullard, R. D. (2007). *Growing Smarter: Achieving Livable Communities, Environmental Justice, and Regional Equity*. Cambridge, MA: The MIT Press.

Burbank, M. J., Andranovick, G. D., & Heying, C. H. (2001). *Olympic Dreams: The Impact of Mega-Events on Local Politics*. Boulder, CO: Lynne Rienner Publisher.

Burcea, G. Ş. (2015). The economical, social and environmental implications of informal waste collection and recycling. *Theoretical and Empirical Researches in Urban Management*, *10*(3), 14–24.

Burke, C. S., Sims, D. E., Lazzara, E. H., & Salas, E. (2007). Trust in leadership: A multi-level review and integration. *The Leadership Quarterly*, *18*(6), 606–632. doi:10.1016/j.leaqua.2007.09.006

Burns, P., & Schapper, J. (2008). The Ethical Case for Affirmative Action. *Journal of Business Ethics*, *83*(3), 369–379. doi:10.1007/s10551-007-9625-8

Burton, N. (2015). *Toyota MR2: The Complete Story*. Wiltshire, UK: Crowood Press.

Busco, C., Frigo, M. L., Riccaboni, A., & Quattrone, P. (Eds.). (2013). *Integrated Reporting: Concepts and Cases that Redefine Corporate Accountability*. New York, NY: Springer-Verlag GmbH. doi:10.1007/978-3-319-02168-3

Butler, H. N. (1989). The contractual theory of the corporation. *George Mason University Law Review*, *11*(4), 99–123.

Cafferata, R. (2014). Management in adattamento. Bologna, Italy: Il Mulino.

Cafferata, R. (2014). *Management in adattamento. Tra razionalità economica, evoluzione e imperfezione dei sistemi*. Bologna: Il Mulino.

Cafferata, R. (2016). Darwinist connections between the systemness of social organizations and their evolution. *Journal of Management a Governance*, *20*(1), 19–44. doi:10.1007/s10997-014-9303-z

Caldarelli, A., Fiondella, C., Maffei, M., Spanò, R., & Zagaria, C. (2011). The common good and Economia Aziendale theory: Insights for corporate social responsibility from the Italian perspective. *Journal of the Asia-Pacific Centre for Environmental Accountability*, *7*(4), 197–216.

Camagni, R. (2008). Regional competitiveness: Towards a concept of territorial capital. *Modelling regional scenarios for the enlarged. Europe*, 33–47.

Camilleri, M. A. (2012). *Creating shared value through strategic CSR in tourism* (Doctoral dissertation). University of Edinburgh, UK.

Capello, R., Fratesi, U., & Resmini, L. (2011). *Globalization and regional growth in Europe: past trends and future scenarios*. Springer Science & Business Media. doi:10.1007/978-3-642-19251-7

Carroll, A. B. (1979). Three-dimensional conceptual model of corporate performance. *Academy of Management Review*, *4*(4), 497–505.

Carroll, A. B. (1991). The pyramid of corporate social responsibility: Toward the moral management of organizational stakeholders. *Business Horizons*, *34*(4), 39–48. doi:10.1016/0007-6813(91)90005-G

Carroll, A. B. (1999). Corporate social responsibility: Evolution of a Definitional Construct. *Business & Society*, *38*(3), 268–295. doi:10.1177/000765039903800303

Carroll, A. B., & Shabana, K. M. (2010). The business case for corporate social responsibility: A review of concepts, research and practice. *International Journal of Management Reviews*, *12*(1), 85–105. doi:10.1111/j.1468-2370.2009.00275.x

Cassandro, P. E. (1969). Il profitto dell'impresa, mezzo e non fine. *Dirigenti Industria*, 7-8.

Cassandro, P. E. (1978). Sul concetto di impresa come "comunità". *Rassegna Economica*, 1.

Cassel, D. (2001). Human Rights Business Responsibilities in the Global Marketplace. *Business Ethics Quarterly*, *11*(2), 261–274. doi:10.2307/3857749

Cavaco, S., & Crifo, P. (2014). CSR and Financial Performance: Complementary between Environmental, Social and Business Behaviours. *Applied Economics*, *46*(27), 3323–3338. doi:10.1080/00036846.2014.927572

Cavalieri, E. (1999). Organizzazioni produttive, aziende e imprese: considerazioni di carattere istituzionale. *Rivista Italiana di Ragioneria e di Economia Aziendale*, 3/4.

Cavalieri, E. (2009). Una riflessione sulle cause e sulle responsabilità della crisi globale. *Rivista Italiana di Ragioneria e di Economia Aziendale*, 5/6.

Cavalieri, E. (2012). Dottrina e organizzazioni produttive verso nuovi modelli di sviluppo. *Rivista Italiana di Ragioneria e di Economia Aziendale*, 1/2.

Cavalieri, E. (2010). *Le nuove dimensioni dell'equilibrio aziendale: Contributo alla rivisitazione della teoria*. Turin, Italy: Giappichelli.

Cavalieri, E., & Ferraris Franceschi, R. (2008). Economia aziendale: Vol. I. *Attività aziendale e processi produttivi*. Turin, Italy: Giappichelli.

Chakravarthy, B. (2010). The sharing imperative. *Strategy and Leadership*, *38*(1), 37–41. doi:10.1108/10878571011009877

Charron, R., Harrington, H. J., Voehl, F., & Wiggin, H. (2015). *The Lean Management Systems Handbook*. Boca Raton, FL: CRC Press.

Chee Tahir, A., & Darton, R. C. (2010). The Process Analysis Method of selecting indicators to quantify the sustainability performance of a business operation. *Journal of Cleaner Production*, *18*(16-17), 1598–1607. doi:10.1016/j.jclepro.2010.07.012

Cheng, J.-H., Yeh, C.-H., & Tu, C.-W. (2008). Trust and knowledge sharing in green supply chains. *Supply Chain Management*, *13*(4), 283–295. doi:10.1108/13598540810882170

Cheng, M. (2016). Sharing economy: A review and agenda for future research. *International Journal of Hospitality Management*, *57*, 60–70. doi:10.1016/j.ijhm.2016.06.003

Chen, H., Noronha, G., & Singal, V. (2004). The price response to S&P 500 Index additions and deletions: Evidence of asymmetry and a new explanation. *The Journal of Finance*, *59*(4), 1901–1929. doi:10.1111/j.1540-6261.2004.00683.x

Chen, S., & Bouvain, K. (2009). Is corporate responsibility converging? A comparison of corporate social responsibility reporting in the USA, UK, Australia and Germany. *Journal of Business Ethics*, *87*(1), 299–317. doi:10.1007/s10551-008-9794-0

Cherubini S., Bonetti E., Iasevoli G., & Resciniti R. (2009). *Il valore degli eventi. Valutare ex ante ed ex post gli effetti socio-economici, esperenziali e territoriali.* Milano, Italy: Franco Angeli.

Cheung, A. (2011). Do stock investors value corporate sustainability? Evidence from an event study. *Journal of Business Ethics*, *99*(2), 145–165. doi:10.1007/s10551-010-0646-3

Cheung, A., & Roca, E. (2013). The effect on price, liquidity and risk when stocks are added to and deleted from a sustainability index: Evidence from the Asia Pacific. *Journal of Asian Economics*, *24*, 51–65. doi:10.1016/j.asieco.2012.08.002

Chikarmane, P. (2012). *Integrating waste pickers into municipal solid waste management in Pune, India.* WIEGO Policy Brief No 8. Retrieved March 5, 2016, from http://www.inclusivecities.org/wp-content/uploads/2012/10/Chikarmane_WIEGO_PB8.pdf

Chin, S. T. S., Raman, K., Yeow, J. A., & Eze, U. C. (2012). Relationship Between Emotional Intelligence And Spiritual Intelligence In Nurturing Creativity And Innovation Among Successful Entrepreneurs: A Conceptual Framework. *Procedia: Social and Behavioral Sciences*, *57*, 261–267. doi:10.1016/j.sbspro.2012.09.1184

Christmann, P., & Taylor, G. (2006). Firm self-regulation through international certifiable standards: Determinants of symbolic versus substantive implementation. *Journal of International Business Studies*, *37*(6), 863–878. doi:10.1057/palgrave.jibs.8400231

Chui, M., Manyika, J., Bughin, J., Dobbs, R., Roxburgh, C., & Sarrazin, H. (2012). *The social economy: Unlocking value and productivity through social technologies*. McKinsey Global Institute.

Cinquini, L., & Marelli, A. (2007). Accounting history research in Italy, 1990–2004: An introduction. *Accounting Business & Financial History*, *17*(1), 1–9. doi:10.1080/09585200601127509

Çıtak, L., & Ersoy, E. (2016). Firmaların BIST sürdürülebilirlik endeksine alınmasına yatırımcı tepkisi: Olay çalışması ve ortalama testleri ile bir analiz. *Uluslararası Alanya İşletme Fakültesi Dergisi*, *8*(1), 43–57.

Claessens, S., Djankov, S., & Lang, L. H. P. (2000). The separation of ownership and control in East Asian corporations. *Journal of Financial Economics*, *58*(1), 81–112. doi:10.1016/S0304-405X(00)00067-2

Clark, C., & Brennan, L. (2012). Entrepreneurship with Social Value: A Conceptual Model for Performance Measurement. *Academy of Entrepreneurship Journal*, *18*(2), 17–32.

Clarke, T. (1998). The stakeholder corporation: A business philosophy for the information age. *Long Range Planning*, *31*(2), 182–194. doi:10.1016/S0024-6301(98)00002-8

Clarkson, M. B. E. (1995). A Shareholder Framework for Analyzing and Evaluating Corporate Social Performance. *Academy of Management Review*, *20*(1), 571–610.

Coase, R. H. (1937). The nature of the firm. *Economica*, *4*(16), 386–405. doi:10.1111/j.1468-0335.1937.tb00002.x

Coca-Cola. (2015). *Coca-Cola supports retail capacity and economic development in Brazil.* Retrieved from https://sharedvalue.org/examples/coletivo-retail-program-supporting-retail-capacity-and-economic-development-brazil

Cochran, P. L., & Wood, R. A. (1984). Corporate social responsibility and financial performance. *Academy of Management Journal*, *27*(1), 42–56. doi:10.2307/255956

Coda, V. (2006). Economia Aziendale: alla ricerca di punti di convergenza. In Società Italiana dei Docenti di Ragioneria e di Economia Aziendale (Eds.), Manifesto dei soci fondatori, in "Appunti per un dibattito sulla cultura aziendale". Academic Press.

Coda, V. (2010). Insegnamenti dalle "crisi di senso". *Sinergie*, *81*, 25–30.

Cohen, B., & Kietzmann, J. (2014). Ride on! mobility business models for the sharing economy. *Organization & Environment*, *27*(3), 279–296. doi:10.1177/1086026614546199

Cointreau, S. (2006). *Occupational and environmental health issues of solid waste management- Special emphasis on Middle-and Lower-Income countries.* The World Bank Group Urban Papers, UP-2. Retrieved January 5, 2017, from http://siteresources.worldbank.org/INTUSWM/ Resources/up-2.pdf

Committee for Economic Development. (1971). *Social Responsibilities of Business Corporations. A Statement on National Policy by the Research and Policy Committee of the Committee for Economic Development.* New York: Committee for Economic Development.

Consolandi, C., Jaiswal-Dale, A., Poggiani, E., & Vercelli, A. (2009). Global standards and ethical stock indexes: The case of the Dow Jones Sustainability Stoxx Index. *Journal of Business Ethics*, *87*(1), 185–197. doi:10.1007/s10551-008-9793-1

Contiu, L. C., Gabor, M. R., & Stefanescu, D. (2012). Hofstedes cultural dimensions and students ability to develop an entrepreneurial spirit. *Procedia: Social and Behavioral Sciences*, *46*, 5553–5557. doi:10.1016/j.sbspro.2012.06.474

Control Risks. (2012). *A new frontier: Oil and gas in East Africa.* Retrieved June 30, 2016, from https://www.controlrisks.com/~/media/Public%20Site/Files/Our%20Thinking/east_africa_whitepaper_LR_web.pdf

Cordos, R. C., Bodea, A., Avasilicai, S., Bacali, L., Pop, C., & Anguelov, K. (2008). *Entrepreneurship.* Cluj-Napoca: Todesco Publishing House.

Cosbey, A., Mann, H., Maennling, N., Toledano, P., Geipel, J., & Brauch, M. D. (2016). *Mining a Mirage? Reassessing the shared-value paradigm in light of the technological advances in the mining sector.* International Institute for Sustainable Development.

Costa, E., & Ramus, T. (2012). The Italian Economia Aziendale and catholic social teaching: How to apply the common good principle at the managerial level. *Journal of Business Ethics*, *106*(1), 103–116. doi:10.1007/s10551-011-1056-x

Costa, J. E. R., & Martí, J. M. R. (Eds.). (2012). *Towards a New Theory of the Firm: Humanizing the Firm and the Management Profession.* Bilbao: Fundación BBVA.

Craig-Smith, N. (1990). *Morality and the Market: Consumer Pressure for Corporate Responsibility.* London: Routledge.

Crane, A., Palazzo, G., Spence, L. J., & Matten, D. (2014). Contesting the value of creating shared value. *California Management Review*, *56*(2), 130–153. doi:10.1525/cmr.2014.56.2.130

Cronin, J. J. Jr, Brady, M. K., & Hult, G. T. M. (2000). Assessing the effects of quality, value and customer satisfaction on consumer behavioral intentions in service environment. *Journal of Retailing*, *76*(2), 193–218. doi:10.1016/S0022-4359(00)00028-2

Cronin, P., Ryan, F., & Coughlan, M. (2008). Undertaking a literature review: A step-by-step approach. *British Journal of Nursing (Mark Allen Publishing)*, *17*(1), 38–43. doi:10.12968/bjon.2008.17.1.28059 PMID:18399395

CSM (Centre for Social Markets). (2001). *Corporate Social Responsibility: Perceptions of Indian Business.* A Report by CSM, Calcutta, India. Retrieved May 10, 2016, from www.csmworld.org/public/pdf/social_respons.pdf

Curran, M., & Moran, D. (2007). Impact of the FTSE4Good on firm price: An event study. *Journal of Environmental Management, 82*(4), 529–537. doi:10.1016/j.jenvman.2006.02.010 PMID:16678334

Dallas, L. (2011). Short-termism, the financial crisis, and corporate governance. *The Journal of Corporation Law, 37*, 264–363.

Das Gupta, A. (2010). *Ethics, business and society*. Singapore: Sage Publications.

Das Gupta, A., & Das Gupta, A. (2005). Corporate social responsibility: the Indian context. In D. Crowther & R. Jatana (Eds.), *Representations of social responsibility* (Vol. 2, pp. 31–73). Hyderabad, India: ICFAI University Press.

Daszyńska-Żygadlo, K., Ryszawska, B., Słoński, T., & Zawadzki, B. M. (2014). *Investors' reactions for sustainability index inclusion –Is CSR a good news?*. Retrieved May 5, 2016, from http://hdl.handle.net/11089/14828

Davenport, E. (2011). *The next catalyst for change: How corporate shared value is reshaping capitalism. CMC Senior Theses. Paper 111*. Claremont College.

Davies, R. J. (2016). *Japanese Culture: The Religious and Philosophical Foundations*. Rutland, VT: Tuttle Publishing.

Davis, J. J. (1994). Good ethics is good for business: Ethical attributions and response to environmental advertising. *Journal of Business Ethics, 13*(11), 873–885. doi:10.1007/BF00871701

Davis, K. (1960). Can Business Afford to Ignore Corporate Social Responsibilities? *California Management Review, 2*(3), 70–76. doi:10.2307/41166246

Davis, K. (1967). Understanding the Social Responsibility Puzzle. *Business Horizons, 10*(4), 45–51. doi:10.1016/0007-6813(67)90007-9

Davis, K. (1973). The Case For and Against Business Assumption of Social Responsibilities. *Academy of Management Journal, 16*(2), 312–322. doi:10.2307/255331

Daw, J. (2013). *What Does Creating Shared Value Mean for the Non-profit Sector?*. Retrieved May 30, 2016 from https://sharedvalue.org/groups/shared-value-initiative-community/what-does-creating-shared-value-mean-nonprofit-sector

Dawar, N., & Chattopadhyay, A. (2000). *Rethinking Marketing Programs for Emerging Markets*. Davidson Institute Working Paper Series. Retrieved on May 28, 2016, from http://eres.bus.umich.edu/docs/workpap-dav/wp320.pdf

De Dominicis, U. (1966). *Lezioni di ragioneria generale*. Bologna, Italy: Azzoguidi.

De Nisco, A., Riviezzo, A., & Napolitano, M. R. (2008). The role of stakeholders in town centre management: Guidelines for identification and analysis. *Journal of Place Management and Development, 1*(2), 166–176. doi:10.1108/17538330810889998

Del Rio, P., & Burguillo, M. (2008). Assessing the impact of renewable energy deployment on local sustainability: Towards a theoretical framework. *Renewable & Sustainable Energy Reviews, 12*(5), 1325–1344. doi:10.1016/j.rser.2007.03.004

Del Rio, P., & Burguillo, M. (2009). An empirical analysis of the impact of renewable energy deployment on local sustainability. *Renewable & Sustainable Energy Reviews, 13*(6-7), 1314–1325. doi:10.1016/j.rser.2008.08.001

Delgado, M., Porter, M. E., & Stern, S. (2010). Clusters and entrepreneurship. *Journal of Economic Geography, 10*(4), 495–518. doi:10.1093/jeg/lbq010

Dell'Acqua A., Morri G. & Quaini E. (2013). *L'indotto di Expo 2015. Analisi di impatto economico*. Milano, Italy: SDA Bocconi.

Della Lucia, M. (2013). Economic performance measurement system for event planning and investment decision making. *Tourism Management*, *34*, 91–100. doi:10.1016/j.tourman.2012.03.016

Deloitte. (2015). *Gambia Steady State Model Analysis*. Deloitte Consulting LLP.

Demailly, D., & Novel, A. S. (2014). *The sharing economy: make it sustainable*. Studies N°03/14. IDDRI.

Dembek, K., Singh, P., & Bhakoo, V. (2016). Literature review of shared value: A theoretical concept or a management buzzword? *Journal of Business Ethics*, *137*(2), 231–267. doi:10.1007/s10551-015-2554-z

Deniz, G. C. (2010). *The Informal Waste Collection Sector and the Waste Pickers; A Case Study in Ankara* (Unpublished master's thesis). Bogazici University, Istanbul, Turkey.

Denning, S. (2011). Why "shared value" can't fix capitalism. *Forbes*. Retrieved from http://www.forbes.com/sites/stevedenning/2011/12/20/why-shared-value-cant-fixcapitalism/

Denning, S. (2012). Is shared value a new mental model for innovation?. *Forbes*. Retrieved from http://www.forbes.com/sites/stevedenning/is-sharedvalue-a-new-mental-model-for-innovation/

Devinney, T. M. (2009). Is the Socially Responsible Corporation a Myth? The Good, the Bad, and the Ugly of Corporate Social Responsibility. *The Academy of Management Perspectives*, *23*(2), 44–56. doi:10.5465/AMP.2009.39985540

Dhanaraj, C., Lyles, M. A., Steensma, H. K., & Tihanyi, L. (2004). Managing tacit and explicit knowledge transfer in IJVs: The role of relational embeddedness and the impact on performance. *Journal of International Business Studies*, *35*(5), 428–442. doi:10.1057/palgrave.jibs.8400098

Di Carlo, E., Fortuna, F., & Testarmata, S. (2015). Boundaries of the business model within business groups. *Journal of Management and Governance*, *20*(2), 321–362. doi:10.1007/s10997-015-9338-9

Di Gregorio, D. (2013). Value creation and value appropriation: An integrative, multi-level framework. *Journal of Applied Business and Economics*, *15*(1), 39–53.

Dias, S. (2010). *Overview of legal framework for social inclusion in solid waste management in Brazil.* WIEGO Research Paper. Retrieved March 5, 2016, from http://wiego.org/sites/wiego.org/ files/publications/files/Dias_Brazil_Legal_framework_social_inclusion_waste_0.pdf

Dias, S. (2012). Not to be taken for granted: what informal waste pickers offer the urban economy. *The Global Urbanist*. Retrieved April 4, 2016, from http://globalurbanist.com/2012/11/27/waste-pickers

Dicken, P. (Ed.). (2011). *Global shift: Mapping the changing contours of world economy* (6th ed.). New York: The Guilford Press.

Dickey, D., & Fuller, W. A. (1979). Distribution of the Estimators for Autoregressive Time Series with a Unit Root. *Journal of the American Statistical Association*, *74*, 427–431.

Dickey, D., & Fuller, W. A. (1981). Likelihood Ratio Statistics for Autoregressive Time Series with A Unit Root. *Econometrica*, *49*(4), 1057–1072. doi:10.2307/1912517

Dijkgraaf, E., & Gradus, R. (2016). *Post separation of plastic waste: Better for the environment and lower collection costs.* Tinbergen Institute Discussion Paper 16-103/VI. Retrieved January 5, 2017 from https://ssrn.com/abstract=2875279

Dilling, P. F. A., Harris, P., & Khoo, B. (2008). The effect of corporate responsibility related information on the capital market: An event study approach. *Journal of Academy of Taiwan Business Management Review*, *5*(3), 119–127.

Dinçer, B. (2011). Do the shareholders really care about corporate social responsibility? *International Journal of Business and Social Science*, *2*(10), 71–76.

Dixon-Woods, M. (2011). Systematic reviews and qualitative methods. In D. Silverman (Ed.), *Qualitative Research. Issues of Theory, Method and Practice* (3rd ed.; pp. 331–346). London, UK: Sage Publications.

Dobrescu, E. M., & Dobrescu, E. M. (2014). Theories Regarding the Role of the Growth Poles in the Economic Integration. *Procedia: Social and Behavioral Sciences*, *8*, 262–267.

Dodd, M. E. (1932). For whom are corporate managers trustees. *Harvard Law Review*, *45*(7), 1145–1163. doi:10.2307/1331697

Doh, J. P., Howton, S. D., Howton, S. W., & Siegel, D. S. (2010). Does the market respond to an endorsement of social responsibility? The role of institutions, information, and legitimacy. *Journal of Management*, *36*(6), 1461–1485. doi:10.1177/0149206309337896

Donaldson, T., & Dunfee, T. W. (1999). *Ties that bind: A social contracts approach to business ethics*. Boston, MA: Harvard Business School Press.

Donaldson, T., & Preston, L. (1995). The stakeholder theory of the corporation: Concepts, evidence and implications. *Academy of Management Review*, *20*(1), 65–91.

Donaldson, T., & Preston, L. E. (1995). The Stakeholder Theory of the Corporation: Concepts, Evidence, and Implications. *Academy of Management Review*, *20*(1), 65–91.

Donnelly, J. (1985). *The Concept of Human Rights*. London, UK: Croom Helm.

D'Orey, P. M., Fernandes, R., & Ferreira, M. (2012). Empirical Evaluation of a Dynamic and Distributed Taxi-Sharing System. *Intelligent Transportation Systems (ITSC), 2012 15th International IEEE Conference on Intelligent Transportation Systems*, 140-146. doi:10.1109/ITSC.2012.6338703

Doz, Y. L., & Hamel, G. (1998). *Alliance Advantage: The Art of Creating Value through Partnering*. Boston, MA: Harvard Business School.

Dredge, D. (2006). Policy networks and the local organizations of tourism. *Tourism Management*, *27*(2), 269–280. doi:10.1016/j.tourman.2004.10.003

Dredge, D. (2010). Place Change and Tourism Development Conflicts: Evaluating Public Interest. *Tourism Management*, *31*(1), 104–112. doi:10.1016/j.tourman.2009.01.004

Driver, M. (2012). An Interview with Michael Porter: Social Entrepreneurship and the transformation of Capitalism. *Academy of Management Learning & Education*, *11*(3), 421–431. doi:10.5465/amle.2011.0002A

Drucker, P. F. (1946). *The Concept of the Corporation*. New York, NY: Harper Collins Publishers.

Drucker, P. F. (1984). The new meaning of corporate social responsibility. *California Management Review*, *26*(2), 53–63. doi:10.2307/41165066

Dudley, N. (2011). Supplement: Angola - Economy - A private key to sustained growth. *The Banker*.

Dugger, W. M. (1989). *Corporate Hegemony*. Westport, CT: Greenwood Press.

Dul, J., & Hak, T. (2008). *Case Study Methodology in Business Research*. Oxford: Butterworth-Heinemann.

Duman, L., Beduk, A., Koyluoglu, A. S., & Kezban, A. (2015). Entrepreneurship Culture at SMEs: A Case Study in Konya. *Procedia: Social and Behavioral Sciences*, *207*, 492–501. doi:10.1016/j.sbspro.2015.10.119

Dumay, J. (2014). 15 years of the journal of intellectual capital and counting: A manifesto for transformational IC research. *Journal of Intellectual Capital, 15*(1), 2–37. doi:10.1108/JIC-09-2013-0098

Dumay, J., Bernardi, C., Guthrie, J., & Demartini, P. (2016). Integrated reporting: A structured literature review. *Accounting Forum, 40*(3), 166–185. doi:10.1016/j.accfor.2016.06.001

Dumay, J., & Cai, L. (2014). A review and critique of content analysis as a methodology for inquiring into IC disclosure. *Journal of Intellectual Capital, 15*(2), 264–290. doi:10.1108/JIC-01-2014-0010

Dunn, D., & Yamashita, K. (2003). A Changed World, Micro capitalism and the Mega-Corporation. *Harvard Business Review, 81*(8), 46–54. PMID:12884667

Durlauf, S. N., & Fafchamps, M. (2004). *Social Capital.* The Centre for The Study of African Economies (No. 214). Working Paper Series.

Dutton, J. E., Dukerich, J. M., & Harquail, C. V. (1994). Organizational Images and Member Identification. *Administrative Science Quarterly, 39*(2), 239–263. doi:10.2307/2393235

EC (European Commission). (2010). *Being Wise with Waste: The EU's Approach to Waste Management.* Retrieved May 15, 2016, from http://ec.europa.eu/environment/waste/pdf/WASTE%20 BROCHURE.pdf

EC (European Commission). (2016). *Turkiye Multeci Krizi.* Retrieved June 30, 2016, from http://ec.europa.eu/echo/files/aid/countries/factsheets/turkey_syrian_crisis_tr.pdf

Eckhardt, G. M., Belk, R., & Devinney, T. M. (2010). Why dont consumers consume ethically? *Journal of Consumer Behaviour, 9*(6), 426–436. doi:10.1002/cb.332

Edenkamp, P. (2002). Insights into how consumers are thinking, how they are acting and why. *Brandweek, 43*(36), 16–20.

Edmonson, A., & McManus, S. (2007). Methodological fit in management field research. *Academy of Management Review, 4*(4), 1155–1179. doi:10.5465/AMR.2007.26586086

EEA (European Environment Agency). (2011). *Recycling Industry Can Boost the European Economy.* Retrieved May 21, 2016, from http://www.eea.europa.eu/downloads/96d2c164-96d6-47d8-bda4-3b856a32747e/1332497451/recycling-industry-can-boost-the.pdf

EEA (European Environment Agency). (2013). *Managing Municipal Solid Waste — A review of Achievements in 32 European countries. Report No. 2.2013.* Retrieved May 12, 2016, from file:///C:/Users/pc/Downloads/Managing%20 municipal%20solid%20waste%20(2).pdf

EEA (European Environment Agency). (2015). *SOER - Cross-Country Comparisons. Waste. Municipal Solid Waste Generation and Management.* Retrieved May 12, 2016, from http://www. eea.europa.eu/soer-2015/countries-comparison/waste

Eisenhardt, K. M. (1989). Building Theories from Case Study Research. *Academy of Management Review, 14*(4), 532–550.

Eisenmann, T. R., Parker, G. G., & Van Alstyne, M. W. (2006). Strategies for Two-Sided Markets. *Harvard Business Review, 84*(10), 92. PMID:16649701

Elkington, J. (1994). Towards the Sustainable Corporation: Win-Win-Win Business Strategies for Sustainable Development. *California Management Review, 36*(2), 90–100. doi:10.2307/41165746

Elkington, J. (1998). *Cannibals with forks. The triple bottom line of the 21st century* (1st ed.). Oxford, UK: Capstone Publisher Limited.

Elster, J. (1998). Emotions and Economic Theory. *Journal of Economic Literature, 36*(1), 47–74.

Epstein, J. (2011). *So you tall this CSR? Or one of its many other names?*. Retrieved from http://www.forbes.com/sites/csr/2011/07/28/so-you-call-this-csr-or-one-of-its-many-othernames/

Erdem, Z. K. (2010). The contribution of renewable sources in meeting Turkeys energy related challenges. *Renewable & Sustainable Energy Reviews*, *9*(9), 2710–2722. doi:10.1016/j.rser.2010.07.003

Ergun, C. (2005). *Yoksulluk ve Enformel Sektor: Cop Toplayicilari Ornegi (Isparta-Izmir Karsilastirmasi)* (Unpublished master's thesis). Süleyman Demirel University, Isparta.

Ernst & Young. (2014). *Creating shared value in Africa: Local content in the oil and gas industry*. EYGM Limited.

Ernst & Young. (2014). *Creating shared value in Africa: Local content in the oil and gas industry*. Retrieved from http://www.ey.com/Publication/vwLUAssets/EY-creating-shared-value-in-africa/$FILE/EY-creating-shared-value-in-africa.pdf

Ert, E., Fleischer, A., & Magen, N. (2016). Trust and reputation in the sharing economy: The role of personal photos in Airbnb. *Tourism Management*, *55*, 62–73. doi:10.1016/j.tourman.2016.01.013

Escudero, G. (2013). Modelos de Empresa y Etica. *Cuadernos Empresay Humanismo, 120.*

Espenson, A. (2014). *5 Companies Doing Corporate Social Responsibility Right*. Retrieved May 20, 2016, from http://www.business2community.com/social-business/5-companies-corporate-social-responsibility-right-0951534#rYj9voqGiqDJ3B3A.97

Essex, S. J., & Chalkley, B. (1998). Olympics Games: Catalyst of urban change. *Leisure Studies*, *17*(3), 187–206. doi:10.1080/026143698375123

Esteves, A. M., Coyne, B., & Moreno, A. (2013). *Local Content Initiatives: Enhancing the Sub-National Benefits of the Oil, Gas, and Mining Sectors*. Retrieved June 30, 2016, from http://www.resourcegovernance.org/sites/default/files/Sub_Enhance_Benefits_20151125.pdf

Ethiraj, S. K., & Posen, H. E. (2013). Do product architectures affect innovation productivity in complex product ecosystems? *Advances in Strategic Management*, *30*, 127–166.

European Commission. (2011). *A renewed EU strategy 2011-14 for Corporate Social Responsibility*. Brussels: European Commission.

European Commission. (2015). *Smart cities*. Retrieved June, 8, 2016, from https://ec.europa.eu/digital-single-market/en/smart-cities

European Innovation Partnership on Smart Cities and Communities. (2013). *Strategic Implementation Plan*. Retrieved April 24, 2016 from http://ec.europa.eu/eip/smartcities/files/sip_final_en.pdf

Eurostat. (2012). *Municipal Waste*. Retrieved May 11, 2016, from http://epp.eurostat. ec.europa.eu/ portal-page-porta./statistics/search_database

Eurostat. (2016). *European Statistics*. Retrieved May 11, 2016, from http://ec.europa.eu/ eurostat/statistics-explained/index.php/Municipal_waste_statistics

Evans, D. S. (2002). *The antitrust economics of two-sided markets*. Available at SSRN 332022

Evans, D. S. (2003). Some Empirical Aspects of Multi-Sided Platform Industries. *Review of Network Economics*, *2*(3), 191–209. doi:10.2202/1446-9022.1026

Extractive Industries Transparency Initiative. (2016). *EITI Progress Report 2016- From Reports to Results*. Retrieved June 30, 2016, from https://eiti.org/files/progressreport.pdf

Ezeah, C., Fazakerley, J. A., & Roberts, C. L. (2013). Emerging trends in informal sector recycling in developing and transition countries. *Waste Management (New York, N.Y.)*, *33*(11), 2509–2519. doi:10.1016/j.wasman.2013.06.020 PMID:23886489

Fama, E., & Jensen, M. C. (1983). Separation of ownership and control. *The Journal of Law & Economics*, *26*(2), 301–325. doi:10.1086/467037

Fang, B., Ye, Q., & Law, R. (2016). Effect of sharing economy on tourism industry employment. *Annals of Tourism Research*, *57*, 264–267. doi:10.1016/j.annals.2015.11.018

Farahani, M. F., Mirzamohamadi, M. H., & Noroozi, N. (2014). The Study On Features Of Informal Education In Post-modernism. *Procedia: Social and Behavioral Sciences*, *136*, 559–563. doi:10.1016/j.sbspro.2014.05.376

Farquhar, J. D. (2012). *Case Studies Research for Business*. Thousand Oaks, CA: Sage Publications. doi:10.4135/9781446287910

Fassin, Y. (2012). Stakeholder management, reciprocity and stakeholder responsibility. *Journal of Business Ethics*, *109*(1), 83–96. doi:10.1007/s10551-012-1381-8

Fava Neves, M., & Dutra de Barcellos, M. (2013). *Value creation, capture and sharing model for food companies, chains and networks (VCCS Model)*. Symposium honouring Klaus Grunert, AU, Arhus.

Feagin, J. R., Orum, A. M., & Sjoberg, G. (Eds.). (1991). *A Case for the Case Study*. Chapel Hill, NC: The University of North Carolina Press.

Fergutz, O., Dias, S., & Mitlin, D. (2011). Developing urban waste management in Brazil with waste picker organizations. *Environment and Urbanization*, *23*(2), 597–608. doi:10.1177/0956247811418742

Ferrari, R. M. (1999). *Small enterprise clusters for local development in transition context: the case of Romania*. Milan, Italy: Bocconi University.

Ferrero, G. (1968). *Istituzioni di economia d'azienda*. Milano, Italy: Giuffrè.

Field, A. (2009). *Discovering Statistics Using SPSS* (3rd ed.). London: SAGE Publications.

Firnkorn, J., & Müller, M. (2011). What will be the environmental effects of new flee-floating car-sharing systems? The case of car2go in Ulm. *Ecological Economics*, *70*(8), 1519–1528. doi:10.1016/j.ecolecon.2011.03.014

Fitzgerald, N., & Cormack, M. (2006). *The Role of Business in Society: An Agenda for Action*. Retrieved May 26, 2016, from https://www.hks.harvard.edu/m-rcbg/CSRI/publications/report_12_CGI%20Role%20of%20Business%20in%20Society%20Report%20FINAL%2010-03-06.pdf

Fjell, L., & Rødland, S. E. (2015). *CSR in international business: Creating shared value* (Unpublished Masters' Thesis). Norwegian University of Science and Technology.

Flyvbjerg, B. (2006). Five Misunderstandings About Case-Study Research. *Qualitative Inquiry*, *12*(2), 219–245. doi:10.1177/1077800405284363

Fombrun, C., Gardberg, N., & Barnett, M. (2000). Opportunity platforms and safety Nets: Corporate citizenship and reputational risk. *Business and Society Review*, *105*(1), 85–106. doi:10.1111/0045-3609.00066

Font, X., Guix, M., & Bonilla-Priego, M. J. (2016). Corporate social responsibility in cruising: Using materiality analysis to create shared value. *Tourism Management*, *53*, 175–186. doi:10.1016/j.tourman.2015.10.007

Forno, F., & Garibaldi, R. (2015). Sharing economy in travel and tourism: The case of home-swapping in Italy. *Journal of Quality Assurance in Hospitality & Tourism*, *16*(2), 202–220. doi:10.1080/1528008X.2015.1013409

Fourie, J., & Santana-Gallego, M. (2011). The impact of mega-sport events on tourist arrivals. *Tourism Management*, *32*(6), 1364–1370. doi:10.1016/j.tourman.2011.01.011

Freeman, R. E. (1984). *Strategic Management – A Stakeholder Approach*. Boston, MA: Pitman.

Freeman, R. E. (1984). *Strategic management: A stakeholder approach*. Prentice-Hall.

Freeman, R. E. (2010). Managing for Stakeholders: Trade-offs or Value Creation. *Journal of Business Ethics*, *96*(1), 7–9. doi:10.1007/s10551-011-0935-5

Friedland, J. (Ed.). (2009). *Doing Well and Good: The Human Face of the New Capitalism*. Charlotte, NC: Information Age Publishing.

Friedman, M. (1970). The social responsibility of business is to increase its profits. In T. Beauchamp & N. Bowie (Eds.), Ethical Theory and Business (pp. 50–55). Upper Saddle River, NJ: Prentice Hall.

Friedman, M. (1970). The social responsibility of business is to increase its profits. *New York Times Magazine*, *33*, 122–126.

Frigo, M. L., & Ramaswamy, V. (2009). Co-creating strategic risk-return management. *Strategic Finance*, *5*(May), 25–33.

Frooman, J. (1997). Socially Irresponsible and Illegal Behavior and Shareholder Wealth: A Meta- Analysis of Event Studies. *Business & Society*, *36*(3), 221–249. doi:10.1177/000765039703600302

Frynas, J. G. (2009). *Beyond corporate social responsibility: Oil multinationals and social challenges*. Cambridge, UK: University Press. doi:10.1017/CBO9780511581540

Fust, A., & Tobias, J. (2014). *Self-Regulation and Entrepreneurial Learning*. Paper presented at the 59th Annual ICSB World Conference, Dublin, Ireland.

Garriga, E., & Melè, E. (2004). Corporate Social Responsibility Theories: Mapping the Territory. *Journal of Business Ethics*, *53*(1-2), 51–71. doi:10.1023/B:BUSI.0000039399.90587.34

Gascon, J. F. (2015). *Creating shared value: Corporate case study in developing countries*. Retrieved from https://www.mcgill.ca/isid/files/isid/gascon.pdf

Gauthier, C., & Gilomen, B. (2016). Business Models for Sustainability, Energy Efficiency in Urban Districts. *Organization & Environment*, *29*(1), 124–144. doi:10.1177/1086026615592931

Gedik, Ş., Miman, M., & Kesici, M. S. (2015). Characteristics and Attitudes of Entrepreneurs Towards Entrepreneurship. *Procedia – Social and Behavioral Sciences*, *195*, 1087-1096.

George, M. L. (2003). *Lean Six Sigma for Service: How to Use Lean Speed and Six Sigma Quality to Improve Services and Transactions*. New York, NY: McGraw-Hill.

Gerdes, P., & Gunsilius, E. (2010). *The waste experts: Enabling conditions for informal sector integration in solid waste management. Lessons learned from Brazil, Egypt and India.* GTZ Deutsche Gesellschaft für Technische Zusammenarbeit GmbH. Retrieved January 10, 2017, from https://www.giz.de/ en/downloads/gtz2010-waste-experts-conditions-is-integration.pdf

Gerring, J. (2007). *Case Study Research: Principles and Practices*. New York, NY: Cambridge University Press.

Getz, D. (2008). Event Tourism: Definition, Evolution, and Research. *Tourism Management*, *29*(3), 403–418. doi:10.1016/j.tourman.2007.07.017

Ghemawat, P. (1991). *Commitment: The dynamics of strategy*. New York: The Free Press.

Gholami, S. (2011). Value creation model through corporate social responsibility (CSR). *International Journal of Business and Management*, *6*(9), 54–57. doi:10.5539/ijbm.v6n9p148

Ghoshal, S. (2005). Bad management theories are destroying good management practices. *Academy of Management Learning & Education*, *4*(1), 75–91. doi:10.5465/AMLE.2005.16132558

Giacalone, R. A., & Wargo, D. T. (2009). The roots of the global financial crisis are in our business schools. *Journal of Business Ethics Education*, *6*, 147–168.

Giannessi, E. (1960). *Le aziende di produzione originaria: Vol. 1. Le aziende agricole*. Pisa, Italy: Cursi.

Giddens, M. (2011). *Investment & pensions Europe: Measuring social impact*. Retrieved from http://www.ipe.com/measuring-social-impact/41198.article

Gildea, R. L. (1994). Consumer Survey Confirms Corporate Social Action Affects Buying Decisions. *Public Relations Quarterly*, *39*(4), 20–22.

Gillespie, N. A., & Mann, L. (2004). Transformational leadership and shared values: The building blocks of trust. *Journal of Managerial Psychology*, *19*(6), 588–607. doi:10.1108/02683940410551507

Girard, L. F. (2006). Celebrating our urban heritage - Innovative strategies for urban heritage conservations, sustainable development, and renewable energy. *Global Urban Development.*, *2*(1), 1–10.

Glynn, M. A. (2008). Configuring the Field of Play: Hao Hosting the Olympics Games Impacts Civil Community. *Journal of Management Studies*, *45*(6), 1117–1146. doi:10.1111/j.1467-6486.2008.00785.x

Golinelli, G. M. (2005). L'approccio sistemico al governo dell'impresa. L'impresa sistema vitale (vol. 1). Padua, Italy: Cedam.

Gomm, R., Hammersley, M., & Foster, P. (2000). *Case Study Method: Key Issues, Key Texts*. Thousand Oaks, CA: Sage Publications.

Goodman, S. A., & Svyantek, D. J. (1999). Person-Organization fit and contextual performance: Do shared values matter. *Journal of Vocational Behavior*, *55*(2), 254–275. doi:10.1006/jvbe.1998.1682

Graafland, J., & van de Ven, B. (2006). Strategic and moral motivation for corporate social responsibility. *Journal of Corporate Citizenship*, *22*(3), 111–123. doi:10.9774/GLEAF.4700.2006.su.00012

Grace, D., & Lo Iacono, J. (2015). Value creation: An internal customers perspective. *Journal of Services Marketing*, *29*(6/7), 560–570. doi:10.1108/JSM-09-2014-0311

Grădinaru, C. (2015). *University education and its contribution to increasing the management system performance of the Romanian companies* (PhD Thesis). Bucharest.

Gradl, C., & Jenkins, B. (2011). *Tackling barriers to scale: From inclusive business models to inclusive business*. Retrieved from https://www.hks.harvard.edu/mrcbg/CSRI/publications/report_47_inclusive_business.pdf

Graf, A., & Maas, P. (2008). Customer value from a customer perspective: A comprehensive review. *Working Papers on Risk Management and Insurance, 52*, 1-37.

Grant, R. M. (2013). *Contemporary Strategy Analysis*. Chichester, UK: Wiley.

Gray, R. (2001). *Social and Environmental Responsibility, Sustainability and Accountability, Can the Corporate Sector Deliver?.* Centre for Social and Environmental Accounting Research, University of Glasgow. Retrieved on May 28, 2016, from www.agenda-scotland.org/documents/ Can%20business%20deliver%20Gray.pdf

Greening, D. W., & Turban, D. B. (2000). Corporate Social Performance as a Competitive Advantage in Attracting a Quality Workforce. *Business & Society*, *39*(3), 254–280. doi:10.1177/000765030003900302

Greeno, J. L., & Robinson, S. N. (1992). Rethinking Corporate Environmental Management. *The Columbia Journal of World Business*, *27*(3-4), 222–232.

GreenPaper EU. (2001). *Promoting a European Framework for Corporate Social Responsibility.* Brussels: Commission of the European Communities. Retrieved on May 28, 2016, from www.btplc.com/Societyandenvironment/ Reports/ GreenpaperonCSR.pdf

Greenwood, M. (2007). Stakeholder engagement: Beyond the myth of corporate responsibility. *Journal of Business Ethics*, *74*(4), 315–327. doi:10.1007/s10551-007-9509-y

Gregori, G. L., Pencarelli, T., Splendiani, S., & Temperini, V. (2013). Sustainable Tourism and Value Creation for the Territory: Towards a Holistic Model of Event Impact Measurement. *Calitatea-Acces to Succes*, *14*(135), 97–102.

Grewal, D., Monroe, K. B., & Khrisnan, R. (1998). The effects of price-comparison advertising on buyers perception on acquisition of value, transaction value, and behavioral intentions. *Journal of Marketing*, *62*(2), 46–59. doi:10.2307/1252160

Groenewegen, J. (1997). Institutions of capitalisms: American, European, and Japanese systems compared. *Journal of Economic Issues*, *31*(2), 333–347. doi:10.1080/00213624.1997.11505921

GTB/ILO (Turkish Ministry of Labour and Social Security/International Labour Organization). (2016). *Geri Dönüşüm Sektöründe Kooperatifçilik Potansiyeli Çalıştayı*, Retrieved January 15, 2017, from http://koop.gtb.gov.tr/haberler/ turkiyedeki-atik-toplayicilarinin-kooperatiflesmesine-yonelik-cok-onemli-adimlar-atildi

Guerrero, L. A., Maas, G., & Hogland, W. (2013). Solid waste management challenges for cities in developing countries. *Waste Management (New York, N.Y.)*, *30*(1), 220–232. doi:10.1016/j.wasman.2012.09.008 PMID:23098815

Gunsilius, E., Spies, S., Garcia-Cortez, S., Medina, M., Dias, S., & Scheinberg, A. (2011). *Recovering Resources, Creating Opportunities. Integrating the Informal Sector into Solid Waste Management.* Retrieved January 7, 2017, from https:// www.giz.de/en/downloads/giz2011-en-recycling-partnerships-informal-sector-final-report.pdf

Gutberlet, J. (2008). Empowering collective recycling initiatives: Video documentation and action research with a recycling co-op in Brazil. *Resources, Conservation and Recycling*, *52*(4), 659–670. doi:10.1016/j.resconrec.2007.08.006

Guthrie, J., Ricceri, F., & Dumay, J. (2012). Reflections and projections: A decade of intellectual capital accounting research. *The British Accounting Review*, *44*(2), 68–82. doi:10.1016/j.bar.2012.03.004

HaberTurk. (2016). *A'dan Z'ye Kagit Toplama Krizi.* Retrieved June 30, 2016, from http://www.haberturk.com/gundem/ haber/1187912-adan-zye-kagit-toplama-krizi

Hahn, R. (2012). Inclusive Business, Human Rights and the Dignity of the Poor: A Glance beyond Economic Impacts of Adapted Business Models. *Business Ethics (Oxford, England)*, *21*(1), 47–61. doi:10.1111/j.1467-8608.2011.01640.x

Haksever, C., Chaganti, R., & Cook, R. G. (2004). A Model of Value Creation: Strategic View. *Journal of Business Ethics*, *49*(3), 291–305. doi:10.1023/B:BUSI.0000017968.21563.05

Hall, P., & Landry, C. (1997). *Innovative and Sustainable Cities.* European Foundation for the Improvement of Living and Working Conditions.

Halme, M., & Fadeeva, Z. (2000). Small and medium-size tourism enterprises in sustainable development networks. *Greener Management International*, *30*(Summer), 97–113.

Halme, M., Linderman, S., & Lima, P. (2012). Innovation for Inclusive Business: Intrapreneurial Bricolage in Multinational Corporations. *Journal of Management Studies*, *49*(4), 743–758. doi:10.1111/j.1467-6486.2012.01045.x

Hamari, J., Sjöklint, M., & Ukkonen A. (2015). The Sharing Economy: Why people participate in collaborative consumption. *Journal of the Association for Information Science and Technology*.

Handelman, J. M., & Arnold, S. J. (1999). The Role of Marketing Actions with a Social Dimension: Appeals to the Institutional Environment. *Journal of Marketing*, *63*(3), 33–48. doi:10.2307/1251774

Hartline, M. D., Maxham, J. G. III, & Mckee, D. O. (2000). Corridors of influence in the dissemination of customer-oriented strategy to customer contact service employees. *Journal of Marketing*, *64*(2), 35–50. doi:10.1509/jmkg.64.2.35.18001

Hartman, L. P., & Werhane, P. H. (2013). Proposition: Shared value as an incomplete mental model. *Business Ethics Journal Review*, *1*(6), 36–43. doi:10.12747/bejr2013.01.02

Hart, S. L., & Christensen, C. M. (2002). The Great Leap. Driving Innovation from the Base of the Pyramid. *MIT Sloan Management Review*, *44*(1), 51–57.

Hart, S. L., & Milstein, M. B. (2003). Creating sustainable value. *The Academy of Management Executive*, *17*(2), 56–67. doi:10.5465/AME.2003.10025194

Hayami, Y., Dikshit, A. K., & Mishra, S. N. (2006). Waste pickers and collectors in Delhi: Poverty and environment in an urban informal sector. *The Journal of Development Studies*, *42*(1), 41–69. doi:10.1080/00220380500356662

Hayes, A. S., & Pereira, J. (1990). Facing a Boycott, Many Companies Bend. *Wall Street Journal, 24*, 1.

Hayes, A. F., & Krippendorff, K. (2007). Answering the call for a standard reliability measure for coding data. *Communication Methods and Measures*, *1*(1), 77–89. doi:10.1080/19312450709336664

Hayes, R. H., & Abernathy, W. J. (1980). Managing our way to economic decline. *Harvard Business Review*, *58*, 67–77.

Hearn, G., & Pace, C. (2006). Value-creating ecologies: Understanding next generation business systems. *Foresight*, *8*(1), 55–65. doi:10.1108/14636680610647147

Heinrichs, H. (2013). Sharing economy: A potential new pathway to sustainability. *GAIA-Ecological Perspectives for Science and Society*, *22*(4), 228–231. doi:10.14512/gaia.22.4.5

Helling, B., & Ajmal, S. I. (2017). *The Year The Rideshare Industry Crushed The Taxi*. Retrieved January 17, 2017, from https://rideshareapps.com/2015-rideshare-infographic/

Helms, M. M., & Nixon, J. (2010). Exploring SWOT analysis – where are we now? A review of academic research from the last decade. *Journal of Strategy and Management*, *3*(2), 215–251. doi:10.1108/17554251011064837

Henderson, J. C. (2005). Planning, changing landscapes and tourism in Singapore. *Journal of Sustainable Tourism*, *13*(2), 123–136. doi:10.1080/09669580508668482

Henten, A. H., & Windekilde, I. M. (2016). Transaction costs and the sharing economy. *Info, 18*(1), 1-15.

Heo, C. Y. (2016). Sharing economy and prospects in tourism research. *Annals of Tourism Research*, *58*, 166–170. doi:10.1016/j.annals.2016.02.002

Herbert, B. (1996). Nike's Pyramid Scheme. *New York Times*, pp. 17-23.

Hern, A. (2015). *Why the Term 'Sharing Economy' Needs to Die*. Retrieved on March 30, 2017 from http://www.theguardian.com/technology/2015/oct/05/why-the-term-sharing-economy-needs-to-die

Hidalgo, C., Peterson, K., Smith, D., & Foley, H. (2014). *Extracting with purpose: Creating shared value in the oil and gas and mining sectors' companies and communities*. Retrieved from http://www.fsg.org/publications/extracting-purpose

Hillebrand, B., Buttermann, H., Behringer, J., & Bleuel, M. (2006). The expansion of renewable energies and employment effects in Germany. *Energy Policy*, *34*(18), 3484–3494. doi:10.1016/j.enpol.2005.06.017

Hills, G., Russell, P., Borgonovi, V., Doty, A., & Lyer, L. (2012). *Shared value in emerging markets: How multinational corporations are redefining business strategies to reach poor or vulnerable populations*. Retrieved from http://www.fsg.org/publications/shared-value-emerging-markets

Hines, P., Holweg, M., & Rich, N. (2004). Learning to evolve. *International Journal of Operations & Production Management*, *24*(10), 994–1011. doi:10.1108/01443570410558049

Hino, S. (2006). *Inside the Mind of Toyota: Management Principles for Enduring Growth*. New York, NY: Productivity Press.

Hirschman, A. O. (1970). The search for paradigms as a hindrance to understanding. *World Politics*, *22*(3), 329–343. doi:10.2307/2009600

Hnatek, M. (2015). Entrepreneurial thinking as a key factor of family business success. *Procedia: Social and Behavioral Sciences*, *181*, 342–348. doi:10.1016/j.sbspro.2015.04.896

Hoeffler, S., & Keller, K. L. (2002). Building Brand Equity through Corporate Societal Marketing. *Journal of Public Policy & Marketing*, *21*(1), 78–89. doi:10.1509/jppm.21.1.78.17600

Hoffmann, V. H., & Busch, T. (2008). Corporate Carbon Performance Indicators, Carbon Intensity, Dependency, Exposure, and Risk. *Journal of Industrial Ecology*, *12*(4), 505–520. doi:10.1111/j.1530-9290.2008.00066.x

Hofstede, G., Hofstede, G. J., & Minkow, M. (2010). *Cultures and Organizations: Software of the Mind* (3rd ed.). New York, NY: McGraw-Hill.

Hong, P., Doll, W. J., Nahm, A. Y., & Li, X. (2004). Knowledge sharing in integrated product development. *European Journal of Innovation Management*, *7*(2), 102–112. doi:10.1108/14601060410534393

Hsiao, T.-Y., & Chuang, C.-M. (2016). Creating shared value through implementing green practices for star hotels. *Asia Pacific Journal of Tourism Research*, *21*(6), 678–696. doi:10.1080/10941665.2015.1068194

Hubert, D. (2016). *The Use of Tax Havens in the Ownership of Kenyan Petroleum Rights*. Retrieved June 30, 2016, from https://www.oxfam.org/sites/www.oxfam.org/files/file_attachments/rr-tax-havens-kenyan-petroleum-rights-100516-en_0.pdf

Human Rights Watch. (2015). *"There is No Time Left" Climate Change, Environmental Threats, and Human Rights in Turkana County, Kenya*. Retrieved from https://www.hrw.org/report/2015/10/15/there-no-time-left/climate-change-environmental-threats-and-human-rights-turkana

Hurriyet. (2016). *Atik Toplayicilar Sirketlesti*. Retrieved January 15, 2017, from http://www. hurriyet.com.tr/atik-toplayicilar-sirketlesti-37290120

Husted, B. W. (2003). Governance Choices for Corporate Social Responsibility: To Contribute, Collaborate or Internalize? *Long Range Planning*, *36*(5), 481–498. doi:10.1016/S0024-6301(03)00115-8

Husted, B. W., & Allen, D. B. (2000). Is It Ethical to Use Ethics as Strategy? *Journal of Business Ethics*, *27*(1-2), 21–32. doi:10.1023/A:1006422704548

Iansiti, M., & Richards, G. L. (2006). *Information technology ecosystem: Structure, health, and performance*. Academic Press.

Iansiti, M., & Levien, R. (2002). *The New Operational Dynamics of Business Ecosystems: Implications for Policy, Operations and Technology Strategy*. Division of Research. Harvard Business School.

Iansiti, M., & Levien, R. (2004). Strategy as ecology. *Harvard Business Review*, *82*(3), 68–81. PMID:15029791

IISD. (1992). *Business Strategies for Sustainable Development*. Retrieved May 8, 2016, from https://www.iisd.org/business/tools/strategies.aspx

ILO (International Labour Organization). (2011). *Children in hazardous work: what we know what we need to do*. International Programme on Elimination of Child Labour (IPEC). ILO. Retrieved 7 January, from http://www.ilo.org/wcmsp5/groups/public/@dgreports/@dcomm/@publ/documents/ publication/wcms_155428.pdf

ILO (International Labour Organization). (2012). *Working Towards Sustainable Development: Opportunities for Decent Work and Social Inclusion in a Green Economy*. Retrieved February 13, 2015, from http://www.ilo.org/global/publications/ilo-bookstore/order-online/books/WCMS181836/ lang--en/index.htm

Imai, M. (1986). *Kaizen: The Key to Japan's Competitive Success*. New York, NY: McGraw-Hill.

Imai, M. (1997). *Gemba Kaizen: A Commonsense, Low-Cost Approach to Management*. New York, NY: McGraw-Hill.

India C. S. R. Outlook. (2015). *A Snapshot of CSR Spend In FY 2014-15' 250 BSE-Listed Companies*. Retrieved September 20, 2016, from http://www.ngobox.org

Ingelsson, P., & Mårtensson, A. (2014). Measuring the importance and practices of Lean values. *The TQM Journal*, *26*(5), 463–474. doi:10.1108/TQM-07-2012-0047

Inkpen, A. C., & Moffett, M. H. (2011). *The global oil & gas industry: Management, strategy & finance*. Tulsa, OK: PennWell.

International Energy Agency. (2014). *World energy outlook 2014*. Retrieved June 30, 2016, from https://www.iea.org/Textbase/npsum/WEO2014SUM.pdf

International Petroleum Industry Environmental Conservation Association. (2013). *Social and economic development*. Retrieved from http://www.ipieca.org/topic/social-responsibility/social-and-economic-development

International Union for Conservation of Nature. (n.d.). *IUCN definitions – English*. Retrieved 2, January, 2017, from https://www.iucn.org/downloads/en_iucn__glossary_definitions.pdf

Ionescu, V. (1999). *Supply-Side Strategy for Productivity, Competitiveness and Convergence between the CEECs and (in) the EU-Romania Case Study*. Academic Press.

Irungu, G. (2015, June 2). Australian explorer pulls out of second Lamu oil block. *Business Daily*. Retrieved June 30, 2016, from http://www.businessdailyafrica.com/Australian-explorer-pulls-out-of-second-Lamu-oil-block-/-/539552/2737918/-/br6rt7z/-/index.html

Isenberg, D. J. (2010). How to start an entrepreneurial revolution. *Harvard Business Review*, *88*(6), 40–50.

Ishikawa, K. (1993). *Introduction to Quality Control*. Tokyo: 3A Corporation.

Ishikawa, K. (1985). *What is Quality Control? The Japanese Way*. Englewood Cliffs, NJ: Prentice-Hall.

ISTAC (Istanbul Environmental Management Industry and Trading Inc.). (2015). *Integrated Solid Waste Management - Strategic Plan 2015-2019*. Retrieved May 28, 2016, from http://www.istac.istanbul/contents/15/WEB_ISTAC_STRATEJI.pdf

ISTAC (Istanbul Environmental Management Industry and Trading Inc.). (2016). *IBB 100 Milyonu Cope Gitmekten Kurtardi*. Retrieved May 28, 2016, from http://www.ibb.istanbul/tr-TR/ Pages/Haber.aspx?NewsID=23017#.V3JR0riLTIU

Istanbul, B. (n.d.a). *BIST Sustainability Index Ground Rules*. Retrieved May 10, 2016, from http://www.borsaistanbul.com/docs/default-source/endeksler/bist-sustainability-index-ground-rules.pdf?sfvrsn=10

Istanbul, B. (n.d.b). *BIST Sustainability Index*. Retrieved May 10, 2016, from http://www.borsaistanbul.com/en/indices/bist-stock-indices/bist-sustainability-index

Jabareen, Y. (2006). A new conceptual framework for sustainable development. *Environment, Development and Sustainability*, *10*(2), 179–192. doi:10.1007/s10668-006-9058-z

Jackson, A. (2008). *EXPO International Expositions 1851–2010*. London, UK: V&A Publishing.

Jacobides, M. (2013). *Creating and Capturing Value in Your Business Ecosystems*. Retrieved from TedXTalk: http://www.tedxthessaloniki.com/index.php/talk_video/creating-and-capturing-value-in-your-business-ecosystems/#sthash.wUfQjlTZ.dpuf

Jacquemont, D. (2014) The organization that renews itself: Lasting value from lean management. In C. Johnson (Ed.), *The Lean Management Enterprise* (pp. 8-15). Retrieved December 12, 2016, from www.mckinsey.com/leanmanagement/2014_lean_management_enterprise_compendium.ashx

Jean, W. A., & Yazdanifard, R. (2015). The review of shared value in contemporary CSR run by two successful companies to sustain the business in recent years. *International Journal of Management, Accounting and Economics*, *2*(9), 1122–1129.

Jean, W. A., & Yazdanifard, R. (2015). The Review of Shared Value in Contemporary CSR Run by Two Successful Companies to Sustain the Business in Recent Years. *International Journal of Management. Accounting and Economics*, *2*(9), 1122–1129.

Jenkins, B., Valikai, K., & Baptista, P. (2013). *The Coca-Cola Company's 5by20 Initiative: Empowering Women Entrepreneurs across the Value Chain*. Cambridge, MA: The CSR Initiative at the Harvard Kennedy School and Business Fights Poverty.

Jensen, M. C. (2001). Value Maximisation, Stakeholder Theory, and the Corporate Objective Function. *European Financial Management*, *7*(3), 297–317. doi:10.1111/1468-036X.00158

Jensen, M. C. (2001). Value maximization, stakeholder theory, and the corporate objective function. *Journal of Applied Corporate Finance*, *14*(3), 8–21. doi:10.1111/j.1745-6622.2001.tb00434.x

Jensen, M. C. (2002). Value Maximization, Stakeholder Theory, and the Corporate Objective Function. *Business Ethics Quarterly*, *12*(2), 235–256. doi:10.2307/3857812

Jensen, M. C., & Meckling, W. (1976). Theory of the firm: Managerial behavior, agency costs, and capital structure. *Journal of Financial Economics*, *3*(4), 305–360. doi:10.1016/0304-405X(76)90026-X

Johannes, E. M., Zulu, L. C., & Kalipeni, E. (2015). Oil discovery in Turkana County, Kenya: A source of conflict or development? *African Geographical Review*, *34*(2), 142–164. doi:10.1080/19376812.2014.884466

Johansen, S. (1988). Statistical Analysis of Cointegrating Vectors. *Journal of Economic Dynamics & Control*, *12*(2-3), 231–254. doi:10.1016/0165-1889(88)90041-3

Johanson, J., & Vahlne, J. E. (2011). Markets as networks: Implications for strategy-making. *Journal of the Academy of Marketing Science*, *39*(4), 484–491. doi:10.1007/s11747-010-0235-0

Johnson, C. (1982). *MITI and the Japanese Miracle: The Growth of Industrial Policy, 1925-1975*. Stanford, CA: Stanford University Press.

Jones, T. M. (1980). Corporate Social Responsibility Revisited, Redefined. *California Management Review*, *22*(2), 59–67. doi:10.2307/41164877

Jones, T. M. (1995). Instrumental stakeholder theory: A synthesis of ethics and economics. *Academy of Management Review*, *20*(2), 404–437.

Jonikas, D. (2013). Conceptual framework of value creation through CSR in separate member of value creation chain. *Bulletin of Geography Socio–Economic Series*, *21*, 69–78.

Jonikas, D. (2014). Value created through CSR measurement possibilities. *Procedia: Social and Behavioral Sciences*, *156*, 189–193. doi:10.1016/j.sbspro.2014.11.169

Jönsson, S., & Schölin, T. (2014). Potentials facilitators of workplace learning in a TPS based company. *Journal of Management Development*, *33*(10), 1004–1018. doi:10.1108/JMD-10-2012-0130

Joshi, Y. C., & Shah, D. (2016). Transforming Corporate Social Responsibility towards Socially Responsible Corporation. *Synergy*, *18*(1), 1–9.

Juran, J. M. (1989). *Juran on Leadership for Quality: An Executive Handbook*. New York, NY: The Free Press.

Juscius, V., & Jonikas, D. (2013). Integration of CSR into value chain: Conceptual framework. *InzinerineEkonomika-Engineering Economics*, *24*(1), 63–70.

Jusevicius, R., & Liugailaite, L. (2013). Smart Development: A Conceptual Framework. *Proceedings of the International Conference on Intellectual Capital, Knowledge Management & Organizational Learning* (pp. 212-219). Retrieved April 10, 2016, from http://web.a.ebscohost.com/ehost/pdfviewer/pdfviewer?vid=3&sid=a7eed2ab-4453-4beb-bbee-cb7a81961fe8%40sessionmgr4003&hid=4109

Kamiya, S. (1976). *My Life with Toyota*. Toyota Motor Sales Company, Ltd.

Kanat, G. (2010). Country report. Municipal solid waste management in Istanbul. *Waste Management (New York, N.Y.)*, *30*(8-9), 1737–1745. doi:10.1016/j.wasman.2010.01.036 PMID:20185290

Kania, J., & Kramer, M. (2011). Collective impact. *Stanford Social Innovation Review*, *9*(1), 36–41.

Kanter, R. M. (2011). How Great Companies Think Differently. *Harvard Business Review*, *89*(11), 66–78.

Kantis, H. D., & Federico, J. S. (2012). *Entrepreneurial Ecosystems in Latin America: The role of policies*. International Research and Policy Roundtable (Kauffman Foundation), Liverpool, UK.

Katayama, H., & Benett, D. (1996). Lean production in a changing competitive world: A Japanese perspective. *Journal of Operations & Production Management*, *16*(2), 8–23. doi:10.1108/01443579610109811

Kavi, K. (2009). The upstream energy value chain. *Oil & Gas Journal*, *107*(45), S9–S11.

Kaya, D. (2006). Renewable energy policies in Turkey. *Renewable & Sustainable Energy Reviews*, *10*(2), 152–163. doi:10.1016/j.rser.2004.08.001

Kaya, D., & Kilic, F. C. (2015). New markets for renewable industries: Developing countries-Turkey, its potential and policies. *Journal of Energy in Southern Africa*, *26*(1), 25–35.

Kay, J. (1997). The stakeholder corporation. In G. Kelly, D. Kelly, & A. Gamble (Eds.), *Stakeholder capitalism* (pp. 125–141). London: Macmillam Press.

Kearney, A. T. (2015). *Creating value by doing good.* A.T. Kearney Inc.

Keay, A. (2008). Ascertaining the corporate objective: An entity maximization and sustainability model. *The Modern Law Review*, *71*(5), 663–698. doi:10.1111/j.1468-2230.2008.00711.x

Keleş, S., & Bilgen, S. (2012). Renewable energy sources in Turkey for climate change mitigation and energy sustainability. *Renewable & Sustainable Energy Reviews*, *16*(7), 5199–5206. doi:10.1016/j.rser.2012.05.026

Kemper, A., & Martin, R. L. (2010). After the fall: The global financial crisis as a test of corporate social responsibility theories. *European Management Review*, *7*(4), 229–239. doi:10.1057/emr.2010.18

Kibor, F. (2014, October 2). Tullow told to unveil exploration plan for Kerio Valley and Elgeyo Marakwet. *The Standard.* Retrieved June 30, 2016, from http://www.standardmedia.co.ke/article/2000136815/tullow-told-to-unveil-exploration-plan-for-kerio-valley-and-elgeyo-marakwet

Kim, W. C., & Mauborgne, R. (2005). *Blue Ocean Strategy.* Boston, MA: Harvard Business School Press.

Kipsang, W. (2016, March 29). Showdown as Elgeyo-Marakwet, Turkana county leaders give terms for exploration. *Daily Nation.* Retrieved June 30, 2016, from http://www.nation.co.ke/news/Leaders-want-title-deeds-before-oil-exploration/-/1056/3137222/-/4hmjhp/-/index.html

Kirmani, A. (1997). Advertising Repetition as a Signal of Quality: If Its Advertised So Much, Something Must Be Wrong. *Journal of Advertising*, *26*(3), 77–90. doi:10.1080/00913367.1997.10673530

Kleemann, L., & Krieger-Boden, C. (2011). *Bridging morale and business through shared value?.* Kiel policy brief / InstitutfürWeltwirtschaftan der Universität Kiel, No. 38.

Kocasoy, G. (2003). *Institutional Structure of the Solid Waste and Landfill Management in Developing Countries.* Paper presented at 9th International Waste Management and Landfill Symposium, Sardinia, Italy.

Koenigsaecker, G. (2013). *Leading the Lean Enterprise Transformation* (2nd ed.). Boca Raton, FL: CRC Press.

Kogut, B. (2000). The network as knowledge: Generative rules and the emergence of structure. *Strategic Management Journal*, *21*(3), 405–425. doi:10.1002/(SICI)1097-0266(200003)21:3<405::AID-SMJ103>3.0.CO;2-5

Kogut, B., & Zander, U. (1996). What firms do? Coordination, identity, and learning. *Organization Science*, *7*(5), 502–518. doi:10.1287/orsc.7.5.502

Kolcuoglu, D. (2010). *Renewable Energy: Turkey's Hope for Energy Independence.* Retrieved October 15, 2016, from http://www.hg.org/article.asp?id=24256

Komninos, N. (2011). Intelligent cities: Variable geometries of spatial intelligence. *Intelligent Buildings International*, *3*(3), 172–188. doi:10.1080/17508975.2011.579339

Kosai, Y. (1986). *The Era of High-Speed Growth. Notes on the Postwar Japanese Economy.* Tokyo: University of Tokyo Press.

Koslowski, P. (2000). The limits of shareholder value. *Journal of Business Ethics*, *27*(1-2), 137–148. doi:10.1023/A:1006438000855

Kowsari, R., & Zerriffi, H. (2011). Three dimensional energy profile: A conceptual framework for assessing household energy use. *Energy Policy*, *39*(12), 7505–7517. doi:10.1016/j.enpol.2011.06.030

KPMG. (2005). *KPMG International Survey of Corporate Responsibility Reporting 2005*. KPMG Global Sustainability Services. Retrieved May 05, 2016, from http://www.kpmg.org

Krafcik, J. F. (1988). Triumph of the lean production system. *Sloan Management Review*, *30*(1), 41–52.

Kramer, M. (2011). *CSR vs. CSV - What's the difference?*. Retrieved May 30, 2016 from http://www.fsg.org/blog/csr-vs-csv-what's-difference

Kramer, M. R., & Tallant, K. (2014). Roundtable on shared value in education. *Stanford Social Innovation Review*. Retrieved from http://ssir.org/articles/entry/roundtable_on_shared_value_in_education

Kramer, M. R. (2009). Catalytic Philanthropy. *Stanford Social Innovation Review*, *7*(3), 29–35.

Kreckova, Z. (2015). Corporate response to concept of shared value. *European Scientific Journal*, *11*(22), 36–45.

Krippendorff, K. (2013). *Content Analysis. An Introduction to Its Methodology*. Thousand Oaks, CA: Sage Publications.

Krishna, C. G. (1992). *Corporate Social Responsibility in India*. New Delhi, India: Mittal Publications.

Kriston, A., Szabo, T., & Inzelt, G. (2010). The marriage of car sharing and hydrogen economy: A possible solution to the main problems of urban living. *International Journal of Hydrogen Energy*, *35*(23), 12697–12708. doi:10.1016/j.ijhydene.2010.08.110

Kroeger, A., & Weber, C. (2015). Developing a Conceptual Framework for Comparing Social Value Creation. *Academy of Management Review*, *30*(4), 513–540.

Krueger, N. F. Jr. (2007). What lies beneath? The experimental essence of entrepreneurial thinking. *Entrepreneurship Theory and Practice*, *31*(1), 123–138. doi:10.1111/j.1540-6520.2007.00166.x

Krzyżanowska, M., & Tkaczyk, J. (2014). Shared Value Creation and Marketing. *Management and Business Administration. Central Europe*, *22*(4), 153–167.

Kumar, R., Murphy, D. F., & Balsari, V. (2001). *Altered Images: The 2001 State of Corporate Responsibility in India Poll. In Understanding and Encouraging Corporate Responsibility in South Asia – Update 1*. New Delhi, India: Tata Energy Research Institute.

Lackmann, J., Ernstberger, J., & Stich, M. (2012). Market reactions to increased reliability of sustainability information. *Journal of Business Ethics*, *107*(2), 111–128. doi:10.1007/s10551-011-1026-3

Lai, F., Zhang, M., Lee, D. M. S., & Zhao, X. (2012). The Impact of Supply Chain Integration on Mass Customization Capability: An Extended Resource-Based View. *IEEE Transactions on Engineering Management*, *59*(3), 443–456. doi:10.1109/TEM.2012.2189009

Landon, S., & Smith, C. E. (1997). The Use of Quality and Reputation Indicators by Consumers: The Case of Bordeaux Wine. *Journal of Consumer Policy*, *20*(3), 285–297. doi:10.1023/A:1006830218392

Langtry, B. (1994). Stakeholders and the moral responsibilities of businesses. *Business Ethics Quarterly*, *4*(4), 431–443. doi:10.2307/3857342

Lan, L. L., & Heracleous, L. (2010). Rethinking agency theory: The view from law. *Academy of Management Review*, *35*(2), 294–314. doi:10.5465/AMR.2010.48463335

Laventure, L. (2016). *How the search for oil is inflaming tensions in Kenya*. Retrieved June 30, 2016, from http://www.aljazeera.com/indepth/features/2016/03/search-oil-inflaming-tensions-kenya-160302094606486.html

Law, C. (Ed.). (1996). *Tourism in Major Cities*. London: International Thompson Business Press.

Lawrence, A. T., & Weber, J. (2008). *Business and Society*. New York, NY: McGraw-Hill Irwin.

Lazonick, W. (2011). From innovation to financialization: how shareholder value ideology is destroying the US Economy. The Handbook of the Political Economy of Financial Crises.

Leandro, L., & Neffa, E. (2012). Is the integration of shared value creation (SVC) with strategy management of productive organizations an innovative approach to environmental challenges faced by companies today?. *International Journal of Business, Management, Economic Research Journal*, *3*(2), 484–489.

Leavy, B., & Moitra, D. (2006). The practice of co-creating unique value with customers: An interview with C. K. Prahalad. *Strategy and Leadership*, *34*(2), 4–9. doi:10.1108/10878570610652581

Lee, M. P. (2008). A Review of the Theories of Corporate Social Responsibility: Its Evolutionary Path and the Road Ahead. *International Journal of Management Reviews*, *10*(1), 53–73. doi:10.1111/j.1468-2370.2007.00226.x

Lee, S. M., Olson, D. L., & Trimi, S. (2012). Co-innovation: Convergenomics, collaboration, and co-creation for organizational values. *Management Decision*, *50*(5), 817–831. doi:10.1108/00251741211227528

Lefebvre, H. (1971). *Everyday Life in the Modern World*. London: The Whitefriers Press.

Lepak, D. P., Smith, K. G., & Taylor, M. S. (2007). Value creation and value capture: A multilevel perspective. *Academy of Management Review*, *32*(1), 180–194. doi:10.5465/AMR.2007.23464011

Letaifa, S. B. (2014). The uneasy transition from supply chains to ecosystems. *Management Decision*, *52*(2), 278–295. doi:10.1108/MD-06-2013-0329

Leth, M., & Hems, L. (2014). *The potential for creating shared value in Australia*. CSV Green Paper. Retrieved from https://static.squarespace.com/static/52045752e4b0330b6437dade/t/52dce083e4b086a63887ccb5/1390207107654/CSV-Green%20Paper_Draft%20for%20Discussion.pdf

Lewis, M. A. (2000). Lean production and sustainable competitive advantage. *International Journal of Operations & Production Management*, *20*(8), 959–978. doi:10.1108/01443570010332971

Liberman, M. B., & Balasubramanian, N. (2007). *Measuring Value Creation and Its Distribution Among Stakeholders of the Firm*. Retrieved May 29, 2016, from http://www.anderson.ucla.edu/faculty/marvin.lieberman/docs/Lieberman-Subra_VCD.pdf

Liker, J. K. (2004). *The Toyota Way: 14 Management Principles from the World's Greatest Manufacturer*. New York, NY: McGraw-Hill.

Liker, J. K. (Ed.). (1998). *Becoming Lean: Inside Stories of U.S. Manufacturers*. Portland, OR: Productivity Press.

Liker, J. K., & Hoseus, M. (2008). *Toyota Culture: The Heart and Soul of the Toyota Way*. New York, NY: McGraw-Hill.

Liker, J. K., & Meier, D. P. (2006). *The Toyota Way Fieldbook: A Practical Guide for Implementing Toyota's 4Ps*. New York, NY: McGraw-Hill.

Liker, J. K., & Meier, D. P. (2007). *Toyota Talent: Developing your People the Toyota Way*. New York, NY: McGraw-Hill.

Liker, J. K., & Ross, K. (2017). *The Toyota Way to Service Excellence*. New York, NY: McGraw-Hill.

Lin, C. H., Yang, H. L., & Liou, D. Y. (2009). The impact of corporate social responsibility on financial performance: Evidence from business in Taiwan. *Technology in Society*, *31*(1), 56–63. doi:10.1016/j.techsoc.2008.10.004

López, L. A., Domingos, T., Cadarso, M. Á., & Zafrilla, J. E. (2014). The smarter, the cleaner? Collaborative footprint: A further look at taxi sharing. *Proceedings of the National Academy of Sciences of the United States of America*, *111*(51), 5488–5488. doi:10.1073/pnas.1420242112 PMID:25503369

Lopez, M. V., Garcia, A., & Rodriguez, L. (2007). Sustainable development and corporate performance: A study based on the Dow Jones Sustainability Index. *Journal of Business Ethics*, *75*(3), 285–300. doi:10.1007/s10551-006-9253-8

Lo, S. F., & Sheu, H. J. (2007). Is corporate sustainability a value-increasing strategy for business? *Corporate Governance: An International Review*, *15*(2), 345–358. doi:10.1111/j.1467-8683.2007.00565.x

Lourenco, I. C., Branco, M. C., Curto, J. D., & Eugenio, T. (2012). How does the market value corporate sustainability performance? *Journal of Business Ethics*, *108*(4), 417–428. doi:10.1007/s10551-011-1102-8

Lynes, J., & Andrachuk, M. (2008). Motivations for corporate social and environmental responsibility: A case study of Scandinavian Airlines. *Journal of International Management*, *14*(4), 377–390. doi:10.1016/j.intman.2007.09.004

Lyon, T., & Maxwell, J. (2008). Corporate Social Responsibility and the Environment: A Theoretical Perspective. *Review of Environmental Economics and Policy*, *2*(2), 240–260. doi:10.1093/reep/ren004

Lytras, M. D., Al-Halabi, W., Xi Zhang, J., Masud, M., & Haraty, R. A. (2015a). Enabling Technologies and Business Infrastructures for Next Generation Social Media: Big Data, Cloud Computing, Internet of Things and Virtual Reality. *Journal of Universal Computer Science*, *21*(11), 1379–1384.

Lytras, M. D., García-Peñalvo, F. J., & Ordóñez de Pablos, P. (2013). Advanced human-computer interaction. *Computers in Human Behavior*, *29*(2), 305–306. doi:10.1016/j.chb.2012.11.018

Lytras, M. D., & Kurilovas, E. (2014a). Special issue on Information and communication technologies for human capital development. *Computers in Human Behavior*, *30*, 361. doi:10.1016/j.chb.2013.11.002

Lytras, M. D., Mathkour, H. I., Abdalla, H. I., Al-Halabi, W., Yáñez-Márquez, C., Wolfgand, S., & Siqueira, M. (2015b). An emerging - Social and emerging computing enabled philosophical paradigm for collaborative learning systems: Toward high effective next generation learning systems for the knowledge society. *Computers in Human Behavior*, *51*, 557–561. doi:10.1016/j.chb.2015.06.004

Lytras, M. D., Mathkour, H., Abdalla, H. I., Yáñez-Márquez, C., & Ordóñez de Pablos, P. (2014b). The Social Media in Academia and Education: Research R-evolutions and a Paradox: Advanced Next Generation Social Learning Innovation. *Journal of Universal Computer Science*, *20*(15), 1987–1994.

Lytras, M. D., Zhuhadar, L., Zhang, J. X., & Kurilovas, E. (2014c). Advances of Scientific Research on Technology Enhanced Learning in Social Networks and Mobile Contexts: Towards High Effective Educational Platforms for Next Generation Education. *Journal of Universal Computer Science*, *20*(10), 1402–1406.

Ma, S., Zheng, Y., & Wolfson, O. (2013). T-share: A large-scale dynamic taxi ridesharing service. In *Data Engineering (ICDE), 2013 IEEE 29th International Conference,* (pp. 410-421). IEEE.

Maczadlo, R. (2015). Creating competitive advantages – The European CSR-strategy compared with Porter's and Kramer's shared value approach. *ECONVIEWS*, *28*, 243–256.

Maersk Oil. (2016, February 3). *Maersk Oil completes acquisition of East African licences* (Press release). Retrieved June 30, 2016, from http://www.maerskoil.com/media/newsroom/pages/maersk_oil_completes_acquisition_of_east_african_licences.aspx

Magee, D. (2008). *How Toyota Became #1: Leadership Lessons from the World's Greatest Car Company*. New York, NY: Portfolio.

Magill, M., Quinzii, M., & Rochet, J. C. (2015). A Theory of the stakeholder corporation. *Econometrica*, *83*(5), 1685–1725. doi:10.3982/ECTA11455

Mahler, A. (2010). *Nigeria: A prime example of the resource curse? Revisiting the oil-violence link in the Niger Delta.* Retrieved June 30, 2016, from https://www.giga-hamburg.de/en/system/files/publications/wp120_maehler.pdf

Mahler, A. (2012). An inescapable curse? Resource management, violent conflict, and peacebuilding in the Niger Delta. In P. Lujala & S. A. Rustad (Eds.), *High-value natural resources and post-conflict peacebuilding* (pp. 391–412). London: Routledge.

Malecki, E. J. (2011). Connecting local entrepreneurial ecosystems to global innovation networks: Open innovation, double networks and knowledge integration. *International Journal of Entrepreneurship and Innovation Management*, *14*(1), 36–59. doi:10.1504/IJEIM.2011.040821

Mansfield, E., Rapoport, J., Romeo, A., Samuel Wagner, S., & Beardsley, G. (1977). Social and private rates of return from industrial innovation. *The Quarterly Journal of Economics*, *91*(2), 221–240. doi:10.2307/1885415

Manville, C., et al. (2014). *Mapping Smart Cities in the EU.* European Commission, Directorate General for Internal Policies – Policy Department A: Economic and Scientific Policy.

Manzanera-Roman, S., & Brandle, G. (2016). Abilities and skills as factors explaining the differences in women entrepreneurship. *Suma de Negocios*, *7*(15), 38–46. doi:10.1016/j.sumneg.2016.02.001

March, J. (1991). Exploration and exploitation in organizational learning. *Organization Science*, *2*(1), 71–87. doi:10.1287/orsc.2.1.71

March, J. G., & Simon, H. A. (1958). *Organizations*. New York: John Wiley and Sons.

Marello, M., & Helwege, A. (2014). *Solid waste management and social inclusion of waste pickers: Opportunities and challenges.* GEGI (Global Economic Governance Initiative) working paper. Retrieved March 3, 2016, from https://www.bu.edu/pardeeschool/files/2014/11/Social-Inclusion-Working-Paper.pdf

Margolis, J. D., & Walsh, J. P. (2003). Misery Loves Companies: Rethinking Social Initiatives by Business. *Administrative Science Quarterly*, *48*(2), 268–305. doi:10.2307/3556659

Markham, S. E., Yammarino, F. J., Murry, W. D., & Palanski, M. E. (2010). Leader-member exchange, shared values, and performance: Agreement and levels of analysis do matter. *The Leadership Quarterly*, *21*(3), 469–480. doi:10.1016/j.leaqua.2010.03.010

Marksberry, P. (2012). Investigating The Way for Toyota suppliers. A quantitative outlook on Toyota replicating efforts for supplier development. *Benchmarking: An International Journal*, *19*(2), 277–298. doi:10.1108/14635771211224572

Marouli, C. (1995). Women resisting (in) the city: Struggles, gender, class and space in Athens. *International Journal of Urban and Regional Research*, *19*(4), 534–548. doi:10.1111/j.1468-2427.1995.tb00527.x

Marshal-Llacuna, L. L., & Segal, M. E. (2016). The Intelligenter Method (I) for making smarter city projects and plans. *Cities (London, England)*, *55*, 127–138. doi:10.1016/j.cities.2016.02.006

Martin, C. J. (2016). The sharing economy: A pathway to sustainability or a nightmarish form of neoliberal capitalism? *Ecological Economics*, *121*(3), 149–159. doi:10.1016/j.ecolecon.2015.11.027

Martin, E., Shaheen, S., & Lidicker, J. (2010). Impact of carsharing on household vehicle holdings: Results from North American shared-use vehicle survey. *Transportation Research Record: Journal of the Transportation Research Board*, *2143*, 150–158. doi:10.3141/2143-19

Martini & Transparency International. (2014). *Local content policies and corruption in the oil and gas industry*. Retrieved June 30, 2016, from http://www.u4.no/publications/local-content-policies-and-corruption-in-the-oil-and-gas-industry/

Masini, C. (1982). *Lavoro e risparmio*. Turin, Italy: Utet.

Mason, C., & Brown, R. (2014). *Entrepreneurial ecosystems and growth oriented entrepreneurship*. Paris: OECD.

Massaro, M., Dumay, J., & Guthrie, J. (2016). On the shoulders of giants: Undertaking a structured literature review in accounting. *Accounting, Auditing & Accountability Journal*, *29*(5), 767–801. doi:10.1108/AAAJ-01-2015-1939

Massiani J. (2015). L'impatto economico dell'Expo, dal sogno alla realtà. *EyesReg*, *5*(4).

Matheson, V. (2006). Economic Impact Analysis. In W. Andreff & S. Szymansky (Eds.), *Handbook on the Economics of Sport*. Cheltenham, UK: Edward Elgar. doi:10.4337/9781847204073.00020

Matsuo, M. (2015). Human resource development programs for knowledge transfer and creation: The case of the Toyota Technical Development Corporation. *Journal of Knowledge Management*, *19*(6), 1186–1203. doi:10.1108/JKM-03-2015-0108

Matten, D., Crane, A., & Chapple, W. (2003). Behind de Mask: Revealing the True Face of Corporate Citizenship. *Journal of Business Ethics*, *45*(1-2), 109–120. doi:10.1023/A:1024128730308

Maxham, J. G. III, & Netemeyer, R. G. (2003). Firms reap what they sow: The effects of shared values and perceived organizational justice on customers evaluations of complaint handling. *Journal of Marketing*, *67*(1), 46–62. doi:10.1509/jmkg.67.1.46.18591

Mayer, J. D., & Salovey, P. (1993). The intelligence of emotional intelligence. *Intelligence*, *17*(4), 433–442. doi:10.1016/0160-2896(93)90010-3

May, M. E. (2007). *The Elegant Solution: Toyota's Formula for Mastering Innovation*. New York, NY: The Free Press.

Mcguire, J. B., Sundgren, A., & Schneeweis, T. (1988). Corporate social responsibility and firm financial performance. *Academy of Management Journal*, *31*(4), 854–872. doi:10.2307/256342

McVea, J. F., & Freeman, R. E. (2005). A Names-and-Faces Approach to Stakeholder Management. *Journal of Management Enquiry*, *14*(1), 57–69.

Mcwilliams, A., & Siegel, D. (2000). Corporate Social Responsibility and Financial Performance: Correlation or Misspecification? *Strategic Management Journal*, *21*(5), 603–609. doi:10.1002/(SICI)1097-0266(200005)21:5<603::AID-SMJ101>3.0.CO;2-3

McWilliams, A., & Siegel, D. (2001). Corporate Social Responsibility: A Theory of the Firm Perspective. *Academy of Management Review*, *26*(1), 117–127.

McWilliams, A., & Siegel, D. S. (2011). Creating and capturing value: Strategic corporate social responsibility, resource-based theory, and sustainable competitive advantage. *Journal of Management*, *37*(5), 1480–1495. doi:10.1177/0149206310385696

Medina, M. (2008). The informal recycling sector in developing countries- Organizing waste pickers to enhance their impact. *Gridlines*. Retrieved March 1, 2016, from https://www.ppiaf.org/ sites/ppiaf.org/files/publication/Gridlines-44-Informal%20Recycling%20-%20MMedina.pdf

Medina, M. (2011). *The informal sector – a driving force for recycling management. Recovering resources, creating opportunities: Integrating the informal sector into solid waste management*. GIZ GmbH (German International Cooperation), Partnership for Recycling Management. Retrieved January 10, 2017, from https://www.giz.de/en/downloads/giz2011-en-recycling-partnerships-informal-sector-final-report.pdf

Medina, M. (2005). Serving the unserved: Informal refuse collection in Mexico. *Waste Management & Research, 23*(5), 390–397. doi:10.1177/0734242X05057698 PMID:16273947

Melé, D. (2009). Integrating personalism into virtue-based business ethics: The personalist and the common good principles. *Journal of Business Ethics, 88*(1), 227–244. doi:10.1007/s10551-009-0108-y

Mena, K. P. B., & Zelaya, N. S. L. (2013). *Creating shared value in the educational sector: The contributions of CSV to the educational sector through social impact organizations* (Master Thesis). Umea School of Business and Economics.

Metcalfe, C. E. (1998). The stakeholder corporation. *Business Ethics (Oxford, England), 7*(1), 30–36. doi:10.1111/1467-8608.00083

Meyer, A. D., Brooks, G. R., & Goes, J. B. (1990). Environmental jolts and industry revolutions: Organizational response to discontinuous change. *Strategic Management Journal, 11*, 93–110.

Meynhardt, T. (2009). Public value inside: What is public value creation? *International Journal of Public Administration, 32*(3-4), 192–219. doi:10.1080/01900690902732632

Michelini, L. (2012). *Social Innovation and New Business models. Creating shared value in low income markets.* Heidelberg, Germany: Springer. doi:10.1007/978-3-642-32150-4

Michelini, L., & Fiorentino, D. (2011). Nuovi modelli di business per la creazione di valore condiviso: Il social e l'inclusive business. *Impresa Progetto - Electronic Journal of Management, 1*(1), 1–20.

Michelini, L., & Fiorentino, D. (2012). New business models for creating shared value. *Social Responsibility Journal, 8*(4), 561–577. doi:10.1108/17471111211272129

Miles, J. A. (2012). *Management and Organization Theory.* San Francisco, CA: Jossey-Bass.

Milliman, J., Ferguson, J., & Sylvester, K. (2008). Implementation of Michael Porter's strategic corporate social responsibility model. *Journal of Global Business Issues, 2*, 29–33.

Minghua, Z., Xiumin, F., Rovetta, A., Qichang, H., Vicentini, F., Bingkai, L., & Yi, L. et al. (2009). Municipal solid waste management in Pudong New Area, China. *Journal of Waste Management, 29*(3), 1227–1233. doi:10.1016/j.wasman.2008.07.016 PMID:18951780

Ministry of Energy and Petroleum. (2016). *Basinal wells.* Retrieved June 30, 2016, from http://www.energy.go.ke/index.php/petroleum-areas-of-interest/file/873-basinal-wells.html

Ministry of Urban Development - India. (2015). *Smart Cities Mission.* Retrieved June, 6, 2016, from http://smartcities.gov.in/

Mishra, S., & Suar, D. (2010). Does Corporate Social Responsibility Influence Firm Performance of Indian Companies? *Journal of Business Ethics, 95*(4), 571–601. doi:10.1007/s10551-010-0441-1

Mitchell, R., Agle, B., & Wood, J. (1997). Toward a Theory of Stakeholder Identification and Salience: Defining the Principle of Who and What Really Counts. *Academy of Management Review, 22*(4), 853–886.

Mitler, D., Rostorfer, D., & Ledbetter, K. (2015). *Water stewardship in Africa: The next frontier for building shared value.* University of Michigan.

Miyazaki, A. D., & Morgan, A. G. (2001). Assessing market value of event sponsoring: Corporate Olympic sponsorship. *Journal of Business Research, 41*(Jan-Feb), 9–15.

Miyungu, J. N. (2014, October 12). Tullow faces worker unrest at Turkana exploration sites. *The Standard.* Retrieved June 30, 2016, from http://www.standardmedia.co.ke/business/article/2000137914/tullow-faces-worker-unrest-at-turkana-exploration-sites

Mizik, N., & Jacobson, R. (2003). Trading off between value creation and value appropriation: The financial implications of shifts in strategic emphasis. *Journal of Marketing, 67*(1), 63–76. doi:10.1509/jmkg.67.1.63.18595

Modell, S. (2009). In defence of triangulation: A critical realist approach to mixed methods research in management accounting. *Management Accounting Research, 20*(3), 208–221. doi:10.1016/j.mar.2009.04.001

Mohammed, M. (2013). *Conceptual framework for corporate accountability in the context of sustainability: A literature review.* Paper presented at the 5th Annual EuroMed Conference of the EuroMed Academy of Business, Montreux, Switzerland. doi:10.1108/EMJB-05-2013-0026

Mohan, A. (2001). Corporate citizenship: Perspectives from India. *Journal of Corporate Citizenship, 2*(3), 107–117. doi:10.9774/GLEAF.4700.2001.su.00012

Möhlmann, M. (2015). Collaborative consumption: Determinants of satisfaction and the likelihood of using a sharing economy option again. *Journal of Consumer Behaviour, 14*(3), 193–207. doi:10.1002/cb.1512

Moldovan, O., & Bocoş-Binţinţan, V. (2015). The necessity of reconsidering the concept of non-formal education. *Procedia: Social and Behavioral Sciences, 209*, 337–343. doi:10.1016/j.sbspro.2015.11.245

Monden, Y. (1998). *Toyota Production System: An Integrated Approach to Just-In-Time.* Norcross, GA: Engineering & Management Press.

Moon, H. C., Pare, J., Yim, S. H., & Park, N. (2011). An extension of Porter and Kramer's creating shared value (CSV): Reorienting strategies and seeking international cooperation. *Journal of International and Area Studies, 18*(2), 49–64.

Moore, C. (2014). *Corporate social responsibility and creating shared value: What's the difference?.* Retrieved from https://sharedvalue.org/sites/default/files/resource-files/CFR-047%20Corporate%20Social%20Responsibility%20White%20Paper_FINAL.pdf

Moore, J. F. (2006). Business ecosystems and the view from the firm. *Antitrust Bulletin, 51*(1), 31-75. Retrieved May 27, 2016, from http://www.antitrustinstitute.org/files/Business%20ecosystems%20and%20the%20view%20from%20the%20firm,%20antitrust%20bu_081320081450.pdf

Moore, J. F. (1993). Predators and prey: A new ecology of competition. *Harvard Business Review, 71*(3), 75–83. PMID:10126156

Moore, M. H. (1995). *Creating public value: Strategic management in government.* Harvard University Press.

Moreno, C. (2015). *Doing Their Part: 3 Excellent Examples of Corporate Social Responsibility.* Retrieved May 20, 2016, from http://lineshapespace.com/doing-their-part-3-excellent-examples-of-corporate-social-responsibility

Moreno-Sanchez, R. D. P., & Maldonado, J. H. (2006). Dynamic model of solid waste management in developing countries. *Environment and Development Economics, 3*(03), 371–391. doi:10.1017/S1355770X06002853

Mukherjee, A., & Nath, P. (2007). Role of electronic trust in online retailing: A re-examination of the commitment-trust theory. *European Journal of Marketing, 41*(9-10), 1173–1202. doi:10.1108/03090560710773390

Mumford, L. (1961). *The City in History.* New York: Harcourt, Brace and World.

Murman, M. E., Allen, T., Bozdogan, K., Cutcher-Gershenfeld, J., McManus, H., Nightingale, D., & Widnall, S. et al. (2002). *Lean Enterprise Value: Insights from MIT's Lean Aerospace Initiative*. New York, NY: Palgrave. doi:10.1057/9781403907509

Murray, K. B., & Montanari, J. R. (1986). Strategic Management of the Socially Responsible Firm: Integrating Management and Marketing Theory. *Academy of Management Review*, *11*(4), 815–828.

Musa, J. I. (2008). Growth prospects of oil and gas abundant economies: The Nigerian experience (1970–2000). *Journal of Economic Studies (Glasgow, Scotland)*, *35*(2), 170–190. doi:10.1108/01443580810870155

Musango, J. K., & Brent, A. C. (2011). A conceptual framework for energy technology sustainability assessment. *Energy for Sustainable Development*, *15*(1), 84–91. doi:10.1016/j.esd.2010.10.005

Mutahi, P. (2015, September 29). Access to information is a fundamental right, so we need laws to make it possible. *Daily Nation*. Retrieved June 30, 2016, from http://www.nation.co.ke/oped/Opinion/Access-to-information-is-a-fundamental-right/-/440808/2888946/-/n8a9eb/-/index.html

Nadler, L. (1984). What Japan learned from the U.S.- that we forgot to remember. *California Management Review*, *26*(4), 46-61.

Nakane, C. (1972). *Japanese Society*. Berkeley, CA: University of California Press.

Namiki, N., & Sethi, S. P. (1988). Japan. In R. Nath (Ed.), *Comparative Management* (pp. 55–96). Pensacola, FL: Ballinger Publishing Company.

Napier, G., & Hansen, C. (2011). *Ecosystems for Young Scalable Firms*. FORA Group.

Narver, J. C., & Slater, S. F. (1990). The Effect of a Market Orientation on Business Profitability. *Journal of Marketing*, *54*(4), 20–35. doi:10.2307/1251757

Narver, J. C., Slater, S. F., & MacLachlan, D. (2004). Responsive and proactive market orientation and new-product success. *Journal of Product Innovation Management*, *21*(5), 334–347. doi:10.1111/j.0737-6782.2004.00086.x

Narwal, M., & Sharma, T. (2008). Perceptions of corporate social responsibility in India: An empirical study. *Journal of Knowledge Globalization*, *1*(1), 61–79.

National Oil Corporation of Kenya. (n.d.). *Oil and Gas Exploration History in Kenya*. Retrieved June 30, 2016, from http://nationaloil.co.ke/site/3.php?id=1

Néron, P. Y. (2013). Toward a political theory of the business firm? A comment on political CSR. *Business Ethics Journal Review*, *1*(3), 14–21. doi:10.12747/bejr2013.01.03

Neves, J. M. d. N. G. V. (2013). *Creating shared value. The case of Nestlé* (Dissertation). Universidade Católica Portuguesa.

Nidumolu, R., Prahalad, C. K., & Rangaswami, M. R. (2009). Why sustainability is now the key driver of innovation. *Harvard Business Review*, *87*(9), 56–64.

Nitobé, I. (2002). *Bushido: The Soul of Japan*. Tokyo: Kodansha International.

Njagi, J. (2016, March 24). Not so fast, say Turkana MPs as they vow to block pipeline works. *Daily Nation*. Retrieved June 30, 2016, from http://www.nation.co.ke/news/Oil-bid-suffers-fresh-hitch-as-MPs-vow-to-block-works/-/1056/3131484/-/us7i92z/-/index.html

Nohria, N., & Ghoshal, S. (1994). Differentiated fit and shared values: Alternatives for managing headquarters subsidiary relations. *Strategic Management Journal*, *15*(6), 491–502. doi:10.1002/smj.4250150606

Nutrire il Pianeta. Energia per la Vita! (2015). Retrieved from http://www.expo2015.org/

Nwagbara, U., & Kamara, H. Y. (2015). Corporate Social Responsibility (CSR) Leadership and Poverty Reduction: The Case of Nigeria and Sierra Leone. *Economic Insights – Trend and Challenge, 67*(2), 21-30.

Nzeadibe, T. C. (2009). Solid waste reforms and informal recycling in Enugu urban area, Nigeria. *Habitat International, 33*(1), 93–99. doi:10.1016/j.habitatint.2008.05.006

Oberndorfer, U., Schmidt, P., Wagner, M., & Ziegler, A. (2013). Does the stock market value the inclusion in a sustainability stock index? An event study analysis for German firms. *Journal of Environmental Economics and Management, 66*(3), 497–509. doi:10.1016/j.jeem.2013.04.005

Odhiambo, M. (2014, June 25). Company rules out payment for land in oil search. *Daily Nation.* Retrieved June 30, 2016, from http://mobile.nation.co.ke/counties/Company-rules-out-payment-for-land-in-oil-search/-/1950480/2361950/-/format/xhtml/-/dtj55d/-/index.html

Odia, J. O. (2016). Foreign direct investments, corporate social responsibility and economic development: Exploring the relationship and mitigating the expectation gaps. In M. Ojo (Ed.), *Foreign Direct Investments, Corporate Social Responsibility, and Economic Development.* IGI Global. doi:10.4018/978-1-5225-0305-7.ch015

OECD (Organisation for Economic Co-operation and Development). (2008). *Environmental Performance Reviews: Turkey.* Retrieved March 3, 2016, from http://www.oecd.org/environment/ country-reviews/environmentalperformancereviewsturkey2008.htm

OECD. (2016). *Collaborative strategies for in-country shared value creation: Framework for extractive projects. OECD Development Policy Tools.* Paris: OECD Publishing.

Ogden, S., & Watson, R. (1999). Corporate Performance and Stakeholder Management: Balancing Shareholder and Customer Interests in the U.K. Privatized Water Industry. *Academy of Management Journal, 42*(5), 526–538. doi:10.2307/256974

Ogrean, C. (2014). Perceptions on the strategic value of corporate social responsibility-some insights from global rankings. *Journal of International Studies, 7*(2), 128–140. doi:10.14254/2071-8330.2014/7-2/11

Ohno, T. (1988). *Toyota Production System Beyond Large-Scale Production.* Portland, OR: Productivity Press.

Okimoto, D. I., & Rohlen, T. P. (Eds.). (1988). *Inside the Japanese System.* Stanford, CA: Stanford University Press.

Omran, M., Atrill, P., & Pointon, J. (2002). Shareholders versus stakeholders: Corporate mission statements and investor returns. *Business Ethics (Oxford, England), 11*(4), 318–326. doi:10.1111/1467-8608.00291

OneSight. (2016). *OneSight Overview Presentation.* Retrieved May 30, 2016 from https://onesight.org

Onida, P. (1971). *Economia d'azienda.* Turin, Italy: Utet.

Onuoha, G. (2016). *A 'rising Africa' in a resource-rich context: Change, continuity and implications for development.* Academic Press.

Orlitzky, M., Schmidt, F. L., & Rynes, S. L. (2003). Corporate social and financial performance: A meta-analysis. *Organization Studies, 24*(3), 403–441. doi:10.1177/0170840603024003910

Orlitzky, M., Siegel, D. S., & Waldman, D. A. (2011). Strategic corporate social responsibility and environmental sustainability. *Business and Society Review, 50*(1), 6–27. doi:10.1177/0007650310394323

Osono, E., Shimizu, N., Takeuchi, H., & Dorton, J. K. (2008). *Extreme Toyota: Radical Contradictions That Drive Success at the World's Best Manufacturer.* Hoboken, NJ: John Wiley & Sons.

Osterwalder, A., & Pigneur, Y. (2010). *Business Model Generation: A Handbook for Visionaries, Game Changers, and Challengers*. Hoboken, NJ: Johan Wiley & Sons.

Othman, S. N., Noor, Z. Z., Abba, A. H., Yusuf, R. O., & Hassan, A. A. (2013). Review of life cycle assessment of integrated solid waste management in some Asian countries. *Journal of Cleaner Production, 41*, 251–262. doi:10.1016/j.jclepro.2012.09.043

Ovadia, J. (2012). The dual nature of local content in Angolas oil and gas industry: Development vs. elite accumulation. *Journal of Contemporary African Studies, 30*(3), 395–417. doi:10.1080/02589001.2012.701846

Owyang, J., Samuel, A., & Grenville, A. (2014). *Sharing is the new buying: How to win in the collaborative economy (Report). Vision CriticalBlog*. Retrieved April 15, 2016, from http://www.web-strategist.com/blog/2014/03/03/report-sharing-is-the-new-buying-winning-in-the-collaborative-economy/

Ozaki, R. S. (1991). *Human Capitalism. The Japanese Enterprise System as World Model*. Tokyo: Kodansha International.

Özçelik, F., Öztürk, B. A., & Gürsakal, S. (2014). Investigating the relationship between corporate social responsibility and financial performance in Turkey. *Atatürk Üniversitesi İktisadi ve İdari Bilimler Dergisi, 28*(3), 189–203.

Ozgen, H. N. (2001). Kentte yeni yoksulluk ve cop insanlari. *Toplum ve Bilim, 89*, 88–101.

Ozsoy, D. (2012). Yeni kent yoksullugu, atik toplayicilari ve temsil sorunsali: Katik dergisi uzerine bir inceleme. *Istanbul Universitesi Iletisim Fakultesi Dergisi, 43*, 105–121.

Palmer, K., Sigman, H., & Walls, M. (1997). The cost of reducing municipal solid waste. *Journal of Environmental Economics and Management, 33*(2), 128–150. doi:10.1006/jeem.1997.0986

Panapanaa, V., Bruce, T., Virkki-Hatakka, T., & Linnanen, L. (2016). Analysis of Shared and Sustainable Value Creation of Companies Providing Energy Solutions at the Base of the Pyramid (BoP). *Business Strategy and the Environment, 25*(5), 293–309. doi:10.1002/bse.1866

Papadolambakis, M. (1988). *Spaces of Freedom: Essays for a Dialectic of Space-making*. Athens: Exantas. (in Greek)

Parr, J. (2007). Spatial definition of the city: Four perspectives. *Urban Studies (Edinburgh, Scotland), 44*(2), 381–392. doi:10.1080/00420980601075059

Parsons, T. (1960). *Structure and process in modern societies*. New York: The Free Press.

Parsons, T. (1961). An Outline of the Social System. In T. Parsons, E. A. Shils, K. D. Naegle, & J. R. Pitts (Eds.), *Theories of Society*. New York: Free Press.

Pascale, R. T., & Athos, A. G. (1986). *The Art of Japanese Management*. London: Penguin Books.

Patro, C. S., & Raghunath, K. M. K. (2016). Corporate Social Responsibility: A Manifestation in FDI. In M. Ojo (Ed.), *Analyzing the Relationship between Corporate Social Responsibility and Foreign Direct Investment* (pp. 215–240). Hershey, PA: Business Science Reference. doi:10.4018/978-1-5225-0305-7.ch014

Pavlovich, K. (2001). The twin landscapes of Waitamo: Tourism network and sustainability through the Landscape Group. *Journal of Sustainable Tourism, 9*(6), 491–504. doi:10.1080/09669580108667416

Payne, A. F., Storbacka, K., & Frow, P. (2008). Managing the co-creation of value. *Academy of Marketing Science Journal, 36*(1), 83–96. doi:10.1007/s11747-007-0070-0

Pearce, D. (1999). Tourism in Paris: Studies at the microscale. *Annals of Tourism Research, 26*(1), 77–97. doi:10.1016/S0160-7383(98)00051-6

Pechlaner, H., Bachinger, M., Volgger, M., & Anzengruber-Fischer, E. (2014). Cooperative core competencies in tourism: Combining resource-based and relational approaches in destination governance. *European Journal of Tourism Research*, *8*, 5–19.

Pechlaner, H., Raich, F., & Beritelli, P. (2010). *Destination Governance. Tourism Review,* 65(4), 4–85.

Peloza, J., & Shang, J. (2011). How can corporate social responsibility activities create value for stakeholders? A systematic review. *Journal of the Academy of Marketing Science*, *39*(1), 117–135. doi:10.1007/s11747-010-0213-6

Peltoniemi, M. (2004). Cluster, value network and business ecosystem: Knowledge and innovation approach. Organisations, Innovation and Complexity: New Perspectives on the Knowledge Economy, (pp. 9-10).

Pepe, C. (2013). Values and corporate responsibility in globalization processes (EMEE vol. 32). Milan, Italy: McGraw-Hill Education.

Pepe, C. (2013). *Values and corporate responsibility in globalization processes*. Milan, Italy: McGraw-Hill Education.

Perrotti, R. (2014). *Perché l'Expo è un grande errore*. Retrieved May 3, 2016, from http://www.lavoce.info/wp-content/uploads/2014/05/Perch%C3%A9-lExpo-%C3%A8-un-grande-errore.pdf

Peterson, K., Rehrig, M., Stamp, M., & Kim, S. (2012). *Competing by saving lives: How pharmaceutical and medical device companies create shared value in global health*. Retrieved from http://www.fsg.org/publications/competing-saving-lives-0

Peterson, E. A. (2013). Compliance and ethics programs: Competitive advantage through the law. *Journal of Management and Governance*, *17*(4), 1027–1045. doi:10.1007/s10997-012-9212-y

Petrovic-Lazarevic, S. (2008). The development of corporate social responsibility in the Australian construction industry. *Construction Management and Economics*, *26*(2), 93–101. doi:10.1080/01446190701819079

Petty, R., & Guthrie, J. (2000). Intellectual capital literature review: Measurement, reporting and management. *Journal of Intellectual Capital*, *1*(2), 155–176. doi:10.1108/14691930010348731

Pfitzer, M., Bockstette, V., & Stamp, M. (2009). Innovating for Shared Value. *Harvard Business Review*, *91*(9), 100–107.

Pfitzer, M., Bockstette, V., & Stamp, M. (2013). Innovating for shared value. Companies that deliver both social benefit and business value rely on five mutually reinforcing elements. *Harvard Business Review*, *91*(9), 100–107.

Pfitzer, M., Bockstette, V., & Stamp, M. (2013). Innovating for shared value. *Harvard Business Review*, *91*(9), 1–9.

Phillips, P. C. B., & Peron, P. (1988). Testing for a Unit Root in Time Series Regression. *Biometrika*, *75*(2), 336–346. doi:10.1093/biomet/75.2.335

Phillips, R., Freeman, R. E., & Wicks, A. C. (2003). What stakeholder theory is not. *Business Ethics Quarterly*, *13*(4), 479–502. doi:10.5840/beq200313434

PiC (Partners in Change). (2004). *Third Report on Corporate Involvement in Social Development in India*. New Delhi: PiC.

Piketty, T. (2014). *Capital in the Twenty-First Century*. Cambridge, MA: The Belknap Press of Harvard University Press. doi:10.4159/9780674369542

Pine, B. J., & Gilmore, J. H. (1999). *The Experience Economy*. Boston, MA: Harvard Business School.

Pirson, M. (2012). Social entrepreneurs as the paragons of shared value creation? A critical perspective null. *Social Enterprise Journal*, *8*(1), 31–48. doi:10.1108/17508611211226575

Pirson, M., & Lawrence, P. (2010). Humanism in Business - Towards a Paradigm Shift? *Journal of Business Ethics*, *93*(4), 553–565. doi:10.1007/s10551-009-0239-1

Plender, J. (1997). *A Stake in the Future: The Stakeholding Solution*. London: Nicholas Brealey.

Plewa, C., Conduit, J., Quester, P. G., & Johnson, C. (2015). The Impact of Corporate Volunteering on CSR Image: A Consumer Perspective. *Journal of Business Ethics*, *127*(3), 643–659. doi:10.1007/s10551-014-2066-2

Pokhrel, D., & Viraraghavan, T. (2005). Municipal solid waste management in Nepal: Practices and challenges. *Journal of Waste Management*, *25*(5), 555–562. doi:10.1016/j.wasman.2005.01.020 PMID:15925764

Poole, E. (2009). Organizational Spirituality - A Literature Review. *Journal of Business Ethics*, *84*(4), 577–588. doi:10.1007/s10551-008-9726-z

Porter, M. (2014). *Created shared value: Becoming a movement.* Shared Value Leadership Summit, New York, NY.

Porter, M. E. (2000). Locations, clusters, and company strategy. In G. L. Clark, M. P. Feldman, & M. S. Gertler (Eds.), The Oxford Handbook of Economic Geography (pp. 253–274). Academic Press.

Porter, M. E., Hills, G., Pfitzer, M., Patscheke, S., & Hawkins, E. (2011). Measuring shared value. *How to Unlock Value by Linking Social and Business Results*, 10-11.

Porter, M. E., Hills, G., Pfitzer, M., Patscheke, S., & Hawkins, E. (2012). *Measuring share value: How to unlock value by linking social and business results.* Retrieved from www.fsg.org: http://www.mesacc.edu/other/engagement/2013Conf/Measuring_Shared_Value.pdf

Porter, M. E., Hills, G., Pfitzer, M., Patscheke, S., & Hawkins, E. (2012). *Measuring Shared Value: How to Unlock Value by Linking Social and Business Results*. Retrieved January 3, 2017, from http://animus-csr.com/docs/Measuring_Shared_Value.pdf

Porter, M. E. (1985). *Competitive advantage: Creating and sustaining superior performance*. New York, NY: The Free Press.

Porter, M. E. (1998). *Competitive advantage-Creating and sustaining superior performance* (2nd ed.). New York: Free Press.

Porter, M. E., Hills, G., Pfitzer, M., Patscheke, S., & Hawkins, E. (2012). *Measuring Shared Value How to Unlock Value by Linking Social and Business Results*. Boston: FSG.

Porter, M. E., & Kramer, M. (2011). Creating shared value: Redefining capitalism and the role of the corporation in society. *Harvard Business Review*, *89*(1/2), 62–77.

Porter, M. E., & Kramer, M. R. (1999). Philanthropy's New Agenda: Creating Value. *Harvard Business Review*, *77*(6), 121–131. PMID:10662001

Porter, M. E., & Kramer, M. R. (2002). The competitive advantage of corporate philanthropy. *Harvard Business Review*, *80*(12), 56–68. PMID:12510538

Porter, M. E., & Kramer, M. R. (2006). Strategy & Society. The link between competitive advantage and corporate social responsibility. *Harvard Business Review*, *84*(12), 78–92. PMID:17183795

Porter, M. E., & Kramer, M. R. (2006). Strategy & Society: The Link between Competitive Advantage and Corporate Social Responsibility. *Harvard Business Review*, *84*(12), 78–92. PMID:17183795

Porter, M. E., & Kramer, M. R. (2006). Strategy and Society. The Link Between Competitive Advantage and Corporate Social Responsibility. *Harvard Business Review*, *84*(12), 78–92. PMID:17183795

Porter, M. E., & Kramer, M. R. (2006). Strategy and society: The link between competitive advantage and corporate social responsibility. *Harvard Business Review*, *84*(12), 78–92. PMID:17183795

Porter, M. E., & Kramer, M. R. (2006). Strategy and Society: The Link between Competitive Advantage and Corporate Social Responsibility. *Harvard Business Review*, *84*(12), 78–92. PMID:17183795

Porter, M. E., & Kramer, M. R. (2011). Creating Shared Value. *Harvard Business Review*, *89*(1-2), 62–77.

Porter, M. E., & Kramer, M. R. (2011). Creating Shared Value: Redefining Capitalism and the Role of the Corporation in Society. *Harvard Business Review*, *89*(1-2), 62–77.

Porter, M. E., & Kramer, M. R. (2011, January-February). The Big Idea: Creating Shared Value. How to reinvent capitalism—and unleash a wave of. *Harvard Business Review*, *89*(1), 2–17.

Porter, M. E., & Millar, V. E. (1985). How information gives you competitive advantage. *Harvard Business Review*, *63*(4), 149–152.

Porter, M., & Kramer, M. (2002). The Competitive Advantage of Corporate Philanthropy. *Harvard Business Review*, *80*(12), 56–69. PMID:12510538

Porter, M., & Kramer, M. R. (2011). Creating shared value: How to reinvent capitalism - and unleash a wave of innovation and growth. *Harvard Business Review*, *89*(1/2), 62–77.

Post, J. E., Preston, L. E., & Sauter-Sachs, S. (2002). *Redefining the Corporation: Stakeholder Management and Organizational Wealth*. Stanford, CA: Stanford University Press.

Prahalad, C. K., & Hart, S. L. (2002). The fortune at the bottom of the pyramid. *Strategy Business Magazine*, 26.

Prahalad, C. K. (2005). *The Fortune at the Bottom of the Pyramid*. Pearson Education Inc.

Prahalad, C. K., & Hammond, A. (2002). Serving the World's Poor, Profitably. *Harvard Business Review*, *80*(9), 48–58. PMID:12227146

Prahalad, C. K., & Ramaswamy, V. (2000). Co-opting customer competence. *Harvard Business Review*, *78*(1), 79–90.

Prahalad, C. K., & Ramaswamy, V. (2004a). *The Future of Competition: Co-Creating Unique Value with Customers*. Boston, MA: Harvard Business School.

Prahalad, C. K., & Ramaswamy, V. (2004b). Co-creation experiences: The next practice in value creation. *Journal of Interactive Marketing*, *18*(3), 5–14. doi:10.1002/dir.20015

Prahalad, C. K., & Ramaswamy, V. (2004c). Co-creating unique value with customers. *Strategy and Leadership*, *32*(3), 4–9. doi:10.1108/10878570410699249

Pramar, S. K. (2012). *Companies Should Implement Their CSR Projects Themselves*. Retrieved June 05, 2016, from http://www.indiacsr.in/en/?p=7797

Preston, L. E., & Post, J. E. (1981). Private Management and Public Policy. *California Management Review*, *23*(3), 56–63. doi:10.2307/41172602

Priem, R. L. (2007). A consumer perspective on value creation. *Academy of Management Review*, *32*(1), 219–235. doi:10.5465/AMR.2007.23464055

Qu, S. Q., & Dumay, J. (2011). The Qualitative Research Interview. *Qualitative Research in Accounting & Management*, *8*(3), 238–264. doi:10.1108/11766091111162070

Ramaswamy, V. (2008). Co-creating value through customers experiences: The Nike case. *Strategy and Leadership*, *36*(5), 9–14. doi:10.1108/10878570810902068

Rappaport, A. (1990). *La strategia del valore*. Milano, Italy: Franco Angeli.

Ravald, A., & Grönroos, C. (1996). The value concept and relationship marketing. *European Journal of Marketing*, *30*(2), 19–30. doi:10.1108/03090569610106626

Raynard, P., & Forstater, M. (2002). *Corporate Social Responsibility: Implications for Small and Medium Enterprises in Developing Countries*. United Nations Industrial Development Organization. Retrieved May 16, 2016, from http://unido.org/userfiles/BethkeK/csr.pdf

Reddy, V., Uitto, J., Frans, D., & Matin, N. (2006). Achieving global environmental benefits through local development of clean energy? The case of small hilly hydel in India. *Energy Policy*, *34*(18), 4069–4080. doi:10.1016/j.enpol.2005.09.026

Réfléchir à la création de mon entreprise. (n.d.). Retrieved from https://www.jesuisentrepreneur.fr/creer-une-entreprise/comment-proteger-idee.html

Reich, R. (2007). *Supercapitalism: The transformation of business, democracy and everyday life.*. Retrieved from http://www.economist.com/node/18330445

Reingold, E. (1999). *Toyota: People, Ideas, and the Challenge of the New*. London: Penguin Books.

Rescher, N. (1969). *Introduction to Value Theory*. Washington, DC: University Press of America.

Resciniti, R. (2008). L'event experience per orientare il sistema di offerta. In R. Resciniti & G. Maggiore (Eds.), *Event experience. Progettare e gestire eventi da ricordare*. Napoli: Edizioni Scientifiche Italiane.

Richardson, H. W., & Nam, C. W. (2014). *Shrinking cities: a global perspective* (Vol. 71). Routledge.

Ringmar, E. (2005). *Surviving capitalism*. London: Anthem Press.

Riordan, C. M., Gatewood, R. D., & Bill, J. B. (1997). Corporate Image: Employee Reactions and Implications for Managing Corporate Social Performance. *Journal of Business Ethics*, *16*(4), 401–412. doi:10.1023/A:1017989205184

Risso, M. (2012). A horizontal approach to implementing corporate social responsibility in international supply chains. *International Journal of Technology Management*, *58*(1-2), 64–82. doi:10.1504/IJTM.2012.045789

Ritchie, J. and Spencer, L. (2002). Qualitative data analysis for applied policy research. *The Qualitative Researcher's Companion*, 305-329.

Robbins, N. (2000). *Position Paper on Emerging Markets and Human Rights*. Retrieved May 28, 2016, from http://ampcapital.com.au/_PDF/adviser/sri/papers/Emerging_Markets.pdf

Robert, K. H. (2000). Tools and concepts for sustainable development, how do they relate to a general framework for sustainable development, and to each other? *Journal of Cleaner Production*, *8*(3), 243–254. doi:10.1016/S0959-6526(00)00011-1

Robinson, R. (2015). 6 inconvenient truths about Smart Cities. *The Urban Technologist*. Retrieved June, 15, 2016, from https://theurbantechnologist.com/2015/02/15/6-inconvenient-truths-about-smart-cities/

Robinson, M., Kleffner, A., & Bertels, S. (2011). Signaling sustainability leadership: Empirical evidence of the value of DJSI membership. *Journal of Business Ethics*, *101*(3), 493–505. doi:10.1007/s10551-011-0735-y

Roca, L. C., & Searcy, C. (2012). An analysis of indicators disclosed in corporate sustainability reports. *Journal of Cleaner Production, 20*(1), 103–118. doi:10.1016/j.jclepro.2011.08.002

Rocchi, M., & Fererro, I. (2014). *Systematic shared value in finance: Expanding Porter's approach.* Working Paper No. 07. Pontificia Università della Santa Croce/University of Navarra.

Roche, M. (1994). Mega-events and urban policy. *Annals of Tourism Research, 21*(1), 1–19. doi:10.1016/0160-7383(94)90002-7

Rossi, J. L. (2009). *What is the value of corporate social responsibility? An answer from the Brazilian Sustainability Index.* Retrieved April 13, 2016, from http://ssrn.com/abstract=1338114

Ruffa, S. A. (2008). *Going Lean: How the Best Companies Apply Lean Manufacturing Principles to Shatter Uncertainty, Drive Innovation, and Maximize Profits.* New York, NY: AMACOM.

Rupp, D. E., Ganapathi, J., Aguilera, R. V., & Williams, C. A. (2006). Employee reactions to corporate social responsibility: An organizational justice framework. *Journal of Organizational Behavior, 27*(4), 537–543. doi:10.1002/job.380

Saarijärvi, H., Kannan, P. K., & Kuusela, H. (2013). Value co-creation: Theoretical approaches and practical implications. *European Business Review, 25*(1), 6–19. doi:10.1108/09555341311287718

Sagalovsky, B. (2015). Organizing for Lean: Autonomy, recursion and cohesion. *Kybernetes, 44*(6/7), 970–983. doi:10.1108/K-01-2015-0020

Sala-i-Martin, X., & Subramanian, A. (2003). *Addressing the natural resource curse: An illustration from Nigeria.* Cambridge, MA: National Bureau of Economic Research. doi:10.3386/w9804

Salau, O., Sen, L., Osho, S., & Adejonwo-Osho, O. (2016). Empirical investigation of formal and informal sectors in waste recycling of the municipal waste management system of developing countries. *Journal of Environment and Ecology., 7*(2), 21–33. doi:10.5296/jee.v7i2.10007

Santi, P., Resta, G., Szell, M., Sobolevsky, S., Strogatz, S. H., & Ratti, C. (2014). Quantifying the benefits of vehicle pooling with shareability networks. *Proceedings of the National Academy of Sciences of the United States of America, 111*(37), 13290–13294. doi:10.1073/pnas.1403657111 PMID:25197046

Santi, P., Resta, G., Szell, M., Sobolevsky, S., Strogatz, S. H., & Ratti, C. (2014). Reply to Lopez et al.: Sustainable implementation of taxi sharing requires understanding systemic effects. *Proceedings of the National Academy of Sciences of the United States of America, 111*(51), 5489–5489. doi:10.1073/pnas.1421300112 PMID:25503368

Sarti, M. (2015). *Tutti I numeri di Expo 2015.* Retrieved July 12, 2016, from http://www.jobintourism.it/job/articolo.php?id_articoli=24040

Satder (Street Waste Collectors Association). (2016). *Geri Donusum Emekcilerinin Sorunlari ve Cozum Onerileri Clistayi.* Retrieved December 20, 2016, from https://www.sokakatik toplayicilari.com/category/calistay/

Sato, M. (2008). *The Toyota Leaders.* New York, NY: Vertical.

Saul, J. (2011). *Social innovation: 5 strategies for driving business growth through social change.* San Francisco: Jossey-Bass.

Schaltegger, S., & Wagner, M. (2011). Sustainable entrepreneurship and sustainability innovation: Categories and interactions. *Business Strategy and the Environment, 20*(4), 222–237. doi:10.1002/bse.682

Scheinberg, A. (n.d.). *Privatisation and the informal sector: Thinking locally, acting globally?*. WASTE, Advisors on Urban Environment and Development, and Wageningen University, Environmental Policy Department. Retrieved January 5, 2017, from http://www.iswa.org/uploads/ txiswaknowledgebase/620431Paper.pdf

Scheinberg, A., Simpson, M., & Gupt, Y. (2010). *Economic aspects of the informal sector in solid waste*. Research report for GTZ (German Technical Cooperation). Retrieved January 6, 2017, from https://www.giz.de/expertise/downloads/gtz2010-en-Economic-Aspects-WASTE.pdf

Scheinberg, A. (2011). *Value Added: Modes of Sustainable Recycling in the Modernisation of Water Management Systems*. Wageningen, The Netherlands: Wageningen University.

Schenk, R., & Blaauw, P. F. (2011). The work and lives of street waste pickers in Pretoria- a case study of recycling in South Africa's urban informal economy. *Urban Forum, 22*, 411-430.

Scherer, A. G., & Palazzo, G. (2007). Toward a political conception of corporate social responsibility: Business and society seen from a Habermasian perspective. *Academy of Management Review*, *32*(4), 1096–1120. doi:10.5465/AMR.2007.26585837

Scherer, A. G., & Palazzo, G. (2011). The new political role of business in a globalized world: A review of a new perspective on CSR and its implications for the firm, governance, and democracy. *Journal of Management Studies*, *48*(4), 899–931. doi:10.1111/j.1467-6486.2010.00950.x

Scherer, A. G., Palazzo, G., & Matten, D. (2017). The business firm as a political actor: A new theory of the firm for a globalized world. *Business & Society*, *53*(2), 143–156. doi:10.1177/0007650313511778

Schifrin, N., & Fannin, Z. (2016). *How Al-Shabab is recruiting young men from Kenya*. Retrieved June 30, 2016, from http://www.pbs.org/newshour/bb/how-al-shabaab-is-recruiting-young-men-from-kenya/

Schmitt, B. (2016). *Nice Try VW: Toyota Again World's Largest Automaker*. Retrieved May 10, 2016, from https://dailykanban.com/2016/01/nice-try-vw-toyota-again-worlds-largest-automaker/

Schonberger, R. J. (1982). *Japanese Manufacturing Techniques: Nine Hidden Lessons in Simplicity*. New York, NY: The Free Press.

Schor, J. B. (2014). *Debating the Sharing Economy. A Great Transition Initiative Essay*. Retrieved April 26, 2016, from http://greattransition.org/publication/debating-the-sharing-economy

Schor, J. B., & Fitzmaurice, C. J. (2015). *Collaborating and Connecting: The emergence of the sharing economy. In Handbook on Research on Sustainable Consumption*. Cheltenham, UK: Edward Elgar.

Schor, J. B., & Fitzmaurice, C. J. (2015). Collaborating and connecting: the emergence of the sharing economy. In L. Reisch & J. Thogersen (Eds.), *Handbook of Research on Sustainable Consumption*. Cheltenham, UK: Edward Elgar. doi:10.4337/9781783471270.00039

Scott-Kemmis, D. (2012). *Responding to change and pursuing growth: Exploring the potential of business model innovation in Australia*. Australian Business Foundation.

Sedita, S. R. (2009). Le organizzazioni project-based. In S. R. Sedita & M. Paiola (Eds.), *Il management della creatività. Reti, comunità e territori*. Roma: Carocci Editore.

Seebode, D., Jeanrenaud, S., & Bessant, J. (2012). Managing innovation for sustainability. *R & D Management*, *42*(3), 195–226. doi:10.1111/j.1467-9310.2012.00678.x

Sembiring, E., & Nitivattananon, V. (2010). Sustainable solid waste management toward an inclusive society: Integration of the informal sector. *Resources, Conservation and Recycling*, *54*(11), 802–809. doi:10.1016/j.resconrec.2009.12.010

Sen, S., & Bhattacharya, C. B. (2001). Does Doing Good Always Lead to Doing Better? Consumer Reactions to Corporate Social Responsibility. *JMR, Journal of Marketing Research*, *38*(2), 225–243. doi:10.1509/jmkr.38.2.225.18838

Sen, S., Bhattacharya, C. B., & Korschun, D. (2006). The Role of Corporate Social Responsibility in Strengthening Multiple Stakeholder Relationships: A Field Experiment. *Journal of the Academy of Marketing Science*, *34*(2), 158–166. doi:10.1177/0092070305284978

Serafeim, G. (2014). *The Role of the Corporation in Society: An Alternative View and Opportunities for Future Research.* Harvard Business School, Working paper 14-110. Retrieved May 21, 2016, from http://www.hbs.edu/faculty/Publication%20Files/14-110_e7a7f1b3-be0d-4992-93cc-7a4834daebf1.pdf

Serenko, A., & Bontis, N. (2013). Global ranking of knowledge management and intellectual capital academic journals: 2013 update. *Journal of Knowledge Management*, *17*(2), 307–326. doi:10.1108/13673271311315231

Sethi, S. P. (1975). Dimensions of Corporate Social Performance: An Analytical Framework. *California Management Review*, *17*(3), 58–65. doi:10.2307/41162149

Shah, R., & Ward, P. T. (2007). Defining and developing measures of lean production. *Journal of Operations Management*, *25*(4), 785–805. doi:10.1016/j.jom.2007.01.019

Shamah, R. A. M. (2013). Measuring and building lean thinking for value creation in supply chains. *International Journal of Lean Six Sigma*, *4*(1), 17–35. doi:10.1108/20401461311310490

Sharma, A., & Kiran, R. (2013). Corporate Social Responsibility: Driving Forces and Challenges. *International Journal of Business Research and Development*, 2(1), 18–27. doi:10.24102/ijbrd.v2i1.182

Shaw, W. H., & Barry, V. (2016). *Moral Issues in Business*. Boston, MA: Cengage Learning.

Sheehy, B. (2015). Defining CSR: Problems and Solutions. *Journal of Business Ethics*, *131*(3), 625–648. doi:10.1007/s10551-014-2281-x

Shleifer, A., & Vishny, R. (1997). A survey of corporate governance. *The Journal of Finance*, *52*(2), 737–783. doi:10.1111/j.1540-6261.1997.tb04820.x

Shmueli, E., Mazeh, I., Radaelli, L., Pentland, A. S., & Altshuler, Y. (2015). Ride sharing: a network perspective. In Social computing, behavioral-cultural modeling, and prediction, (pp. 434-439). Springer. doi:10.1007/978-3-319-16268-3_55

Siegfried, J., & Zimbalist, A. (2002). A Note on the Local Economic Impact of Sports Expenditures. *Journal of Sports Economics*, *3*(4), 361–366. doi:10.1177/152700202237501

Signitzer, B., & Prexl, A. (2007). Corporate sustainability communications: Aspects of theory and professionalization. *Journal of Public Relations Research*, *20*(1), 1–19. doi:10.1080/10627260701726996

Signori, S., & Rusconi, G. (2009). Ethical thinking in traditional Italian Economia Aziendale and the stakeholder management theory: The search for possible interactions. *Journal of Business Ethics*, *89*(3), 303–318. doi:10.1007/s10551-010-0391-7

Simon, H. A. (1964). On the concept of organizational goal. *Administrative Science Quarterly*, *9*(1), 1–22. doi:10.2307/2391519

Singer, A. E. (2010). Integrating ethics and strategy: A pragmatic approach. *Journal of Business Ethics*, *92*(4), 479–491. doi:10.1007/s10551-009-0176-z

Singh, R., & Bhagat, K. (2004). Corporate Initiatives in Indian Agriculture. *Indian Management, 43*(2), 72–79.

Sirin, S., & Ege, A. (2012). Overcoming problems in Turkeys renewable energy policy: How can EU contribute? *Renewable & Sustainable Energy Reviews, 16*(7), 4917–4926. doi:10.1016/j.rser.2012.03.067

Slater, S. F., & Narver, J. C. (1995). Market Orientation and the Learning Organization. *Journal of Marketing, 59*(3), 63–74. doi:10.2307/1252120

Slater, S. F., & Narver, J. C. (1998). Customer led and market-oriented: Lets not confuse the two. *Strategic Management Journal, 19*(10), 1001–1006. doi:10.1002/(SICI)1097-0266(199810)19:10<1001::AID-SMJ996>3.0.CO;2-4

Smith, A. (2006). After the Circus Leaves Town: The Relationship between Sports Events, Tourism and Urban Regeneration. In K. Smith (Ed.), *Tourism, Culture and Regeneration* (pp. 69–84). Oxon, UK: CABI Publishing. doi:10.1079/9781845931308.0085

Smith, J. B., & Colgate, M. (2007). Customer value creation: A practical framework. *Journal of Marketing Theory and Practice, 15*(1), 7–23. doi:10.2753/MTP1069-6679150101

Società Italiana dei Docenti di Ragioneria e di Economia Aziendale (SIDREA). (2009). L'oggetto degli studi di Economia Aziendale. In Atti del I convegno Nazionale su 'La Ragioneria e L'Economia aziendale: dinamiche evolutive e prospettive di cambiamento'. Milan, Italy: Franco Angeli.

Somavia, J. (2000). Business: Its Direct Stake in Putting Human Needs First. *UN Chronicle, 37*(2), 42.

Soriano-Meier, H., & Forrester, P. L. (2002). A model for evaluate the degree of the leanness of manufacturing firms. *Integrated Manufacturing Systems, 13*(2), 104–109. doi:10.1108/09576060210415437

Speiss-Knafl, W., Mast, C., & Janse, S. A. (2015). On the Nature of Social Business Model Innovation. *Social Business. An Interdisciplinary Journal, 5*(2), 113–130.

Spitzeck, H., & Chapman, S. (2012). Creating shared value as a differentiation strategy – the example of BASF in Brazil. *Corporate Governance, 12*(4), 499–513. doi:10.1108/14720701211267838

Sroka, W. & Lorinczy, M. (2015). The perception of ethics in business: analysis of research results. *Procedia – Economics and Finance, 34*, 156-163.

Stake, R. E. (1994). Case studies. In N. K. Denzin & Y. S. Lincoln (Eds.), *Handbook of Qualitative Research* (pp. 236–247). Thousand Oaks, CA: Sage Publications.

Stake, R. E. (1995). *The Art of Case Study Research.* Thousand Oaks, CA: Sage Publications.

Stålberg, L., & Fundin, A. (2016). Exploring a holistic perspective on production system improvement. *International Journal of Quality & Reliability Management, 33*(2), 267–283. doi:10.1108/IJQRM-11-2013-0187

Stokes, R. G., Köster, R., & Sambrook, S. C. (2013). *The Business of Waste: Great Britain and Germany, 1945 to the Present.* Cambridge, UK: Cambridge University Press. doi:10.1017/CBO9781139225663

Stubbs, W., & Cocklin, C. (2008). Conceptualizing a Sustainability Business Model. *Organization & Environment, 21*(2), 103–127. doi:10.1177/1086026608318042

Sulmasy, D. P. (2001). Four Basic Notions of the Common Good. *St. John's Law Review, 75*(2), 303–311.

Sulopuisto, O. (2016). *Why Helsinki's innovative on-demand bus service failed.* Retrieved May 15, 2016, from http://citiscope.org/story/2016/why-helsinkis-innovative-demand-bus-service-failed

Sultangazi (District municipality). (2015). *Sokak Toplayıcılari Geri Donusum Sistemine Kazandirildi*. Retrieved January 10, 2017, from http://www.sultangazi.bel.tr/tr/guncel-haberler/sokak-toplayicilari-geri-donusum-sistemine-kazandirildi_231

Sundaram, A., & Inkpen, A. (2004). The corporate objective revisited. *Organization Science*, *15*(3), 350–363. doi:10.1287/orsc.1040.0068

Swartout, N. L (2016). *Exxon Mobil local content program*. Being presentation at the UNCTAD, Nairobi, Kenya.

Székely, F., & Knirsch, M. (2005). Responsible leadership and corporate social responsibility: Metrics for sustainable performance. *European Management Journal*, *23*(6), 628–547. doi:10.1016/j.emj.2005.10.009

Szmigin, I., & Rutherford, R. (2013). Shared value and the impartial spectator test. *Journal of Business Ethics*, *114*(1), 171–182. doi:10.1007/s10551-012-1335-1

Tadesse, T., Ruijs, A., & Hagos, F. (2008). Household waste disposal in Mekelle city. Northern Ethiopia. *Journal of Waste Management*, *28*(10), 2003–2012. doi:10.1016/j.wasman.2007.08.015 PMID:17936609

Tagliaventi, M. R., & Mattarelli, E. (2006). The role of networks of practice, value sharing, and operational proximity in knowledge flows between professional groups. *Human Relations*, *59*(3), 291–319. doi:10.1177/0018726706064175

The BIE and the Universal Expositions | Expo Milano 2015. (2015) Retrieved on March 7th 2016 from http://www.expo2015.org/archive/en/learn-more/the-history-/the-bie-and-the-universal-expositions.html

The meaning of EXPO Milan 2015. (2015) Retrieved January 14, 2016, from http://www.expo2015.org/archive/en/learn-more/the-history-/the-meaning-of-expo.html

Tinsley, R., & Lynch, P. (2001). Small tourism business network and destination development. *International Journal of Hospitality Management*, *20*(4), 367–378. doi:10.1016/S0278-4319(01)00024-X

Tirole, J. (2010). *The theory of corporate finance*. Princeton University Press.

TMEF (Turkish Ministry of Environment and Forestry). (2008). *Waste Management Action Plan 2008-2012*. Retrieved February 20, 2016, from http://www.cygm.gov.tr/cygm/files/eylemplan/ atikeylemplani.pdf

TMSIT (Turkish Ministry of Science, Industry and Technology). (2014). *National Recycling Strategy Document and Action Plan 2014-2017*. Retrieved February 20, 2016, from http://www.resmigazete. gov.tr/eskiler/2014/12/20141230M1-12-1.pdf

Tokgöz, N., & Önce, S. (2009). Şirket sürdürülebilirliği: Geleneksel yönetim anlayışına alternatif. *Afyon Kocatepe Üniversitesi İİBF Dergisi*, *11*(1), 249–275.

Tolliday, S., & Zeitlin, J. (Eds.). (1986). *The Automobile Industry and its Workers: between Fordism and Flexibility*. Cambridge, UK: Polity Press.

Toma, S.-G., & Marinescu, P. (2013). Social responsibility versus corporate social irresponsibility. *Economy & Business*, *7*(3), 109–115.

Toyota Foundation. (1974). *Prospectus and History*. Retrieved March 31, 2016, from https://www.toyotafound.or.jp/english/profile/history.html

Toyota Mobility Foundation. (2016). *Mobility Issues*. Retrieved December 29, 2016, from http://www.toyotamobility-foundation.org/en/ projects/

Toyota Motor Company. (2016a). *Toyota Precepts: The Base of the Global Vision*. Retrieved March 31, 2016, from http://www.toyota-global.com/company/toyota_traditions/company/apr_2012.html

Toyota Motor Company. (2016b). *Guiding Principles at Toyota*. Retrieved March 29, 2016, from http://www.toyota-global.com/company/ vision_philosophy/guiding_principles.html

Toyota Motor Company. (2017a). *Toyota Global Vision*. Retrieved January 3, 2017, from http://www.toyota-global.com/company/vision_philosophy/toyota_global_vision_2020.html

Toyota Motor Company. (2017b). *Sustainable Management Report*. Retrieved January 3, 2017, from http://www.toyota-global.com/sustainability/report/ar-smr/pdf/sustainable_management_report16_fe.pdf

Toyota Motor Corporation. (2006). *Toyota Code of Conduct*. Retrieved March 31, 2016, from http://www.toyota-global.com/company/history_of_toyota/75years/common/pdf/code_of_conduct.pdf

Transforming our world: the 2030 Agenda for Sustainable Development (Resolution adopted by the General Assembly on 25 September 2015). (2015). Retrieved November 28, 2015, from http://www.un.org/ga/search/view_doc.asp?symbol=A/RES/70/1&Lang=E

Transparency International. (2016). *Corruption Perceptions Index 2015*. Retrieved June 30, 2016, from http://www.transparency.org/cpi2015#downloads

Treviño, L. K., & Nelson, K. A. (2011). *Managing business ethics. Straight talk about how to do it right* (5th ed.). New York, NY: Wiley.

Tsai, W., & Ghoshal, S. (1998). Social capital and value creation: The role of intrafirm networks. *Academy of Management Journal*, *41*(4), 464–476. doi:10.2307/257085

TUIK (Turkish Statistical Institute). (2012). *Municipal Solid Waste Statistics*. Retrieved March 1, 2016, from http://www.tuik.gov.tr/PreHaberBultenleri.do?id=16170

TUIK (Turkish Statistical Institute). (2013). *Municipal Solid Waste Statistics*. Retrieved March 1, 2016, from http://www.turkstat.gov.tr/PreHaberBultenleri.do?id=15844

TUIK (Turkish Statistical Institute). (2014). *Municipal Solid Waste Statistics*. Retrieved March 1, 2016, from http://www.tuik.gov.tr/PreHaberBultenleri.do?id=18777

Tullow Oil P. L. C. (2014). *Tullow in Kenya*. Retrieved June 30, 2016, from http://www.tullowoil.com/Media/docs/default-source/operations/tullow-kenya-profile.pdf?sfvrsn=2

Tullow Oil P. L. C. (2016). *About local content*. Retrieved June 30, 2016, from http://www.tullowoil.com/suppliers/about-local-content

Turan, N. G., Coruh, S., Akdemir, A., & Ergun, O. N. (2009). Municipal solid waste management strategies in Turkey. *Waste Management (New York, N.Y.)*, *29*(1), 465–469. doi:10.1016/j.wasman.2008.06.004 PMID:18644708

Turban, D. B., & Greening, D. W. (1997). Corporate Social Performance and Organizational Attractiveness to Prospective Employees. *Academy of Management Journal*, *40*(3), 658–763. doi:10.2307/257057

Turkishtime. (2014). Şirketlerde Sürdürülebilirlik. *Turkishtime*. Retrieved May 1, 2016, from http://www.turkishtimedergi.com/genel/sirketlerde-surdurulebilirlik/

Tuttle, L. (2009). Ankara Recycling Association, Turkey. In M. Samson (Ed.), Refusing to be Cast Aside: Waste Pickers Organizing Around the World (pp. 15-16). Cambridge, MA: Women in Informal Employment: Globalizing and Organizing (WIEGO).

Tyler, D., & Dinan, C. (2001). The role of interest groups in England's emerging tourism policy network. *Current Issue in Tourism*, *4*(2-4), 210–252.

Uber. (2017). *uberPOOL Share your ride and save*. Retrieved January 18, 2017, from https://www.uber.com/ride/uberpool/

Ukolov, V. F., Solomatin, A. V., Solomatin, Y. V., Chernikov, S. U., & Ukolov, A. V. (2016). Food-sharing economy pattern comparison in UK and Russian markets. *International Business Management, 10*(18), 4268–4282.

Ulaga, W., & Eggert, A. (2006). Value-based differentiation in business relationships: Gaining and sustaining key supplier status, *Journal of Marketing, 70*, 119-136.

UNEP (United Nations Environment Program). (2005). *Solid Waste Management*. Retrieved May 25, 2016, from http://www.unep.org/ietc/Portals/136/SWM-Vol1-Part1-Chapters1to3.pdf

UNEP (United Nations Environment Program). (2015). *Global Waste Management Outlook*. Retrieved May 25, 2016, from http://www.unep.org/ietc/Portals/136/Publications/Waste%20Management/GWMO%20report/GWMO%20full%20report.pdf

UN-HABITAT (United Nations Human Settlements Programme). (2010). *Solid Waste Management in the World's Cities*. Retrieved February 5, 2016, from http://unhabitat.org/books/solid-waste-management-in-the-worlds-cities-water-and-sanitation-in-the-worlds-cities-2010-2

United Nations Development Programme. (2008). *Creating Value for All: Strategies for Doing Business with the Poor*. New York: United Nations Development Programme. Retrieved May 30, 2016 from http://growinginclusivemarkets.org/media/gimlaunch/Report_2008/GIM%20Report%20Final%20August%202008.pdf

United Nations Development Programme. (2015). *Human Development Indicators*. Retrieved June 30, 2016, from http://hdr.undp.org/en/countries/profiles/KEN

United Nations. (2015). *Global Sustainable Development Report 2015 Edition*. Advance Unedited version. Retrieved March, 2016, from https://sustainabledevelopment.un.org/content/documents/1758GSDR%202015%20Advance%20Unedited%20Version.pdf

United Nations. (2015). *Transforming Our World: The 2030 Agenda For Sustainable Development, A/RES/70/1*. New York: United Nations.

United Nations. (n.d.). *Home. Sustainable Development Knowledge Platform*. Retrieved from https://sustainabledevelopment.un.org/

USEPA (United Stated Environmental Protection Agency). (n.d.). *Wastes - Non-hazardous Waste – Municipal Solid Waste*. Retrieved February 5, 2016, from https://archive.epa.gov/epawaste/nonhaz/ municipal/web/html/index.html

Vadastreanu, A.M., Maier, D. & Maier, A. (2015). Is the Success Possible in Compliance with Ethics and Deontology in Business?. *Procedia – Economics and Finance, 26*, 1068-1073.

Vaidyanathan, L., & Scott, M. (2012). Creating shared value in India: The future for inclusive growth. *Vikalpa: The Journal for Decision Making, 37*(2), 108–113.

Van der Borgh, M., Cloodt, M., & Romme, A. G. L. (2012). Value creation by knowledge-based ecosystems: Evidence from a field study. *R & D Management, 42*(2), 150–169. doi:10.1111/j.1467-9310.2011.00673.x

Van Marrewijk, M., & Were, M. (2003). Multiple Levels of Corporate Sustainability. *Journal of Business Ethics, 44*(2/3), 107–120. doi:10.1023/A:1023383229086

Van Zeeland, A. J. W. M. (2014). *The Interaction between Popular Economy, Social Movements and Public Policies: A Case Study of the Waste Pickers' Movement*. Geneva, Switzerland: United Nations Research Institute for Social Development.

Varadarajan, P. R., & Menon, A. (1988). Cause-Related Marketing: A Coalignment of Marketing Strategy and Corporate Philanthropy. *Journal of Marketing*, *52*(3), 58–58. doi:10.2307/1251450

Velasquez, M. (1992). International Business, Morality and the Common Good. *Business Ethics Quarterly*, *2*(1), 27–40. doi:10.2307/3857220

Vigano, E., & Mattessich, R. (2007). Accounting research in Italy: Second half of the 20th century. *Review of Accounting and Finance*, *6*(1), 24–41. doi:10.1108/14757700710725449

Vilanova, L. (2007). Neither shareholder nor stakeholder management: What happens when firms are run for their short-term salient stakeholder? *European Management Journal*, *25*(2), 146–162. doi:10.1016/j.emj.2007.01.002

Visser, W. (2013). *Creating shared value: Revolution or clever con?*. Retrieved from http://www.waynevisser.com/wp-content/uploads/2013/08/blog_csv_csr_wvisser.pdf

Visser, W. (2006). Revisiting Carroll's CSR pyramid: An African perspective. In E. R. Pedersen & M. Hunicke (Eds.), *Corporate citizenship in developing countries: New partnership perspectives* (pp. 29–56). Copenhagen: Copenhagen Business School Press.

Visser, W. (2008). Corporate social responsibility in developing countries. In A. Crane et al. (Eds.), *The Oxford handbook of corporate social responsibility* (pp. 473–479). Oxford, UK: Oxford University Press.

Visser, W. (2010). The age of responsibility: CSR 2.0 and the new DNA of business. *Journal of Business Systems. Governance and Ethics*, *5*(3), 7–22.

Visser, W., & Kymal, C. (2015). Integrated Value Creation (IVC): Beyon Corporate Social Responsibility (CSR) and Creatong Shared Value (CSV). *Journal of International Business Ethics*, *8*(1), 29–43.

Visser, W., Matten, D., Pohl, M., & Tolhurst, N. (2007). *The A to Z of Corporate Social Responsibility*. London: Wiley.

Vogel, D. (1986). The Study of Social Issues in Management: A Critical Appraisal. *California Management Review*, *28*(2), 142–152. doi:10.2307/41165191

Vogt, H. (2014, August 19). Violence Imperils Kenya Port Project: Land Disputes, Terrorism Threaten Plan to Turn Coastal Region Into Economic Hub. *The Wall Street Journal*. Retrieved June 30, 2016, from http://www.wsj.com/articles/violence-imperils-kenya-port-project-1408490217

Voicu, B. (2010). *Capital social în România începutului de Mileniu: Drumeț în țara celor fără de prieteni?*. Iași: Editura Lumen.

Voicu, B. (2008). Riscurile politicilor de dezvoltare bazate pe formarea capitalului social. *Sociologie românească*, *VI*(1), 11–25.

Voicu, B., & Voicu, M. (2009). Volunteers and Volunteering in Central and Eastern Europe. *Sociologia*, 539–563.

Voicu-Dorobanțu, R. (2014). A conceptual approach to entrepreneurial ecosystems and applied algorithms. *Advances in Applied Mathematics*, 397-406.

Von Liel, B. (2016). *Creating Shared Value as Future Factor of Competition: Analysis and Empirical Evidence*. Wiesbaden: Springer Fachmedien. doi:10.1007/978-3-658-12603-2

Waddock, S. A., & Graves, S. B. (1997). The Corporate Social Performance - Financial Performance Link. *Strategic Management Journal*, *18*(4), 303–320. doi:10.1002/(SICI)1097-0266(199704)18:4<303::AID-SMJ869>3.0.CO;2-G

Wagner, S. M., & Lindemann, E. (2008). Determinants of value sharing in channel relationships. *Journal of Business and Industrial Marketing*, *23*(8), 544–533. doi:10.1108/08858620810913353

Wainwright, O. (2015). *Expo 2015: what does Milan gain by hosting this bloated global extravaganza?*. Retrieved October 20, 2016, from http://www.theguardian.com/cities/2015/may/12/expo-2015-what-does-milan-gain-by-hosting-this-bloated-global-extravaganza

Wallman, S. M. H. (1999). Understanding the Purpose of a Corporation: An Introduction. *The Journal of Corporation Law*, *24*(4), 807–818.

Wang, S. (2014). On the Relationship between CSR and Profit. *Journal of International Business Ethics*, *7*(1), 51–57.

Wang, Z., Sharma, P. N., & Cao, J. (2016). From knowledge sharing to firm performance: A predictive model comparison. *Journal of Business Research*, *69*(10), 4650–4658. doi:10.1016/j.jbusres.2016.03.055

Warhust, A. (2001). Corporate Citizenship and Corporate Social Investment: Drivers of Tri-Sector Partnerships. *Journal of Corporate Citizenship*, *1*(1), 57–73. doi:10.9774/GLEAF.4700.2001.sp.00008

Warner, M. (2011). *Local content in procurement: Creating local jobs and competitive domestic industries in supply chains*. Sheffield, UK: Greenleaf Pub.

Wartick, S. L., & Rude, R. E. (1986). Issues Management: Corporate Fad or Corporate Function? *California Management Review*, *29*(1), 124–132. doi:10.2307/41165231

Watts, M. (2004). Resource curse? Governmentality, oil and power in the Niger Delta, Nigeria. *Geopolitics*, *9*(1), 50–80. doi:10.1080/14650040412331307832

WCED. (1987). *Report of the World Commission on Environment and Development: Our Common Future*. Retrieved April 13, 2016, from http://www.un-documents.net/our-common-future.pdf

Weaver, D. B. (2000). A broad context model of destination development scenarios. *Tourism Management*, *21*(3), 217–224. doi:10.1016/S0261-5177(99)00054-0

Weaver, D. B. (2005). The distinctive dynamics of exurban tourism. *International Journal of Tourism Research*, *7*(1), 23–33. doi:10.1002/jtr.521

Weaver, D. B. (2012). Organic, incremental and induced paths to sustainable mass tourism convergence. *Tourism Management*, *33*(5), 1030–1037. doi:10.1016/j.tourman.2011.08.011

Werner, W. (2009). Corporate social responsibility initiatives addressing social exclusion in Bangladesh. *Journal of Health, Population, and Nutrition*, *27*(4), 545–562. doi:10.3329/jhpn.v27i4.3401 PMID:19761088

Werther, W. B. Jr, & Chandler, D. (2011). *Strategic corporate social responsibility: Stakeholders in a global environment*. Los Angeles, CA: Sage.

Wheeler, D., Colbertm, B., & Freeman, R. E. (2003). Focusing on Value: Reconciling Corporate Social Responsibility, Sustainability and a Stakeholder Approach in a Network World. *Journal of General Management*, *28*(3), 1–29. doi:10.1177/030630700302800301

Whelan, G. (2012). The political perspective of corporate social responsibility: A critical research agenda. *Business Ethics Quarterly*, *22*(4), 709–737. doi:10.5840/beq201222445

Whelan, G. (2013). Political corporate social responsibility: Some clarifications. *Business Ethics Journal Review*, *1*(10), 63–68. doi:10.12747/bejr2013.01.10

White, T., & McBurney, D. (2012). *Research Method* (9th ed.). Belmont, CA: Wadsworth.

WIEGO (Women in the Informal Economy Organising and Globalising). (2000). *Women in the Informal Economy*. Cambridge, MA: WIEGO.

WIEGO (Women in the Informal Economy Organising and Globalising). (2014). *The Urban Informal Workforce: Waste Pickers/Recyclers*. Retrieved March 3, 2016, from http://wiego.org/sites/ wiego.org/files/publications/files/IEMS-waste-picker-report.pdf

Wilburn, K., & Wilburn, R. (2014). Demonstrating a commitment to corporate social responsibility not simply shared value. *Business & Professional Ethics Journal*, *33*(1), 1–15. doi:10.5840/bpej20144216

Williams, M., & Bowdin, G. A. J. (2007). Festival evaluation: An explanatory of seven UK arts festivals. *Managing Leisure*, *12*(2-3), 187–203. doi:10.1080/13606710701339520

Wilson, D. C., Araba, A. O., Chinwah, K., & Cheeseman, C. R. (2009). Building recycling rates through the informal sector. *Waste Management (New York, N.Y.)*, *29*(2), 629–635. doi:10.1016/j.wasman.2008.06.016 PMID:18701272

Wilson, D. C., Velis, C., & Cheeseman, C. (2006). Role of informal sector recycling in waste management in developing countries. *Habitat International*, *30*(4), 797–808. doi:10.1016/j.habitatint.2005.09.005

Wilson, F., & Post, J. E. (2012). Business Models for people, Planet (&Profits): Exploring the Phenomena of Social Business, a Market Based Approach to Social Value Creation. *Small Business Economics*, *40*(3), 715–737. doi:10.1007/s11187-011-9401-0

Wilson, J. M. (2003). Gantt charts: A centenary appreciation. *European Journal of Operational Research*, *149*(2), 430–437. doi:10.1016/S0377-2217(02)00769-5

Windsor, D. (2013). Corporate social responsibility and irresponsibility: A positive theory approach. *Journal of Business Research*, *66*(10), 1937–1944. doi:10.1016/j.jbusres.2013.02.016

Womack, J. P., & Jones, D. T. (2003). *Lean Thinking. Banish Waste and Create Wealth in Your Corporation*. New York, NY: Free Press.

Womack, J. P., & Jones, D. T. (2007). *Lean Solutions: How Companies and Customers Can Create Value and Wealth Together*. London: Simon & Schuster.

Womack, J. P., Jones, D. T., & Roos, D. (1991). *The Machine that Changed the World: The Story of Lean Production*. New York, NY: Harper Perennial.

Wood, D. J. (1991). Corporate Social Performance Revisited. *Academy of Management Review*, *16*(4), 691–718.

World Bank, Social Capital Initiative. (1998). *Social Capital Initiative Working Paper Series*. Retrieved from http://go.worldbank.org/IVEBAGOF20

World Bank. (2012). *Urban Development Series. What a Waste. A Global Review of Solid Waste Management*. Retrieved April 5, 2016, from http://siteresources.worldbank.org/INTURBAN DEVELOPMENT/Resources/336387-1334852610766/What_a_Waste2012_Final.pdf

World Business Council for Sustainable Development (WBCSD) & SNV Netherlands Development Organization. (2008). *Inclusive Business: Profitable Business for Successful Development*. Geneva: WBCSD & SNV. Retrieved May 30, 2016 from http://wbcsdservers.org/wbcsdpublications/cd_files/datas/business-solutions/social-impact/pdf/InclusiveBusiness-ProfitableBusinessForSuccessfulDevelopment.pdf

Wu, J. J., Chen, Y. H., & Chung, Y. S. (2010). Trust factors influencing virtual community members: A study of transaction communities. *Journal of Business Research, 63*(9-10), 1025–1032. doi:10.1016/j.jbusres.2009.03.022

Yardimci, S., & Saltan, A. (2007). Geri donusumun gorunmeyen yuzu. *Toplum ve Bilim, 108*, 206–238.

Yigit, I. (2015). Survival tactics of waste paper pickers in Istanbul. *Journal of Ethnic and Cultural Studies, 2*(1), 1–14.

Yildiz, S., Balahorli, V., Hosoglu, F., & Sezer, K. (2014). Waste management in the metropolis of Istanbul - Waste incineration and energy production facility in Istanbul Waste Management. *Vivis, 3*, 265–275.

Yin, R. K. (2012). *Applications of Case Study Research* (3rd ed.). Thousand Oaks, CA: Sage Publications.

Yin, R. K. (2014). *Case Study Research: Design and Methods* (5th ed.). Los Angeles, CA: Sage Publications.

Yoneyama, E. (2007). Phenomenology of life, Zen and management. *Society and Business Review, 2*(2), 204–217. doi:10.1108/17465680710757411

Young, G. (2012). *Strategic corporate social responsibility and small to medium businesses in Australia.* Creative Commons.

Young-Ybarra, C., & Wiersema, M. (1999). Strategic Flexibility in Information Technology Alliances: The Influence of Transaction Cost Economics and Social Exchange Theory. *Organization Science, 10*(4), 439–459. doi:10.1287/orsc.10.4.439

Yunus, M. (2007). *Creating a World Without Poverty: Social Business and the Future of Capitalism.* New York: Public Affairs.

Yunus, M. (2010). *Building Social Business: The New Kind of Capitalism that Serves Humanity's Most Pressing Needs.* New York: Public Affairs.

Yusuf, S. (2009). From Creativity to Innovation. *Technology in Society, 31*(1), 1–8. doi:10.1016/j.techsoc.2008.10.007

Zadek, S. (2004). The path to corporate responsibility. *Harvard Business Review, 82*(12), 125–132. PMID:15605571

Zamagni, S. (2010). La lezione e il messaggio di una crisi annunciata. In *Crisi economica, crisi antropologica. L'uomo al centro del lavoro e dell'impresa*. Rimini, Italy: Il Cerchio.

Zappa, G. (1950). Il reddito di impresa. Giuffré Editore.

Zappa, G. (1927). *Tendenze Nuove negli studi di Ragioneria, Opening Speech of the Academic Year 1926–1927.* University of Venice.

Zappa, G. (1954). La nozione d'azienda nell'economia moderna. *Il Risparmio, 8*, 1255–1278.

Zappa, G. (1956). *Le produzioni nell'economia dell'impresa. Tomo primo.* Milan, Italy: Giuffré Editore.

Zelizer, V. A. (2010). *Economic Lives: How Culture Shapes the Economy.* Princeton, NJ: Princeton University Press. doi:10.1515/9781400836253

Zimbalist, A. (2015). *Circus maximus: The Economic Gamble behind Hosting the Olympics and the World Cup.* Washington, DC: Brookings Institution Press.

About the Contributors

Mario Risso is Full Professor of Management and he is Dean of School of Economics at the Niccolò Cusano University- Rome (Italy). He holds a PhD in Banking and Finance from University of Rome Tor Vergata, a Master in Asset Management and a Master in Retail Management. He holds University Degree in Business Administration, from University of Rome "Tor Vergata". He is a member of the Editorial Team of "Symphonya. Emerging Issues in Management" (http://symphonya.unimib.it/) and a member of the Scientific Advisory Board of the International Journal of Economic Behavior. He is a Managing Editor of the series "Essays in Management Economic and Ethics". His main research interests embrace retailing, global supply chain management, corporate social responsibility, international business. He is the author of several books and articles published in international journals including International Journal of Technology Management and International Journal of Applied Behavioral Economics.

Silvia Testarmata Associate Professor of Business Administration at the Niccolò Cusano University of Rome, Italian Chartered Accountant and Statutory Auditor. She obtained her Ph.D. degree at the University of Rome "Tor Vergata" and taught at the University of Rome "Tor Vergata", LUISS University and Link Campus University before joining the Niccolò Cusano University of Rome in 2013. She teaches Business Administration, Accounting and Financial Reporting I and Accounting and Financial Reporting II in university degrees as well as in executive education. Currently she is Faculty member of the Ph.D. programme in Governance and Management for Business Innovation of the Niccolò Cusano University and Editorial Board Member of the Journal of Investment and Management and Journal of Business and Social Review in Emerging Economies. In addition, she serves as Editorial Review Board Member for several journals as follows: Accounting and Financial Control; Geopolitics under Globalization; International Journal of Human Resources Development and Management; International Journal of Sustainable Entrepreneurship and Corporate Social Responsibility and International Journal of Managerial and Financial Accounting. She is also member of many academic associations of accounting, business and management issues. Her field of expertise are in governance and management, financial accounting and reporting, business planning. Her current research interests are strategy, business models and value creation, corporate disclosure and social accounting, ethics and CSR in organizations. She attends as a speaker at many international conferences and she is author of several articles and books. Recently she has published articles in Journal of Management and Governance (2016); Journal of Public Budgeting, Accounting & Financial Management (2014); Corporate Ownership and Control (2013 and 2014); Corporate Board (2012); International Journal of Public Administration (2010).

* * *

Veli Akel is an Associate Professor of Finance at Faculty of Economics and Administrative Sciences in Erciyes University, Kayseri, Turkey. Assoc. Prof. Akel teaches Capital Markets, International Finance, Portfolio Management, Corporate Finance and related courses. He received the B.S. degree in Business Administration, Erciyes University, 1998, M.S. degree in Finance, Anadolu University, 2001, and PhD degree in Finance, Erciyes University, 2006. His main research areas focus on financial contagion, neural networks, institutional investor and capital markets.

Nurcan Kilinc Ata holds PhD degree in economics department from University of Stirling in United Kingdom. She focused on renewable energy policies and their impacts on installed capacity in developed and developing countries. Her research interests are energy economics (Renewable Energy Sources), energy market, energy policy, environmental economics, and econometric analysis (Demand Forecast). Her current interests lie in the nexus of energy policies and energy investment, particularly focusing on energy and environmental econometric modeling. Also, she worked as foreign trade analyst, researcher, assistant professor in a wide variety of business, academia, and research center such as import-export analysis, renewable energy sources application and evaluation, energy policies, forecasting market share analyze for natural energy sources. She has over 7 years of academic and international research experience. She has conducted and participated in European research projects. Since 2005, she has produced over a dozen publications in a diversity of formats and presented at a number of national and international conferences. At a personal level, she is a very energetic person who likes to take initiative and engage people in motivating and interesting. Outside of work, she enjoys travelling, meeting with her friends, and cooking.

Nuray Cakirli is a PhD candidate at the University of Goettingen, Department of Agricultural Economics and Rural Development. She received her Master's degree in Sustainable Resource Management at the Technical University of Munich, where she carried out her Master's thesis on the Waste Prevention Strategies, within the EU FUSIONS (Food Use for Social Innovations) Project. Her current research at the University of Goettingen focuses on adoption of technological innovations in organic agriculture. She is broadly interested in sustainable agri-business practices, food quality and safety management systems, organizational theories, resource management, agricultural and food waste management, and extension services.

Levent Çıtak is an Associate Professor of Finance at the Faculty of Economics and Administrative Sciences in Erciyes University, Kayseri, Turkey. Assoc. Prof. Çıtak teaches Corporate Finance, Financial Management and Investment Project Analysis. He received B.S. degree in Business Administration from Erciyes University in 1993, MBA with a major in Financial Management from Pace University, NY, USA in 1997, and PhD degree from Dumlupınar University in 2003. He has published papers in academic journals on corporate governance, determinants of financial performance, market efficiency.

Emiliano Di Carlo, Ph.D., is Associate Professor of Business Administration at the Department of Management and Law, at the University of Rome "Tor Vergata" and Executive Vice-director of the Master in Anticorruption at the University of Rome "Tor Vergata". His research interests are in the fields of finance and governance of business groups, business strategy, accounting and financial management of firms and local governments, international accounting standards, corporate governance, conflict of interests, corruption, corporate social responsibility, business ethics.

Ersan Ersoy is an Associate Professor of Finance at the Faculty of Economics and Administrative Sciences in Nevşehir Hacı Bektaş Veli University, Nevsehir, Turkey. He teaches Corporate Finance, Capital Markets and Portfolio Management. He received B.S. degree in Business Administration from Anadolu University in 1999, MBA degree in Finance from Anadolu University, Eskisehir, Turkey in 2002 and PhD degree from Erciyes University in 2011. He has published papers in academic journals on derivatives, corporate governance, dividend policy and determinants of financial performance.

Fabio Fortuna is the Chancellor of the Niccolò Cusano University of Rome, Former Dean of the School of Economics, Full Professor of Accounting and Ph.D. Coordinator of the Ph.D. in Governance and Management for Business Innovation of the Niccolò Cusano University. Currently, he is member of various scientific committees and editorial boards in the field of business and management issues. He is the author of many publications on business administration, accounting and finance. His fields of expertise are in business administration, accounting and finance. His current research interests are corporate governance, corporate social responsibility and corporate disclosure in organizations. He has published several articles and books. In particular, he is co-author of the widely recognized article on business models published in the Journal of Management and Governance in 2016.

Alessandro Giosi took his Ph.D. in Public Management and Governance at University of Rome of "Tor Vergata" in which he covered the position of Assistant Professor. Since 2014 is Associate Professor in Accounting at Lumsa University of Rome in which is Chief of the MsC in Marketing & Digital Communication. He teaches Business Administration and Business Planning. He is member of the Italian Association of the Business Administration Professors (SIDREA) and of the European Group of Public Administration (EGPA). His mains interests research are: accounting of both private and public entities, financial analysis and corporate governance. He is author of publications on both national and international journals. He is senior consultant in government accounting and professor in training programs.

Cătălin Grădinaru is a University Assistant at The Faculty of Administration and Business, University of Bucharest, for Entrepreneurship, Introduction to Business and Services Marketing at the bachelor study level. He has a Licence in Business Administration and a Masters Degree in Business Consulting after having completed his studies at the faculty he teaches at and a PhD degree in Economics from the School of Advanced Studies of The Romanian Academy, the Department of Economic, Social and Legal Sciences. He started teaching since 2012 and has shown a great interest in his research related to the role played by education in universities, companies and, generally speaking, in a welfare state. He is also devoted to promoting the concept of entrepreneurship in Romania, conducting studies in this field of activity and guiding his students to this endeavor. He is also promoting a spirit of social responsibility and volunteering through the associations he is part of.

Samuli Kortelainen is a postdoctoral researcher at Lappeenranta University of Technology, Finland. His research interests are in utilizing computational research methods in strategic management. He is also an academic entrepreneur and helps companies to make better decisions through utilizing modern computational techniques.

Aino Kuitunen is a doctoral candidate from Lappeenranta University of Technology at the department of International Business, Marketing and Entrepreneurship. She has a M.Sc. (agriculture and forestry) degree from Environmental economics and natural resource management with multidisciplinary studies. Previously she has been working for instances such as WWF Finland, Finnish meteorological institute and University of Helsinki in several research projects where the emphasis has been on climate change mitigation and adaptation. Her research interests include sustainable energy investments, urban challenges and equitable market design. Currently she is doing research about the investors' perception of carbon risk which is also the topic of her thesis.

Lauri Lättilä (D.Sc. [Tech.] from Lappeenranta University of Technology) works as the COO of SimAnalytics. His work concentrates on building scalable, mathematical models which are data adaptive by nature. His research interests lie in the domain of combining simulation and mathematical models with various optimization and machine learning frameworks.

Miltiadis D. Lytras is a Research Professor in the American College of Greece, with a research focus on Cognitive Computing, information systems, technology enabled innovation, social networks, computers in human behavior, semantic web, knowledge management and technology enhanced learning, with more than 150 publications in these areas. He serves as the Editor in Chief of the International Journal on Semantic Web and Information Systems, http://www.igi-global.com/ijswis (Indexed in SCI, Thomson Reuters, Impact Factor 2016: 1.5) and the Editor in Chief, International Journal on Knowledge Society Research, http://www.igi-global.com/ijksr

He has served as leading guest (co)-editor of 45 special issues inpeer reviewed International Journals most of them indexed in SCI/SSCI Thomson Reuters.

Paul Marinescu is a University Professor at The Faculty of Administration and Business, University of Bucharest. He has a Licence in Cybernetics after he graduated The Academy of Economic Studies in Bucharest and a PhD in Economics from The Romanian Academy. He teaches Project, General and Change Management at The Faculty of Administration and Business, University of Bucharest. His interests relate to the development of students' careers and aims at improving educational system.

Christina Marouli studied biochemistry (B.A.), Urban and environmental policy (M.A.) and sociology (PhD) – with a specialisation in environment and social inequalities – in the United States. Her doctoral research dealt with urban environment, gender and class in Athens, Greece. She has worked as a consultant and a free lance researcher on environmental and occupational safety health issues in the private sector. She has extensively taught on environmental protection, environmental education, occupational safety and health, sociology and environmental management. She has experience on environmental education - creating modules, training / educating and doing research, in the context of NGOs and at higher education (undergraduate and graduate) institutions. She was also awarded a Fulbright award in the context of which she collaborated with a Turkish professor doing research on multicultural environmental education programmes. In addition, she has worked on women's and children's issues in the context of her Non-Governmental Organizations (NGO) work as director of Save the Children, Greece and responsible for development education at the YWCA). She was a co-founder of the Emergency Research Center (NGO). In the recent years, she has also worked for the European Commission as a monitoring expert for LIFE projects in Greece and Cyprus. She has been teaching - since its inception in 2010 - at the Environmental Studies Program of Deree – American College of Greece (ACG), to the design of which she actively participated. At ACG, she initiated the Center of Excellence for Sustainability and she has been its Director since its inception in fall 2011.

James Odia, PhD, an associate professor in the Department of Accounting in the University of Benin, Nigeria where he currently teaches and researches on strategic management accounting and corporate sustainability.

Nickanor Owuor studied in Kenya before proceeding to India where he did his Bachelor of Commerce degree (1997-2000) at the University of Calicut, Kerala, and MBA (2001-2003) from the same university. He also holds a Post Graduate Diploma in International Business (Pondicherry University) and Higher Diploma in Software Engineering. Nick started teaching at Egerton University in Kenya. He taught there from 2003-2006 and upon invitation by the Government of Ethiopia, he also served in Ethiopia from August 2006 to August 2007. While there, he taught at University of Hawassa. From Ethiopia Nick went to Tanzania where he taught at Mount Meru University from September 2007 to October 2009. Since December 2009 he has been at University of Kurdistan- Hewlêr in the Business and Management Sciences Department. He is currently pursuing PhD Higher Education: Research, Evaluation and Enhancement, from Lancaster University, UK.

Chandra Sekhar Patro is currently an Assistant Professor at Gayatri Vidya Parishad College of Engineering (Autonomous), Visakhapatnam, India. He has Ph.D in Faculty of Commerce and Management Studies from Andhra University, India and post-graduate degree in Master of Commerce (M.Com.) from Andhra University, Master in Financial Management (MFM) from Pondicherry University, and also MBA (HR & Finance) from JNT University. Mr. Patro has over 9 years of teaching experience in higher education. Mr. Patro has gained very good knowledge in Human Resource Management and Accountancy/Finance subjects. He has published number of research papers in reputed National and International Journals and also presented papers in National and International Conferences.

Cătălin Ploae, Ph.D., University lecturer at the Faculty of International Business and Economics of Bucharest University of Economic Studies, holds a Ph.D. in International Business from the Bucharest University of Economic Studies, a Post Doc in Economics from the Romanian Academy and an MA in Marketing from the University of Lille, France. His research interests span from the topics of his Post Doc dissertation and Ph.D. thesis (intercultural management) to innovation and sustainable endeavors, with the constant of community involvement, increase of economic, environmental and social sustainability. He has been member in 4 R&D projects with topics ranging from the development of interdisciplinary research in educational system to economic sustainability and the assessment of Romanian agriculture sector. He is member of the Royal Economic Society, World Economics Association, the Romanian Scientific Society of Management and the Society for Romanian Studies. He was involved in 7 national and international projects that were co-financed by the European Union. He was a visiting professor to the University of Auvergne, France. He is the author/co-author of 5 books, 1 book chapter, 2 ISI Thomson peer-reviewed articles, 12 International peer-reviewed articles, 15 articles published in conference proceedings.

K. Madhu Kishore Raghunath is currently pursuing Ph.D in Management from National Institute of Technology-Warangal, India. He has post-graduate degree in Management. He has over 4 years of teaching experience in higher education. Mr. Madhu has good knowledge in Finance and Marketing subjects. He qualified CBSE NET and also TS&AP SET. He has published several articles in repute National and International journals and conferences. He has post-graduate degree in Management. He has over 4 years of teaching experience in higher education. Mr. Madhu has good knowledge in Finance and Marketing subjects. He qualified CBSE NET and also TS&AP SET.

Patrizia Silvestrelli is Associate Professor of Business Management since 2015 at the Department of Economics and Law of the University of Macerata (Macerata, Italy). She earned a magna cum laude Degree in 1997 at the School of Economics "G. Fuà" of the University of Ancona where she gained also the Ph.D. Degree in Business Organization and Management in 2001. She was visiting Ph.D. student for three semesters at the Darla School of Business of the University of South Carolina (USA) where she accomplished the research project for her thesis. She earned the Assistant Professor position in 2004 at the Business School of the University of Rome "Tor Vergata" where she taught until 2010, when she moved to the University of Macerata. Patrizia's research interests are addressed to investigate some significant issues in tourism management, like sustainability, hospitality innovation and cultural heritage enhancement. In previous publications, she dealt with internationalization issues, focusing on strategic paths and organizational structures for international companies. In particular, she carried on a study about worldwide evolution of consumer electronic industry and strategies implemented by companies operating in that sector, like delocalization, product innovation, promoting and selling. Patrizia Silvestrelli actually teaches General Management and International Management (undergraduate courses) and International Marketing (graduate course). In the past, she taught several courses as International Trading, Organizational Behaviour, Production & Logistic, Tourist Marketing, Heritage Management. She is also lecturer in Masters, Ph.D. and training courses both at academic and professional level. She is member of the Faculty (Department of Economics and Law), Student Career Council, Course of Study Board, Master in Marketing e Direzione Aziendale Executive Committee (University of Macerata), Master in Management delle attività turistiche e culturali (University of Roma "Tor Vergata").

Aytug Sozuer is a lecturer of international business and entrepreneurship at University of Yalova, Turkey. He has a doctoral degree in Business Management and Organization from Istanbul University. Before joining academia, he worked at several multinational companies as a specialist in sales and exporting. His academic research fields of interest include governance, inter-firm relationships, and start-ups.

Banu Tanriover finished PhD in the department of economics at Karadeniz Technical University in Turkey. Tanriover is working in the department of economics at Osmaniye Korkut Ata University in Turkey as Assist. Prof. Her research areas are macroeconometrics, business cycles theories, asymmetric cycles and the persistence of economic shocks, and time series analaysis.

Sorin-George Toma is Professor of Entrepreneurship and Strategy at the Faculty of Administration and Business, University of Bucharest, where he teaches in the undergraduate and postgraduate programs. He has a Licence in Electromechanics from the Naval Academy Constantza, a Licence in Marketing from the University of Economic Studies Bucharest, a Licence in Sociology from the University of Bucharest, a M.A. degree in Sociology from the University of Bucharest, a M.B.T. from Carl Duisberg Koln, two Ph.D. degrees in Economics from University of Economic Studies and Sociology from the University of Bucharest and a post-Ph.D. degree from the Romanian Academy. His research interests relate to the role of entrepreneurship in economic development, the relationships between corporate social responsibility and sustainability, and between strategy and creativity. He currently leads the Business Consulting master program at the University of Bucharest.

Nina Tura (M.Sc. Tech.) is a technology Ph.D. candidate in the School of Business and Management at Lappeenranta University of Technology in Finland. She has been conducting research and teaching at Lappeenranta University of Technology since 2012. Currently she is working in the department of Industrial Engineering and Management. She has been working in multiple research projects focusing on sustainability strategies, sustainability-oriented innovations and circular business. Her primary research goal is to increase the knowledge regarding the challenges of managing the value of sustainable-oriented innovations which is also the topic of her Doctoral Thesis. Her additional research interests include strategic management, environmental technology and sustainability.

Roxana Voicu-Dorobanţu, Ph.D., is Associate professor in the Faculty of International Business and Economics, Bucharest University of Economic Studies in Bucharest, she holds a PhD in Economics and a postdoctoral degree at the Romanian Academy. She has been specialized in research and education institutions, at a national and international level, and is a visiting professor with the University in Sczeczin, Poland and Edinburgh Napier, United Kingdom. Member of several international organizations in economic research, she is Vice- President of the English Speaking Union Romania. Roxana has coordinated both national and multinational research teams, including in a specialized research center, and has participated in more than 15 research and R&D projects. She also has an active participation in business, through her consultancy, risk management and restructuring endeavors. Her interests lie in regional and community development, business ecosystems, innovation and sustainability. She is the author of more than 20 peer-reviewed articles, of two books (one published nationally and one internationally), and more than 30 papers presented in international conferences.

Eleonora Zaccaro received her Master's Degree in Business Communication, Marketing and new media from Lumsa University in Rome in November 2016. In April 2016 she was hired as a Content Stratgey and Social Media Assistant for Persol and Sunglass Hut at Luxottica Group in Milan. She is now currently working as a Global Communication and Digital Media Specialist at Calzedonia Group in Verona.

Index

G

H

I

K

L

M

N

O

P

Q

R

S

T

U

V

W

www.ingramcontent.com/pod-product-compliance
Lightning Source LLC
LaVergne TN
LVHW062115300926
849161LV00010B/2463